THE HISTORY OF IRVINE

The device on the title page is the coat of arms of the Royal Burgh of Irvine.

THE HISTORY OF IRVINE

Royal Burgh and New Town

JOHN STRAWHORN

JOHN DONALD PUBLISHERS LTD
EDINBURGH

© Cunninghame District Council 1985

All rights reserved. No part of this publication
may be reproduced in any form or by any means
without the prior permission of the publishers,
John Donald Publishers Ltd., 138 St Stephen Street,
Edinburgh, EH3 5AA

ISBN 0 85976 140 1

Exclusive distribution in the United States of America
and Canada by Humanities Press Inc., Atlantic
Highlands, NJ 07716, USA

Phototypesetting by H.M. Repros Ltd., Glasgow
Printed in Great Britain by Clark Constable (1982) Ltd.

Preface

'The more one studies Scottish history the more one feels convinced that the first requisite for the writing of real Scottish history is that there should be all over the country an intensive study of local history: and only when the results of such study are available will the historian be able to undertake that wider synthesis which will provide a history of modern Scotland.' George Pratt Insh, *The Study of Local History*, 1932.

For long enough professional historians turned up their academic noses at locally produced histories. They had nothing but contempt for the enthusiastic amateur, lacking historical training or perspective, who magnified the importance of local events, who delighted in legend, genealogy, anecdote, and parochial trivia. Some experts, however, have been sensible enough to realise that within the most amateurish local publications may be found nuggets of useful detail embedded in the dross, and that others have been works of considerable scholarship, like Arnold McJannet's *The Royal Burgh of Irvine*, published in 1938. Disregard for local history, however, still survives. Over the last fifteen years the *Scottish Historical Review* has failed to mention any new publication relating to Ayrshire, although well over a hundred books and pamphlets have been produced locally during that period, fifty of them currently in print, as catalogued by the Ayrshire Federation of Historical Societies. Yet it is generally accepted that research in the central records must be complemented by local studies. The recent establishment of a Scottish Local History Forum suggests that at last local history has become respectable.

Why a new history of Irvine? For all its undoubted merits, McJannet's work requires revision and amplification. Although he meticulously studied a wide range of available sources, local prejudice denied him access to the municipal records of the burgh whose history he was writing. Also, since his time new evidence has been unearthed and new interpretations have been suggested by historians. Perhaps the most serious criticism is that McJannet ignored recent history. As did James Paterson, historian of Ayrshire, who in 1863 could announce that 'With the rebellion of 1745 may be said to have ceased all that is interesting in the history of Scotland'. Yet, as Dr. Insh reminded, 'Without a study of the nineteenth — and of the twentieth century — Scottish history is a house without a roof'. Another thing, we are now more interested in social history, which Insh pioneered: 'not a record of tribal wars and of antiquarian memories but a history of the Scottish people ... We want to know not alone how the Norman castle came into being, but also how the modern tenement and cottage were evolved'.

As a former student of Dr. Insh, I honour his memory by seeking in this book to follow his precept: 'Our business is to explain just how this locality came to be what it is at the present day'.

The idea for a new history of Irvine came from Cunninghame District Council. The present author was commissioned and granted all necessary facilities and absolute literary freedom to tell the story in his own way. Arrangements were made with John Donald Publishers Ltd. to produce a volume at a price which would ensure the widest possible circulation. For its imaginative initiative Cunninghame District Council deserves full credit.

Acknowledgement to members and officials of Cunninghame District Council for their enthusiastic support is recorded at the end of this book; also to all others who assisted in the gathering of information, and in the process of publication.

This book has been written by a historian as a contribution to Scottish history. Some who have no particular interest in Irvine should find in its pages material which illuminates the story of our country's social developments. Most readers naturally will be people with a special regard for Irvine. We hope that those who are older residents will find this a faithful portrait of the burgh of which they are so proud. We hope that Irvinites who have left their native town will recall past scenes and events with nostalgia, and note with interest how much of the old survives amid more recent changes. In particular we hope that young people growing up in the New Town, and those coming to make their home here, will through this book come to appreciate more fully that Irvine is a lively community with long and continuing traditions.

JOHN STRAWHORN, 1985

Contents

Preface	v
PART ONE: THE BEGINNING	1
Chapter	
ONE Origins	2
TWO Early Days in the Burgh	8
THREE The Burgh Council	20
FOUR Church and Castle	28
FIVE Feuds and Factions	38
PART TWO: GROWTH	49
SIX Some Progress	50
SEVEN The Council and the 18th Century	64
EIGHT Commercial Growth	76
NINE Church and School	86
TEN John Galt's Irvine	94
PART THREE: THE 19TH CENTURY	107
ELEVEN The Coming of Reform	108
TWELVE Little Change	123
THIRTEEN Little Progress	132
FOURTEEN A New Beginning	144
FIFTEEN Industrial Town	155
PART FOUR: THE 20TH CENTURY	167
SIXTEEN A New Age	168
SEVENTEEN The First War and After	180
EIGHTEEN The Small Burgh and the Second War	193
NINETEEN Mid-Century	204
TWENTY From Burgh into New Town	216
Sources and Acknowledgements	234
List of Provosts	244
List of Events	246
Present-day street plan	248
Index	250

Part One
The Beginning

ONE

Origins

No one can tell exactly when or how Irvine began.

It is known that people have been living in the neighbourhood for some six thousand years. To the north at Ardeer, and to the south at Shewalton, evidence has been unearthed of the presence of mesolithic people. Numerous finds of microliths — stone-made heads of harpoons, knives, and the like — are witness to visits from wandering groups of these coastal hunters seeking a bare livelihood in what was then an Arctic climate. At Ardeer and Shewalton there have been found traces of later settlers of the Neolithic, Bronze, and Iron Ages on what were obviously attractive sites for colonisation.

But in the intervening area where Irvine later grew up, archaeological remains are few. At Bartonholm a solitary flint scraper was found by John Smith. In his *Prehistoric Man in Ayrshire* he described it as 'perhaps the most ancient article which has been found in Ayrshire'. He also noticed near Snodgrass a perforated stone sinker, such as a fisherman might have used. And he measured and recorded four considerable mounds, two on Irvine Moor, one at Girdle Toll which had been levelled in 1852, and at Lawthorn. Perhaps these were constructed by some prehistoric peoples, perhaps they are of later date, perhaps merely natural features. Near the heart of Irvine is another prehistoric puzzle. Where the river now flows there was once, it is claimed, a circle of standing stones. Some were presumed to have been swept away by the encroachment of the river; others were removed, despite popular protests, when the weir was constructed in 1895; one solitary boulder remains in the river, in the shadow of the modern bridge. This 'Granny Stane' takes its name, according to fanciful theory, from Apollo Grannicus, the sun god; Grannos, a god of thermal springs; or Grianaig, a Celtic fish-goddess.

What complicates the picture of Irvine's origins, and perhaps explains the scarcity of archaeological finds, is the fact that the rivers have changed their courses and the sea has also receded. Within living memory the River Garnock altered its channel near Bogend. At some much earlier period, it is claimed, the Garnock found its way into the sea near Stevenston. The River Irvine before a spate in 1769 turned north at Warrix, passed by Newmill, and joined the Annick Water below Moats Hole. This old course, known as the Auld Water Gang, can still be traced alongside the Warrix interchange on the by-pass. It has been presumed that the River Irvine originally followed a different route from there to the sea. And there has been much argument about where the seacoast was at different periods. 'Within the memory of persons now alive, the sea has receded considerably on this coast', it was stated in the New Statistical Account of 1837. It is certain that in prehistoric times the sea came much further inland than it does now. When the River Irvine changed its course near Warrix, the spate uncovered the remains of a whale. This, it has been estimated, was beached there about four thousand years ago, when the first colonists were already settled at Ardeer and Shewalton. Some ribs of this whale later adorned local gardens, Irvine weavers used the vertebrae as weights, and parts were presented to the Hunterian Museum at Glasgow University.

Recent palaeogeographical research suggests a maximum sea level some five thousand years ago (High Water Mark of Spring Tide [HWMST] around 12 to 13 metres Above Ordnance Datum [AOD]). With the sea reaching inland as far as Warrix, we can visualise a great bay between Ardeer and Shewalton, with the coastline not far from Stanecastle. Calculating an average 0.2m per century drop in sea level, there would follow a rapid recession of the sea over two thousand years; another two thousand years when change in the coastline was less noticeable; with a further considerable recession during the last five hundred years.

During most of the Christian era there would thus be little significant alteration in the coastline. At the time of the Roman occupation (c.100 AD, HWMST around 6.5m AOD) the great bay would be reduced in size, but the Garnock would still enter it south of Kilwinning, and the estuary of the Irvine would be somewhere north-west of Shewalton. The sites of Bartonholm and Irvine would be on the coastline. Behind Irvine the great lagoon of earlier times would have become a loch, first noted in the 13th century,

The coastal site now occupied by Irvine was under water five thousand years ago. The shore at that time was near the line of the present bypass road.

reduced to three smaller lochs by the 17th century, and finally drained at the end of that century.

It has been conjectured that the Romans must have had a port at Irvine. Fortlets near the sea have been found elsewhere, above Largs and near Girvan. It has been guessed that a military road from their fort near Loudoun Hill extended down the Irvine Valley to the coast. What the Romans called Vindogara Sinus may have been the great bay between Saltcoats and Troon or between Saltcoats and Ayr, or the smaller but now-vanished bay at Irvine. If they had a port at the mouth of the Irvine, no trace remains of the site, and a few Roman coins discovered form inconclusive evidence. The River Irvine then entered the sea somewhere south of its present estuary. Long afterwards in 1760 Richard Pococke, coming from Kilwinning and passing Irvine, 'crossed the river, observed a tumulus, and some works that were much like a Roman camp'. The conjectured Roman port may have been there near Shewalton, or it may have been north about Marressfoot. These areas were at that time exposed, but later eroded away by the northern meanderings of the River Irvine, then replaced by fluvial sediment, which covered any remains. Another possibility is that the Romans may have had a fort away from the shore at Stane. That name is first recorded in 1363 but it is (possibly) much older, and (maybe) commemorating an earlier and (perhaps) Roman stone-built structure.

We can be more certain that between 1000 AD (HWMST 5m AOD) and 1600 AD (HWMST 3m AOD) the castle, harbour and church of the new town of Irvine lay on the open coast. The first maps we have showing details of the local area appear in the great Amsterdam Atlas of Johannes Blaeu published in 1654. That of Kyle shows the familiar modern coastline with the Rivers Irvine and Garnock converging as they do now. That of Cunninghame, also surveyed by Timothy Pont at least a

4 *The History of Irvine*

The Granny Stane, one of Irvine's prehistoric puzzles, is in the river below the New Town Shopping Centre. Since 1895, when the weir was constructed down-river, only the tip of this massive boulder is visible.

half-century before, curiously shows what the previous situation may have been like. One authority thinks this map to be 'engraved without much care ... possibly erroneous', but to another 'it appears to make geological sense'. The map shows a wide bay with Bartonholm on the coast, an unnamed island at Ardeer, and the River Garnock entering this bay south of Kilwinning. It is tempting to speculate a closure of the gulf between Stevenston and Ardeer forcing the waters of the River Garnock south, and the confluence of the two rivers producing accelerated silting north and west of the old harbour of Irvine, which thus lost its previous wide access to the sea. There were repeated complaints in the 17th century of the harbour's silting, and a search for alternative arrangements. This may suggest that the crisis was a result of recent dramatic change; or the culmination of a protracted development for which there is no recorded evidence before the 16th century.

There is mention of 'Strathyrewen in Galwegia' in two charters of the 12th century (c.1130). But that, if it indeed refers to our area, is a reference to the valley rather than this particular place. More definite is the appearance of 'Hirun' in Benedict of Peterborough's chronicle under the year 1184.

Thereafter the name occurs in written records in variant forms, Irewin, Ervyne, etc., approaching the modern spelling in the 17th and 18th centuries. The derivation of the name has caused argument. Most commentators agree that the town takes its name from the river. Clear river, west-flowing river, and the river with the green banks have been offered as interpretations. Some have wondered if Irvine took its name from Vindogara or from St. Inan. A quite different theory is that the town was founded by a man called Erin Erinvine, whose surname meant 'brave westland man'. But there is no proof that that supposed father of King Duncan had anything to do with this area. It is accepted that the Irvine family came from another place of that name in Annandale.

The first settlement, which possibly took its name from the river, may have been a prehistoric pagan religious site where the Standing Stones are reported to have been, on ground near the sea, perhaps then an island, which at a later date was converted into a Christian settlement. Ninian was at Whithorn in the year 397 and Columba at Iona from 563. Fragmentary remains of stone crosses suggest that Christianity had reached South Ayrshire in the 5th century. Place names and legends are dubious evidence, but evidence which we must needs make use of, for we have no other information. Certain early saints are associated with the Irvine area. Ninian himself had an altar dedicated to him long afterwards in Irvine Church, a chapel at Dundonald Castle, and there is a St. Ninian's Isle in the Garnock below Kilwinning. Irvine Church also had an altar to St. Conval, an Irish missionary who came to assist Mungo in the late 6th century. He had associations also with Inchinnan, Cumnock, and Kirkconnel. And there was in 17th-century Irvine a High Street tenement called Convalls Walls. St. Bride or Bridget is commemorated by name in Arran, West Kilbride, at Brydeskirk near Stanecastle, and the St Bryde's well by the Drucken Steps. But the Celtic saint whom tradition most closely associates with Irvine was Inan, or Evan, who is reported to have continued missionary work initiated with Conval. Inan's name is found in the parishes of West Kilbride, Dundonald, and Beith, and perhaps he was one and the same as the saint after whom Kilwinning is said to be named. Adam King's Kalendar of 1588, which is reputedly based on much older sources, firmly declared that Inan was preaching at Irvine in the year 839, and it is also claimed that Inan died here. There was once a well named after him in Fullarton, south of the present harbour. But the more famous Chapel Well beside the River is associated with him only by those blessed with an uncritical imagination. Yet tradition insists that Inan had a close association with Irvine. McJannet in his *Royal Burgh of Irvine* vividly recreates the scene of an early Irvine. 'It was no doubt, near the mouth of the river Irvine, in the neighbourhood of which the influence of the ancient British church predominated, as has been narrated, that he set up his muinntir, a few huts made of mud and wattle, a church, and, near at hand, a cattle steading, and he would doubtless also possess "a plough of land". There, assisted by his disciples, among them artisans and students, and under the protection of the local chief, he carried on his missionary work.'

But while associating Ninian, Conval, Bridget, and Inan with Irvine, it is well to remember that the connection of a saint with a place often originated in a medieval dedication. The cult of a saint obviously does not necessarily imply his local presence at some past time. Nevertheless it can surely be asserted with confidence that sometime in the 5th century or after a place of Christian worship was created, and later, in the 12th century, was incorporated into the diocesan organisation instituted by David I; as Irvine Parish Church, it is first mentioned in 1233.

Irvine Castle is mentioned in the chronicle attributed to Benedict of Peterborough under the year 1184, indirectly, when he tells of 'A certain fountain of running water changed to blood near the church of St. Vinin [i.e. Kilwinning] in the western district of the land of the King of Scotland, below Cunningham, not far from the castle of Hirun [i.e. Irvine]'. To understand how this castle came to be established it is necessary to look at the background of political and administrative developments in south-west Scotland.

At the time of the Romans this area was inhabited by a British tribe called the Damnonii. In the Dark Ages which followed, a kingdom called Cumbria or Strathclyde emerged. Within it there were sub-kingdoms like Kyle, reputedly named after a King Coilus. Cunninghame was another. Much wider than the present administrative district, it comprised the whole of modern Ayrshire north of the River Irvine. In the case of Cunninghame, the origin of the name is even less certain. It has been variously explained as King's house, land of milk pails, land of rabbits — none at all convincing. Someone called Proc is supposed to have been a local chief during this period. And there was a possible visitation by the legendary figure of Arthur, that later-romanticised British cavalry chief. Certain it is that there were invasions and immigrations — the local Welsh-speaking Britons being met by Gaelic-speaking Scots from Ireland and Argyll, English-speaking farmers coming from the Lothians and beyond, and Viking Norwegians from the sea.

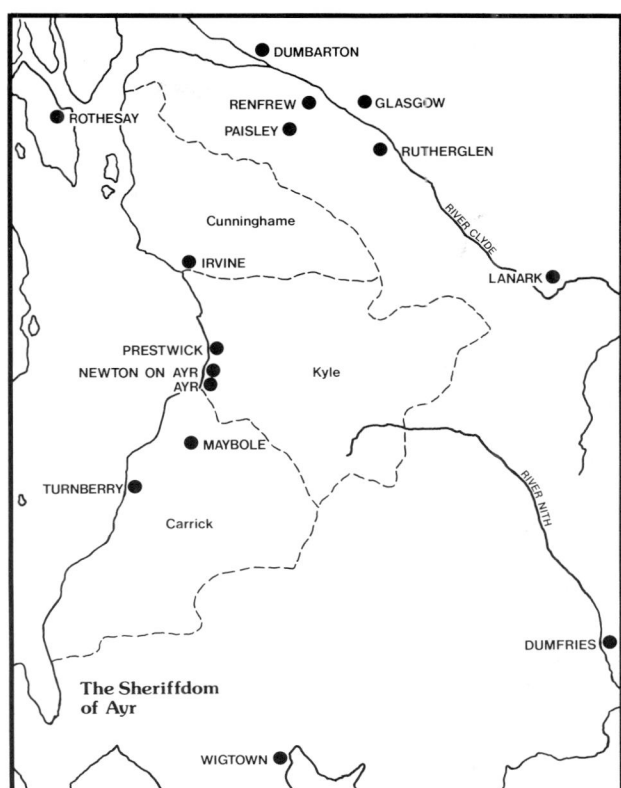

In historic times, this area became part of the Kingdom of Scotland, and the Bailiary of Cunninghame was made part of the Sheriffdom of Ayr.

The end of the Dark Ages can be marked from 1034 when Duncan of Strathclyde inherited from his grandfather Malcolm the kingdom of the Picts, Scots and Lothian. In the early centuries of the Middle Ages which followed, Strathclyde was absorbed into the Kingdom of Scotland. The invasion and annexation of Galloway in 1160 and the repulse of the Norwegians at Largs in 1263 are two notable incidents in the assertion of effective royal authority in the south-west. Slowly but systematically successive kings extended their influence — David I (from 1124), Malcolm IV (1153), William the Lion (1165), Alexander II (1214), Alexander III (1249-1286). These kings of Scots, to provide effective control over their territories, recruited outside help. Generous grants attracted prospective settlers from furth of Scotland — footloose warrior barons from Norman England and France, churchmen, and later merchants. Hugh de Morville, of Norman origin, was offered land in Lothian and Lauderdale, and was made Constable of Scotland, and he or his son Richard de Morville was made Lord of Cunninghame and Largs. The Breton, Walter Fitzalan, became Steward of Scotland with lands in Renfrewshire to which was added the northern part of Kyle. The rest of Kyle was retained in royal hands, on the uneasy border with the semi-independent state of Galloway, from which Carrick was detached.

To manage these territories, wooden motte-and-bailey castles were erected. The advance into the south-west is marked by the construction of Irvine Castle sometimes before 1184 by the de Morvilles; Walter Fitzalan making his local headquarters at Dundonald; and William the Lion's new castle at Ayr in 1197.

Typically, the de Morvilles organised the lordship of Cunninghame on a feudal basis, retaining the area round Irvine for themselves. They rewarded with grants of land their followers, who included Arthur of Ardrossan, Philip de Horsey, Richard de Barclay, Simon de Beaumont (all in Ardrossan), Robert Croc (West Kilbride), Hugh de Eglinton (Kilwinning), and others in Largs, Giffen, Stewarton, Kilmaurs, Kilmarnock, and Loudoun — covering the entire area north of the River Irvine. These retainers maintained themselves on the proceeds of their baronies. They built their own castles. As vassals they owed allegiance to their overlord, rendering homage and military aid as required, paying suit in the bailiary court of Cunninghame at Irvine.

Again typically, the de Morvilles fostered the development of the church. Tyronensian monks of that reformed Benedictine order were brought from Kelso to set up Kilwinning Abbey. For their maintenance they were amply endowed with lands and became responsible for fourteen parish churches throughout Cunninghame. Which of the de Morvilles was responsible for the foundation of Kilwinning Abbey and when remains uncertain. Various years between 1140 and 1191 have been postulated: the most recent investigation suggests sometime between 1184 and 1189 and the founder as Richard de Morville.

The same uncertainty surrounds the date of the foundation of the Burgh of Irvine, whose promoter must have been one of the early lords of Cunninghame. The first lord, Hugh de Morville, was succeeded by his son Richard de Morville (1163–1189) whose son William de Morville followed. William's daughter Helena married Roland, lord of Galloway, whose successors were thus lords both of Galloway and of Cunninghame. Alan, son of Roland, married Margaret, who was of the royal house, a niece of two kings and cousin of two others. Their daughter Devorguilla married a John Balliol whose son through descent from his royal grandmother Margaret was able successfully to claim the throne in 1292. So under King John the lordship of Cunninghame became an appanage of the Crown. After Bruce's victories and his accession as Robert I, he awarded Balliol lands and the lordship of Cunninghame sometime between 1316 and 1320 to his grandson Robert the Steward who would himself succeed as first of the Stewart kings in 1371.

Which of the lords of Cunninghame was responsible for the foundation of the Burgh of Irvine has always been obscure. Claims have been made for an earlier date than can reasonably be maintained. An early 19th-century writer in the New Statistical Account declared that 'Irvine ranks amongst the most ancient of the royal burghs of Scotland'. More recently, McJannet took the view that 'Irvine was not only the oldest burgh in Ayrshire, but, as a royal burgh, was also earlier in date of erection to Ayr'. Alas for local patriotism, painstaking research has forced reassessment. Ayr's date of foundation has been exactly determined as 1205. It has also been convincingly proved that a document which seems to suggest that there were already burgesses in Irvine at that date could not in fact have been from the year 1205: it must be a copyist's error for 1295 or 1305. Assertions that Irvine was from the beginning a royal burgh must also founder. Not till the 15th century was there a precise distinction between a royal burgh and a burgh of barony. Before that all were simply 'free burghs' with a variety of privileges conferred irrespectively of whether the burgh was held by king, bishop, abbot, earl or baron. There is, besides, a more widely argued debate on the origins of burghs in general, whether they grew out of existing settlements beside a church, castle, or river crossing, or as deliberate creations of a new community. Burghs were, in fact, the 'new towns' of the Middle Ages. In Irvine there should be no difficulty in accepting that while in many places a 'new town' could be created on a greenfield site, here is an example of a new town grafted onto an existing community. Indeed, by a curious parallel, the 20th-century New Town of Irvine was planned to absorb the two burghs of Irvine and Kilwinning. In the case of the medieval 'new town' of Irvine, it seems likely there were already two village settlements — one beside the parish church, the other beside the castle to the north. Between them the Burgh of Irvine was laid out with the precision expected from planners of all periods of history.

There is a slim possibility that a burgh was formed here in the reign of David I, but it seems more likely that the original creation was sometime in the reign of Alexander II, i.e. between 1214 and 1249. A passing reference to the 'town' of Irvine in a document of 1230 might imply that a burgh had not yet been formed, and if so fix the date as possibly after 1230 but certainly before 1249. The Charter from King Alexander II, though since lost, we can presume granted royal permission for the lord of Cunninghame of that time — William de Morville? — to set up a burgh at Irvine. This would have been on the same terms as Walter Fitzalan had in 1180 received a royal charter making

Prestwick the first burgh in what became Ayrshire. The burgh of Ayr itself was created also by King William the Lion in 1205: it was on crown land and was granted the special privilege of collecting tolls throughout Cunninghame and Kyle.

Though Irvine must have originated as a baronial burgh, it eventually achieved the status of a royal burgh. But the process was a tortuous one. When John Balliol, Lord of Cunninghame, became king in 1292, his burgh of Irvine became in a sense a king's burgh; and in 1304 Edward I of England as his overlord extracted from Irvine the fee normally paid by a king's burgh. Irvine was presumably still subject to tolls levied by the Burgh of Ayr, though we can guess that opportunity was taken to claim exemption. This anomalous position was of course legally resolved when John ceased to be king. Robert I's grant of Cunninghame to his grandson gave the latter the powers of lordship 'as well within burgh as without'. This confirms that after the brief period as king's burgh Irvine had by 1320 reverted to the status of a baronial burgh. Nevertheless, Irvine disputed the continued claim of Ayr to collect toll. The situation was apparently resolved by a Charter of Robert I in 1322. There was confirmation that Irvine should enjoy the burghal rights as granted 'in a Charter made for that purpose to the said burgesses by Alexander the Second of venerable memory'. And the additional award was made 'to the said burgesses and their successors that they be altogether acquit and perpetually free from the toll which before our present grant they were wont to pay in our burgh of Ayr'. Ayr, however, was a king's burgh ('our burgh' in the Charter) while Irvine was not one ('the said burgh' in the Charter), and so despite the specific exemption in Irvine's 1322 Charter, Ayr continued to press its claims against what it must have regarded as an upstart baronial burgh. That it continued as such was confirmed when in 1367 Robert the Steward as lord of Cunninghame delegated to Sir Hew of Eglinton the offices of Bailie of Cunninghame and Chamberlain of the Burgh of Irvine. When Robert succeeded as king in 1371, the elevation of his Burgh of Irvine to a special status was not automatic — Prestwick, another burgh belonging to the new king continued its inferior role, as did Newton-upon-Ayr which had been created a burgh in that century. But exceptionally, and just a year after his accession, Robert II awarded Irvine a new Charter.

The Royal Charter of 1372 was obviously prompted by three petitions from the burgesses of Irvine, each of which won a favourable response from Robert II. First, there was a satisfactory settlement of the long-standing dispute with Ayr. A special inquiry confirmed that the baronies of Cunninghame and Largs were subject for purposes of trade to the Burgh of Irvine, thus implicitly rejecting Ayr's claim to a commercial monopoly over the whole county. Secondly, Irvine's status as a king's burgh was defined by having 'all liberties and privileges, as freely fully and honourably as any burgh within our kingdom'. Thirdly, to promote the further development of Irvine's trade, there was a grant of the liberty of guild and the right to appoint guild brethren. In a Letter of Protection circulated in advance to other authorities — including no doubt the Burgh of Ayr — there was the strict instruction 'that in no manner ye presume to vex, oppress, or disturb the said burgh, burgesses, or community', and Irvine's status as a king's burgh was explicitly confirmed in its description by Robert II as 'our burgh' — the first recorded use of this phrase by a king in respect of Irvine. The generous settlement was due less to the philanthropy of a well-disposed monarch than to his urgent financial needs. This western burgh, in existence since at least 1249, had after a troubled century firmly established itself; the monarchy could expect to benefit fiscally from its continued progress. For this the burgh required the security of commercial autonomy, scope to trade freely at home and abroad, and its merchants the authority to constitute themselves as guild brethren and manage the burgh's affairs. They were already prosperous enough to secure from the king what was a satisfactory contract. Robert II's 1372 Charter thus elevated Irvine to that special status that would soon be formally described as that of a royal burgh. Occasionally thereafter and until the 16th century the Burgh of Irvine had to take legal action against infringements of its rights by the Burgh of Ayr, the Sheriff of Ayrshire, and the Bailie of Cunninghame. But the 1372 charter proved a reliable safeguard, and for additional security the Burgh of Irvine took the precaution of obtaining Charters of Confirmation and Letters of Protection from a series of later monarchs.

TWO

Early Days in the Burgh

The only survival of the early Burgh is the property divisions which can still be traced in the form of ancient walls in the area round the town centre. The layout of the 13th-century new town was necessarily influenced by the topography of the land and the trackways which traversed it. On the neck of land between the great inland loch and the estuary of the river to the west, the church occupied a commanding site on one of the sandy hills which overlooked the river. To the north, the castle guarded the cove where a little harbour was surely already in existence. Halfway between the church and the castle a shallow depression formed a gully through which the surplus waters of the loch drained out to the river and the sea. The course of a path from the castle to the church is followed still by the West Road and Hill Street, continuing past the Chapel Well to ford the river. More important were the routes which led from all parts of Cunninghame to converge on Irvine Castle which was the headquarters of that territory: down the valley and via East Road, heading towards the Seagate; from the north, also skirting the loch, came other ways. There was also that long-distance route coming up the coast from Ayr and the south, crossing the river at the Puddleford and, by way of what is now the Kirkgate, making towards the north.

For the planners of the new Burgh of Irvine the most attractive available site was the level tract of land sheltering behind the sandy knolls. The first phase of development was laying out there a broad thoroughfare, sixty to eighty feet wide and designed for market purposes. The market cross — first mentioned in 1260 — was located opposite the narrow Kirkgate. The main thoroughfare at the north-west end made a ford crossing of the stream, then narrowed after it turned to breast the hill, bypass the Castle, and make a northern exit.

Plots of land were pegged off, presumably beginning on the level central area adjacent to the market place. Settlers who would colonise the new Burgh were attracted — not only Scots, but English, Flemings, Normans and Scandinavians were usual among such immigrants. Persons with sufficient capital to set up as merchants and craftsmen were offered tempting terms, with land granted on burgage tenure. Each incomer was allotted a Burgh toft — about $\frac{1}{4}$ acre of a tail rig, perhaps 500 feet long, behind a 20-foot frontage on the main thoroughfare. The land was granted in perpetuity, with a rent-free period to allow the building of a timber dwelling and the enclosure of the toft with a dyke. Additional land on the Back Riggs was also available for clearing and cultivation. In return for a fixed annual rent to the Burgh's superior, and modest assistance in guarding the Burgh, the new burgess enjoyed security of tenure and extensive privileges — scope to develop his business, exemption from tolls, liberty to trade freely throughout the kingdom, and the protection of the Burgh Court.

The new Burgh attracted not only merchants and craftsmen who could set themselves up as burgesses. Lesser folk came to work for them, rarely achieving the rank of burgess but referred to as mere 'indwellers'. A third group were substantial landowners from different parts of Cunninghame and even beyond who felt it worthwhile to acquire a property in this district capital. Some at least chose the rather smaller tofts on the south side of the market, backing on to the sand hills. Their townhouses held on burgage tenure gave them, though absentees, the rank of burgess as 'uplandis men'.

How rapidly Irvine grew after the first Charter grant (sometime before 1249) can only be conjectured. Despite the political disturbances associated with the Wars of Independence, the Burgh seems to have made marked progress. In 1324 one burgess, Thomas Baxter, was prosperous enough to donate the annual rents from eight of his properties towards the support of a chapel in the parish church, and his example was followed by others in succeeding generations. By 1372 the burgesses were sufficiently well-off to secure from Robert II the new Charter with its recognition and augmentation of their privileges. In the next century the Burgh of Irvine acquired a range of facilities which will be described later. It has been calculated that by 1517 Irvine's population had reached 1,000. Ayr had between 1,500 and 2,000. Only five

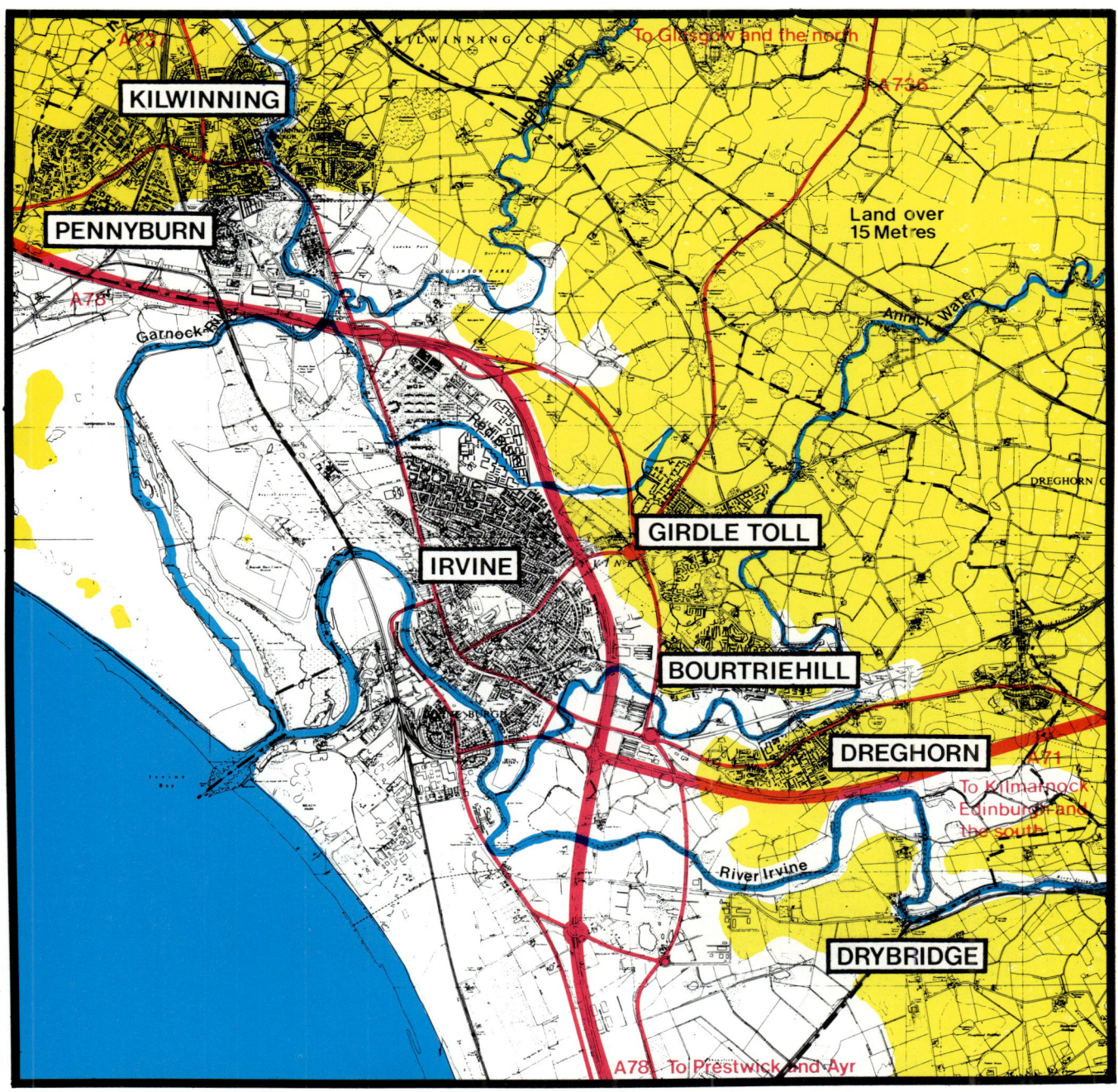

Irvine is situated in the south west of Scotland, on a lowland area where the River Irvine enters the Firth of Clyde, forming a joint estuary with the River Garnock. The Burgh of Irvine and the other communities named have since 1967 been part of Irvine New Town.

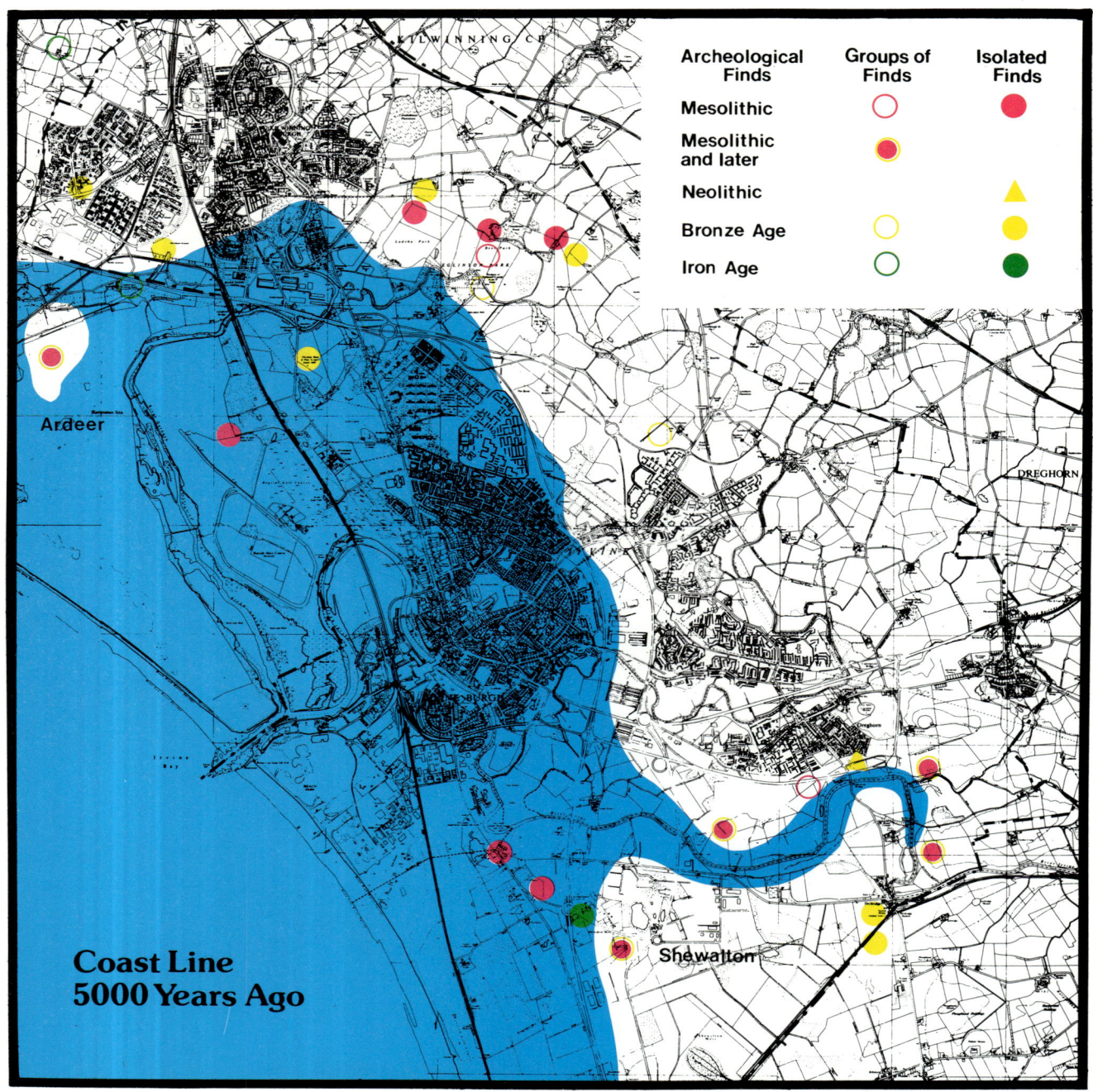

Favoured sites for prehistoric peoples were Ardeer and Shewalton. In each place mesolithic people, the earliest settlers, were followed by others in the succeeding neolithic, bronze, and iron ages. Not far from Ardeer, other remains have been found around Stevenston, and by the Lugton Water at Eglinton. Near Shewalton, remains have also been found beside the River Irvine by Dreghorn. But in the vicinity of Irvine — then under water — finds have been few.

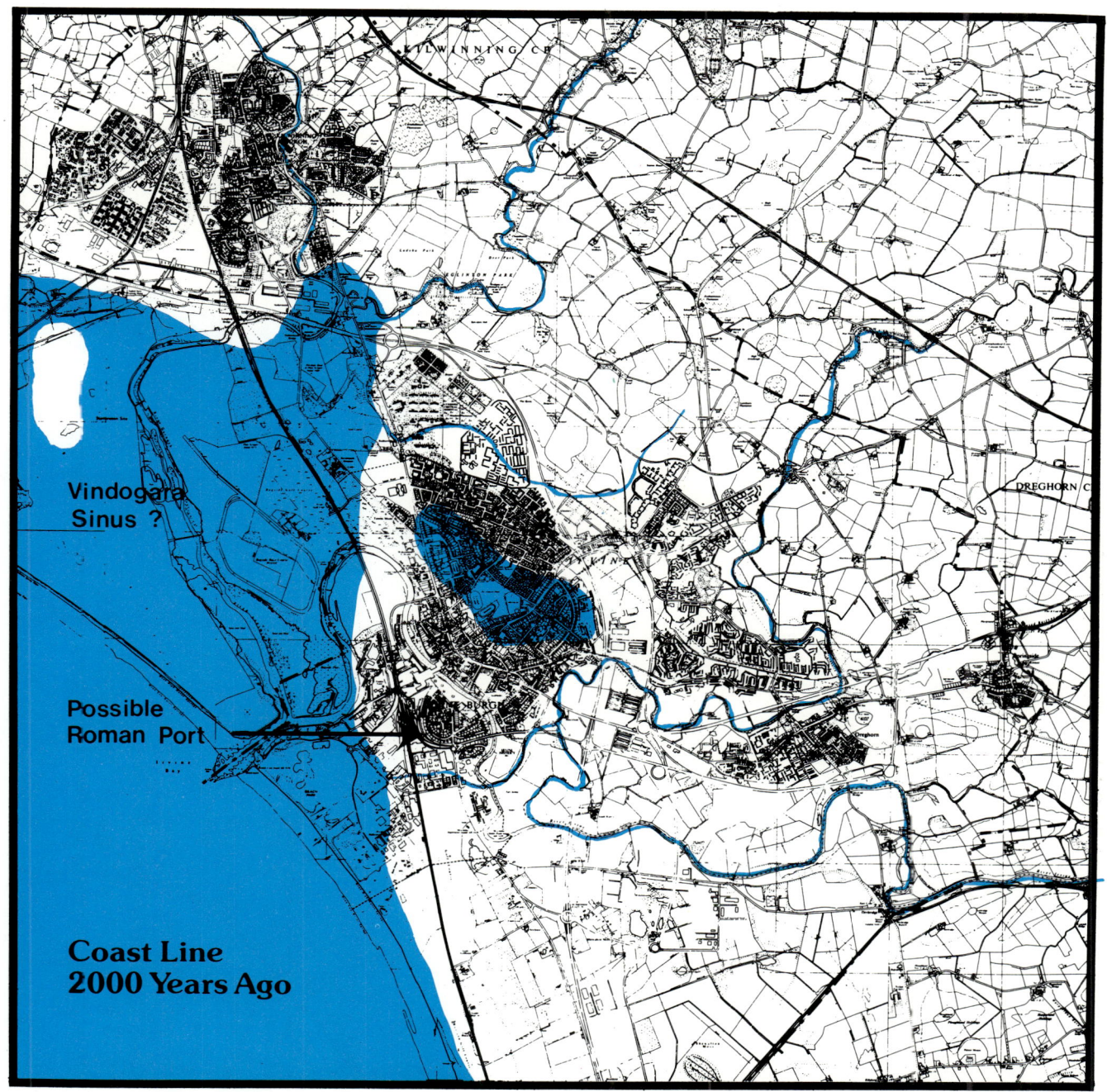

Two thousand years ago, the sea had receded from Knadgerhill and Stanecastle. Most of Irvine had emerged from under water, but a loch would continue for many centuries.

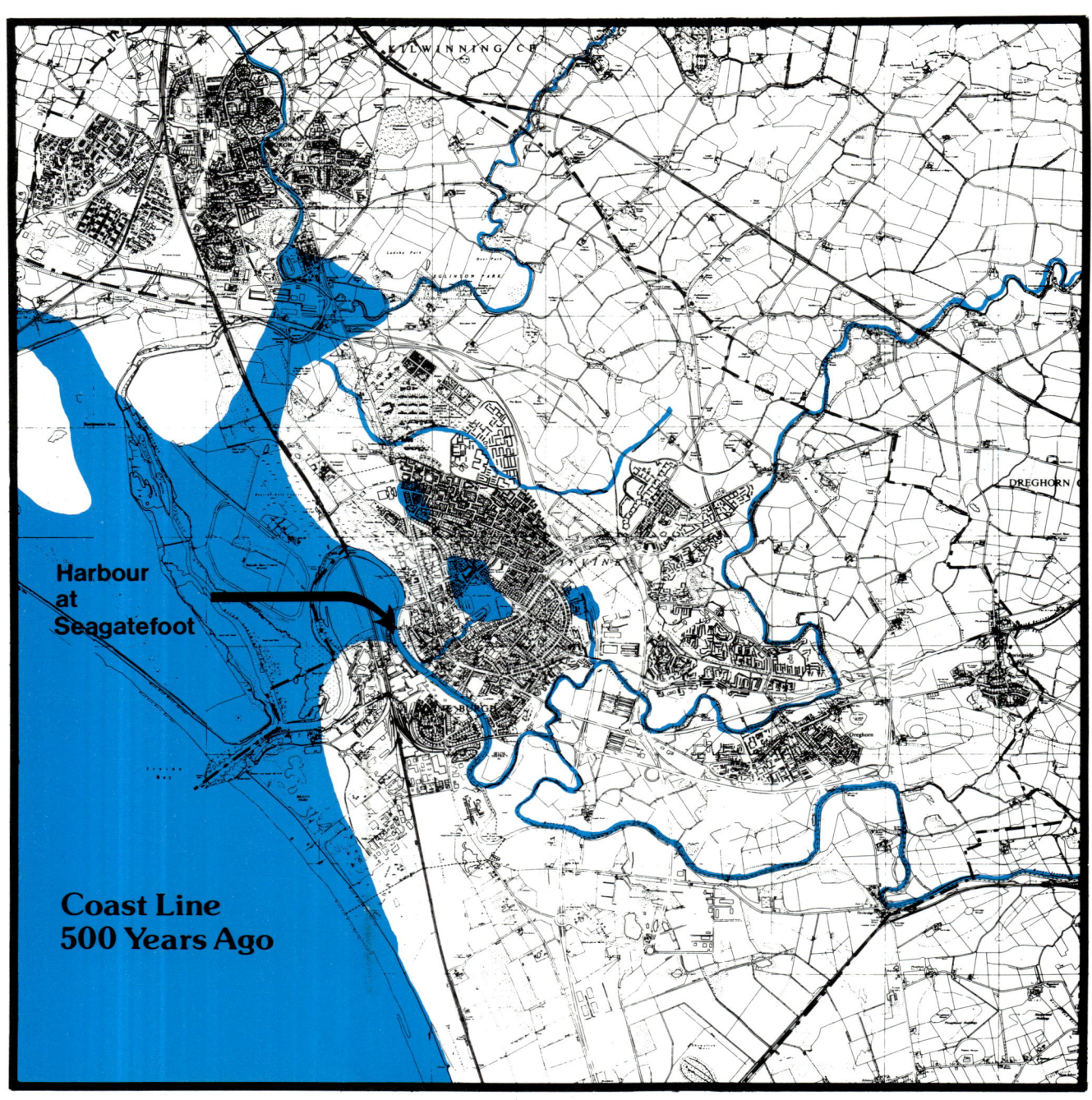

Five hundred years ago, Irvine had become established, facing the open sea. Small areas of loch still survived behind the town. The estuaries of the rivers Garnock and Irvine were in process of silting up.

Scottish towns held more than 5,000, with Edinburgh outranking them all with less than 300,000 inhabitants — all at a time when the total population of Scotland was around 800,000.

The extension of the Burgh's built-up area — the 'biggit land' — may be measured by passing references to properties in those various legal documents which happen to have survived. Although these were written in the quaint medieval Latin of local notaries, we can identify certain modern streets. High Street appears as the street of the market ('in vico Fori', 1324), the great street ('in magno vico ex parte orientali vici regi', 1452), and the king's street ('vici regii', 1455). We can note its northern extension into what is now Eglinton Street, for this is separately described as the street that leads to Kilwinning ('vici qui ducit as Kilvynryne', 1506). Seagate can be clearly identified ('in vico marino', 1419; 'viam, que ducit ad mare', 1506). Castle Street — once known as 'the Paith' — may be one of the vennels upon the Knowe ('super collam vulgo lie Know', 1617). At the other end of the Burgh what was to become the Glasgow Vennel was then known as Smithy Bar ('in locc qui dicitur ly Smethy Barr', 1426). Kirkgate has an early mention ('in vico ecclesie', 1324) as does the Kirk Vennel ('vennellam ecclesiasticam', 1419). What is sometimes referred to as a common vennel (e.g. 'communem vennellam', 1419) cannot always be located, but there is precise mention of that one leading from the Kirkgate down to the Puddle Ford ('vinellam que ducit ad aquam de Irwin', 1426). Building had extended to Mount Musart ('supra ly Mount Musart', 1426) to form as another vennel what is now Hill Street ('vinellam dictam Monkmosart', 1541). Further north, West Road seems to have existed as Sandyhill ('monte arenosa', 1477) and perhaps also as Sandgate ('ly Sandgat', 1499; 'via arenosa', 1542). Here too was a common way or passage leading to the Green ('viam communem sive passuagium qui itur ad viridarium', 1616). The Green itself is first mentioned in 1499. Even the less attractive, low-lying, and cramped borders of the open drain that bisected the Burgh were built upon to form what was then called the Grip ('le Grip', 1477) and afterwards Chapel Lane. Its westward extension was also built up ('vennellam que descendit ad vadum fratrum', 1477; 'viculum qui ducit ad aquam', 1508). And here too is the first mention of the Bridgegate ('via pontis', 1506). There is one isolated mention of a Friarsgate ('the frere zet', 1540) which may have been an alternative name for Bridgegate or Kirkgate.

High Street has perhaps always been known by that name. The various Latin forms cited above may simply have been attempts at translation, though it is possible that the designation was indeed Marketgate, Meiklegate, or King's Street. Kirkgate, Seagate, and Bridgegate are accepted names of long standing. It is of course incorrect to presume that 'gate' implied a barrier. The appropriate usage of 'gate' or 'gait' survives in the Scots proverb of 'gang your ain gate' and old-fashioned English expressions like 'walking with an awkward gait'. It means a walk, or in this case a street leading to the kirk, to the sea, to the bridge. Oddly, the name Sandgate has failed to survive. Of the lanes called vennels, only the Kirk Vennel retains the old name. The vennel on what was variously called Hill Mosard, Mount Musart, Makmusarthill, McMisserthill, Mizarhill, and Monmisarhill lost not only the name of vennel but also the mysterious designation — perhaps from Mount Mizar in Psalm 42 — to become simply Hill Street. By contrast, the vennel which was originally called Smithy Bar or Smiddy Bar was named Glasgow Vennel only from the 18th century. Of the tracks which skirted the town, that stretch on the west which led towards the harbour may have been called Sandgate, but the first houses built there were described as on Sandyhill, known later as Hamil Hill (after a 17th-century burgess) and as McFarlane's Hill (in the next century). Across it ran the Westbackside, or West Back Way. This became the West Back Road, and like its partner the East Back Road, acquired in 1895 the present more euphonious abbreviated name. One old name which long survived was the Gryp, the Grup, the Gruipe Guitter, 'the vennel or stank commonly called the Grip' (1616). When the loch was drained in 1698, the stream through the Grip dried up. It was later renamed Chapel Lane, but the old name continued in use. One short lane leading from it into the Bridgegate was sometimes known as the Wee Grip. The other from the Grip towards the bridge took the name of Rotten Row, another term whose interpretation has inspired much speculation.

Each medieval Burgh for its security required an encircling wall and gateways called ports where the main thoroughfares entered the built-up area. Each burgess for private as well as communal security erected a dyke at the end of his toft — here nothing as elaborate as a military fortification but sufficient to prevent the illicit access of packhorses or mounted men. Fragments of such walls may still be traced. A similar function was required of the gateways, to keep out unwelcome visitors. That Irvine's ports were not very substantial in construction is apparent because in 1499 an inquiry had to be held to decide where they were! It is certain that the Townhead Port was situated at the end of High Street just before the Kirk Vennel and the Smithy Bar — marking the eastern bounds of the town. It seems possible that in the first instance there was a west port at the other end of the market precinct, just before Bridgegate turned off, with the Gruipe Gutter stream lying then outwith the built-up area. Or perhaps it was just beyond, where the highway crossed the stream. Later, as

10 *The History of Irvine*

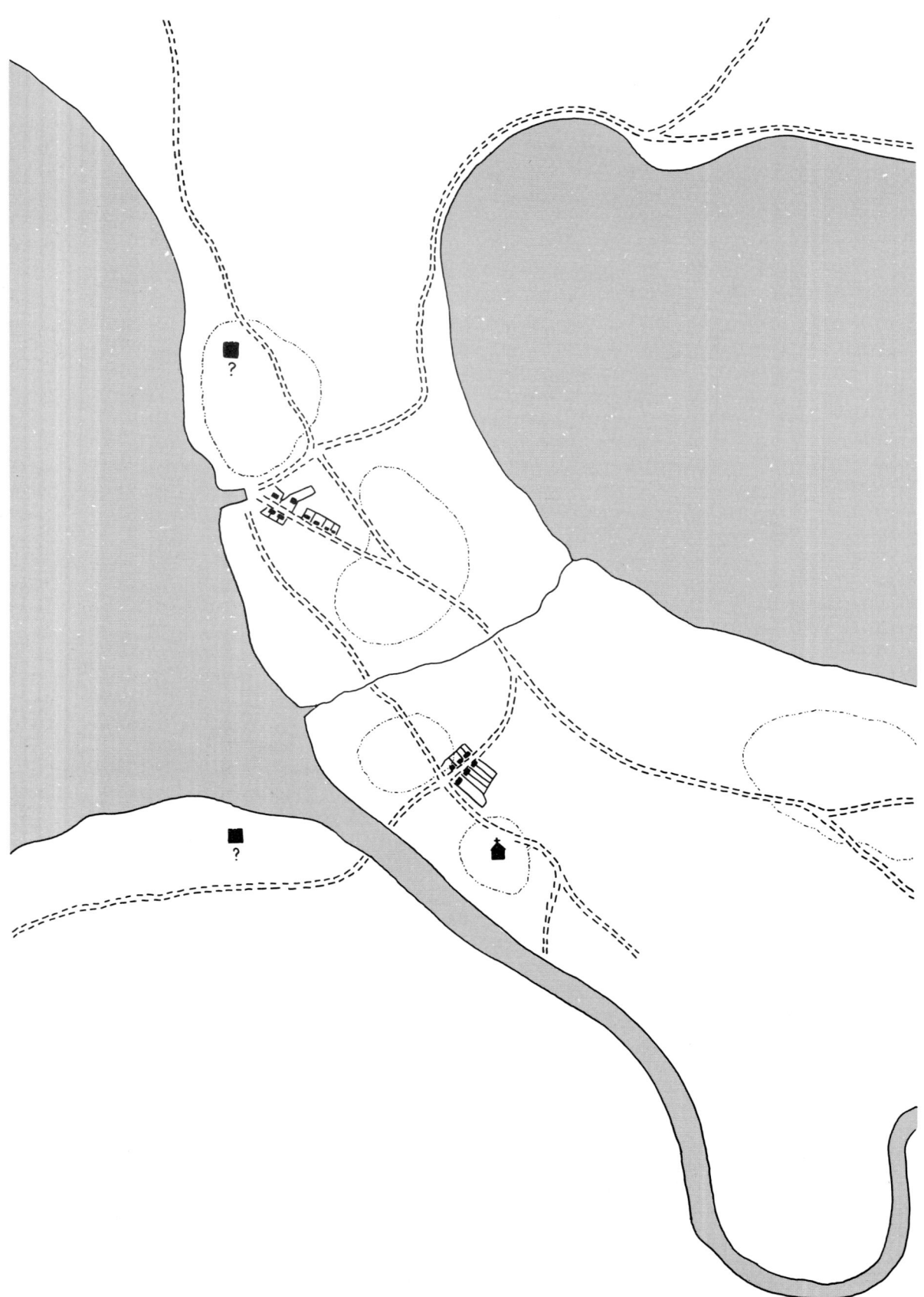

Early Days in the Burgh 11

Irvine Old Parish Church occupies the site of an earlier church. There may have been a place of worship here since the 5th century. On the river below is the ancient Puddleford.

the Burgh was extended, the port was sited further along Eglinton Street beyond the Seagatehead — variously known as the West Port, the North Port, or the Townend Port. At the Tailor's Straun the town's officers on parade used to lower their halberts, long after the gateway had gone. Access to the Burgh via Seagate, Bridgegate and Kirkgate must also have been controlled, perhaps by yetts or simple gateways. The ports were opened daily from dawn till the evening curfew, and tolls were charged on incomers arriving to buy and sell at the market.

The market cross was, as McJannet appropriately remarked, 'the focus of the Burgh, the point at which all its activities converged, the meeting place of the burgesses, the spot at which proclamations must be made, at which important acts must be done, the scene of public rejoicings of all kinds, and the dreaded theatre of punishment and shame'. Only the site survives, marked by cobbles on the roadway, of what is said to have been a magnificent cross. The 1914-18 war memorial erected nearby in the style of a typical Scots mercat cross suggests what it may have looked like.

A tolbooth was erected soon after 1386. In that year Robert II supplemented his earlier Charter by another generous grant — that of an area 40 feet long and 30 feet broad on the king's highway, for a nominal rent. There the burgesses might erect 'a decent and fair house, in which they may hold their public and private councils, that it may be a court house'. The original structure was eventually extended to form an impressive two-storey building, with walls four feet thick, and crowned by a tower. The Council room, court house and prison were reached by a flight of steps rising up from beside the market cross. At the other, western, side of the tolbooth was the Tron, or burgh weighing machine.

When a bridge was first erected at Irvine goes unrecorded. Though Ayr had its bridge as early as the year 1236, there would seem to have been none here at the end of that century, on the evidence that Wallace engaged the English at a ford crossing. Perhaps a first timber structure would date from the 14th century. If the burgesses could build a tolbooth in 1386, they could surely have afforded a bridge. The present Auld Brig over the Ayr may have been constructed in 1491, and it is possible that Irvine soon sought to emulate its rival royal burgh. 1506 provides the first mention of the Bridgegate, which implies the existence of a bridge of some sort. A bridge is first recorded in 1533, and it is guessed that is was of stone. In 1578 the whole of Ayrshire was required to contribute to its repair, and there was a dispute until Ayr agreed to pay its stent for 'mending of the Brig of Irvine'. For repairing the 'decayit brig' in 1589 the burgh was empowered to levy pontage tolls on all who crossed the bridge. These petty customs payable at a

Site plan, 1200. It is difficult to imagine how different in the 13th century was the site where Irvine would be established. The river emptied into a wide bay. Inland was a great loch. On the isthmus between were low hills — contours shown at 45 feet or 15 metres above present sea level. The highest point was occupied by a church (first recorded in 1233). To the north the Lords of Cunninghame had a wooden castle (noted in 1184) perhaps at Gallowsknowe overlooking the cove. The land across the river in Kyle belonged to the Fullarton family (whose first recorded member died in 1280). The line of ancient tracks may be guessed.

12   *The History of Irvine*

A stone tower castle at the Seagate dating from the 14th century was followed by the 16th century 'Palace'. This is the earliest picture, drawn by John Ainslie in 1790 for the Eglinton Estate Plan Book.

bridge toll bar were leased annually by public roup. Just a few years later Timothy Pont could mention favourably that 'neir to ye toune the River Irwyne is over passed by a faire stone Bridge'.

Before there was a bridge, and indeed afterwards, the river was easily though less conveniently crossed by fords. The Chapelford was at the foot of Chapel Brae ('viam discendendo ad aquam de Irwin', 1572) beside the Chapel Well, and has only a passing mention ('the common vennel leading to the Chapelfurd and Golfhills', 1616). The Puddleford was approached on the western side of the church — 'at the head of the Kirkgate ... the common vennel called the Puddingfuird' ('vocatum lie Puddingfuird', 1620). This was an obvious principal approach to the town from the other side of the river. This ford was, according to tradition, the site of Puddlie-deidlie, a skirmish between Wallace and the English. Explanations of the name range from 'deadly-fight' to 'holy steps', and the name is sometimes given as Puddliedoodly. The 'holy steps' (pas de Dieu) may have been stepping stones used by the Carmelite friars on their way to Irvine Parish Church. The stepping stones themselves may have been derived from the old circle of Standing Stones, of which the Granny Stane alone survives some yards downstream. Just below where Irvine Bridge was built, there was the Friars Ford ('vadum fratrum', 1477) associated with the Carmelite friars from Friars Croft on the Fullarton bank and leading by the Grip into the town. After 1695 when the transport of coals across the bridge was prohibited, this ford under the name of the Carford was used by the 'cars' as the coal carts were called. Not far downstream was the Marress ford, which led across from the Towns Green, and where stepping stones were laid in 1853.

The opposite bank of the river was, of course, outwith the burgh and indeed beyond the bounds of Cunninghame. Fullarton was part of the parish of Dundonald and within Kyle Stewart. It was occupied in the late 13th century by Alan de Fowlertoun, who received it from the High

West Road follows an early path from the harbour at Seagatefoot leading towards the church.

Stewards, the superiors of the northern part of Kyle. This Fullarton estate was later extended to the east and south, to include Shewalton, part of Dreghorn, Gailes, Crosbie, Troon and other properties in the neighbourhood. Sometime in the 14th century one of the Fullarton family provided the Carmelite friars with the lands known as Friars Croft. The first lairds of Fullarton had their residence hereabouts. Some say where Fullarton Place later led on to Irvine Bridge; some would locate it upriver nearer to Puddleford. George Foullertoun, who held the lands from 1430 till 1471, was more often known as Laird of Crosbie. It was probably he who moved the family seat to Crosbie, where it remained till a new Fullarton House was built near Troon in 1745. Among George's possessions, Marress is first mentioned (1464). From the 13th century the Fullartons had extensive fishing rights, defined as 'from the Trune to the water mouth of Irvine, and thence up the water as far as the lands of Fowlertoun go'.

Where the water mouth was has been much disputed. Robert Whyte in his thoughtful lectures always argued that 'though Pont in his map of Irvine dated about 1600 shows the river flowing into the sea without making its last loop, and also shows the mouth of the Garnock about two miles north of the mouth of the Irvine ... yet ... the river entered the sea in 1600 in roughly the same place as today and so too did the Garnock. The harbour might vary with the state of the river, the state of tides, and with the size of vessels, but the barmouth was approximately where it is today'. He cited as evidence that in 1572 the burgh purchased that piece of the Marress where the railway bridge now crosses the river; a lease of 1602 from John Darleith of the salmon fishing in the mouths of the two rivers, which Whyte thought unlikely if these were two miles apart; and the fact that by 1700 the lands of Bogside were being eroded by the river. He concluded that 'if at one time the sea lapped the walls of Seagate Castle, it must have been many centuries

The path from harbour and castle towards the church crossed Mount Musart by what is now Hill Street.

before'. But the street past the Castle was called Seagate — and not Rivergate. It seems unlikely that a burgh like Irvine would be sited at a spot without open access to the sea. Examples could be found of other trading ports which were adversely affected by the recession of the sea. Pont's map and other early charts certainly suggest that at some recent period Irvine harbour was less confined. Paterson in his County history rightly describes this area as 'an extensive tract of low marshy lands, many hundred acres of which, at no distant period, were overflowed promiscuously with the waters of this river and the tides of the ocean'. We can perhaps reconcile the existing evidence by suggesting the lands of Marress and Bogside emerging from the sea as salt-flats, then reclaimed land, in the 14th and 15th centuries; their convergence creating the problems first noted in the 16th century; with later difficulties as the rivers meandered over the flat lands beside their estuaries.

The first contemporary piece of evidence is from an English military report written between 1563 and 1566: 'The Town of Irrewing; being a burrow towne, eight myles Northwartes from Are, fare waye over the sandes And having a porte and haven, not verye good, being but a faddome three quarters at the full sea, A narrow Incomyng, through a bank upon both sydes, and a barred haven'. Only a few decades afterwards Timothy Pont supplemented this: 'Irrwyne Toun, this the head burrough and chieffe porte of ye country of Cuninghame the port and harbry being now much decayed from quhat it was anciently being stopt with shelves of sand wich hinders the neir approch of shipping'. Neither of these documents mentions a river whose course was blocked; both imply a port to which acess was impeded by drift sands. So did the complaint of the Burgh Council in 1596 that the water mouth was 'overblawne and fillit with sand'. Some time later in 1655 Thomas Tucker confirmed this, describing the port of Irvine as 'at present clogged and almost choaked up with sand, which the Westerne Sea beats into it'.

In 1572 the Council of the Burgh initiated some action. Several years before in 1546 John Foullartoun had sold Shewalton to Edward Wallace and in 1566 had similarly sold to him and John Wallace of Dundonald the lands of Marress, together with the fishing in the water mouth of Irvine as far as the bridge. In 1572 the burgh entered into a contract with them to secure a piece of the Marress to form a quay 'for lowsing and lading of thair ships, boats and merchandise, and the merchandise of whatsover others that shall happen to resort towards the said burgh, upon the foresaid lands of Marress on other side of the Water of Irving with a sufficient gait and passage through the foresaid lands'. They might dam the river if they wished to divert its course provided the arable land of Marress was not affected. It proved difficult to implement this scheme, however. Though granted the revenue from the customs for five years after 1579, collection proved awkward. William and Hugh Scott, though 'custumars' deriving their livelihood from the levy on exports, refused to contribute. Commissioners appointed to discuss possible improvements failed to report, and their successors of 1590 were equally unproductive. In 1594 the Council sought 'support to the buying and bigging of ane harbery'; in 1596 they proposed a new port for Irvine on the Island of the Little Cumbrae; in 1608 they settled on Troon as an alternative. Provost Archibald George was instructed to go to Edinburgh to engage a master of works. James Weir, a miller from Stevenston, was put in charge of the work and instructed to bring two picks, twelve wedges, and a little iron mell. Indwellers — those not of burgess rank — were conscripted. The town was divided into five quarters, and each house had to furnish one man for one day's work each week. But 'their new erectit herbere called the Trone' proved unsatisfactory and was abandoned. Imposts devised to assist the various schemes seem to have been

When Bridgegate House was built in 1973, a passage through the modern building perpetuated the ancient right-of-way linking harbour and church.

insufficient. As the 17th century advanced, renewed efforts were made to renovate the existing facilities at Irvine.

Despite the obvious difficulties, the harbour always continued to operate. Indeed Bishop Leslie, writing in 1578, referred to its 'commodiousness … nocht mekle inferiour to Air'. Sir William Brereton in 1636 thought it 'daintily situate upon a navigable arm of the sea'. Though he found Irvine had only three or four vessels, the biggest not exceeding 16 tonnes, Renfrew had no more, and those only 5 or 6 tonnes each; Glasgow had only a dozen ships in all, half of them admittedly much bigger, from 100 to 150 tonnes.

Through the harbours of the royal burghs were imported goods that only the feudal landlords and burgess merchants could afford — wines from Bordeaux; spices, fine cloth, and luxury items bought in the Netherlands; raw materials for the craftsmen, bar iron from Sweden, timber from Norway; salt suitable for fish curing from Brittany and Spain; and grain in times of dearth. Such goods were handled by Irvine merchants for sale throughout Cunninghame. Although there are no surviving records, there are passing references to French ships at Irvine in 1499, 1524 and 1577; and in 1617 a local vessel was lost on a voyage to France with Provost Andrew Tran aboard. Exports were what could be produced locally. Fragmentary customs records for 1519-22 indicate that the products exported from Irvine were hides, woollen cloth, salmon and herring. There would also be trade with Ireland and the Western Highlands in cattle and various locally-manufactured items, and in 1542 comes a first mention of twenty tons of coals being shipped from Irvine.

The hides for export were processed by the skinners of the

High Street was from the beginning of the burgh a broad thoroughfare designed for market purposes.

burgh, while the cordiners worked in leather. The websters of the town and country wove plaiding or coarse woollen cloth, with waulkers or fullers doing the finishing, and the tailors making up garments for local use. Other goods for the local market were manufactured in wood by the wrights or squaremen, and in metal by the smiths and hammermen. The other principal craft in the burgh was that of the coopers, whose barrels were necessary for the export of salted fish. Timothy Pont reminds us that 'ther is plentey of salmons takin in this River', and many went for export. Herring fishing was also important, and in the 15th and 16th centuries the fishing fleet from Irvine, in little open galleys operated by four men in each, was plying in Loch Fyne and other waters of the West Highlands. While most of the catch went to the local market, barrels of salt herring found their way to the Continent: 1481 was a peak year, with £45 worth of fish exported — seven times as much as Ayr.

That the merchants who handled all this trade were extending their business was seen when in 1532 John Mure, bailie and later provost, took over two 'bornys' or storehouses at the Townhead. That commerce was augmenting the local population is seen by the development of the town mills where all meal for foodstuffs had to be processed.

The first mention of a mill is in 1391. This was the Howmill or Hairsmill on the banks of the Irvine at Milgarholm. This property did not belong to the burgh, but a lease was taken of what was for a time the only 'burrowmill'. Sometime before 1555 an additional mill had to be provided. The Lochmill was erected on burgh land at Lochwards, deriving its power from water which drained from the loch into the Annick. Some of the water passed along the Headless Lady's Gott. There Irvine's only ghost was to be found — apart from the piper who walks the mythical tunnel between Seagate and Stane castles. Very close by Lochmill there was another mill, on the bank of the Annick itself. It may have been quite old when it is first mentioned in 1642 as the Water Mill. The Water Mill became known as the Slate Mill. Since *schlut* is the Dutch word for lade or water-course, this has suggested an origin for the name. But in fact the change of name may have followed the slating of the mill in 1680. How the mills were managed is explained on the occasion when all three were

Old walls, as behind 37 High Street, mark boundaries which are over seven hundred years old.

leased by the burgh in 1659 to Robert Galt and his family who were 'honest yeomen folks, fermourers, and mylners'. Their income would be derived from 'all manner of corn, beir (barley), wheat, peas, rye, and other stuff grindable growing and that shall happen to grow upon the ground of all lands whatsoever belonging to the said burgh'. As was customary, all persons were 'thirled' to a mill and bound to have their meal ground there, the miller being recompensed by keeping some of it as 'multures'. Much further up the Annick Water was the Friersmill which served the landward part of the parish. Somewhere on the other bank of the Irvine in Dundonald Parish there was a Fullarton Mill, perhaps the Wackmil marked on Pont's map of Kyle, and also Shewalton Mill. Of Irvine's three mills, only the Slate Mill survived. The drainage of the loch eventually put Lochmill out of business. Howmill was left high and dry by a change of the river's course. It was replaced by Newmill in Dreghorn parish, which not very long afterwards suffered the same fate.

By the 16th century the town of Irvine was extending towards the mills, with building in the Townhead beyond its earlier confines. The town was not only growing but changing in character. Only slowly, however, were the wooden houses replaced. There was a Sklate Hall (1419); and a house in the Seagate 'now roofed with tiles' ('nunc tegulati', 1542) which suggests also a stone-built building. In 1599 the town was 'decayit with sudden fire', possibly involving that part of the High Street opposite the tolbooth, judging by the number of 'waste' properties noted there in Robert Broun's protocol book of 1613–20. In 1617 stone was still sufficiently uncommon for 'two tiled tenements' to be noted. In 1649 the town was again ravaged by fire, a recurrent danger when houses were made of wood. But the necessary rebuilding probably involved an increasing use of stone. In the royal charter of 1601 the burgh was granted formal power to have a quarry, and it is possible that Duntonknoll was then worked. In 1577 the Earl of Eglinton contracted with a glass wright in Glasgow for the glazing of windows in his properties including those in Irvine.

The central area of the town had become congested. Houses fronting the High Street in particular were being extended with storehouses and back tenements erected down the tailrigs with access through closes. The highway itself was probably encroached upon, as forebooths were erected. The new stone buildings with their gables facing the street were often fronted with wooden extensions, the Timmerland being the last survivor of this pattern. One back tenement on the east side of the High Street had (1617) a hall, two other rooms (called the chamber of dice and the turnpike chamber), a kitchen, and stable. Another property on the opposite side had (1619) a fore tenement, under and above, with a back gallery, and two back lower houses in the close of that tenement, extending to thirty-four feet, with hall, bedchamber, and cellar. Another tenement in the Kirkgate (1616) had two back houses and a forebooth or shop — the first mention of a shop as such. By 1664 the Council was renting four such shops at the tolbooth.

Some of the 16th-century houses were impressive enough to have individual names. At the corner of High Street and Kirkgate was one known as Roxburgh, known to have had a beautifully panelled interior and wide open fireplaces. Probably on the same side of High Street were the Kanest, Lople, and Sklate Hall, with St. Wissing near the Bridgegate corner. On the opposite side near the cross was Convall's Walls. Some of these were townhouses for the landed gentry of Cunninghame. The Earl of Eglinton had not only Seagate Castle, but another house nearby, later called Castlepark, in the street which now bears his name. The Earl of Glencairn for a time owned Roxburgh. The Abbot of Kilwinning held Lople and an adjoining house. Others were possibly owned by the other great lords of Cunninghame — Boyd of Kilmarnock and Campbell of Loudoun — and certainly by the lairds of Caldwell, Giffordland, Lyne, Robertland, Annahill, and Stane; and by the lairds of Gadgirth, Adamton, and Barnweil in Kyle. An inventory was made in 1499 of the house of Craufurd of Giffordland, which suggests a measure of limited comfort. There were two dinner tables ('twa met burdis'), five benches ('a lang sedile' and 'iiii formys'), kitchen equipment ('twa pottis and a pane, a baike stule, and twa tubbis, ii barellis and a pipe', 'a ladile, a tyne stop'), three chests for storage ('ii kists' and 'ane ark'). There were five beds ('three ruche beddis', 'ii fedder beddis') with bedding ('ii bolstaris, also iii pare of schetis, ii blanketis, and thre coddis [i.e. pillows] and a covering'). There was 'ane irne chymne' with 'a tangis' to mend the fire. Some indication of contemporary costume may be derived from another inventory, that of the possessions of a distant cousin of the Earl of Eglinton, John Montgomerie of Brigend, an old blind bachelor who died in Irvine in 1612. He owned a chest, containing a fustian doublet cut out upon taffeta, a pair of red scarlet breeks, one coat, one pair of breeks of brown cloth, one pair of old breeks called of cloth of silver, one cloak of brown French cloth, one velvet hat, a pair of pistols, and a string of silk. These were valued

Chapel Lane, otherwise 'the Grip'. This formed the northern boundary of the early burgh. Along it flowed 'the Gruipe Gutter' draining waters from the loch.

at £14 Scots, a fraction of the sterling equivalent, and like other sums in early records difficult to assess by modern values.

The people of the early burgh must remain shadowy characters. Names of certain burgesses appear in an indenture of 1260, a church grant of 1324, and in the Exchequer Rolls for 1391. Persons are still for the most part designated by Christian name only. In the church grant, for example, the donor is 'Thomas, called Baxter, burgess of Irvine', and proprietors of neighbouring lands include 'William son of Henry son of the vicar', 'Isabella daughter of Rodger son of Fergus', 'James of the Crag', 'Martin son of Walter the cook', 'William son of Roger the Mount', 'William of the Stodegarth'. There is however Reginald Urry, perhaps a descendant of Adam Urry who witnessed the 1260 indenture. By the 15th century surnames have become usual as in another church grant witnessed by 'Hugh Clerk, John Fleming, Thomas Wilson, John Williamson, Michael Wilson, Alan Clerk, Adam Boyman, and Robert Boyman, burgesses'. By the 16th century documentation has become sufficient to attempt a fragmentary reconstruction of certain careers, like that of John Mure, the first recorded provost in 1540. He was perhaps one of the Mures of Caldwell, possibly a descendant of the 'young John Mure', a burgess mentioned in 1419, 1426, 1446, and 1445. Another of the same name had a house on the north side of the Bridgegate in 1506. The man who would become provost first appears definitely with a dozen others against whom there was a complaint in 1524 'for the wranguis defrauding of our soverane lordis costumis of their merchandice and guids sauld be thame to Frenchemen'. This indicates that he was one of Irvine's leading merchants, who were objecting to the mode of paying customs on their exports. By 1528 he was one of the burgh's two bailies; he was provost in 1540 and 1542; two years later he had reverted to bailie. We know that his residence was in the Kirkgate, and we can presume he was the John Mure who also had two houses in the Seagate (one of them new-tiled), others at Brigend and Montmisarthill, storehouses at Townhead, and a seventh property at the Cross beside the Fleshmarket, next to that called Convall's Walls. He also had land by the road leading to the Annick and another patch beside Chapel Brae. He or another of the same name was acting as a notary in 1557 and 1572. He was married to Jonet Howie and died sometime before 1615. A daughter Margaret died soon after, and his properties passed to his son Quintin. There was a John Mure in 1601 described as a skipper, another of 1699 who was a notary, and a third of 1668 who was a tailor. One of these was in 1645 a councillor, perhaps some relation of Irvine's first provost.

In 1540 when John Mure was provost, the bailies were Robert Scott and Steyn Tran. Scott was provost in 1543, and Stephen Tran followed between 1552 and 1557. Also a merchant with extensive properties, he founded a notable local dynasty. Patrick Tran was provost from 1591–3 and again in 1600. Patrick's eldest son Andrew was bailie from 1611 until he was promoted provost late in 1617. His tenure lasted only a few months. He set off for France on *The Gift of God* of which he was part-owner. It was lost with all aboard. Another of the family, Robert Tran, was a councillor in 1608. Still another, Robert Train from Irvine, became Minister of Eaglesham in 1635. In 1665 there is note of 'Maisteris Robert Tron schoolmaister of this brugh'. In August 1670 the burgh accounts allowed just over £1 to pay for 'The magistrats with Mr. Robert Trans some four mutchkins of wine and ane chapin of beir and tobacco and pypes'. A modest tribute perhaps to the Tran family for over a century of service to the royal burgh.

THREE

The Burgh Council

The origins of the town council are obscure. The earliest documents refer only to 'the burgesses and community of Irvine' who after 1386 had the tolbooth wherein to hold 'their public and private councils'. But regularly constituted councils apparently did not as yet exist. The crown required agents in the royal burghs, and certain burgesses were selected, originally to suit royal purposes, but coming to act as representatives of the burghal community. Two bailies are to be found in many burghs by the 14th century, and John of Glassauch and John Sakeschaw are mentioned as bailies of Irvine in 1391. An alderman is recorded in 1514, a provost in 1539, and in 1540 John Mure is named. There was a town clerk in 1502 called Thomas Young. The first specific mention of a council is in a royal letter of 1529 to 'the ballies counsale and communite of our burgh of Irwin'. The whole body of the burgesses was apparently by 1537 concerning itself in an annual choice of councillors at the court following Michaelmas. Such elections by 'ane multitude ... of simple persons fremen' was not to the liking of the crown. There was an instruction that the choice be made only by 'the best and wourthiest of our said burgh'. The 1372 charter had indeed authorised the creation of a guild, with the wealthier merchants forming such a privileged caste among the burgesses. But no merchant guild as such developed here, and all burgesses were casually regarded as guild brethren. An Act of 1469 ruled that in burghs each new council should be chosen by the old, and in 1537 this parliamentary legislation was belatedly enforced upon Irvine, introducing a system which would prove to be long lasting. The less affluent craftsmen did in fact later win some limited representation, but control of the council was effectively in the hands of the wealthier merchants. The franchise was restricted, and the status of burgess was privileged. No other was legally entitled freely to trade or carry on business within the burgh.

The powers of the early burgh council were extensive and, as will become apparent, differed considerably from the functions of a 20th-century local authority. The council had a wide judicial responsibility. The burgh court held in the tolbooth had power over cases ranging from theft to manslaughter, if committed within the burgh whether by burgess, indweller, or visitor. A burgess could claim the right to be tried within his own burgh. To secure such 'repledging' involved periodic disputes with other judicial authorities. For example, in 1459, 1460 and 1472 certain burgesses of Irvine had their charges transferred from the court of justice ayre of the king held in the burgh of Ayr. In 1539 the sheriff of Ayr and the bailie of Cunninghame were reproved for similarly infringing the judicial liberties of the burgh of Irvine. In 1586 a burgess on trial at the High Court of Justice in Edinburgh had his case remitted to Irvine following evidence presented by John Broun, the first person to be described as 'procurator' for the burgh. Punishment in those days might involve an *unlaw*, as a fine was called; a short spell of incarceration in the gaol for debtors and such; public exposure in the stocks, cuck-stool, jougs, or branks; with the possibilities of flogging, branding, mutilation or execution. Whenever the burgh lacked a hangman, that duty had to be performed by the younger bailie. The Gallows were presumably on that knoll, the Gallows Knowe, which was levelled early in the 19th century — north of the burgh on the edge of the Moor, behind where Heathfield was later built.

The council also had fiscal responsibilities. The king was entitled to revenue from a royal burgh — the annual rents which the burgesses owed their superior; the petty customs levied at the ports and at the market; and the great customs collected at the harbour. The first two — the 'burgh-mails' — for convenience were converted into a fixed 'feu-ferme' payable to the crown by the burgh, arranged in the case of Irvine in 1413. Collection of the great customs — levied on certain exports — was delegated to a burgess nominated as custumar or customs officer, but evasion was so common that in 1527 the crown here adopted the alternative method of leasing the right to collect these harbour customs. In addition to such recognised payments to the king from the burghs, what were originally regarded as exceptional levies developed into a tax imposed on landowners and on the burghs. The surviving stent rolls for 1535–37 reveal incidentally that among the Scottish burghs, Ayr ranked tenth and Irvine sixteenth. Such taxes were naturally unpopular. In 1570 the provost and bailies were instructed to 'chairge the inhabitaris off oure said burgh of Irwin to convene and elect certane persones to stent thair nychtbouris ... undir the paine of rebellioun'. In 1580, despite a complaint about the hardship involved for 'a nowmer of thame that was puir men', Irvine burgh was required 'to tax everie ane within the samin according to thair habilitie', which — if it were ever implemented — would have required a local income tax.

There were other impositions. To assist the king in his times of need involved more than financial assistance. Each burgess was expected to equip himself with arms for the defence of the burgh, and there were periodic 'wappin schewings' on Irvine Moor. In 1514 the burgh had to provide vessels and mariners for James V's expedition against the Lord of the Isles, and just a month later to send all fencible men with arms to assist in war against the English. Similar requisitions are recorded for later years and no doubt occurred earlier too, often straining the burgh budget. Another requirement, later prized as a constitutional right, was originally regarded as an irksome duty — representation at parliament. A commissioner from Irvine seems to have attended the Perth parliament of 1430; certainly attendance is recorded for 1469; and Irvine burgh continued to send its own member — usually the provost — until the extinction of the Scots parliament in 1707. As one of his duties, the Irvine commissioner for 1592 was required to attend with 'our nobilitie and estaittis' at Holyrood in prospect of the birth of a royal prince. The association of the monarch with this one of his seventy royal burghs could only occasionally be immediate. Robert II, that benefactor of Irvine, retired to spend the last two years of his long life at Dundonald Castle, and it has been guessed that between 1388 and 1390 he 'frequently visited Irvine'. So did Robert III, his successor. In 1400, when in Irvine, he sealed a charter to the burgh of Ayr — as did James II in 1458. And in 1405 Robert III purchased some furnishings in Irvine for Dundonald Castle. In 1506, 1507 and 1512 James IV visited Irvine. Later, on 2nd August 1563, Mary Queen of Scots, after spending a day and night at Eglinton, travelled on to Ayr. As she passed through her burgh of Irvine she may well have been offered the loyal greetings of the council. The fertile imagination of later generations has conceived some colourful but quite fictional ceremonial, supposedly derived from this occasion.

The Council had perforce as agent for the crown or on its own initiative to attend to various necessary duties. In 1500, because of a visitation of 'the pest or plague', entry was restricted. Again in 1545 Mary Queen of Scots, 'understanding that her burgh of Irvine was infected with a contagious plague', granted the council special powers because 'divers lieges and inhabitants of the burgh put themselves in opposition thereto, whence the said pestilence would apparently infect the whole country'. In 1599 aid was sought by the council when the burgh was 'decayit ... with sudden fire'. Apart from such emergencies, the council was regularly involved with such public utilities as the tolbooth, the bridge, and the harbour. From time to time it had to concern itself with everyday nuisances, and increasingly so as the town grew it had to attend to what were then called the 'commone werkis'. But those functions which would much later become the main business of a local authority, of providing environmental and other services, were as yet peripheral to the activities of the council. The early burgh was not an agent of public welfare, but a corporation with landed and commercial interests, whose purposes were economic rather than social.

The burgh territory was a considerable area. The council was responsible for the built-up area, the 'biggit land', otherwise the 'terra burgalis'; the cultivated lands of the Back Riggs forming the 'terra campestris'; and also the 'terra communis' which included land between the Red Burn and the Annick Water and may originally have comprised almost all of Irvine parish.

The 'terra burgalis' was composed of the tofts which came to form the town of Irvine, granted on burgage tenure to those who became burgesses. These tofts could be inherited, disposed of to other incomers, or acquired by some burgesses who were prosperous enough eventually to control a number of properties. In each case the transfer of land required the approval of the council, symbolised in a ceremony of conveyance. Details of several hundred such transactions are recorded in the protocol books of two local notaries — Cuthbert Simpson (1499–1513) and Robert Broun (1613–20). The provost or a bailie met the parties concerned on the land itself. The grantor returned the land to the burgh, whereupon a new infeftment was made, and the new occupant took formal possession by seizing a handful of earth and stones — the process of 'sasine'. Any incomer thus acquiring land in the burgh had to become a burgess by paying the 'burgess fine' — which also was paid at a reduced rate by any indweller who inherited or purchased a burgage holding. Some incomers were even able on occasion to pay such a fine for the sole purpose of trading freely within the burgh. But in 1595 such 'outtintoun burgesses' were deprived because they 'duellis nocht nor makis nocht actuale residence thairinto and ar traffiqueris as friemen'. The extensive list included persons from all parts of Cunninghame, from Largs to Newmilns.

Burgesses holding tofts within the 'terra burgalis' could

22 *The History of Irvine*

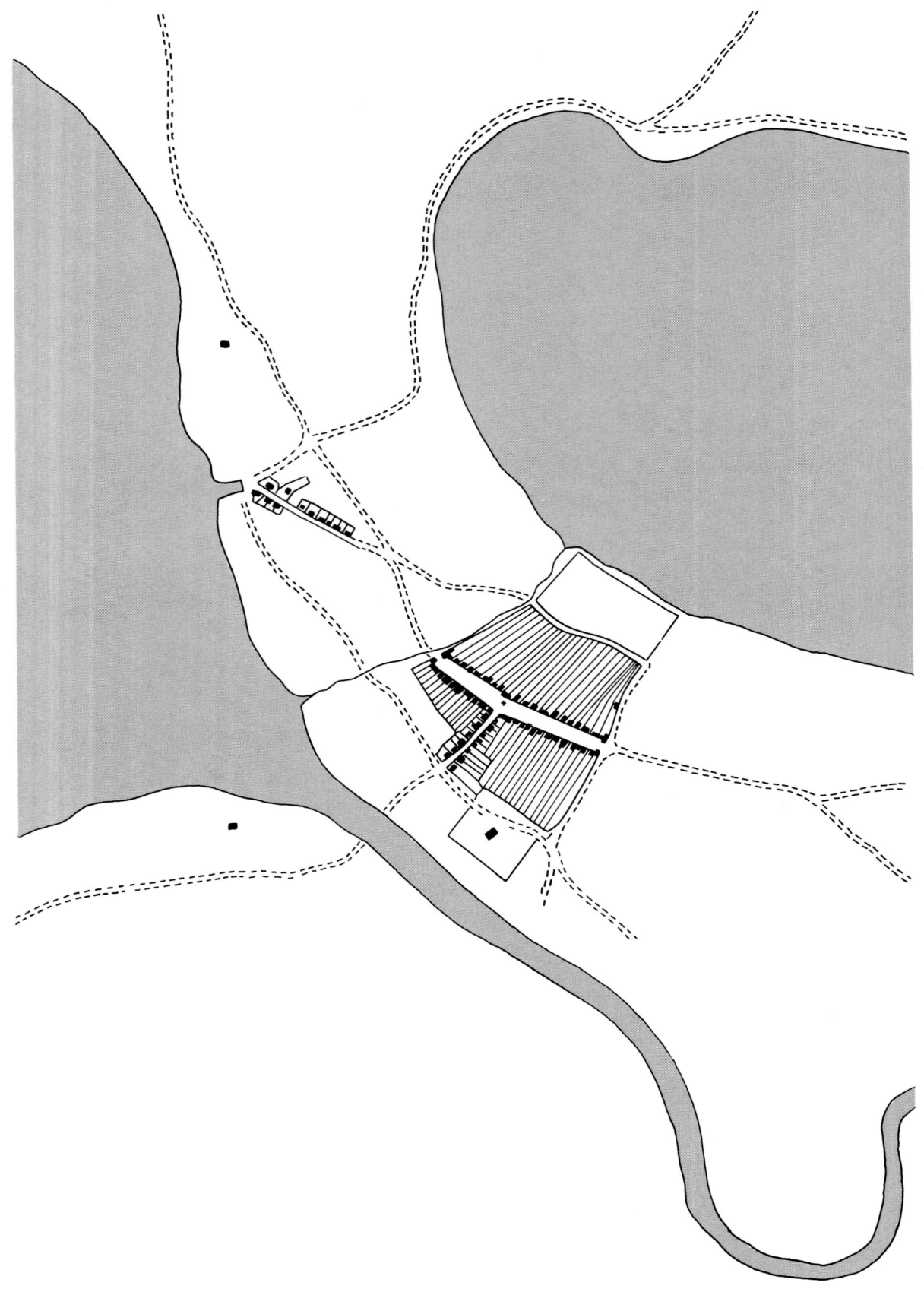

The centre of the burgh was the Cross, first mentioned in 1260, and still marked on the roadway outside the Town House. The old market cross was demolished in 1694, but the 1914-18 War Memorial was imaginatively designed as a replica.

The tolbooth was erected soon after 1386 and later extended to contain council chamber, court room, and prison. Beside it, as this 19th-century drawing shows, was the tron or weighing machine.

share in the cultivated land on the precincts of the town which formed the 'terra campestris'. The original Backriggs lay to the east beyond what became known as the East Back Road, between the 'biggit land' and the loch. As the town extended into the Sandyhill area, an additional area was brought under the plough beyond the West Back Road. Later as Townhead was built up, new Back Riggs were formed on both sides of the road behind the building plots. By the 17th century a further area had been reclaimed beyond the loch in a tract of land stretching from Dunton Knowe towards Hayholm. This 'Toune's Land' was leased by roup to burgesses. It illustrates the operation of the runrig system whereby there was a periodic redistribution of the better 'infield' and the poorer 'outfield' land. Seventy-eight acres were divided into twenty-six lots, each containing an acre of infield and two separated acres of outfield, and in 1668 'the samen was given out to the Inhabitants be lott for the ensweing sevin years'. While in the first instance the Backriggs formed a necessary source of produce to feed a largely self-sufficient community, as commerce increased and some burgesses concentrated on mercantile pursuits, such land might be neglected. So in 1430 the burgh of Irvine thought fit to apply an Act anent Waste Burgh Lands — 'By taking of earth and stone of the said lands ... at the fourth court, if the lands shall not have been redeemed ... [such waste lands shall] remain in free heritage and property of the community of the said burgh for ever'.

On the 'terra communis' the townsfolk found pasture for their cattle. The extensive Moor to the north of the Burgh was the most convenient location for this long-surviving practice. by 1782 there were only thirty-six beasts — burgesses paid 8/- per cow, and others 15/-. Provost John Paterson remembered the last Towns Herd, William

Town plan, 1300. When a burgh was established, probably by William de Morville between 1230 and 1249, this 'new town' was planned on the flat sheltered area behind the church. Burgage plots were laid out on both sides of the wide Marketgate or High Street. By 1300 the first phase of development was complete. The river was crossed at the Puddleford, where William Wallace reputedly encountered the English (c. 1297).

High Street was an enclosed area, extending only as far as what became Bridgegatehead.

Houston, blowing his horn along the High Street in the year 1833. Traditionally the two Towns Herds sounded their horns to collect the cattle in time for the opening of the ports at five in the morning, and brought them back just before curfew. Grazing, however, was only one of the uses of the common land. It was the source of building materials — timber for house-building (and making furniture), straw and heather for thatch, turves for roof ridges, and the common land provided fuel — peat, broom and heather, plus wrack from the seashore.

Although there is no surviving cartulary evidence, it is probable that the burgh was originally endowed with an extensive tract of land comprising almost all of Irvine parish, and indeed beyond. The remote upland area seems to have been disposed of at an early date. Armsheugh was certainly part of the burgh territory. In 1260 Sir Godfrey de Ross was paying twice yearly to the burgh for 'Hormissock'. In 1361 Sir Hew de Eglinton acquired 'Hormishaw' and the adjacent lands of Doura, Patterton and Balgray. Of these three others, there is no proof of the burgh's superiority, but centuries later in 1664 the council noted that the 'few duty' for 'Ormescheoch' was 'long awand'. Part of Armsheugh in 1260 was already under the plough; part was still the Wood of Langhurst. The burgesses retained certain rights to pasture their cattle and to cut timber. Not long afterwards in 1295 or 1305 (not 1205 as formerly supposed) the burgesses ratified the transfer of twenty acres of land somewhere in the same area from Bryce de Eglinton to his younger brother Ralph. Some miles further off and now in the parish of Kilwinning is the significantly named Burrowland, from which the 17th-century burgh of Irvine received feu duty. It continued to appear long afterwards in the burgh records, sometimes under the alternative name of Montaber (Mount Tabor?). Nearby and also in Kilwinning parish was Groatholm, among Irvine burgh lands in 1689. Closer, in 1417 there was a dispute with William Francis of Stane regarding a piece of moorland, perhaps Knadgerhill, which is was confirmed did in fact belong to the burgh. In 1664 the burgh was receiving feu duties from the lands of Roddinghill, Holehouse and Friersmyln, but it is uncertain whether this superiority existed before these church lands were secularised in the 16th century. While there is doubt about just how extensive was the original burgh territory, a confirmatory Charter from James VI in 1601 indicated that the burgh was still a considerable landowner. The burgh was then in possession of lands most of which were situated around the perimeter of the steadily diminishing loch. To the north was the Gallowmure. To the east was Knadgerhill, then Newmure, and what was called Hiemyre. To the south beside the Annick Water were Weirisholme and Guildelandys. Between the town and the loch, at the head of the Smiddy Bar, were the Inner and Outer Bogfaulds, also known as Bogflatts. A rental of 1642 added some smaller patches of what may have been reclaimed from the loch. West of Knadgerhill was Busland or Bushlands, and Spittalmeadow. To the south-east were Scottswards or Lochwards (also known as Loch mill wards, Overwards, or simply Lochlands), Rood Meadow (sometimes Red or Rood Meadow), and Dalrymple wards. West of the Bogfaulds was the Braid Meadow. All these lands had been feued out. By contrast, Patoun's Thorne next to Scottsward is mentioned as being held in burgage tenure, suggesting that this had been part of the Backriggs. Other lands being feued were included in a 1664 list. These comprised the Twa Faulds near the Braid Meadow; Chappell and Chapelland east of the church, and some unidentified plots: St. James land, perhaps the same as a

High Street was extended towards Seagate. Near Seagatehead, at the beginning of Eglinton Street, was the Townend Port.

later St. John's land; McUnstanhill, which if not in error for what was later Kairde's Yairds west of McMusarthill may have been near the West Back Road; where also the Sandierig was presumably, and possibly also what is called Cowpers land. In addition to these lands which were feued out in perpetuity for fixed annual payments, other parts were 'sett' for short periods. These were recorded for 1664. Gooslone was presumably that extensive area later variously known as Goatfields, Gottfields, Goalfields and latterly Golffields. Further downriver, beyond the bridge, there was the Town's Green on reclaimed land, and 'the gras of the Grein' was 'sett' or leased. Across the river, actually outwith the burgh, the land of Marress had been purchased in 1572, later corrupted to Murray's Land. Inland, Rottenbog beside the Glebe Aiker was adjacent to Knadgerhill. Crocefurd was on the Red Burn on the way to Bartonholm. Redburn itself and Bogside were remoter parts of the Town Moor. Other plots leased out by 1689 were Kidsneuk near Redburn; Divet Park near Busland; and the unidentified McFade's Rig. Continued leasing of other parts of the Moor in the 18th century brought protests, and indeed riots. What was considered a sufficient area remained, though a mere fragment of the originally extensive 'terra communis'.

The primary function of the burgh council was to organise the markets and fairs which were indeed the basic reason for the burgh's existence.

To the markets farming folk of Cunninghame brought what they had for sale. By the end of the 16th century this was accounted a most productive area. Timothy Pont mentions good pasture for cattle; a plentiful supply of moorfowl, waterfowl, partridges and hares; and fish, particularly good trout, from the burns and loch. He noted that by liming their lands the industrious inhabitants had enriched their pastures and were already specialising in dairy farming, supplying butter to 'a grate pairt of ye kingdome'. The whole of Cunninghame was thickly populated 'so that one may much wonder how so small a bounds can contain so well so many people having no trade to live by but their husbandry and the rent arising from the ground except a few living on the sea coast by fishing'. Originally Irvine provided the only market within

Cunninghame. Burghs of barony catering for local trade were formed at Newmilns (1491), Kilmaurs (1527), Saltcoats (1529), Kilmarnock (1592), Largs (1595), Fairlie (1601) and Kilbirnie (1642). In 1538 the burgh of Irvine, while recognising poor chapmen 'that bears their pakkis upoun thair bakkis', sought a ban on those who organised illegal open markets 'upoun all sondayis at the paroch kirkis of Kilmarnock, Beith, Dalry, Largis and utheris kirkis within Cunynghame and sellis hyde, woll, skynnis, claith, meill, malt, fische, flesche, and chepmen heldis plane buthes and sellis all maner of small marchandice and cramry wair'. In 1617 and later they took specific action against the burgh of Kilmarnock for infringing Irvine's privileges of foreign trade.

It was worthwhile coming to the market of Irvine, for here could be purchased the products of the Irvine craftsmen. Although the new burghs of barony did have the privilege of carrying on crafts, the royal burghs of Irvine and Ayr were the only significant manufacturing centres, each with a range of trades. When in 1646 the council of Irvine burgh granted a seal of cause to the Incorporated Trades, this was a mere formal recognition of already well-established crafts. The Smith craft included the hammermen, not only blacksmiths but all other workers in metal. The Websters were the weavers of coarse woollen cloth, with whom the Tailors were associated. The Cordiners were the shoemakers and other workers in leather. The Skinners dealt in skins and hides, and there was at least one glover among them. The Wrights worked in wood — joiners, carpenters, squaremen or builders. Last were the Coopers making barrels and other wooden vessels.

While the craftsmen depended on the markets and fairs for sale of their products, these occasions were dominated by the merchants whose business involved both buying and selling, dealing in local commerce at the markets, and at the fairs involved in trade with other parts of Scotland and abroad. Foreign trade was a monopoly of the royal burghs, and the Irvine merchants — though they never formed themselves into a guild as the 1372 Charter had authorised — were powerful enough to control the council and manage the burgh in their own interests.

The usual original grant to a burgh was of a weekly market and an annual fair. It is not recorded when additional grants were made to Irvine. But — an indication of the burgh's progress — in James VI's Charter of 1601 it was confirmed that Irvine had the right to two weekly markets and three fairs each year. At the markets — on Monday and Friday — regular business was done around the Cross and fixed sites nearby in High Street. At the fairs all the main thoroughfares must have been crowded with temporary booths erected by travelling chapmen. The fair in August was always the most important. It may have originated with the pagan celebration of Lammas, converted to a Christian festival. It would seem to predate the year 1386 when land for building the tolbooth was granted by Robert II in return for an annual rent of one silver penny payable at the feast of the Assumption of the Blessed Virgin on 15th August. On 14th August 1540 Provost John Mure and Bailies Robert Scott and Steyn Tran proclaimed the royal protection 'upon the fayr eyne of the assumptione of our Ladye'. Thus Marymass is first described as held on the Festival of the Blessed Virgin Mary. In 1572 the Earl of Eglinton was allowed to 'keep the heid faire' on 15th August. In 1578 two fairs were listed, the first beginning on 15th August 'quilk is the first Ladie-day', the next on 8th September 'quilk is commonlie callit the latter Ladie-day'. Since these were only twenty-three days apart, and with harvest imminent, the second was to be postponed till 23rd October. In fact it was a supplement, for in 1601 the three fairs were 13th to 16th August; 7th to 10th September; and 23rd to 25th October. There were adjustments in 1693 and afterwards.

The prosperity of Irvine cannot properly be judged by an examination of the burgh finances. This was certainly so by the 18th century when corruption had become endemic in the affairs of the royal burghs. But a superficial analysis of the earlier burgh accounts does reveal something of the extent and character of the council's activities in the 17th and preceding centuries. Each year after the Michaelmas selection of a new council, an appointment was made of a provost, two bailies, procurator fiscal, and the 'thesaurer', that councillor who would be responsible for the burgh finances during the ensuing year. For the year 1593–94 income was £342 Scots and expenditure £353 Scots. In a much later but more informative year (1664–65) the income ('rents and casualties') amounted to £1508 Scots, around £128 in sterling. The expenditure ('dischairge') was £1420 Scots or £118 sterling. These figures are not in themselves particularly significant, but it is interesting to assess the relative importance of the constituent elements. The extensive burgh lands which had earlier been leased out in perpetuity for fixed annual payments produced what, as a result of inflation, was now the miserable sum of £43. Burgh fines which were the entry fees for new burgesses brought in £46. Unlaws amounted to £122, ranging from penalties imposed in the burgh court to levies on members absenting themselves from council meetings. The main single source of income was £726 from 78 acres of arable 'Toune land'. £184 came from the rent of the burgh mills. £276 was derived from a variety of items rouped for short fixed periods — various pastures and meadows, the grass of the town green, the bridge tolls (£22), the petty customs derived from the markets and fairs (£79), the great

At the east end of the burgh the Townhead Port was flanked on one side by the Kirk Vennel and on the other by Smiddy Bar, later called the Glasgow Vennel.

customs collected at the port — the 'water baillieship' (£65), and the 'teinds of cobbills' charged on fishing boats (£16). Since 1560 the town had also acquired £110 in church teinds to be applied thereafter towards the upkeep of church and school. The bailies were customarily responsible for collecting the Burgh Mails or burgage rents. These with the petty customs also due to the crown had in 1413 been commuted into a fixed 'feu-ferme' payment, and the surplus accruing formed the basis of the Common Good, into which other burgh profits might also be paid. Separately stentmasters were appointed to collect from the burgesses their contributions towards the increasingly frequent national tax levies and the more occasional levies by the council for various purposes. The expenditure of the Irvine council is less easy to calculate. It included payments to the crown; remuneration to officials — who were the councillors themselves apart from the common clerk; wages of lesser persons such as the drummer, bell-ringer, sergeant or court officer, and halberdiers; after 1560 the salaries of parish minister and schoolmaster; increasing sums spent on public works; and a regular and apparently lavish amount spent on hospitality.

The royal burgh of Irvine was proud and prosperous enough to acquire its appropriate recognition as a body corporate. On the common seal of the burgh (which was attached to official documents) the arms are portrayed. The earliest surviving seal (1552) represents the Virgin and Child on one side; on the other a lion chained between two trees. On the walls of the tolbooth at some time or other — possibly the 17th century — were engraved the royal coat of arms and those of the burgh, with a lion crowned sejant affronte, in his dexter paw a sword proper, in his sinister paw a sceptre, with the motto 'Tandem bona causa triumphat' — 'A good cause triumphs in the end'.

FOUR
Church and Castle

It has been claimed that the church of Irvine was founded by Inan, who is said to have died there in the year 839. In fact, there is no solid proof of who founded the church; and there may have been a place of worship there from the 5th century onwards. That first church must have been on the site of the present church, or nearby where there was a later Chapel to St. Mary. A second church is reputed to have been built early in the 12th century, presumably around the same time as the castle. The first documented reference to the parish church of Irvine is the year 1233 when it so happened that a dispute over a piece of land was settled in a court of law held here ('in parrochiali ecclesia de Yrewin'). This parish church was one of those within the deanery of Cunninghame and part of the diocese of Glasgow. It became attached to Kilwinning Abbey which collected its revenues from the parish, and was responsible for staffing the church. The church of Irvine was dedicated to the Blessed Virgin Mary, and the festival of Her Assumption on 15th August is still the time of Marymass. Perhaps significantly, this is very near 18th August when the festival of St. Inan might once have been celebrated.

The medieval church building which survived till the 18th century occupied the same site but was smaller in area than the present one. It was of the traditional cruciform plan, with nave to the west and chancel to the east. It had small lancet windows and a steeple or tower containing a bell. Inside there was the high altar, and at various dates were added other altars in little side chapels off the north and south aisles. The medieval church of Irvine must have become a rather splendid edifice. There were eventually altars to St. Katherine and St. Ninian (first noted 1419), St. Mary and St. Michael (1446), St. Peter (1455), St Conval, St. Stephen and St. Sebastian (1477), St. Salvator and St. Thomas (1506), St. John and St Christopher (1541), St. Nicholas (1542) and to the Holy Trinity and the Holy Blood (also first noted 1542). In addition there was a separate Chapel to St. Mary on the Bank beside the river (1452). These various altars were endowed by local benefactors who made provision for chaplains to serve them. There were at least seven chaplains thus assisting the parish priest.

While the priest was appointed by Kilwinning Abbey, the selection of chaplains was normally in the hands of the burgh council.

The first recorded church grant (1324) was by Thomas Baxter of annual rents for a chaplain to celebrate divine services for the souls of himself, his wife, and his family. William of Cunninghame, vicar of Dundonald and son of the lord of Kilmaurs, similarly made provision for his father, mother, and relations (1419) and also for King James I and the royal family (1426). Lady Alice Campbell of Loudoun also provided (1446, 1452) masses for the royal family and her own. In fuller detail, this mortification required that the chaplains involved should 'make continual residence' and should not 'keep a wench or concubine'. And for the granting of sasine, the image of St. Michael was led in procession to the lands donated by Lady Alice. Finlay Park endowed a new altar (1455) and stipulated a daily mass, with special anniversary services. William Stoupishill, another burgess (1477), provided an altar with a silver cup overgilt with gold and a missal book. He required 'seven chaplains, the better singers of the foresaid church, solemnly celebrating the said obit or anniversary'. Before each such service the parish clerk should ring the church bells and the burgh bellringer toll the town bell. The bailies should attend the mass and afterwards distribute food and drink to the older and feebler persons of the town. James Chalmer of Gadgirth made a further grant (1502). Rankin Broun endowed another altar (1506). So did Alexander Scott (1541), a churchman in Corstorphine who bequeathed his various properties in Irvine, 'trusting in the help of heaven, and inflamed with zeal of the highest devotion ... for the help, salvation, and relief of my own soul, and the souls of my father, mother, brothers, sisters, forefathers, kinsmen, friends, benefactors, my parishioners, and of all and sundry those persons from whom I have received any good in life, which neither by office nor benefit I have fully recompensed, and of all faithful souls as well of the living as of the dead'. He made provision for 'a chaplain endowed with the sacred order of priesthood, of my own kindred and blood in

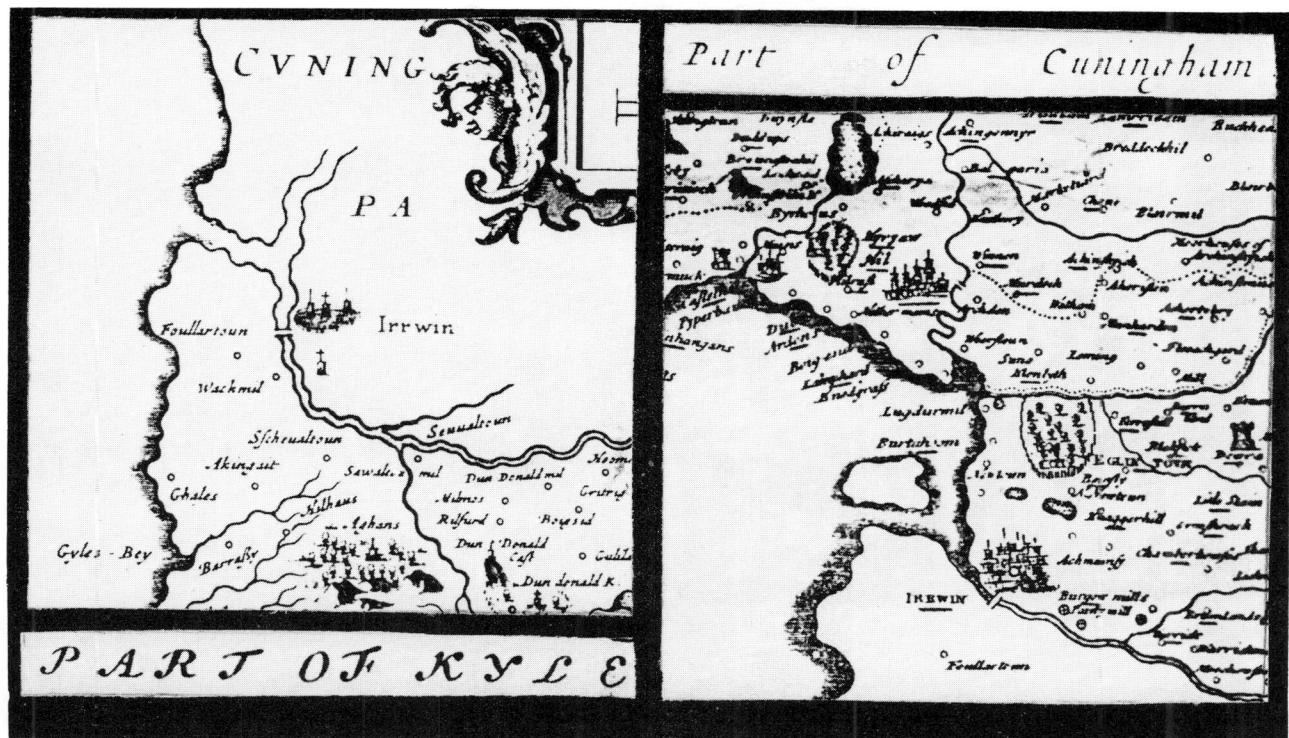

Blaeu's Atlas of 1654, based on information from Timothy Pont, shows Irvine on two of its maps. The map of Kyle shows the present-day coastline. That of Cunninghame, which may have been drawn earlier, shows the river flowing into the sea near the heart of Irvine.

preference to others of foreign blood, sufficiently instructed in the Gregorian chant'. He should be present at every church service, clothed in a surplice. He should celebrate mass at his altar daily at seven in the morning and 'after every mass there celebrated, still clad with the sacred priestly robes, directing his looks towards the place of sepulchre of my ancestors, alone and by himself, or associated with another, he shall be bound honestly and devoutly to say and sing the psalm De Profundis, and in the end the verse Requiescant in pace; and Domine exaudi orationem, et., and Clamor etc, etc., Oremus cum collecta, Absolve quaesumus animas, etc., with sprinkling of the holy water, together with Placebo and Dirige, with nine lessons for the souls aforesaid, on every sixth weekday of every week'. He made further arrangements for requiem masses, with wax candles lit and placed on the fine cloth covering the tomb of his ancestors. The sacristan would toll the great bells of the church, and a handbell would be rung throughout the town. Gifts of money, food and drink would be distributed to thirteen poor persons. Fearfully, he warned the chaplain appointed not to 'publicly keep or cohabit with any concubine or loose wench, or frequent taverns, dicing, prostitutes, harlots or any one perchance night-walking, or in any way mingle with brawlings, branglings, or disputes in public, or anyhow be accustomed to any insolencies or debauched manners that may cast a note or stain upon the clerical honour'.

These church grants afford us glimpses of the role played by the medieval church in Irvine. Daily life was punctuated by ecclesiastical ceremonies. The fact that the rentals of over ninety properties were dedicated to the maintenance of chapels at the church is a memorial not only to piety but to the considerable wealth acquired by the church and its influence on local affairs. The text of the church grants supplies occasional references to individual chaplains. We find some living in the High Street, like sir John Marschale who died just before 1452 — the designation of 'sir' signifies a cleric. In that year two other chaplains had their dwellings in the Kirkgate. In 1528 Mr. Thomas Scot — the designation 'Mr.' indicating that he was a master or university graduate — became chaplain at St. Mary of the Bank. He lived beside the Grip and held other lands in the burgh. Details of parish priests are sparse, but the work of diligent medievalists has produced names which deserve to be listed: Robert de Deyn as vicar of the parish church of Irvine sometime before 1394 was followed by Mr. John

Seagatefoot, site of the original Irvine harbour, on the coast before the 16th century.

Stewart, then perhaps Hugh Raa (before 1405), Mr. Robert Storm (1409), Mr. John Clerici (1409), Sir Lawrence Train (1438), Mr. Archibald de Crawford (1439), Mr. William Hog (1439), Mr. Thomas Ramsay (1475), Mr. Thomas Brown (1488). Sir Thomas Auld (1499), Mr. Thomas Scott (1510), and John Nechell (1541) followed as curates. The last vicar, at the time of the Reformation, was Mr. Thomas Andro.

As well as the secular clergy who administered the parochial services, the regular clergy were represented here by the 'Frere Kirk besyd Erwin'. These were the Carmelite friars whose priory was in Fullarton on the opposite side of the river from the Royal Burgh, actually within the parish of Dundonald. This was one of the ten Carmelite houses in Scotland. The Carmelites are an order of mendicant or begging friars, called also White Friars from the white plaited cloak worn over their brown habits. Founded at Mount Carmel in Palestine by a crusader of the 12th century, the order reached Scotland in the reign of Alexander III. This makes improbable one claim that they arrived in 1240. More likely it was in the 14th century. The founder was one of the Fullartons of Fullarton, possibly Adam Foullertoun who was knighted in 1346. At any rate the Carmelites were well-established in 1399 when his grandson and successor undertook to maintain their convent, which included a chapel and cloister. From later sources we learn that the priory was some fifty yards west of the Old Place of Fullarton and not far from where Cunninghame House is now situated. On the eight acres of Friars Croft they had gardens and an orchard. Indeed in 1501 James IV made payment to 'the French gardiner passand to Irewin for wyne treis', which suggests that experiments in the cultivation of vines were being carried on. Adjacent to Friars Croft on land called Dyets Temple the friars had a malt kiln. On the land of Marress they had pasturage for their sheep. They could go into Irvine by the Friars ford or by following a path upriver cross to St. Mary's Well beside the chapel. That things did not always run smoothly is evident from an agreement of 1412 with Rankin Foullertoun after 'sundry tymes great debaitt and stryfe betwixt the said worshipful Lorde and our ffrers dwellande in the said house of Irrwyne, sume for willfullness, and sume for defaute of knawlegde'. The patronage and support of the Carmelites by the Fullartons was confirmed, and there was to be no further unwarranted interference. The convent in Fullarton, like the parish church of Irvine, was dedicated to the Virgin Mary, and the friars were specifically designated in 1426 as 'of the Order of the blessed Mary, mother of God, of Mount Carmel'. They served through devotion, preaching, and fund raising. They were the recipients of gifts and legacies from local and more distant benefactors. James IV on several occasions made overnight stops here on pilgrimage to Ladykirk and to Whithorn, and made appropriate donations. The friars were not authorised to hold property save their place of dwelling. They seem to have disposed of a tenement in the Kirkgate (1542). They collected annually six bolls of grain as multures from Armsheugh, Roddinghill and Holehouse, which lands were thirled to the Friersmyln on the Annick. The first recorded prior is William Coker (1412), followed by Friar Alexander (1426), John Wallace (1480), Edward Boyd (1499), John Graham (1510), Donald Randall (1528), and finally Robert Burn.

After the Reformation, perquisites were transferred to the Burgh Council. Previously in 1558 Robert Burn, the last prior of the convent, had feued the lands of Friars Croft and Dyets Temple to John Fullarton of Dreghorn. The feuing of church properties had become a common practice, but this transaction would seem to hint at a closure. Demolition of the buildings must soon have followed, with the materials perhaps used for the making of the Marress quay in 1572 or for the repair of the bridge in 1578 and 1589. Nothing seems to have remained by 1600 when Timothy Pont wrote that 'Neir to ye toune the River Irwyne is over passed by a fair stone Bridge, neir to wich wes formerly a frierry of ye order of ye Carmalites founded of old by the Laird of Foulartoune'.

Within the Burgh of Irvine there were Templar tenements belonging to another religious order. The Knights Templars — the Poor Knights of Christ and of the Temple of Solomon — were a crusading military order founded in the 12th century for the protection of pilgrims. They were awarded properties in all the Royal Burghs of Scotland, with the rents contributing to the revenues of the order. Each temple house was marked with the sign of the cross, was held free of all burdens, and was supposed to provide sanctuary. When the order was suppressed in the 14th century, its properties throughout Scotland were conveyed to the Knights of the Order of the Hospital of St. John of Jerusalem. The Hospitallers, whose headquarters in Scotland were at Torphichen, possessed by the 16th century more than a score of temple tenements in the Irvine area. These included properties at Gailes, Montaber, Redburn, Dreghorn, Perceton, and Dyets Temple in Fullarton Within the royal burgh there may have been sixteen, reduced by 1600 to eleven. There were two in the Kirkgate, two in High Street, one in Bridgegate, and one of the others was Templedean on the east side of Smiddybar. After the Reformation the lands of the order passed into lay hands. By 1609 the superiority of the Temple lands throughout Cunninghame was acquired by Robert Montgomerie of Hessilhead and retained by that family till 1720. In 1895 the town council had to expend £5 to acquire the superiority of that Temple tenement south of the Fleshmarket which had been purchased for building the new Town House.

There is mention of a chapel to St. Bridget ('capelle sancte Brigide') near Stanecastle in 1417. Two centuries later the 'twenty shilling lands of old extent called Brydskirk' are recorded, but with no mention of a chapel. It has been supposed that this chapel was secularised 'centuries before the days of Knox'. By the time of the First Statistical Account, Stanecastle was 'said to be the remains of an ancient nunnery'. This tradition was expanded into romantic fiction by John Galt for his novel *Ringan Gilhaize*. One remaining place requires note. While all religious establishments were responsible for providing such facilities as they could in the way of lodging for travellers. alms for the poor, and care for lepers and other infirm persons, there were also hospices or spittals offering specialised provision. Within Ayrshire there were at least five spittals, at Prestwick, Ayr, Symington, Fail and Maybole. There may have been others at Mauchline, Stewarton, Kilmarnock and Irvine. The slender evidence for this last is the existence of a piece of land called Spittal Meadow (1542). Yet the site would seem a likely one, where a main road from the north-east crossed the Red Burn at the Drucken Steps on the outskirts of the Royal Burgh. Further down the burn there was also a Cruceford or Crossford near the templar land of Redburn. To the east of the burgh Redmeadow or Roodmeadow may also have had a religious association. There is finally one mysterious reference to Black Friars ('Tempill of the blak freris in Irrwine at the frere zet', 1540).

There was a castle at Irvine in 1184. Exactly where cannot be firmly stated. The castles being built in Scotland in those days were small wooden towers set up on large earthen mounds called mottes. There were five mounds in the vicinity, two on Irvine moor to the north of the present town, one at Bartonholm, and another two on the higher ground to the east. Of these Gallows Hill and Lawthorn might be possible sites, for a motte hill was often also a court hill where justice was administered. But if there was an original wooden castle, say on the Gallows Hill in the 12th century, or nearby on a lower position, it was on this last site by the Seagate that a stone castle was constructed in the 13th or 14th century. This included a watch tower commanding the harbour. Part of it was retained and incorporated in the third castle designed in the later 16th century. Since this was a mansion house rather than a castle, McJannet called it 'the Palace', which fell into disuse in the 18th century and survives as an ancient monument.

The existence of a castle in the Seagate in the early days of the burgh must be presumed. When the Norwegians sailed up the Firth of Clyde in 1263 on the way to eventual defeat at Largs, they made landings on the Ayrshire coast. The castle at Ayr was stormed, and possibly also that at Irvine, although there is absolutely no evidence one way or another. Not very long afterwards, during the Wars of Independence, the castle at Ayr — possibly still of wooden construction — was garrisoned by the English and destroyed by Bruce. The castle at Irvine, on the other hand, played no recorded part in those wars, though it has been accorded by local repute a subsidiary role in that preliminary encounter described as 'the battle that never was'. In 1296 Edward I of England sent a punitive expedition to Scotland following his deposition of King John Balliol. The following summer it was necessary to send a second expedition under Sir Henry Percy, who came up Nithsdale to Ayr. An assembly of dissident Scots assembled near Irvine, led by a number of magnates including the earl of Carrick, Robert Bruce. Percy advanced towards Irvine (coming along the route now followed by the bypass) and took up position, it is believed, on Tarryholm beside the Irvine Water. According to the Chronicle of Walter of Guisborough, 'The army of Scots was on the other side of a small loch and they could see each other'. The loch was what was perhaps even then known as Trindlemoss and later as Scotts loch. The Scots were encamped on Knadgerhill, involved in argument among

32 *The History of Irvine*

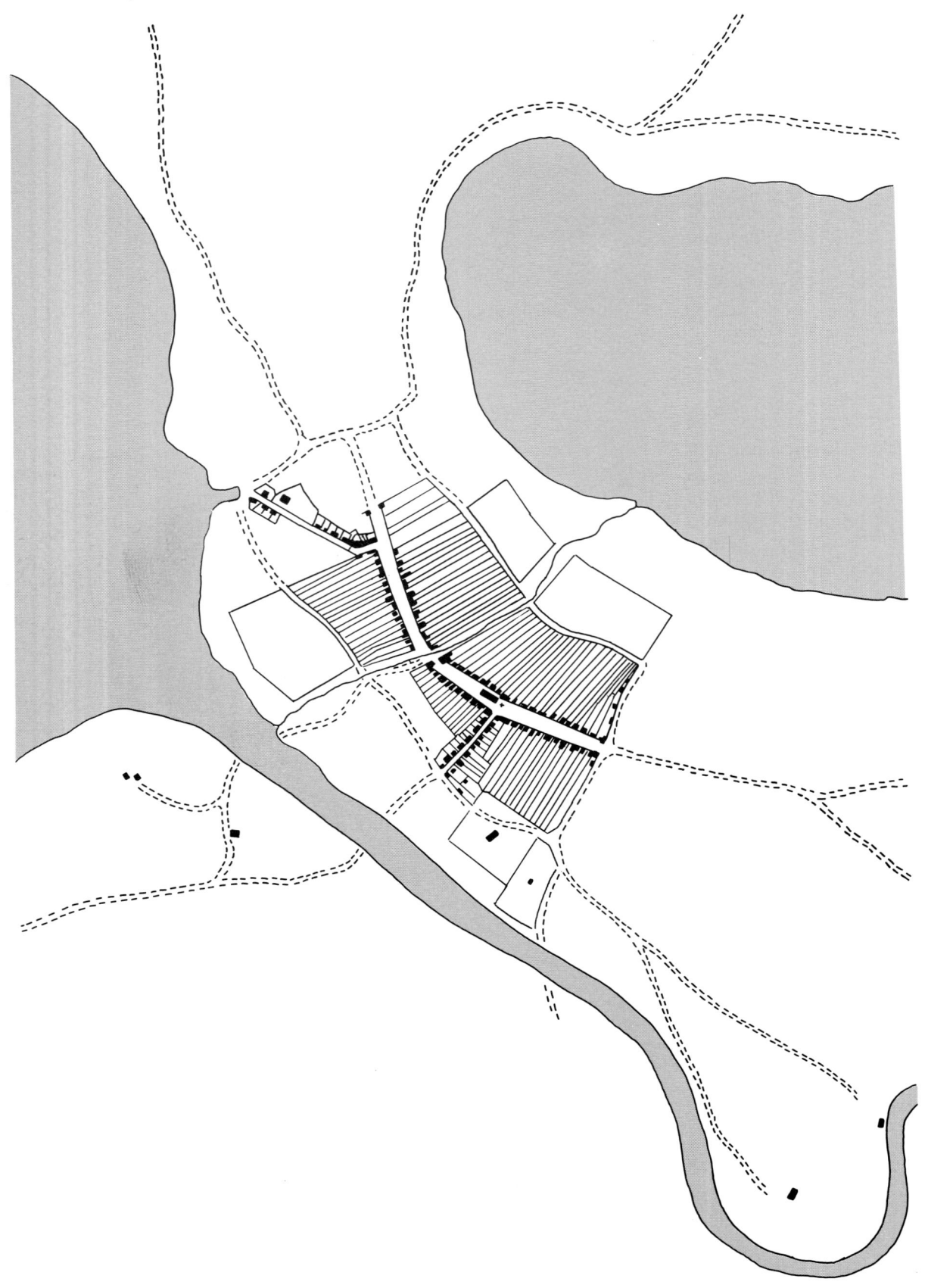

Church and Castle 33

Kirkgate, linking church and market place, followed an ancient track which was integrated into the burgh plan.

themselves, and they decided to submit without a fight. The 'Site of Scottish Camp' where this capitulation took place on 9th July 1297 is commemorated by a monument beside the entrance to what is now the cemetery at Knadgerhill, and a plaque on the wall of Seagate Castle boldly asserts that here was signed what is termed 'the Treaty of Irvine'. William Wallace, who had initiated the revolt at Lanark in May, was mustering his forces in Selkirk Forest in July as a prelude to his victory at Stirling Bridge in September. McJannet mistakenly presumed that Wallace was at Knadgerhill, though he 'bore no share in the capitulation'. Ex-provost P.S. Clark in 1940 devloped that historical romance. When the nobles and their followers capitulated, Wallace and the remnants of 'the army of the common people' withdrew, crossed the river, and attacked the English army in the rear in a 'daring venture'. Looking downriver from the new Golffields footbridge which he was inaugurating, Clark elaborated his imaginative narrative: 'The fight at the ford was a tremendously strenuous one ... one of the most important initial steps in the ultimately successful struggle for Scottish independence'. In cold fact, William Wallace was not at Irvine in 1297 or later. But, if folk memory can be accepted, he may have come down from Riccarton at an earlier date, for tradition claims that on one occasion he successfully ambushed an English cavalry force seeking access to the burgh by the Puddle ford — the Puddlie-deidly, the deadly fight. Nothing further is known about Irvine's part in the Wars of Independence, though Edward I is reputed to have camped there for eight days in 1300. P.S. Clark, however, was able to invent some details in his later speeches: 'It was from here that Bruce marched with his men to engage the English at the Battle of

Town plan, 1400. After Robert II's 1372 charter, Irvine was equipped with a tolbooth (1386) and became firmly established as a royal burgh. Houses and back riggs now extended towards Seagate, where a stone tower castle was built (after 1366). Over the water Fullarton Old Place was also built, and a Carmelite priory founded on reclaimed land at Friars Croft, linked to the town by the Friars Ford. Upriver the Howe Mill was operating (before 1391).

At Seagate, Sir Hew of Eglinton in 1366 may have built the square stone tower which was incorporated in the 16th-century building and is visible in this photograph of 1901.

Bannockburn' and the Moor was 'granted to the town for all time by King Robert the Bruce as a thanks-offering for the services rendered by the town at Bannockburn'.

After the fighting was over, the de Morville lands and properties which had passed into Balliol hands were disposed of by the new King Robert I. The ownership of the castle of Irvine at that period may help to explain its obscure history. Belonging originally to the de Morvilles, it would be smaller than William the Lion's royal castle at Ayr. When possession of the castle at Irvine passed to the lords of Galloway, one can presume some neglect by an absentee landlord. When the castle became crown property under Balliol and then Bruce and his Stewart successors, there was no incentive to extend it. The castle of Ayr, important enough to be garrisoned by the English and destroyed by Bruce, was never rebuilt. Robert II chose instead to reconstruct Dundonald Castle as a royal residence. Already in 1367 Robert II had delegated to Sir Hew of Eglinton the offices of Bailie of Cunninghame and Chamberlain of Irvine. Perhaps it was Sir Hew who replaced a decayed wooden castle with a stone-built tower fitted to guard the haven of the growing burgh that had been placed under his care and which Robert II would soon elevate in status.

The third and still-surviving Seagate Castle was certainly a creation of the Eglinton family. It was constructed by Hugh, third earl of Eglinton (1564–85), probably after his marriage to Margaret Drummond in 1562, and possibly in 1565. The initials of the married couple along with the Montgomerie and Drummond coats of arms appear on two bosses in the vaulting of the entrance passageway. The architecture is typical of the period around 1570. Like so many of the castles then being built, it was capable of defence in emergency, but it was primarily a palace or place or mansion house in Scottish Renaissance style. The older castle, which may have occupied much the same area, was cleared, leaving only the portion of a tower in the north-west corner. The ground floor of the new structure contained kitchen and guard chamber, with two vaults on the other side of the covered entrance passage, and the windows are small, sometimes mere slits. But the first floor, reached from the back courtyard by a spiral staircase, provided two large apartments and a great hall; and there were other chambers on a second floor which is now gone. The upper windows are large, with elegantly sculpted surrounds. These and the large fireplaces and the rich furnishings we can envisage are an indication of the new wealth of the 16th-century lords. So too is the impressive gateway, with its embellished late-Gothic rounded arch. The plaque more recently affixed to the outside wall records not only the Treaty of Irvine of 1297 which is supposed to have been signed here in a previous building, but also an alleged visit of Mary Queen of Scots in 1563. The records state explicitly that she stayed at Eglinton on 1st August and the next day rode on to Ayr. If on her way through Irvine she chose to stop at the new-built Seagate Castle — if indeed it had been rebuilt then — it must have been a fleeting visit.

Planned as a domestic building, this Seagate Castle would never be garrisoned, but provided a town house for occasional residence by members of the Eglinton family. There is a tradition that in the 17th century it was occupied by one George Gemmell of Craigfoot, a royalist persecutor of the Covenanters. There are less credible stories of underground passages leading to Stane and to Dundonald Castle. By the 18th century it ceased to be occupied at all. The tenth earl had the roof removed to provide timbers for a church in Ardrossan parish. In 1760 Richard Pococke described it as ruinous. It became a haunt for smugglers and gangrel bodies and a convenient quarry for building stone. Despite some repairs in 1810, it suffered severe storm damage in 1839; decay continued until 1883 when the debris was cleared to allow antiquarian appraisal of what remains Irvine's oldest building.

In the earlier part of its history a Constable was in charge of the castle, on behalf of an absentee lord and as his judicial agent. Timothy Pont describes Philip de Horssey, son-in-law of Richard de Morville, as possessor of Bartonholm and holding such a post as representative of the lord of Galloway ('Janitor Comitis Gallovidiae'). Between 1391 and 1425 Thomas de Vauce was Constable with an annual salary of two merks from the crown, which was deducted by the bailies from the burgh's return to the exchequer and paid directly to the Constable. In 1428 John de Brakanrig through his wife inherited the post, which by 1438 was transferred to Thomas Spark of Bartonholm, described both as Constable and as Keeper of the prison of Irvine. After fifty-one years Thomas Spark sold to William Cunningham of Craigens the lands of Bartonholm and Snodgrass, together with fishing in the Garnock and the office of Constable. Payment of the traditional two merks annually apparently ceased in 1596, and with it the post of Constable.

Sir Hew of Eglinton, when he was appointed Bailie of Cunninghame and Chamberlain of Irvine, in 1367, acquired Seagate Castle. He was of a family supposed to have held the estate in Kilwinning parish since the 11th century. 'The gude Schir Hew' was a noted poet, one of the makars 'who was cunning in literature, curious in his style, eloquent and subtle, and who clothes his composition in appropriate metre, so as always to raise delyte and pleasure'. This courtier-poet had a wife closely related to the Steward, who when he succeeded as King Robert II in 1371 retained his intimate associations with this corner of his kingdom. To royal patronage Sir Hew added good fortune. In 1357 the barony of Ardrossan by inheritance was added to that of Eglinton. Then Sir Hew's daughter married Sir John Montgomerie of Eaglesham, whose family had held that Renfrewshire estate for nine generations, since the 12th century. Sir John Montgomerie had distinguished himself at the battle of Otterburn. After his father-in-law's death in 1380 his estates included Eaglesham, Eglinton and Ardrossan. Inheriting also the offices of Bailie of Cunninghame and Chamberlain of Irvine, he was a powerful figure. His grandson Sir Alexander would become Lord Montgomerie in 1449, and the third lord Hugh was created first earl of Eglinton in 1508. The Montgomeries would become involved in a bitter feud for dominance over Cunninghame, and they would play an influential role in the affairs of the Royal Burgh of Irvine.

In his capacity as Bailie of Cunninghame and Chamberlain of Irvine, Sir Hew of Eglinton obtained possession of Seagate Castle and yard, but no other properties locally. The area comprising Irvine parish which had belonged once to the de Morvilles had been previously disposed of. The Burgh of Irvine had originally been awarded much (if not all) of it. Some had later been handed out by the Bruce to reward supporters, at a (literally) peppercorn rent — that for Bartonholm was one pound of pepper, for Stane two pounds of white pepper, and for Bourtreehill four chalders of meal and one pound of pepper. By Sir Hew's time there were four small baronies in the upland part of Irvine parish, each of about 300 acres — Balgray, Armsheugh, Stane and Bourtreehill. On the laigh lands there were half-a-dozen smaller properties of varying sizes — Broomlands, Tourland, Chalmerhouses and Milgarholm on one side of the burgh, Bogside and Bartonholm on the other. Each of these was occupied over the generations by a bewildering succession of owners, sometimes local lairds, sometimes representatives of the leading Ayrshire families. Most in due course became part of the great Eglinton estate.

Balgray, though acquired by Sir Hew of Eglinton in 1361, seems to have been relinquished soon afterwards and went through many hands until in 1768 it was divided among four bonnet lairds. Armsheugh, over which the Burgh for long claimed superiority was, with the farms of Roddinghill and Holehouse, disposed of by Bruce. By 1600 it was in the hands of the Montgomeries of Skelmorlie and with their other lands incorporated in the Eglinton estate in 1796. Stane was owned in 1417 by William Francis, whose daughter married a son of the first earl of Eglinton. This

Seagate Castle was rebuilt about 1565 by Hugh, 3rd earl of Eglinton, as a mansion in the Scottish Renaissance style. Its ruins were cleared in 1850, when this drawing was made.

William Montgomerie built Stane Castle, and in 1570 his grandson sold it to the third earl. Brydeskirk, presumably at one time church land, was occupied by a branch of the Barclay family and later incoporated into Stane. The story of Bourtreehill is a complex one. While the lands were granted to and sometimes occupied by certain persons, the superiority seems to have been held by others. In 1363 Robert the Steward granted to Alan of Blair the annual rent (noted in the previous paragraph) in return for a pair of gilt spurs or twelve silver pennies at Whitsunday yearly, if asked. In 1817 the twelfth earl of Eglinton inherited Bourtreehill, but his successor sold it.

On the smaller properties on the lower reaches of the Annick Water, Tourland was held by a succession of lesser lairds. Broomlands belonged to John Peebles, a provost of Irvine who died in 1596. Later it passed to a cadet branch of the Eglinton family, one of whom — Charles Montgomerie, a Glasgow merchant — constructed an elaborate genealogical table to prove that he was in fact the heir male to the Eglinton family. In the 1780s he sold Broomlands to Robert Hamilton of Bourtreehill, with which estate Broomlands was thereafter incorporated. Further downstream Chalmerhouses, otherwise Chamberhouses or Thornliebank, was held by a succession of proprietors. Before the Reformation Milgarholm belonged to Kilwinning Abbey and in 1603 passed to the earl of Eglinton. Associated with it was Howe mill, and there is a record of John Stewart (1469), and John Hair (1479) after whom the mill was sometimes called Hair's mill. By 1640 there were three proprietors of Milgarholm, while the Howe mill was in the hands of the earl. Oddly, on one occasion in 1678 the Burgh presented the miller with a blue bonnet, surely a relic of a feudal due. Even more oddly, in the 19th century above the doorway of Milgarholm was a stone bearing the royal arms of the United Kingdom. During the 18th century Milgarholm belonged to Provost John Cumming, after whom it was named — temporarily — Cummingfield.

Of the small properties to the north of the Burgh, Bartonholm was at one time (according to Timothy Pont) in the possession of Philip de Horssey, son-in-law of Richard de Morville. Between 1438 and 1489 it was held by Thomas Spark. Since John Cathcart is also credited with possession in 1439 of the lands of Bartonholm, it would seem that here too there was some division of ownership. This is confirmed later. Though William Cunningham of Craigens in 1498 acquired Bartonholm along with the office of Constable, in 1640 both Patrick Spark and Margaret Cunningham are recorded. By 1651 an Irvine merchant called Adam Fullarton had taken over, and the last representative of this branch of the Fullarton family in 1852 sold Bartonholm to the earl of Eglinton. Pont's map of Cunninghame shows Bartonholm on the shoreline. Snodgrass, which William Cunningham purchased along with Bartonholm (1498) and which passed to the earl of Eglinton (1528), was shown by Pont as on the Stevenston bank of the Garnock estuary. These lands and others adjacent known as Bogside and Culterland were much affected by the recession of the sea and the later meanderings of the Garnock river. They must have been augmented both by reclamation and by encroachment on the lands of the burgh muir. John Mure 'of ye Bogsid of Irwin' is noted in 1490. In 1643 Hugh Blair succeeded his father Bryce in the land of Boigsyde and Culterland. Later in that century the Burgh was leasing out the lands of Bogside, Kidsneuk and Redburn. Before 1807 Bogside had become part of the Eglinton estate, to which Bartonholm was added in 1852, thus completing the territorial expansion of that estate into Irvine parish which had been proceeding since the 14th century.

FIVE

Feuds and Factions

From the 15th until the 18th century various political circumstances resulted in periodic disturbances afflicting Irvine. First, the burgh could not escape involvement in the long and bitter feud between the Montgomeries of Eglinton and the Cunninghams of Kilmaurs. The background to this conflict, which extended from 1488 to 1609, may be briefly explained. Both families had been steadily extending their possessions and their influence. In addition to the Eglinton estates of Ardrossan, Kilwinning and Eaglesham, members of the Montgomerie family had acquired lands in different parts of Ayrshire. Similarly from their base at Kilmaurs, branches of the Cunningham family had become established throughout north Ayrshire and inherited Glencairn lands in Dumfriesshire and other parts of Scotland. Members of the leading Ayrshire feudal families were now powerful enough to become active participants in national politics, and win enhanced status. Sir John Montgomerie's grandson Alexander was in 1445 created first Lord Montgomerie, and the third Lord Hugh was made first earl of Eglinton in 1506. In 1450 Sir Alexander Cunningham was created Lord Kilmaurs and in 1488 made earl of Glencairn. In times when royal authority was weakened, it was inevitable that rival factions should come into conflict.

The quarrel between the Montgomeries and the Cunninghams became focused on the office of Bailie of Cunninghame, with control over the bailiary court at Irvine. The grants of Robert the Steward to Sir Hew of Eglinton in 1367 of this office on a hereditary basis were now challenged by the other family, who asserted a prior claim, that their ancestors had been awarded the hereditary bailieship as thanes of Cunninghame under the de Morvilles. Compromise still seemed possible in 1425 when, as part of a marriage settlement, Sir John Montgomerie granted to Sir Richard Cunningham 'the Balzery of Conyngham, with al the profytis pertenande til it, for the terme of his life'. But after the latter's death in 1446 his heir was reluctant to relinquish the office, and the dispute became inflamed, bursting into violent conflict in 1488.

This was only one of several Ayrshire feuds, which resulted in the assassination of leading figures — like James, Lord Boyd (1484); Sir Hugh Campbell of Loudoun, Sheriff of Ayr (1527); and Sir Thomas Kennedy of Culzean (1601). The Eglinton-Glencairn feud produced others, and involved the townsfolk of Irvine in the periodic 'slaughters, spulzies and quarrels'. Not unexpectedly, in the breakdown of law and order, there were other instances of violence in the burgh. A chronological list of incidents summarises the complex story of the feud:

1488 Kerelaw Castle, a Glencairn stronghold in Stevenston parish, attacked and burned down by Montgomeries.

1489 For the next ten years the holding of the bailiary court at Irvine suspended because of clashes between the rival factions.

1491 John Spark of Bartonholm broke into and claimed possession of Templar tenement in Kirkgate.

1497 Cuthbert, son of Lord Kilmaurs, led attack in Irvine on Hugh, Lord Montgomerie.

1498 Assassination in Irvine of Martin Makeachne by Lord Montgomerie.

1499 Cuthbert, Lord Kilmaurs, seized Irvine tolbooth, his followers committing 'treason, fire-raising, rape, slaughter, common theft and forethought felony'.

1505 William Cunningham of Craigens wounded in attack by John, Master of Montgomerie (eldest son of Lord Montgomerie).

1507 John, Master of Montgomerie, wounded.

1510 Arbitration failed.

1511 Affray in Irvine led by Montgomeries — John Scott, burgess, seized, put in tolbooth, then in stocks; theft of pots, pans, plates and pewter vessels from house; Mrs. Scott struck and hair pulled out 'in great quantities'.

1513 After Battle of Flodden, another attempt at arbitration.

1517 William Cunningham, Master of Glencairn, wounded John, Master of Montgomerie, and killed three others.

1520 John, Master of Montgomerie, killed in 'Cleanse the Causeway' affray in Edinburgh supporting the faction of Earl of Arran against the Earl of Angus.

1522 At bailiary court in Irvine Earls of Eglinton and Glencairn ordered to cease mustering of men-at-arms.

1523 Temporary reconciliation. 'The said earls, masters, their kin, friends, and servants, that are now present in this town, shall take each other by the hands and remit to each other the rancour of their hearts, and either of them shall bring their friends, that are

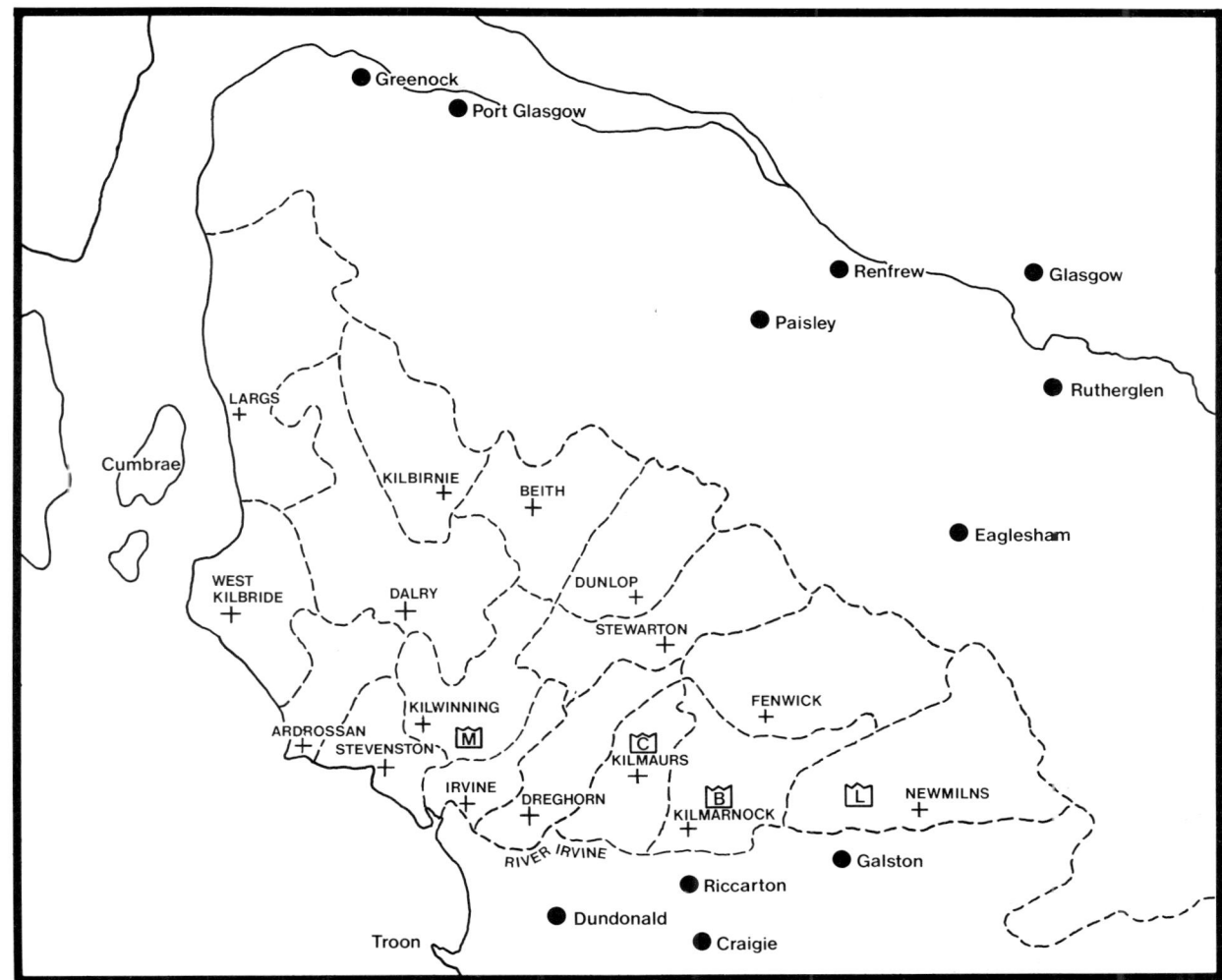

Cunninghame from 1488 to 1609 was a battleground in the bitter feud between the Montgomeries of Eglinton and the Cunninghams from Kilmaurs. This map of the Bailiary of Cunninghame shows parish centres and the principal strongholds of the Montgomeries (M), Cunninghams (C), Boyds of Kilmarnock (B) and Campbells of Loudoun (L).

absent, to the tenth day of April next to come in Irvine, and cause them to shake hands'.

1526 Assassination of Edward Cunningham of Auchenharvie, followed by that of Archibald Cunningham of Waterstoun.

1527 Eglinton Castle attacked and destroyed by William, Master of Glencairn; muniments burned; Montgomeries took refuge at Ardrossan.

1529 Complaint by burgh of Irvine against Hugh, earl of Eglinton for 'divers tymes cumin upon thame for thare slauchter in thair aune houssis with drawin knyffis and siclike has invadit thame upon our hie streit and uther wais in grete skayth to thame'.

1530 Farty led by William, Master of Glencairn, killed Gabriel Sympill near Armsheugh.

1533 William Montgomerie of Stane with violence seized from the house of John Rankine, burgess of Irvine, 'ane tyde kow (cow in calf), ane stirk (steer), ane mete almery (meat cupboard), tua brasin pottis (brass pots), thre pewdir dischesis (pewter dishes), ane veschel almery (dresser?), ane mete burd (dining table), ane irne spete (iron spit), ane pan' plus loads of coals, turves, and peats.

1536 Assassination of Master Matthew Montgomerie, chaplain.

1547 Neil Montgomerie of Lainshaw killed in Irvine by Robert, Master of Boyd, who took refuge at Bogside.

1555 Assassination of John Montgomerie in Irvine.

1557 Another complaint by the burgh of Irvine against Hugh, earl of Eglinton, who 'with ane grite cumpany of folkis ... nocht allenerlie [only] stoppit and maid impediment to the said complenaris in halding of thair fair and uptaking of their custumes and dewiteis thairof bot alsuae crewellie invadit thame for thair slauchter and hurt and woundit civers of thame'.

1574 Trial by Magistrates of Thomas Snodgirs for murder of his wife.

1579 Trial by Magistrates of William Porter for murder of Andrew Dickie.

1585 Perhaps arising from the feud, Ninian Barclay, burgess of Irvine, guilty of 'the mutilatioun of Johnne Broun, burges of Irrving of his rycht leg committit within the said burgh'.

1586 Assassination of Hugh, fourth earl of Eglinton, shot with a pistol, beside the Annick near Stewarton. In the ensuing violence Robert Cunningham of Giffen shot near Dunlop; Alexander Cunningham of Montgreenan shot at his own gate; Sir Robert Montgomerie of Skelmorlie and his son killed in Paisley; John Cunningham of Clonbeith pursued, found hiding in a chimney in Hamilton and cut to pieces.

1587 James VI took action against the various feuds. Robert, Master of Eglinton, and James, Earl of Glencairn, cautioned.

1601 William Cunningham of Tourlands beheaded in Edinburgh following his seizure of the house of Cunninghamhead.

1606 At meeting of parliament in Perth, affray between the Setons (kinsmen of the Montgomeries) and the Cunninghams. This was a late outburst — royal power was now sufficient to end the era of feuds.

1607 Perhaps associated with the feud was a final atrocity when Hugh Garven, notary and town clerk of Irvine, was killed by John Montgomerie, brother to the laird of Skelmorlie, and William Montgomerie, writer in Irvine.

1609 William Montgomerie imprisoned in Irvine but released by armed force of magistrates and burgesses.

1609 Thomas Boyll from Largs complained that Bailie John Barcley and Town Clerk William Caldwell attacked him with swords and put him in the stocks; and the following year further complained of another arrest without warrant.

The feud was formally concluded on 16th March 1609 when the privy council brought together representatives of the Montgomeries and Cunninghams, and they 'choppit handis togidder in taiken of a constant friendship'. After Alexander Seton succeeded as 6th Earl of Eglinton in 1615, he commended James VI for his 'Royal wisdom and admirable dexterity in taking away all divisions, and reconciling all deadly feuds between your subjects in this kingdom'.

Concurrently with the Eglinton-Glencairn feud, and associated with it, were Montgomerie claims which infringed the liberties of the royal burgh of Irvine. When in 1498 James IV awards Hew, Lord Montgomerie, special powers and renewed recognition as Bailie of Cunninghame and Chamberlain of Irvine, this was not only an affront to the Glencairn faction, but a threat to the burgh, since he was specifically entitled to 'hold Courts of Bailiery and Chaimberlaincy within the Burgh of Irwyne'. In 1517 James V seemed to extend this office of justiciary, and Lord Montgomerie, now earl of Eglinton, felt free to treat Irvine as the superior of any baronial burgh would. In 1529 and 1557, the protests of the royal burgh, as noted above, received crown support. In 1569 James VI confirmed the burgh's judicial powers; in 1572 the earl of Eglinton was specifically advised; and in 1573 a contract stipulated in detail their respective jurisdictions. The burgh was responsible for all crimes and offences within the burgh. Eglinton had a limited interest, 'having the use and rycht of the keeping of the heid fair of the said burgh halding yeirlie at our first termeday quhilk is the xv day of August past memour of man'. He had the right to collect those customs due from the fair and to hold a court thereafter, solely to deal with 'faltis and complaintis'. Having thus thwarted interference by Eglinton, the burgh in 1594 was able also to reject a royal nominee for the post of town clerk, asserting its 'undoubtit rycht to elect and creat all officeris within Burgh'.

The independence of the royal burgh thus seemed secure by the beginning of the 17th century. Eglinton's control of the Marymass fair was accepted amicably. Annually on the eve of the fair, as Bailie of Cunninghame the earl presented to the magistrates gloves which were exhibited outside the tolbooth as a symbol of the king's peace. And the occasion was marked by appropriate refreshment in 1686: '14 August. Item The Magistrates the tyme of their receaving their gloves from the Bailyie of Cunninghame three chapins of wyne and ane pynt of aill and ane pype'.

One isolated affray in the year 1670 illustrates, however, that times were still disturbed. Some horses belonging to Sir Alexander Cunninghame of Robertland were seized for debt and brought for sale at Irvine cross. Sir Alexander complained to the earl of Eglinton as Bailie of Cunninghame. A party of twenty men, well mounted, with swords, pistols and plate sleeves, arrived in Irvine to recover the horses. Sir Alexander forced his way into the house of Arthur Hamilton, the town clerk. Some Irish mechants in the street seemed to be laughing at the proceedings until Alexander Kennedy, one of Robertland's men, threatened them with a pistol, when they took refuge in a shop. Provost James Blair arrived on the scene and remonstrated, but was threatened with a naked sword. Whereupon some of the townsfolk picked up some wooden poles lying nearby and knocked Kennedy off his horse. John Reid, a towns officer, emerged from the tolbooth with his halbert and felled Kennedy with it. Several shots were fired by Robertland's party before they rode off. Kennedy died nine days later. The towns officer was committed to the tolbooth, but exonerated. The halbert which killed Kennedy was still in use in the 19th century — but for ceremonial use only.

Religious dissensions commenced while the feuds were still going on, and continued to produce civil disorders throughout most of the 17th century.

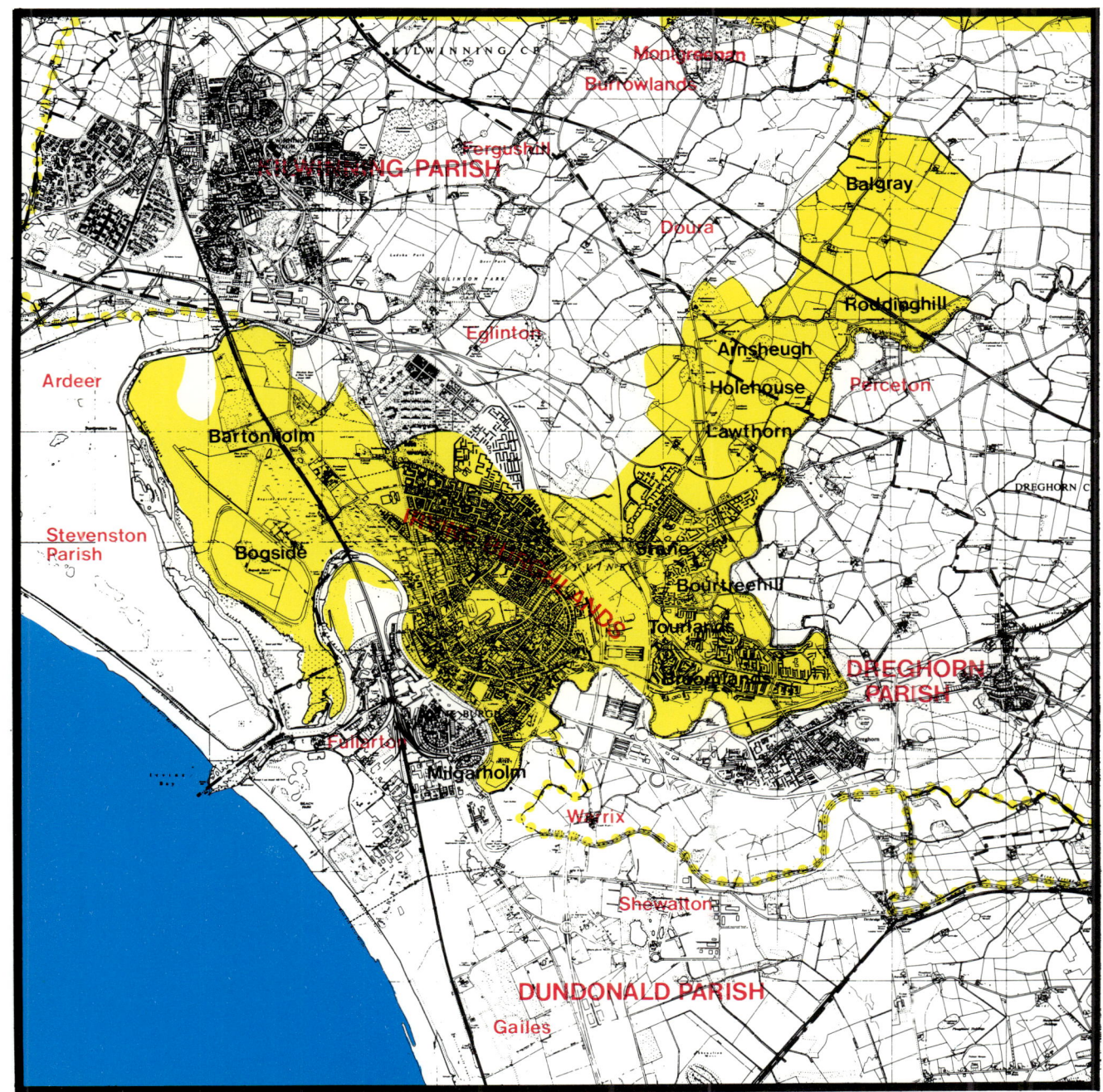

Irvine and adjacent parishes. The Burgh of Irvine may originally have owned the whole of Irvine parish (as well as several properties in Kilwinning parish, including Burrowland). The various small estates formed within the parish are marked, as well as major estates of the adjoining areas.

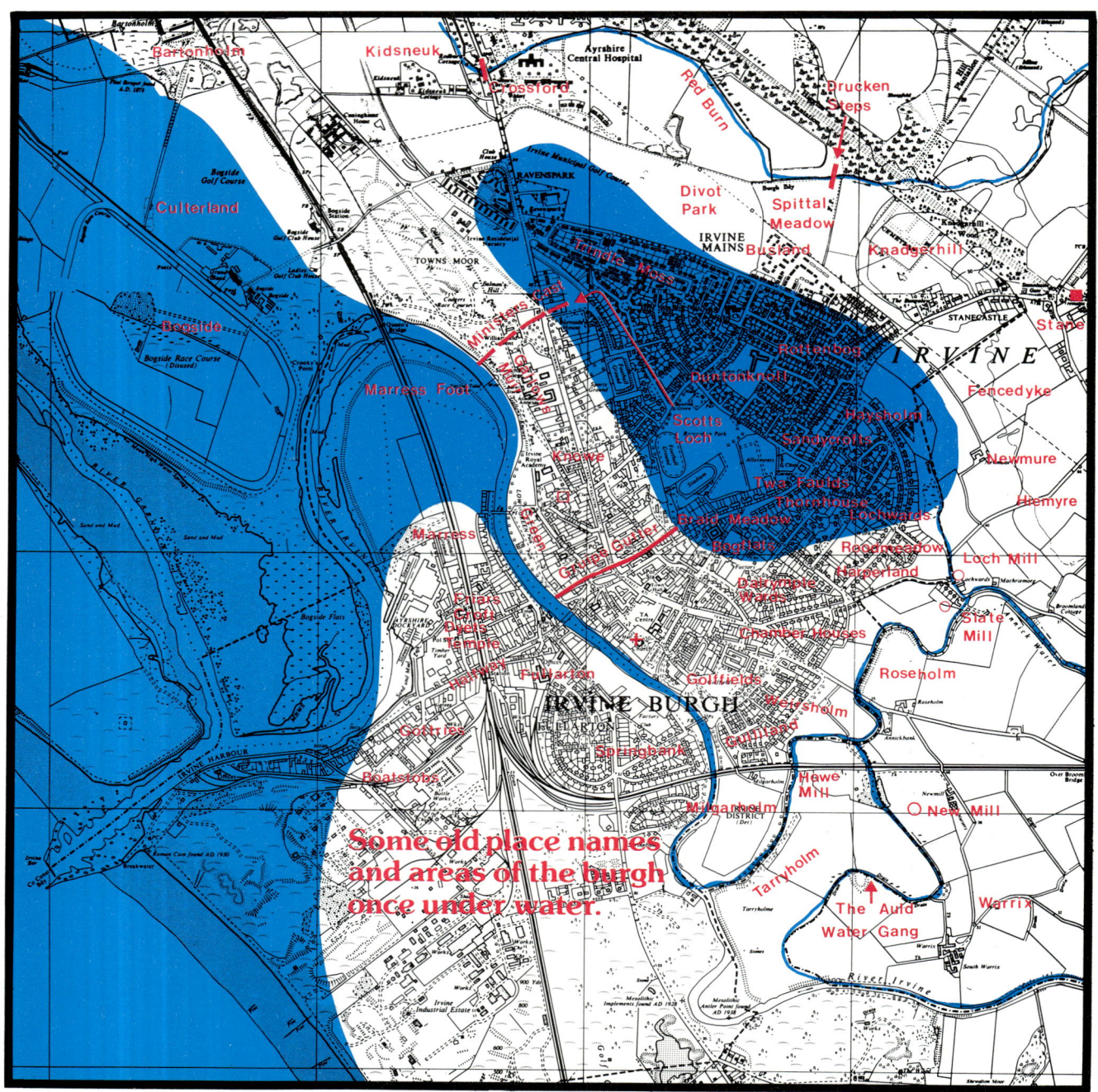

Old Place Names. The records mention places whose locations are in many cases unknown to residents of the present day. They may also be unaware of the areas which were under water at the time the burgh was formed in the 13th century. Scotts Loch (which included the area of the present Recreation Park) was not drained till 1691.

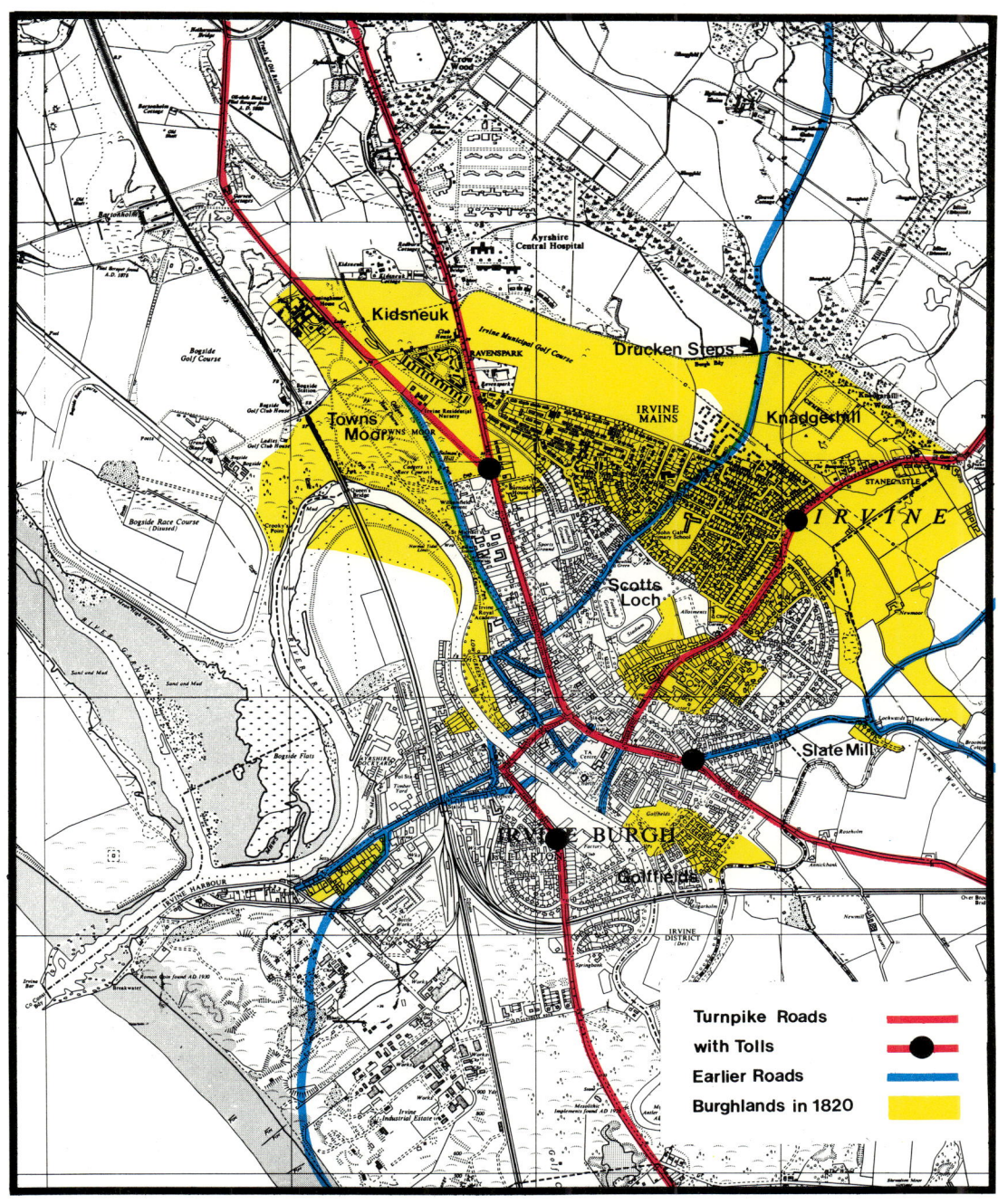

Roads. Until the 18th century un-made tracks provided difficult passage for horsemen and pack animals. Coaches and carts became common on the toll roads built after the Ayrshire Turnpike Act of 1767.

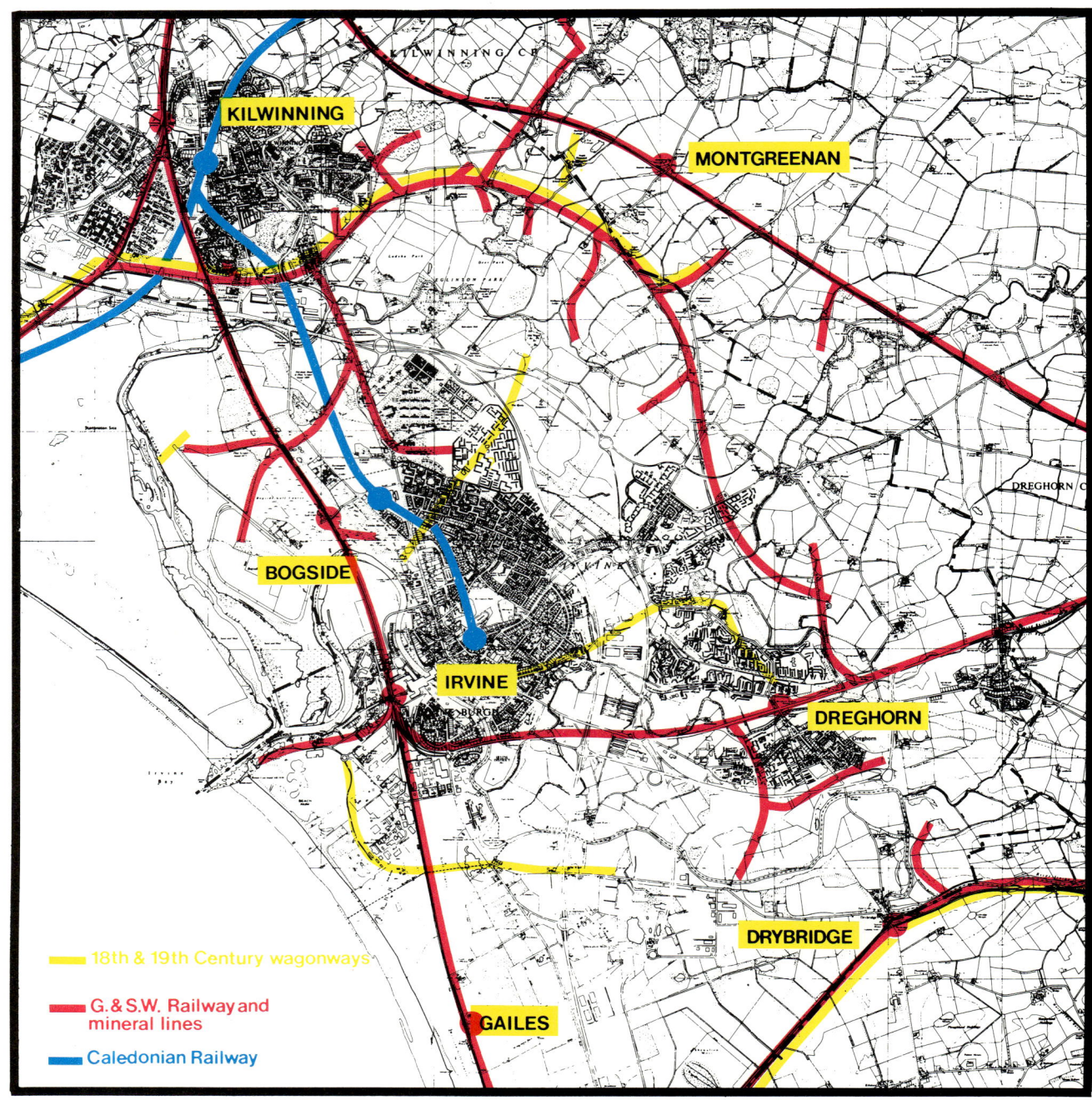

Railways. In the 19th century railways provided rapid transport for passengers and goods traffic. Waggonways to transport heavy loads like coal were superseded with the opening of a railway line to Ayr (1839) and Glasgow (1840), followed by a network constructed by the Glasgow and South Western Railway Company; and (1890) by the rival Caledonian Railway Company.

Eglinton Castle, destroyed in 1527, was rebuilt. It was depicted by John Ainslie in 1790, before the more familiar later mansion house was erected.

The overthrow of the Roman Church in 1560 was less dramatic than used to be supposed. The political developments leading up the Reformation indeed inhibited the Eglinton–Glencairn feud between 1557 and 1586. What occurred in 1560 was essentially a political revolution in which the Lords of the Congregation, with Protestant sympathies and English support, challenged the royal authority of Mary of Guise, regent for Mary Queen of Scots and representing the Roman Catholic and French interests. The parliament of 1560, which included both the earls of Eglinton and Glencairn — with Provost Robert Barclay presumably the commissioner for the royal burgh of Irvine — ratified and approved the Confession of the Protestant faith 'as hailsome and sound doctrine, groundit upon ye infallibill trewth of God's Word'. Hugh, 3rd earl of Eglinton, who convoyed Queen Mary back from France in 1561, was less than enthusiastic. He fought for her at Langside in 1568, reputedly supported by a contingent of Irvine's carters. In defiance of the new edicts, mass was still being celebrated privately at Eglinton in 1570. Alexander, 5th earl of Glencairn, who like his father was a strong supporter of the pro-English Protestant cause, was entrusted with the 'casting down' of religious houses in the west of Scotland. But at Kilwinning Abbey the destruction seems to have been confined for the most part to the choir, the monks' part of the church. It has been concluded that 'the amount of dislocation brought about by the religious settlement of 1560 has frequently been exaggerated in the past'. This is certainly true of Irvine.

The parish chuch of Irvine was certainly not 'cast down' but with altars and images removed was retained and adapted for Protestant worship. The revenues of the chaplainries and certain annual rents belonging to the Carmelite friars were by 1572 transferred to the burgh council, to whom were entrusted those educational and welfare responsibilities which will merit fuller mention in the next chapter. The reluctance (reported in 1572) of some forty burgesses to pay to the Council annual rents previously devoted to the maintenance of the chaplains may suggest some opposition to the new Order. Though priests were forbidden to celebrate mass, they were permitted to retain their stipends for the rest of their lives. Thomas Andrew, who was the incumbent vicar at Irvine, went over to the new church. So did many other Ayrshire priests, as is evident from the continued payment of their full stipends without deduction of the 'thirds of benefices'. Thomas Andrew indeed was in 1572 allowed to feu to Peter Brown of Burrowlands the glebe lands adjacent to the church. It was found necessary, however, to appoint as parish minister John Lynd (1565) who was found 'unsufficient', Robert Hamilton (1567-68), then John Young (1570-89). Thomas Andrew acted as their associate 'Vicar of Yrwing

42   The History of Irvine

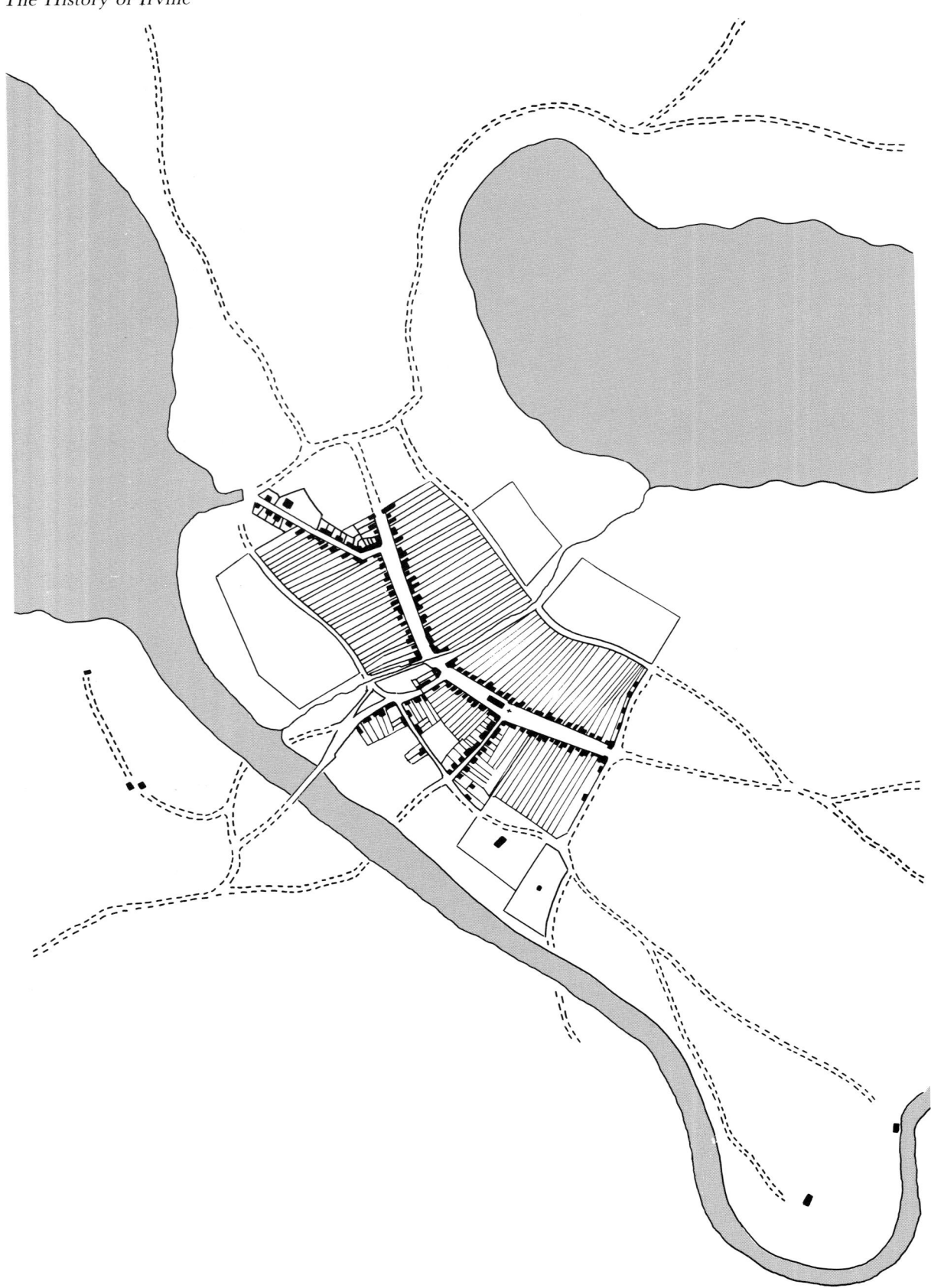

By the 16th century some houses were built of stone. The usual style was with a gable fronting the street, as in this solitary surviving example at the corner of High Street and Kirkgate.

and reader there'. The last Carmelite prior in Fullarton, Robert Burn, seems to have continued in a similar capacity as 'reader at Dundonald and Crosbie'. Even if the new doctrines of Protestantism were advocated only by a minority of zealots, there had been widespread agreement within the old church that reform was necessary, and the ecclesiastical changes were easily accomplished and in this area at least almost universally accepted.

In 1583 William Strang was appointed, as colleague to John Young and presumably as successor to Thomas Andrew. The provost and bailies made the presentation, and provided a stipend and a dwellinghouse. They were also responsible for the church and churchyard, ensuring that 'the place of burial may be honestlie keipit fra horse, swyne, and uther bestial'. Mr. Strang was to take services 'twyce everie Sonday publiclie in ordinar teching, likewyse upon the Waddinsday and Fryday as neid requyris'. The council would co-operate with the elders now chosen to form a kirk session 'for mantenans of the disciplin of the kirk, and to punise vicis [wrong-doers] according to the godlie actis of parliament, especially contemneris of the Word, sacramentis, and al them that wilfullie and obstinatlie absentis themself from preching of the Word chiefle upone the Sabbath day'.

Discipline involved rebuke before the congregation 'in the place of publict repentance'. The earlier kirk session records have not survived, but it appears that of the seven deadly sins, one in particular always specifically engaged the attention of what Burns later called 'the houghmagandie pack'. In 1615 Irvine was one of the several churches in which penance had to be done by the lady of Kilbirnie for abduction and her son for rape. And

Town plan, 1500. For a population of around a thousand persons, there was now building in Bridgegate, on Mount Musart, and beyond Seagatehead. Land was reclaimed from the loch of Trindlemoss, on the Green (first mentioned 1499), and at Marress (first mentioned 1464). Prosperity is indicated by the generous grants which embellished the church. A stone bridge had been built, and George Fullarton moved his residence to Crosbie.

that church censure seems then to have been applied to persons of all degrees is further evident by the sixth earl of Eglinton himself having to occupy the penance stool for the sin of fornication.

The kirk session seems not to have required to concern itself with recusancy — though Strang's successor, William Scrimgeour (1588-1618), was in 1610 accused of 'harbouring John Campbell alias Father Christostome, ane known trafficquing priest'. Its attention was directed towards what were regarded as pagan practices. The pre-Christian festival of Beltane was an occasion for merrymaking still in 1610 when 'ye younkeiris [youngsters] of the toun went out to thair May play with the provest and bailyeis'. In 1618 the earl of Eglinton made gifts 'at my Lady's command ... to the puir folk on the grene of Irwing the first of May' and also 'to the town pyper and drum'. In 1658 Kilmarnock kirk session took action against 'a number of vaine wantoun lasses summondit for their lasciviose and scandalous carriadge, in promiscuous dancing with men, in mutual kissing and giveing ribbons as favours to the men, upon Whitsunday, in the town of Irvine, in the time of preaching'. Similar action must have been taken by Irvine kirk session against any traditional festivities associated with the Marymass fair. For Marymass may then have incorporated pagan Lammas ceremony as well as the celebration of the Assumption — and all popish festivals (including Christmas and Easter) were to be prohibited.

More serious — and terrifying in its impact — was the action taken against the alleged practice of witchcraft. The Reformed Church in 1563 regarded this as a matter of urgency, and the requisite Act cited Exodus xxii, 18, and Deuteronomy, xviii, 10-12. In 17th-century Irvine more than twenty persons were executed for witchcraft.

In the spring of 1618 the Irvine vessel *The Gift of God*, on a voyage to France, was wrecked on the coast of Cornwall. Nearly all aboard were lost, including the part-owner Provost Andrew Tran and the skipper John Dean, burgess. News of the disaster was brought by John Stewart, a vagabond, before the only two surviving sailors arrived home. It was well known that there was ill feeling between John Dean's wife and Margaret Barclay, wife of her brother-in-law Alexander Dean. From the evidence of her eight-year-old servant girl, a daughter of Isobal Insch or Taylor, a prosecution for witchcraft emerged. Margaret Barclay had been heard to wish ill luck to the departed ship. Under torture she and Isobel Shearer or Crauford revealed that clay figures had been moulded (with a fair-headed figure representing the provost). In company with Stewart and the two Isobels, Margaret Barclay had cast the figures into the sea in the presence of the Devil in the shape of a lap dog. John Stewart hanged himself in his cell. Isobel Insch flung herself down from the church belfry where she had been confined. Margaret Barclay and Isobel Crauford were strangled and burned at the stake.

In 1650 seventeen witches from various parts of Cunninghame were similarly executed at Irvine, twelve in March, five in June. Others were apparently dealt with in 1662 and 1682, the last a spaewife who discovered a thief by divination. The presbytery of Irvine, to which all the parishes of Cunninghame were attached, supervised the persecution, and were represented at the executions. Though Hugh, 7th earl, had some misgivings, the Countess of Eglinton could in 1650 write, 'God Almighty send a good trial to all the witches, and send a hot fire to burn them with'. It has been said that the Irvine witches were burned at a spot beyond the Townhead, near Springfield. Witches were certainly associated with this locality, because nearby at Patons Thorn the Devil in shape of a black foal appeared to Margaret Barclay and her associates. The usual place of execution was at the Gallowsknowe, to the north of the town and west of Heathfield. Just below that place, in the river, was a deep pool called the Witches Plumb, presumably where witches were ducked to test whether the Devil would save them from drowning.

There had been no recorded opposition to the establishment of the Reformed Church; its disciplinary rule was unchallenged; but there came much vexatious dispute about church government and organisation.

For the maintenance of the ministry it had been hoped to inherit the resources of the old church. But most of the church lands had been feued out already, as happened with Kilwinning Abbey under the commendatorship of Gavin Hamilton (1550-1571). Revenues passed into lay hands too, and indeed all the properties and receipts from Kilwinning Abbey were acquired by the earl of Eglinton in 1603. The minister of Irvine's stipend was uncertain, and for long he was without a manse or glebe, despite a promise of the town council in 1631 to make provision. The earls of Eglinton also in 1603 acquired the patronage of the church of Irvine with power to appoint its ministers. This was deemed by some to limit ecclesiastical independence. While the presbyterian system of kirk sessions and presbyteries remained intact, the assertion of royal control over the church by the appointment of bishops produced resentment against episcopacy. Tentative moves by James VI and the policy of Charles I involving the introduction of a prayer book in 1637 succeeded in uniting members of all classes in defence of presbyterian principles and forms of worship. The period of relative calm since the ending of the feuds was succeeded by an era of civil and religious discord which continued intermittently for the next fifty years.

Radical presbyterianism made its impact on Irvine

The Timmerland was typical of houses extended into the street and sometimes creating congestion. This building occupied the Bridgegatehead corner into the 19th century.

following the arrival in 1618 of David Dickson, presented as parish minister by Alexander Seton, 6th Earl of Eglinton. David Dickson was a man of great ability and integrity, and such a powerful preacher that the church had 'great crowds at the dores and in the streets'. Even on Mondays the church became filled with those attending market. In the large hall of his dwellinghouse at the west corner of the Kirkgate and High Street the bearded figure of Dickson was often found with groups assembled for prayer and counsel. In 1621 he was temporarily suspended for his criticisms of prelacy. Later he began to organise opposition to Charles I throughout Scotland and, following the National Covenant, the minister of Irvine was made in 1639 the Moderator of the General Assembly of the Church. To exercise his leadership more effectively he left Irvine in 1642 to become professor at Glasgow University, then Edinburgh. Others from Irvine also played a leading role in the political and military struggles which ensued, including especially Provost Mr. Robert Barclay whose career and family background require some attention.

The Barclays were a well-established local family. There was a towns officer (Alexander Barclay, 1595), a teacher (Mr. David Barclay, 1611), a witch who was executed (Margaret Barclay, 1619), a servitor to the earl of Eglinton (Ninian Barclay, 1645); assorted burgesses including a tailor (John Barclay, 1619), and a mason (Archibald Barclay, 1615); a bailie (John Barclay, 1608), and no fewer than four provosts between the 16th and 18th centuries — Robert Barclay, 1559; Ninian Barclay, 1602, 1616-17; Mr. Robert Barclay, 1639-41; 1642-44; 1648-49; 1655-59; William Barclay, 1729. There were also Barclays who were lairds of Brydeskirk, Perceton, Warrixhill, and Warrix in Dreghorn parish; and Ladyland and Kilbirnie not far off. The fact that there was Over Perceton and Inner Perceton (with Barclays in the latter), Warrixhill (sometimes called Perceton-Cunninghame which passed to a Barclay), as well as Warrix in two lots (only one of which was owned by Barclays) has naturally caused some confusion. It would seem that from the original Barclays of Ardrossan came the Kilbirnie branch, whence the cadets of Ladyland and from them the Barclays of Perceton; from whom came those of Brydeskirk and of Warrix. The merchant burgess family of Irvine who gave the burgh its provosts were owners of Warrix (but not of Perceton as has sometimes been surmised).

The Barclays of Perceton, deriving from a Robert Barclay who acquired it in the 15th century, produced — after an uncertainly recorded genealogy — that Robert

Barclay who succeeded about 1660 and was created a baronet in 1668. Sir Robert Barclay of Perceton had close Edinburgh connections — he was a bailie of that city and acquired two wives from there. But he retained his association with Irvine, helping to build a new quay (1677), regularly enjoying the council's hospitality as did his son, 'Perston young and old' (1669-86), sailed from Irvine in his own ship (1689), and died in 1694. The third baronet, Sir Robert Barclay, was a Jacobite who died in exile; another grandson, David Barclay, was ennobled by Frederick the Great. As well as Sir Robert Barclay of Perceton, there was Mr. Robert Barclay of Brydeskirk who died in 1616, and whose son David sold it to Ninian Barclay, an Edinburgh merchant.

Robert Barclay, provost in 1559, was possibly father to Ninian Barclay who in 1585 was involved in feuding and the 'mutilation of Johnne Browne', became a councillor in 1601, and died during his second term as provost in 1617. His eldest son, Ninian, succeeded to Warrix, and the widow Marion Ross and her three sons shared the various burgh properties. There was a tenement on the east side of High Street called Dunwodyes (two along from one owned by another Ninian Barclay!), another on the west side next to Roxburgh, other two in the Kirkgate and the Bridgegate, plus various lands — Scottiswards, land east of Roodmeadow, St. James land, land and barns on the west side of the road leading to the Annick. Robert, the second son, shared in these, and also benefited when his younger brother Hew died in 1619. Robert became a graduate and was always appropriately designated as Mr. Robert Barclay. As a 'Paedagouge' he was employed as a tutor by Lord Lorne, later Marquis of Argyll, who in 1630 was enrolled as an honorary burgess of Irvine, and whose brother from 1642-1645 held the short-lived title of Earl of Irvine. Not long afterwards Mr. Robert Barclay began in 1639 his four terms as provost of Irvine. As Irvine's commissioner in parliament, and no doubt under Argyll's patronage, he was one of those sent by the Scots parliament to negotiate with Charles I in London, and continued to play a prominent role in public affairs till the Restoration of Charles II in 1660. Locally he may have been involved in the evacuation of Glasgow University, in 1646 because of the plague, to Irvine. One of the students involved was Lord Neil Campbell, Argyll's son; Colin Campbell, another student and kinsman, died here. After 1660 Mr. Robert Barclay was leeted again for the provostship but not chosen (1666, 1667) and refused further nomination to the council (1669). He rented 'his rig' (1664) and 'ane aiker of infield land' (1668). He continued to associate with councillors at tavern meetings (1670), and died in 1679. He was wealthy enough to have endowed his youngest daughter with twenty thousand merks plus various properties, when in 1668 she married James Boyle, a later provost.

Mr. Thomas Barclay's elder brother, Ninian Barclay of Warrix, was followed by another Ninian Barclay whose son, William Barclay of Warrix, became provost in 1729. He is chiefly celebrated because his younger daughter Jean had two bastard weans to the town clerk James Marshall; and the death of his son Dr. Robert Barclay in Buenos Aires was followed by extended litigation.

While Provost Mr. Robert Barclay was pursuing his important political activities Alexander, 6th earl, described as 'the pious Eglinton', and renowned as 'Greysteel', fought in the armies of the Covenant till 1650, followed by ten years as a prisoner of war. A younger son, Robert Montgomerie, continued the fight against Cromwell, while James Fullarton of Fullarton and Crosbie was in 1650 involved with the extremist Western Association. Meanwhile, within Irvine itself, during the ministries of Hew Mackaile (1642-50) and Alexander Nesbitt (1650-69) there were sufferings to be borne. There were periodic levies and requisitions. There were 'widows, orphans and lame souldiers' to be assisted. In 1645 when Montrose's highlanders were near, many townfolk 'fled and transportit thameselves, thair wyffes, bairnes, servands, familie guids and geir yea even as we say bag and baggage so much as they were habile to get transportit to Yrland or uthir partes beyond sey'. During the Cromwellian occupation English troops were garrisoned at Eglinton and in the tolbooth.

The Restoration of Charles II in 1660 seemed to promise peace. The burgh motto, 'Tandem bona causa triumphat' (Yet a good cause triumphs in the end), was supposedly originated at this time to commemorate the triumph of the royalist cause. Yet paradoxically it was ambiguous enough perhaps to afford inspiration to others — those who were soon compelled towards violent resistance to Charles II's reintroduction of episcopacy. That king's insensitivity to Scottish feelings, most obvious in his ecclesiastical policies, is also instanced in his award to an English family of the title of Viscount Irvine, which they held from 1670 until 1778, without any local connections. In 1662 ex-provost Mr. Robert Barclay (who is reported to have had some involvement in the negotiations for the restoration of Charles II) was fined £1,200 for his share in the previous rebellion. Ex-provost John Reid was fined £600. Others including ex-provost Allan Dunlop and town clerk Robert Brown were sued for their part in an attack on Drumlanrig in 1650. Such recriminations were resented.

In 1666 armed Covenanters set out from Ayrshire for Edinburgh. This Pentlands Rising was crushed, and prisoners taken were returned for execution in Irvine, Ayr and Kilmarnock. William Sutherland, a Highlander and the Irvine hangman, boldly refused to perform the task despite severe pressures. Eventually a prisoner at Ayr did the job, fortified with brandy and a promise of release. The two Covenanters thus executed at Irvine on the last day of 1666 were James Blackwood and John McCoull.

There is no note of Irvine's involvement in the later rebellions of 1679 (Drumclog and Bothwell Bridge) and 1680 (Airdsmoss). Through these unhappy times the burgh suffered from impositions, occupation by the Highland Host in 1678, and interruption of normal burgh procedures. Councillors refused to 'take the test' and could not validly exercise their duties. In 1677 the inhabitants held meetings in the church to elect a committee to manage the town's affairs. In 1682 the privy council had to intervene and arbitrarily nominate a council. In 1687 members of the family of Wallace of Shewalton, who were sympathetic to the new king James VII, were brought in to form a council. A further difficulty was that in 1681 the tolbooth was found insufficient to accommodate all persons arrested for attending conventicles — those clandestine religious services which Irvine had known on occasion since the time of David Dickson. The royal authorities made several attempts at reconciliation. George Hutcheson (1669-74), then a Mr. Shaw (1674-76?), John Stirling (1676-84) and William Hamilton (1684-88), though favouring presbyterian principles, were prepared to serve as 'indulged ministers' under supervision. Of these, Hutcheson was accounted an effective preacher, who delivered a series of forty-five sermons on Psalm 130; personally, with 'large and open countenance, [he] was merry and facetious in conversation, and of an amiable, companionable, and friendly disposition'. Eventually toleration was extended to allow those who refused to attend a parish church which was under episcopal control to worship as they wished. In 1688 a house at Seagatehead was accordingly fitted out by the town council — but never required.

The toleration brought back to Irvine Patrick Warner, son of a local burgess. One of two boys who were trained as ministers, Patrick Warner came back to Scotland from India in 1677, became a field preacher, then sought refuge in Holland. In 1688 he was ordained minister of Irvine. Not long afterwards James VII and II was ousted in the Glorious Revolution by William of Orange, who in due course abolished prelacy and recognised the presbyterian rule of the Church of Scotland. Patrick Warner while in Holland had advised the Prince of Orange so to do. Thus Irvine can claim its share in the church settlement which finally concluded the Killing Times.

Patrick Warner ministered till 1708. Among his other works was the improvement of the lands he acquired —

THE

GENUINE DECLARATION

OF

William Sutherland,

HANGMAN AT IRVINE;

WHEREIN HIS

KNOWLEDGE OF THE SCRIPTURES, HIS COURAGE, AND
BEHAVIOUR TOWARDS THE PERSECUTORS,

AND THEIR

BARBAROUS TREATMENT OF HIM AT AIR,

ARE PLAINLY SET FORTH.

———

EDINBURGH:
PRINTED BY AND FOR D. WEBSTER AND SON,
HORSE WYND.
1821.
Price Threepence.

Two Covenanters were martyred in 1666. But William Sutherland, the Irvine hangman, refused to execute them.

more fully detailed in the next chapter. He retired to his estate of Ardeer, 'now aged above 60, my strength decayed, and my voice too weak for so numerous a congregation'. During the vacancy which followed Mr. Warner's retiral, a minister who was expected to preach one Sunday did not appear. William McKnight, a native of Ireland and recently licensed as a minister, happened to be making an overnight stay in Irvine, and was invited to preach. He was liked so well that a deputation was sent to Eglinton, and the earl agreed to his presentation. The ministry of William McKnight (1709-50) belonged to a new and more pacific chapter of church history.

Part Two
Growth

Six

Some Progress

Despite the civil and religious disorders listed in the previous chapter, everyday life was able to proceed with only occasional interruption. More surprising, economic and social advances were being made in the 17th-century burgh.

Timothy Pont, in his description of Cunninghame around 1600, could write: 'This countrey is beine of a longe tyme verry peacable except somequhat in the late age troubled with ye intestine broyles of ye housses of Glencairne and Eglintone and ther adherents wich ar nou in effect all forgottin and by ressone of ye long peace it hes injoyed from forraine invasione it is become verry civill and weill cultured'. The low ground was 'fertill and full of profitt'. The greater part of Cunninghame was 'much enriched by the Industrious inhabitants lymeing of ther grounds, quherby the pasturs heir since this experiment wes practised is become much more luxuriant then befor'. The whole area was specialising in dairy farming, and yields were three times as good as in adjacent areas. Recent research has revealed that in the neighbourhood of Kilwinning farming practice was being improved. The traditional runrig system had been modified and the periodic reallocation of arable land among tenants abandoned. Pont noted how populous the area was. Indeed it can be described as relatively overpopulated, which explains the emigrations to Argyll and Ulster at this period; possibly this contributed also to the various social disturbances. Yet the landowners benefited from what amounted to an agricultural revolution. The great lords could afford to build new tower houses which provided comfort as well as protection — of Cunninghame's 35 castles, 18 were built or rebuilt in the 17th century. The feuing of church lands allowed many sitting tenants to acquire their own farms and set themselves up as bonnet lairds. So Pont could remark how Cunninghame was 'marvelously weill beutified with goodly buldings and edifices of Noble and gentlemen, and ye duellings of the yeomanrie verry thick poudred over the face of this countrey, for all ye most pairt weill and comodiously planted and granished'.

The new commercial farming brought an increase in marketing which benefited the royal burgh of Irvine. There is evidence that in the late 16th century some burgesses were affluent enough to engage in land speculation, providing mortgages for lesser lairds in adjacent parishes. In the 17th century Irvine, despite its various problems, grew considerably. While the rival burgh of Ayr increased in population from an estimated 1,500 to 2,000, Irvine was growing even more quickly from 1,000 to 1,500.

It is possible to assess the advances made, with the assistance of the town council minutes which survive from 1595 more or less intact. The 'sett' or constitution of the burgh provided for a council of 15 merchants, to whom were added two representatives of the trades after 1646. Each year just before Michaelmas the old councillors chose the new. Two merchants might be replaced or continued, at the pleasure of the council. The two deacons representing the incorporated trades had to be changed yearly. On the Monday after Michaelmas the old and new councillors together elected the provost and two bailies, who might not hold office for more than two years in succession. On the next Friday various other officials were appointed by the new council.

The addition of two craftsmen to the council was the culmination of a long campaign by the trades for representation. Various Acts of 1556, 1564 and 1581 had never been implemented locally, and a complaint lodged by local craftsmen with the privy council in 1611 proved ineffective. Indeed the local ringleaders, a saddler and a smith, were put in the stocks and threatened with further penalties. But as a sign of the growing power of the craftsmen, they won their Seal of Cause in 1646 establishing the Incorporated Trades and allowing representation on the council by deacons of two crafts, who were, however, selected by the council.

Membership of the council was not always welcomed, particularly in the period of religious dissension after 1660. In 1665 six burgesses refused to accept nomination, and the officers of the burgh were ordered to 'incarcerat them within the said tolbuith therin to remain ay and quhill they and either of them accept of ther said electione as counsellouris'. In 1679 eight members of the old council seeking to be quit of their responsibility nominated 'absent persons or seamen who were nearly always absent'. The difficulty was that councillors were required to make a declaration accepting the episcopal church arrangements. With no councillors validly appointed, a meeting was held in the church to try to resolve the problem. The 1680 election was again declared irregular. In 1687 James VII prohibited further elections and nominated a council composed of reliable men — including William Wallace of Shewalton and five others of that family. In 1689, after the Glorious Revolution, the burgesses were directed to elect a new council by the customary method.

The office of provost could be an onerous one — in 1670 Provost James Blair was almost killed trying to prevent an affray — and the provost was usually awarded the additional responsibility of representing the burgh in parliament. The intrusion of William Wallace as provost in 1687 was perhaps not altogether unacceptable, because he was a burgess who combined mercantile with landed interests. Other provost-lairds of this period were John Peebles of Broomlands; Ninian Barclay of Warrix; John Scott who owned Clonbeith in Kilwinning parish and those local lands which resulted in Trindlemoss acquiring the name of Scotts Loch; Alexander Cunningham of Collellan in Dundonald parish; and Thomas McGoun of Smithston in Kilwinning parish.

The office of treasurer also had its difficulties. A councillor was responsible for the accounts for one year only, yet he was dependent on the efficiency of his predecessors. In 1665 there was an awkward situation with the 'lait thesaurer quha reported no diligence anent the auditing of his accompt of the teind, quhairupon the Magistratis and Councell ordeins him to remain in prisone and quhill he mak payment'. In 1667 the council in desperation ordered all previous treasurers save one 'to be presentlie incarcerat within the tolbuith quhill they mak their thesaurers accomptis'. More systematic auditing was introducing in 1680.

Another councillor was appointed as fiscal. This could be an unpopular job, sometimes entrusted to one of the craftsman councillors. Later of course a lawyer had to be appointed. After 1657 there was a division of labour when another councillor was appointed as dean of guild with the responsibility for civil as distinct from criminal business. Other councillors were appointed to act with nominated burgesses as visitors for inspecting markets and mills, birleymen to settle boundary and similar disputes, and stentmasters to collect taxes. The bailies were both magistrates in the burgh court and collectors of the rents. All these elected officials were entitled to a fee for their services. The post of town clerk was an appointment for life. Robert Broun the notary held it for sixty years from 1612 until 1672. A predecessor, Hew Garven, was murdered in 1607, and there are numerous other examples of officials being assaulted when performing their duties.

In the 17th century the burgh employed four towns officers. In 1601 'officeris claythis' were purchased, and in 1688 there was another order for red cloth and furnishings for their uniforms. The sergeant or macer was responsible for summoning parties to compear in the burgh court. Others performed the duties of hangman, drummer and piper, bellman, and night watch. In 1681 there was an account for 'polishing, mending and dressing of the officeris halberts and for ane hors lock for the stocks'.

The town council met as occasion required. There was an instruction in 1669 'to meet each Friday at ten hours at the ringing of the bell'. From year to year they carried out what was normally routine business. New burgesses were elected on payment of the appropriate fine, and occasionally honorary burgesses. In 1665 they were persuaded to create as burgesses various lords and their retainers, numbering 69 in all. Monetary penalties called unlaws were collected from persons incarcerated in the tolbooth, whether for debt or slaughter. It is perhaps a sign of improving standards of behaviour that minor offences were dealt with, like throwing stones 'qhuairwith ane child was hurt in the lip' (1664) and 'horrid cursing' for which the punishment was 'to be imprisoned till next market day and then to be taken to the Cross, and have a paper put on his face and to have rotten eggs cast at him' (1690). In support of the discipline of the church a woman guilty of adultery was banished from the burgh (1666), as was the town drummer for bigamy, 'harbouring and entertaining of two wives or whores'. Others were fined (1602) for irregular marriages.

That there was increased business at the markets and fairs is suggested by the appointment of inspectors and the creation of the post of dean of guild. Placards listing the petty customs were displayed on market days, and in 1691 it was found necessary to revive the 'Michaelmas Laws' regulating business. Forestalling or selling before the market officially opened was prohibited (1669). Baxters (bakers) were required to put their mark on loaves, which had been found often under weight (1677). Prices were fixed for candles and bread (1666). Action had to be taken against 'unfree traffiqueris', non-burgesses who traded illegally (1606). There were complaints about landward fleshers and unfree weavers and tailors. In 1668 weights 'found light' were impounded. And, to avoid the necessity of travel on a Sunday, the Monday market was moved to Tuesday (1690).

Attention was devoted by the Council to the 'common

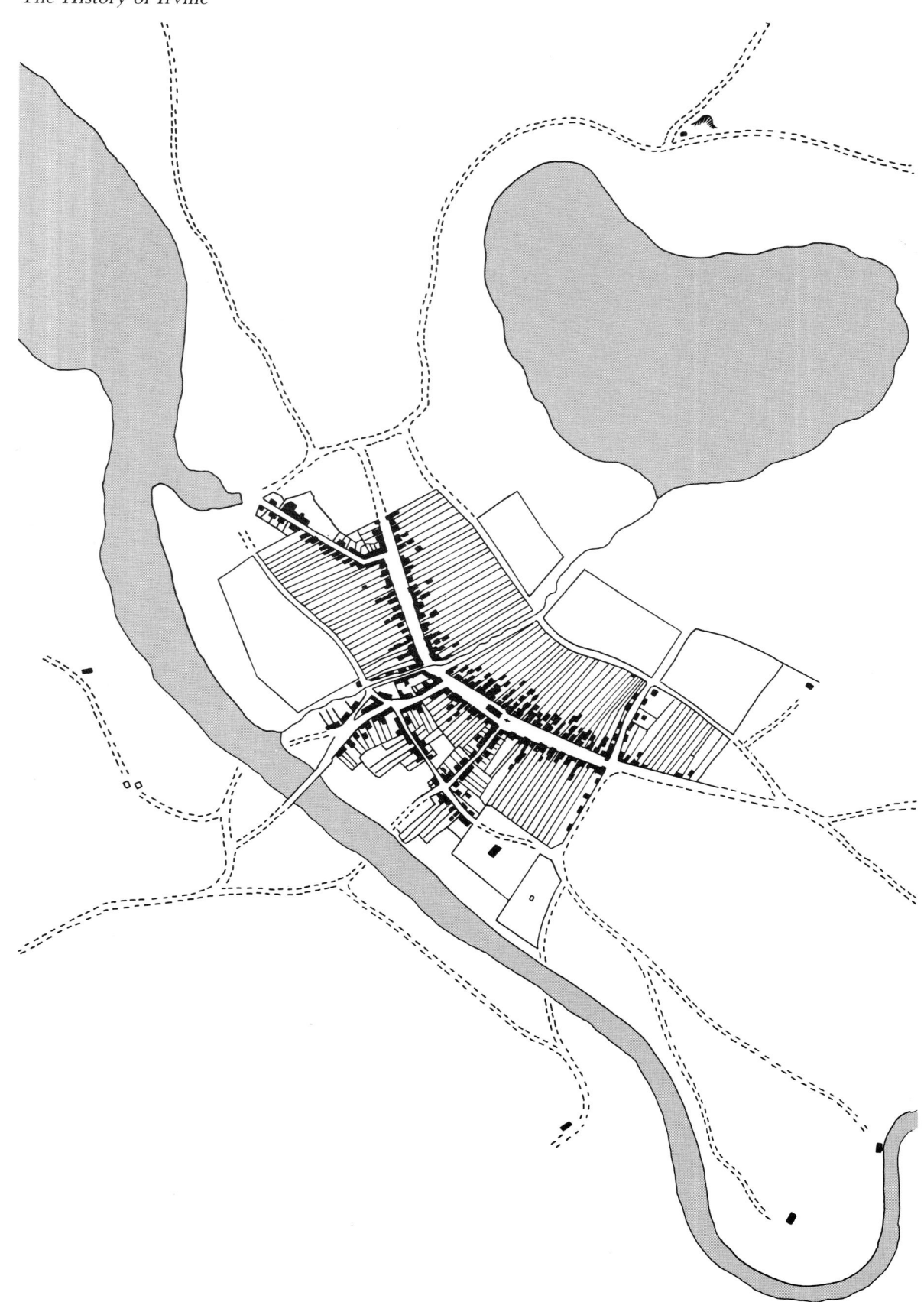

werkis'. The inhabitants were required to sweep the 'calsay' in front of their dwellings and to clear away the middens they had deposited there (1665). As the town extended in area, an increased water supply became necessary, especially after the Grip Gutter dried up. In 1695 the inhabitants near Seagatehead obtained permission to dig a well there, the first of many that were sunk later. The fires which swept the town in 1599 and 1647 were followed in the latter instance by an appeal throughout the presbytery of Irvine for aid in rebuilding. In 1677 a regulation was made against using candles in premises where linen was being worked, but this was probably ignored — as it was in the famous fire in a heckling shop much later in 1781.

For the better management of the burgh's extensive lands, burgesses were required to produce their charters (1601), repair their back dykes (1665) and fence their properties (1686). Revenue increased throughout the century, but so also did the demands of the royal exchequer. Rather than impose what would have seemed exorbitant stents, Irvine like other royal burghs in the second half of the 17th century began to borrow heavily to pay for its commitments. To lend money to the burgh in an age before banks were available was convenient for merchants and landowners, and profitable too. But it involved the royal burghs in what became chronic insolvency. In 1692 Irvine admitted to the Convention of Royal Burghs that while its Common Good amounted to £1,790 Scots, its total liabilities were £11,636. Continued feuing of burgh land was used to bring slightly more in annual returns, but the initial payment — the grassum — might disappear as a perquisite to the magistrates. The annual roup of lands for pasture and of dues to be collected afforded another opportunity for personal profit. To prevent deception it was required that auctions should be announced 'by tuck of drum' and concluded at the 'running of sand glass'. Yet councillors were often able to arrange successful bids. In 1665, for example, the provost won the right to collect the dues from fishing boats and the following year also the harbour dues and the grazing on the Rotten Bog.

There is ample evidence that business was expanding in the 17th century. It has already been noted how the built-up area of the town was being extended, with shops opened, the meal mills busy, and the markets and fairs apparently flourishing. Specialisation, another sign of progress,

The Incorporated Trades won their Seal of Cause in 1646, an indication of the growing importance of manufactures.

appeared in the vicinity of the Cross with mention of a Fishmarket (1609) and a Fleshmarket (1620). There was also a Mealmarket, where a notable improvement was made. 'The ordinary sheltering place of Victual Mercat ... is now changed and altered so that the meall corne and other graines ... are now exposed to raine wind and weather whereby the victuall is greatly damnified.' Royal permission was obtained to levy an additional petty duty on grain, several properties near the Cross were purchased, and a Market House was erected in 1694 for storage and sale of grain. In the process, the old mercat cross of the burgh disappeared for ever. The council ordered 'The Cross to be taken away, and the stones to be applied

Town plan, 1600. Despite civil and religious conflicts, Irvine continued to grow. The church was adapted for protestant worship (1560), a burgh school at Kirkgatehead was endowed (1572), Seagate Castle was rebuilt (1565), and Duntonknowe quarry provided for new stone-built houses. With the best sites now occupied, the Grip and Hamilhill were used, back tenements added in High Street, and building extended into Townhead. Recession of the sea created a major problem, and in 1572 the council purchased Marressfoot for a new quay to handle Irvine's growing trade.

The Powder House was built about 1642 for storage of locally manufactured gunpowder.

towards erecting the meal market house, now a-building, in respect there is a great want of freestone for that work, and that the Cross, being of an old fashion, and inconvenient, doth mar the decorum of the street'. No trace was left, but it seems to have been quite a substantial structure.

The tolbooth itself underwent some improvements in the 17th century. In 1672 the gable was rebuilt, various insignia were probably added at this time, and in 1681 the old steeple was replaced. That the tolbooth was supplied with a clock is clear from payments to the 'knockkeiper' in 1601. In 1686 a new town clock with two dials was purchased from David Buchanan of Gorbals. In the steeple a new cast bell was also installed in 1637. A local tradesman was paid an annual fee for attending to the clock and bell. In 1667 his duties were defined: 'to dress the Toune knok for ane yeir to come and to ring the Tolbuith bell according to the ancient custome tuice ilk day during the said space (except upon the sabbath day) viz. at fyve hours in the morneing and ten hours at night and to ring the secund bell ilk sabbath conforme to old use'.

Necessary work was undertaken at the bridge and harbour. By 1665 the 'fair stone bridge' described by Pont was requiring repair. The pillars had become undercut and the arch weakened so that the bridge had become unsafe. The privy council agreed to an increase in bridge tolls, and the Earl of Eglinton who assisted in securing this grant was rewarded with free passage over the bridge. The roup of the bridge dues which produced only £22 Scots in 1665 increased to £106 Scots the following year, and contributed to the £1,000 Scots spent on extensive repairs. A contract was made with 'quarriers for winneing of stanes for reparatioun of the brig', and the work of reconstruction was accomplished by John Smyth, a Kilmaurs mason, whose efforts were so much appreciated that he was made an honorary burgess. In 1668 timber dismantled from the bridge was sold. In 1681 the road surface was improved by the 'calsaying' of the bridge. In 1695 posts were erected to prevent damage by heavy traffic, which was forced to use the Car ford.

Similarly in the 17th century a lot of attention was devoted to harbour improvement. It should be pointed out that evidence submitted in applications for grants must sometimes be treated with suspicion, by historians as well as the authorities more directly involved. There seems to have been some exaggeration in the council's petition of 1665 that the bridge was 'unpassable to man or beast', and in their description of the harbour in 1613 as 'by the force and violence of the sea altogidder ruinated and decayit'. In fact, the council successfully surmounted the various difficulties in providing adequate facilities. The establishment of a quay at Marress in 1572 must have been of limited value. Proposals in 1584 for an alternative port on the Little Cumbrae came to nothing. Troon was used for a few years after 1608. But the Marress quay seems to have been used until 1665 when with 'the Watter of Irving changeing its channell' a plan was devised 'to cutt throw the lands of Marreis at that place callit the docke, for making of ane harberie at ane neir cutt'. The inhabitants were conscripted to 'goe out by quarters ilk day for cutting thereof', with absentees to be fined. Whether this cutting of a new channel or canal was accomplished is uncertain. In 1669 arrangements were made for 'a bowie to be made upon the bar', which may mean that some sort of lighthouse was erected. In 1677 the inhabitants were again called upon that 'the haill stanes lying at the ends of the bridge be taken to the shore for the laying of a Kasey [causeway] for the good of the harbour, and ease and advantage of vessels'; and later that year 'to take stones out of the water for the laying of ane key at the Bar'. William Fullarton of Crosbie and Sir Robert Barclay of Perceton contributed 'for helping to build ane key at the Bar'. From this I conclude that in 1677 the harbour was moved to its present site opposite the mouth of the Garnock. At the same time a new road was laid out to that harbour from the bridge — called 'the lang Calsay' and later the Halfway, otherwise Haafway or road to the sea. In 1691 the river was allowed to revert to its former channel, the quay at the bar was rebuilt, and to aid navigation the mouth of the Garnock was dredged.

Trade was obviously expanding. A recent study of this period has concluded that Ayrshire was 'an area as progressive as any in Scotland. It lay on the awakening face of the country ... It looked first to Ireland ... It maintained a European trade as wide as the seas between Stockholm and

The harbour was moved in 1677 to its present location, handling small sailing vessels, as it did when this photograph was taken late in the 19th century.

Bordeaux ... It looked already to America'. A sign of the expanding trade of the Ayrshire ports was the division some time in the 1670s of the coast into the two separate customs precincts of Ayr and Irvine. That of Irvine included Saltcoats, where Robert Cunningham of Auchenharvie constructed a new harbour between 1684 and 1700 — itself an indication of expansion. The nature of the trade of this north Ayrshire precinct is indicated in the customs registers for the years 1681–86. Though incomplete, they list arrivals and departures involving Ireland (169;402), England (0;1), Norway and the Baltic (5;1), and France (11;8), as well as a considerable unrecorded traffic with other Scottish ports.

In the return of 1692 (which it has been judged was 'made with the intention of stressing the poverty of the town') Irvine reported that they had only eight small ships, of which one had been lately lost. In the five preceding years they had a ship of 70 tons from France with salt and brandy; one of 30 tons from Norway with tar and timber; a share in two others; and their small 20-ton ships traded with Ireland mainly in wool and foodstuffs.

The preponderance of trade with Ireland reflected a continuing but expanding trade, exporting wool, cloth, stockings, coal and miscellaneous manufactured goods, and importing leather, horses, cheese and butter. There were restrictions on the importation of Irish grain, often evaded, and waived because of the bad harvests between 1696 and 1700. There was also a considerable passenger traffic. At the beginning of the century Ulster was colonised with Protestant settlers. The protocol book of Robert Broun records a number of Irvine burgesses who had thus emigrated. Sir William Brereton was told in 1636 that ten thousand Scots had moved to Ireland in the previous two years. This was clearly an exaggeration, but nearer the truth was the supplementary information that most had embarked at Irvine in parties of a hundred at a time, and three hundred on one tide. From about the same era began a contrary tide, what would eventually become a flood of Irish beggars, despite attempts to exclude these unwelcome immigrants. In 1681 an Irish theatrical company of thirty persons en route to Edinburgh was held up at Irvine because of such restrictions.

Trade with Scandinavia was limited to the importation of timber, tar, and iron. The traditional commercial links with Holland and France were adversely affected by war, government restrictions and piracy. In 1636 a German and an English pirate were sentenced to death at Irvine, commuted to banishment. In 1643 the Irvine ships *James of Saltcoats* and *Providence* were commissioned to hunt for pirates on the Irish Sea. In 1689 the aged Sir Robert Barclay, sailing on his own ship, the *Barbara*, from Irvine to Bristol was taken by a French privateer but saved by an English frigate. Protectionist policies limited trade with France almost entirely to the importation of salt for fish curing. Nevertheless there was no apparent shortage in the taverns of Irvine, because the town accounts, taking 1680 as an example, include bills for claret, sack, Rhenish wine, and aquavita or brandy.

That fishing remained an important enterprise is indicated by the regular rouping of the 'cobble teinds'. Conservation of salmon stocks was attempted in 1581 when the magistrates were fined for 'slauchter of reid fische and of fry of all fische'. In 1602 there was an attempt to prohibit Ayr and Irvine fishers who used 'sandeill pokes' which destroyed the herring fry. In 1607 Ayr and Irvine fishermen retaliated by attacking Saltcoats and cutting down the masts and sails of their rivals' boats. In 1622 James Kennedy of Culzean was appointed to preserve the pearl fishing in the waters of Irvine, Ayr and Girvan.

Ships little bigger than fishing boats were now venturing across the Atlantic. Two such ships from Ayr were of only 28 and 14 tons. Records do not tell the full story of what was an illicit trade with the English colonies, and it has been guessed in the case of Ayr that 'returns were deliberately falsified to make the burgh appear poorer than it really was'. That Irvine ships may have crossed the Atlantic is perhaps hinted at by the fining in 1637 of several unlicensed merchants who were selling tobacco. An opportunity to invest in transatlantic trade came in 1696 with the Company of Scotland's Darien colonial scheme. Subscriptions of £100 were made by the burgh and eleven other persons: Provost Thomas McGoun, Alexander Cunningham, William McTaggart, John Thomson and Edward Kerr, merchants; William Hamilton, lawyer; William Cunningham, apothecary; George Monro, clerk of Cunninghame; Zacharias Gemmell of Bogside; Rev. Patrick Warner; and Maria Stirling, daughter of a former minister. This investment of £1,200 was small compared with Ayr's £2,800 and Kilmarnock's £1,800. Ayrshire contributed £19,450 out of the total capital of £400,000 Sterling. It was perhaps fortunate for Irvine that they were canny folk, and only these few made a minimum investment in what turned out to be a disastrous enterprise.

The craftsmen of the town shared in the undoubted expansion of trade. After 'crying in ane mutinous and hostile way against the magistrates' they won recognition and, as already mentioned, obtained from the council a Seal of Cause in 1646 which formally acknowledged the Incorporated Trades. It is perhaps significant to note the order in which the several crafts were listed: Smiths including Hammermen; Websters; Tailors; Cordiners; Skinners; Wrights including Joiners and Carpenters; Squaremen; and Coopers. Note was also made of the waulkers or fullers of cloth who were not as yet sufficient in number to form their own guild. There is specified in the Seal of Cause 'the full number of Sevin crafts'. The waulkers never achieved a separate identity. Indeed the skinners and coopers seem also to have failed to become established on their own, for later in the century the minutes both of the council and the Trades refer only to five. The hammermen who in 1645 had hoped to obtain their own 'right of deaconrie' were thirteen in number. All this suggests perhaps a hundred master craftsmen who with their journeymen, apprentices and families might form about a third of the estimated burgh population of 1,500.

In the Weavers Book under 1646 there was a suitable inscription:

> God prosper thou this Seal to us
> And grant us a right use of it
> So shall we fear and reverence
> Thy gracious will and providence.

The Hammerman Book of 1647 echoed the sentiment:

> Lord be our guide and us conduct
> And teach us thy right way
> That we may fear and know thy laws
> For now ever and for aye.

The Seal of Cause made provision for mutual charitable aid, with contributions kept in 'the box'. But its principal purpose was to maintain the customary control of admission to each trade through supervision of apprentices, and the employment by masters of approved journeymen. Standards of workmanship were maintained by debarring unauthorised and consequently unreliable persons. While at a later date the monopolistic powers of craft guilds were seen to be restrictive, in the 17th century they effectively encouraged expansion.

The Incorporated Trades in 1646 also secured the privilege of having two of their deacons appointed to the council. The choice was made not by the Trades but by the council. Indeed the council regarded the Trades as subordinate to their authority. In 1657 there was a confused dispute in which the council claimed a share of the crafts' admission fees, and the Trades in reply asserted that they were entitled to a deacon convener. Ill feeling persisted. In 1668, when the Trades purchased a mortcloth to be used in the burial of members, the council prohibited its use. The common mortcloth had to be hired from the kirk session,

The 'Halfway' was laid out in 1677, leading to the new harbour. It was renamed Montgomery Street in the late 19th century, just a generation before this photograph of 1907.

which depended on this revenue to support poor persons, who might include widows and children of tradesmen. The next year certain deacons were incarcerated in the tolbooth for daring to choose their own boxmaster — as the deacon convener was called. It was pointed out that the deacons of the five crafts had to submit a leet of three from whom the council made choice. Yet by 1673 (when their records begin) the Trades were choosing their own boxmaster, after 1718 called deacon convener. The crafts were enjoying an enhanced social status by the end of the 17th century. Their loft or seat in the west end of the church was at a considerable distance from the pulpit. They wished to bring it forward to the side of the council seat. That place was occupied by 'such as are unfitt to occupy such ane place, and being of the rabble doe often creat disturbances'. In 1693 the council agreed to a Trades Loft being brought forward beside the council seat which should, however, be raised to a higher level.

To the traditional staple trades of working in wool, leather, wood or metal were added new local enterprises in the 17th century. One of the hammermen, possibly an armourer, must have established a bell foundry, for in Irvine there were cast several bells — for the Over Tolbooth in Ayr (1616), Irvine Tolbooth (1637), Maybole (1696) inscribed 'Albert Danel Geli afrenchnan', and Kilmarnock (1697) with a similar inscription. There is record of another novel manufacture in the early 17th century. An instruction by James VI for the provision of powder magazines in all royal burghs seems to have been implemented in Irvine, for in 1643, 1644 and 1646 orders were met for large quantities of gunpowder. Saltpetre was derived from deposits in byres, stables and doocots. This would be stored at the Powder House in the Golffields, whose construction has thus been attributed to the year 1642. The range of occupations was being extended. The Incorporated Trades would include those weavers apparently now specialising in linen; there would be more masons among the squaremen wrights, and in 1685 a slater became a burgess. There was a surgeon called Tobias (c.1653) succeeded by James Frank (1683), John Hutchison (1685) and the well-to-do apothecary-surgeon William Cunningham (1695). There were brewers and tavern-keepers who were well patronised by the councillors in the course of their duties. During fifteen months between January 1686 and May 1687 Janet Garven was paid nearly £400 Scots for such refreshments.

In the 17th century also began the intensive working of local coal. Exports to begin with were inconsiderable, some 20 tons (1542) and 66 tons (1623). These may have come from the neighbouring parish of Kilwinning, for in 1681 when ten loads of coal were wanted for a bonfire, they were purchased from Alexander Hamilton, 'coal greve at Corshill heugh'. Coal heughs were the earliest shallow opencast workings. In 1686 Irvine council initiated its own municipal enterprise. They were perhaps stimulated by the success of the pioneering work of Robert Cunningham of Auchenharvie in nearby Stevenston parish. John Wallace, described as a 'Coal Ingineer', was engaged to make a survey and sink a pit. He was appropriately welcomed on 4th January: 'Some of the Councill being sent by the Magistratis to entertaine Mr. Wallace when he came to seek the coal'. There was a tavern bill 'that night when he came, for aill and brandy, tobacco and pipes', then further bills for the next three days and others before he departed in the autumn. At the end of May a suitable site had been obtained somewhere near Doura, on the skirts of Irvine parish, on the upland area beyond Armsheugh. Hired 'toune workeris' on 7th June were 'setting doune the first shank of the heugh'. They were supplied regularly with ale, bread, and cheese, and there was extra ale (and brandy for the magistrates) when they 'gott their first coall' on 7th September. A second seam was reached on 15th September, the 'thickest coal' on 28th October, and another 'new cord' by 7th December. The works at Doura were apparently soon abandoned, but by 1692 further exploration of the tounlands was made, with the Incorporated Trades actively interested. Sinkings were made at Knadgerhill, Newmure, and by the owners of the lands of Lochmill. Regular loads must have been brought down to Irvine and to the harbour, either via the Drucken Steps or by Stane, skirting the shores of the Scotts Loch. In 1688 the council implemented a statutory right to levy a duty on coal exports, and the 'Coal Barrel' was rouped. The tacksman was entitled to make charges ranging (in 1691) from 4/- on ships of less than 20 tons to 8/- on those above 30 tons. Coal was brought from Kilwinning pits, and Fergushill set up its own coal yard at the quay. So considerable was the traffic that damage to the bridge seemed possible, and the coal carts had to use the Car ford across the Irvine Water.

In their 1692 report Irvine Council lamented that 'ther inland trade is very inconsiderable'. This is another obvious misrepresentation to excuse unwillingness to contribute to an appeal from the Convention of Royal Burghs. For the carriers of Irvine with their packhorses were busy transporting loads to and from Glasgow and other places. They were sufficiently numerous in 1670 to form what became the Carters Society. That date — which seems credible — appears on their flag along with the motto 'Once in the year we ride in State'. This is perhaps a reference to the Marymass Fair and the horse races now associated with that event. To supply the carriers there was presumably an increased number of smithies. There were two as far back as 1419, probably at the appropriately named Smiddy Bar, one at Seagatehead (1618), and another later on the East Back Road. To facilitate transport a bridge at Redburn was repaired (1689), and another over the Annick was built or rebuilt (1695) on the route to Kilmarnock. At the same period, with the draining of the loch, it would become feasible to provide two more direct links on the way to Glasgow, one by Quarry Road, the other by Ballot Road beyond Smiddy Bar, which would be renamed Glasgow Vennel. On the other main thoroughfare leading from the burgh, that across the bridge and leading towards Ayr, a signpost was erected in 1692: 'post to be put up at north side of Airgate mouth for directing strangers'. There was an attempt at 'mending of the calsays' (1679). The surface of these roads, however, was not likely to be much better than in 1619 when the 6th Earl of Eglinton's coach and horses had to be accompanied to Glasgow by six of his most able tenants to assist it on its way.

One further indication of improved communication was the development of the royal mail under Charles II, supplemented locally in 1665. 'The Magistrats and Council of this brugh taking into ther consideratioun the benefit that may redound to the inhabitants thereof be setling ane common weeklie foot post for procureing of Intelligence from abroad, for keeping up commerce and traid, Have therfoire unanimouslie maid choise of Alexander Wintun to be common post of this brugh, quha is weeklie to depairt towardis Edinburgh upon the Tuesday morneing, and to returne thereto upon the Saturday following.' For this he would be paid £10 quarterly, plus for each letter 2/- from townsfolk and 4/- from others. And he would be supplied with 'ane badge to be maid to him with the tounes arms'.

The complaint in 1692 that 'ther inland trade is very inconsiderable' seems altogether unfounded. What really irked was that in the general increase of trade they were not able to maintain the local monopoly to which the royal burgh felt legally entitled. The quite spectacular 17th-century growth of Kilmarnock seemed a threat to their interests. In 1617 two Kilmarnock traders hawking their wares in Irvine were arrested, but had to be released. In 1658 Irvine took action, which proved unsuccessful, against Kilmarnock for infringing the privileges of the Royal Burgh. All over Scotland the royal burghs were on the defensive. In the 1692 report to the Convention of Royal Burghs, Irvine cited seven burghs in Cunninghame,

The Burgh School, first mentioned in 1572, continued at the Kirkgatehead until 1816. Thereafter it was occupied by two free schools, by weavers, and by the fire brigade.

'which are very prejudiciall to them in point of trade, and serve the most pairt of the countery with goods by retaill and that ther houses are better and more of them than many royal burghs, particularly Kilmarnock'. In 1700 the two old rivals, Ayr and Irvine, joined forces to protest that 'the trade of Kilmarnock in import and export to France, Holland, Norway, Virginia, and Ireland and other forraigne parts has been above half of the trade of both of the Burghs of Ayr and Irvine'. In fact, though Irvine merchants could no longer claim the whole of the Cunninghame hinterland as their own special reserve, the port and town of Irvine did benefit from its new and continuing function as a port for Kilmarnock and — until mid-18th century — for Glasgow. Irvine apparently felt no threat from the new port established just up the coast at Saltcoats. Nor was Irvine incommoded when William Fullarton sought and obtained a charter in 1707 to establish on the other side of Irvine bridge a burgh of barony of Fullarton, with a Wednesday market and annual fairs in July and November.

By the end of the 17th century the Burgh or Irvine was involved in the agrarian changes which brought improvement to the lands in the environs of the town as to Cunninghame in general. In 1688 lime was being quarried on the Low Green. On the burgh moor (1695), to improve the pasture for cattle, whins were cut down and sheep and horses prohibited. On those farms operating on burgh lands — Knadgerhill, Newmoor, Fencedyke and Hiemyre — there were various stipulations requiring good management. When Knadgerhill was leased in 1698, the tenant was required to plant two trees for each one he cut down. The continued silting of the loch afforded opportunity for reclamation of what had been called in 1587 the 'new fond land'.

The draining of the diminished loch was the most notable project of the late 17th century. It has been said that English soldiers during the Cromwellian occupation brought new ideas to local farming. More definite is the evidence of Dutch examples, including a knowledge of drainage methods acquired by Rev. Patrick Warner when in exile in Holland. In 1691 Warner, now parish minister of Irvine, and the owner of family properties, purchased from Walter Scott of Clonbeith the 'loch of Irving and lands thereof, of old called Trindlemoss, thereafter called Scott's loch, with the bounds, fishings, and fowlings thereof, and the north quarter of the meadow, called the Braid Meadow, with two other meadows, all lying continguous to the loch within the territory of the burgh'. He also obtained permission to cut ditches or 'gotts' which can still be traced on modern Ordnance Survey maps. What was long afterwards known as the Minister's Cast drained waters north and west past where Williamfield was later built, to fall into the River Irvine as Jenny's Burn just above where the weir now is. As a result the 'stank' known as the Grip Gutter dried up, which was a benefit to the town. More important, the loch and swamp behind the town became valuable farm land. The success of Warner's experiment stimulated others afterwards similarly to drain the southern area into the Annick Water, and the Loch Mill went dry. With the loch thus drained, more direct roads could be formed. A new Quarry Road led to Duntonknowe. And Glasgow traffic could take the Ballot Road — said to be named from an old ball game of bulleting or throwing bowls played there.

The process of rebuilding the town in stone was advanced with the exploitation of Duntonknowe quarry. In 1664, in a search for suitable stone, quarries were 'assayed'. When the bridge was rebuilt in 1666, 'quarriers for winneing of stanes' were engaged, probably at Duntonknowe. In 1668 'the Quarrell hoil' is mentioned. In 1672 it was leased to the towns officers, James and Thomas Spark. In 1681 the council provided 'to the men that wrought in the Dunton Know quarrall at the said proveists ordar for drink'. Yet local resources had to be supplemented by importing stone from Saltcoats, Cumbrae, and 'the Craig'; the shortage of freestone meant, as we saw, the use of the old mercat cross in building the meal market; and a Kilmaurs mason had to be brought in for repairing the bridge. The burgh accounts also list payments for 'sax thousand sklaits and the ffaught therof ffor the use of the toune'. This followed 'the sclating of the mill' in 1681 — a good deal of work was done at all three mills in this year. The kirk was still partially thatched — two loads of foggage were supplied that year. But 'sklaitters' were employed there in 1619, a 'glassenwright' was also there for twelve days in 1681, and in 1697 the windows were all glazed. With the work also at the bridge, harbour, tolbooth, and mealmarket, masons were busy in Irvine in the last decades of the 17th century.

Other social advances are less easy to assess. While warlike pursuits were dying, one 'old antient practeis' was reported in 1665. The council annually arranged for 'the Paippingoe to be sett up and that whasoever burgessis pleasit to adres thamselffs thairto with thair bowis and arrows for schooting thairat'. At Kilwinning the papingo — a decorated wooden bird — was put up on the tower of the abbey; at Irvine it was possibly placed high on the tolbooth. The archery contest was held each May, and 'whosoevir sould ding the samyn doun sould be captain and have ane Benne or Scarff consisting of the value of twelff pundis Scotts or thairby'. The other traditional local sport of horse racing is also first noted in 1630. There is a puzzling reference to a new stob to replace one cut down 'in the bak syd of the Sandgait port' for 'weying of all ryderis thairat that sud rin at the silver coop furneist out yeirlie betuix the Erl of Eglintoun and this burgh'. In 1636 there was an eight-mile race twice round a circuit north of the town over burgh and Eglinton land. A silver cup was presented 'mutually and equally alike on both their charges' by the 6th earl and the burgh council. Eighty-one country gentry subscribed sufficient capital to provide a monetary prize, and other prizes were financed by the stakes contributed by the entrants. While there is no indication of when this race was run, in 1694 the council provided a silver tumbler as a prize for a race to be run on the last Tuesday of October. If there were races associated with Marymass in the 17th century, or if the carters were involved, there is no record.

Though the kirk prohibited the celebration of holy days, traditional ceremonies associated with Beltane in May were being enjoyed in 1610, 1618 and 1658; and Hallowe'en and Yule certainly continued to be celebrated. The council paid for bonfires in 1662, 1670 and 1681. On the first occasion they consumed '2 quarts aill, 5 quarts of aill, 2 quarts and a choppein wyn, two dozen of glasses at the benfyrs'. On the last they paid for ten loads of coal 'quhilk were burnt upon the 29 May', which was the birthday of the King. It is tempting to wonder if the townsfolk had the opportunity to enjoy a dramatic performance by the thirty Irish actors held up in Irvine in July 1681.

Despite the doctrinal disputes which vexed the Church in Scotland in the 17th century, and the resentment at innovations in church government, regular worship continued, and the kirk sessions as established after the Reformation operated without interruption. The maintenance of the kirk and kirkyard in each parish was the concern of the heritors (landowners), and the burgh council as chief heritor in the parish of Irvine assiduously attended to its responsibilities. It paid for repairs to the church building, repaired the kirk dyke and provided a stile at the south entrance to keep out beasts. In 1669 it provided 'green cloth with laces and facing of silk to cover the fore seat of the magistrates seat with the pulpit at the town's expense' and also repaired 'the scholars sait'. The patronage and the right to nominate the minister was held by the earl of Eglinton, and he was responsible for collecting from landowners the teinds that furnished the minister's stipend. The council, though not able to provide a manse,

The Elephant Inn, Eglinton Street. At a malt barn here in 1646 Glasgow University conducted its classes when there was plague in the city.

paid the rent of the dwelling occupied by the minister. And the council co-operated with the kirk session not only in matters of discipline, but in the provision of poor relief and education. We can guess that councillors often were elders as well, so that co-operation could be close.

The Protestant kirk inherited from its predecessor a charitable concern for the support of those who were aged, infirm, orphaned, and without family support. Acts of small benevolence to the needy are recorded in the council minutes of 1601: 'to by a schirt to a pure man', 'to a cripill for a horse'. In 1602 there were payments to a weaver and tailor for 'the Frensche manes sark and claithes', perhaps a shipwrecked seaman. In 1653 there was aid for the impoverished wives of soldiers. In 1662 the council paid to send 'twa poor boys' as apprentices in the wool manufactory that the 7th earl of Eglinton had set up at Montgomeriestoun — the Cromwellian citadel at Ayr which the earl obtained a charter to develop as a self-contained burgh beside the county town. In 1676 there was a bequest for the poor from William Crumbie. Poor persons might be licensed to beg through the parish, but incomers proved an embarrassment. In 1601 a woman was fined for receiving 'sturdie beggeris', and in 1668 the town drummer publicly warned inhabitants against harbouring vagabonds.

To extend educational provision was a prime concern of the Reformed Kirk, which envisaged parish schools where all might learn how to read the scriptures, and burgh schools which especially could prepare for university those needed to staff the new church. There had been a church school in Ayr since the 13th century, and it is possible that in this other royal burgh there had also been established a sang schule with music and Latin for the boys of the church choir and potential priests. No records survive to indicate if in Irvine, as in Ayr, the 16th-century burgh council was involving itself in such a church school which after the Reformation could be converted into a burgh school. The earliest documentary evidence is an award by James VI in 1572 to the burgh council of Irvine of the revenues of the church's former chaplainries plus the multures of the Carmelite friars towards the foundation of the King's school of Irvine ('fundatio nostra Scole de Irwing'). The school then, or soon afterwards, was in a house at Kirkgatehead, on the right-hand side of the entrance to the kirkyard.

The master of a burgh school, in the words of John Knox, should be 'such a one as is able at least to teach Grammar and the Latin tongue, yf the Toun be of any reputation'. The earliest surviving minutes of Irvine Town Council (1595) mention a schoolmaster, and within five years they were planning to appoint also a doctor — an assistant who in 1652 described his duties as teaching 'the children which were learning to read and wryt'. The Irvine master had an annual salary of 25 merks (1600), increased to 30 merks (1633), considerably augmented after 1646, and before 1696 amounting to 200 merks. In that last year the Scots Parliament fixed a statutory minimum of 100 merks and a maximum of 200 merks, which remained operative until 1803. The Irvine Council was equally generous to the doctor whose salary rose from 40 merks (1652) to 120 merks (1689). These basic salaries were of course supplemented by the fees paid by pupils and by the 'casualties' which the kirk session contributed for various duties. The master acted as session clerk and sometimes reader in the kirk. The doctor was the precentor who led the praise and was indeed described (1633) as 'doctour and musiciner'. The keeping of a register of baptisms and marriages was another church duty for him, and there were arguments about payment for this.

Agreement of council and session was essential in making appointments. In 1689 when the latter took the initiative in selecting a doctor and precentor, the council readily ratified their action. Previously in 1685 when the council sacked a master, the session were resentful at not being consulted. From references in council minutes it is possible to compile a list of some 17th-century masters: James Birrell (1600, 1609), David Barclay (1611), Robert Ramsay (after graduation in 1618 and until he became minister of Dundonald in 1625), Thomas Garven (1626), Robert Tron (1665), Patrick Cumming (1671, 1678), James Wilson (discharged 1685), William Clerk from Beith (1686, 1688), Alexander Orr (1689), Matthew Lindsay (1690), Matthew Couper from Ochiltree (1690), John Cumming (1692, resigned 1699), and Bailie John Nisbet (1699–1704). The doctors recorded are: Hew Ross (1652, 1656), James Hay (1665, 1669), William Wallace (died before 1686), Archibald Crawford (1689, 1690), John Woodside (1692), Gavin Houston (1692), William Davidson (1694), Andrew Cumming (noted for his 'extreme pains and diligence', 1697, but who resigned along with the master, 1699), and Charles Murkland (1699). On one occasion we are afforded a glimpse of detail. It was perhaps to celebrate the appointment of a new master in 1689 that the parties adjourned to a tavern: 'the Magistrats and the clerk with the young Schoolmaster two chapins of wine and two chapins of ail and tobacco and pyps'.

What the school at the Kirkgatehead looked like can be deduced from repair bills and other passing references. It was a thatched cottage with shuttered windows, probably of but-and-ben style. Of its two apartments, one was a classroom. The other may have been a second classroom or the home of the doctor. The master had a separate dwelling whose 'maill' was paid by the council. Inside the classroom the only furniture was the teacher's desk and chairs. The floor was probably of earth, though by 1745 it was covered with paving stones. The schoolyard was at the back, enclosed by a stone dyke.

Fortuitously we have a first-hand account of what school life was like in 17th-century Irvine. Robert Ramsay, when he went to Dundonald as minister in 1625, drew up plans for a school there, but these so-called Dundonald Regulations were based on his experience in the Irvine burgh school where he had been master. Each day the school assembled at 7 a.m. (or later in winter at sunrise); there were intervals for breakfast from 9 till 10 and for dinner between 12 and 1; the 'hour of skailing' was 6 p.m. (or earlier in winter at sunset). School met six days each week, and on Sundays it was also required 'that the scholars be present at the sermons on the Lord's Day, that they sit round about the master silent, hearkening modestly and reverently'. Each schoolday opened and closed with prayer; on Monday morning the pupils were examined on the content of the previous day's sermon; on Saturday there was another half-hour of religious instruction; and each evening for homework there was some item of scripture to be memorised. Once a quarter at least the minister and other gentlemen visited the school to inspect if work was being satisfactorily performed. For the bright boy — the lad o' pairts — Latin was provided. For this pupils came into school earlier than the others, and were given exercises to do while the rest of the school were all taught reading together, the older children helping the younger ones. Religion and reading were the only subjects for most. A few parents could afford an additional fee for an hour's writing lesson each morning, with the master providing pens and examples to be copied. Pupils were also to be taught 'good manners' and 'gestures of courtesy' and to avoid 'skarting of head, arms, etc.' Discipline was severe. 'Lenity, allurements, commendations, fair words, some little rewards' had to be supplemented with 'striking some on the loof (palm) with a birch wand, belt, or pair of tawse, others on the hips ... but none ... on the head or cheeks'. Among the pupils there was a 'common censor' and a 'clandestine censor' to report misbehaviour to the master, such as 'unlawful or obscene pastimes such as may readily defile or rent their clothes or hurt their bodies' or playing in the kirkyard. To relieve the 'continual bensall (pressure) of learning' and for 'sharpening their ingynes (wits)' the pupils were allowed some little time off for recreation — Tuesday, Thursday and Saturday afternoons, two hours in summer, one in winter — which would lighten somewhat their monotonous regime.

That there was a demand for schooling is clear from the protest to the council by master and doctor in 1665 'against severall persons that keipps schooles in the brugh, to the utter wraick and decay of the comone schooll'. The council prohibited competitors who took away fee-paying pupils from its own school. It did, however, allow children under six years of age to be taught in private schools. In 1665 it permitted James Porter to 'teach youth the airt of arithmetik, ciphering, singing of musick, and learning youth to rectifie their wreitings, provyding he does not prejudge the grammar schoole in teaching of youth to read or learne Scotts or latine or weitt or doe ony uther thing quhilk the maisters of the grammar school were in use to do'. In 1698 the council further permitted private provision of a more liberal curriculum when Mary Turner was allowed to teach 'such airts as are taught to children in Edinburgh'.

Universal literacy was slow to achieve. In 1567, of the 216 Scottish barons who agreed to a Bond of Association, only sixteen 'signed with their hands at the pen'. That none of the twenty-five Ayrshire barons involved could do so has suggested a general lack of education before that time. On the other hand it must be pointed out that some few landowners of Cunninghame were not only literate but noted for their poetic achievements — Sir Hew of Eglinton in the 14th century, followed by Alexander, 5th Earl of Glencairn (1512-1574), Hew Barclay of Ladyland (1545-1597), and Alexander Montgomerie of Hessilhead (1545-1611, author of the celebrated 'Cherry and the Slae'). This tradition was continued after the Reformation by Sir William Mure of Rowallan (1594-1657) and William Hamilton (1665-1751) from Kilwinning — the Hamilton of Gilbertfield who later inspired Burns. Within the royal burgh literary interests were not yet awakened. Original composition was restricted largely to religious dogmatics, like the works of Rev. David Dickson, and the 'Reasons against Abolishing penal statutes against papists' by the town clerk John Hamilton in 1686. Some of the craftsmen might be moved to attempt verse — as quoted above — but in the Seal of Cause of 1646 three of the twelve craftsmen could not even sign their names. The burgh school concentrated on the teaching of reading, and only a minority learned to write. But it was also preparing some students for university. Throughout the century the churches within the presbytery of Irvine provided bursaries 'to maintain some students and scholars which have nothing to maintain themselves with'. In 1698 Irvine Town Council made grants to two local students at university.

Relations between Irvine and Glasgow University were close. In 1626 the council subscribed £100 Scots toward its redevelopment. In the same year a native of Irvine became Principal of the University. John Strang was born in 1584, a son of the manse, but left Irvine at the age of four with his widowed mother. From Kilmarnock he went on to follow a distinguished career in church and university. As Principal he added to his staff in 1642 as professors of divinity the ministers of Irvine and Kilwinning, David Dickson and Robert Baillie. When in 1645 plague struck Glasgow, the university was evacuated to Irvine. The staff comprised the Principal, the two professors, and four regents, one of whom was James Dalrymple of Stair. For the next two sessions classes were conducted in a malt barn on the west side of Eglinton Street, later occupied by the Elephant Inn. An annual payment of £372 was made to 'John Grahame, Maltman, for furnishing of the hous and for the intertenement of the Principal, Maisters, and Bursoris at Irving'. After the university returned to Glasgow and John Strang retired in 1651, he was succeeded as Principal by Robert Ramsay, the former master of Irvine burgh school. The educational and social record of the 17th century, paralleling the economic growth of the burgh, signifies that — despite the ecclesiastical dissensions — this can be accounted an era of some progress.

SEVEN

The Council and the 18th Century

For earlier centuries one can only guess at the circumstances which lay behind recorded decisions of council. From the beginning of the 18th century we can detect the existence of rival factions, cliques with temporary common interest rather than commitment to any programme or principle, as with political parties of a later age. With negotiations in hand for a union with England, the choice in 1702 of a commissioner to represent Irvine in the Scots parliament produced a violent schism in the council, and a disputed election, boycotted by some members, and with another councillor kidnapped to prevent his attendance. Alexander, 9th earl of Eglinton, becoming provost in 1702, initiated that long period when earls and their nominees exerted control over the affairs of Irvine. At the time of the Union, while some local merchants and members of the Trades were opposed — just how many cannot be assessed — in 1707 the commissioner for Irvine, Bailie George Monro, joined with Provost John Mure of Ayr and another 31 of the 62 burgh members to vote for the Act of Union in what turned out to be the last session of the Scots parliament. Monro, as clerk to the bailery of Cunninghame, was obviously an agent for Eglinton. It has been alleged that support for the union was accomplished by bribery — an accepted feature of 18th-century politics. Certainly the burgh and the eleven other local persons (including Monro) who had invested in the Company of Scotland were promised compensation. And many welcomed union because it offered the opportunities of a common market, by free trade with England and the English colonies across the Atlantic.

In the new United Kingdom parliament, the royal burghs of Scotland could not expect individual seats. But Irvine council's elected commissioner, with those from the burghs of Ayr, Rothesay, Inverary, and Campbeltown, would meet to choose an MP for the new constituency of Ayr Burghs. The opportunities for personal profit were obvious in electing a member when there were only five voters.

The other privileges of the royal burghs were guaranteed by the Act of Union. Its constitution or 'sett' continued, as re-defined for Irvine in 1710: 'Their councill consists of fifteen merchants, including the provost, two baillies, dean of gild, and treasurer, and two trades, making in all seventeen. They elect their magistrats, viz. the provost and tuo baillies, yearly, the first Munday after Michalmass; and the Friday preceeding they leit the magistrats, and do put tuo on the leit to the old provost and four to the tuo old baillies, and the Friday preceeding that they elect their new councill, and on the Friday after the election of the magistrats they choose their dean of gild, treasurer, clerk, fiscall, officers, visitors of mercats, birlamen, etc. and are obliged yearly to change tuo merchants and tuo trades. And the provost and tuo baillies are not to continue above tuo years'. Despite periodic demands that some sort of public poll be introduced, this system by which the council made up its membership by co-option continued unchanged until 1833.

The domination of the merchants was resented by the Trades, who led opposition to the council's continued feuing of the Moor. In 1707 there was an unsuccessful protest. In 1743 they were accused by the council of 'encouraging and countenancing a mob that happened in the place last spring' which had apparently threatened to pull down Provost Glasgow's house. In 1749, when the magistrates granted long leases of parts of the Moor — 'barren ground entirely useless' — to members of the council, the Trades' lawsuit against them again failed, and there was another riot, and a 'throwing down of a dyke at the town end'. In 1753 part of the Moor was leased to a Linen Company, six of whose partners were councillors. There was a third riot, those arrested were rescued from the tolbooth, the new enclosures were broken down, and a protracted lawsuit followed.

In 1756 the ruling faction — apparently outwith Eglinton's control — was overthrown by means of a conspiracy, the only means possible when there were no public elections. 'A scheme was formed to overthrow the very sett of the Burrow', and one of the leading protagonists was John Cumming of Milgarholm, physician to the 10th earl of Eglinton. Cumming was involved in numerous commercial enterprises including shipping, fishing, brewing and linen manufacture. At the meeting of 17th

September Provost James Campbell made the usual formal request 'to the members to have their Eye on proper persons to be taken in and put out'. The selection meeting convened on 24th September at 10 o'clock and waited till 2 p.m., since only nine councillors had turned up 'tho called upon at the Door three times by one of the officers'. It seems that the absent councillors had been abducted. John Smith, a Trades councillor, was able to turn up, though he had been 'forcibly and in a riotous and outrageous manner carried off out of the Town under cover of night... dragged to the house of Charles Dalrymple of Orangefield, scratched on the face, blooded, bruised, and cruely maltreated by a bandittie'. At the council meeting six new merchant councillors were selected and two new Trades councillors. In the new council the provost was Mr. John Cumming, physician; the dean of guild was Mr. William Cunningham, rector of the grammar school; and Thomas Brown, architect, was treasurer. There were protests. The election had been held on the wrong day — arising from the change of the calendar by Act of Parliament in 1752. More important, it was obvious that six of the councillors were not merchants. But the Court of Session eventually accepted the election as valid.

To secure themselves, the new faction persuaded Alexander, 10th earl, to become provost in 1760. To advance Eglinton's local interests and exert influence in the choice of a member of parliament were sufficient inducement. A few months before the 10th earl's murder at Ardrossan in October 1769 the town clerk Alexander Nisbet resigned. He felt he could no longer continue because of 'the confusion of the Town's affairs from the arbitrary measures that have been and may still be pursued by several men in this Council who have attained an exorbitant influence which I cannot comply with'. A new faction seems to have seized control, with whom Archibald, 11th earl of Eglinton became associated.

This clique was accused of voting into the council no fewer than five country gentlemen rather than indwelling burgesses Though four councillors had to be replaced annually, it was asserted that 'thirteen may be said to remain forever as they always take in two silly persons to shift'. Whereas formerly deacons of crafts had always been chosen as the Trades councillors, 'the junto, to secure themselves, took up tradesmen who had not arrived at that dignity... of so mean a rank that one of them, for many years past, could not afford to keep either apprentice or journeyman, but drove the shuttle for the poorest subsistence'.

Charles Hamilton was the dominant figure of the period. He was born in 1704, son of the laird of Ladyland in Kilbirnie parish. He came to Irvine as a tide waiter and in 1740 was enrolled as a burgess. He rose to become Collector of Customs — for after 1707 this was no longer a responsibility of the burgh but of the government excise officers. As Collector of Customs for the port of Irvine and responsible for the coast from Troon to Largs he had a staff of fourteen. Salaries and fees brought him in a considerable hundred pounds a year. From his elder brother he inherited the estate of Craighlaw in Wigtownshire. to which he added Garvoch in Renfrewshire, and local properties. In 1750 he became a councillor in Irvine. In the same year he acquired a feu at the quay and a lucrative monopoly for the Ship Inn of the sale of liquor at the harbour. He resided at a house at the corner of High Street and Glasgow Vennel which later became the Porthead Tavern. He was wealthy enough to become first in the district except the family of Eglinton to drive a closed carriage. A nephew of William Hamilton of Gilbertfield who inspired Robert Burns, he befriended that young poet during his short stay in Irvine. He was provost for six two-year terms between 1758 and 1781, and died in 1783.

From 1786 to 1832 the provost was always an earl of Eglinton, alternating with other members of his family. The 11th earl (1769-96), like his murdered brother whom he succeeded, was closely involved in the improvement of the Eglinton estate, and despite membership of the House of Lords and other London interests, maintained a valuable association with Irvine, where they had both begun their schooling. Hugh, 12th earl (1796-1819), who had become provost while only laird of Coilsfield, rebuilt Eglinton Castle, but his schemes for developing a harbour at Ardrossan were not to Irvine's advantage.

This period of Eglinton influence over Irvine burgh was one when coincidentally a traditional superiority was brought to an end. In 1747, after the Jacobite rebellion and to reduce the power of Highland clan chiefs, an Act abolishing heritable jurisdictions brought to an end various hereditary rights throughout Scotland. The lordship of Cunninghame with the right to hold a bailiary court in Irvine was abolished — in return for £7,800 of compensation — and with it the earl of Eglinton's superiority over the Marymass fair. Not that there was any suspicion of the loyalty of Eglinton or indeed the burgesses of Irvine. On the occasion of the 1715 rebellion, Alexander, 10th earl, reviewed six thousand loyal Ayrshire volunteers on Irvine Moor, after a march along High Street. The burgh of Irvine was represented by trained bands, plus a company of artillery with three pieces of cannon. Similarly in 1745 a Town's Company of Volunteers was formed. Sir Robert Barclay, third baronet of Perceton, was a solitary jacobite sympathiser, who died in exile in 1717. Like the earl of Kilmarnock on the latter occasion, he found no local support.

Not that the Union had proved an unqualified success.

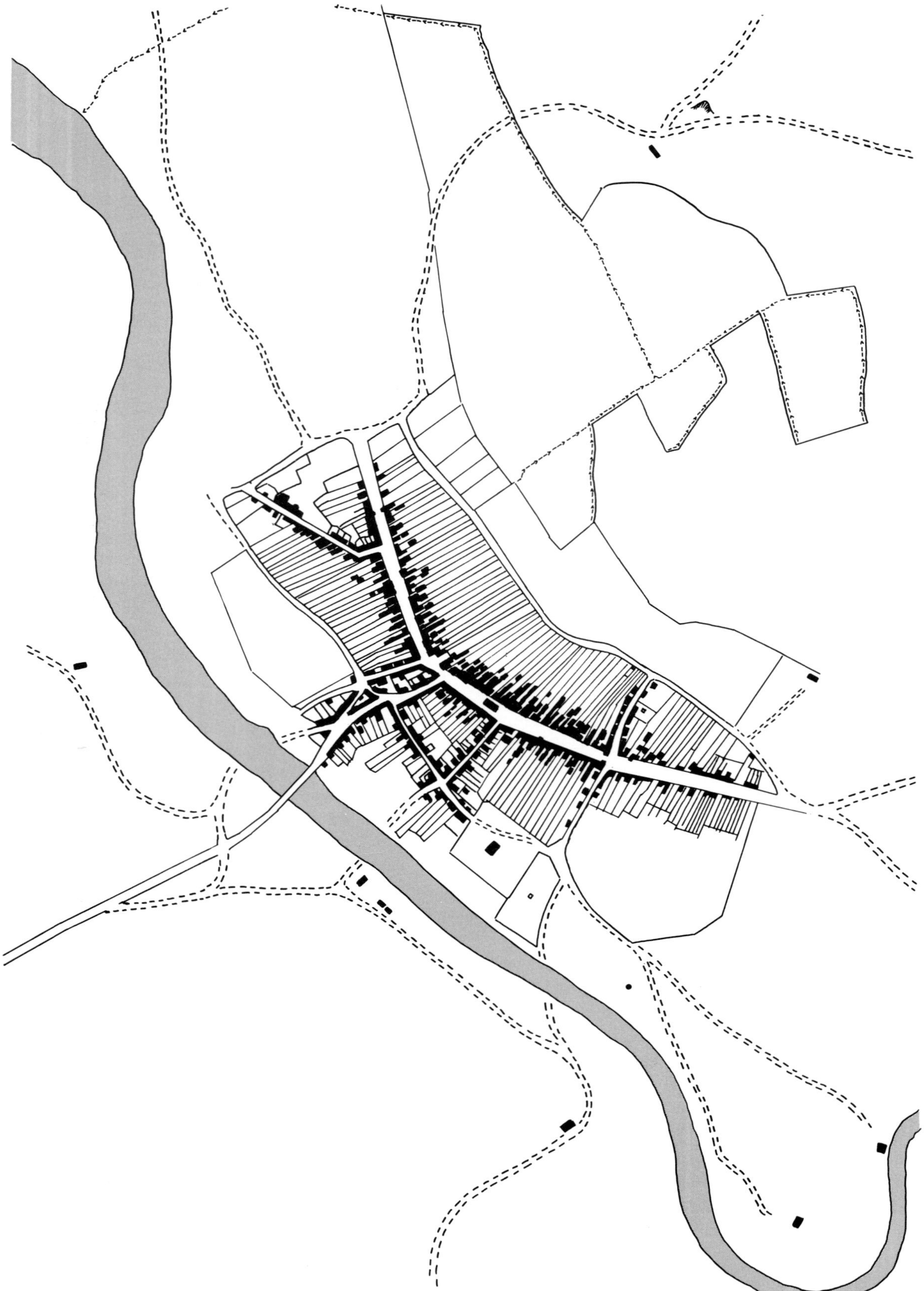

66 The History of Irvine

On the Moor the Carters Society, formally constituted in 1753, held their races, viewed by the council from Magistrates Hill. Other parts of the Moor were feued by the council in the 18th century, which provoked a series of riots.

There was no immediate increase in trade. Fiscal adjustments indeed had produced a Salt Tax which penalised the fish curers. Even more unpopular was the Malt Tax which increased the price of ale. Increasing customs duties on imports to English levels resulted in a vast expansion of contraband trading. Saltcoats was a convenient spot at which salt smuggling became concentrated. The 'free trade' in a wider range of more profitable articles was carried on all along the coast of the Firth of Clyde. The open shore between Troon and Irvine was a favourite location. A report from Irvine explained that 'as the Isle of Man is so situated, and that as it is... about twelve hours' sail from this port, it is now more than ever become the greatest storehouse or magazine for the French and other nations to deposit prodigious quantities of wines, brandies, rum, etc., coffees, teas, etc., and other Indian goods and all manner of goods and merchandises that pay high duties... which are afterwards carried off in small boats and wherries built for that purpose, and smuggled upon the coast of Scotland to an enormous degree'.

In 1712, when certain Irvine burgesses were cited by the Justices of the Peace at Ayr for the long-established offence of illicit importation of grain from Ireland, Irvine town council unsuccessfully sought to have them repledged to their own burgh court according to the ancient practice, which was however judged to have fallen into desuetude. In 1722 some sailors and their wives broke into Irvine Customs House and carried off 36 casks of brandy, 'many of which they hid in houses in the burgh; some of the casks were got back much damnified'. By 1731 smuggling had become so prevalent that troops were stationed at Irvine

Town plan, 1700. In the 17th century Irvine's population had rapidly increased to more than 1,500. The old town centre was becoming congested, and there were extensions into the Townhead and across the river on the Halfway. Progress is exemplified by recognition of the Incoporated Trades (1646), formation of the present harbour (1677), an improved tolbooth (1672), and a meal market (1694). The drainage of Scotts Loch (1691) signified agrarian improvements. Plans were made by William Fullarton for a separate burgh of barony (1707) over the river. While earlier town plans are based on conjecture, we can gauge the situation in 1700 by reference to Roy's map of 1747-55.

Porthead at the corner of Glasgow Vennel was the home of Provost Charles Hamilton, an outstanding figure of the 18th century.

and other nearby places 'for the assistance of the officers of the Customs'. In 1733, when contraband goods were seized, a body of forty to fifty armed men from Beith broke into Irvine Customs House to recover them. Knowing of the existence of 'brandy holes' for the concealment of smuggled goods, the authorities made a search, and twelve casks of brandy were discovered in one of the magistrates' houses. An armed mob made another attack on the Customs House in an unsuccessful attempt to save them.

In 1744 there was a formal declaration of intent: 'The Magistrates and Town Council of this Burgh having seriously considered that the smuggling and using uncustomed goods especially tea, brandy, and other foreign Spirits has drained this Country of its ready money, sunk the value of our grain, and must inevitably terminat in the ruin of the nation if not quickly prevented, They therefore firmly Resolve and heartily Recommend to the whole Inhabitants to Exert themselves to the utmost in their power in putting a speedy and effectual stop to so great evil by abstaining from the use of all unentered Tea, brandy, and other foreign Spirits in their own houses or in Taverns, And by Assisting all his Majesty's officers in Detecting and Seizing all kinds of such goods, And appoint this Solution to be publicly Intimat by beat of Drum and in the newspapers'. They did not, however, go so far as the farmers of Fullarton who recommended a total abstinence from 'that foreign and consumptive luxury called tea' which was a drink fit only for the 'weak, indolent, and useless'.

Yet the 'free trade' continued unabated. In 1764 it was estimated that goods to the value of £20,000 were smuggled annually into Irvine Customs precinct which extended from Troon to Largs. Certain customs officers were found to be acting in collusion with the smugglers. When a cargo was run at Troon, four casks of spirits were laid aside for each of these officers, to remain untouched till the remainder were uplifted. Later in 1764 when an attempt at seizure was made, the customs officers were beaten off by a band of a hundred mounted men armed with sticks, accompanied by some women who loaded up all the carts which had assembled on the shore. In 1768 when the river was in flood, a party of smugglers boldly fought their way with their goods across Irvine bridge. In 1769 a vessel from Dublin was boarded by twenty men who overpowered the revenue guards and carried off the goods.

While the acquisition of the Isle of Man by the UK government in 1765 directed a serious blow to the trade, Robert Burns in 1783 could write that there was still 'a great trade of smuggling carried on along our coasts, which, however destructive to the interests of the kingdom at large, certainly enriches this corner of it' and indeed was the only thing flourishing in that year of recession when 'this country has been, and still is decaying very fast'. What really brought the smuggling trade to an end was an expanded and more efficient excise service — in which Burns himself became enrolled — and the long French wars.

Local volunteer forces were raised when the establishment was threatened in 1688, 1715, and 1745. During the various French wars recruits for the regular army were enlisted, and troops billeted in the town, requiring the Council to appoint a quartermaster. In 1781 plans were made for rebuilding the Powder House, and this was accomplished by 1801. This 'Pouther Magazine' was 'for the Safety of the Inhabitants and Town itself... The necessity of which magazine was more observable now than ever from the great quantity of Pouther kept by the Military Quartered in Town'. When later a French invasion seemed possible, the West Lowland Fencibles were raised in 1793, and an Ayrshire Militia in 1797. Both of these had local units, commemorated by plaque and colours in the parish church still. More real was the threat to shipping in wartime. In 1777 it was imperilled by the raids of John Paul Jones, and in that year three American privateers captured the Irvine brig *Jean and Peggy* en route from Dublin. In 1779 and 1780 the council offered generous bounties to encourage local sailors to enlist in the Royal Navy. But recruits could be obtained only by impressment, especially in the latter years of the century. John Galt vividly described in Irvine 'the pressgang, headed by their officer, with cutlasses by their side, and great club-sticks in their hands... Then we heard the driving of the bludgeons on the doors, and the outcries of terrified women; and presently after we saw the poor chased sailors running in their shirts, with their clothes in their hands, as if they had been felons and blackguards... Then came some three or four of the pressgang with a struggling sailor in their clutches... Syne came the rest of the gang with their officers, scattered as it were with a tempest of mud and stones, pursued and battered by a troop of desperate women and weans, whose fathers and brothers were in jeopardy'.

Apart from such occasional crises, everyday life continued its normal course, with the town council extending its activities. The dean of guild was more important than ever before, annually selecting those who would form his guild court of twelve councillors. Originally dealing with market regulations and merchants' disputes, in a growing town some supervision of the building of houses became their increasing concern. There were new paid officials. The town clerk, dependent previously on the rental of the Clerk's Acre, was in 1786 awarded £5 per year. There was now also a factor responsible for revenues and accounts, and a harbourmaster, both jobs offering additional perquisites for some councillors. In addition to

John Galt, born in 1769, from memories of his Irvine childhood recounted tales of the smugglers and the press gang. A plaque at the Bank of Scotland in High Street marks the place of his birth.

the four town's officers, the drummer, and two herds, from 1755 six inhabitants were enrolled as part-time constables, increased to twelve in 1787. Three others were nominated as 'foresters'. And a quartermaster arranged for billeting of soldiers. Alexander Cunningham in 1726 was appointed Town's Surgeon, and granted Surgeon's Acre off Ballot Road in recompense for 'furnishing the indigent poor with drugs'. Other, older posts were still filled, like visitors to the markets, birlaymen, and stentmasters. A decision in 1766 to prohibit 'hawkers and peddlars' must have proved impossible to implement. A new Fleshmarket of 1740 was not successful as it became polluted with blood and dung, and most preferred the butchers' practice of slaughtering beasts outside their shops. Within ten years it was rouped as a storehouse.

The council's headquarters, the tolbooth, was extensively reconstructed in 1745. In 1740 it had been

The tolbooth, renovated in 1745, as delineated by the Ordnance Survey of 1859.

struck by a thunderbolt, with one prisoner killed and several injured. Thereafter it was 'in a very tottering condition'. The walls of the north-west end were rebuilt and the roof was renewed. A new town clock was installed in 1755, with four dials and gilded hands. The improved tolbooth was later described as 'a very stately fabric about 80 feet long, 27 feet broad, and two stories in height, with a steeple at one end rising about 80 feet high'. Upstairs, reached from the entrance at the south-east end under the steeple, were the guardroom, then the council chamber and court room, then the courthall prison with three cells. The guardroom was a windowless dungeon. This, called officially the Outer Prison, but familiarly known as the Black Hole, was where criminals were kept in chains. Debtors and those guilty of other civil offences were kept in the other cells, which were barred and locked. But they could not be fettered, they were allowed visitors, and they were a constant worry to the council, who became liable for their debts if they escaped.

In 1719 ex-provost Samuel Moor of Ayr was incarcerated here for debt, but made his escape, followed by others even after the tolbooth's reconstruction made it more secure. Responsibility was heavy for the town's officers, who had other duties, like Walter Scot, appointed as executioner in 1751. He was not kept busy with hangings — there was a rare execution in 1755 of a woman at the Tron, graphically recreated in John Galt's The Provost. But he had also 'to keep out all the foreign poor and rake the streets and keep them clean' and also 'prevent dogs getting into the Church on the Lord's day in time of divine service'. After two prisoners escaped in 1771, the council appointed a gaoler, which was a full-time job, for the prison was at

One Mile six furlongs from ye Parish Kirk of Kilwinning

Great improvements in agriculture were made in the 18th century by landowners, by Irvine town council as well as the earls of Eglinton. Redburn, one of the farms portrayed in the Eglinton Estate Plan Book of 1790.

times crowded. In 1796 the council had difficulty finding accommodation for their annual celebration of the King's birthday. After this, the downstairs premises were altered. While the Great Council Room was retained upstairs, downstairs the three shops and a 'laigh chamber' provided storage for the fire engine, an Ordinary Council Room, and an office for the town clerk. Previously he had a room next to the Meal Market in a building erected by Benjamin and Joseph Cochrane, wine merchants, which was nicknamed Parliament House either because of its grandeur or because so much political business was done there.

The rebuilding of the tolbooth was only one example of the construction undertaken by the council involving also harbour, bridge, church, school and mill, other improvements in what would later be called environmental services, and various projects of municipal enterprise — all of which will be described in the next two chapters.

The council was conscious of the importance of its extensive burgh lands, and did much in the 18th century to develop them. Alexander, 10th earl of Eglinton, who succeeded as a boy of six, began while in his twenties those schemes of improvement on his own estate which earned him the title of 'reviver of agriculture in Ayrshire'. But even before Earl Alexander had initiated his pioneering activities, in 1742 Irvine council was offering allowances to tenants who 'inclose with dyke and ditch planted with thorns and saughs'. Two years previously indeed, David Crawford had offered 'to inclose Groatholm and another acre of lotted land betwixt that and the road from Duntonknow and Stanecastle'. In 1741 Charles Hamilton got an extended tack of Spittalmeadow by promising to enclose it. The council itself in 1748 enclosed Redburn and also the 'part of the moor at the back of Duntonknoll to Charles Hamilton's Divotpark and bounded by a ditch down the moor and the Coal road'. In 1749 they agreed that 'the Inclosing of the Townlands would be very beneficial to the Inhabitants and ornamental to the place' and envisaged the total conversion into good pasturage of the Moor which was 'a barren field almost quite covered with whins'. There was effective popular resistance to encroachment of the inhabitants' grazing ground. But in 1750 it was possible to enclose part of the Back Riggs on the west side of the town, the Six Riggs and a Half on what was now called McFarlane's Hill, along the 'Westbackside'. In 1755 Braidmeadow acquired new dykes and ditches. When leases of the farms of Knadgerhill and Newmure ran out, the lands were 'to be enclosed with dyke and ditch and

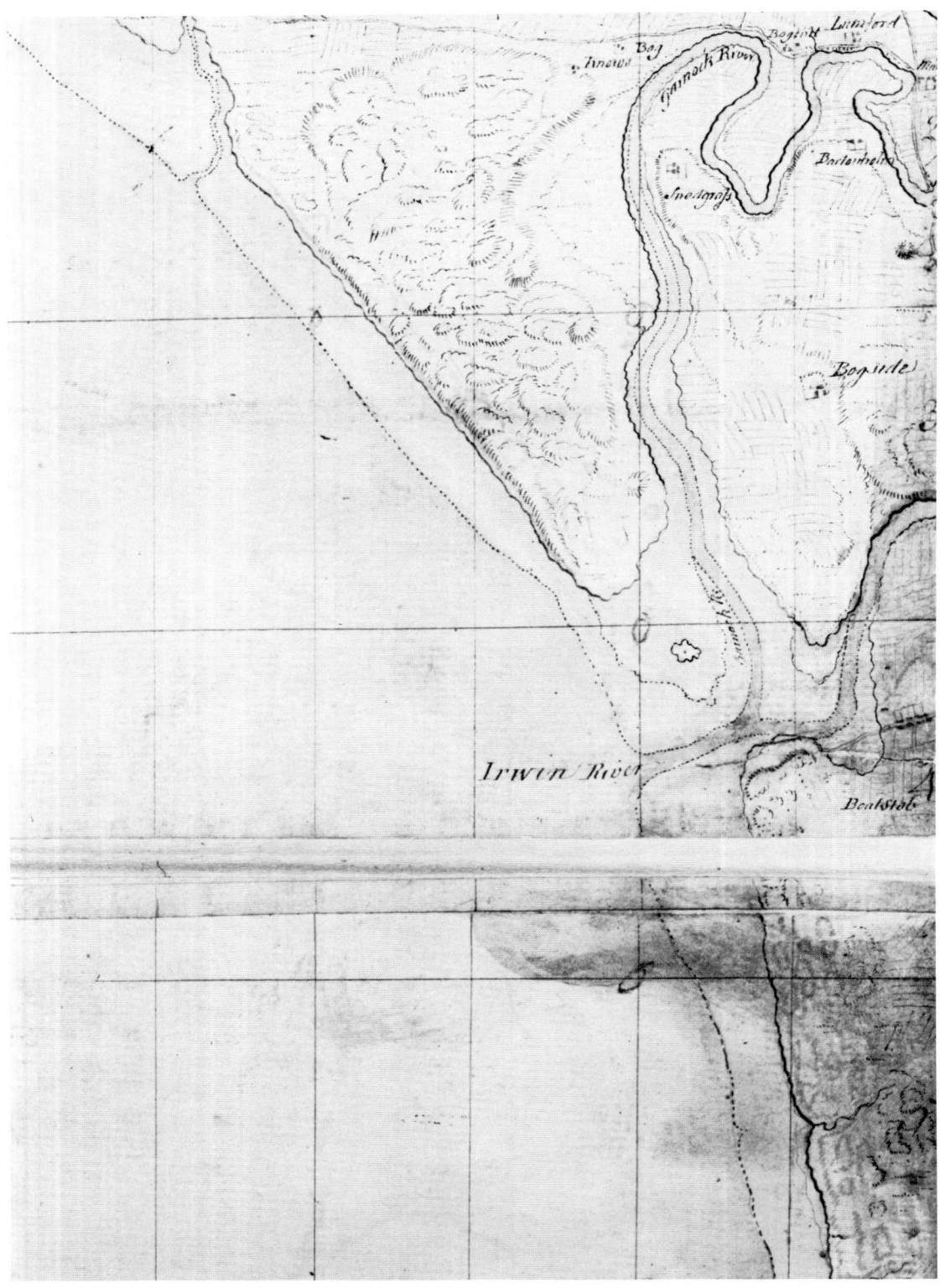

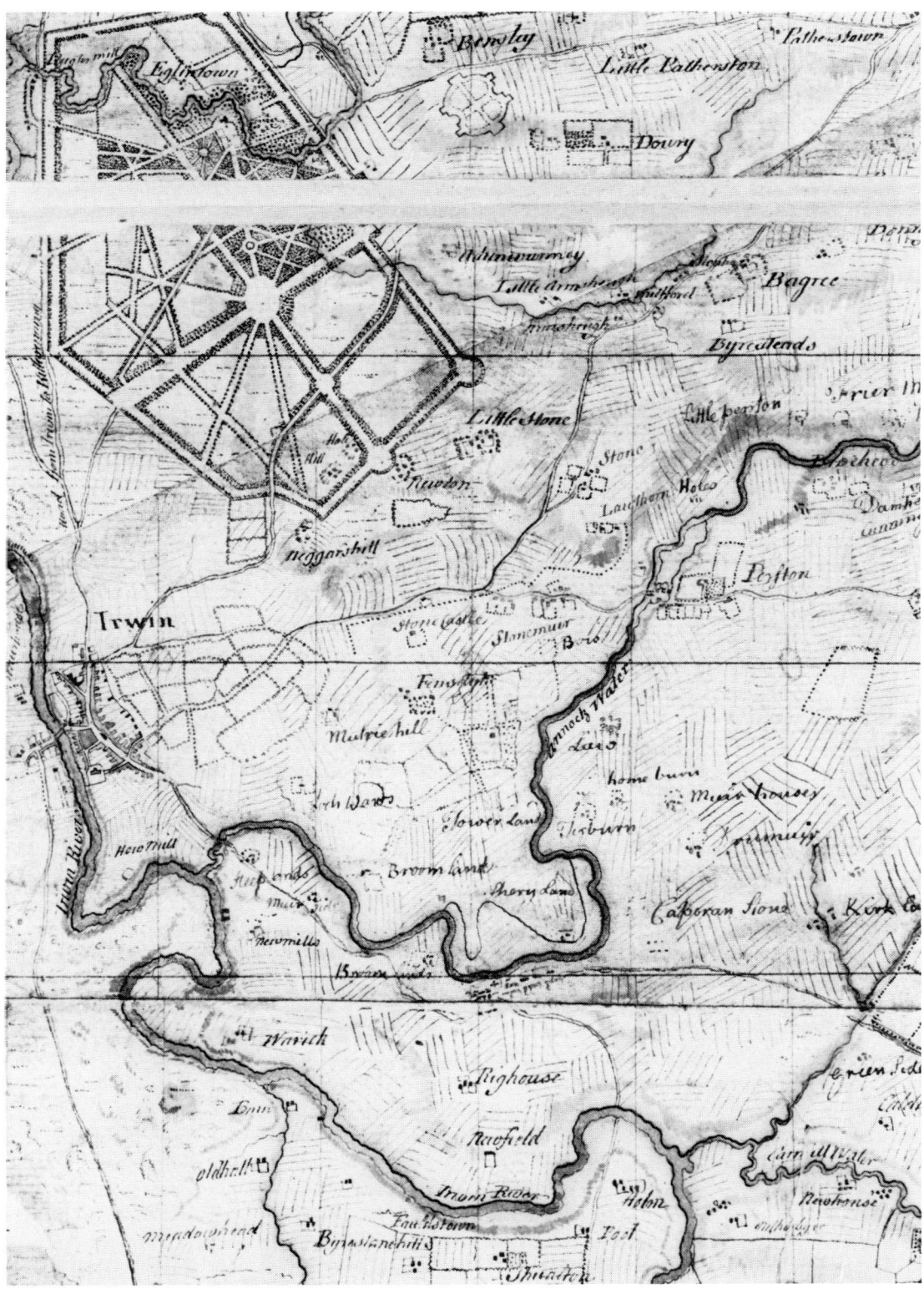

Irvine is first depicted in detail, in the middle of the 18th century, on this map which formed part of General William Roy's Military Survey of Scotland.

thorns'. In 1761 it was reported that the 'low ground of the Knadgerhill from the Drunken Steps near Higgins house southwards and to the east to the march with Stane Castle has been surveyed and laid out in eight plots'. Two years later it was decided 'to inclose the east part of the common from the Minister's Cast or Gott to Redburn bridge'. In 1769 there was a further 'inclosure of the east side of the common from Mr. Warner's ground to Divot Park'. While much of the newly enclosed land provided grazing and arable fields let to town's inhabitants, additional farms were created. In 1702 there had been at Newmure a house with separate spense, barn, and byre, the roofs all thatched with straw, and at Knadgerhill a similar steading. In 1778 it was arranged that the tenant of Kidsneuk might build a 'dwelling house upon the farm with a Barn, Byre, and Stable'. In 1788 Bailie John Campbell, who had a tack of Haysholm, 'made a Garden of the Inclosure' and built on it a 'little dwelling house for his tenant'. Later in 1815 the farm of Irvine Mains would similarly be formed. On what remained of the Moor in 1782, there were grazed only 36 cattle belonging to townsfolk.

Some areas of townland had been disposed of in previous generations. The area of the Scotts Loch had been sold to Patrick Warner of Ardeer, and the adjacent lands of Lochwards (otherwise Scotswards or Barclaywards), Dalrymple Wards, and Roodmeadow similarly disposed of. Fencedyke, including the old Hiemyre, was sold to Montgomerie of Broomlands. But the council compensated by acquisitions. In Fullarton, Marressfoot had been obtained in 1572, while in 1750 Friars Croft and Dyets Temple were purchased for £535. Gulliland was obtained from the kirk session in 1759, Chapelbrae from John Allan in 1761, and part of the Golffields in 1781 from George Fullarton of Bartonholm in exchange for part of the Moor.

The improved lands could be set on a tack or lease, usually for nineteen years. There was always the temptation, however, to seek a profitable 'grassum' and feu away land in perpetuity. This was acceptable when small plots for building houses were involved, as at Friars Croft and the Westbackside. But feuing areas of the Moor aroused opposition. In retrospect it can be judged a shortsighted policy — as when the burgh of Ayr in 1754 rouped the entire lands of Alloway extending to 2,300 acres for £7,190. Such feuing of burgh lands always aroused suspicion of shady dealing.

John Galt, in *The Provost*, presented a picture of the municipal politics of 'Gudetown'. He suggested that as the 18th century advanced, corruption had become somewhat less blatant. But the councillors still seemed to benefit personally whether the burgh was collecting or expending money. When land was feued, they 'got their loofs creeshed with something that might be called a grassum, or rather, a gratis gift'. When a paid job of work had to be done, the procedure was 'just to put whatever was required into the hands of one of the council, who got the work done in the best way he could'. The councillors felt they were 'free to indemnify themselves in a left-handed way for the time and trouble they bestowed in the same'. There was 'jooking and wising in a round-about manner to accomplish their own several wills and purposes... although it was the custom to deduce reasons from out the interests of the community, for the divers means and measures that they wanted, to bring to a bearing for their own particular behoof, yet... the cloven hoof of self-interest was now and then to be seen aneath the robe of public principle'.

An insight into how the council conducted its business is incidentally revealed in some bills for 1720 which happen to have survived. On 7th January, when the provost was 'penning an address', he charged a tavern bill for 3/5. The next day, when the magistrates and councillors signed it, it cost £1/3/0 for seven pints and a chopin of ale and two double gills. On 12th January, when the address was despatched, there was a further 2/4 for two chopins of ale and a sheet of paper. And later, in 1785, after the school extension was completed, the council had 'Dinner at openin the Gramar Scoull'. This function was in the Crown Inn, whose owner, Bailie James Shaw, charged £1.5.0. As well as the meal (14/-), there were consumed two bottles of port (6/-), two bottles of sherry (5/-), punch (7/6), four bottles of porter (1/4) and seven bottles of beer (1/2).

How the unreformed burgh was operating is further revealed in those financial records which towards the end of the 18th century are available in a more complete form. The factor's accounts for 1795-96 list income ('Articles of Charge') as teinds, feu duty, and rents. The teinds (some £20) were originally levied to provide the minister's stipend. Feu duties (£30) were the small returns from those lands which had been leased in perpetuity. The major item was rent (£570). Most of this (£500) was rent from land — farms like Knadgergill, Newmure, and Kidsneuk let to tenants, and numerous 'parks' leased for grazing or cultivation, with small allotments of 'potato ground'. There was also income (£70) from the petty customs of the markets and fairs, from the meal market and the flesh market ('the Shambles'), the mill, harbour and anchorage dues, the washing house, Duntonknowe quarry, the working of coal, three shops under the tolbooth, and roup of seats in the magistrates' loft in church. With other minor contributions such as sale of five burgess tickets and interest from the Ayr Bank, and £60 cash in hand, income amounted to some £690. Expenditure was detailed under 'Discharge'. Salaries and fees required around £150 — the stipend of the parish minister, payments to the two school masters, the town clerk, the factor (William Templeton), the quartermaster (David Sillar), officers, bellman, clockmaker, and keeper of the fire engine, with two guineas to Dr. Fleming for 'medicines to poor patients'. Tradesmen's bills amounted to £120, including £70 for repair of the church roof. Another £100 went on miscellaneous expenses — cleaning the streets, purchasing constables' batons, claret and bread for the sacraments, engraving burgess tickets, travelling expenses of a candidate for the post of sewing mistress, a charge for translating some burgh charters, drink at the King's birthday (£14), and £3.15.6 towards Marymass Fair races. The remaining major expenditure was more than £200 interest paid on the burgh's loan debt of £4,750 at $4\frac{1}{2}$ per cent, and there was a surplus of £120 over the year. As the council reported some years later to a House of Commons Select Committee, street lighting, wells, and all improvements could be provided from the town's funds without any assessment of the inhabitants being necessary.

The factor's accounts were audited by a committee of eight councillors, including the treasurer and bailies, whose involvement in collection and disbursement of funds had now disappeared. The burgh factor was also collector of cess and taxes and thus responsible for a separate set of accounts. The cess or land tax was levied on lands, houses, trade, and ships. To assist in making the assessments, the council annually appointed stentmasters, eight councillors and four others. In the year 1795-96 the factor collected over £80 cess plus £150 for the newfangled taxes on windows, inhabited houses, male servants, carriages and horses. A required £225 was transmitted to the Receiver General, leaving an 'overplus'. The council were able to report to the House of Commons Select Committee on Royal Burghs that by 1818 they had accumulated a sufficient surplus to require no collection of cess that year, and that the affairs of this royal burgh were in good order.

EIGHT

Commercial Growth

In the first half of the 18th century Irvine enjoyed a remarkable period of expansion. So rapid was the growth that by mid-century this had become Ayrshire's biggest burgh, with a population in the town of around 3,000 as compared with Ayr's 2,000 and Kilmarnock's 2,500. In 1760 Irvine could claim to have become Scotland's third most important port. Out of the nation's 999 ships, Port Glasgow and Greenock together had 327; Leith had 79; and the precinct of Irvine had 77. That figure for the 'Port of Irvine', it must be admitted, included those from Saltcoats, which had also become a busy harbour. So Irvine's status was much more modest than the statistics would seem to suggest. Yet its growth was impressive enough. From the eight small ships of 1692 it had built up a fleet of 32 by 1770. In 1794 Irvine had 52 ships, eight over 100 tons including two at 150 tons, and in all 3,835 tons. By comparison Saltcoats had 37 ships totalling 3,409 tons, fourteen of them over 100 tons and the biggest 192 tons.

This notable progress was made possible by the council's persistent and sustained efforts to develop the port. Despite work in 1706 at 'removing the shelves, and maintaining the harbour' it was still judged in 1734 to be 'in a miserable condition and in danger of going to Ruine'. But the next year the river was deepened and cleaned. In 1739 there was a major enterprise in 'Enlarging the Key or Breakwater' with the formation of a stone-built jetty. This was supplemented in 1755 with 'palings' on both banks to 'confine the river' and 'scour the Channell'. Whenever the recalcitrant river breached its banks, as in 1743, 1745, 1748, 1752, and later in 1767 and 1769; immediate repairs were undertaken. The wreck of an old vessel *The Dutchess*, which 'does great hurt', was removed in 1748. Ballast when brought in was carefully disposed of. A lighter for dredging was acquired in 1751 and a 'balast boat or gabbert' got from the Broomielaw in 1756. John Smeaton was invited to make a report on Irvine harbour in 1760, and after the big flood of 1769 major reparations were undertaken, aided by £150 which Provost Charles Hamilton obtained from the Convention of Royal Burghs. Earlier in 1750 he had taken a feu at the quay, in 1755 in association with three other councillors he erected a storehouse, and in 1767 a row of warehouses was built. In 1759 John Webb took a feu from Patrick Boyle of Shewalton to form a shipbuilding yard at 'the Brae'. That the harbour was busy is evident from the Rules and Regulations for Masters of Ships which the council adopted in 1775 to consolidate the various instructions given to the 'Shoarmaster', or harbourmaster, an official first appointed in 1731.

In 1723 an English visitor described Irvine as a tolerable seaport with 'upon the Key, a good Face of Business, especially the Coal Trade to Dublin'. By 1744 there was such a demand for coal by waiting vessels that the shoarmaster had to devise a system of priorities to ensure a quick turn-round. In 1760 Richard Pococke found 'a pretty good harbour, and they have a great trade in fishing, and in exporting coal to Ireland called Scotch coal'. It was later recalled by Rev. James Richmond that when the coal boats arrived 'they blew a large horn, which was fixed to a post at the quay by an iron chain: and, upon this signal, the country people loaded their coal poneys or small horses, and carried down what quantities were required'. By 1791 the volume of exports had increased to 24,000 tons annually, and the coal traffic was on a more organised basis, and the major coalmasters had coal rees at the quay where they held stocks ready for loading. By this time, as the Statistical Account for the various parishes records, Irvine harbour was handling coals from a much wider hinterland. There was coal from local pits — those of the burgh when they were operating, as described later; from Broomlands; and from Bartonholm where a 'fire engine' was installed just before 1798 to drain these deep pits. A little came from the three small pits in Kilwinning parish at Easter Doura, Laigh Fergushill, and Montgreenan. Earlier in 1771 the earl of Eglinton had a pit and feued from Irvine burgh an 'avenue from the Circle at the Mains down to the river' with permission to make roads, waggonways, and breastworks and coal rees on the river side. A major contribution came from Dreghorn parish, where Warrix was producing 11,000 tons a year, most of it for the Irish trade. Some also came from Busbie and Thornton in

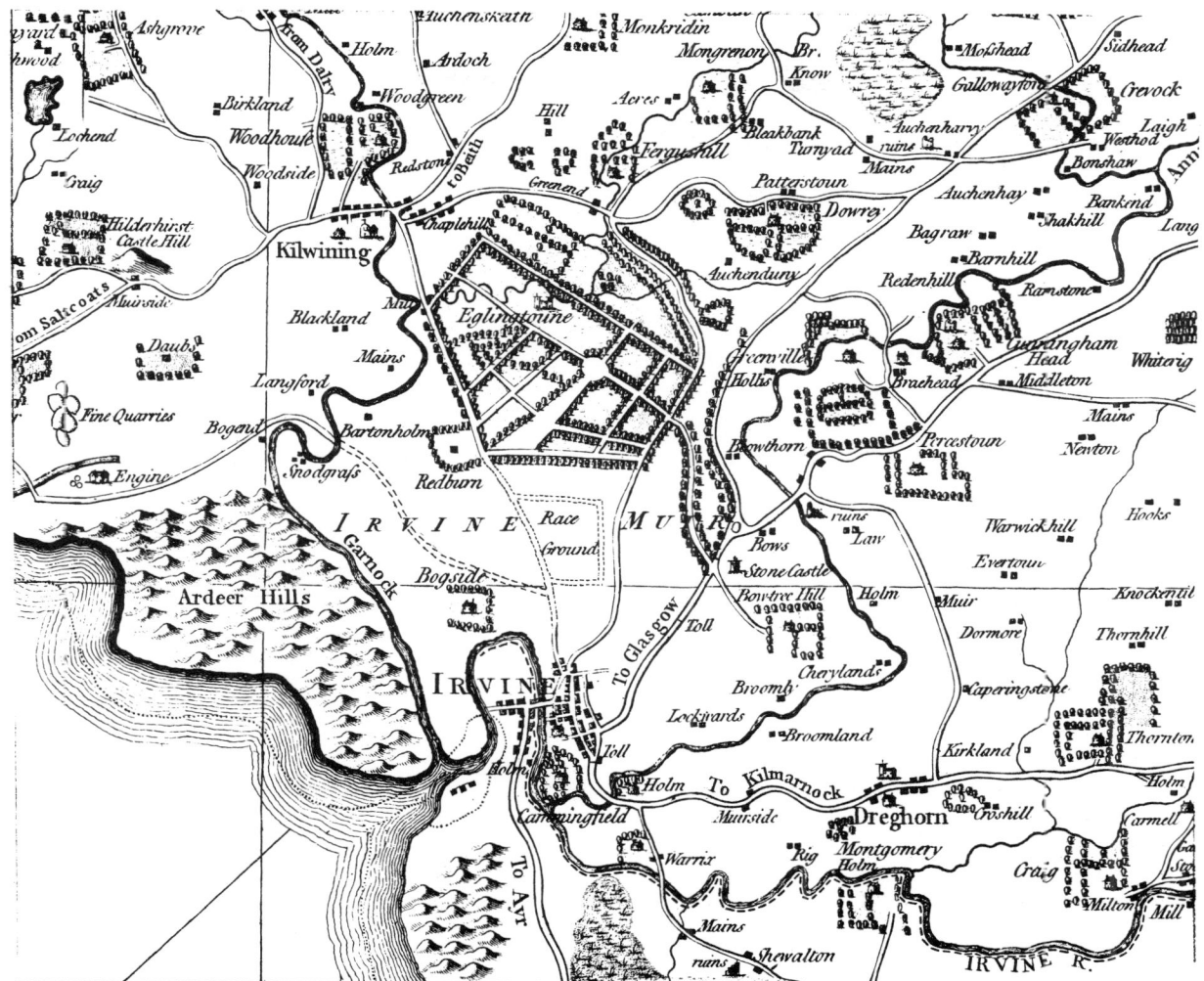

Armstrong's Map of 1775 shows Irvine as Ayrshire's largest town, with a population of 3,000, supplied by new turnpike roads, and surrounded by estates which have been improved and beautified by plantations. The earl of Eglinton had a Race Ground on part of Irvine Moor.

Kilmaurs parish. In Dundonald parish, some was brought from Tarryholm and Shewalton, much more from the Fairlie pits at Romford. From Kilmarnock, 3,000 tons was annually carried seven miles from the Caprington pits at Riccarton. After 1778 a very substantial increase was achieved from two pits at the Misk in Stevenston parish, whose combined annual output was 10,000 tons. Two short canals were cut from them to the Garnock and the coals were floated right down to Irvine harbour. For the bulk of the trade, coals were conveyed in small coal carts with a capacity of some eight hundredweights. Irvine itself had sixty carters, as well as carriers plying to Kilmarnock, Paisley, Greenock, and Glasgow in general merchandise.

The coal traffic was only part of Irvine harbour's burgeoning trade. After 1707 when the American trade was opened to Scottish enterprise, Irvine shared with Greenock and Port Glasgow the handling of the annually swelling bulk of merchandise for Scotland's commercial and manufacturing capital of Glasgow. While Irvine's traditional trade continued (1,618 barrels of herrings were exported in 1715), there was new business (107,533 pounds of tobacco were re-exported in 1720). The larger ships carrying the bulk of the tobacco and later the cotton had to go upriver — Irvine could handle only with difficulty vessels over 80 tons and nothing over 250 tons. But for some smaller ships it was more convenient to avoid the trip up the Firth and unload at Irvine, which was no further away from Glasgow than Greenock was.

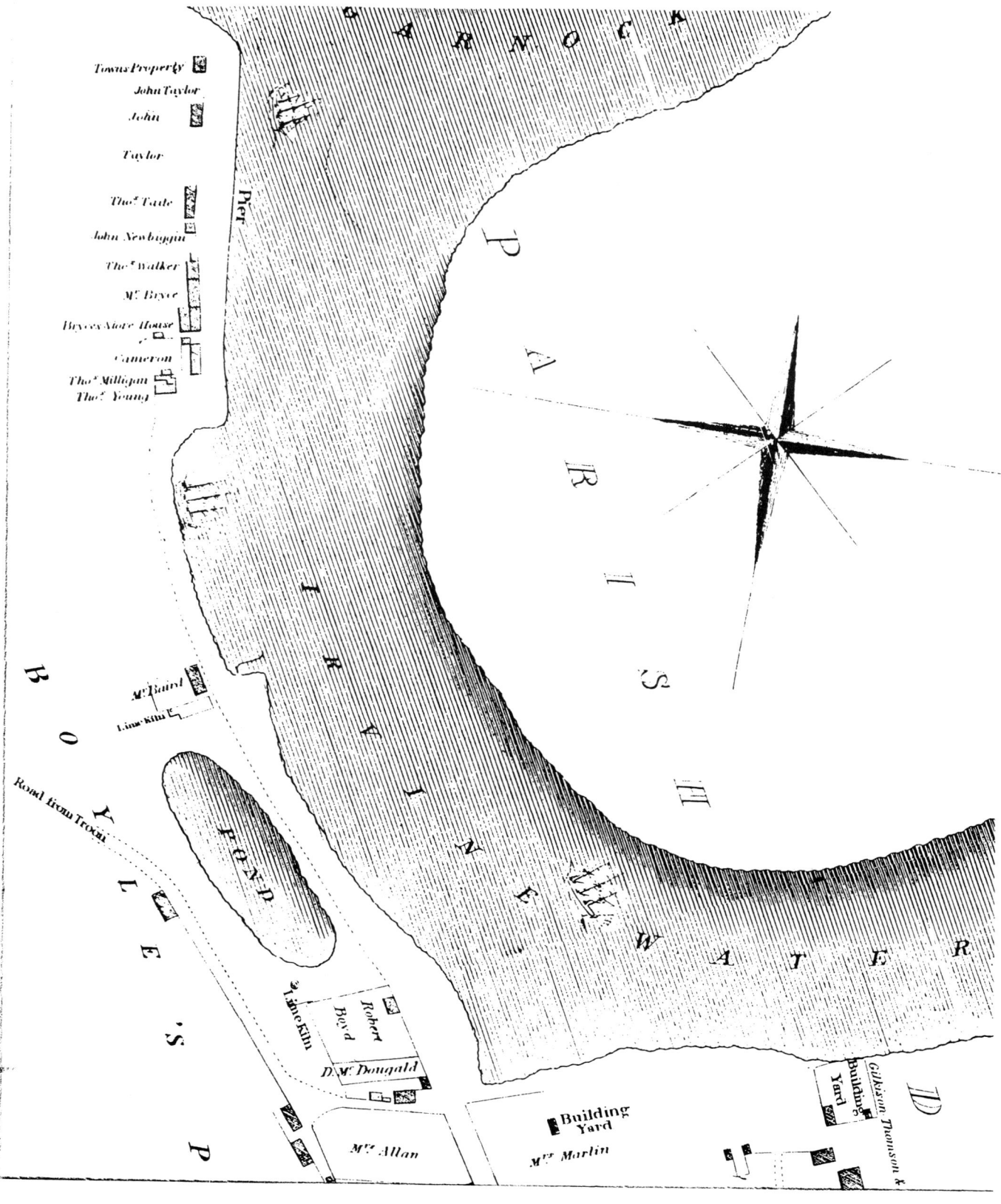

Of the 32 vessels belonging to Irvine in 1770, the dozen larger ones visited their home port only once during a twelve month period, obviously involved in long-distance trading. Some, though only between 60 and 100 tons, must have been crossing the Atlantic to the West Indies and Virginia. Tobacco was being re-exported to Holland. There were occasional Mediteranean voyages. All the other smaller ships made four or five calls in the same period, engaged in Irish and coastal traffic, and at the fishing. In the same year there were nearly fifty visiting vessels. Half-a-dozen which came into Irvine several times look like Saltcoats coal boats, two bringing 'slates in, coal out', 'dales in, coal out'. Most were sloops, gabberts and other small boats visiting once on coastwise business. There were the two Greenock packet boats which shared a route with Irvine's own packet boat. There were another half-dozen larger vessels calling in once, some no doubt bringing in American imports.

Irvine lost most of its Glasgow business after 1773 when the dredging of the Clyde made that inland city itself a seaport. But Irvine remained busy with the export of textiles from Paisley and Kilmarnock, and importing hemp, iron, and wood from the Baltic countries, hides and skins from Ireland, and great quantities of grain and other foodstuffs for the whole of the south-west of Scotland. Indeed, though Glasgow's foreign trade was severely hit during the American war, that of the port of Irvine (including Saltcoats) continued to grow because of the Irish traffic. It has been assessed that in the 1780s, in terms of export tonnage, Irvine was the second most important port in the country, and in the import trade it was third or fourth. By 1794 Irvine itself had 52 ships, and 42 of these were new ships not named on the 1770 list. Irvine was now equipped with a fleet of larger vessels. These ships were manned by 305 sailors, all local men. Many others had emigrated to the West Indies, America, and the Far East as sailors, shipmasters, storekeepers, and planters. By this time, however, Irvine's commercial lead was threatened. Between 1789 and 1791 the quay was extended. But Ayr's harbour was also being modernised, and its 33 vessels of 1790 increased to 54 by 1807 as compared with Irvine's 52. Ayr's population had grown to 4,000 while Irvine's had had a more modest increase to 3,500 in a half-century. More seriously, the future of Irvine's coal trade would be threatened by the construction of the new ports at Ardrossan (1806) and Troon (1808). And inland at Kilmarnock there had been a spectacular growth of manufacturing which raised its population in the second half of the 18th century from 2,500 to 6,000. Herein lay the failure of Irvine's achievement. It prospered for a time on a commerce which proved short-lived. It failed to develop effectively its own local industry. As Rev. James Richmond aptly noted in the Statistical Account, writing in 1791, 'Manufactures, as yet, are not carried on here to any extent'.

This was not for want of trying. Local businessmen on their own initiative, or through the agency of the town council, commenced a number of enterprises. But in the 18th century there were too many abortive efforts and failures, as we shall now see.

Following its first coalmining enterprise in 1686 at Doura, and sinkings in 1692 at Knadgerhill and Newmure, for a time the town council became discouraged. In 1702 one shank at Newmure had to be abandoned because of 'oversight, neglect, or mismanagement'. £400 was borrowed to set down a new shank alongside to reach the coal which was known to be thirty fathoms underground. No workable coal was found, so the burgh sold off its 'windlasses, mouth graith, barrs, picks, shovells, spades, jows (?), and timber' to John Hamilton who was sinking a shank at Shewalton. Whether or not the private pit on the land of Lochmyln continued is unknown. Certainly in 1704 coal was being worked at Fergushill by Bailie Gray and his partners as a private venture. In 1717 Provost William McTaggart became involved with Saltcoats shipmasters in the Auchenharvie Coal Works. McTaggart in 1719 actually went to London to purchase for Auchenharvie a Newcomen steam pump which was the second to be installed in Scotland. Before he abandoned his interest in Auchenharvie, he had taken over Fergushill in 1721, where in 1725 a waggonway was constructed, also second in Scotland. In 1728, after giving up Auchenharvie, he planned to work the coal on the burgh lands of Irvine. But another generation was to pass before the town council revived its interest in coalmining.

In 1761 there was a 'Sudden and excessive rise in the price of Coalls from four pence to five pence per load at the Coall Pits in the neighbourhood'. For the benefit of the inhabitants and the export trade the council decided again to 'make trial for finding Coalls in the Town's grounds', and ex-Bailie Adam Dickie was authorised to collect voluntary contributions. Investors were promised 10% on any profits, and there was to be 'no allowance for drinking except what was bestowed to workers' — to allay the justified fears of investors who were acquainted with the council's tavern bills!

Early in 1762 the voluntary contributions were used to make a sinking on the Town Green near Seagatefoot. In April the council borrowed £100 to provide an air shank. In the first week of production (3rd–10th July) three 'coallers'

The harbour as developed in the 18th century is shown on Wood's Town Plan of 1819.

Between 1762 and 1768 the town council sank pits on the Low Green, on the Moor (where the Academy was later built) and over the water at Marressfoot. The account books for 'the Grean Coalls' give details of this early municipal enterprise.

had an output of 99 loads. By October fourteen men were employed, producing a peak of 473 loads of coal and 223 creels of 'cullm' (small coals) in one week. In 1763, to compensate for dwindling output, a third shank was sunk in the Green, requiring another loan of £100. Production continued to fluctuate, but by the end of 1764 eleven colliers reached a new weekly peak of 555 loads (now being sold at 6d. per load. Locally there would be, as in nearby Kilwinning, eight loads to the ton. In 1765 the workers complained that they could not work in the present shank any longer 'for want of air'. But because 'the working of the Coall has already been very serviceable in supplying the Shipping with Coalls for exportation', there was further borrowing, and two new shanks were set down 'in the Muir' at the spot where the Academy was later to be built. By the end of 1765 there was a weekly output of 699 loads — the colliers always seemed to do particularly well the week before the New Year celebrations. In 1766 a sixth and seventh shank on the other side of the water at Marressfoot helped maintain this level of production, and at the end of that year there was an all-time weekly record of 804 loads from fifteen colliers. But 1767 brought a decline. The council was finding 'the Coall trade was not so flourishing'. In June 1768 work was abandoned because it 'cannot be any longer carry'd on by the Community to any advantage'. It was planned to roup 'the Coall Work', and in 1769 equipment was disposed of.

The enterprise was far from being a failure. The books showed a total income (£3267) which was marginally greater than expenditure (£3208). The profit of £59 was suspiciously small. An audit produced another £100 from Bailie John Reid who had been keeping the books and was found to have made several overpayments to himself. In the last year coals were being sold at the harbour for 7½d per load. Production expenses were 2d. per load to the colliers, 1¾d for carriage to the harbour, and oncost above and below ground was the variable which determined profitability.

Oncost above ground at the outset comprised the wages of two men ('6 days at the Click', 4/- each), payment for 'watching the Coalhill 7 nights' (3/-), a gin boy (3/-), plus upkeep of the horse which turned the gin for raising the buckets ('buckies'). The horse required oats, peas, straw, and hay cut on the Green or at Redburn, kept in a stack. The gin required occasional lubrication with 'butter and oil... for the whorles'. As the work expanded, eight surface workers were needed, and from July 1766 Frances Clark took charge at 10/- per week. There were two gin boys and a groom. There was more work at 'coupan water', discharging water raised in the buckets into a 'waterwear' that drained into the river. Sometimes a 'kart' of 'light coalls' or 'hard coalls' had to be purchased from a pit at

A view of Irvine as seen in 1820 by George Robertson from his house at Waterside. It shows the spire of the tolbooth, the parish church, and the bridge, all recently rebuilt.

Tarryholm suitable 'for givien light to the men in Morning'.

When shanking was in progress, a dozen other men were specially engaged (around 6/- each for '6 nicks at shanking'). Their picks and boring tools ('jumphers') had to be sharpened. Timber had to be cut at Eglinton to make the 'barrs'. Powder and powder horn, with candles, had to be purchased for blasting and 'borring the hard stone'. Clay had to be brought from Broomlands for 'motting the shank' when a sinking went down through sand. One special problem arose in January 1768 of 'cutting down ice on sides of shank and clining when thaw came', similar to the expense just a year before in 'cleaning the snaw of the Coalls'. There was a bonus for the shankers, 'to the men to drink upon Saturday night, 1/6', with more 'that night the coal was got', and in one obviously awkward situation '1 bottall of Aquvitie to the men that went Doun the pit'.

Underground the colliers' wages fluctuated according to their output. There was a basic payment of 2d. per load of coal worked — very occasionally raised when the going was particularly difficult. Members of the colliers' family, we can presume, had to assist in the work. There is no specific mention of females being involved; children were certainly required, and latterly there were special payments of 'putter boys wages' with 6/- divided among five lads who drew the hutches. The colliers supplemented their basic wage with oncost payments for non-productive jobs. The stoop-and-room technique of extraction was followed, and there were payments for 'biggan about the Stupes' and 'redding a room'. One pit had a 'main Road'; another had two levels, the 'east levan' and the 'wast levan'; still another worked the 'high and lach (laigh) coalls'. From the main galleries there were 'ducks' or sloping side passages which had to be 'redd' (tidied), as had the 'sink bothan' (sump) and the 'Borr and Gattan' (?). There was 'laying a piece of wood over a Gatton', and 'reding Rafrie' (?). Other work to be done was 'drawing the Mind' (driving forward the mine), 'biggan fallen roof', 'barring the coall' (putting up roof supports), 'blasting the Gaw' (breaking through a whin dyke), and always 'drawing the dirt'. In addition to payment for hewing and oncost work, the colliers were for a long time each awarded '1 load faircoalls at 3d. each', perhaps fire-danger money, and latterly also 'geat coalls for each man keeping their own road right'. John Brown, oversman from 1766, got a special responsibility element of 2/6 weekly which brought his wage up to around 15/-. Some other colliers collected only 6/-, just about what craftsmen in the burgh were then earning.

The 'coallers' were highly skilled experts who were brought in specially. To begin with there was a 'quest of Coallers in Stinson (Stevenston) and Ayr', and later on John Brown was paid 6d. to cover the travelling expenses of one from Glasgow. The contract was sealed appropriately with 'new comed coallers to drink'. Each week, too, a shilling or so was expended 'to drink to Coallers on Saterday'. There were similar occasions at Ne'erday and at the Marymass Fair: '1762, 21st August: To Bread and Drink to the Coallers after the Preade (parade) on Maramess fair'. Three years later there were 'expencis in Trysting Bunnets' to provide two colliers with bonnets 'at the perade'. In 1767 the expenditure was more specifically detailed: 'to the workers on the fair day, to Drink 13/-, to bread and chise 4/-'.

Although the colliers could at times be relatively well-off, their conditions of work were of course difficult. On two occasions, when the magistrates ventured on an inspection, they had to sustain themselves with 3/- and 9/2 for liquor. Ventilation was always a problem. Hence 'putting up a Door and Biggan up some througharts for Air', 'a new door for convoying air through the levans', and 'a big Rone for conving Air throo the pit'. Indeed the final closure of the pits came when the 'Coallers went from the work for want of air'. In 1763 two men died because of 'bad air'. Fire damp was especially dangerous when candles were used for illumination. One collier was paid 2/6 weekly as 'fairsman' who went 'through the work every morning befor the men went down for fear of fair [fire]'. Despite this, on at least fourteen occasions men were burnt, and Dr. Fleming had to be sent for. There was one 'great fall', and some men may have been entombed in 1765 when '2 men went doun the old pit to Chap to the men in the douck'. There were purchases of oil, salve, and spirits 'to the men that was burnt', with 'drink to the Coallers that day the 4 men was burnt to make them to go down to the work again'. On four occasions they had thus to be given drink 'to Incuradge them'. Sometimes a 'pension' of 1/- or 2/- was paid for a week or two to an injured miner.

Although elsewhere miners were sometimes still indentured for life, and this legal slavery was not eliminated until the Acts of Parliament of 1775 and 1779, the colliers in the Irvine pits seem to have been free miners. Of the three colliers engaged in the initial working, Bryce Blair was injured in the first week, got a week's pension of 1/- and then was apparently discharged; Robert Frew worked for three months; George Anderson continued until 1767. Of the fourteen men employed at the end of 1765, only four were among the ten discharged when the works closed in 1768. That there was such a high turnover of staff is an indication of the local difficulties, the availability of jobs in other pits in the area, and their liberty to come and go freely.

After the town council abandoned its municipal enterprise in coalmining in 1768, in 1770 it granted the tack of the coal in Marressfoot to Alexander Fairlie, factor of the 11th earl of Eglinton. In the following year a similar tack of the coal in the Moor was taken by a Mr. Beaumont, probably John Beaumont from Newcastle, who was extending his east of Scotland coal interests into Ayrshire. After abortive trials, he relinquished his lease, which in 1785 was taken up by a company composed of Bailie James Shaw, two merchants, a shipmaster, and William Templeton, the local bookseller. Others, including the Incorporated Trades, invested money, and the council could claim every twelfth load as its rental. The company 'sett down a Pitt in the East Part of the Moor and had a Shank at the North West of the Inclosed Common'.

The records of 'the Muir Coal' indicate that a coal grieve, from three to five 'Cleeksmen', and two gin boys were employed on the surface. Underground there was an oversman (on a fixed 12/- wage), and at one point 19 'Coalhewers'. Some of these occasionally earned over £1 but usually less than 10/- weekly, based not only on coal cut but on what was sold. There was the traditional payment for weekly drink 'on the Count table' and 'drink to the Coalhewers per order the last day of the old year'. From time to time there was 'Ale and Whisky to the Carters' and 'Brandy to the Carters who brought the Hay'.

Throughout the first half of 1786 output was usually between 500 and 700 loads a week, sold to the town at 6d. a load, or 'to the shore' at 7d. But in July water halted production. Two gins with double buckets could not cope, and the company, already over £1000 in debt, could not afford a steam pump or 'fire engine'. The company struggled on till it was wound up in 1789. In 1791 William Young, an Irvine man who was overseer of the Coalwork at Warrix, obtained from the council a tack of the 'Malting Coal and Common Fire Coal' on the west of the Redburn road to Kilwinning, including the Green, Gallowsknowe, Marressfoot, and Kidsneuk, at a fixed annual rental. Thereafter Irvine town council took no active part in the working of coal.

By chance there survives a vivid description of a local pit

Fullarton Street was laid out in 1776, within the burgh of Fullarton which had been created in 1707.

by Charles Hutcheson, a thirty-one-year-old Glasgow merchant who made a holiday trip to Arran in the summer of 1783. Before embarking at Irvine, he 'agreed to step out of our way and view... the coal works at the Warricks... the Engine is a Curious piece of Mathematics, we however were Soon Satisfied therewith, for there is something dreadful in the Operation, and is ready to Scare a Stranger (which I believe proceeds from the consideration that the Ground is all Boss below) — the motion of the Lavers over ones head — the dreadful and disagreeable noise of the Steam bursting from the Boilers and the Gushing of the water raised by the Engine from the Pit, which added to the frightful appearance of the miners, hoisting now and then out of Heugh, all them as black as little Devils — the Sight was rather awful than pleasing'.

The council retained its monopoly of corn milling. By 1791 the eventual situation was explained: 'There is one mill belonging to the town, and at a little distance from it, on the water of Annock. It pays, of yearly rent, about £60. The inhabitants are thirled to this mill, and pay 6d. per boll for grinding oats and malt'. A century before there had been three mills, and their story in the 18th century is complex and at times difficult to decipher. The Howe Mill at Milgarholm, which the burgh had once leased, though affected by a change in the river's course in the 17th century, was apparently for a time restored as a waulk mill for processing of cloth. Fullarton of Bartonholm planned to reconvert it into a cornmill, but his new dam was swept away about 1800 and the scheme given up. The Loch Mill must similarly have ceased to function following the draining early in the 18th century of the loch which fed it. Perhaps to compensate for this loss, the council in 1737 allowed the surgeon John Gemmel of Tourlands to erect a windmill at Gallowsknowe, but this was abandoned in 1748. The remaining Town Mill was that known as the Slate Mill, but never so named in the records; indeed this mill is often most confusingly described as the 'Town's Mill of Loch Mill' or simply as Loch Mill, no doubt because the two buildings were so close together as to be regarded as one unit. In 1742 there was installed a 'big steel miln sometime ago made in Kilmaurs', also small steel mills. These had rollers and were generally used for crushing malt for brewing or distilling. Here perhaps was the 'old Waulkmill at and contiguous to Lochmill' which Alexander Edwards, tobacconist and councillor, sought to convert into a snuffmill in 1755. And in 1765 a 'Brewerie was in great forwardness of being set up' at this location.

A new situation arose as a result of the great flood of 1769. An old beggar woman (it is said) was rudely turned away from the waulk mill at Milgarholm, and foretold that in retribution the river would foresake the mill within twenty-four hours. The spate, when it came, made for the River Irvine a new more direct course south of Tarryholm. The lower reaches were swamped with 'immense quantities of sand' and the harbour choked by the 'great inundation'. The old channel was left dry, and with it Newmill in Dreghorn parish, which was later converted into a brewery. Milgarholm was no longer on the main stream but supplied only with the lesser and insufficient waters of the Annick. Fortunately the Town Mill was not affected, and survived as the solitary corn mill. A new kiln was provided in 1774, improved roller mills for grinding malt in 1786, and in 1794 fanners were installed for winnowing grain. The mill was for the convenience of the inhabitants: it was not developed as a commercial enterprise.

The town council became involved, though more indirectly, in an attempt to develop large-scale production of linen at a time when that was still Scotland's principal textile. In 1749 a Linen Company was formed with the intention of establishing a factory in which a large number of handlooms would be installed. Forty persons contributed £50 each. With five of these partners being councillors, it was easy to secure the co-operation of the council in allocating part of the Moor as a site. As John Galt remarked of a similar occasion, 'nothing could be more manifest than but there was some joockerie cookerie in this affair'. As a preliminary a row of workers' houses was erected. The company was allowed to make use of the stones and timber from the old windmill. But when a further area of the Moor, extending from Castle Street as far as the Minister's Cast, was fenced off, there was a 'great Clamour among the lower sort of the Inhabitants'. The Incorporated Trades took a principal part in this opposition, defending popular rights to the Moor, and no doubt also the threatened vested interests of the weavers' trade, for large-scale production of linen would offer dangerous competition for the domestic weavers. But what became known as 'the Factory Park' was acquired for bleaching. Work was carried on for eight years, with limited success. The Linen Company's chances were thwarted by the overthrow of the old council in the 1756 conspiracy as described in chapter seven. The company was dissolved, and in 1757 Charles Hamilton was able to purchase, for £480, the workers' houses, which were later converted into muslin weavers' shops.

An expansion of the woollen and linen manufacture as carried on by the traditional domestic spinners and weavers is suggested by waulking of cloth being done at Lochmill before 1755 and at Milgarholm a few years after. There was bleaching at the Golffields in 1750, and a year later a bleachfield was set up as a commercial undertaking, at Braidmeadow, by John Innes and Company. Flax is said to have been 'retted' in pools in the River Irvine. On Marymass Monday there were the annual sales of wool and lint (linen).

In the last two decades of the 18th century the new cotton weaving became Scotland's main manufacture. In Irvine there were handloom weavers of muslin at Burns Street and in the new and appropriately named Cotton Row beyond the Glasgow Vennel. About 1788 a Glasgow company set up a tambour works, paying 70 girls from 1/3 to 2/- a week in that intricate embroidery work. In 1790 spinning jennies were installed in another factory employing 80 hands. And another two small spinning factories, employing about 50 each, were erected 'in the suburbs'. This suggests that the vested interests of the Trades were forcing new businesses to go over into Fullarton, outwith the burgh, just as at Ayr the new industries became established over the water in Newton. In 1792 an approach was made to the council to allow the establishment of a water-powered cotton spinning factory where the Minister's Cast entered the River Irvine on the Moor but, significantly, this, it seems, was not approved.

All in the way of manufactures that the Statistical Account could report for 1791, in addition to the new cotton businesses, were 'three small shipbuilders, a tan work, a rope work, and a bleachfield. One whisky still which consumes about 950 bolls of malt yearly. One small brewery'. The shipbuilding yards on the river west of Friars Croft were small in scale. The rope work was also in Fullarton, near the Puddleford, operated by Hugh Garven. The tan works, set up at the Seagatefoot in 1762 by William Burns from Kilwinning, was abandoned before 1812. The small distillery, and the brewery (perhaps at Lochmill), seem also soon to have disappeared.

The Incorporated Trades enjoyed some benefit from the general commercial expansion. In 1719 their boxmaster had been recognised as deacon convener. Although in 1743 a petition to revise their constitution was refused by the council because of 'late instances of Arrogance and Insolence', in 1756 the new council agreed to a Charter of Confirmation, 'on condition that the Trades at the call of the Magistrates assist in quelling the riots and tumults'. The new charter recognised the six Trades of smiths, weavers, tailors, wrights, cordiners, and coopers. The coopers had been reinstated as a corporation in 1755 after a long period when their craft organisation had lapsed. In 1723 the barbers and wigmakers, who had their own charitable society with a membership as high as some of the Trades, had also been granted incorporation, but this seems to have proved ineffective. The skinners, a seventh trade listed in the old Seal of Cause of 1646, had never become properly constituted.

The carters, whose flag suggests they formed a society in 1670, became formally constituted in 1753 with 106 members. Rates of hire were formulated — $2\frac{1}{2}$d a mile for a packhorse, 4d for one to ride, 10d a mile for use with a chaise. There was a box for charitable purposes, with ten overseers coming from the 'town-heid', 'town-end', 'brigget', and 'bridgend'. And, as will later appear, there were arrangements for the 'Draff Race' at Marymass. Although the carters were in 1775 granted a loft in the new kirk, and had a substantial membership, yet in 1780 the council refused official incorporation, since this was not a craft of manufacturers.

The Incorporated Trades were proud of their privileges, particularly their possession of the Trades Loft in the church, obtained in 1693. In 1709 there was a dispute as to which Trade should have precedence in going into kirk — and the council diplomatically ruled that it should be as they were listed in the Seal of Cause. In 1726 the Trades insisted that no member should occupy the foreseat in the Loft 'but such as have Hats under penalty of 5/-'. Such records as survive indicate the shoemakers in a dispute over the workmanship of 'a pair of pumps' (1767) and one fined (1777) for striking a fellow-member. The hammermen, who were smiths, protected the interests of the master craftsmen by prohibiting journeymen from 'working to themselves on Saturdays, or any other time' (1719). Anyone admitted to the craft must first produce a specified 'say-piece' (essay piece), and specimens noted (1725) were 'a copper skelet' (small kettle) and 'a white iron mill' (snuff box). Such requirements are specified in the Charter, with details of payments for admissions, Trades Loft fees, and subscriptions for the maintenance of poor and aged members and their wives and bairns. How the individual crafts were organised is revealed by the fact that the hammermen, for instance, had an annually elected executive committee consisting of a deacon, two masters, two key-masters, two say-masters, fiscal, clerk and officer. Their affluence and sociability is hinted at by the Incorporated Trades making payment in 1725 'for a treat to the magistrates and gentlemen of the town'.

By 1791 the membership of the Trades was assessed as 116 weavers, working in wool or flax; 27 tailors; 56 shoemakers; 24 smiths; 80 masons and wrights; and only 7 coopers. In addition, the Statistical Account shows that the town had 'a great many grocers and small hucksters shops, and four or five hardware shops'. There were also 10 maltsters, 6 master butchers, 7 bakers, 6 cloth merchants, 2 chandlers, 2 saddlers, 3 copper smiths, 4 tinkers, as well as one physician, 3 surgeons, 5 writers or lawyers, 2 druggists, and 6 barbers. There were 150 coal hewers, most of them probably living in the town.

To meet the needs of the new economy, banks were instituted. The first to be set up locally was in 1786 as a branch of the Ayr Bank of Hunters & Co. James Hunter, son of an Ayr provost, had served with the county's first bank, John McAdam & Co., founded in 1763. This was taken over in 1771 by Douglas, Heron and Co., which collapsed disastrously in 1772. The cashier, James Hunter, with four relatives, founded his own less pretentious Ayr Bank in 1774, and branches in Irvine and Maybole. The Irvine branch was operated from 1786 to 1804 by its manager Alexander Cunningham from his house opposite Seagatehead. His successor, James Crichton (1804–1817), moved it to a more central site in High Street, then Alexander Paterson (1817–67) to premises opposite the Bridgegatehead where Bank Street was later made. Also in 1786 the recently formed Paisley Bank opened an Irvine branch, originally at Bridgegatehead, and after 1804 further along High Street, between the Kirkgate and Kirk Vennel, when Robert Montgomerie became manager.

In this new economy there was still need for the traditional markets and fairs. It was felt necessary in 1796 to supplement the tron with a 'Stillyard' for weighing hay and loaded carts. Though Rev. James Richmond did not mention markets in the Statistical Account, he was probably thinking of them when he did write that 'the principal commodities are linen, cloth, horses, wool, etc.' Marymass, which concluded with the races on Friday and Saturday, began with the important sales of wool and lint (Monday) and the horse fair (Wednesday). Yet the old burghal community based on local crafts and local trade was in process of being superseded.

NINE

Church and School

During the long ministry of Rev. William McKnight (1709-51) the church continued to occupy a prominent role in the life of the community. The bitter religious dissension of previous generations had exhausted itself, and sectarianism did not become prominent in Irvine until the latter part of the 18th century.

The demolition of the medieval Church of St. Mary and its replacement by a new parish church in 1773 marked the end of an era. Earlier in 1721 the old steeple was 'in great hazard of falling down' and had to be dismantled. Some of its masonry was used in making a well in the Bridgegate; its bell was hung up on a tree in the kirkyard, then installed in the tolbooth. In another way the old church was proving inadequate. In 1722 forms were provided for seating some of the congregation; in 1736 the first of a series of assistant ministers was appointed to help shepherd the augmented population of burgh and parish. The number of 'examinable persons' grew from around a thousand in 1700 to 3,100 in 1761. During the ministry of Rev. Charles Bannatyne (1751-73) increased expenditure on repairing the fabric of the old church culminated in his laying the foundation of a new building. The costs — which amounted eventually to £2,500 — were the responsibility of the heritors. These were the landowners of the parish, with the town council as the prinicpal heritor paying three-quarters of the total. The new church was larger than the old one, and part of the old graveyard had to be taken in. The church measured eighty feet by sixty, with walls raised to forty feet high.

Above it was erected in 1778 a steeple 150-feet high with spire and weather cock. This was a copy of the Adam steeple of St. Andrew's Church, Dundee. In 1797 Provost Hugh, earl of Eglinton, added a twenty hundredweight bell brought from London. Later in 1803 the Volunteers donated a clock for the steeple, designed by John Watt, a local clockmaker. The contractor for the building of the church was Bailie David Muir, who paid his masons ten pence a day working on the walls and a shilling when on the steeple. Inside, the pulpit was on the north-west side, fronted by a desk for the precentor, and below that two pulpit pews for officiating elders. The 'Big Kirk', as it became known, was able to seat a congregation of 1,770. Lofts were provided for the principal heritors — Eglinton, Bourtreehill, and the magistrates; others were rouped to Bartonholm, the Incorporated Trades, the Sailors, and the Carters. In the rest of the galleries and on the ground floor, pews were constructed and allocated by public auction. Preference was given to the minor heritors, and provision was made for those who could not afford their own seats. In the centre of the floor area there were two rows of seats where communion tables could be erected for the twice-yearly sacraments. At each of the four doorways was a 'brod' or box for offerings, which were devoted to poor relief.

The orderly allocation of seats brought to an end the unseemly squabbles which were frequent in the old church. Attempts were made to reduce the other disorders that marred 18th-century church services. When in 1775 the Carters Society sought to obtain a loft, they promised to remain seated till the magistrates left the kirk and to 'behave themselves decently and orderly and making no noise with their book boards or folding boards'. In 1792 a fine of 2/- was imposed on anyone falling asleep on a front seat during the two-hour-long services. Provost John Paterson recalled as an apprentice about 1807 when the Trades Officer was armed with a long rod to give sleepers a prod, and if that proved ineffective to bang it down on the bookboard. In general, church discipline continued to be applied by the kirk session.

The authority of the kirk session became less effective as the community grew and altered in character. This was the established church, with the town council still sending its own representative to the annual meetings of the General Assembly of the Church in Edinburgh. But dissatisfaction with church government and doctrine persuaded numbers throughout Scotland to withdraw their allegiance. The first secession of 1733 had little impact in Irvine. The parish minister, Rev. William McKnight, was prepared in 1742 to welcome to his house and pulpit the Methodist missionary George Whitefield. Yet Whitefield's great

Irvine Parish Church was rebuilt in 1773 at a cost of £2,500. The steeple was added in 1778, and in 1798 a bell was provided by Hugh, earl of Eglinton, who was also provost of Irvine.

open-air rally, with five thousand of an audience near the Powder House in the Golffields, stimulated an evangelical enthusiasm which was not fully satisfied by the established church. When only a few years later in 1751 McKnight died and the earl of Eglinton presented Rev. Charles Bannatyne from Arran as his successor, this was not to the taste of those who felt that the wishes of parishioners should be consulted. When a Relief Church was formed in 1752 'for the relief of Christians... and their natural right to choose a pastor', the dissidents began meeting at the Golffields and by 1773 had sufficient support to erect their own Relief Kirk in the West Road at the foot of Hamil hill, and to support their own chosen ministers — James Jack (1777-82), Hugh White (1782-83), and Peter Robertson (1784-1819). Other seceders who had been travelling to Kilmaurs were able to form their own congregation in 1792, meeting in the kiln or malt barn at the corner of Glasgow Vennel and East Road. In 1809 they built a church nearby in Cotton Row, with Alexander Campbell as their first minister (1809-43). This Burgher Kirk belonged to the Associate Synod formed in 1747 following a schism among the Seceders. Around the same time a number of independents established a Baptists' meeting house in the Bridgegate before obtaining George Barclay as minister (1808-38). Over in Fullarton there was as yet no church of any kind. Between 1771 and 1776 Brother and Sister John Montgomery attempted to set up a church of the Moravian Brethren at the Braid Close in the Halfway associated with the one in Ayr, but their missionary efforts were unavailing and they returned to Ireland with their later-famous son James Montgomery who was born here. Of the growing number of Irish immigrants, many were Ulster protestants. Those few who were of the old faith were not especially welcome, for in 1779 the town council formally protested at the parliamentary repeal of penal laws against Roman Catholics. Such went apparently without any spiritual guidance locally until 1822. Provost John Paterson, however, has an enigmatic note under the year 1797: 'Barney Cloas. Journeyman to Jas. Russel, shoemaker paid his dues to the Trade. He was a well known character and kept a pub in the Guild Closs. He used to officiate as an R.C. Priest'. That the established church remained

On the Golffields, beside the Powder House, the Methodist missionary George Whitefield held an open-air rally in 1742. This early 19th-century print shows the spot, changed only by a rebuilt bridge (1748); the Washing House (1749); the new parish church (1773) with its first manse (1821); and houses across the water in Fullarton Street (1776).

acceptable to the majority of believers was perhaps due to two circumstances. When Rev. Charles Bannatyne's death in 1773 caused a vacancy, the earl of Eglinton agreed to the presentation of Rev. James Richmond, who was the choice of the council, the kirk session, and 228 heads of families. And in 1783 religious extremism was brought into disrepute by the Buchanite Delusion which erupted in the Relief Kirk.

In 1782 there was ordained to that church Hugh White, originally a licentiate of the Church of Scotland who had been exposed in America to the free-love doctrines of the 'Shaker' sect. In the early summer of 1783 he invited Mrs. Elspeth Buchan to his home in Seagate. An orphan born in Banffshire, Elspeth Simpson followed a disordered career with a history of religious hysteria, deserted her husband, and formed a mystical association with White. He was the 'Manchild' and she the 'Woman' of Revelations, commissioned to announce the second Coming of Christ. White was deposed for heresy, but there were sufficient adherents to hold meetings in a tent in White's Seagate garden, then in the Glasgow Vennel house of Patrick Hunter, a prosperous lawyer and merchant whose crooked back earned him the nickname of 'Humphy Hunter'. Robert Burns described the Buchanites: 'Their tenets are a strange jumble of enthusiastic jargon, among others, she pretends to give them the Holy Ghost by breathing on them, which she does with postures and practices that are scandalously indecent; they have likewise disposed of all their effects and hold a community of goods, and live nearly an idle life, carrying on a great farce of pretended devotion in barns and woods, where they lodge and lie all together, and hold likewise a community of women'. Twice Mrs. Buchan was driven out of town by riotous mobs; twice she returned. Then in May 1784 the town council formally banished her and forty-five followers. A disorderly crowd accompanied them from Seagate and along the High Street through the Cow Fair, then in progress. Young John Galt remembered them 'singing psalms as they went, shouting and saying they were going to the New Jerusalem'. They left by Kilmarnock road and migrated via Mauchline towards Kirkcudbrightshire, where they established themselves as a community. There Mrs. Buchan, 'the Friend Mother of the Lord', died in 1791. Her corpse was preserved by those who awaited a resurrection. Many of

Objections to the presentation of ministers to the parish church by the earls of Eglinton led to the formation of a separate congregation who erected their own Relief Church in 1773.

her dispirited adherents drifted back to Irvine. Some returned to the fold of the established church, including Mrs. Hunter who in 1787 'professed her sorrow on account of being misled by the errors of Mrs. Buchan and desired to be restored to Christian privilege'. The Relief Kirk recovered from the Buchanite controversy. In 1788 they had to take down and rebuild their church more securely. By 1791 there were 240 adherents, increasing to 600 by 1818 when the church was enlarged to accommodate 930 worshippers. The Baptists had only 40 members, though there was room for 450 in the church they built in West Road in 1808. The Burgher Kirk had places for 800. There was thus a total of 3,950 seats in the various places of worship. This was for a community in 1820 of 6,370 — 4,398 in Irvine parish plus 1,972 in Fullarton. Clearly many families had abandoned a church connection, even allowing for unshepherded Roman Catholics, a score or so of Methodists, a few Anti-burghers, and some Reformed Presbyterians (otherwise Cameronians or McMillanites) who had no local place of worship.

Since the established church could now claim only a fraction of the population, its powers of discipline were losing their effectiveness. While early in the 18th century the kirk session records are filled with detailed inquisitions of offenders, followed by public rebuke before the congregation, later there is an obvious weakening of authority. In 1785, for example, there were ten cases of antenuptial fornication: the parties were simply admonished and absolved by the session. Two irregular marriages were similarly disposed of. Public penance was reserved for five cases of adultery. By the end of the century private rebuke was the norm for all offences. And the kirk session gave up its annual meeting for privy censure, when the elders confessed their own sins. There is further evidence of a slackening of traditional restrictions. In 1734 the shipmasters were censured for 'profaning the Lord's day by unnecessarie lousing their vessels'. In 1794 the barbers were protesting that they could not attend church 'by their Customers requiring them to shave and dress them on the Lord's day'. By 1814 Bailie Fullarton was lamenting about people 'strolling through the streets and fields in an idle and disorderly manner upon the Lord's day'. In the same circumstances the kirk session found it increasingly difficult to exercise effectively its traditional responsibility for poor relief. This involved aid for orphans and for those who were aged and infirm but had no family to sustain them. In 1746, for example, the session granted 8d weekly to one who had 'grown old and infirm so that he cannot work as usual and is in a starving condition'. From time to time the council made exceptional grants to other

James Montgomery, the 'Christian Poet', was born in 1771, son of Moravian missionaries, in the Halfway — which was later renamed in his honour. His birthplace, 26 Montgomery Street, is now demolished.

deserving cases — in 1741 'to blind John Smith to buy clothes'. Special church collections were arranged in times of crisis, as to repair fire damage at the Townhead in 1733, and after a devastating hailstorm in 1734. But an augmented population depending on a fluctuating trade was increasingly vulnerable, and Rev. James Richmond in 1791 noted that 'the poor of this place have greatly increased within these fifty years'. The most necessitous were by that time being awarded from 6d to 2/6 per week. In 1807 there were 34 on the permanent roll of paupers. Richmond also remarked how the enlargement of farms had dispossessed cottars, who crowded into town and became a burden. The extent of vagrancy can be assessed by the thousand beggars who assembled at the funeral of the 9th earl of Eglinton in 1729 to share in the £50 charity then distributed. In 1750 Irvine town council, complaining that the town 'has of late been much pestered with foreign poor', authorised the town officers to try to keep them out. In 1758 an abortive plan was mooted to erect a poorshouse, to be financed by a poor tax levied 'according to Trade and Circumstance' and upon lands proportionate to valuation. In times of dearth, as in 1740, the council borrowed to bring in a cargo of victual from London. In 1777 there was a meal mob, as described by John Galt in *The Provost*. In 1800 the council allocated some of its income from rents to aid a committee purchasing meal for the poor, and the next year similarly supported a 'Public Kitchen'.

The better-off members insured themselves against times of difficulty by contributing to friendly societies. The Incorporated Trades, the Carters and the Sailors Society were joined by others. An Irvine Friendly Society was formed in 1785, and in 1820 there were sixteen such local organisations with a membership of 1,113. They also assisted their less fortunate brethren in various ways. From time to time there had been generous gifts to the session: the property of Gulliland from Hugh Brown of Milgarholm in 1691; a mortification from James Blair, Glasgow merchant, in 1709 to support four paupers; £30 annual interest from Bailie John Gray, surgeon, in 1784 to assist poor scholars; £300 towards the poor from Mr. Stewart, a druggist.

The social responsibilities of the kirk session still included support for the town council in the provision of education. Here, too, the 18th century brought difficulties and valiant attempts to surmount them, but not till the early years of the 19th century would a real new beginning in education be possible.

Throughout the 18th century the council consistently sought to provide good schooling at the premises in Kirkgatehead. They generously provided the master with the statutory maximum annual salary of 200 merks, augmented by scholars' fees, their Candlemas offerings, income from boarders, and fees as session clerk. He taught Latin, writing and music. He was assisted by the doctor, who was also relatively well paid with 120 merks and his payment by the session for acting as precentor in the church. In 1746 a third master was added to the staff. The school itself was improved in 1724 with 'new lights and desks'. Although in 1750 it was 'in danger of falling', it was completely rebuilt 'according to a new plan'. This new school had two large rooms measuring 30 by 17 feet, separated by a vestibule over which a bell turret was erected, and an extension was added in 1783.

Despite these efforts, the council found it difficult to staff the school effectively. Mr. John Thomson, who came from Kilmarnock in 1704 to replace James Hislop as schoolmaster, had to be dismissed after five years for non-attendance, 'whereby their school was entirely broke'. There followed a series of less well-qualified masters, none of whom lasted long — James Stewart (1710), John Spark (1714), John Fullarton (1715), James Smith (1717, 1720), and William Cumming (1723). There was a similar rapid turnover of doctors: Peter Aird (1704), William Cumming (1720), John McIver (1723), Francis Scott (1724), William Jack on whose death Alexander Galt was appointed (1735), William Dickie, (1737), Mr. Henderson (who 'made great progress in accomplishing severally in singing some new Church tunes', 1758), John Gemmill (1761), and James Carfrae (dismissed, 1776).

William Cunningham, appointed master in 1726, proved more reliable. In 1729 the Presbytery 'found that the first class translated a part of the Greek Testament into Latin, and some of the Roman authors into English, answered the questions put to them, and translated many English sentences into elegant Latin with great dexterity.

THE

DIVINE DICTIONARY;

OR, A

Treatise indicted by Holy Inspiration,

CONTAINING

The FAITH and PRACTICE of that PEOPLE (by this world) called BUCHANITES, who are actually waiting for the second coming of our Lord, and who believe that they, alive, shall be changed and translated into the clouds, to meet the Lord in the air, and so shall be ever with the Lord.

And there appeared a great wonder in heaven, a woman.—REV. xii. 1.

Written by that SOCIETY.

DUMFRIES:
Printed by ROBERT JACKSON, 1785.
Price Ninepence.

In 1784 the Relief Church was disrupted and the town scandalised by Mrs Elspeth Buchan, whose doctrines were explained in this contemporary booklet.

They found also a sett of globs and mapps, for instructing students in the elements of geography and astronomy and that the masters teach arithmetic and navigation to such as desire instruction therein'. During Cunningham's long term of office the school was rebuilt, he adopted the new title of rector, he became a prominent member of the town council in 1756, and served school and community till his death in 1766 at the age of seventy. His tombstone described him as 'a gentleman of distinguished ability, piety, integrity, and learning who discharged the duties of his important office with diligence, fidelity, and approbation upward of forty years'. William Dickie, who

Among the Buchanites expelled from Irvine in 1784 was Andrew Innes who died in 1846, the last survivor of the sect.

served with 'fidelity and care' as doctor from 1737, succeeded him and continued as master until 1783. But it was clear that good assistants were difficult to find, and even more difficult to keep. When it was decided to appoint a third master, Mr. James Baillie, who came in 1746 from Mauchline 'to teach English after the modern way', went off to Ayr in less than a year. His successor, Mr. James Kempt from Aberdeen, proved 'troublesome and litiginous' and had eventually to be dismissed in 1759. It would be tedious to list the continued difficulties with these English masters, and no doctors seem to have been appointed after 1777, thus reducing the staff again to two.

There were high hopes of a new beginning in 1783. Mr. James Robertson Muir was appointed rector at £18 sterling plus the usual emoluments, with 4/- from each pupil per quarter. Mr. Benjamin Maul, a native of Dailly who had been parish schoolmaster in Muirkirk since 1773, became master responsible for English, writing, and arithmetic at £10 per annum plus fees. The smaller room in the school used for teaching English was enlarged by extending the south-east gable. A bequest from the late Bailie John Gray would provide schooling for some poor children. In addition to the prescribed subjects, bookkeeping, mathematics, geography, and French were offered. Responsibility for these seems to have fallen to Maul, who was obviously an enthusiastic teacher. In his home in Hill Street he and his wife — a relation of Burns' friend John Lapraik — kept boarding pupils. The number of these had however dwindled since before the American War when William Cunningham had often more than a score of pupils from across the Atlantic. Muir seems to have been less energetic. In 1791 he had only thirty boys as compared with Maul's seventy. After Maul's early death in 1797 at the age of 49, the school lost its reputation, and parents were bringing in teachers to set up private schools. Around mid-century several 'strangers' had attempted to set up such schools in the town, and the council's dispute with their English master Mr. James Kempt was that he had abandoned the grammar school and begun to teach Latin privately, which was considered a threat to the monopoly of the master of that school. In 1759 the council had protested when a Mr. George Leslie proposed setting up 'in Mary McKelvie's house' to teach Greek, Latin, French, arithmetic, writing, bookkeeping, navigation and mathematics. There was no objection to private elementary schools. Indeed in 1732 the kirk session began subsidising one at Stane. And the council was willing enough to encourage schooling of a type which the grammar school could not provide. From 1773 the council appointed a series of schoolmistresses to teach girls needlework. There was no objection when David Sillar set up in East Road what became a popular school of navigation. By the time of the Statistical Account there were several such private schools.

In 1797 David Sillar was unsuccessful in his application to become Maul's successor as English master. The classically orientated studies of the grammar school were proving unpopular, yet no one could halt the decline. By 1800 so few were being enrolled that Muir shut up the school for several months and 'deserted it'. At this low ebb, the council eventually in 1811 persuaded Muir to resign with the offer of an annuity of £25. Looking to Ayr, where the old burgh school had recently (1796) been converted into an academy, they started planning a similar new school for Irvine. On the advice of the rector at Ayr they replaced Muir by James Lockhart Brown from Falkland in 1812. While at Ayr a lavish £80 a year was provided, here only £30 could be offered. But with his other emoluments, he would finish up not far short of the parish minister who had a stipend of £40 plus meal plus eight acres of glebe, and better than the Relief minister's £70 a year in full. William Clark had been appointed English Master in 1804 at £15 plus fees of 4/6 per quarter for reading, writing, and arithmetic at 3/- for reading only.

Despite its various shortcomings, the old burgh school at Kirkgatehead offered opportunity and in the 18th century had some notable alumni. Alexander, 10th earl of Eglinton (born 1723), succeeded to the title at the age of six and attended Irvine school until 1737 when he was fourteen. His younger brother Archibald (born 1726), who would become 11th earl, was his school fellow. Less reputable was James George Semple (born about 1750). The son of a customs officer, he was an able scholar who distinguished himself in Latin and Greek. 'An elegant figure, a person exceeding well made, and [with] a genteel deportment', he won the 'esteem and favour' of the opposite sex, which resulted in his 'abdication of Irvine'. In London he won the hand of a wealthy young lady, whose family rescued her from Semple and arranged for him to go to Russia, where his charms made him aide de camp to Prince Potemkin in the Crimea in 1776. Escaping from his numerous frauds and deceptions, he made his way back to London, posing as an agent 'on his Majesty's service with expresses of the most important and serious nature'. Back in England he continued his career as confidence-trickster, cheating 'peers and publicans', and claiming the friendship of Prime Minister William Pitt and other notables. Eventually this 'Prince of Swindlers' was caught and confined in Newgate prison, tried at the Old Bailey in 1786, found guilty of felony, and sentenced to transportation. There were more praiseworthy former pupils, details of whose careers are more fully outlined elsewhere in this book. David Boyle of Shewalton (born 1772) went from Irvine school to become a famous lawyer. Henry Eckford (born 1775) would help build the US Navy. John Galt (born 1779) went to school there at the age of eight, but moved to Greenock two years later. John Allan (born 1779) became a merchant in Virginia; he adopted Edgar Allan Poe (born 1809) and brought him to Irvine in 1815 to begin his schooling in the last year of the old school at Kirkgatehead.

Those who were pupils of Mr. Benjamin Maul between 1782 and 1797 were fortunate indeed. Among the burgh factor's accounts are payments made to William Templeton for books supplied to the English school, which reveal a stimulating range being requisitioned by Maul. For the youngest pupils there was not only a series of 'penny

James George Semple from Irvine won national notoriety in the 18th century as a confidence trickster.

books' for reading, but sets of 'small picture books' and copies of 'Three Hundred Animals'. As well as 'Psalm Books' there were 'Song Books'. 'Watt's Catechism' was supplemented by *The Pilgrim's Progress*. Two books on better writing were available. For older pupils Milton was followed by more recent poets: Pope, Thomson, Gray, and Young. There were 'Trajedys and play books' and Goldsmith's 'Essays'. Prose works purchased included biographies, Anson's *Voyages*, Defoe's *Robinson Crusoe*, and Swift's *Gulliver's Travels*. And most remarkable was the recognition of recent Scottish literature with four copies of 'William Wallace', presumably Hamilton of Gilbertfield's version, three copies of Allan Ramsay's 'Gentle Shepherd', another two 'with music', and one copy of 'Ferguson's Poems'.

TEN

John Galt's Irvine

When John Galt was born in 1779, his 'Gudetown' was in process of rapid growth and change. Irvine burgh's population doubled in the first half of the century, and in the next fifty years numbers continued to increase from 3,000 to 3,500, with another two thousand on the other side of the river. How this was affecting the town was suggested by Rev. James Richmond in the Statistical Account: 'This increase has chiefly taken place in the suburbs or annexed part of the parish, the numbers in the town having rather decreased, owing to the taking down of some old houses, each of which contained many families; whereas the new ones built in their place are occupied by one or two families at most'. The town centre with so many old wooden houses was being renewed. In 1734 there had been another great fire, with the 'houses being pulled down in order to prevent the further spreading of the fire'. In 1776, 'because so many inhabitants are building houses', the council leased Duntonknoll Quarry, whose working required the installation of a steam engine in 1805.

Wood's Town Map of 1819 reveals how the town was extended. The main thoroughfare was built up completely from Townhead in the south-east to what was later named Burns Street at the other end. Bridgegate, the Grip (now Chapel Lane), Mount Musart (now the Hill), and Kirkgate were fully occupied. The Vennel (formerly Smiddy Bar and not yet officially Glasgow Vennel) extended into Cotton Street, and houses were being erected on East Backway. Better-class residences were being set up on attractive sites overlooking the river and along the Kilwinning road. In the 'suburb' of Fullarton the working class was accommodated in increased numbers in new houses 'mostly of one storey, with finished garrets'. Halfway was built up on both sides along its length, with feus planned by the council to retain a clear 'view of the Harbour from the head of the Bridgegate'. In 1776 Fullarton Street (later nicknamed Soor Milk Raw) was laid out by Colonel William Fullarton of Fullarton, who in 1808 was succeeded by his second cousin Colonel Stewart Murray Fullarton of Bartonholm. Marress and the farmland around belonged to the Boyles of Shewalton who had acquired it from Edward Wallace in 1715.

Trade and increased traffic required improved thoroughfares. A first requirement was an improved bridge, and between 1748 and 1753 a new one was built by Thomas Brown for £350, with four semi-circular arches each of forty feet span. Since wheeled vehicles were still uncommon, the new bridge was very like its predecessor. It was only eleven feet wide, with low parapets for the benefit of the swinging packs on horses' backs, and a widened passing place in the middle. There was a smaller bridge over the Annick, rebuilt in 1720. The other over Red Burn was described by the earl of Eglinton as 'a few sticks covered with earth, which is ready to break down by the weight of any carriage', and the council replaced it in 1777.

A general improvement in communications was effected by the Ayrshire Turnpike Acts of 1767 and 1774. The first of these provided for twenty-two roads 'much frequented by travellers, but ... impassable in winter for wheel carriages and horses'. These included four main routes which served Irvine. They would be turnpiked, with tollgates erected and the revenues applied to road improvement. The old road from Ayr — still used thereafter by those seeking to evade paying tolls — followed the shore, with 'a dangerous quick sand on the road at the foot of Pow Burn'. It approached Irvine near the harbour by the Gottries (or Guthries) road and reached the bridge and ford crossings by what (after Halfway was laid out) became the Back Road, later Loudoun Street. The new turnpike road came by Gailes and entered by what became Fullarton Street. Similarly the older northern exit from Irvine across Gallowshill towards Bartonholm was superseded by the turnpike which took a more direct line via Redburn. From Townhead and across the Annick went the turnpike through Dreghorn, to Kilmarnock, or by a branch to Tarbolton and the south. To the north-east went the fourth main route, towards Stewarton and to Glasgow. On these roads, toll bars were erected at the south end of Fullarton Street; beside Williamfield; beyond the Townhead past the junction with East Road; and near Stane. How the new roads were made and repaired by statute labour is shown in the Minutes for 1776 of the Road Trustees, who 'call out the Inhabitants and others Lyable, to perform their actual service upon the Road betwixt the Town of Irvine and the Stain Castle Toll Bar'. Exemption was not allowed, save by arranging for substitutes who would 'accept of money from those willing to pay, in place of performing their work'. Landowners had roads built on their own estates to link up with the turnpike main routes. In 1780 Sir Walter Montgomerie Cunningham made one from Greenvale, as Annick Lodge was then called. In 1799, to protect his new policies, the earl of Eglinton closed the old road beyond the Drucken Steps, providing a diversion by Knadgerhill.

Through the second part of the century the council was vigorously involved in improving the thoroughfares within the burgh. This required, regrettably, the destruction of the two old ports in 1756. They were 'in a ruinous condition', and the now dangerous 'arches of both ports' were removed. Because the High Street was so broad at the Cross, the tolbooth could be retained, though the householders nearby in 1794 had to remove 'the large stones which are standing at some doors' — the louping-stanes for the convenience of horsemen. Similarly, so that the Bridgegate could be 'made straight and regular', two sheds were demolished in 1756, as was a house at Townhead in 1763 which encroached on the street. Feuars were required (1752) to causeway the road from their houses to the middle of the highway, and most years the council spent money on road works: in what was called Ballat or Bullet Road (1754), Bridgegate (1756), roads to Stane, Lochmill and the harbour (1757), Townhead and Stanecastle (1759), High Street and passages (1765), repairing holes in High Street (1767), road to the mill (1785), Boyle's road to Marress (1789), Seagate (1793), beyond Townhead (1794), from the bridge by Halfway to the quay (1809). In 1794 the dean of guild was instructed to remove all timber and rubbish from the streets.

The town that John Galt was growing up in was one of busy streets — carts carrying coal and general merchandise, merchants and hawkers thronging the High Street markets, coaches beginning to ply each Monday, Wednesday and Friday to Glasgow and Ayr. A noisy place, with vagrants and sailors frequenting the popular taverns which multiplied from 24 to 38 in the last third of the century. A place filled with the smells of horse manure, tanning of leather, and cattle being butchered in the streets. A town of crowds — meal mobs, redcoats, pressgangs, smugglers, fairs, and the Buchanites whom the infant John Galt witnessed being driven out of town. For the growing boy there were the delights of playing in the yard around the fine new church, exploring the vennels and closes, investigating the now ruinous Seagate Castle, crossing the new bridge to enjoy the quayside scenes, roaming amongst the whins on the Moor and into the woods of Eglinton. 'No man ever had a happier childhood than mine,' he recalled. 'It was a morning dewdrop glittering in the rising sun.' John Galt was observant enough to note, and realise in retrospect, what was going on during his ten years of childhood there from 1779 till 1789. From his mother he learned the Scots speech, and from his grandmother and the other old women in the close heard of the old days and the changes they had experienced. Even after he left his native place he seems to have kept in touch and was aware of the continuing changes until he returned to receive the freedom of the burgh in 1825.

The growing town required an improved supply of water. The inhabitants at Seagatehead had sunk a well there (1695), as did those of the Bridgegate, using stones from the church steeple (1722). These and the older one at the Cross were converted into pump wells by the Council (1740). Other public and private wells were sunk. In the Townhead were the Port Well, the Whiskey Well, and the Tollbar Well. There was one at Kirkgatehead, and the Black Well by the Puddleford. There were others in Glasgow Vennel and Cotton Row. At the other end of High Street were the Grip Well and the Townend Well beyond Seagatehead beside Bachelors' Walk. Washing of clothes was done at the Gallowswell, at Seagatefoot's later Slaughterhouse Well, at Chapel Well, or on the Golffields beside the Tanzie Well — perhaps a corruption of St. Anne or St. Inan. There the council erected a washing house in 1749 measuring 35 by 15 feet for washing and bleaching. In 1763 they acquired from William Allan the land of Chapel with its well, and the little wash-house on the site of the old chapel of the Bank.

The town could not escape the continued visitation of epidemics. The Statistical Account reported that in 1760 many had died of the 'bloody flux'. Smallpox came in 1781, again in 1784 when 54 died, and in 1790 with another 57 deaths. 'Inoculation here, till of late, was not in general practice.' There was also a 'fever' which killed 24 in 1791, and a less serious 'influenza'. Some assistance was afforded by one physician, three surgeons, and two druggists resident in 1791. The other continuing danger in a cramped town was fire, particularly when the old regulations of 1677 were ignored by the increasing number of textile workers. When Burns' heckling shop was burned down in 1781, there is no mention of a fire engine. But one was acquired soon afterwards. From 1784 John Galt, a mason, was being paid for 'keeping the water works' and checking it once a month. The council charged 5/- for the 'water engine frequently asked for filling vessels with water when new or repaired'. What sort of vessels were involved is not clear. After Galt's death in 1793 he was replaced by Thomas Milliken, and in 1807 public subscription provided an additional larger 'Water Engine for

96 *The History of Irvine*

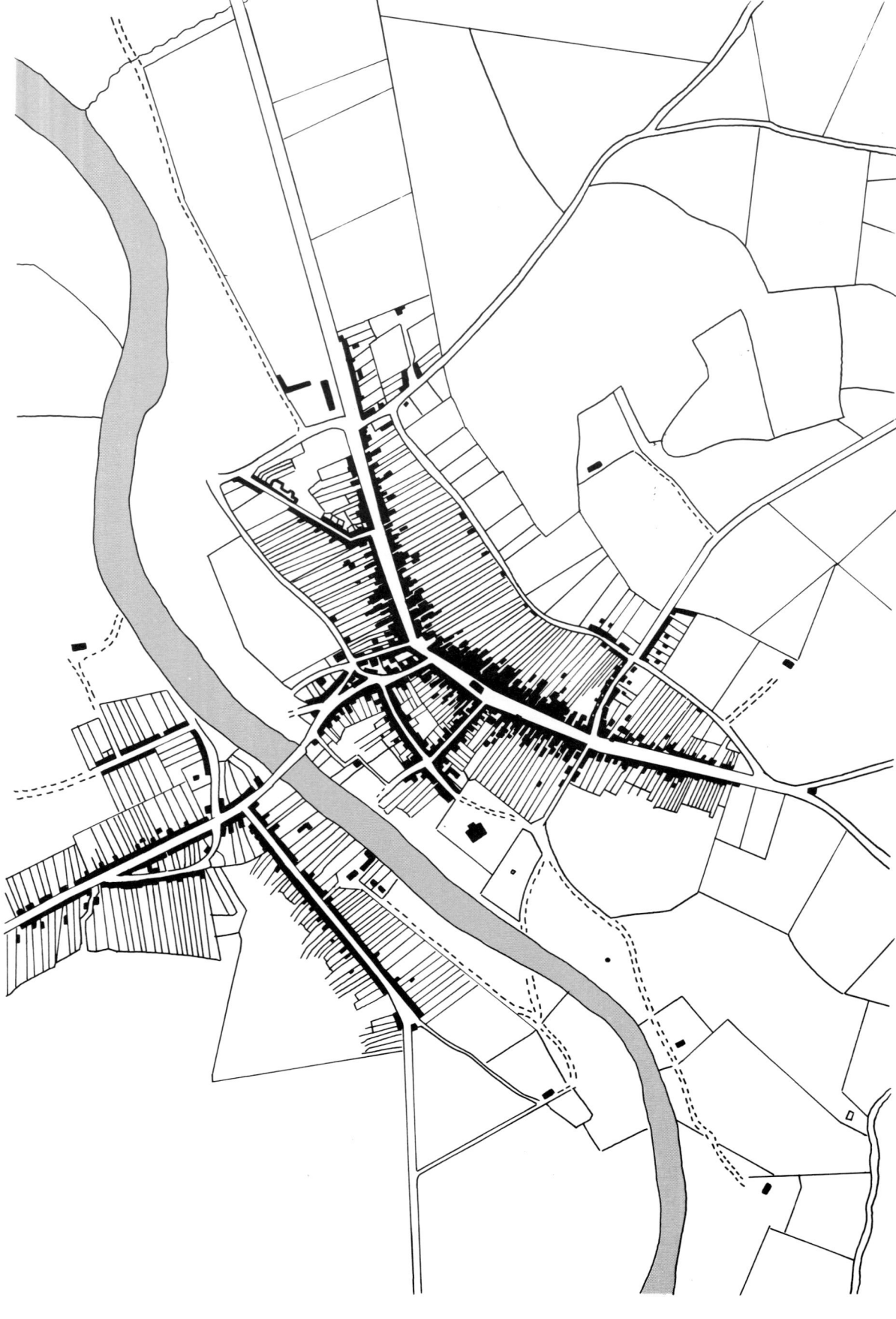

The Glasgow Journal *in 1753 advertised Marymass Fair, the management of which was acquired from the earl of Eglinton in 1747.*

extinguishing fires', stored below the tolbooth. In 1791 inhabitants were urged to keep their chimney vents clean and free from soot, and because so many chimneys had recently gone on fire, a fine of 5/- would be imposed for neglect. Another public improvement had been proposed in 1740 — 'to Erect ten publick Lamps to light the streets in the winter time at the Town's expense'. This seems not to have been implemented until 1804, when there was a public subscription 'for enlightening the Town' and the council agreed to provide oil and maintain the lamps.

These improvements brought a sense of wellbeing which Rev. James Richmond reflected in the Statistical Account:

'Perhaps in no sea-port town of the same extent are the inhabitants more sober and industrious than in this. They are social and cheerful but seldom riotous, it being very unusual for many persons to be seen upon the street after 12 o'clock at night. The people, in general, are in easy circumstances; many of them are wealthy... there has not for many years been an instance of bankruptcy among them, one or two incomers only expected. They are humane and generous... and this perhaps is one reason of the streets being so much infested with vagrant poor'. Richmond noticed also that the people of Irvine were 'remarkably hospitable... happy in each other's society,

Town plan, 1800. After a spectacular 18th-century growth, over 3,000 people were crammed into the increasingly congested burgh. Nearly 2,000 others now lived across the river — Colonel William Fullarton had laid out Fullarton Street (1776), while feus in Halfway, Waterside, and Friars Croft were provided by Irvine Town Council. The burgh itself was enhanced by an improved tolbooth (1745), a new bridge (1748), and a rebuilt parish church (1773), with places of worship for Relief, Baptist, and Burgher congregations (1773, 1808, 1809); and the burgh school was replaced by an academy (1816) — all revealed in detail in Wood's Town Plan of 1819.

John Galt was born in 1779 in the middle flat of this house at the north end of High Street, and spent his first ten years here — 'No man ever had a happier childhood'.

and entertain frequently and well. Their entertainments are more substantial than showy; though in this, upon occasions, they are by no means defective'.

The Marymass Fair was now the highlight of the burgh's social life. When the earls of Eglinton lost their heritable jurisdiction in 1747, the council must have seized this opportunity to demonstrate their now-untrammelled control over the fair with appropriate pageantry. Because of the statutory calendar change in 1753, an advertisement was inserted in the *Glasgow Journal* which reveals the new management: 'By order of the Magistrates and Town Council of Irvine. The annual fair of the said burgh, commonly called Marymass Fair, which formerly began the first Tuesday of August, and continued all that week, is this year to be kept the third Monday of August, new style, and yearly in all time coming, upon that day, and to continue the following days of that week'. What went on at the fair can be guessed from passing references. On one occasion, in 1804, there was a riot 'last Marrimass Saturday' when five persons were each rewarded with a pound for assistance in quelling it. Normally the fair was opened with the magistrates inspecting the market stalls, which were increasingly augmented by sideshows. There was a parade of the Trades, led by the town's officers in their scarlet livery, carrying their halberds, and lowering them as a salute on passing the old port. In this parade each carter was to participate, 'mounted on horse back with his best clos and good bleu bonnet'. The Carters Society was formally constituted in 1753 also. They have, of course, claimed a greater antiquity. The carters' flag bears the date 1670. It is asserted that their predecessors fought for Queen Mary at Langside in 1568. And one Irvine carter asserted: 'When the Ark was ready, Noah and his household flitted into it, and wha ever saw a flitting without a carter?' To the carters in 1753 was devolved the responsibility of riding the marches, to mark the burgh bounds. Possibly as a recompense for this, the council made annual contributions towards the races which were held on Friday and Saturday. By 1794 the usual two guineas was supplemented by 8/- 'for Ribbons on Marrimass Saturday' to bedeck the winning horses; and another 8/- 'for drink to the Constables at Marrimass'. The carters had their own 'Draff Race' for the draught horses, with a fine if they did not participate, and a deduction for the charity box if they won a prize. These Marymass races would be held on the old racecourse at Ravenscroft as shown on Armstrong's 1775 map. Before the institution of Bogside Races on a new course by the 12th earl of Eglinton in 1808, the carters may have laid out their own 'Cadgers Race Course' on the burgh moor, for in 1793 the council paid £1.10/- to 'John Watt as expense making the new Horse Course'.

Other sports of the 18th century are less easy to find notice of. Archery, popular till the 17th century, seems to have died out until it was revived in the 19th century. In 1738 the young earl of Eglinton won a prize at Irvine for shooting with 'powder and ball', and such contests were no doubt continued later in the century by the Volunteers. There was presumably curling, perhaps golf (at the Golffields), and possibly bowling. For indoor recreation outwith the home, the increased number of inns provided not only for drinking but also facilities for meetings and functions. The Trades, the Carters, and the Sailors Society would sometimes meet in such places. Annually on the first Monday after Michaelmas, each craft had its business meeting, followed we can presume by the now-traditional 'wee pie'. A greater celebration followed with the 'Big Pie', after the installation of the new Deacon Convener of Trades. Ritual and fraternity were also to be found in the Freemasons. There was a lodge in 1757, which became defunct, but was followed by Lodge Irvine St Andrews, founded in 1780 and meeting in the Wheatsheaf Inn in High Street. There were also the Kings Arms, the Eglinton Arms and the Crown Inn managed by Bailie Shaw. Robertson in 1820 noted 'two Head Inns, as they are called... very respectable... both have large rooms for public meetings'. A glimpse of social life in Irvine is

Edgar Allan Poe came in 1815 at the age of six to stay in Bridgegate House, which looked across to Rotten Row.

afforded by Charles Hutcheson, who kept a journal of his stay in 1783. Irvine he found a place whose streets 'are Elegant, Clean, and Handsome, and their Relief and Parish Churches are Surprisingly fine... a receptacle of Kind, Humane, Polite, Hospitable people. Being Strangers to Affectation, their manners are unfettered with the schackles of restraint, reserve, or distance'. He made some acquaintances, and 'Hearing there was a Company of Strolling players in Town I went with Several Irvine bucks to see *Douglas*'. This he found disappointing, but 'In company with two or three Irvine bucks we called upon the Players at their Quarters and finding them to be entertaining enough in their own Line, we treated them with Several bottles of Porter. Garrick and Mrs Siddons furnished us with an hour's talk'. But again he was disappointed with the finish: 'Having now and then a Song between hands we Spent this Evening but with little Satisfaction (to myself) for the greater part of their Songs were Calculated for foxhunters, Drunkards, Debauchees, or Fools'.

This was the Irvine which produced a group of celebrated sons. The first was James Montgomery, born in 1771 in the Halfway, son of the Moravian missionary. He left with his parents when he was little more than four years old. All he remembered of his native place was hearing of a great flood, and the King's birthday when all the windows were thrown open when the soldiers fired a salute. Montgomery was destined to have a notable career as a journalist, lecturer, poet, and hymn writer, and his death was marked with a spectacular funeral procession in Sheffield in 1854. When he returned to Irvine as an old man of seventy, he was feted and presented with the freedom of the burgh.

Davie Boyle was born in Boyle's Parterre in the High Street in 1772. His father was the Hon. Patrick Boyle of Shewalton, third son of the second Earl of Glasgow and a prominent local landowner. David Boyle grew up in Irvine, became an advocate in 1793, Solicitor General and MP for Ayrshire 1807–11, Lord of Session and Justiciary 1811, Lord Justice Clerk 1811–41, and Lord Justice General and President of the Court of Session in 1841–52. In 1837 he succeeded his brother, Colonel John Boyle of the Ayrshire Militia, to the estate of Shewalton, where he was buried in 1853. His tombstone records that he was 'universally revered in public and beloved in private life'. He was

Robert Burns came to Irvine in 1781 at a formative stage in his career. His stay has been commemorated by Irvine Burns Club (formed in 1826) and by Pittendreigh Macgillivray's statue on the Moor (erected in 1896).

The Heckling Shop in Glasgow Vennel where Robert Burns worked at the flax. Here inspected by a group of 19th-century figures including Maxwell Dick the inventor. The Heckling Shop was restored as part of the Glasgow Vennel project of 1983.

remembered as the judge who sentenced to death three radicals for treason in 1820 and Burke the body-snatcher and murderer in 1829. A statue was erected to his memory in 1867, appropriately at the east end of the High Street, but it was later removed to Seagatefoot.

Nearby in the High Street between the tolbooth and Templeton's bookshop lived the Eckfords. Henry Eckford was born there in 1775, was trained as a ship's carpenter, and emigrated to Quebec at the age of fifteen. From there he moved to New York as naval architect and manager of the Brooklyn Navy Yard, and his work earned him fame as one of the creators of the US Navy. Galt, who knew him, recounted how by 'some sinister trick in the management of the company... Eckford lost his fortune'. He moved to Turkey to superintend the Sultan's dockyards, and he died in Constantinople in 1832.

Still in the same decade, on 2nd May 1779, John Galt was born in a three-storey tenement further along the High Street near Seagatehead. The middle flat was tenanted by William Galt, a ship's captain, who was able to afford tutoring for his son. Not till the age of eight did he begin school, and he did not stay there long. Though a big lad, he was awkward and delicate, and his daydreaming was taken for dullness. But he did well at private lessons in the school in the evenings, tutored probably by the able Benjamin Maul. At home he was a voracious reader. And as he later remarked, 'memory occasionally carries me back to transactions that must have happened when I was very young'. When William Galt became master of a West Indiaman, he flitted to Greenock with his wife and the four children. Ten-year-old John went to school there, started as a clerk at the age of sixteen, then moved to London in 1804. Various unsuccessful business ventures were accompanied by the writing of stories, plays, and travel books. Then followed a series of Scots novels which made his reputation and eventual fame — *The Ayrshire Legatees*, 1820; *Annals*

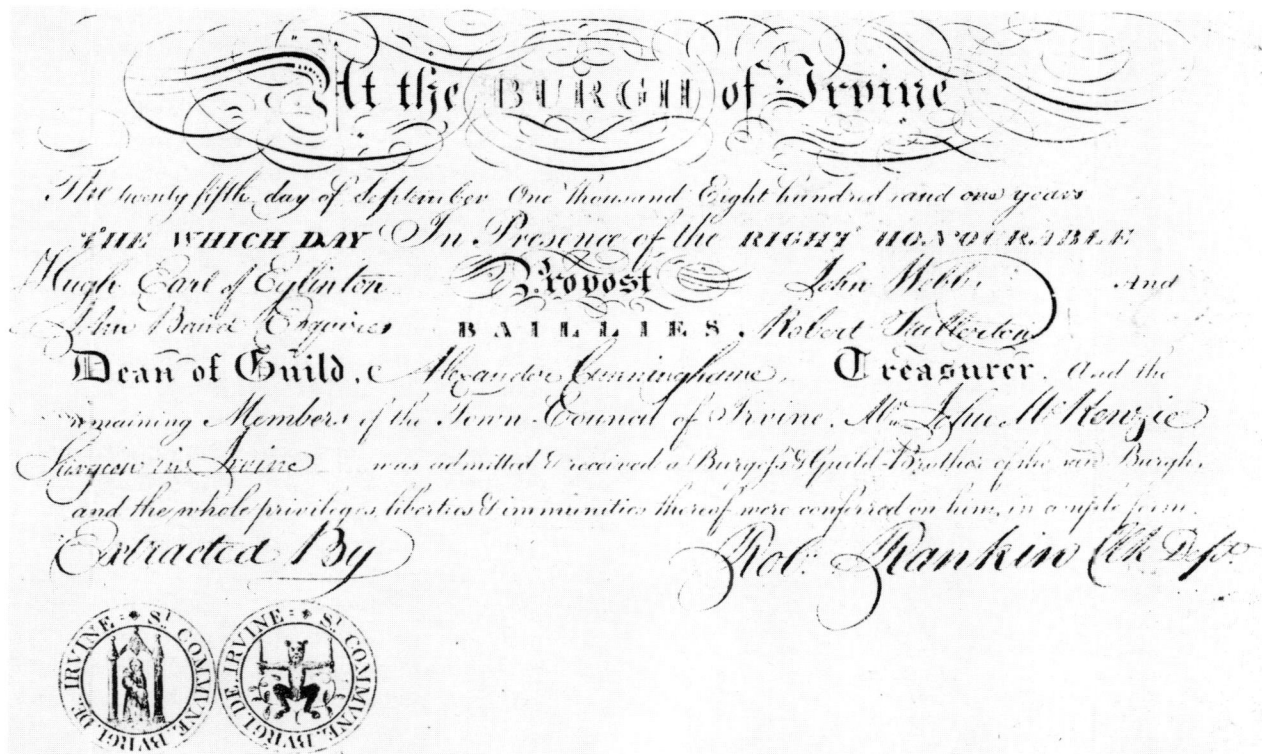

Dr John Mackenzie and David Sillar, two associates of Burns, both played a prominent part in Irvine municipal life. Here is shown Mackenzie's burgess ticket.

of the Parish, 1821; *Sir Andrew Wyllie, The Provost, The Entail,* 1822; *Ringan Gilhaize,* 1823; and *The Last of the Lairds,* 1826. For the next three years he was in Ontario as superintendent of the Canada Company's land improvement schemes, and in 1827 he founded the town of Guelph. But this colonial project ended in failure, as had all Galt's other business ventures. In 1834 he retired to Greenock, producing again some memorable shorter items among his mass of hack writing. There he died in 1839 at the age of sixty. In 1825 he had revisited Irvine, meeting to his surprise old Bailie Fullarton who had been his model for Provost Fawkie in *The Provost*. At the council meeting of 16th September it was noted that 'the requisite committee of the Magistrates and council had last week conferred the freedom of the Burgh upon John Galt Esquire now of the City of London, he having made Oath de fideli and paid the Stamp Duty of which the meeting approve'.

At the back of John Galt's High Street birthplace was a little house where a lesser figure was born. Bryce Gulliland, about ten years older than Galt, was carried off by the pressgang, but rose to be flag lieutenant on the *Royal Sovereign* and fell with Nelson at Trafalgar.

A distant relative of the novelist's father was another William Galt, a merchant whose home was the two-storey Bridgegate House, just west of Hill Street. A nephew, John Allan, went to Virginia to become a tobacco merchant. John Allan and his wife adopted the child of an American actor and a London actress. This Edgar Allan Poe, born in Boston in 1809, came in 1815 to stay with Aunt Mary Galt at Bridgegate House. Though the six-year-old enjoyed trips to Arran and Kilmarnock, he found the regime of kirk, school, and Bridgegate oppressive to his peculiar nature, and after only a few months he was sent to London. In 1820 he returned to America to produce the poems and short stories which made him famous, dying in 1849 after a neurotic and unhappy life.

Earlier, when John Galt was a two-year-old, an even more famous figure made a brief stay in Irvine. Because this occurred at such a formative stage in the career of Robert Burns, a detailed study is necessary. For evidence we have his own autobiographical letter written in 1787, which is haphazard, disorganised, with accuracy seeming sometimes to be sacrificed to dramatic effect. We have a little information from his brother Gilbert and some other friends. We have also witnesses from Irvine who many years later contributed recollections at first or second hand or repeated local hearsay.

In 1781 Robert Burns was a twenty-two-year-old

The town council minutes record the freedom of the burgh awarded in 1826 to John Galt by Bailie Robert Fullarton — whom Galt had satirised in his novel *The Provost*.

bachelor, living with his parents, three younger brothers, and three younger sisters on the farm of Lochlea in Tarbolton parish. Both he and brother Gilbert agreed that he had been 'bashful and awkward', but he was a lively thinker who was fond of reading and had tried his prentice hand at poetry. What prompted Burns's decision to come to Irvine? Typically, he himself passed it off as a casual and sudden choice: 'Partly through whim, and partly that I wished to set about doing something in life, I joined a flax dresser in a neighbouring town'. Gilbert is more precise: 'He became anxious to be in a situation to marry... He began therefore to be thinking of trying some other line of life'. Obviously the family farm could not support them all, and when he began a formal courtship of Alison Begbie early in 1781, he must have been planning to go off with her as a married man. Gilbert explained how he and Robert had been growing flax, and went on: 'In the course of selling it, Robert began to think of turning flax-dresser, both as being suitable to his grand view of settling in life, and as subservient to the flax-raising'. Robert defined exactly the nature of the business. It was not only 'to learn the trade' but also to 'carry on the business of manufacturing and retailing flax'. The flax-dresser was to be 'my Partner', which suggests that some capital was invested. It is uncertain when he left Tarbolton for Irvine. A letter of 12th June mentions that the affair with Alison Begbie was ended, but there is no mention of a move. It can be presumed that he was still in Tarbolton for the seventh meeting of the Bachelors Club on 25th June and his first masonic meeting on 4th July, and that he departed for Irvine soon afterwards. Of the flax-dressing in Irvine, Burns summed up: 'This turned out a sadly unlucky affair'. He attributed the failure to his partner, whom he described as 'a scoundrel of the first water who made money by the mystery of thieving'. This has been explained as either by smuggling or receiving stolen goods. Tradition has it that this Alexander (or Samuel) Peacock was a half-brother of his mother. Samuel Peacock had a house in the Glasgow Vennel. Opposite it was Templedean (or Bog Ha' as it was later known), which belonged to Joseph Francis, Maltman. In its grounds was the heckling house, which must have been rented by Peacock. One room was a workshop, and the other a stable where Burns perhaps made his bed. He found better lodgings, renting a room and doing for himself down the Vennel in another house (also now rebuilt). A further tradition is that after a quarrel, he and Peacock split up. He still lived in the Glasgow Vennel. But he took another room to start heckling on his own account. This is said to have been along the High Street beyond the Kings Arms Hotel in a close named after Montgomery Boyd, baker.

During his stay in Irvine he became unwell. Fortunately it was not the smallpox which ravaged the town that year. Gilbert blamed it on the dull, dusty, and harassing new job, 'neither agreeing with his health nor inclination'. Burns himself described is as 'my hypochondriacal complaint being irritated to such a degree, that for three months I was in a diseased state of body and mind'. He was well enough to be in Tarbolton to be passed and raised at the masonic meeting on 1st October. But later he was so bad that his father came down to visit him. On 27th December he wrote home that he was little better, and alarmingly announced that 'ere long, perhaps very soon, I shall bid an eternal adieu to all the pains, and uneasiness and disquietudes of this weary life'. But he rather spoiled the melodramatic effect by saying he was in need of more oatmeal, that he was too busy to visit them at New Year — 'work comes so hard upon us' — and mysteriously mentions 'some other little reasons which I shall tell you at meeting'.

Burns suggests he did little reading during his stay in Irvine. He mentions several volumes that 'gave me the idea of novels', which can only mean he was toying with becoming a novelist himself. We know he was specially interested in prose composition: 'Rhyme, except for some religious pieces... I had given up'. It is to this time of illness and depression in Irvine that a group of solemn and melancholy pieces has been attributed, none of lasting significance. The cheerier song 'No Churchman am I', with its praise of 'a big belly'd bottle', may have been composed for his Irvine masonic brethren. And there is a distinct possibility that it was in William Templeton's bookshop, behind the Tron, where he hunted for new ballads and songs, that he encountered Fergusson's poems which later 'strung anew my wildly-sounding, rustic lyre with emulating vigour'.

Despite his 'three months' of illness, he had opportunity, it seems, for some happier occasions. As he said, 'From this adventure I learned something of town life'. If he participated in the Marymass Fair in the week beginning 20th August, it has gone unrecorded. He certainly attended the parish church under Rev. James Richmond, who was under the impression that he had taken his first communion there, though once again there are no records to substantiate this. Older residents later declared that he argued about doctrine, adopting a Calvinist point of view. He also had some association with members of the Relief congregation, and three years later when it was convulsed by the Buchanite controversy he claimed that he had been 'personally acquainted with most of them'. Among these would be Patrick Hunter who lived in the Glasgow Vennel. As a freemason, he would make some friends at the recently formed Irvine Lodge. He almost certainly met Provost Charles Hamilton, who lived in the High Street just at the foot of Glasgow Vennel. Hamilton was clearly an ill man by then. 10th April, 1781 was his last attendance at council, apart from the formal meeting on 1st October, and he would die in 1783, aged 78. But if relations with the father could not have been close, he struck up a firm friendship with the son, John Hamilton, then a medical student. William Templeton the bookseller was another councillor, beginning his first term at Michaelmas 1781. Ex-provost Dr. John Cumming of Milgarholm also claimed an association. It has indeed been suggested that Cumming and Hamilton, both involved in manufacturing and bleaching textiles, had something to do with Burns's coming to Irvine.

There was one particular and lasting friend, to whom Burns devoted more space in his autobiographical letter than to any other person. Richard Brown, a twenty-nine-year-old sailor, after an adventurous early life was back in his native Irvine for a spell before getting a ship of his own and making a success of his career. How Robert Burns made the acquaintance of this rather more experienced young man is unknown. He was certainly a freemason, and may even have been another of his mother's distant relatives: 'I formed a bosom-friendship with a young fellow, the first created being I had ever seen... This gentleman's mind was fraught with courage, independence. Magnanimity, and every noble manly virtue... I loved him, I admired him... I strove to imitate him... His knowledge of the world was vastly superior to mine, and I was all attention to learn'. Long afterwards Burns exaggerated when he wrote to Brown, 'You are the earliest friend I now have on earth, my brothers excepted'. In this he did an injustice to David Sillar, with whom he had previously walked and talked in Tarbolton as he now did with Brown in Irvine. To Brown he later wrote: 'Do you remember a Sunday we spent in Eglinton woods? You told me, on my repeating some verses to you, that you wondered how I could resist the temptation of sending verses of such merit to a magazine; twas actually this that gave me an idea of my own pieces which encouraged me to endeavour at the character of a Poet'. This occasion when the idea of publication first occurred to Burns is commemorated by a tablet erected in 1927 by Irvine Burns Club inscribed, 'The Drukken Steps (St. Bryde's Well) — Eglinton Woods — favourite walk 1781–82 of Robert Burns and his sailor friend Richard Brown', with an appropriate quotation.

This 'wild, bold, generous young fellow' had other things to teach Robert Burns: 'He was the only man I ever saw who was a greater fool than myself when Woman was the presiding star... he spoke of a certain fashionable failing with levity, which hitherto I had regarded with horror. Here his friendship did me a mischief'. Later Brown, grown old in respectability, hotly denied that he had led Burns astray. Yet Gilbert, in whom Robert confided, had no doubt that it was in Irvine that his brother 'contracted some acquaintance of a freer manner of thinking and living... whose society prepared him for overleaping the bounds of rigid virtue'. Burns's phrase about Brown teaching him a 'fashionable failing' the biographer James Currie transcribed as 'illicit love', and in this Burns almost certainly served his apprenticeship in Irvine.

One Irvine lass whose name has been linked with Burns was Jean Gardner, said to have been the daughter of John Gardner, a butcher who lived in the Seagate. The Gardners were members of the Relief congregation, whose minister was a near neighbour. Jean Gardner became a follower of Mrs. Buchan, and left Irvine with her. It was one of the Buchanites who later said that she had been acquainted with Burns. It has been argued that Burns continued his friendship with her for a time after he had left Irvine, and that when he wrote his 'Epistle to Davie' and referred to 'my darling Jean', this was Jean Gardner rather than Jean

Armour from Mauchline as is more generally assumed. After the Buchanite sect broke up, Jean Gardner did not return to Irvine, but married another of the group, emigrated, and died in Philadelphia in 1793. The details are puzzling, the more so as John Gardner, flesher, actually died in 1768. He owned three houses in the Seagate and the park called Spenshill. Half was inherited by the elder of his two daughters, Jean Gardner, who was already then a widow, and surely too old in 1781 to have an affair with Robert Burns. That her deceased husband was a shipmaster called Alexander Armour, whose widow might be designated Mrs. Jean Armour, may have contributed to the confusion. Two others have an even more shadowy association with Burns's stay in Irvine. Betty Smith, a local lass, took part much later in the little traditional ceremony when Burns took possession of Ellisland farm. Mary Campbell, his 'Highland Mary', is said to have worked in Irvine as a young servant girl at some time or other.

The one with whom Robert Burns may have had a passionate affair was Jean Glover. Born in Kilmarnock in 1758, daughter of a respectable handloom weaver, she was clever and sharp-witted, but her physical charms and fondness for gaudy attire led her astray. She had a fine voice and became a vagrant, singing and playing her tambourine to eke out a living. She was apparently well known in Irvine — perhaps she was there at the Marymass Fair of 1781 — and latterly she went to Ireland where she died in 1801. Burns later praised a song of hers, 'Coming through the Craigs of Kyle', which he 'took down from her singing as she was strolling thro' the country, with a slight-of-hand blackguard'. When, where, and in what circumstances he did not relate, but it was very likely in Irvine, and he knew her well enough to describe her bitterly as 'not only a whore but also a thief'.

The dramatic climax to the Irvine chapter of Burns's life came with the burning down of the heckling shop at Hogmanay, so vividly described in his autobiographical letter: 'and to finish the whole, while we were giving a welcoming carousal to the New Year, our shop, by the drunken carelessness of my Partner's wife, took fire and was burnt to ashes; and left me, like a true Poet, not worth sixpence. I was obliged to give up business'. Here too there is doubt about what actually happened. Tradition insists that Burns had broken with Alexander and Sarah Peacock before this. It has been claimed that the fire was actually at Montgomery Boyd's Close up the High Street. And another allegation is that the fire was started by Burns himself accidentally upsetting a candle. Gilbert had nothing to say about the fire. He simply recorded that Robert 'wrought at the business of a flax dresser in Irvine for six months, but abandoned it at that period, as neither agreeing with his health not inclination'. As for Burns being left 'like a true Poet, not worth sixpence', according to Isabella Burns he did not come home from Irvine until three months later in March 1782 — to begin another chapter of his eventful life. Despite uncertainties and conjectures, it can fairly be claimed that in Irvine Robert Burns indeed 'learned something of town life', widening his social experiences and extending his literary vision. When in 1826 Irvine Burns Club was established, two of its founders were close associates of the poet who also came to Irvine, but who stayed longer and became prominent personalities of the burgh.

David Sillar was a year younger than Burns, son of the tenant farmer of Spittalside in Tarbolton parish. First a herd boy, then a ploughman, for a time he filled in as a teacher in the parish school, then set up a little private school of his own at Commonside a few miles away. He became friendly with Robert Burns sometime before May 1781 when Sillar belatedly joined the Tarbolton Bachelors Club. He was competent on the violin, was something of a poet, and Alexander Tait the Tarbolton versifier apostrophised them as 'twa rantin', rhyming billies'. The reason for Sillar's departure for Irvine in 1783 is perhaps explained by Tait: 'The lass grew blae, she did lament; The man in black for Davie sent'. In Irvine David Sillar set up as a grocer in one of the shops under the tolbooth, but by 1786 he was evicted for debt, and on three other occasions he was in financial trouble, with a brief incarceration in the tolbooth prison. In 1789 he published fifty of his own *Poems*. He was no mere imitator of Burns, but a prolific and competent versifier in his own right. An attempt to make a literary career in Edinburgh failed, and he returned to Irvine and to teaching. He set up a school of navigation in East Back Road (near the later Industrial School) and was successful enough to earn from it an income of around £100 a year. We find him as one of the six constables in 1787. In 1795 he was appointed, on the recommendation of the Incorporated Trades, as quartermaster for the burgh. In 1797 he was on the leet for the post of English master in the burgh school. He had married a local widow and set up house in the High Street on the site now occupied by the post office. Affluence came after 1811 when he inherited the fortunes two younger brothers had made in the lucrative West African trade. He was able to lend £1,000 to the council, and a donation to the new academy earned him a life directorship. He was an original shareholder in the Irvine Gas Light Company. He was chosen to be a councillor in 1815, and a bailie from 1819 to 1821, and he remained a councillor till his death in 1830 at the age of seventy. His tombstone in the churchyard is appropriately inscribed with a quotation from Burns's epistle to 'Daintie Davie'.

John Mackenzie was a surgeon trained in Edinburgh.

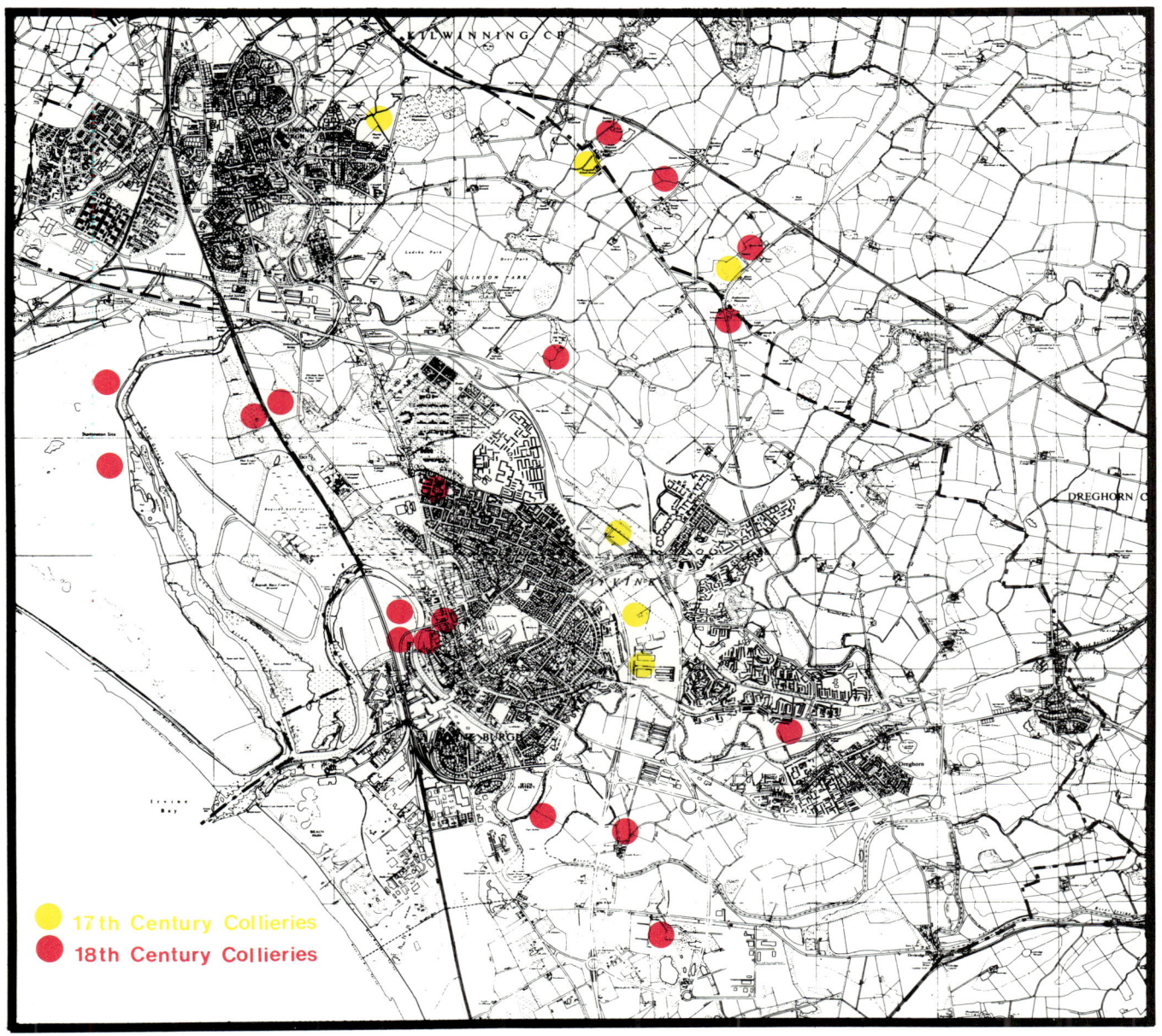

- 17th Century Collieries
- 18th Century Collieries

17th and 18th century collieries. There is mention in the early 16th century of coal being worked on Kilwinning Abbey land, and 20 tons exported from Irvine harbour (1542). Irvine town council attempted workings near Doura (1686) and at Knadgerhill and Newmure (1692). Others in the 17th century were exploiting coal at Corsehill and Lochmyln.

In the 18th century there were various attempts to extend operations. Irvine town council had pits at the Low Green (1762), nearby on the Moor (1765) and at Marresfoot (1766). These were abandoned, but under lease coals were worked at Marressfoot (1770) and on the Moor (1785–89). Elsewhere within the parish Bartonholm was worked (1797) and Sourlie (before 1790). Nearby in Dundonald parish coal was worked at Shewalton (from 1702) and Tarryholm (1765). In Dreghorn parish there was a pit at Warrix (1783) and possibly Broomlands (1791). In Kilwinning parish Fergushill was worked (from 1704); various others around mid-century; one near Eglinton Mains (1771); by the end of the century Laigh Fergushill, Montgreenan, and East Doura were the only ones operating. From Stevenston parish coals were brought to Irvine harbour from two pits at Misk (1778).

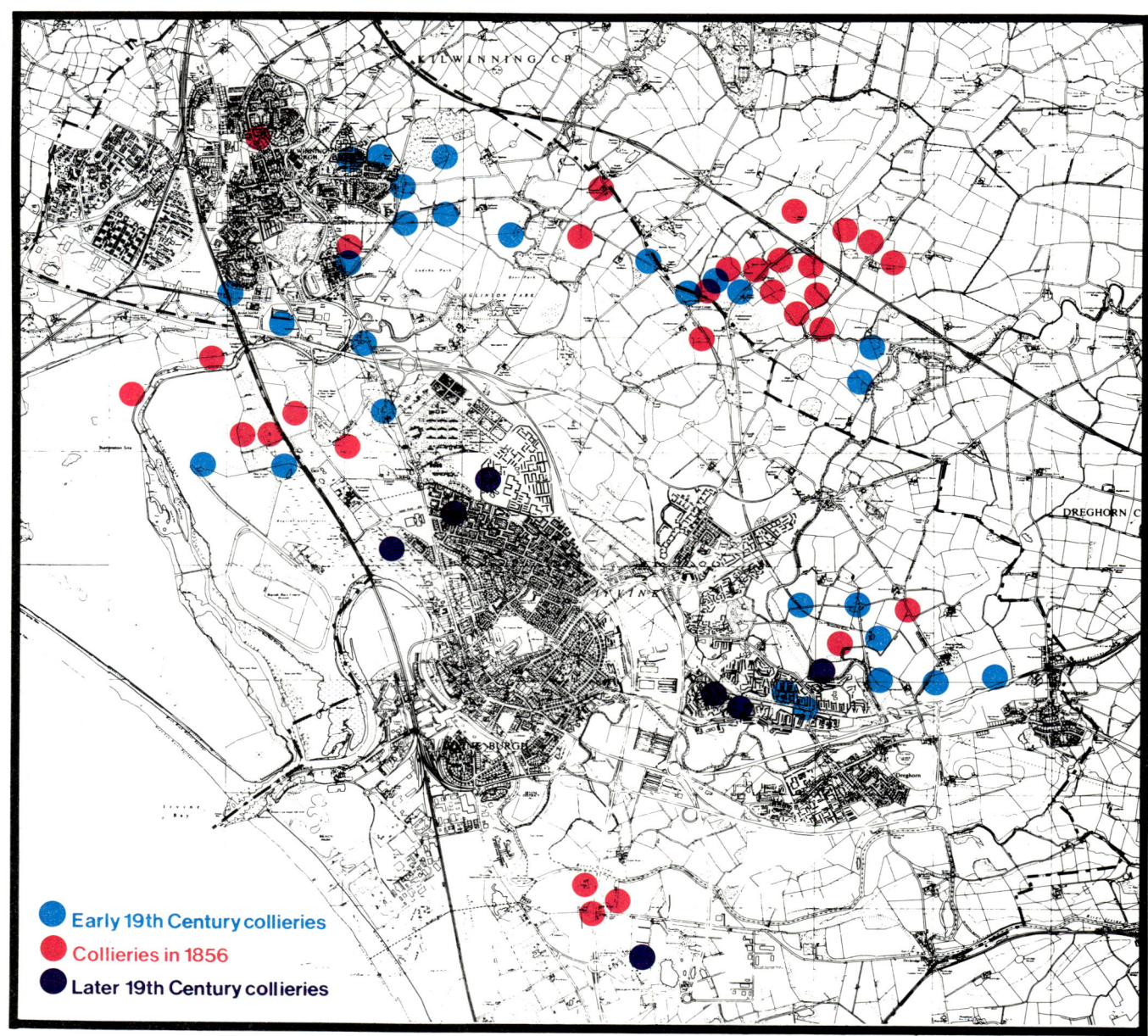

- Early 19th Century collieries
- Collieries in 1856
- Later 19th Century collieries

19th century collieries. In the early 19th century, workings at Bartonholm (from 1797), Snodgrass (1802) and Longford (1815) were interrupted by flooding (1833–53). To the south Shewalton was (from 1814) further exploited, and near Dreghorn a new pit was opened (1838). The main developments were in those parts of Kilwinning parish closest to Irvine, undertaken by the earls of Eglinton and others: at Nethermains and Redstone (1820), Corsehill and Doura (1829), Monkredding and Montgreenan (before 1842). In 1842 those being worked there were Doura, Fergushill, Redstone, and Ladyha.

In mid-century, the Ordnance Survey of 1856 shows 28 pits in the vicinity of Irvine. Most were in that area including Corshill (6), Fergushill (1), Doura (4), and Annick Lodge (2). Nearer were those at Bartonholm (2), Nethermains, and Redburn; others on the opposite side of the Garnock; and at Dreghorn.

The later 19th century brought closure to most of these. Though others were opened, the total number was reduced to twelve by 1874. There were pits on Irvine Moor and at Ravenscraft (1866–88). Lady Sophia Pit was opened in 1883, named after the eldest daughter of the 14th Earl of Eglinton. There were further developments near Dreghorn and new working at Shewalton.

- ★ Collieries in 1908
- ● More Recent
- ▲ Open Cast

20th century collieries. At the beginning of the 20th century, nineteen pits were working, as shown on the 1908 Ordnance Survey map. Few were opened thereafter. Most closed down in the period between the wars, including Bartonholm (1928), Bogside (1929), Redburn (1930), and Eginton's Lady Sophia (1930).

When the coal industry was nationalised in 1947 the only local pits surviving were at Warrix and Shewalton, both soon after closed.

The history of mining in the area is that of a series of small-scale and often short-lived enterprises exploiting the most accessible seams and then abandoning the workings, sometimes leaving no record of their operations. When the New Town was formed in 1967, original plans had to be radically altered once the extent of coal workings and the risk of subsidence in certain areas was realised. The opportunity was taken to extract coal at Sourlie by open-cast methods (1983–86).

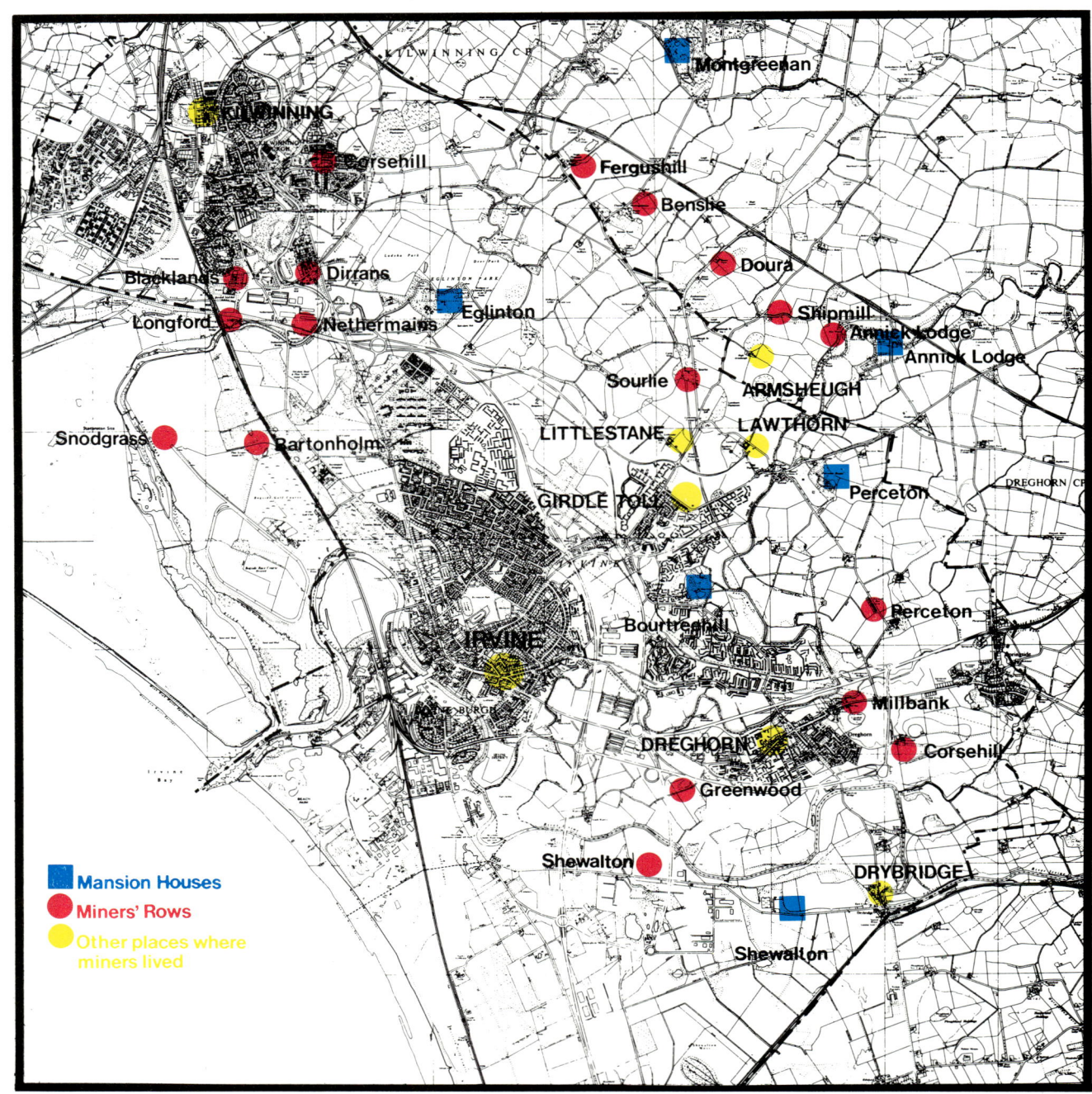

Mansion Houses and Miners Rows. Landowners augmented their incomes from rents by exploiting the mineral resources of their estates. Some of them initially managed their own enterprises, but by the middle of the 19th century it was customary to lease the working to coalmasters. In 1873 the Earl of Eglinton collected £32,504 in rents plus £9,520 in mineral royalties.

   The colliers originally lived in established communities like Irvine or were lodged in convenient farm buildings. Early in the 19th century miners rows were built at Bartonholm, Snodgrass, Nethermains, Doura, Sourlie, and Shewalton. Others built later included Perceton Rows, built for John Macredie, which in 1842 was awarded a Highland Society prize for its superior design with kitchens (18½ x 12 feet) supplemented by two small rooms (each 9 x 6 feet) for lodgers or washing.

   The 20th century has seen the breakup of many great estates, including Eglinton whose castle fell into ruin after 1926. The mansion houses of Perceton, Annick Lodge, and Montgreenan have survived. All the miners rows have gone, with a new community established in 1934 at Girdle Toll as part of Ayr County Council's re-housing scheme.

He was brought to Mauchline by Sir John Whitefoord of Ballochmyle, acquired sufficient landed property to become a freeholder with a parliamentary vote, and married Helen Miller, daughter of the host of the Sun Inn, and one of the 'six proper young belles' of Burns's poem. He attended Burns's father in his last illness at Lochlea, and was a masonic brother and patron to the poet. When Sir Hugh Montgomerie of Coilsfield became 12th earl of Eglinton in 1796, he persuaded Dr. Mackenzie to remove from Mauchline to Irvine, granting him the life rent of Seagate house in the High Street and an annuity of £130 per annum to continue at Eglinton those medical services previously given at Coilsfield. At Irvine, Mackenzie acquired the land of Lochwards, built up his general practice, and in 1824 was awarded the degree of MD by Edinburgh University, his *alma mater*. Meanwhile Mackenzie had been enrolled as a burgess in 1801; in the same year joined the council, on which the earl was provost; in the next year became a bailie, and latterly was treasurer and dean of guild. He served on the council till 1828, when, now a widower, he retired to Edinburgh. There he died and was buried in 1837, with a commemorative stone erected in Irvine churchyard.

When in 1825 John Galt was awarded the freedom of the burgh, David Sillar and John Mackenzie were both involved as councillors. And when just a few months later in June 1826 it was decided to form an Irvine Burns Club, among the twelve original subscribers were these two and five other members of the town council, plus the town clerk, and the Convener of Trades — a sufficient indication that the men who ran Irvine had a pride in their cultural heritage.

Part Three
The 19th Century

ELEVEN

The Coming of Reform

Modern readers of *The Provost* notice particularly the financial 'jookerie cookerie' in the affairs of 'Gudetown', and the records of Irvine amply confirm that corruption characterised the unreformed royal burgh. Yet John Galt was aware that the self-interest of the councillors was accompanied by an enlightenment which contributed to the municipal progress which he so vividly chronicled in his novel. On the eve of the great Reform Act of 1832, when a deputation of inhabitants petitioned Irvine council to call a public meeting, that council deemed it 'unnecessary' since it felt itself to be fully aware of the 'sense of the community'. As indeed it did, for though not directly accountable to an electorate, it was never out of touch with public opinion. In the generation before the Reform Act the council was in fact closely involved with various local bodies specially constituted to provide improved facilities of various kinds.

That was first obvious in the provision of poor relief. The council had always co-operated with the church in this, but a swollen population experiencing periodic trade depression suffered crises of a novel magnitude. The established church cared for as many as possible. In 1820 that church was expending £460 towards the poor, provided by the church collections (£95), fines, fees, and rent of mort cloth at burials (£52), rent and interest from bequests (£92), and voluntary donations from magistrates, merchants, and heritors in lieu of a poor tax (£221). There were eighty paupers on the church's permanent roll, with as many occasional recipients on the 'watering roll' for alms after each sacrament; another thirty to thirty-five were provided with badges authorising them to beg through the parish. The other churches willingly did what they could. The council was unable itself to provide much complementary provision when the town was 'much infected by stranger Beggars'. In 1800, because the poor were suffering severely from high prices and a scarcity of meal, a committee was formed including not only representatives of church and council, but also other inhabitants. £25 from the town's rents was earmarked for emergency relief, repeated the following year to support a 'public kitchen which has been established for supporting the poor'. Such voluntary co-operation was exercised on later occasions. In 1814 a fund was raised to purchase coals for the poor, and this was continued annually, with 299 recipients in 1819, and 800 loads distributed in 1831. Also in 1816 the earl of Eglinton called a meeting of 'Heritors and respectable inhabitants' because of 'the distresses of the Labouring poor and to devise some means of finding employment for them'. This also became an established organisation. In 1826 the money subscribed paid for the employment of seven married men, twenty younger men between sixteen and twenty, and thirty-two boys over the age of ten. In 1829 unemployed weavers were given work at the quay and the quarry. In 1832 the 'unemployed operatives' themselves organised a public meeting and the council gave £20 to help. In 1826 Lady Jane Montgomerie made an innovation by organising a bazaar to raise funds for the unemployed.

Voluntary initiative of a different sort occurred when the 'present distressed state of the country' seemed to threaten revolution. The Ayrshire Yeomanry, raised in Carrick in 1798, was in 1817 enlarged by the formation of a second regiment with volunteers from Cunninghame and Kyle, and the local troop of about fifty men were joined by another hundred to be stationed at Irvine in November 1817 because of the political unrest. In 1820 they were supplemented by an Armed Association of the Inhabitants to 'preserve the peace of the town', and the council contributed £42 towards the purchase of uniforms.

There was an earlier instance of the council's willingness to devolve its responsibilities to a voluntary body, and the creation of what became a lasting institution. In 1813 the council took a principal part in calling a public meeting, for its school at the Kirkgatehead had 'long been complained of, not only on account of its being situated so near the Church, but also for the want of room to accommodate the Scholars'. The council was willing to grant a new site at the north end of the town, thirty-one unemployed men were given work levelling the Gallows knoll north of Spence Hill, and contributions were invited for 'a society for the education of youth within the said Royal Burgh of Irvine'.

The foundation stone of the new academy was laid on 22nd April 1814, with a procession of two bands, freemasons, councillors, clergy, trades, subscribers, and 370 pupils — those from the grammar school under James Lockhart Brown, from the English school under William Clark, and from the recently founded Free School under James Neil. The building, designed by David Hamilton of Glasgow, was opened on 3rd July 1816, when it was decreed that there should be 'a Holiday to the Pupils in all time coming' each 10th December, the birthday of Hugh, 12th earl of Eglinton. In 1818 a royal charter was obtained by the earl in his own right and as provost. By its terms Irvine Academy was to be administered by directors including the earl of Eglinton, eleven councillors, and all who had subscribed £50 or more. In fact, while the town council contributed £1,600, other subscribers supplied only £500. This was an inauspicious start, followed by a series of disappointments.

The academy was staffed initially by the teachers of the old Kirkgatehead school: J.L. Brown, rector; William Clark, English master; and Ebenezer Clark, assistant. In 1819 the directors were appalled by an 'outrageous attack made upon the Windows of the Academy by some evil-disposed persons'. This vandalism continued, the result of Townend weavers playing 'at the Ball', copied by schoolboys who were also guilty of throwing stones, and there was 'lenity' in punishing the miscreants. There were hopes of an improvement in the academy's reputation when Daniel Stewart succeeded as rector in 1826. He hoped to implement the original scheme of providing 'additional Teachers in the different branches of Science'. In 1820 drawing classes were started by a Mr Bruce, and in 1826 James Dick was appointed as Drawing Master. Plans to appoint a commercial teacher were seen by James Clark as a threat to his income from fees. There was a 'violent quarrel' at a public meeting in 1829 when Clark exchanged 'most uncourteous epithets' with Stewart and challenged him to a duel. All this had 'a baneful effect upon the minds and morals of the pupils'. Litigation confirmed Clark's rights, but in 1830 he departed. Thereafter his successor, Allan MacNab, would concentrate on English, while James McConnell as a new commercial teacher would be responsible for writing, arithmetic, and bookkeeping. Because of such difficulties, little came of the initial hopes that students would be attracted to Irvine, which was described as 'healthy and possesses advantages as a place of education for youths superior to any other in the county'. The academy's accommodation for 455 pupils in its seven rooms was not stretched. In 1820 there were fewer than 400. As many went to the other schools in the town. There were five or six private schools where 260 children had elementary education in reading, writing and arithmetic; a Free School set up in 1814 provided for 80 more; a sewing school supported by the council took up to 30 girls for plain seam and coloured work; and there was a boarding school for young ladies. The academy itself was little more than an elementary school, for only 48 took Latin or Greek, and 36 studied other advanced subjects such as mathematics. Although the council subsidised the academy by paying the masters' basic salaries, providing gates and railings, and supplying globes for geography teaching, yet the directors had to charge high fees, which contributed to the limited success of the new regime in education.

The need for a new system of management also inspired the council to obtain parliamentary consent in 1826 for 'an Act for widening and improving the Bridge of Irvine, making streets communicating thereto, and for more effectually enlarging, deepening, improving, and maintaining the Harbour of Irvine'. Control of the harbour passed to trustees who included fourteen councillors, seven shipowners, and the Convener of the Trades. The council had long manfully coped with the silt brought down by the two rivers and recurring crises of flooding and floating ice, and extensive embankments had been constructed (1824). Merchants and shipowners were worried by competition from the earl of Eglinton's new harbour at Ardrossan. At Irvine, up to sixty vessels could be berthed, but those over a hundred tons could not cope with a bar which had only seven feet of water, and nine and a half at spring tides. There was opportunity for the new harbour trustees to undertake major improvements. Alas, the chance was missed. The trustees contented themselves with the existing harbour dues and made no attempt to increase them to finance what might have been advantageous in the long term. More far-seeing were the Bridge Trustees, who were the five Magistrates, the Convener of Trades, and six of the County Road Trustees. The old bridge, built between 1748 and 1752, only eleven feet broad, was widened to twenty-five feet, and the pontage tolls which paid for this very necessary improvement were removed by 1850. Powers were used to try to remove obstructions from the narrow Bridgegate, and to lay out the new Bank Street and thus find work for the unemployed in 1828.

Another public utility was created in 1829 by the Irvine Gas Light Company, when local enterprise with a capital of £3,250 set up a gas works in Ballot Road. The town council's oil lamps had illuminated the main streets since January 1805. Now the gas company contracted to erect, in the first instance, thirty cast-iron street lamps. As the mains were extended through the town, gas lighting was installed in the church and churchyard (1831) and the academy (1832); and the Crown Hotel was lit by gas when Archibald William, 13th earl of Eglinton, was entertained on 25th September 1832 to a 20th birthday dinner, and presented with the freedom of the burgh. The gas mains were later

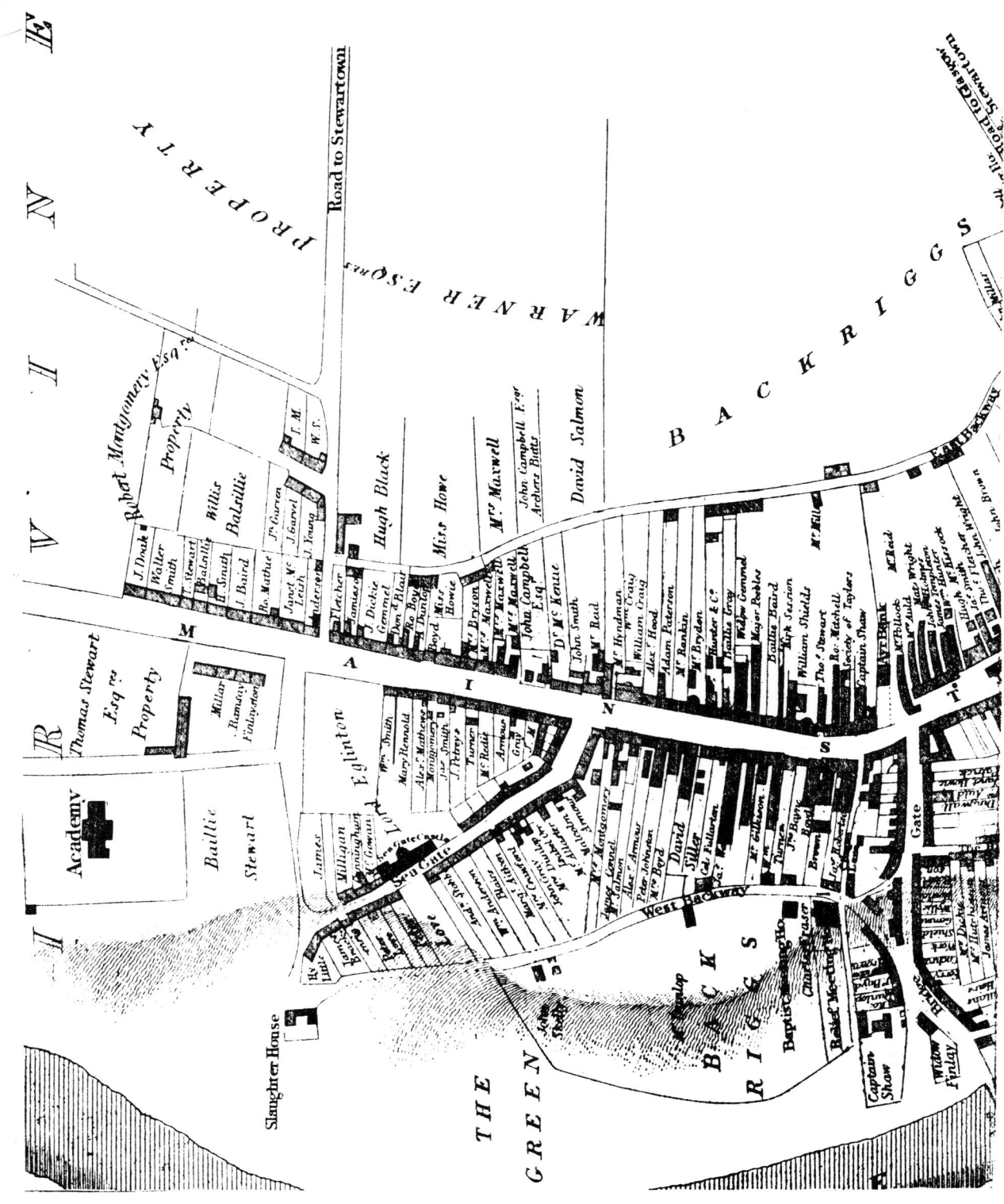

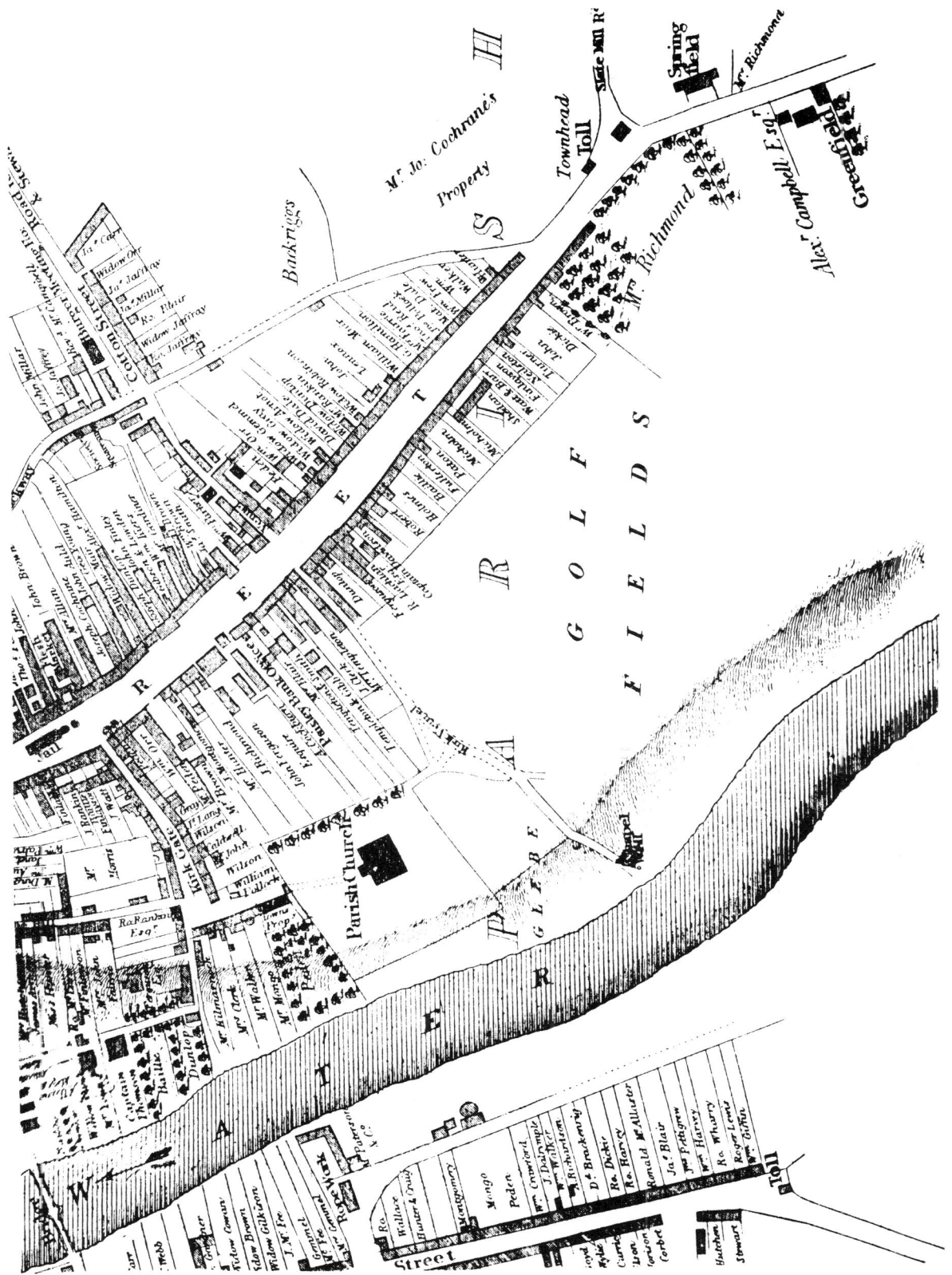

Wood's Town Plan of 1819 shows the Tolbooth (jail) and Flesh Market; four places of worship; the new Academy; and residences of prominent persons like David Sillar, Dr John Mackenzie, and Bailie Fullarton.

112 The History of Irvine

extended to Waterside and Friars Croft (1836) and the Harbour (1851).

Around this time a panic seized Irvine, first noted when the council minutes of 1826 recorded 'very distressing depredations that had lately been committed in the Church Yard of Irvine by the disinterring and carrying away the bodies of the dead'. A Society of inhabitants for watching the churchyard had already been formed. The council gave it donations of £10 for several years, with a reward of £20 (never claimed) for discovery and apprehension. Yet there were allegations, later recalled by Provost John Paterson, of a 'regularly organised party' who supplied corpses to Glasgow University. Suspicion fell on Councillor John Fletcher, a surgeon who lived in the Parterre in High Street, and on Robert Stein, a Glasgow carrier whose yard was just over the wall in Kirkgate. Another was William Anderson who lived in the Seagate; his butcher's yard backed on to the West Road which is still associated in popular tradition with the body-snatchers. Also implicated was the sexton, town's officer James Wilson, who lived in West Road and was building a new dwelling there, later known as 'the Resurrectionist House'. In December 1826 he was dismissed 'as the Council were all aware of the reasons why'. Dr. Mackenzie was the only councillor who dissented from a unanimous decision. Wilson had been responsible for the kirkyard, and the weavers who now occupied the old schoolhouse at Kirkgatehead set a trap, hiding coins below the turf of new graves. When these were found to be missing, a large crowd assembled, opened up the graves, and a dozen were found to be empty. Provost Paterson was later informed that 'the resurrectionists seemed to have generally only dug a hole at the head of the graves, and after knocking out the end of the coffin, drew out the corpse'. Thereafter, for security, corpses were tied into coffins by 'strong iron, $\frac{1}{2}$ inch wire put round the neck, middle, and feet, and fastened by nuts on the outside to the bottom of the coffin'. Later in 1831 the Squaremen Society supplied strong mortsafes at a guinea a time. Also a Watch House was constructed, on wheels, but generally sited near the entrance to the Trades Loft on the east side of the church. Each night three of the inhabitants armed with oil lamps and blunderbusses guarded the churchyard, and shotmarks on headstones bore witness to nervous watchmen. Yet Paterson believed there might have been some substance to the panic. Eye witnesses reported one attempted intrusion into the churchyard. Darnshaw near the old castle of Auchenharvie was cited as the collecting point for corpses from neighbouring parishes, which could be sold in Glasgow for £10 each. One corpse held in Glasgow College for dissection was actually identified and returned to Irvine for reburial.

Irvine Academy was opened in 1816, to replace the old burgh school at Kirkgatehead.

Another emergency arose in 1831 when again the initiative was taken outwith the council. As an epidemic of cholera was threatened, a local Board of Health was constituted, under the lead of Captain John Brooks. With pools of stagnant water on various properties seen as a hazard to health, the council was persuaded to spend over £300, provide drainage by laying a covered sewer to serve High Street, Kirkgate, and Kirk Vennel, and to attend to the 'filthy and abominable state' of the slaughterhouse at the Seagatefoot. Sporadic efforts were made to improve the inadequate water supply, more than ever necessary in an age when tea was replacing ale as the principal drink. Of the existing sources, only the Chapel Well was thought good enough for 'Tea water'. In 1831 a new pump well was provided at Kirkgatehead; and a private well in Cotton Row was taken over, though it was 'not to be used on Sabbaths during Divine Service in the Burgher meeting house'. In 1832 an additional well was provided in High Street, probably the one which some wag nominated as the Whiskey Well to distinguish it from the older and ambiguously named Port Well.

Early in 1832 cholera reached the West of Scotland. The Board of Health, with subscriptions from the inhabitants (and seven guineas from the council), provided the poor, who were especially threatened, with gifts of clothing and a soup kitchen. In February a woman from Glasgow brought infection and death to the nearby colliery village of Doura. With Irvine now under threat, the Board of Health planned for an emergency hospital, seeking the use of the old school, and settled for the old ropeworks at the far end of Halfway. In June the council was sufficiently alarmed to set up an

---

Wood's Town Plan of 1819 included that area in Dundonald parish where 2,000 people now lived. Friars Croft and Halfway belonged to Irvine Town Council. The area inherited by Colonel Stewart Murray Fullarton in 1808 would soon be acquired by the Duke of Portland. The other major proprietor was Colonel John Boyle of Shewalton who would be succeeded in 1837 by his brother, Lord Justice David Boyle.

official Board of Health under the authority of the Privy Council. Wisely, Captain Brooks and his associates were included among the members. On 31st July a woman died in the Halfway of what was diagnosed as cholera. The next day six constables were appointed, with Peter Anderson (Long Pate) as chief constable. They were to guard the approaches to the town, and when need arose to fumigate houses, destroy infected clothing, and inter the dead. Three women were hired as nurses to assist in the emergency hospitals at Halfway and Springbank. A doctor was brought down from Glasgow at three guineas a week to assist Drs. Walker and King. An attempt was made to postpone the proposed day of rejoicing to celebrate the passing of the Reform Act. The Carters Society was persuaded to abandon the Marymass procession. The 'customary dancing parties' during Fair Week were to be discouraged, and public houses were to shut early. The magistrates were asked to remove from Mr. Dunlop's Inn an Itinerant Exhibition of Wax Figures. Kilmarnock shoemakers were to be admitted to Irvine only if they had medical certificates. By October the crisis was over and the Board of Health could be disbanded. In Kilmarnock, 250 had died, in Ayr 190. Irvine escaped lightly. The Register of Burials records that 'their Died in the months of August and September about 21 persons of that Disease the Cholera'. This was fewer even than at Doura, where there were thirty deaths.

These accounts of diverse topics have one common feature, that of groups of inhabitants becoming organised on a voluntary basis to share with the unreformed council the provision of better public services. The council, of course, continued to exercise its traditional responsibilities.

In 1808 the iron spire and weathercock of the Tolbooth were blown down by a gale. They were replaced by a conical spire designed by Willis Balsillie, surmounted by a vane in the shape of a sloop made by Tinkler Robertson. The new superstructure reminded the 12th earl of Eglinton of a candle-snuffer: 'Damn it, ye have clapt an extinguisher on it'. A more pleasing alteration was made the following year when David Hamilton, the Glasgow architect, designed a new outside stairway at the eastern entrance. But the premises, though picturesque, were cramped and inadequate. Upstairs off the court room were three cells where debtors were lodged, and on the other side below the steeple the guard room and Black Hole where criminals were confined. Here in 1811 Lord Macdonald of the Isles was lodged after a brawl at the Carpenters Ball. So too in 1814 was Private John McManus of the 27th Regiment of Foot, who had quarelled with and shot Allan Hutton, a weaver, near the Tron, for which he was hanged at Ayr. Also in 1814 a vagrant who stabbed Patrick Warner of Ardeer was imprisoned before a sentence of transportation.

Congestion occurred in the post-war depression when because of the large number of debtors it was necessary in 1816 to employ a night watchman. Two years later, with 27 persons in the three debtors' cells 'which afforded a much less area than was provided by Law for Negroes in the Middle passage', permission of the Court of Session was obtained to use the court room also as a prison. The councillors submitted to the 'privations and hardships' of meeting in the Clerk's Chamber below. What aggravated the problem was that Irvine as a royal burgh was responsible for accommodating prisoners for the whole of north Ayrshire including Kilmarnock.

The council complained that 'they had so much exhausted the funds of the Burgh by building a New Academy and improving the Harbour, that it was quite impossible for them to undertake the building of a new Jail'. Other exceptional expenditure was incurred in taking over the old tannery at Seagatefoot as a slaughter house (1812) and rebuilding the town mills (1827). Yet in 1818 as they were pleading poverty (to the Court of Session) they boasted (to a Parliamentary Committee on Royal Burghs) that all improvements were paid from the town's funds without any assessed levy, and such a surplus had been built up that in that year no cess had to be collected. George Robertson confirmed this in 1820. The cess paid to the Exchequer, now reduced to some £50, was 'all that the inhabitants have to pay towards Burrough Taxes in Irvine. All public expense, in every other respect, are defrayed from the Town's funds: such as the building of edifices, church, school, prison, bridge, etc., and keeping them in repair, the causewaying of the streets, the public wells and the public lamps, even the minister's stipend, and school salaries, are furnished free to the inhabitants. Circumstances, it is believed, not to be paralleled in any other Burgh Royal or other town in the kingdom'.

In 1832 'the affairs of Irvine may be considered as comparatively prosperous'. The council was employing a town clerk (£20), factor (£30), gaoler (£30), billet master (£7), gaol surgeon (£4.4/-), two town's officers (£6 each), town drummer (£7), and bell-ringer (£5.10/-). The collector of taxes received no salary, but as the cess annually paid to government was £58.10/- and the amount raised was about £74, and 'as no surplus appears in the accounts of the town, the whole must be retained by the collector, who had thus 25 per cent for collection'.

The burgh was still a wealthy landowner. Of the 2,644 Scots acres of the parish of Irvine, Eglinton in 1820 now held almost a half — Armsheugh, Stane, Bourtreehill, Bogside, and Snodgrass — amounting to some 1,200 acres. Balgray was divided among four proprietors (Thomas, Robert, and William Reid, and Robert Dunlop), and nearer the town were four small surviving estates —

In Kilwinning Road in the early 19th century wealthier local businessmen built substantial villas and moved from the increasingly congested High Street.

Towerlands (John Webb), Chalmershouses (Robert Glasgow), Howmill with Milgarholm (John Hoggarth), and Bartonholm (Colonel Fullarton). None of these eight properties was more than 80 Scots acres, and together they amounted to some 600 acres. Another hundred acres or so can be accounted by Lochwards (Dr. Mackenzie and Robert Rankin), Scotts Loch (Patrick Warner), Dalrymplewards (Bailie Thomas Stewart) and other smaller lots the burgh had feued. The remainder, extending to more than 750 Scots acres, formed the burgh lands. Most of this was now leased on tack. The farms of Knadgerhill, Newmure, Haysholm, and Kidsneuk were joined by the new farm of Irvine Mains (1815), and smaller enclosures were let for cultivation or grazing. By the end of the 18th century, the policy of alienating burgh lands had been abandoned by the council. The once extensive Burgh Moor was now reduced to around 100 acres 'in natural condition', so little used for grazing that by 1833 the town herd would become redundant. Rents from land formed the most important item of burgh revenue — £530 in 1778 (63%) and £870 in 1808 (81%); by 1832 it was £1,137 out of £1,498. Rents per acre by 1820 locally averaged 24/7 in Irvine parish with 27/4 for cultivated land. This was a result of the agrarian improvements, and the town council enjoyed the benefit of improved commercial farming. The farms of the parish of Irvine supplied a town which had now become almost entirely dependent on purchased foodstuffs, by growing oats (480 acres), potatoes (156), some beans (54), barley (42), wheat and rye (23), turnips (32), and also hay (210) and grass (1,415) to maintain 266 milk cows, 244 other cattle, 92 pigs, 90 sheep and 165 horses. By 1841 there was an increased specialisation in dairying, and the New Statistical Account reported 370 dairy cows, only sixty horses, and about a hundred men and women farmworkers on land which was now being let to tenants at around £2 per acre.

In the vicinity of the town there was feuing of land for housebuilding. Beyond Townhead, villas were erected at Springfield and Greenfield before 1819 on land obtained from Chamberhouse. Some inhabitants of the town were able to dispose of parts of their extensive burgage plots for the building of houses in East Back Road and the salubrious sites west of Hill Street overlooking the river. The council, however, was the main vendor. Colonel Fullarton of

Bartonholm and others took feus along West Back Road. Across the water Halfway and Back Road became completely built up, with better-class housing in Waterside and Friarscroft. Around 1820 a new development was of large houses in their own grounds along Kilwinning Road: Cottagefield, Hamilfield, and Ravenscroft (1819) on one side; Stewarthall, Heathfield, and Williamfield on the other. This last was built in 1821 for Robert Macredie, captain of an East India Company ship, son of William Macredie of Perceton whose grandfather had acquired that estate in Dreghorn parish from the Barclays in 1720.

Further feuing was possible in Bank Street after that new throughfare was made in 1828 by the Bridge Trustees, to complete the plan of improved access to and from the harbour. The council was of course involved, as it was in the maintenance of existing roadways. In 1801 the earl of Eglinton as provost proposed lowering the level of High Street from Seagatehead to the Grupe, because the declivity made it unsafe for horsemen. Halfway, the road to the harbour, was renewed (1810) and provided with sidepaths or pavements (1812), and other streets were provided with syvers (1812). Minor roads were repaired, like the Grupe (1812), and Castle Street down to Seagatefoot (1823). In 1816, to provide work for the unemployed, a footpath was laid 'on the back road on the west side from Miss Campbell's chaise house north to the saw pit'. In 1829 a major project was commenced, to improve the streets generally by laying square causeway stones, one or two hundred yards each year. Meanwhile the streets were kept cleaner by rouping refuse to farmers who could use the dung (1806), and dunghills were removed from Sandy Potts by the churchyard gate in Kirk Vennel (1821). The main streets were now illuminated at night with oil lamps (1805), followed by gas (1829).

The burgh retained its partnership with the parish church. Annually the council continued to exercise its statutory right of appointing a burgh representative to attend the General Assembly of the Church in Edinburgh. In 1811 it fulfilled its responsibility for repairing the church roof, which in 1830 had to be removed and a new one raised six feet, with iron pillars replacing the old wooden supports. The earls of Eglinton remained patrons, and after Rev. James Richmond's death chose Rev. James Henderson (1805-20), then Rev. John Wilson (1820-44), who was remembered wearing a surtout of fine black broadcloth, and the high collar, starched cuffs and tall silk hat of that period. He was the first to occupy the manse which was built on the glebe in 1821. Successive councils had long insisted that churches within royal burghs need not be supplied with manses. Defeated in this, in 1822 they showed a new reluctance to pay for the communion elements, according to tradition. At this period the teinds, which were intended to help maintain the parish church, amounted to little more than £20 annually, and some of the landowners were now refusing to pay them to the council. With so many inhabitants (and some councillors) no longer belonging to the established church, there was a natural weakening of the bond. But the community retained its predominantly protestant character. Of the 125 Irish households listed in the local 1820 census and widely distributed throughout the town and Fullarton, most had attached themselves to the Established Church (62) and the other places of worship. There were only 30 households described as Roman Catholic, a mere 2% of the total population. There was a certain community of interest among those of the Big Kirk, the Relief, Burgher and Baptist Kirks, and the score of Methodists. In 1812 a Bible Society was formed with about sixty members. In 1819, 527 young persons attended evening Sunday schools 'superintended by many well disposed elderly people of various religious persuasions'. In 1826, £100 was bequeathed by Major Davidson for supporting a Sabbath School. In 1829 the council willingly subscribed three guineas to help Rev. John Wilson provide an assistant to counter 'the extreme ignorance as to religion that prevailed among a very numerous class of his parishioners about Bartonholm and Sourlie'. In 1831 a 'number of gentlemen' established a non-denominational Town Mission to give 'religious instruction etc. to the Poor', and the council contributed £5 annually — supporting yet another of those various voluntary bodies which were in fact usurping the traditional authority of the town council.

Early in the 19th century Irvine's population reached 6,000. At the second decennial census in 1811 there were 3,910 in the burgh proper and 1,972 in 'the suburbs' on the other side of the river. These figures included 160 militia billeted in the town and 450 seamen, and in addition to that total of 5,882 there were 488 in the country part of Irvine parish. Quoting these figures, George Robertson praised the town where he had made his home: 'Many of the houses are constructed in a handsome stile, and nearly all have excellent gardens in the back ground. There are several lesser streets or lanes in various directions which are narrower, but the buildings in general not incommodious, whilst they also have each their gardens attached. In the immediate vicinity, some elegant villas have lately been erected, more especially on that sloping bank to the southward, near the river, from whence the prospect is delightful'. George Robertson, who came from Linlithgow as factor to Eglinton, retired to Bower Lodge in Waterside, became a councillor (1812-19), and wrote *Rural Recollections* and books on Ayrshire before his death in 1832 aged 74. Earlier, the fastidious William Aiton had praised Irvine as 'a clean, open, fine looking town'. A later

Hamilfield was purchased by John Smith, a solicitor whose daughters — Mrs Lewis and Mrs Gibson — won academic renown for the discovery and translation of a Syriac gospel manuscript.

commentator described it as 'a rendezvous of the leisured class... The broad and beautiful High Street was a suitable promenade... when gentlemen were known by their pigtails and powder and when ladies dressed as fantastically and scrimpily as they do at present... Never more will be seen the powdered hair, the three cornered hats, the knee breeches, and the lace which at one time gave such an embellishment to the streets of Irvine'.

Appropriately, in 1807 Hugh, 12th earl of Eglinton (1798–1819), laid out a new race course at Bogside. He and his son each put up £50 prizes, and Irvine town council contributed twenty-five guineas, then fifty guineas, and continued this annual contribution even in 1820 despite the 'present distressed state of the country'. The principal meeting was for three days near the end of June, 'attended by a large portion of the noblemen and gentlemen of Ayrshire and neighbouring counties, and frequently by many from different parts of England'. William Aiton personally recalled the gatherings in the principal inns throughout the day, assemblies at night, and the ball and supper at Eglinton Castle on the last night of the Bogside races each year 'in which the usual taste, hospitality, and urbanity of manners of the noble family are displayed'. The Town Moor also offered opportunities for hunting and fowling (1808), and annual permits were issued. Rabbits had been introduced by Robert Cunningham to Auchenharvie after 1770, and pheasants to Eglinton soon afterwards by the 12th earl. Archery was practised off the East Back Road until 1822 when the Society of Archers obtained a feu for butts west of the academy. There was much curling in 1822 when the frost and snow were at their most severe since 1795. The shore also provided scope for the healthful craze of seabathing, especially popular between Saltcoats and Largs.

The extension of social facilities in Irvine was noted by George Robertson, who listed for the town, in 1819, 49 shops and 53 houses of entertainment, with two Head Inns with large rooms for public meetings. There was a Coffee

Room (where the Board of Health met in 1832). There was a daily stage coach to and from Glasgow, and thrice weekly between Ayr and Greenock. Literary interests were catered for by John Templeton, who continued his father's bookshop on the north side of High Street. Printing and publishing began on the opposite side of the street in 1814. In 1783 John Mennons had founded the *Glasgow Advertiser* (later the *Glasgow Herald*); had made an unsuccessful venture as coalmaster; and had then renewed his journalistic career in Irvine. He produced an *Irvine and County of Ayr Miscellany* (1814–15), the *Irvine Mercury* (1815), and several other publications. After his death in 1818 the business was acquired by Edward Macquiston, who published Robertson's *Topographical Description of Cunninghame*. He was followed in 1820 by Maxwell Dick, a young man of ingenuity as well as culture, who had come from Paisley and started as a bookseller on the opposite side of the street not far from Templeton's, before taking over from MacQuiston. Robertson's *Ayrshire Families* was the first of a long list of publications. An early attempt by Dick to start a cheap weekly newspaper failed (because of the newspaper tax), but from 1858 he produced an *Ayrshire News Letter*. In 1824 Dick had become a town councillor, continuing a lively career lasting till his death in 1870. The popularity of reading was further evidenced when in 1831 the subscribers to Irvine Library leased from the council a shop under the Tolbooth, at £3 per year. Musical interests were also extending. There were two bands in 1814 in the procession to found the new academy. In 1830 the *Ayr Advertiser* reported in Irvine a 'Concert of vocal and instrumental music given by several gentlemen', with the proceeds donated to the Indigent Sick Society of Irvine. Other cultural interests are revealed by the presentation of the freedom of the burgh to John Galt in 1825 and the formation of Irvine Burns Club in 1826. Not long after in 1834 John Kelso Hunter found temporary employment as a portrait painter here and could remark, 'I set the society of Irvine above that of any place I have ever seen'.

For the well-to-do, Irvine must have been a pleasant place, despite occasional disturbances, like the shearers rioting at the Bridgegatehead during Marymass (1804), robbery at Redburn by the highwayman John Withrington (1814), the murder in High Street of Allan Hutton by Private John McManus (1814), threats of a radical rising (1817, 1820), and panics induced by body-snatching (1826) and cholera (1832).

Irvine continued to be a nursery for boys of budding abilities. Daniel and Alexander Macmillan were two brothers whose father, Duncan Macmillan, was a carter who lived in the Townhead and attended the Baptist Church. They received an elementary education at the academy. Daniel, born in Arran in 1813, was apprenticed to Maxwell Dick before he was eleven, beginning at 1/6 a week, and served in that bookshop for seven years. Alexander, born in 1818, was by the age of sixteen in charge of a school in East Back Road, connected with the Burgher Kirk. Daniel continued as a bookseller in Stirling, then Glasgow, whither his brother had also moved as a teacher. Then to London, where they both ran a bookshop in Aldergate Street, whence sprang the still-renowned publishing firm of Macmillan.

Although Irvine was continuing to grow, the county town of Ayr had recovered its lead, while both had been outstripped by Kilmarnock. In 1811, as against Irvine's 5,900 of a population, Ayr had now 6,300, and Kilmarnock had reached 10,000. This trend would mean that while Kilmarnock and Ayr grew into large towns, Irvine would continue as a poor third. The omens were foreseen when Rev. James Richmond wrote in 1791 that 'Manufactures, as yet, are not carried on here to any extent'. Robertson in 1820 went further: 'The manufacturing interest does not appear to be in a prosperous state; on the contrary it seems to be declining'.

True, the harbour continued to do good business. In 1819 it had 87 vessels from 15 to 208 tons (totalling 7,265 tons) manned by 517 seamen. In that year it cleared 247 coastwise vessels and 415 to foreign ports, and exported 25,000 tons of coal. Saltcoats, with only 13,000 tons exported, had failed to keep pace. But the new port of Troon with 23,000 tons was a serious rival, and Ardrossan harbour, nearing completion, would offer another challenge which could not be met. Robertson noted that 'The larger vessels now, instead of completing their loads by means of lighters, beyond the bar, take in no more than they can safely navigate over it, and go at once to Ardrossan harbour where they fill up their cargo, at less trouble, and without any danger from want of water'. The Duke of Portland's railway, along which horses pulled carts of coal from the pits near Kilmarnock to his port of Troon (1808), was a herald of further change. The earl of Eglinton's proposal for a branch from it to Irvine (1816) was not taken up, and his further proposal (1819) for a railroad of eight miles from Sourlie and Doura to Ardrossan threw Irvine council into a panic. Renewed efforts to find workable coal in the burgh lands were unrewarding. George Taylor was unsuccessful (1819–21). John Brown of Ayr followed (1826) but had to abandon his Marress pit in 1829. Fortunately William Taylor, who had leased Bartonholm in 1797, was not deterred by the harassment of paying tolls on coals taken by road to Irvine, and devised a short wagonway to the Garnock (1811) to float his coals in lighters down to Irvine harbour. In 1814 he also acquired Boyle's Shewalton pits and made a three-mile railroad through Oldhall, Newhouse and Gailes to Irvine. Although

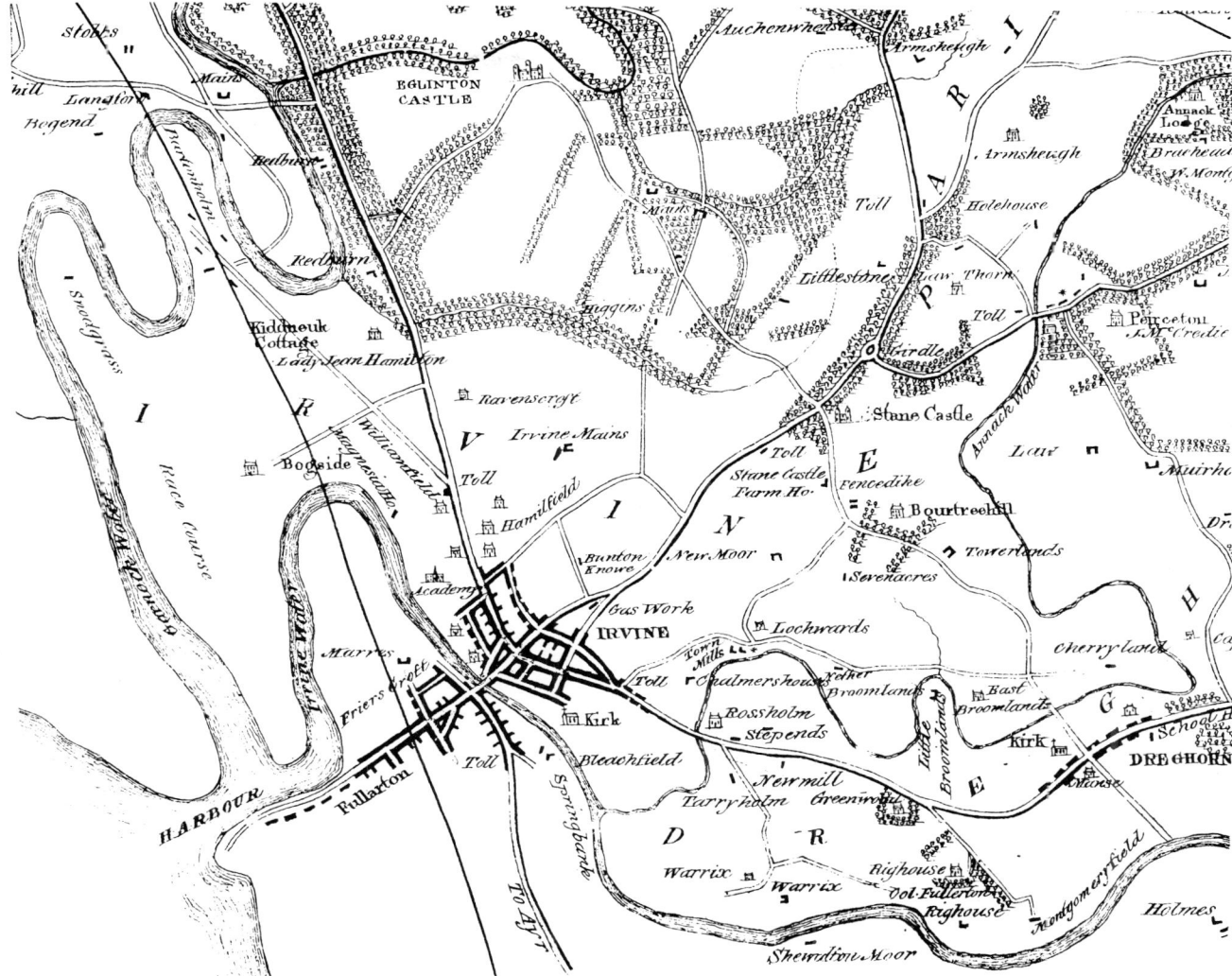

Aitken's Map of 1829 shows Irvine in its rural enviroment. The projected railway line, laid ten years later, would not significantly alter the town, which ceased to grow in the first half of the 19th century.

he himself went bankrupt, by 1820 this line was carrying twenty-eight wagons taking a ton each, three times daily, to the harbour. Significantly, the character of Irvine's trade was now quite restricted. Of 768 sailings in the year 1823, all but a dozen were boats taking out coal and coming back in ballast. The other few were handling a minor coastwise traffic in oats and timber.

Some people seemed to be doing well enough, on the evidence of items noted by Robertson. Hunter's Bank and the Paisley Bank were joined in 1815 by a Savings Bank for persons of modest means, which in 1819 held £1,240 for 219 depositors. In 1830 the Ayrshire Banking Company set up a branch in Irvine, with William Gillies as manager. There were also sixteen friendly societies, whose 1,113 members could afford thus to insure themselves. It is also a measure of the prosperity of some people that '2 or 3 societies established themselves among the higher classes, are for the relief of those poor people who are unconnected to any society'. Robertson also complacently noticed that the crafts of the burgh, though 'limited to the natural demands of the neighbourhood, remain nearly in their usual circumstances'. The six Incorporated Trades continued to safeguard the interests of their members, although their traditional monopolies were obviously being eroded. The deacons of all the Irvine Trades in 1832 unanimously admitted that 'the exclusive privileges were not only of no value to the incorporated tradesmen themselves, but in many instances most injurious to the trade and prosperity of the community'. Those masters entitled to be incorporated as squaremen included (in 1819) 42 wrights, 41 masons and 30 carpenters, plus slaters, plasterers and coachmakers. The hammermen had 20 blacksmiths, along with saddlers, watchmakers, coppersmiths, tinsmiths, and one silversmith 'who also draws in landscape and engraves in wood'. The weavers included the few customary workers in wool and linen, but most of the 602 total were unincorporated muslin weavers, employed by Glasgow and Paisley merchants. There were 34 tailors and 72 shoemakers. The last of the Incorporated Trades, because of the decline in herring fishing, now contained only seven coopers. Among the 49 shopkeepers were 12 bakers, 11 fleshers, and 'an assortment of dyesters, wigmakers, house painters, haberdashers'. There were five surgeons and one physician, and eight lawyers.

One group less prominent in the town itself were the colliers, who had formerly tramped out to the pits, but for whom the coalmasters now provided mining villages, more convenient in some respects, but segregating the workers and their families in tied accommodation. Doura, Sourlie, Bartonholm and Shewalton colliers' rows were all created in the first two decades of the 19th century. The local parish census of 1820 showed 26 households of colliers at Bartonholm, about as many in smaller settlements at Sourlie (6), Lawthorn (5), and Armsheugh, Shipmill and Littlestone (4 each). There were 38 collier households in the town, most of them (24) in Townhead.

As Robertson realised, manufacturing industry in Irvine was not prospering. The cotton trade which had been introduced in the 1780s was languishing. The spinning jenny which had employed 80 girls and the tambour work for 70 others had both closed down. The handloom weaving of muslins, which gave work for 390 in 1811, suffered periods of acute depression, and severe unemployment locally in 1819 and from 1829 to 1832. Shipbuilding had also decayed. Only one of three yards survived. Messrs. Gilkinson, Thomson & Co., however, launched their biggest ship ever in 1814, the 309-ton *Montreal*. And in 1819 they built a 169-ton brigantine *Jean* for Alexander Allan, the Saltcoats shipmaster, which became the first of the Allan transatlantic shipping line. Duncan McDougall had a smithy and machine shop at the corner of Gottries and Harbour Street. This was started about 1801, making anchors and, after 1827, chain cables. But apart from this there is little that can be reported. There were two tanneries and two ropeworks; and the Meadow Bleachfield; in 1826 David Gray opened a brewery at the Green; at Duntonknoll in 1805 a steam engine was installed by Willis Balsillie, the builder who leased the quarry; the Powder House was rebuilt in 1801; and the Magnesia House on the moor may have been the site of an abortive experiment to produce magnesia in saltpans during this unpromising period.

Yet there was no lack of inventive genius in early 19th-century Irvine. James Beaumont Neilson (1792-1865) came to Irvine in 1814 as engine wright at William Taylor's Shewalton colliery, where he laid down the railroad to Irvine harbour. He married Barbara Montgomerie from Irvine in 1815, and at the smithy in Kirkgatehead he carried out successful experiments on the smelting of iron. Later as manager of Glasgow gasworks he won recognition as the inventor of the Hot Blast which revolutionised the iron industry. Irvine can also validly claim credit for the invention of the screw propellor by James Steadman (1790-1865), a local carpenter and cabinetmaker. While still an apprentice, his interest in natural history took him to Eglinton woods. His study of birds led him to attempt a flying machine. His study of fish gave him the idea of rear propulsion for ships. How this could be accomplished was suggested in 1816 from observation of a spinning wheel. William McCririck, a gunsmith, contributed ideas of his own, and over the next decade they collaborated in constructing a number of models. In 1830 such a model was taken by another associate, Maxwell Dick, to London. There one of the engineers to whom it was shown pirated the idea — so it was alleged — and the screw propeller was patented in another's name, without credit or benefit to James Steadman. Maxwell Dick, bookseller, publisher, freemason, Burnsian, and magistrate, was also a talented inventor. In 1827 he devised a snow plough; in 1829 he experimented with a suspension railway at Gailes; in 1832 he invented a bed, warmed by hot water pipes, for the benefit of those infected with cholera; he was involved also in designing the screw propeller and a suction dredger; he showed a telegraph insulator at the Great Exhibition of 1851; and in 1856 he was experimenting with guano and artificial fertilisers on land he sold when the Poorhouse was built. Another who contributed to technological advance was Dr. William Montgomerie. A native of Irvine, when resident in Singapore in 1843 he discovered that Malayan gutta percha was suitable for the manufacture of rubber.

Frustration at local economic difficulties no doubt contributed to the widespread feeling that political reform was urgent — both an extension of the parliamentary franchise and the introduction of burgh elections. During 1817 and 1818 petitions were presented to parliament from almost all the royal burghs in Scotland, including Irvine, alleging mismanagement of municipal affairs through the negligence, ignorance and corruption of the self-elected councils. Irvine burgh council itself received such a petition from 'a number of persons' advocating an alteration of the sett or burgh constitution. The council was not particularly illiberal, and had, as previous pages have shown, sponsored

The King's Arms and the Eglinton Arms. In 1820 these 'two Head Inns, as they are called, are very respectable. Both have post-chaises, and both have large rooms for public meetings'.

or co-operated in various progressive measures for the benefit of the town. Several councillors accepted the desirability of reform, and the Trades councillors in particular obviously had the backing of reformers outside the council chambers. Many moderate reformers, however, were alarmed by the extremists who seemed to threaten revolution. The council was unanimously committed to constitutional principles, as confirmed by the humble addresses it presented to members of the royal family on all appropriate occasions. When the reform movement revived in 1830, and the Incorporated Trades of Irvine asked the magistrates to call a public meeting, the council agreed to meet the Trades for a discussion. In March 1831 the Trades took the initiative in organising an 'Illumination' in support of the Reform Bill then before the House of Commons. The Trades, led by two bands, and followed by an 'immense body of inhabitants', marched in torchlight procession through the town. Bonfires were lit, and every reformer had a candle burning in his window. 'The whole town and suburbs were in a splendid blaze', it was reported in the *Ayr Advertiser*. When this first Reform Bill failed in its final passage through the Commons, King William IV, using his royal prerogative, called a general election. Trades and council combined to send a loyal message of approval to the king, and organised another procession to celebrate the birthday of the monarch who was nicknamed 'Reform Bill'. When Thomas Kennedy of Dunure stood for re-election as MP for Ayr Burghs with a slogan of 'The King, Reform, and Kennedy', the council appointed Bailie Orr as its commissioner, committed to his support. When the new House of Commons passed a second Reform Bill, but the House of Lords rejected it, there were widespread protests, voiced in the case of Irvine at another public meeting when several members of the council 'resolved that they will no longer act under a system which is so much as variance with the sentiments they have expressed on the subject of reform'. A third Reform Bill was introduced in December 1831, forced through the Lords, and passed on 7th June 1832, followed by a Scottish Act on 17th July. On 10th August 1832, despite the cholera, Irvine had its day of rejoicing for the Reform Act. In the procession, in which the Trades were joined by others from Kilmarnock and Stewarton, the various crafts were represented by tableaux, as was customary. The shoemakers had King Crispin and his Queen. The tailors had two members representing Adam and Eve, naked apart from aprons painted with fig leaves. Four weavers were richly costumed as Indian emperor, empress, prince, and princess.

December 1832 saw the first General Election under the extended though still very restricted franchise. In the counties it went to proprietors of land valued at £10 per annum and well-off tenants paying £50 per annum. In the burghs, no longer were members chosen by delegates from groups of councils, but by those householders whose property was valued at the quite considerable £10 per annum. In the county election for Ayrshire, the Tory Colonel William Blair of Blair (who had won the 1831 election by 73 votes to 36 under the old franchise) was ousted by the Whig Richard Oswald of Auchincruive (2,152 votes to 324 under the new franchise). In the Western District of Burghs seat (Ayr, Irvine, Campbeltown, Inveraray, with Oban replacing Rothesay), the Whig T.F. Kennedy was re-elected with 375 votes, the Radical Dr. John Taylor gaining 164, and the Tory James Cruikshanks a mere 33. Within Irvine (whose precise electoral boundaries had now for the first time to be defined) there were 201 persons on the electoral roll. Of the 186 who voted, the public ballot revealed Whigs in the lead with 91 for Kennedy, but almost as many for more Radical reform with 87 for Taylor, and only 8 Tory votes.

1833 was the year of Burgh Reform. Parliament passed three acts for Scottish burgh reform, and the first Town Council Elections were to follow on the first Tuesday in November.

The council then elected was less dramatically changed than might have been imagined. The Eglinton influence had already diminished. Hugh, 12th earl, had been a councillor from 1787 to his death in 1819 at the age of 80, but the grandson who succeeded was a minor, and was not eligible. Earl Hugh's two younger brothers had joined him on the council and continued to share the provostship until 1831. They left behind on the council their nephew, William Montgomerie of Annick Lodge. But this last of the Montgomeries was displaced as provost at Michaelmas 1832, with the council heeding a plea of the Incorporated Trades for 'a Resident Provost whose principles are friendly to Reform'. When the £10 householders cast their votes in the first municipal election in November 1833, two newcomers headed the poll — David Gray, brewer, and William Gillies, banker — and Daniel Stewart, academy rector, was also among the eight newcomers. But the majority of the council of seventeen were products of the old regime. Six of the old council were re-elected, including Maxwell Dick, bookseller, and William Gray, grain merchant — who became the new provost even though his son had received most votes in the election. Another three had previously served on the unreformed council, including Thomas Garven as Convener of Trades. Well-off business and professional people, elected by well-off householders now, continued to manage the affairs of the royal burgh of Irvine.

TWELVE
Little Change

Historians have chosen 1832 as a key date in political and constitutional development, with what they have described as the Great Reform Act. They have seen this as beginning a period of economic and social progress. Yet for the generation which was growing up in Irvine when Victoria became queen in 1837, the first thirty years of her reign brought few significant changes to the town. Not till the approach of the Second Reform Act of 1867 did Irvine begin new developments, with a quickening of political controversy and changes in the work and life of its people.

While one of the burgh reform acts of 1833 insisted on the election of town councillors by the £10 householders, another by which a burgh might introduce a new 'Police system' was not adopted locally. Under its provisions, existing burghs might extend their powers over watching ('police' in the modern sense), lighting, paving, cleansing, water supply and other matters, and levy an assessment for these purposes. Further acts of 1850 and 1862 similarly providing for such a system of 'police commissioners' were neither of them locally accepted. A proposal to adopt the 'new Police Act' was turned down by Irvine town council in 1863 by nine votes to seven.

In one local sense, 1835 may in retrospect mark the end of an era, with the death on 13th January of ex-Bailie Fullarton at the age of 95, a councillor for forty-two consecutive years. Robert Fullarton seems to have come originally from Rothesay, and spoke with a strong Highland accent. He lived at Townhead, carried on a business as a candlemaker, was elected a councillor in 1790, served as a magistrate in the period 1791-1827, deputising for the earl of Eglinton as provost when senior bailie, and provided John Galt with a model for 'Provost Pawkie'. When serving on the bench, he would lecture offenders, telling them that 'their promises wad fill the chawmer, but their performances wad a' gang into a snuff box'. Every day he had some public duty to perform, and every afternoon he could claim a dram at the expense of the common good fund. Provost John Paterson recalled his going about accompanied by his wee dog Chance, and that the academy got a holiday for his public funeral.

The councils elected after 1833 differed little in composition or function from those on which Robert Fullarton had served. The annual elections were on the first Tuesday of November, a few weeks after the former Michaelmas meetings. Of the seventeen councillors (eighteen after 1852), six retired annually, their replacements chosen by a small electorate of less than two hundred substantial businessmen; really not very different in consequence from the old council replacing four of its number by co-option.

After each election the procedures were little different. The councillors chose a provost (though now for a three-year term of office); two bailies (three after 1852); a dean of guild; and a treasurer. After these magistrates were decided upon, the council made the other traditional appointments. James Johnston, town clerk since 1818, was continued till his death in 1853. His successor, David Gray, had an interesting career. Born in 1800, his father a bailie, he began his legal training with town clerk James Innes at age thirteen. In 1826 he abandoned the law to start a brewery, entered municipal politics in 1833 and served as councillor and magistrate for nineteen years. When Johnston died, David Gray was persuaded to accept appointment as town clerk, which post he occupied for the next twenty-four years (1853-77), taking on a bank agency also.

Also appointed, as before, were: factor; fiscal; billet master; stentmasters; visitors of the tron and bread market; visitors of the flesh market; birleymen; foresters; constables; constables for the shore; three town officers; drummer; jailor. In 1837 the officers were supplied with great coats, and the town drummer with a pair of leggings, drawers and a new hat, and it was voted to continue the customary processions to church of the magistrates accompanied by the officers with their halberts. One burgh officer in 1862 was entrusted with the ringing of the town bell at 5.30, 5.55, and 10 a.m., the church bell at 6 and 8 p.m., and on Sundays as required. The council continued to elect annually a burgh representative to attend the General Assembly of the Church, and others to an increasing number of new public bodies.

Bailie Robert Fullarton, councillor for 42 years, was the subject of John Galt's novel *The Provost*. His death in 1835 marked the end of an era.

The long-established practice of enjoying public celebrations survived. There was a dinner in the Kings Arms for the coronation (1838), another for Victoria's marriage to Albert (1840), and 'a comfortable meal for the poor' after the birth of a royal prince (1841). Later there were illuminations and fireworks when that Prince of Wales was married (1863). Annually there was a dinner in the Eglinton Arms after the examinations at the academy, and each new council for some years celebrated its election with 'a public meeting' and 'music at the expense of the burgh', when those 'invited by circular' drank the health of the new councillors. It was agreed to support the revived Bogside Races (1836), but the annual subscription to the Carters Race was discontinued (1834) and Marymass went into a period of decline. Then, with the Carters Society on the verge of dissolution (1851), the council agreed to renew its co-operation in 'the annual and very ancient amusements of the Marymass'.

Regular meetings of the council were still held, on the first Tuesday of each month. An experiment with evening meetings at 7 p.m. was abandoned in 1844 after two years' trial, and there was a reversion to the traditional 10 a.m. assemblies. In that year, however, burgesses and electors were allowed as spectators, and from 1864 newspaper reporters were admitted — a convenience for the *Ardrossan and Saltcoats Herald* (founded in 1853). The council, and the small select electorate it represented, was unwilling to venture on radical innovations. There are occasional hints of rancour in the recorded minutes, but on few local issues does the council seem to have been split on party lines. Some of the councillors, however, played an active part in parliamentary elections. Lord James Stuart held Ayr Burghs from 1834 to 1852 as a Liberal against declining Radical opposition. His successor, E.H.J. Crawford of Auchenames, also Liberal, had as his local agent Alexander Robertson of Whitehurst (provost 1846-50, 1864-66). From 1852 there was a new challenge from Conservative parliamentary candidates, who had strong support on the council under Thomas Campbell of Annfield's long provostship (1850-64).

The routine business of the council continued on traditional lines. The river bank required constant attention, especially after the great flood of 1852. Streets were repaired, and after 1847 the burgh recovered from the Road Trustees entire responsibility for roads within its bounds. There were repeated but desultory efforts to widen Bridgegate, the 'chief entrance' to the town. Carts were purchased (1842, 1853) 'for carrying away the sweepings and rubbish from the streets'. A proposal to 'macadamise' the High Street was turned down (1834), although this system was adopted later (1856) for the Townhead, 'Macadamised by a bed of broken Metal laid above the present Causway'. Use of the Puddleford by horses was now prohibited (1836) to safeguard access to the Puddly Well or Black Well. All the public wells were repaired (1835 and later). An attempt was made (1836) to get local insurance companies to contribute to the upkeep of the fire engines. There were three hand carts, which were fitted with shafts for horses to pull (1852). A new fire station (1860) was provided for them at the old school in Kirkgatehead. A new slaughterhouse was built (1843) at Seagatefoot, to the north-west of the old one, which was proving a public nuisance.

Improved management is indicated by the formation of various council committees. A committee to examine accounts was instituted in 1833 — by 1840 the burgh revenue was £1,676 and expenditure £1,567. After 1837 supervision of the town lands was devolved to an agricultural committee which was kept busy with the upkeep of farms, letting of the Green for grazing of cows, hiring molecatchers, repairing dykes, and beginnng tile draining (1835). How detailed their work was is revealed by the strict instructions in 1852 that Knadgerhill 'shall now be

Little Change 125

In 1832 Irvine's boundaries were defined for parliamentary elections: 201 voters from within this area helped choose an M.P. for Ayr Burghs. Irvine town council's municipal jurisdiction did not extend beyond the river until 1881.

conducted by a three shift rotation, providing always that the tenant shall be bound to manure each green crop with at least Forty good carts of good dung to the Acre'. In 1840 a law committee was formed to deal with property transactions. Feus for housebuilding were arranged, and in 1866 ground was advertised in Kilwinning Road 'to induce people to build and reside here'. In 1851 Bogside Flats were acquired from the earl of Eglinton in exchange for land he wanted at Knadgerhill to create a new entrance to his policies. In 1865 the law committee drew up standing orders for the conduct of council meetings. The Dean of Guild Court continued as before to deal with property disputes, and was given the new statutory responsibility for weights and measures. Various *ad hoc* committees were appointed. The re-appearance of cholera in 1834, 1849, 1852 and 1867 resulted in a drainage committee, later a 'sanatory committee' and others for 'superintending the public works'. There was a committee to arrange for the extension of the churchyard in 1857. The town mill was modernised with a steam engine (1836) and other improvements, making it (1837) 'in point of architecture and machinery... unequalled in the county'. But the bankruptcy of one miller (1836) and the absconding of another (1854) showed that things were not going well, and a mill committee was formed.

The original purpose of the burgh had been to organise markets and fairs, and this still remained an important function. A new fair was instituted (1836) on the first Wednesday in January, which became mainly a horse fair supplementing the Cow Fair in May and the Marymass

Trinity Church, designed by the unorthodox Edinburgh architect T.F. Pilkington, was opened in 1863 for the congregation of the Burgher Kirk.

Rev. Dr William Robertson, the celebrated preacher who led his congregation from Cotton Row to the new Trinity Church.

Fair in August. A midsummer cattle fair on the moor was also proposed (1845). A new steelyard or weighing machine 'as in neighbouring collieries' was installed near the Cross (1839). In 1841 there were weekly grain markets and monthly cattle markets.

Some changes had to be implemented by the council, acting as agents for parliament, which was increasingly concerned with various social problems.

The Prisons Act of 1839 focused attention on Irvine Tolbooth. From 1817 until his death in 1840 the gaoler was Alexander Langlands, a strong man, six foot six and a half inches tall. In 1835 he was himself jailed for debt. During Langland's term of office John Kelso Hunter was able to take in whisky to the debtors who were holding a dance — an indication of how lax conditions were. In 1840 the newly constituted County Board for Prisons considered building a new prison in Irvine. It was decided, however, that criminals and debtors alike were henceforth to be incarcerated at Ayr, and the tolbooth cells would provide only temporary accommodation for persons apprehended. The magistrates were even more anxious to shed another traditional responsibility when in 1853 James McGorran was found guilty in Edinburgh of the murder in Irvine the previous year of a man called McGuire. He was sentenced to be hanged at Irvine on 8th June. Irvine town council pled that all executions should take place in the county town: the crisis was resolved when McGorran's sentence was commuted to 'banishment for life'.

As well as growth of crime, the other critical problem was acute poverty, with which the agencies of church and burgh could no longer effectively cope. Locally in 1834 a joint committee was formed of council, heritors, and representatives of all the churches. Each congregation would support its own poor, the others would be maintained by a fund raised by assessment. In 1841 there were 75 paupers of no religious denomination, whose relief cost £396. During the provostship of W.B. Salmon (1841-45) work for the unemployed was provided by further levelling of the Moor, but leaving the knoll which was designated Salmon's Hill, and later Magistrates' Hill. The council also gave its support to a Public Dispensary set

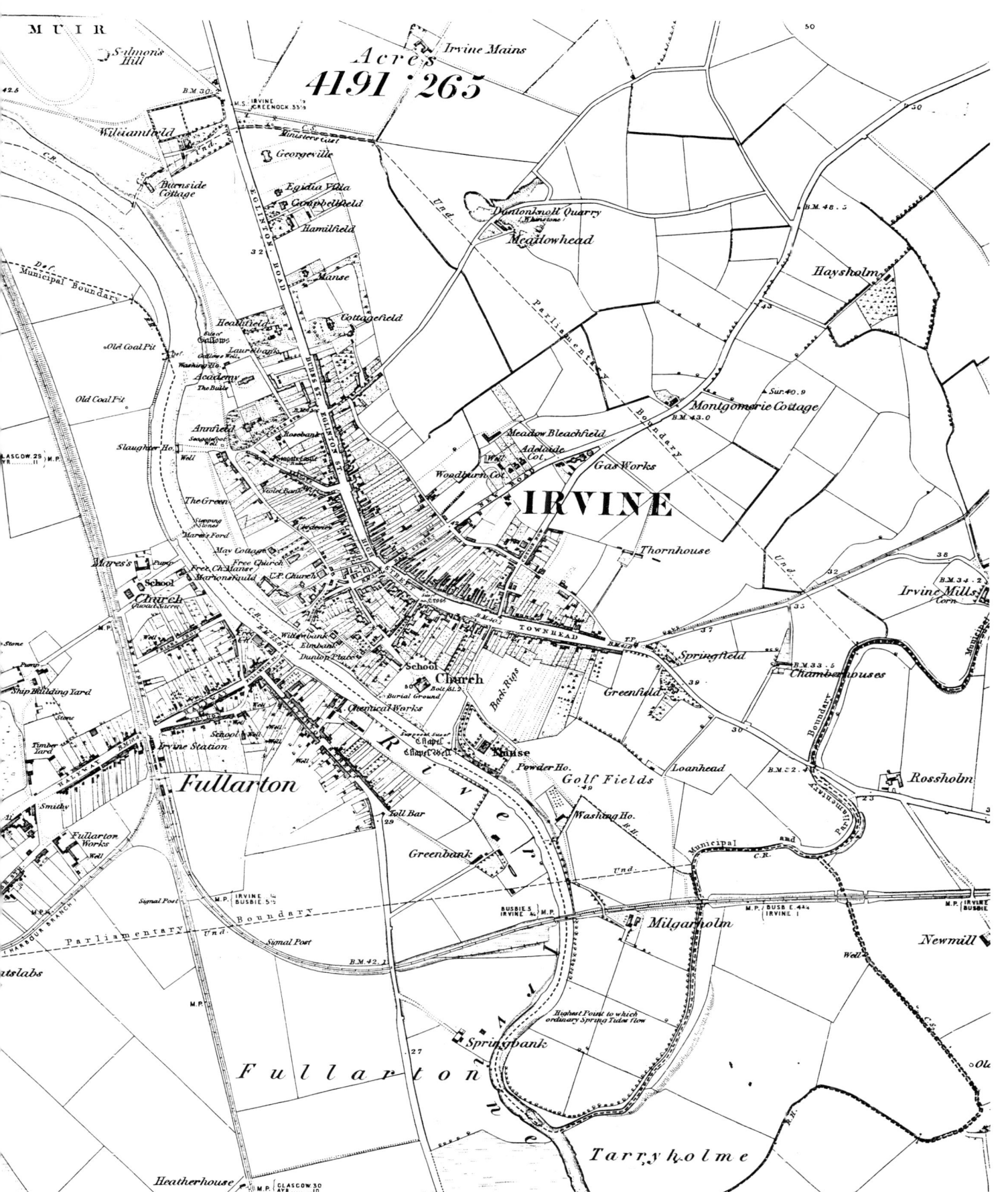

The first Ordnance Survey map shows Irvine in 1857, little changed in the first half of that century.

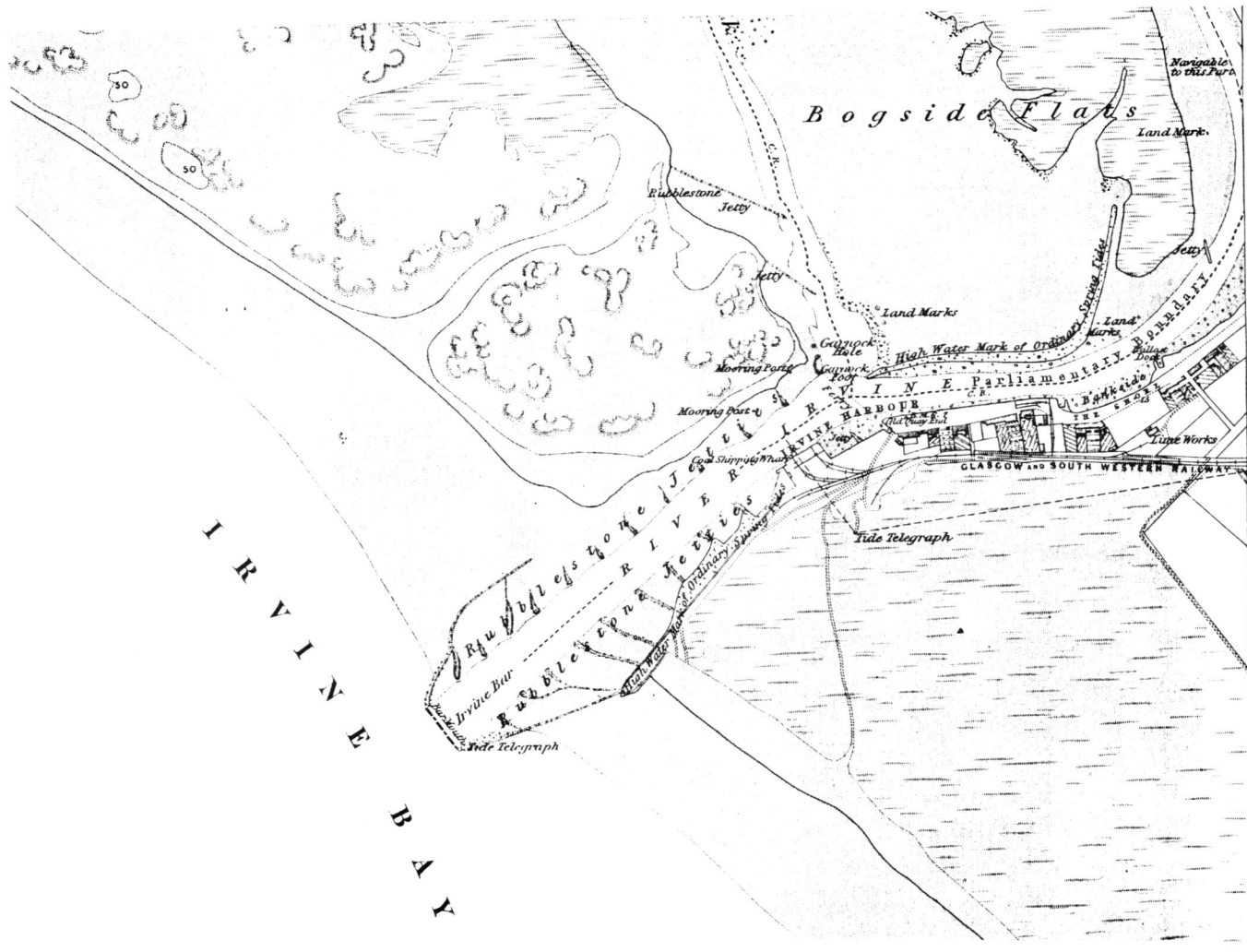

The harbour in 1857 was still small, handling coal exports principally.

up in 1836. It continued to aid a very few exceptional cases, like a 'late tailor' in 1842, 'burdened by old age and infirmity and extreme poverty'. But church dissension after 1843 rendered co-operation more difficult. Parliament, however, stepped in. The 1845 Poor Law Act required the formation of partially elected parochial boards with powers of assessment and allocation of relief to 'aged and other friendless impotent poor'. Boards for Irvine and Dundonald parishes, on which the magistrates were represented, were now responsible for poor relief. The powers of the parochial boards were later extended to deal with public health nuisances. In 1854 north Ayrshire boards co-operated in establishing a Cunninghame Combination Poorshouse at Bogside Road, Irvine. In 1866 there was a proposal to erect a fever hospital at Cotton Row. The numbers of paupers maintained by Irvine Parochial Board were 119 in 1859 (paid from 6d to 3/- weekly) and 176 in 1864.

Meanwhile the council was much concerned in 1845 at the 'great failure which has taken place in the potato crop in this neighbourhood, and generally'. Later it supported funds to assist widows and children of soldiers killed in the Crimean War (1854) and the Indian Mutiny (1857). Over a period of years it organised soup kitchens and provided work for the 'large body of the handloom weavers... destitute of employment and in very necessitous circumstances'. The council minutes record such necessary provision in 1843, 1847, 1851, 1854, 1857, 1858 and in each of the five years of the American Civil War (1861–65) which ruined the Scottish cotton trade and caused distress among the Irvine weavers. In 1865 the council sent an address of condolence to the U.S.A. following the

An early photograph shows goods being unloaded at the Wee Dock.

assassination of President Abraham Lincoln. Aid for the poor was augmented by generous benefactions — in 1846, £300 from Edward Connell, a native of Irvine who had done well in Manchester; more from the Ferguson Bequest in 1856; and £500 from Robert Rankin Holms in 1866. The most notable benefaction came from John Ferguson, who was born in Irvine in 1787. His father, the owner of a small coastal vessel, died in 1802. The widowed mother, Mary Service, lived in straitened circumstances in Fullarton Street, then High Street, supported by her five brothers who were all doing well in America. Each died intestate, and John Ferguson found himself the heir to nearly a million and a quarter pounds. He set himself up as a landowner in Wigtonshire, and when he died in 1856, half a million pounds was set aside for educational and religious causes of one kind or another throughout the six western counties of Scotland. In addition, £1,000 went to Irvine Academy, £1,000 to the poor of Irvine, £1,000 to the poor of Halfway, and £10,000 to the aged of Irvine. Some local people benefited from personal bequests, to which has been attributed the building of some of the villas in Kilwinning Road.

In 1846 another act of parliament formally brought to an end the exclusive rights of burgesses in royal burghs. This was a formality, since possession of a burgess ticket was now a legal anachronism. The Incorporated Trades had long since abandoned claims to monopoly in manufacturing, and henceforth survived purely as social and charitable bodies. But although certain inhabitants no longer need enrol as burgesses, the council retained and exercised the privilege of creating honorary burgesses on whom was bestowed the freedom of the burgh. Two sons of Robert Burns had thus been honoured in 1844 on a visit to the town — Major James Glencairn Burns and Lt. Col. William Nicol Burns. They were followed by the earl of Derby (1855), Lieutenant Nicol Graham, a local hero of the Crimea (1856), Captain James Brown for rescuing a shipwrecked crew (1857), Lord Brougham (1860), and the Earl of Eglinton (1864).

Other acts of parliament dragged Irvine into line with modern needs. In 1854 compulsory registration of births, marriages and deaths superseded the inadequate and incomplete church registers. In the same year the Valuation Act introduced a uniform system of rating on property, allowing regular assessments for a steadily widening range of services. In 1853 the Forbes-Mackenzie

Act tackled the wide-spread drunkenness of the time by licensing premises and limiting hours of opening. Meanwhile the creation of a regular police force was being considered warily. In 1839 the Ayrshire Commissioners of Supply had initiated a county force with a head constable and three constables at Beith, Girvan, and Newmilns. Irvine made do with its part-time enrolled constables, for whom the council supplied a police office in one of the tolbooth shops in 1836. A plan to extend the county force was denounced in 1841 as 'this unnecessary and objectionable measure' by William Montgomerie of Annick Lodge. Yet thirty constables for Ayrshire were then enrolled and doubled in number in 1857, and in 1860 the County Constabulary erected a Police Station in Irvine behind the old Fleshmarket. No longer was it necessary to call upon the military in time of political crisis and social disorder. In 1842 a squadron of Ayrshire Yeomanry had to be quartered in Irvine 'for the purpose of preventing disturbances at the neighbouring collieries during the late strike', and the freedom of the burgh was awarded to their commanding officer, Sir James Boswell of Auchinleck. They were also always on duty at parliamentary elections. Yet those who were without a vote and sought further extension of the franchise made only verbal protests locally. Members of the Radical Association of Irvine who had followed their candidate Dr. John Taylor of Ayr into the Chartist movement renounced in 1838 the use of physical force. The Irvine Chartist Association seems to have been short-lived and ineffective.

What was really exercising public attention during this period was the ecclesiastical controversies culminating in the Disruption of the Church of Scotland in 1843. And this, too, was nothing significantly new, but only the culmination of a century-long process of fragmentation of the presbyterian establishment.

During the early years of the 19th century the established church seemed to be coping well enough in Irvine, under two able ministers. Rev. James Richmond and his successor Rev. John Wilson (1804-44) each became doctors of divinity. For the growing numbers now dwelling over the water, ecclesiastically within the parish of Dundonald, a new congregation was formed. On a site granted by Colonel John Boyle of Shewalton, Fullarton Chapel of Ease was opened in 1838, with Rev. David Wilson as minister. The dissensions which split the national church in 1843 had a minimal effect on Irvine Parish Church. Only one elder and some members were lost to Rev. John Wilson's congregation. In Fullarton Church, however, Rev. David Wilson himself left, taking with him all the elders and most of his flock. There remained only 86 members in 'the puir wee kirk' of Fullarton. Recovery was slow, under a series of short-lived ministries — Revs. John Scoular (1845-51), John Paterson (1851-54), Archibald Fleming (1854-56) and A.M. Crawford (1857-70). In Irvine Parish Church, Rev. Andrew Browne (1844-53) was followed by Rev. James Somerville (1853-93), an eloquent and beloved preacher who had been chosen by the congregation, to whom the earl of Eglinton had delegated his right of presentation.

Meanwhile the Free Church had become firmly established. Fullarton Free Church was built in 1844 on the river bank near the site of the old Carmelite friary. Rev. David Wilson ministered effectively until his death in 1881. With appropriate magnanimity he encouraged his members from the Irvine side of the river to set up their own church. They met first in 1847 in Hamilhill chapel, then in 1849 built Irvine Free Church in West Road. Under their first minister, Rev. William Cousin (1850-59), whose wife, Anne Ross Cundell, was another of Irvine's notable hymn writers, this typical Free Church was organised on the presbyterian pattern with a kirk session exercising its disciplinary, pastoral and charitable functions. Under Rev. R.S. Macaulay (1860-1900) the membership of 'the wee kirk on the hill' doubled.

The presbyterian establishment was now split in two; and there were the other elements which had seceded in the previous century. The Relief Church locally had experienced various difficulties. There was the Buchanite schism of 1783; the need to rebuild their church in 1788; and in 1800 quarrels and resignations over the establishment of a Sunday school and the introduction of new psalm tunes by the precentor. Yet before the death of Rev. Peter Robertson (1784-1819) there was such a revival that it was found necessary to enlarge the church building. Rev. Archibald McLaren (1821-41) continued the good work, but a dispute over a successor left wounds for Rev. James Drummond (1844-67) to heal. The other Secession congregation was the Burgher Kirk in Cotton Row. Under its first minister, Rev. Alexander Campbell (1809-43), a hearty and portly man, that church grew 'first outwardly, then upwardly'. It was from him that Irvine Burns Club received the gift of six original manuscript Burns poems which his wife had inherited from a previous husband. The Burghers (of the Associate Synod which in 1820 helped form a United Secession Church) called as their second minister Rev. William Bruce Robertson (1843-86), one of the outstanding figures in Irvine's ecclesiastical history. 'Robertson of Irvine' became widely known as preacher, pastor, hymn writer, man of letters, and in 1869 doctor of divinity. Under his charge, from the plain and homely building on the outskirts of the town, the church moved into a new and imposing edifice on an elevated site beside the bridge in the heart of Irvine. With the name of Trinity Church, it was equally novel in character. Designed by

T.F. Pilkington, it was cruciform in pattern, in Venetian Gothic Style, with variegated colour in the stone, and ornate throughout. The site was gifted by a member of the established church, and there was a procession of magistrates and councillors for the laying of the foundation stone. It opened for worship in 1863. Its 170-foot spire was completed in 1869 when Provost John Paterson and Rev. Dr. Robertson climbed the scaffold to the top and had a 'fine view of Town and Country around'. This original steeple was soon found to be too heavy, and was shortened in 1870. From the beginning Trinity was a United Presbyterian church, for in 1847 the United Secession and Relief denominations had come together nationally to form the United Presbyterian Church. Thus Irvine had two congregations each of the Established, Free, and United Presbyterian churches.

There were also the independent Baptists, whose congregation was served by Rev. George Barclay (1808-38), then his son-in-law Rev. John Leechman. Meeting first in the Bridgegate, by 1801 they moved to West Back Road, then in 1839 built a new church in the Groop. From 1836 there was another short-lived group about whom little is known — perhaps congregationalists or Glassites — the United Gospel Church under Rev. Robert Smith in their Hamilhill chapel at the west end of the Groop. About this time too (1837) there was an Apostolic Church under Rev. R. Cassels Howden, following the heretical doctrines of Rev. Edward Irving — and in some respect these Irvingites resembled the Buchanites of an earlier generation. Another more lasting religious group emerged from the great evangelical revival of 1859. In 1860 James Holmes began holding services in Bower Lodge, originating a group of Christian Brethren who soon moved to Boyd's Hall in High Street. In 1866 the Methodists had a Wesleyan chapel in Bridgegate.

Among the denominations the original bitterness of dissension sometimes continued to rankle, though instances of friendly co-operation were also marked. There were joint services to mark the tercentenary of the Reformation in 1860. Old principles were sometimes modified — in 1834 the town council refused to object to Sunday deliveries by the letter carriers. An old antipathy was revived with the immigration into the West of Scotland of poor Irish of the Roman Catholic faith. Hostility was engendered by those other immigrants from Ulster who brought anti-Catholic fears with them. Roman Catholic emancipation in 1829 and later parliamentary enactments served only to arouse suspicions, and prejudices flared up from time to time. When in 1860 the French schooner *Success* of Nantes was wrecked on Irvine bar, popular opinion forbade Rev. W.B. Robertson's plea that the seven French sailors should be interred according to the rites of their church. By 1864 there was a locally organised group of Orangemen. Since 1822 mass had been said every two months in the Kings Arms by Father William Thomson from Ayr, and after 1845 monthly by Father Thomas Walker from Kilmarnock. Father John McLachlan, who succeeded in 1853, acquired Hamilhill chapel as a place of worship. This seems originally to have been a three-chimneyed salt-store which was sneeringly called 'the lum kirk'. There an organ was installed, whose music startled the Relief congregation at worship just across the way. Father William FitzGerald came in 1862 as Irvine's first parish priest after an interlude of three centuries. He was a twenty-six-year-old curate brought from Dalry, and was responsible also for Kilwinning; although he worked hard and zealously, his mission among 'the poorest of the poor' was a difficult one. Father Osmund Maguire (1868-70), a distinguished Passionist, was more successful, but he was moved after only two years.

With Irvine in the 1860s having no fewer than nine separate places of worship, it is clear that religious division was an important feature of town life. Equally clearly, the energies and moneys devoted to church building and congregational work indicated that religion still meant much to the people of Irvine.

THIRTEEN

Little Progress

The general character of the town changed little throughout the first half of the 19th century. There was no significant alteration in the built-up area of the burgh proper between the time of Wood's Town Map (1819) and the first Ordnance Survey (1857). The confines of the old royal burgh contained around 4,000 inhabitants. Additional numbers were accommodated in the Halfway and Fullarton part of the parliamentary burgh and in the mining villages of the landward part of Irvine parish. The earliest views of Irvine, which date from this period, show a town little affected by recent alterations. The principal streets (for which the council acquired name plates in 1852) were Burns Street, Quarry Lane, Eglinton Street, Seagate, High Street, Townhead, Glasgow Vennel, Kirk Vennel, Kirkgate, Hill Street, Bridgegate, and Bank Street. The biographer of Rev. Dr. W.B. Robertson, writing in 1888, could refer to 'the Dutch quaintness of its principal street ... a strange medley of crowstepped gable ends, thatched cottages, last century mansions with outside stairs, and new buildings for banks and shops and residences of well-to-do burghers ... it wore for the most part the aspect of a sleepy hollow ... at most hours of the day, a cannon ball might have been fired along the High Street without peril to life or limb'. Some years earlier James Dobie of Beith described 'This neat, compact and well conserved ancient burgh ... its entire population would seem to be easy, quiet and satisfied — a very *beau ideal* of aristocratic fixidity'. That some very old dwellinghouses still survived is attested in 1840 by the town council's prohibiting the removal of turf from the Moor for the repair of thatched roofs.

The most important new buildings were the banks. In 1843 Hunter's Bank was incorporated in the Union Bank which in 1858 moved from Bank Street to High Street, building new premises in Venetian style in place of the house where John Galt had been born. The Ayrshire Banking Company was adjacent, incorporated in the Western Bank in 1845, after whose failure in 1857 the Clydesdale Bank took over. Further down High Street, between the Kirkgate and Kirk Vennel, was the Paisley Bank which in 1837 became part of the British Linen Bank. Nearby between Kirkgate and Bridgegate the Royal Bank of Scotland was built in Italianate style in 1858. The bankers occupied an important place in municipal and social life. Alexander Paterson was a partner in Hunter's Bank, he and his son John continued as agents of the Union Bank, and both served on the council. Provost William Gillies was agent of the Ayrshire Banking Company. His successor in the Clydesdale Bank, J.A. Rankine, was another councillor, who moved to the Royal Bank, where he was followed as agent by David Gray, town clerk. At the Paisley Bank 'Banker Bob' Montgomerie (who succeeded his father in 1814) was also Collector of Customs. He was joined, then replaced, in the British Linen Bank by William McJannet and subsequent members of that well-known family. The Savings Bank, founded in 1815, continued to provide for 'industrious mechanics and servants', and had deposits of £1,050 in 1839.

Only the well-to-do could afford to send their children to Irvine Academy, which became a select school. By 1868 there were 160 scholars who paid £460 in fees, nearly £3 on average. The school had accommodation for 500, and around 1820 it had a roll of between 300 and 400, but by mid-century the number was rarely above 200. Perhaps half of these came from outwith the town, and all three masters took in boarders. Special provision for girls was made in 1851, with a 'part of the playground to the south of the Academy exclusively for the use of the misses', and two years later the town council provided there a 'place of convenience for females'. The town council not only paid the salaries of the masters, but accepted responsibility for repairs and improvements. In 1851 it appointed a janitor and provided a house for him, taking over the coal money the scholars previously gave the teachers in addition to their fees. The janitor was required 'to keep a strict surveillance over the pupils ... to prevent quarrelling and all improper language and behaviour ... and to report all offenders'. A special problem arose in 1852 when the rector decided to join the Free Church. He gave up his post as session clerk of the parish church. There was a move to have him removed from the Academy, but it was ruled that the requirement

This print shows the leisurely High Street scene of the early 19th century.

that masters of parochial schools must belong to the established church did not apply here, so he retained his rectorship. In 1853 John Ferguson presented medals, supplementing the annual prizes awarded by the town council. In 1856, £1,000 from the Ferguson Bequest supplied bursaries for pupils going on to university. Almost all that one former pupil, John Paterson, recalled about the academy was the skeleton of Jean Swan who had been hanged in 1760 for the murder of her bastard bairn. On one occasion this relic of the last person executed in Irvine was strung up 'so that if you opened the door unawares, Jean, or all that was left of her, clasped you in her arms'. Another provost, George Brown, remembered various games like shinty, hares and hounds, 'dooking' in the river, and less familiar ones like 'hammer the block' and 'Geordie Bungell'. This last another former pupil, Rev. David Landsborough, described: 'The part of the green in a line with the Academy building was considered the centre; half the boys occupied it, the other half ran across it — those who were caught and touched three times on the head joined those in the centre, and the running went on till all had been caught'. Each year at the end of June were the annual examinations, spread over two days, when the classes were inspected by all the clergymen in the town assisted by ministers from neighbouring parishes, in the presence of the council, directors, parents and friends. At the end of the second day there was a grand procession of teachers and guests to the Eglinton Arms Hotel for a public dinner with toasts and songs.

Although the roll was small — 130 in 1867 compared with Ayr's 375 and Kilmarnock's 227 — Irvine Academy had become specialised. There were only a dozen pupils less than eight years of age, and most were over the age of twelve — 57 boys and 18 girls out of the total of 99 boys and 31 girls. The higher fees from such senior pupils earned a good living for three masters who served over a long period. George Paulin was rector for thirty-three years (1844–77). Rev. George Corsan was English master for nearly thirty (1834–63). John White was commercial and later mathematics master for thirty-two years (1834–66). None of this notable trio was a graduate, though all seem to have been good enough teachers, and White was outstanding enough to be awarded an honorary doctorate. He was the author of several textbooks (as well as slim volumes of verse

134 *The History of Irvine*

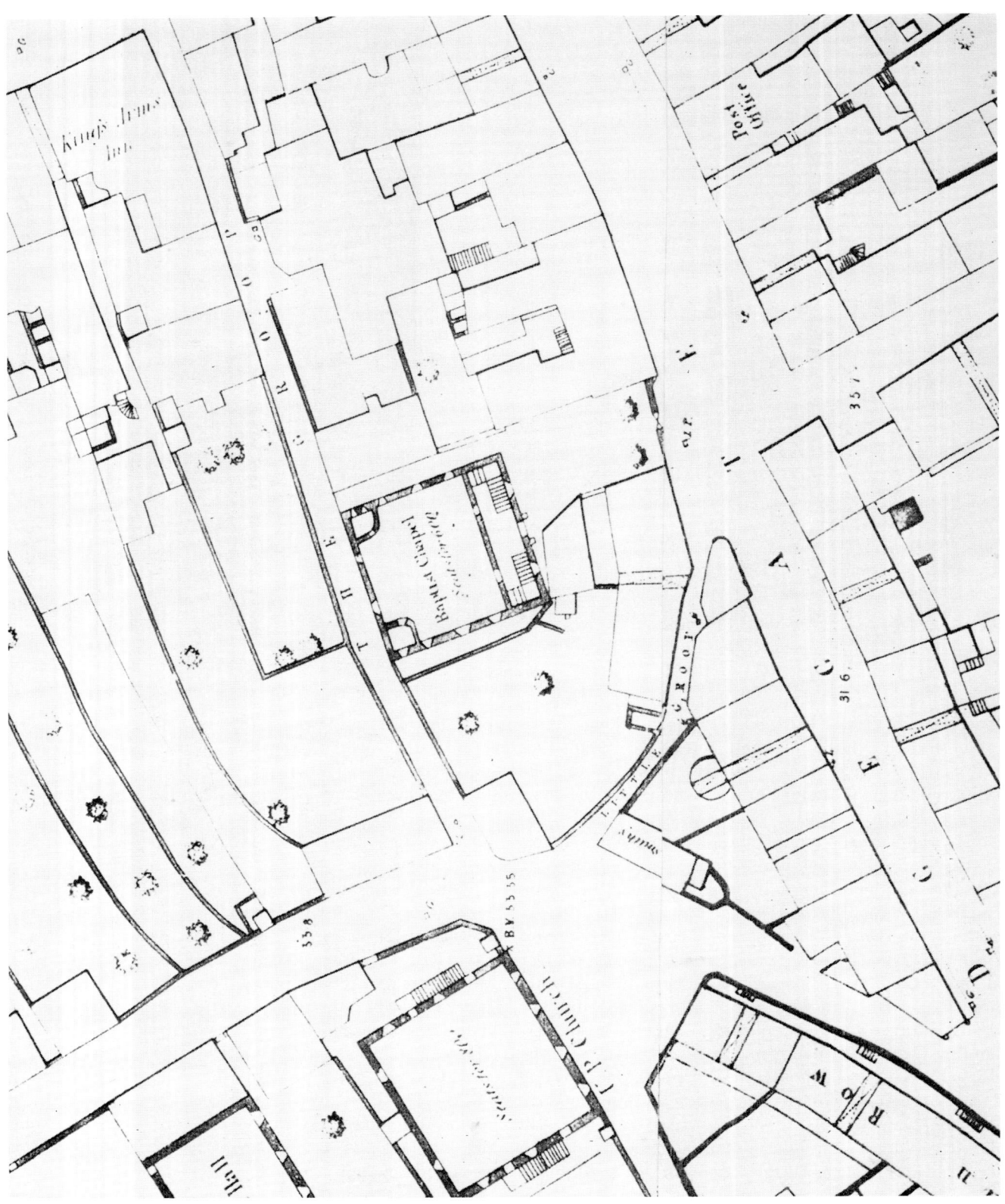

The area around Bridgegate, depicted by the Ordnance Survey in 1859, became increasingly a bottleneck for traffic.

Fullarton Church's first minister, Rev. David Wilson, had an adjoining school built in 1840, operating the 'Madras' system of teaching by monitors.

and essays), and in 1845 was allowed to take over the rector's mathematics classes. These he taught so successfully that he had inscribed on a board a list of former pupils who had distinguished themselves, including thirty-six prizewinners at Glasgow University. Among them was William Jack (1834–1924), a native of Stewarton who was brought up in Irvine, who became Inspector of Schools, then editor of the *Glasgow Herald,* then for thirty years Professor of Mathematics at Glasgow University. Dr. White was an enthusiast for archery, fishing, and music, a Conservative and churchman, fond of snuff and practical jokes. He was also a hard taskmaster who kept the pupils boarding at his home in Bank Street at their studies even on Marymass Saturdays till after noon. In 1855, a typical year, he enrolled 183 pupils in his classes for writing, arithmetic, mathematics, bookkeeping, and drawing. Corsan had 160 learning English composition and grammar, elocution, history and some elementary science. Paulin had only 80, mostly taking geography, some Latin and French, and a few for Greek, German, or Italian.

Because 'the benefits conferred by our High Academy were exclusively confined to the wealthier portion of our townsmen', provision was made by 'working men of Irvine' who erected their own Commercial Academy at Seggans Bank in West Back Road in 1833. The building cost £215, and a teacher was engaged at £60 a year, who taught not only elementary subjects but also Latin for modest fees of 2/- to 2/6 per quarter. The Commercial Academy flourished for some years, with 150 pupils in 1840. But it had to close down in the depression of 1858, leaving Irvine without 'a school where the children of the merchant and artisan class can receive a cheap and efficient education'. The children of the indigent poor were better catered for. There was the Free School which had been started in 1814, with the ministers of the three local denominations participating. Its original 80 pupils increased to 120 by 1840. This school began in a barn at the north end of East Back Road, then obtained one of the two rooms of the old Kirkgatehead school. Better accommodation was acquired after 1844 in Hamilhill chapel, but in 1858 they had to move back to Kirkgatehead. Another Free School was formed in 1839 when William Lyle, a spirit dealer in Halfway, left money for that purpose. A private school — in Fullarton Street — actually in the old townhouse of Fullarton burgh — run by Ebenezer Clark, a former Academy assistant, was taken over, and

Loudoun Street School was opened after the formation in 1843 of Fullarton Free Church, with which Rev. David Wilson was now associated.

this Lyle's Free School became well-established, taking another 120 children. In 1844 the Countess of Eglinton endowed a school to provide instruction for 80 girls in reading, sewing, and knitting, at the modest charge of 2d per week. The council made available the room weavers had occupied in the old school building at Kirkgatehead for Lady Eglinton's school.

Some of the churches made their own provision. For a time the Burgher Kirk had its own school in East Back Road. In 1840 there was a school associated with the Hamilhill chapel, taking the name of Hamilhill Academy. In that year Fullarton Church opened a school for 150 pupils, taught according to the Madras or monitorial system as invented by Dr. Andrew Bell. After the Disruption of 1843 Fullarton Free congregation set up its own school in Loudoun Street to 'serve the community and become a seat of learning to the inhabitants'. In 1869 Father Osmond Maguire opened a school for fifty Catholic children, but it did not last long. There were several smaller 'private educational establishments' together taking some 100 pupils in 1840. Government grants to assist the erection of elementary schools became available after 1833,

and further local aid could be obtained from the Ferguson Bequest of 1856. Thus augmented, a public subscription converted the original Free School into Irvine Public and Industrial School. New premises were erected in 1857 on a site donated by the council in East Back Road behind the old Fleshmarket. The fees were originally 1d per week, where necessary paid for by the parochial board. Examination by an H.M. Inspector in 1862 found the children ragged, dull, and inanimate and the teaching unsatisfactory. But in 1865 Alexander Lumsden was appointed master, and with a female assistant he enrolled 230 children, with an average attendance of 185, making it the largest of the six public schools in the town.

Recreation was still mainly a prerogative of the prosperous middle class, but there are obvious signs of others enjoying new facilities. The Society of Archers had their butts beside the Academy (till 1852), and under the name of the Irvine Toxophilic Society they competed annually in their Robin Hood uniforms for awards presented by the earl of Eglinton. Cricket was being played at the Golffields in 1835 — to the annoyance of those who patronised the Washing House. In 1855 an Irvine Eglinton

The Public and Industrial School, erected in East Road in 1857, survives as a community centre.

Cricket Club was formed, and also an Irvine Trades Club and a Junior Club. Games were played on the Moor till 1866, when coal workings and mineral sidings interfered with the cricket pitch which was in the middle of the Cadgers Race Course. They then moved nearer Townend. The craze for cricket was at its peak in 1862 when there were four local clubs. Some local ladies were playing croquet (1864) while, not to be outdone, the Irvine miners in 1864 challenged those from Annick Lodge to a 'rounders' contest. Another example of working-class participation in sport was a national quoiting contest held in Irvine in 1861. In the 1850s there was already a bowling green between High Street and East Back Road (where the large car park is now). It 1853 it got new turf from Bogside Flats, which also supplied several other clubs in the Glasgow area. In 1866 it was superseded by the new and better nearby Winton Bowling Green, with a fine club house and a curling pond behind. There was curling on various ponds, like the Auld Water Gang, though in 1845 the council turned down a request to form one on the Green. In the severe winter of 1867 there were contests between the Burgh Curling Club and the Stanecastle Club, and skating was also popular. In summer there was sea bathing. In 1845 a local coach hirer ran a 'buss' to the beach with fares of 6d per person or 1/6 for a family. The Moor was described in 1856 as a 'healthful recreation ground'. Public seats were provided at the Golffields (1865) and at the Green (1866). Immediately after erection they were 'marred and blotched by the knives of some thoughtless youngsters'. In 1866 Maxwell Dick put forward in council an imaginative proposal to dam the river and form 'an ornamental sheet of water'. Less expensive amenities were provided with zinc drinking cups at all the public wells (1857).

For social occasions there were (in 1857) eight substantial inns in High Street plus the Albert Hall in West Back Road. William Walker from Fullarton Street made a living as a musician and for many years held dancing classes (1820, 1849). The Incorporated Trades had their annual functions in the Eglinton Arms. In this period, under Deacon Convener Walker McLachlan (1843–45), the Trades were resuscitated as benefit societies and acquired insignia, and the coopers and tailors revived. The Carters also extended their conviviality and later in the century were contributing sixpence each to provide widows at New Year with a bottle of whisky and a currant bun. The freemasons of Lodge Irvine St. Andrew's commemorated their patron saint by a dinner each November, followed by a torchlight procession. In 1862 they acquired their own Masonic Hall in Kirkgate. Irvine Burns Club celebrated the centenary of the Poet's birth in 1859 by organisaing a dinner in their

The magnificent Eglinton Castle, built for Hugh, 12th earl of Eglinton, who succeeded in 1798.

favourite venue, the Kings Arms, a supper in Albert Hall, and a ball 'in the Royal Academy'. There was also a procession of carters, trades, and freemasons which visited Glasgow Vennel, the birthplaces of Montgomery and Galt, and Seagate Castle, halting at each place to sing 'Auld Lang Syne'. In the same year, seventy-five gentlemen enrolled in the newly constituted Irvine Company of the Ayrshire Rifle Volunteers, while another sixty formed a coastal battery of the Ayrshire Artillery Volunteers. They proudly paraded at the local celebrations for the marriage of the Prince of Wales in 1863. Later that year they mustered when intimation was received of an official visit to Irvine of the Channel Fleet — which turned out to be a hoax. Because of the Volunteers, rifle shooting superseded archery, and the local club from 1864 hosted the West of Scotland Rifle Association annual contests at Irvine. The Rifle Volunteers also organised their own brass band, which had to be dissolved after a political row in 1865 when they turned out to welcome the newly re-elected Liberal M.P.

The *Ardrossan and Saltcoats Herald* (which reported the various local functions) complained in 1858 that 'so low has the desire for intellectual entertainment fallen in Irvine, that no lecturer, however great his name, or fame, can command a house'. The Albert Hall provided popular programmes like Sam Cowell, comedian (1858), a demonstration of Mesmerism (1863), and Mr. Butterworth's company of Christy's Minstrels (1867), and there was a visit to the town of Sanger's Circus and Menagerie (1862). On the other hand, there were (in 1837) a Newsroom, a Subscription Library, Maxwell Dick's Circulating Library, and a Coffee Room. The Athenaeum was formed in 1850 to provide a reading room. There was the Montgomery Young Men's Literary Association (1858). There were proposals (1862) to hold 'evening classes for the working people', and a series of lectures 'for working men' was arranged in the Baptist Chapel (1863). In 1867 the solicitor William McJannet founded the Irvine and Fullarton Literary Institute. There was a Choral Union, and there were musical performances at the soirées which the various churches organised both for adults and children. In 1857 Rev. W.B. Robertson organised a Sabbath School outing for nearly two hundred children conveyed by carriage to a Dreghorn farm. By 1860 there were annual Hogmanay treats for the Free School children who were each given an orange, a bun, and a book. Other events illustrate the changing social life. Irvine

Horticultural and Agricultural Society held its first Flower Show on Thursday 9th July 1857. In 1864 the drapers decided to close earlier, at 7 p.m. on weekdays and 9 p.m. on Saturdays; in 1866 a general Merchants Holiday for shopkeepers was arranged for the first time. Around this time photography came to Irvine. There is mention of a visiting professional photographer in 1860. Then there arrived a nephew of Jean Armour, Robert Burns Brown, who lived in Springfield and set up an artist's studio in Bank Street. His son Hugh, precentor of Fullarton Free Church, became a photographer.

New Year and Marymass were the two popular festivals. At the former in 1863 it was reported that 'Throughout the night shoutings were frequently heard from those who had been attending the several weddings of which Hogmanay is so prolific ... a few cases of drunkenness, chiefly among the young'. Two years later there were no fewer than nineteen Hogmanay weddings. Marymass now began on an August Wednesday with a feeing fair, but by 1864 it was noted that few now turned up in the Bridgegate to seek harvest work, where formerly there had been crowds of Highlanders, and latterly Irish. For the rest of the week High Street from Bridgegatehead to Porthead was thronged with stalls — 'Nutshooters, Bagatelles, Wheels of Fortune, Auctioneers, Flyboats, Merry-go-rounds, etc., etc., with a whole host of dealers in hard and soft goods'. On Thursday the carters chose their captain for the year. On Saturday crowds arrived in Irvine by road and rail, estimated (1859) from ten to twelve thousand 'chiefly comprised of the working class'. At noon the carters conveyed the councillors to the Moor for the horse races. These they watched from the knowe called 'Salmon's Hill' (after William Salmon, saddler and provost 1841–45), later as 'the Magisterial Bench' (1863), and eventually as 'Magistrates Hill'. Round about were (1865) seventeen tents selling liquor, six selling pies, and twenty selling tarts and biscuits, plus fruit barrows and shooting galleries. After the races the procession returned to the council chambers for the singing of the National Anthem. In 1864 the participants were reported for the first time calling at Seagate Castle to sing 'Auld Lang Syne' — as they had done five years before on the occasion of the Burns Centenary. They left behind on the Moor what the *Glasgow Herald* in 1867 described as 'scenes of drunkenness and dissipation that have disgraced the town'. Marymass had long since lost all its religious associations; it had apparently not yet become associated with Mary Queen of Scots. A tradition was concocted around this time of a 'Lady Mary of Eglinton' supposedly kidnapped by a Viking knight, whose head she cut off, and with the aid of a cabin boy brought the ship safe home to Irvine. And there was even reference to a fictitious 'St Merri'.

The celebrated Eglinton Tournament of 1839 was organised by Archibald William, 13th earl.

Irvine was still a place to which the county gentry sometimes resorted. After the magnificent new Eglinton Castle was completed in 1802, the masquerades and balls hosted by the ageing 12th earl Hugh were complemented by the Bogside Races which he initiated in 1808. His grandson Archibald William succeeded as 13th earl in 1819 aged only seven, and the races lapsed between 1824 and 1838. Then the course was extended, steeplechasing was introduced into Scotland, and the following year the earl organised the grandiose Eglinton Tournament. Archibald William in 1840 succeeded to another earldom and as Earl of Eglinton and Winton ran winning horses in the St Leger (1842, 1847, 1849) and the Derby (1849). In 1852 he was appointed Lord Lieutenant of Ireland, and in his absence Bogside Races again lapsed. He died in 1861 after a golf match at St Andrews. Archibald William, 14th earl, a young man of twenty, revived Eglinton's social life. A keen foxhunter, he founded the Eglinton Hunt in 1861. In 1867 Bogside Races were again revived and the Scottish Grand National Steeplechase was instituted. In 1885 flat racing under Jockey Club rules was added, and by the time of the 14th earl's death in 1892 there were meetings at Bogside in April, July, August, and September.

The climax of Eglinton's glory was of course the famous Tournament which the 13th earl planned for three days in August 1839. This marvellous piece of pageantry, which is said to have cost him £40,000, brought to Irvine the cream of polite society. In the Castle grounds were erected pavilions, grandstands and canopies. In medieval splendour, Tudor-costumed figures assembled to watch the jousting of armoured contestants. At the opening ceremony on Wednesday 25th, Lady Jane Seymour as Queen of Beauty was led to her throne by a bodyguard of fifty Irvine archers. This was inauspiciously heralded by a

The railway station, opened in 1839 and improved in 1874.

torrent of rain, the tilting which followed was accompanied by further deluges, and the banqueting pavilion was flooded. On the second day outdoor activities had to be abandoned. On the third day the sun shone on the final jousts and a mêlée, and the earl as Lord of the Tournament concluded the events with a banquet and ball. James Paterson, the county's historian who attended, described the occasion as 'one of the most gorgeous spectacles ever witnessed', and to commemorate the event the earl was later presented with the massive and magnificent silver Eglinton Trophy, now displayed in Cunninghame House, Irvine. Paterson recalled that 'the demand for accommodation in Irvine, Kilwinning, Ardrossan, and Ayr, predicated the vast concourse of people'. In the Parterre, High Street, lodgings were found for Prince Louis Napoleon (later Emperor Napoleon III of France). At Irvine, Paterson 'found the streets crowded with people, pouring in from all quarters, while the array of vehicles of every description had never before been witnessed in the burgh'. People came by coach, carriage, and steamboat from Glasow. From Ayr, crowds came by railway, for the line to Irvine had timeously been opened just a fortnight before. It was indeed symbolic that this nostalgic re-creation of a vanished feudal past should be marked by the arrival of the steam train, that trademark of 19th-century industrial progress.

The coming of the railway had been prefaced by an abortive experiment with a steam locomotive in 1816 on the Duke of Portland's line from Kilmarnock to Troon. In 1828 the 13th earl of Eglinton sought to supplement his grandfather's uncompleted Ardrossan-Glasgow canal with a railway, which was opened in 1831 between Ardrossan and Kilwinning, with an extension to Doura and Fergushill. Growing interest is evidenced by Maxwell Dick's experiments with a suspension railway at Gailes in 1829. A company was formed in 1836 with a scheme, never implemented, for a line from Quarry Lane in Irvine to join the Ardrossan railway at Nethermains. There was support for the Glasgow, Paisley, Kilmarnock and Ayr railway company, which was authorised in 1837 and commenced construction of the Glasgow-Ayr line. This would provide Irvine with a railway station in Fullarton by the Halfway. Irvine town council was involved in the sale of a portion of Marressfoot; authorising bridges over Halfway and the new street beside Fullarton Church; and enrolling extra constables to deal with the construction workers who created disturbances in the town on Saturday evenings and Sundays. Treasurer Thomas Campbell obtained a contract for the bridge over the river at Bogside which (to commemorate Victoria's coronation) was named Queen's Bridge, but became more popularly known as Campbell's Bridge. The line was opened from Ayr to Irvine on 5th August 1839, and all the way to Glasgow a year later on 12th August 1840. It was several years before a branch was laid to Irvine harbour (1847) where a new wharf was built. And it was only after a threat of competition from the rival

Caledonian Railway Company that the line from Kilmarnock to Irvine was completed (1848). By this time the other main line had been pushed from Dalry to Kilmarnock (1843) and south by Dumfries to Carlisle (1850). Irvine was now part of the network of the Glasgow and South Western Railway Company which was incorporated in 1847. As an incidental consequence, in 1848 Irvine town clock had to be put forward $17\frac{1}{2}$ minutes to correspond with Greenwich (and railway) time; and from 1853 the electric telegraph at the station brought Irvine into close communication with the outside world.

Yet the initial impact of the railway was limited. To begin with, passenger services were few. In 1850 there were only four trains daily from Irvine to Ayr, four to Glasgow, and two to Kilmarnock. Nor did Irvine obtain a full share of the mineral traffic which formed the main element of the railway business. Coal from the mines north of the town went to Ardrossan, and after 1846 also to Eglinton Iron Works at Kilwinning. These works were supplied by Doura, Fergushill, Perceton (to which the railway was extended in 1848), Bartonholm, and Redburn. The coal from up the valley went mostly to Troon. The branch line to Irvine from Kilmarnock, opened in 1848, did not connect directly with that to the harbour. In 1854 Patrick Mure Macreadie had to lay a tramway from his Perceton pits past Newmoor down to Townhead. Where elsewhere the arrival of the railway was followed by a quickening of industrial growth, for Irvine initially it merely provided improved transport facilities — for Eglinton Tournament and for the traditional commerce.

Cotton continued as the principal manufacture. The New Statistical Account of 1840 listed 400 handloom weavers making from 5/- to 14/- weekly, 200 females earning 3/- a week as winders, and as many as 2,000 doing ornamental needlework, stitching from seven in the morning till near midnight for less than 1/4 a day. The uncertainties of the trade brought periodic depressions, the necessity for relief measures as noted in the last chapter, emigration (for which aid was sought in 1843), and eventual collapse following the American Civil War (1861-65). The New Statistical Account mentioned no other local industry, for indeed there was little else of consequence.

At the harbour the shipbuilding yard was operated by a sequence of unsuccessful owners — Charles Samson who built tea clippers; Peter Murchie; Calderwood and Co. from Ardrossan; a cooperative company of local businessmen; Clark Marr and Co; Ebenezer Ballantyne. Adjoining the harbour three separate firms had sawmills. Nearby was the small smith and machine works which Duncan McDougall had established to make (after 1827) ships' chains and cables. The Sluices behind the quay had

In 1861 the old Tolbooth was demolished, to be superseded by the Town House, opened in 1862.

been drained (1839-42) by the council in association with Lord Justice Boyle. In this area there were limeworks. Beside the railway station were the railway works. And three other businesses were established, presumably after the opening of the harbour branch of the railway in 1847. There (as recorded in 1867) were the Irvine Foundry of John Stewart and Sons; the Fullarton engineering and machine works of Dick, Dean and Co; and the Western Iron Works where Joseph Twibill made steam boilers. In Fullarton Street where there had been a ropework, then a distillery, a Mr. McClintock from Glasgow established a naphtha works in 1852. Elsewhere a new Ropeway was operating behind the junction of East Back Road and Bank Street adjoining the Meadow Bleachfield. The only other manufactory was David Gray's Brewery beside the Green. And there was Duntonknoll Quarry, continuing to supply good building stone and 'very superior oven soles', but William Balsillie gave up the lease in 1867. After an interval it was re-opened and continued the production of the 'famed oven soles' into the 20th century.

In 1850 the council was willing to sell sand from the Moor to the Glengarnock Iron Company. But when in 1853 Robert McGavin, a local man now based in Glasgow, proposed establishing an ironworks beside the river and adjoining the railway, some councillors thought it would be a 'nuisance', there was a petition against it, and the scheme fell through. Significantly, almost all that can be discovered about various industrial establishments is from complaints made in council meetings. On several occasions the council discussed the Fullarton Chemical Works, 'the effluvia from which caused an intolerable nuisance'. It seems clear that councillors and the small electorate they represented were many of them antagonistic to industrial developments which might spoil the traditional character of their town.

A reporter of the *Ardrossan and Saltcoats Herald* concluded (in 1858) that 'Irvine is fast retrogressing'. How Irvine was falling behind was obvious at the harbour. By 1840 timber was being imported from America and grain from Ireland, but exports were restricted to coal. A new wharf to serve the new railway branch of 1847 was the only major development. Significantly, Troon, which had ranked as a creek of Irvine, was in 1863 constituted as the head port, and Irvine reduced to subsidiary status. Irvine, however, was retained as an important lifeboat station. A lifeboat of sorts had been acquired in 1833, replaced in 1861 by the thirty-foot self-righting *Miss Pringle Kidd* named after the donor — one of the RNLI's nine boats on the Scottish coast.

Troon was now exporting 140,000 tons of coal annually, Ardrossan 60,000 tons, Ayr 60,000 tons, and Irvine only 44,000 tons. Irvine harbour was ill-equipped to handle more than it did; the railway could not supply it so well; and in an era when coal was being exploited with increased intensity, the area around Irvine had limited production. In 1842 John Macredie set up a colliery village at Perceton. The collapse of an old shaft at Newmoor (1851) perhaps reminded the council of its possible resources. In 1854 it made unsuccessful bores at Knadgerhill and Irvine Mains; the following year at Ravenscroft and Golffields; and later searches near Bartonholm and Bogside (1859) and Kidsneuk (1863). Offers to lease the coal of the town lands were not taken up until 1866. Meanwhile the workings of Colonel Fullarton had been flooded in 1833, the mining villages of Bartonholm, Longford, Snodgrass, and Nethermains laid under water, and the mines closed for twenty years until they were purchased and drained by the 13th earl of Eglinton. Working conditions around this time can be deduced from a report on Shewalton colliery (1842) where Samson and Co. were extracting coal from seams of 2 feet 4 inches to 2 feet 10 inches at a depth of 11 to 36 fathoms. No females were employed; there were 80 adults plus 17 boys between the ages of 13 and 18, and 12 younger children. Some of them, aged seven and eight, were trappers. Other boys from the age of nine were drawers, pulling four hundredweight bogeys three hundred yards. The New Statistical Account for the same period (Parish of Dundonald, 1841), referring to the miners, speaks of 'much destitution, both temporal and spiritual', which it attributed to 'the proverbial thoughtlessness of this clan of labourers'.

Hints of a new beginning for Irvine can be detected in the 1860s. The erection of a new Town House in 1862 signalled a new spirit in the council which would find further fulfilment after the 1867 Reform Act.

The ancient tolbooth, which had been found wanting as a prison by the County Board in 1840, was becoming so dilapidated by 1856 that the council decided to replace it. Provost Campbell argued for the repair of the old fabric, but because he was 'somewhat overbearing ... he encountered much opposition' and the scheme went ahead against his wishes. A site near Bank Street was considered, but eventually the old Fleshmarket was chosen just behind the old tolbooth. Plans of James Ingram, a Kilmarnock architect, were chosen, for a large and handsome Italianate edifice to cost £4,000. In 1860 the foundation stone was laid by Bailie John Niven — the provost would have nothing to do with the project and stayed away, so there was no entertainment after the ceremony. The new Town House, which was opened in May 1862, had a handsome clock tower and belfry, terminating in an octagonal steeple, later to be surmounted by the old vane in the shape of a sloop taken from the old tolbooth — in all 120 feet high. Within the new Town House the arms from the old tolbooth were preserved. It was further embellished with busts of James Montgomery and John Ferguson, and portraits of Bailie Fullarton, John Ferguson, the earl of Eglinton, and (after his death in 1864) Provost Thomas Campbell. The Town House provided a meeting place not only for the council and burgh court, but for the JP Court, Road Trustees, and the Presbytery. Accommodation was provided for the Collector of Customs and for Irvine Reading Room. The Hall was made available for the horticultural show, the dancing academy, the Choral Union, and various concerts and balls. No longer was there a need for prison cells, for the new Police Station of 1860 was available to the rear.

The old tolbooth was demolished in 1861 and the stones used for the repair of the river bank. The High Street was enhanced by the installation of an ornamental pump at the Cross Well in 1862. In 1866 the Tron was removed, as 'an obstruction to the street and of little farther use to the public'. It had become 'used chiefly as a seat for miners'. And in 1867 a statue of Lord Justice Boyle, sculpted by John Steelle, was unveiled by Rev. Dr. W.B. Robertson outside Boyle's Parterre, his birthplace.

Irvine's population had grown throughout the first half of the 19th century, doubling from 3,500 to 7,500. But it was far less than the fourfold expansion of Ayr (4,000 to 17,600) and Kilmarnock (6,000 to 21,400). Furthermore, while these two thriving towns successfully coped with the collapse of the cotton trade and continued their increase, Irvine suffered an actual decline in population in the '50s and '60s. By 1871 Kilmarnock (23,700) and Ayr (18,000) had left Irvine (6,900) far behind. Whether the reasons included geographical accident or lack of local initiative, the result was that Irvine was now a poor third in the league of Ayrshire burghs. From this more modest base began a new phase of expansion in the last decades of the 19th century.

FOURTEEN

A New Beginning

A new era in political development began in 1867. The Reform Act of that year extended the franchise to all ratepaying householders plus some lodgers. For Irvine this meant that the number eligible to vote in municipal elections increased from fewer than 200 to more than 500, and in the parliamentary burgh (which included Fullarton) from 271 to 611. The introduction of the secret ballot in 1872 eliminated the possibility of intimidation by employers and (more particularly in the country areas) by landlords. The municipal burgh was extended in 1881 to include all of the parliamentary burgh, and after the 1884 Reform Act there were 1,232 electors.

A mass electorate was for the first time involved in politics. Nationally the Liberals were triumphant during the ministries of Gladstone (1868-74; 1880-85; 1886; 1892-94) and Lord Rosebery (1894-95). In the Ayr Burghs constituency the Liberal ascendancy which had lasted since 1832 was broken in 1874. After twenty one years as MP, E.H.J. Crawford was defeated by Sir William Cunninghame, 'a Tory of the Tories' as the *Ayr Advertiser* described him — though by only fourteen votes. In 1880 the seat was easily recovered for the Liberals by R.F.F. Campbell. But with the secession from the Liberal Party of the Liberal-Unionist opponents of Irish Home Rule, then of working-class supporters who turned to Keir Hardie's new Independent Labour Party, the seat became a marginal one. It was retained by the Liberals under Rev. J. Sinclair in a by-election in 1888; won by the Conservative J. Somerville in another in 1890; recovered for the Liberals (with a majority of seven) by W. Birkmyre (1892-95); then held for the Conservatives by C.L. Orr Ewing in 1895 and 1900.

How party politics divided Irvine can be seen in 1868 when 296 local voters helped re-elect the Liberal candidate, but nearly as many — 211 — preferred his Conservative opponent. After the secret ballot in 1872 it was no longer possible to calculate the exact local votes, but in 1880 there was an estimated Liberal majority of 150 among Irvine voters. The issues were never purely political. In 1874 the Liberals were accused of trying 'to exclude religion from the schools', and the Conservative victory was greeted in Irvine when 'the orangemen at once got out their flags, and two enthusiastic Tories went post haste to the Iron Works for their band'. In municipal elections the two political parties were not officially involved. In 1880 the Irvine Conservative Association decided it was 'not within the province of the association to take part in municipal affairs'. Sometimes, of course, there intruded what the *Irvine Herald* called 'questions of Imperial concern'. But local issues and personalities usually counted more than parliamentary programmes. In 1873 there were fourteen candidates for seven seats. Liberals came first and seventh, with the Conservatives winning the other five places. The council was not clearly divided on party lines. Provost John Paterson, a prominent Conservative, was one of the pioneers of municipal progress who in his term of office (1872-78) sponsored the waterworks and other notable schemes of improvement. In the 1874 general election, while he wore the blue rosette, Bailies Orr and Wyllie sported the red rosette of the Liberals, and Bailie Goudie did not actively participate. Election meetings could be lively occasions, with Jamie Sloan actively participating in the heckling. Sloan, born in Kilmarnock about 1850, had apparently studied law and literature but turned into a drunken ne'er-do-well and a noted 'character', known as 'the Irvine orator'.

Irvine was deeply affected by a series of parliamentary enactments, reforms initiated both by Liberal and Conservative governments. The Public Health Act of 1867 extended the powers of burghs and parochial boards. The Roads and Bridges Act of 1878 abolished road tolls. The Local Government Act of 1889 created county councils, while that of 1894 converted parochial boards into parish councils. A general oversight of what was now being called local government passed to the Scottish Office which, with the post of Secretary of State, was created in 1885.

Irvine Town Council in 1867 was still not adapted to operate effectively as an agent of social improvement. It remained a kind of medieval corporation, whose range of interests is reflected in its nine committees — auditing of

Marymass became increasingly a social occasion, with shows in the High Street until 1920.

accounts; town house; agricultural; law; streets, wells, and lighting; churchyard; mill; coal; parish roads. But significant local alterations were made in 1870, 1874 and 1881 which transformed the administration of the burgh.

The first decisive step was taken in 1870 when the magistrates and councillors formallly constituted themselves as a Local Authority. They undertook to exercise, in place of the parochial board, responsibilities under the Nuisance Removal Act of 1856 and the Public Health Act of 1867. Four years later, extended powers were acquired when the council adopted by 14 votes to 2 the General Police and Improvement Act of 1862 — the Lindsay Act which their predecessors had been unwilling by 9 votes to 7 to take advantage of in 1863. Thereby the councillors became from 1874 also Police Commissioners. As such they had no responsibilities for the constabulary — as might now be imagined — but they were empowered to implement certain policies of improvement. The so-called police commissioners were in fact political commissioners. This rather complicated system of three separate bodies — Town Council, Local Authority, and Police Commissioners, each with the same membership and overlapping responsibilities was operated with the so-called Local Authority dealing especially with water, drainage, nuisances, and public health in general and the Police Commissioners concerning themselves with streets, lighting, and associated matters. Their powers covered the municipal burgh — that is, the royal burgh east of the river, but taken to comprehend also those areas across the water which the burgh owned and supervised. Electors in the Halfway and Fullarton part of the parliamentary burgh sought unsuccessfully in 1865 to become included, but had to remain under the care of Dundonald parochial board until amalgamation received parliamentary approval in the 1881 Irvine Burgh Act, whereby the municipal burgh was extended to the parliamentary boundaries and divided into six wards for electoral purposes. Eighteen councillors would continue to represent this extended burgh, with four bailies now. All seats were rendered vacant at the 1881 municipal election. Only seven of the old councillors stood for re-election. Four were successful, to be joined by no fewer than fourteen new members. This reconstituted council continued to manage the affairs of the old royal burgh, and operate as Local Authority and Police Commissioners. Further powers for making improvements were conferred by the 1881 Act and another Irvine Burgh Improvement Act of 1895.

The changing system of local government required professionalism in its administration. From the beginning of the burgh the duties of town clerk had been undertaken by a local notary or lawyer. The post of fiscal, originally allocated to one of the councillors, from the 18th century

John Paterson, a distinguished provost responsible for various innovations and improvements. Interesting facts about old Irvine are to be found in Provost Paterson's notebook, which has survived.

required also someone with legal training, by the 19th century known as procurator fiscal. Similarly the post of burgh factor, created in the 18th century, was a job (and possibly a lucrative one) for a councillor. In 1860 a banker, William McJannet, was appointed; followed in 1883 by his son A.C. McJannet, who in 1886 acquired the new title of Burgh Chamberlain and continued in office till his death in 1922. The newly constituted Local Authority was required to appoint a Medical Officer. For the entire period when this post was occupied by local doctors there was Dr. William Wilson (1876-1916), then his son Dr. James Wilson (1916-50). The parochial board's inspector of poor was made Sanitary Inspector. When a Superintendent of the Water Works was later appointed, he became also Sanitary Inspector, and in due course Burgh Surveyor as well, all jobs requiring technical skills. Annually at the formal meeting of the council following the municipal election, such appointments were recorded. This was shown to be a formality after 1872 when it was confirmed that such were in fact permanent appointments for life. In that year there was a furious row when the business of the council was 'in a manner at a standstill'. The town clerk, David Gray, had decided to appoint James Dickie as his deputy. The council argued that he could not do so without their previous approval, and threatened to replace him. But the law ruled that the council was not entitled to dismiss a town clerk provided he was performing his professional duties in an efficient manner, and thus security of tenure for burgh officials was implicitly recognised. When David Gray retired in 1876, his deputy James Dickie took over, and another long period of tenure followed.

Some older appointments had become obsolete, like birleymen and foresters, while stentmasters disappeared after the Valuation Act of 1854. Although the County Constabulary now policed Irvine, part-time constables under the burgh's own chief constable survived until 1868. The appointment of councillors and others as visitors of the flesh stalls and the bread market ceased also in 1868. There were still weekly grain markets, but like the fairs they were of dwindling commercial significance. The Cow Fair was moved from High Street to the Low Green in 1872 and by 1890 was defunct. The Horse Fair at Townend similarly decayed. And Marymass had become increasingly a social occasion.

Business of the town council proper was centred on the Common Good. Income in 1871 was £2,829, expenditure £2,324; borrowing amounted to £21,000, but assets were valued at £59,000. These were the royal burgh's lands and properties, which required administration. Hence such varied items as dealing with rabbits at Duntonknoll (1876) and rats there too (1892); damage to the Low Green by Sangers Circus (1880); the introduction of wire fencing at Newmoor (1868); maintenance of the Marress ford (1877); protection of mussels in the Garnock against depredations by Ayr fishermen (1869, 1887, 1891); purchase of Dalrymplewards (1874) and Harperland (1874); granting use of the Moor for annual camps of the Royal Renfrew Militia (from 1875), the 4th Battalion of the Argyll and Sutherland Highlanders (after 1881), and other units; trying to dislodge pigeons from the Town House roof (1874), replacing the cracked bell (1889), and installing as a weather vane the sloop which had adorned the old tolbooth (1896); discontinuing the use of the Powder House (1880); administering the Hugh Watt bursaries for able and deserving students (from 1873); a new bequest for the aged from Robert Holmes of Barloch (1886); and another from John Spiers for the deserving poor (1899). As a principal heritor of the parish, the council had to help with repairs of the parish church and was involved in extensions of the churchyard in 1858 and 1885 — Dundonald parochial board provided a separate burying ground off Ayr Road for those in Fullarton. Irvine council still elected annually a burgh representative to attend the General Assembly. The procession to the parish church for worship continued. In 1872 this 'ancient custom' was regarded as 'almost obsolete', nevertheless it survived. In 1880 the council decided to attend on the first Sabbath of each quarter instead of monthly 'as before'. On the first Sabbath of that year they went to the Free Church of which Provost Watt was a member.

The council continued its annual subscriptions to provide coals for the poor. Work was provided for the unemployed (1875, 1877, 1879, 1885) and for those suffering from the miners' strike of 1894. Support was given to soup kitchens supplied by the earl and countess of Eglinton. Aid was offered toward those wounded in the Franco-Prussian War (1870) and victims of famine in India (1874, 1879). When the South African War broke out, eight volunteers were sent off with gifts (1900). The new town bell was pealed for the relief of Ladysmith and Mafeking, and when Pretoria was captured Irvine 'gave itself up to a wild delirium of joy'. Free use of the town hall was granted to various congregations whose churches were being repaired, to the UP Presbytery for meetings (1875) and for the Glasgow-Irvine dinner (1878). There were donations to the Rifle Association, the Irvine Farmers Society for their Cattle Shows (from 1873), the Literary and Social Institute for the purchase of books, a Regatta Club (from 1874), the Ornithological Society for its first annual show (1884), towards Bogside Races, to Eglinton Hunt (till 1874), and Marymass.

For a number of years from 1866 the grant to the committee of the Carters Society was fiercely argued, because of the practice of letting tents on the Moor for the sale of liquor on Marymass Saturday. In 1869 the council banned this sale, and for a number of years 'the Tent Question' became a major issue in municipal politics. By 1877 the prohibitionists on the council were strong enough entirely to ban the tents, but two of the magistrates granted a special licence. At the subsequent election in November four of the six retiring councillors failed to win re-election, and the poll was topped by ex-Provost George Brown who re-entered local politics to enforce the ban. The customary celebration for councillors and friends was held after this election, but when the Kings Arms submitted the bill, the council by nine votes to five ordered that payment should be made personally by those councillors who had been present. From 1878 and for the next forty-two years the usual £20 was granted for the Marymass races, but on condition that no liquor be on sale; and entertainment by the council afterwards was given up. The custom of publicans bringing out drinks to the passing parade possibly originated at this time, to sustain those proceeding towards the Moor where no liquor was available. The

A much-needed piped water supply was provided in 1878, thanks to Provost John Paterson. An old street well can still be seen at Sandy Potts in Kirk Vennel.

Irvine Herald noted how the character of Marymass was changing. On the Wednesday there was still a market with over two hundred horses (in 1874). But the booths offering goods for sale had been almost superseded by the travelling shows. At the races, the ribbons of red, blue and green once awarded by the council as prizes were now worn by the carters as decorations. And despite the prohibition it could be said (1881), 'there is always plenty of liquor going at the races on the present teetotal principle'. Alas for George Brown's attempt to reform the Marymass Fair which had, as he lamented, 'a Popish beginning and a worse ending'.

The tradition of granting the freedom of the burgh was continued. There was an award to Alexander Macmillan, the London publisher (1870); William Somerville from Gloucestershire whose father-in-law came from Irvine, and who gifted a new lifeboat *Isabella Frew* and a boathouse for it (1874); Alexander Mackenzie, the Canadian prime minister who re-visited Irvine (1875) where he had worked as a stonemason and attended the Baptist church before emigrating in 1842; Sir Archibald Campbell, commanding officer of the Argyll and Sutherland Highlanders, which trained annually at Irvine (1892); and John Speirs, who

The harbour tug *George Brown* operated from 1887 to 1957. It was named after a provost whose ban on the sale of liquor at Marymass Races lasted from 1878 to 1920.

presented the Burns Statue (1893). Also in 1875 the council acquired a gold medal and chain to adorn Provost Paterson at the Mansion House dinner as a guest of an Ayrshire-born Lord Mayor of London. Public lamps erected outside the provost's home are first mentioned in 1869. Annual payments were still made to provide the burgh officers with ceremonial garb. It was decided (1894) that 'the immemorial usage of ringing the bell at eight o'clock p.m. should be continued'. Obviously the traditions of the royal burgh were being maintained. A new tradition was introduced under Provost Paterson when the Local Authority began annual inspections of the new waterworks. This Water Trip became a regular occasion, despite one councillor's objection in 1877 to the incidental expenses, and his attempted refusal to pay water rates because of this.

But while the town council continued their ancient procedures, when they met in a different capacity as a Local Authority (after 1870) and as Police Commissioners (after 1874) there appeared a new urgency in their deliberations as they commenced a vigorous policy of social advance.

The first major innovation was the provision of a water supply. In 1851 Dr. William Gray in his role as a magistrate and 'an advanced Liberal' had proposed, but without success, 'the obtaining of a plentiful supply of good and wholesome water'. In 1866 there was a similarly disappointing response to Maxwell Dick's scheme to provide an 'inexhaustible supply' from a reservoir to be formed at Duntonknoll quarry. The public and private pump wells were proving inadequate for the growing town, and though new ones were sunk, an analysis made in 1867 indicated that some were polluted with sewage. The water, too, was hard and not very suitable for washing clothes, so that rainwater had to be collected in barrels for this purpose. Charles Murchland, in his *Irvine Herald* which appeared in 1871 as the first local newspaper, ran a series of articles advocating a supply of gravitation water. In 1873 the Local Authority held a public meeting at which a resolution was carried to introduce such a scheme. Provost Paterson, who was in the chair, recalled an irrelevant (but revealing) comment made in the discussion, about women who would 'sine the Chantie in the Glasgow Vennel well and take away as much as made the parritch'. After this meeting, the project of a new water supply was approved by the Local Authority — but only by the provost's casting vote. His wisdom was confirmed when an analytical chemist in 1874 reported: 'I have never before examined so large a number of doubtful waters from any one locality'. A provisional order was obtained in 1876; plans were prepared by James Leslie, an Edinburgh engineer; and £45,000 was borrowed from the Public Works Loan Commissioners. Dykehead in the parish of Dalry was chosen for a reservoir, and a ten-inch main brought filtered water six miles to Irvine and (by arrangement with the Dundonald parochial board) to Fullarton. In August 1878 the water was turned on by a silver key, and a gala day concluded with fireworks, and banquets in several halls. Water was now available in street wells and (for some) indoor taps. The Police Commissioners set up public urinals (1879), provided street hydrants for the fire engine (1882), and troughs for horses (1888). The mains reached Eglinton Castle and Bartonholm (1884), Gailes (1891) and Stanecastle (1897). Arrangements were made to supply Kilwinning (1878), Nobel's Explosives Works at Ardeer (1881), Stevenston and Saltcoats (1885), and military camps on Irvine Moor. In 1888 the reservoir was enlarged, and from 1879 to 1900 annual consumption increased from 1.3 to 223.5 million gallons.

Provision of water supply was not enough. The death rate continued high with outbreaks of infectious diseases. There were epidemics of typhoid fever (1884), scarlet fever, typhus, diphtheria, enteric fever (1886), measles (1889), whooping cough (1892), smallpox (1893), with rabies (1894) and renewed threats of cholera (1871, 1892). House building was not keeping pace with growing population, particularly in the 1870s, and there was gross overcrowding. The numbers of persons per room, as revealed in the decennial census reports from 1861 to 1901, were as follows: 1.8, 1.68, 1.72, 1.66, 1.63. Conditions were indeed worse in some other Ayrshire burghs, but the Local Authority of Irvine was particularly concerned in 1889 at overcrowding in Fullarton Street. They found they had no powers except where there was 'danger to the health of the inmates or as to create a nuisance'. Occasionally they were able to close down some particularly objectionable premises. They could require improvements in the growing number of lodging houses, including the notorious Elephant Inn in Eglinton Street. They regularly inspected dairies and bakehouses where infectious diseases might breed. The Local Authority was urged on by the Board of Health in Edinburgh, which alleged that in Irvine (1884) 'the execution of the Public Health Act has not been as energetic as it should have been'.

The parochial board for Irvine had in 1866 proposed building a fever hospital in Cotton Row. In 1871 the new Local Authority also considered such a hospital but decided against, 'as they are satisfied that no patient would go into it'. They pointed to the little 'Sickhouse' which five or six years previously the Dundonald parochial board had opened near the shipyard in Halfway — possibly the old

William Henderson set up his Chemical Works in 1871 and laid the foundation for Irvine's industrial future. This cartoon portrait is from *The Bailie,* a Glasgow magazine which described Henderson's residence at Williamfield as 'a princely mansion'.

cholera hospital. That was sufficient, because it was 'seldom occupied arising solely from the aversion of patients to go to it'. But the Local Authority discovered there were powers for the compulsory isolation of fever patients. In 1882 they spent £350 and purchased the Halfway Sickhouse, which was staffed by a Keeper and his wife. In 1885 they acquired a 'cab' for the transport of patients. In 1891 the new Ayr County Council suggested a joint district fever hospital, but after three years' protracted arguments as to whether it should be sited in Kilwinning or Irvine, the scheme collapsed. Instead the Irvine Local Authority improved its own little hospital, provided a wooden annexe for smallpox patients in 1893, and replaced the old 'cab' with an ambulance fever van in 1897. In 1896 a matron was appointed, to be assisted by one nurse and a domestic servant.

An essential preventive measure was an improved

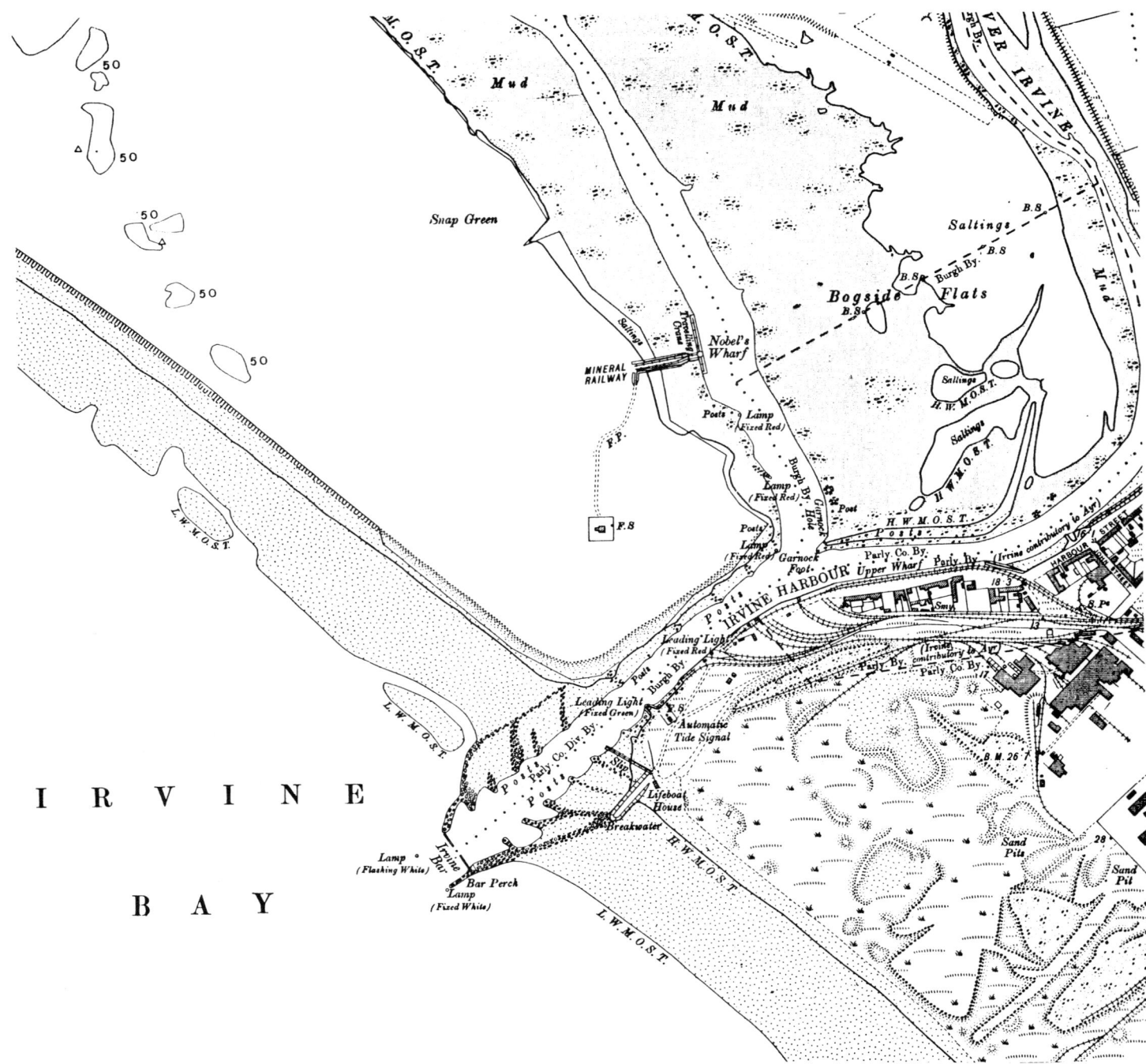

Henderson's Works and the extended harbour as shown on the Ordnance Survey map of 1908.

system of drainage. The town council had laid some old square drains in the 1830s and 1840s. In 1876 the Irvine Local Authority in collaboration with that for Dundonald parish planned a joint scheme with main sewers discharging into the river. In 1883 East Back Road which was unprovided was supplied with a sewer draining towards the Annick Water. In 1888 the old drains in Eglinton Street and Kilwinning Road were renewed, and in 1893 High Street was similarly accommodated. House owners were encouraged to provide an indoor water supply, with water closets connected to the main sewers. As an example, the fever hospital acquired a WC in 1889. Effluent was discharged into the river, and when the weir was constructed in 1896, arrangements had to be made for 'interception and diversion of sewage'. With the main drains now debouching nearer the harbour, conditions there in dry weather were 'very offensive', and the Local Authority in 1899 considered the possibility of a septic tank for treatment of the effluent. But it was a long time before anything was done.

With increased use of water closets, farmers no longer would find it profitable to contract for the removal of ashpits which hitherto had provided rich manure for their fields. In 1882 a burgh dust cart was acquired and depots for manure and ash established at Springbank and beside the gasworks. By 1892 the Local Authority was able to insist on the removal of ashpits from behind private premises, and suggested zinc pails for household rubbish. In 1895 the site of the old gasworks — replaced by a new and bigger installation nearby — became a burgh depot. By 1899 half-a-dozen carts had been purchased, and a staff of seven men under a newly appointed Superintendent of Cleansing collected refuse for dumping along the river banks.

While these various public health provisions were made by the Local Authority, the councillors as Police Commissioners were concerned with more positive measures to maintain the streets and improve the character of the town. In this respect the Local Authority's Sanitary Inspector and Superintendent of Water Works was also the Police Commissioners' Superintendent of Works — by 1899 the Burgh Surveyor.

When in 1881 the bounds of the municipal burgh were extended, the Police Commissioners became responsible for the maintenance and lighting of the streets of the Halfway and Fullarton districts. Gailes Road (later renamed Portland Road) was formed into a street. John Street and Peter Street (later Gottries Road) were taken over. In the older part of the burgh Bank Street, East Back Road, Quarry Lane, and Bridgegate were widened. When some houses in this last were demolished in 1896, Councillor Archibald Kirkland — a man before his time — suggested building 'Working men's houses' to rehouse those displaced. Irvine bridge, which had been taken over from the Bridge Trustees in 1881, was provided in 1887 with iron latticework sides which widened it to 38 feet. In 1886 a footbridge was erected near the Marress ford. In 1882 streets were provided with name plates, and houses numbered, continued in 1895 when some streets were renamed, like East Road and West Road. Halfway had since 1882 become known as Montgomery Street, after the poet and hymn writer who had been born there. The streets were lit throughout with gas, and in 1895 there was an experiment with incandescent burners. In 1897 there was an unsuccessful attempt to take over the privately managed gas company as a municipal undertaking. Proposals from a London company of electrical engineers (1890) were not taken up, and nothing came of Councillor Robert Yule's suggestion (1892) that a turbine wheel should be installed at the town's mill to supply electric lighting for the streets. Permission was however granted to the National Telephone Company in 1886 to erect poles, and this private enterprise set up a telephone exchange at the *Irvine Herald* office in High Street. In 1893 it had 23 lines — to the Eglinton Arms (Telephone Irvine No. 1), the police office, several major firms, coal agents at the harbour, and extending to four numbers in Dreghorn, Perceton, Kilwinning and Stevenston.

There were other signs of change: 'Tar Macadam composite pavements' were considered in 1895; in 1897 one householder laid his footpath in concrete; and in 1899 the Commissioners took over responsibility for all pavements. Increased traffic required the hire of a steam road roller (1897), and a new kind of road transport was anticipated in a letter of 1895 from the Secretary of State regarding 'Locomotion on Highways'. Yet for this growing town the Police Commissioners regarded the old fire engine as sufficient, renewing hoses and requiring quarterly exercises by the volunteer brigade. How inadequate was proved when the town's mill went on fire in 1899. The water mains did not run this far, the hoses could not be extended, and buckets of water could not save the building. Thus ended the old burgh corn mill.

The Harbour Trustees — now twenty-nine members eighteen of whom were required to be town councillors — were operating with increased vigour. In 1856 they spent £1,100 on the purchase of a steam tug *Scottish Maid,* in 1871 replaced by *The Irvine,* and in 1887 by the *George Brown.* In 1857 they increased harbour dues and considered the possibilities of deepening the harbour. In 1867 they acquired new powers and the town council stood security for a loan of £10,000. In 1869 a dredger was purchased which deepened the harbour and the bar. In 1870 they extended their powers for improvement. And as trade was beginning to show a substantial growth, an act of

1873 permitted a massive programme of harbour development, for which they could borrow up to £265,000. The berthage was extended to 1,160 feet, and there were six steam cranes, the two largest each capable of handling 100 tons of coal per hour. In 1886 it could be reported that 'a great improvement has been effected by the extension of the wharf in 1873 and other works; and the trade, which had fallen off, has since revived'. Coal remained the principal export, 189,000 tons by 1899 — although, to keep things in perspective, Ayr, Ardrossan, and Troon that year each exported over 400,000 tons. Other cargoes of miscellaneous items were being handled, including carpets, tanned leather, and tree plants. Imports were of oats, butter, and linen cloth; with timber, hides, and other raw materials. Between 1878 and 1888 exports increased from 70,000 to 136,000 tons, and imports from 24,000 to 69,000 tons. Through the harbour entrance ships were passing into the Garnock to supply the dynamite works which Alfred Nobel started at Ardeer in 1872. And in Irvine itself new chemical works were rising in the vicinity of the harbour.

Irvine town council by virtue of its purchase of Marressfoot in 1572 had possession of land along the left bank of the river and in particular the shore where the harbour was formed. Fullarton lands passed into the ownership of the Dukes of Portland in 1805. The great area to the south of the harbour was part of Shewalton estate. There had been a longstanding dispute with Irvine town council over the precise boundaries in the harbour area: this was amicably settled in 1874 by agreement with Lord Justice Boyle. Here, on the Boatstabs lands belonging to Shewalton, extensive feus were made available for the new industrial undertakings.

In 1871 William Henderson set up his chemical works, importing Spanish ores, producing sulphuric acid, bleaching powder, and caustic soda, and extracting copper by a process he had himself devised. Within twenty years between two and three hundred men were employed on the twenty-seven acre site, and Henderson kept personal and constant control with the aid of telegraph wires extending from the works to his home at Williamfield, which he extended.

William Henderson was a most remarkable man. A contemporary referred to his 'ability, determination, and dogged perseverance'. A recent study of Scottish industrial enterprise has described him as a pioneer of metallurgical chemistry and commented that 'as inventor and industrialist he was not far short of greatness'. Born in Glasgow in 1827, in 1848 he patented a new 'wet' process for extracting copper. In 1863 he helped form a British Metal Extracting Company which obtained from Spanish pyrites the sulphur and copper for which there was great industrial demand. In 1866 Sir Charles Tennant set up the Tharsis Sulphur and Copper Company which mined the ores and utilised the patents of Henderson, who amalgamated and became a director in 1868. After two years Henderson quarrelled with Tennant and set up his own Seville Sulphur and Copper Company. He chose Irvine as the site for his new works, almost simultaneously with Alfred Nobel's choice of the other side of the estuary at Ardeer for his other type of chemical undertaking. At Henderson's wharf in Irvine harbour were unloaded pyrites from Spain, salt from Cheshire, and limestone from Ireland. Skilled men were brought from the Newcastle area, other workers from Ireland. Beside Henderson's Works grew up a waste heap of 'blue billie' — the iron oxide residue. Henderson had devised a process for the extraction of iron from this, though it could not be used locally. He never ceased to invent. He planned to use that waste and local sand to manufacture glass and cement, and experimented in making concrete railway sleepers. Henderson's Works, set up in 1871 with copper as its principal product, was joined a year later by a second undertaking in which he had an interest. On a sixteen-acre adjacent site the Eglinton Chemical Company manufactured bichrome which was used in paints and in tanning. Beside it was also set up the Irvine Chemical Works on ten acres, with 140 workers producing sulphuric acid, caustic soda, and bleaching powder. In 1890 these businesses together with Tennant's St. Rollox Works at Glasgow were combined with others elsewhere to form the giant United Alkali Company. By that time Henderson was dead. He had won wide respect in Irvine, involving himself in various organisations so far as his frequent foreign visits allowed. The *Irvine Herald* saw him as a future provost when the extension of the burgh in 1881 would make him eligible. But in that year, at the age of fifty-four, he died in London on the way home from Spain. In less than ten years he had laid the foundation for Irvine's industrial future.

In the same vicinity as the works which William Henderson had created, a Gas Residual Products Company made use of residue from Ayrshire gasworks to distil naphtha and other products. In 1881 J.B. Lindsay and Co. laid pipes from the docks to convey tar to their new works. In 1891 Alexander Walker began the manufacture of various chemical products. For this great new chemical complex it was argued in 1890 that 'a more suitable place could hardly be got... as the acid and chlorine fumes, easily perceptible in the near neighbourhood, are quickly dissipated by the fresh breezes of the firth'. In fact, the Local Authority had to make repeated complaints about the 'continued escape of noxious vapours from the Chemical Works', and Irvine became familiar with a sickly sweet smell from the prevailing south-west winds.

The Caledonian Railway Company provided Irvine with an alternative railway station, the terminus in Bank Street. Services operated from 1890 to 1930.

Around the harbour were other industrial developments. D. McGill and Co. took over the shipbuilding yard in 1886, employing thirty to fifty men in building and repairing, with a new dock capable of taking vessels up to a hundred feet in length. J.H. Gilmour took the yard over (1892-94), then Irvine Shipbuilding and Engineering Company (1898-1904). In 1899 they constructed twelve vessels totalling 3,410 tons. The Irvine Smith and Machine Works under Malcolm McDougall, great-grandson of the founder, were still making chains and cables. Stewart's Iron Works continued general foundry and engineering jobs. They were joined in 1873 by the larger Irvine Forge Company, employing fifty to seventy men making engine and ship forgings; in 1876 by the Harbour Forge Company with thirty to forty men on similar work; and in 1883 Messrs. Laird and Son moved from Port Glasgow to take over the Fullarton Works where seventy men manufactured wooden blocks for ships' riggings. In 1881 brass founding was begun in the Bridgegate by David Flanagan, who moved to Cochrane Street in 1902. Timber work was also flourishing, with three small firms amalgamated under Provost William Breckenridge. He was partner in Matthew Wright and Nephew Limited, took over the business of John Wright (a cousin and another provost), then that of C. and R. Samson. Great logs were unshipped at the harbour and floated across to the sawmills at the timberyard.

The chemical works and some of the other industrial establishments were served by railway sidings. The passenger railway station was itself much improved in 1874. And the Vale of Clyde Railway Workshops expanded. By the end of the 19th century this area adjacent to Irvine harbour had become one of Ayrshire's main industrial centres, offering employment for well over a thousand men.

The *Irvine Herald* in its second issue (11 March 1871) noticed 'The Signs of Progress' — 'Perhaps at no time previous has Irvine shown as many signs of energy, enterprise, and prosperity as at the present time'. The town council was now enthusiastic about encouraging new industries, advertising feus for 'Public Works' in 1878 and later years. The range of occupations of the councillors elected in 1881 is revealing. There were two defined simply as manufacturers, two as timber merchants, and one as a rope-spinner. These were no doubt committed to industrial expansion, and most of the others would also hope to benefit from the growth of the town. There were two builders, one painter, three grocers, one grain dealer, a ham curer, a draper, a shipmaster, and a mariner; the remaining two are vaguely described as merchant and residenter. Characteristically, in 1883 the council invested £500 from the Common Good to acquire shares in the Lanarkshire and Ayrshire Railway. This was a subsidiary of the Caledonian Railway Company, rival of the Glasgow and South Western Railway Company. A line was planned through Kilwinning and Irvine towards Troon and Ayr to compete with the existing Glasgow and South Western line. In fact only a single track was constructed from Kilwinning through Bogside to a terminus in Bank Street. But it provided an alternative railway station, one right in the heart of Irvine, and hopes of new industrial development in that vicinity. When the bill authorising the railway was passed by parliament in 1884 there was a bonfire and over-enthusiastic crowds in Bank Street, with further celebrations at the opening of the new railway station on 2nd June 1890.

In fact industrial developments on this side of Irvine were limited. Gray's Brewery continued, under new management from 1875, following the retiral of the lawyer-councillor-town clerk who had founded it. In 1879 John Cowan converted a long-established business of candlemaking into a soap factory at Thornhouse — 'an offensive trade' but situated well clear of the built-up area. In 1890 William Kerr was importing cigars and making cigarettes. In 1881 an aerated water manufactory was established beside the Golffields, which Archibald Buchanan took over, then turned into a steam laundry in 1899. Anticipated major developments near the new Bank Street Railway Station did not materialise. William Holmes, who had been building coaches in Fullarton Street, moved to new premises in Bank Street in 1890. In 1891 Robert Kerr set up the Caledonian Foundry beside Quarry Lane. Nearby Duntonknoll quarry continued. But that was all.

The new railway encroached on the site of the old ropeworks. Soon the adjoining Meadow Bleachfield closed down, as did the other bleachfield over the river in Fullarton. The old trades were dying. In 1890 there were still a dozen elderly men continuing as handloom weavers, working at shawls and light mixed fabrics. In 1896 the loom of John Fulton was removed from the last weaving shop — the final demise of what had once been Irvine's main manufacturing business.

By fortunate coincidence the era of new industrial enterprise saw a renewal of coal working on the burgh lands. In 1866 Alexander Simpson of Wishaw sank a pit on the Moor, then a second one near Ravenscroft. From a wharf by the river 'punts or scours' took loads down to the harbour, and there was a mineral branch to the main railway line, which drove away the cricketers and required realignment of the Carters' race course. In 1873 John Paterson and Co. took over the lease, and in 1880 Messrs. Merry and Cunninghame. In 1882 they produced 17,000 tons, yielding the Common Good some £600 in royalties. Even though the seams were worked out and the two pits closed in 1888, there were alternative developments. The 13th earl of Eglinton had re-opened the Bartonholm pits in 1854. His successor, landlord of nearly 24,000 acres around Eglinton, was taking (in 1872) not only £37,000 from rents, but £9,500 in mineral royalties. In 1883 this 14th earl sank the Lady Sophia Pit, Eglinton No.1 just beyond Irvine Mains. And in 1886 the Bourtreehill Coal Company sought permission for their Broomlands No.9 Pit to work the coals under Newmoor. The Inspectors of Mines' Report for 1874 listed nine companies operating twelve coalmines in the vicinity of Irvine — Burgh, Eglinton, Redburn, Bartonholm, Doura, Fergushill, Monkredding, Annick Lodge, Perceton, Armsheugh, Bourtreehill, Shewalton.

During the period from 1871 to 1901 Ayrshire enjoyed a natural increase (excess of births over deaths) of 100,000. The actual increase was only 50,000. There was thus a net loss to the county of another 50,000. Some had moved to other parts of Britain and many emigrated. The actual increase in Irvine's population — from 6,886 (1871) to 9,618 (1901) — was around 40%. This was in the same category as Kilmarnock and Ayr — nearly 50% each — and much greater than the county average of 27%. In the larger burghs, although there were severe losses by emigration in the last decades of the 19th century, population was augmented not only by a high birth rate and a declining death rate, but by a flood of incomers finding work in expanding industries. In 1901, 18% of the inhabitants of Ayrshire were people who had been born elsewhere in Scotland; 2% were from England; and 4% were Irish-born, to whom may be added the locally born families of the 11% Irish-born of 1851. The proportions were probably greater in towns like Irvine. Clearly the contrary floods of emigrants and immigrants were changing the character of Irvine's people in the last decades of the 19th century. When in 1872 George Brown resigned, the *Ardrossan and Saltcoats Herald* commented that 'under his Provostship the Burgh has awakened from the sleep of a century'.

FIFTEEN

Industrial Town

'Irvine had changed, and changed for the worse.' Thus the biographer of Rev. Dr Robertson described the town of 1878. 'Great chemical works had been established by the harbour, which had darkened the air, and filled the quiet streets with unfamiliar faces, and sometimes with uproarious crowds.' What accentuated the difficulties of social change was that Irvine was now experiencing industrial expansion in an awkward period when Britain's commercial supremacy was beginning to suffer from foreign competition. The town council, seeking to deal with the public health problems of the growing town by measures detailed in the previous chapter, was also concerned about social problems. With the town so crowded, in 1872 it complained of the 'congregation of idlers at and near the Bridgegatehead'. Like its predecessors on other occasions in the past, it was worried in 1880 at 'the great number of vagrants'. The registrar's vital statistics for 1871 revealed an illegitimacy rate of 11.4%. *The Ardrossan and Saltcoats Herald* of 1872 reported the noise, swearing, and fighting when the Irvine public houses on Saturday evenings 'vomit out their drunken contents'. In 1873 the County Constabulary created a separate Irvine Division and increased the local force to a superintendent, sergeant, six constables, and a detective officer. In 1888 the magistrates implemented the new Public Houses Act and enforced early closing at 10 p.m. instead of the previous eleven o'clock. In 1892 special measures had to be taken to clear the streets of 'loose paper and refuse material being deposited on them on Saturday nights'. In 1887 there was 'damage and annoyance caused by michievous youths in the Burgh' including obstruction of footpaths, abuse of catapults, writing on walls, interfering with wells, and the breaking of street lamps. The number of reported crimes and offences doubled between 1868 and 1878, only partly attributable to increased police efficiency. By the end of the century they had doubled again. In 1897 there were 491 crimes and offences reported within the burgh of Irvine, 238 of them being breaches of the peace. At that time Irvine had eight inns and hotels, twenty-two public houses, and thirty-five spirit dealers, a total of sixty-five drinking places, 7.15 per thousand of the population. In Ayrshire only Kilwinning had a higher proportion.

There were other causes of disturbance. The political rivalries which produced a Gladstone Club (1883) and a later Unionist Club resulted also in less reputable outbursts of violence at election times. In 1868 special constables had to be enrolled when the burgh was 'much disturbed by Party feelings'. These were in fact sectarian in character, for in 1872 at the opening of the Orange Hall the great procession involved 'violent Party feeling... but no occasion for the interference of the Police'. At Marymass in 1896 there was complaint of 'the singing of Obscene songs on the streets'. With bigger crowds, traffic had to be diverted from High Street at the fairs after 1888. Additional congestion and periodic disturbances were the result of the summer military camps on the Moor. In their first year, 1875, there were street brawls involving the 'wild militiamen' who were branded as 'a regiment of roughs'. By 1900 it was estimated that nine thousand soldiers were encamped in the locality, not counting those at Gailes. The general impression is of the old sleepy burgh rudely awakened.

This was a congested town of overcrowded tenements and narrow closes. Off the west side of High Street, Skinners Close led from the Clydesdale Bank to West Road, and Bruce's Close was near Bridgegatehead. On the other side Pawkie Close and Smiddy Close still survive. Purdie's Close went past the old bowling green, also leading to East Road, as did Coopers Close. Boyd's Close was beside the Eglinton Arms. Much further along, the Jail Close adjoined the Town House, and the Swan Close led past the Swan Inn into Glasgow Vennel. Leading off Bridgegate were Bowmie's Close, Rotten Row, and the Wee Grip.

Some of the 18th-century and older properties were still occupied. There were other survivals from the past. Although one old relic disappeared when the Gallows Well was filled up in 1885, the dilapidated ruins of Seagate Castle were conserved. By authority of the earl of Eglinton the accumulated rubble and rubbish were removed in 1883 and 1884 and trenched into the Low Green. At the same time the council made available its muniments and contributed towards their publication. And Marymass continued in its traditional forms.

There were even halfhearted hopes for 'Irvine as a Coast Resort' — the title of a less than encouraging article in the *Irvine Herald* of 1898. Previously (in 1866) the *Ardrossan and Saltcoats Herald* had noticed one obvious disadvantage: 'Strangers visiting Irvine receive very unfavourable impressions concerning the town, from their walk through that part of it, between the Railway Station and the burgh'. Even more insalubrious was the route through the harbour industrial area to the distant beach, sufficient to explain Irvine's failure to compete with Ayr, Prestwick, Troon and Saltcoats in attracting holiday visitors. In 1891 the town council turned down a proposal to erect 'a Bathing Shelter at the Sea Shore'. Yet there were efforts to improve the town's amenities. Trees were planted along the river banks and on Kilwinning Road. In 1896 John Speirs presented to the burgh a statue of Robert Burns by Pittendreigh Macgillivray. It was unveiled by Poet Laureate of the time, Alfred Austin. The site on the Moor was enhanced by flower beds and seats provided by the Police Commissioners. Concurrently the scheme envisaged by Maxwell Dick in 1866 to improve the river was revived, and the Victoria Weir opened in June 1897 despite the flood of a week before. The ceremonial occasion to celebrate the Queen's Diamond Jubilee was followed by 'Aquatic and Land Sports'.

The river as it passed through the town was enhanced. Pleasure boats for hire were brought from Troon. There was bathing, with measures for 'preventing indecency'. But the removal of large stones in the river by blasting (1897, 1899) was complained of, and the Grannie Stane was saved. Angling was affected, now that the tide no longer reached up to Milgarholm. Provost Paterson listed the various pools in the river: The Witches Plumb below the Minister's Cast; the Wee Plumb below the Academy; the Sodgers Plumb and the Tarry Plumb below the churchyard and above the Puddleford; the Auld Dam between Milgarholm and Springbank; Peat Hole above the entry of the Annick; Hurlingford Pool opposite Warrix where the river left its ancient course; on the Annick the Moats Hole (otherwise Mowat's Hole) between Gulliland and Tarryholm; and the Gulden Wells at the turn immediately above.

The general picture is of a town where middle-class interests were still being maintained, but with increased working-class participation. Apart from the better-quality residential accommodation in the more select areas, the standard of housing was abysmally poor, and the pressures of gross overcrowding were only partially relieved by the new water supply and drainage facilities. Yet wages were improving, and even the poorest had rather more leisure than previous generations. Joiners and cabinetmakers in 1872 earned little more than a pound (23/- or 24/-) for a sixty-hour week. Local miners in 1874 were paid 4/- to 6/- per day. Masons building Bank Street School in 1874 at 8½d per hour might earn nearly £2 per week. The burgh officer in 1895 received a rise from £56 to £60 per year. Unskilled burgh workers were that year paid less than £1 per week (19/-) but had their work time cut from 57 to 48 hours per week.

The shops in the town centre, some of them fashionable enough to acquire roller sunshades (1895). Hoardings for advertisements were put up in the Bridgegate (1893). Aerated waters were on sale (1880), and there were ice cream shops — whose Sunday opening annoyed church folk (1896). Twenty-seven local insurance agencies (1886) indicated thrift, and three local newspapers were a measure both of widespread literacy and interest in local affairs: the Saturday *Herald* (1871), Saturday *Times* (1873), and the Friday *Express* (1880). The Irvine and Fullarton Property Investment and Building Society (1873) with a capital of £55,000, and £22,000 advanced to members on security of heritable property, is an index of business advance. There was parallel working-class initiative. Irvine and Halfway Provident Co-operative Society, formed in 1862, had after seven years annual sales of £1,113 and a dividend of two shillings in the pound. It was superseded in 1873 by Irvine and Fullarton Cooperative Society, which, though it had only eighty-nine members and sold £47 of goods weekly (1875), became more firmly established.

The development of a vigorous local press was due to Charles Murchland. A native of Saltcoats, he took over Maxwell Dick's business in 1870 and instituted the *Irvine Herald* in 1871. He had 'great business capability, sound judgement, strong commonsense, and earnest desire for the public welfare'. He was also 'a delightful man, with a fund of reminiscences'. From his press there issued also Train's book on the Buchanites, an Irvine edition of John Galt's novels, and other works of local interest. A prominent unionist, freemason, and Burnsian, he was involved in various other ventures, from promoting a supply of gravitation water to participating in a cooperative attempt to revive the shipyard. Inevitably he was elected to the council and became provost (1898–1904). He managed the *Irvine Herald* until his death in 1926. Throughout that period (from 1872) it had as a competitor the *Irvine Times* which the *Ardrossan and Saltcoats Herald* produced to retain its local readers. Also in 1880 there appeared the short-lived *Irvine Express* which after six years was incorporated in the *Ayrshire Post*.

It is summer, and many of these children of the 1890s go barefoot. Further along the cobbled High Street is the statue of Lord Justice Boyle — known to the children as 'the Black Man'.

Extension of recreational activities can be observed. Throughout the year there were functions organised by established and predominantly middle-class groups like the Incorporated Trades, Lodge St. Andrew, and the Burns Club, the last of which, said the *Irvine Herald* of 1871, 'shows life once a year'. There was still an annual dinner to celebrate the birthday of the earl of Eglinton. New select occasions were the Farmers Ball instituted in 1870 and meetings of the Glasgow-Irvine Society. This originated in a reunion of Irvine natives in Glasgow and was formally constituted in 1869 with sixty-five members meeting socially and extending charity to less fortunate Irvine folk living in the city. Less exclusive gatherings were now common, with soirées and penny readings organised by the churches, temperance societies and other bodies. The attractions of licensed hotels and public houses were hardly countered by the British Workman's Public House (1881) — a temperance hotel with hot and cold baths. The Good Templars Hall erected in Bank Street in 1871 provided a venue for many popular gatherings. Earlier in 1867 the old Baptist chapel in the Groop was converted by William McJannet into a Literary and Social Institute, with rooms for reading, games and public meetings. It opened with a soirée (evening concert), organised penny readings (combining literary and musical items), and in 1871 had a Diorama (of lantern slide) for six nights. Other popular entertainments were provided by Bostock and Wombell's Menagerie in High Street (1874) and by touring companies like J. Colbourne Trinder's wooden-built People's Theatre, in Cochrane Park, beyond the railway, for six weeks in 1898. On the Low Green there were (in 1899) a gipsy tent and a gospel tent, beside the cabin for boat hirers, and (in 1900) a circus and also Harry Goddard's portable Scotia Theatre.

The Literary and Social Institute provided library facilities. It superseded the old Irvine Reading Room which in 1889, after an existence of 'over eighty years', had only eighteen members and closed down after discontinuing its lease of a room in the Town House. There was a painting class in the town hall (1898). For those with musical tastes

Scene in the Bridgegate. To the left is Hill Street, to the right beyond the Pawnshop is the Wee Grip.

the old Choral Union was revived in 1871 and converted into a Choral Society which met in the parish church for weekly practices for its annual concert. In 1893 an Irvine Male Voice Choir ran a series of concerts supported by an amateur orchestra. In the same year a burgh brass band was formed. There was a short-lived dramatic club in 1881, others in 1889, and in 1898 yet another Irvine Dramatic and Musical Association. Irvine's cultural life was limited, however, by the fact that so few of the town's able sons who went on to university returned to make a career there. And though it was uncommonly difficult for girls to pursue a similar path, there is the notable instance of the twin daughters of John Smith of Hamilfield, a local lawyer who lived in Hamilfield from 1844 until his death in 1867. Agnes and Margaret, born in 1843, went on to advanced linguistic studies in London, then both married ministers at Cambridge. As Mrs. Lewis and Mrs. Green they toured the Middle East, and in a monastery at Sinai discovered in 1892 the palimpsest of an ancient Syriac gospel, which they were able to translate. For this they were each awarded the degree of doctor of divinity, the first women ever so distinguished. But any list of natives who earned successess elsewhere would signalise also Irvine's loss. Those who won some recognition in the arts were David Keir (1802-64) in stained glass; George Henry (1858-1943), Andrew Allan (1863-1942), Scott Munro Orr (1874-?) as painters; Joseph De Monti (1819-84) for organ music; and Robert Bruce Mantell (1854-1928) who became America's leading Shakespearean actor.

Outdoor recreations for the mass of the population remained limited. Those who had gardens could compete at the annual horticultural shows from 1857, while similarly the Ornithological Society (established 1874) catered for fanciers of poultry, pigeons, canaries, and — collie dogs! The railway and the Clyde steamers offered the opportunity for cheap day trips. As an example, in August 1873 John Paterson and Company treated their three hundred miners to a pleasure excursion by rail to Greenock for a cruise to the Gareloch. In June 1899 the burgh workers and fire brigade had a holiday trip, with the town council donating a total £2 towards the expenses. Nearby Bogside offered the attractions of a day at the races, and stimulated local interest in horse racing. When in 1884 the Grand National at Liverpool was won by a horse owned by a local man, H.F. Boyd, the town bells were rung. But participation in sport was too expensive for most folk. Cricket and golf were being played on the Moor in 1888, and Vineburgh Cricket Club were allowed to level an area for their matches. John Fulton Millar not only encouraged cricket, but stimulated some of the players to form a dramatic club. Thirteen enthusiasts formed Irvine Golf Club in 1887, which moved from the Moor to Bogside in 1890, had an eighteen-hole course by 1891, and with the support of Glasgow businessmen who became members built a clubhouse. The Rifle Association continued its existence. The musketry range in the dunes south of the harbour was used both by the units at summer camp and by the local Volunteers. From 1871 these were attached to the Royal Scottish Fusiliers, and in 1892 they opened a new drill hall in East Road. Winton Bowling Club was also well-established. There was a rowing club in 1873 and an amateur swimming club in 1889. Regularly from 1872 there was a regatta at the harbour, with races for sailing boats, ship boats, pleasure rowing boats, punts, and — to make involvement comprehensive — a miners' race with boats propelled with pit shovels. Facilities for boating were enhanced by construction of the weir in 1897. But plans for a pond for curlers and skaters came to nothing. Anglers in 1898 were complaining about poachers trawling and netting in the Garnock and the Annick. A new activity was catered for by Irvine Cycling Club (1895).

The sport which suddenly became a popular craze was the new Association football. In 1872 there was a Football Match in which Irvine Academy defeated Ayr Academy by two goals to one after a two-hour match — but the new code was still not adopted. In 1875 'arrangements were made for organising a complete Football Club, under Association Rules'. Saturday afternoon practices on the Moor were begun by this Irvine Football Club. In 1876 they were playing against a rival Irvine Portland Club, but could only manage a draw of 1-1, even though they had a team of twelve players. Irvine FC in 1878 organised annual sports, and as Irvine Athletic FC played at Meadowpark, then Cochrane Park in 1888. When an Ayrshire Junior Football Association was formed in 1889, among its twenty-four

Montgomery Street in the 1890s, with the Gushet House at the Loudoun Street corner.

members was an Irvine Rangers Club, which in 1893 won both the Ayrshire and the Irvine and District Cups. In 1896 an Irvine and District Juvenile Association followed, and among its eight clubs were Irvine Britannia, Irvine Winton, and Irvine Meadow. The following year this last joined the juniors. And Irvine Meadow laid the foundations of a long and successful career by winning the Ayrshire Cup in their second season (1899), the Irvine and District Cup (1900), and by recovering the Ayrshire Cup (1901). How popular football had become is indicated by the formation of a team of lady footballers in 1896 — the ladies also had a cycling club the next year. Among the younger ones, organised sports began with the Irvine Academical Athletic Club's first meeting in 1884; and a local company of the Boys' Brigade was formed soon afterwards, certainly before 1895, and by 1899 a second company was added.

All this reveals a period of almost bewildering changes in social life. One old custom was sustained by a donor providing children at Hallowe'en (1872) with apples for dooking and nuts for cracking. Earlier in the same year a new custom of Valentine's Day cards was noted in the local press. Christmas enjoyed a new popularity that year with cards for sale and books for presents. And because the school vacation did not include 25th December, there was what the *Ardrossan and Saltcoats Herald* called a 'pupils' strike'.

It remains to examine the status of the churches in this different community; and also the new educational provisions that were being made.

By the second half of the 19th century the established church had lost its dominance. The United Presbyterian and Free Church congregations were vigorous and enthusiastic forces within the community, and indeed their eventual fusion nationally in 1900 created a United Free Church which was in many ways more influential than the established Church of Scotland.

Trinity United Presbyterian Church was something new. Erected in 1863 under the inspiration of Rev. W.B. Robertson, its architecture and its very name symbolised a ritualism which must have appalled the traditionalists. Within a few years he had introduced Christmas services in

Fullarton Street, nicknamed Soor Milk Raw. Irvine Local Authority ordered thatch to be removed from all roofs before Whitsunday 1903.

an appropriately decorated church, yet this innovation was accepted without resistance. Though illhealth forced Robertson's resignation in 1879, his work was continued by Rev. W.S. Dickie. In the Relief UP Church, Rev. Henry Reid (1868-86) initiated less drastic changes, exemplified by the replacement in 1872 of the traditional metal communion tokens by cards, and the replacement of the Fast Days by preparatory services in 1875. Under Rev. John Gray (1886-96) the church building was modernised (1890), and active work was continued by Rev. Robert Pollock (1896-1903).

At Fullarton Free Church, during the long and effective ministry of Rev. David Wilson the original building was replaced in 1873 by a new and bigger one on the same site. He had two vigorous successors — Revs. James Kelly (1881-95) and James Macluskie (1895-1902) who also conducted the Mure Mission which was set up at the harbour in 1888. At Irvine Free Church, Rev. R.S. Macaulay was minister for forty years (1860-1900). Miscellaneous innovations included the formation of congregational societies like the YMCA and the Band of Hope; the introduction of hymns into worship (1882); the discontinuation of private baptism (1886); allowing female members help choose elders (1882); and use of collection bags for offerings (1899). In 1900 this became the Mure United Free Church, named in honour of the Misses Mure of Perceton, two sisters whose generosity extended to both of the local Free churches.

Similar vitality was obvious outwith the presbyterian churches. There was a congregation of the Evangelical Union under Rev. Robert Paterson (1867). The Salvation Army arrived in 1882. The Christian Brethren opened their new Waterside Mission Hall in 1896. The small Baptist congregation were able to make headway despite unusual difficulties. In 1867 they had to sell off their chapel in the Groop. They had had as pastor 'Dr. Porteous', an impostor who made a career here and in America as a pretended minister. Revival came with Rev. George Short (1872-75) and Rev. James Blackie (1876-81). They worshipped in the Good Templars Hall until the handful of dedicated adherents built a new Baptist Church in Bank Street (1879). Then came another setback when Rev. Archibald Kerr had to be dismissed (1895).

Enthusiasm which overlapped denominational barriers was evinced in evangelical revivals in 1859, 1878, and especially in 1874 when Moody and Sankey were welcomed to the Parish Church. There was the Temperance Revival of the 1870s, gaining strong support from Liberals and Free Churchmen. The Good Templars founded a lodge and built their hall in 1871. Ten years later the British Workman's Public House, already mentioned, was opened in Harbour Street as another teetotal institution. For the 'lapsed masses' the Foundry Boys were organised in 1871, meeting first in the Glasgow Vennel Mission Hall and, as numbers grew, moving to the Industrial School, then the Institute Hall.

Irvine Parish Church did not remain unchanged. In this period of transition the harsh Calvanism of earlier generations mellowed, and congregational life significantly changed. Although the earl of Eglinton was patron, he allowed the congregation to make their own choice of minister in Rev. James Somerville (1853-93). He was noted for his 'silver-toned eloquence' and became a doctor of divinity in 1887. He married a daughter of Provost Campbell, had a family of fourteen, and was a much-respected member of the community, enjoying 'popularity with all classes'. In 1874 parliament abolished patronage in the Church of Scotland, so that Somerville's successor was chosen by the congregation by statutory right. This was Rev. Henry Rankin (1893-1928), who had arrived in 1891 as one of the series of assistant ministers whom the session through the century employed as town and parish missionaries. Able and vigorous, he wrote several religious works and a study of *Burns and Irvine*. He survived his retiral to die in 1937.

Throughout this period worship within Irvine Parish Church was transformed step by step. The interior of the church was first altered with the removal in 1854 of the old table seats used for communion, and the entire area was reseated in 1896. Memorial tablets on the walls were added to those which had been set up since 1754. A first stained glass window, to the memory of the 13th earl of Eglinton, was followed by six more later in the century. In 1873 a baptismal font was gifted by the 14th earl of Eglinton. The previous year, custom was modified by new postures in worship — the old practice of standing for prayer and

The Academy, built in 1816, was taken over in 1872 by the School Board, which planned a replacement.

sitting while singing reversed. In 1878 communion cards replaced tokens. In 1878 also came the most dramatic change with the installation of an organ.

Since 1856 there had been a choir (or 'band') under the enthusiastic precentor Robert Lee, who had taken over in 1852 after the resignation of George Paulin, last of the schoolmaster session clerks and precentors. Now in 1878 Joseph Hinchcliffe was appointed organist and choirmaster. In 1882 a paid soprano was appointed. In 1884 the council purchased hymn books for the magistrates' loft. The soprano was replaced by a choirmaster (1886-1910), after which the organist was also choirmaster. Other less important changes were the installation of hot water pipes in 1866, and the introduction of collection bags in 1897. More noteworthy was the abandonment of Fast Days in 1882 and the replacement in 1886 of the traditional diet of Sunday morning and early afternoon worship with a morning service at 11 a.m. and an evening service at 6.30 p.m. There was a significant innovation in 1881 with a wedding held within the parish church, 'a ceremonial seldom seen in a Presbyterian Church'. Obviously Irvine Parish Church was being transformed in character, and adjusting to new conditions. Its continuing vitality was revealed in 1896 with the opening of a church hall in new buildings erected on the site of the old burgh school. As compared with Irvine Parish Church, that of Fullarton, though erected to *quoad sacra* status in 1874, continued to find things difficult under Rev. John Gregor (1870-74); Rev. William Workman (1874-75) who was able to introduce a harmonium; and Rev. Joseph Paton (1876-1902).

The changing character of church life in Irvine is further instanced by the firm re-establishment within the community of the Roman Catholic faith. When Father Thomas Keane arrived in 1870, he was appalled at the inadequacies of the Hamilhill chapel — 'too small and most unsuitable for a Catholic place of worship... cries of children from below... dungpits and privies... no schoolhouse... less than one in five go to Mass... no sodalities to foster and propagate devotion... about eighty apostates among the three hundred and fifty Catholics... Opened eight years ago it has not advanced, rather it has retrograded... it requires extraordinary efforts to save it'. As a mature and experienced parish priest, Father Keane made these necessary efforts. He inspired his flock in Irvine (350), Bartonholm (70), Annick Lodge (120), Doura (60), Overton (70), Fergushill (80) and Kilwinning (300). He opened Sunday schools and started sodalities. In 1872 he purchased St. Winin's hall in Kilwinning, which would in 1878 be detached to form a separate parish. When in 1875 the Albert Hall fell vacant, he was able to purchase it and the little house adjoining to form the Church of St. Mary and a presbytery. By 1879 the new church was extended to seat 320. With five hundred books of his own Father Keane

162 The History of Irvine

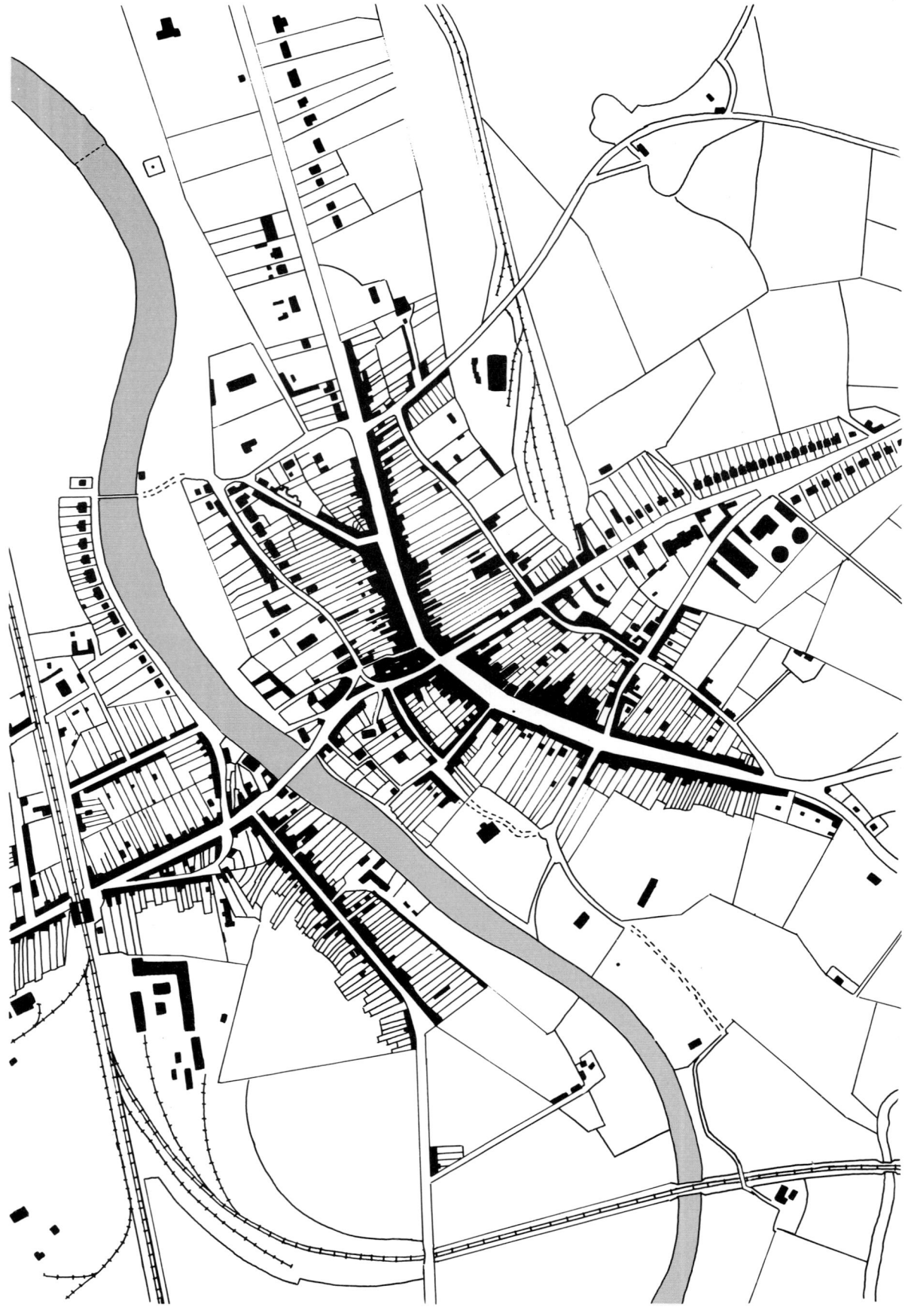

started a library and reading room. After this notable advance, Father Keane's successor Father Henry Murphy stayed only a year, then was deposed by the Bishop for his involvement in Irish politics. Father Ambrose Graham (1880-88) undertook another major development required for the growing Catholic community. In 1883 a new chapel-school was built further along West Back Road, with an adjoining presbytery, half the cost borne by that generous benefactor the Marquess of Bute. This new Church of St. Mary accommodated four hundred, doubled when the school-room partitions were opened. Fathers John Woods (1888-97) and Frederick Letters (1897-1911), though vexed with the problems of a building that was difficult to heat, and a school which it was awkward to staff, established the Church of St. Mary as an accepted element in Irvine's ecclesiastical life.

Dissension among the various congregations diminished. Instead there was cooperation in evangelical, charitable, educational, and anti-drinking activities. There was, however, some unpleasantness in 1873 when a pamphlet by the new Baptist minister stirred up controversy over the practice of adult baptism. Sectarianism appeared in 1872 when an Orange Hall was erected in Kirkgate, the first in Scotland. There was then an Orange demonstration and march, 'a gala day, and such a day as our old town has not witnessed since 1832'. But most of the five thousand participants were from visiting Orange lodges, there was praise for the 'turn-out of the working-class in such excellent holiday attire', and there was 'no occasion for the interference of the Police'. More notable was the general increase of secularism. Sunday delivery of letters continued despite protests in 1834 and later in 1887. Also in 1872 the *Ardrossan and Saltcoats Herald* reported on the Wednesday Fast Day before Communion when the shops were shut and the churches open: 'The religious aspect of the day seems to have disappeared... We listened to one lad going along the street whistling, which among the youth in days gone past was held to be a very great profanation'. In 1882 the churches accepted the inevitable and Fast Days were discontinued because of the 'increasing tendency on the part of many to disregard it as a day of preparation for the observance of the ordinance of the Lord's Supper'.

How many were now without a church connection was revealed incidentally in a census of membership and attendance in 1876. The Parish Church (843) and Fullarton Church (434) gave the established church a membership which still outnumbered that of the other congregations — Free (207), Fullarton Free (214), Trinity UP (340), Relief West UP (273). There was less enthusiasm apparent in the established church congregations, where attendance was only 733 as against 1,074 for the others. Making allowance for some 350 Roman Catholics and 71 Baptists, the total church membership for the Irvine churches was less than 3,000 — in an area where there were around 5,400 adults in a population of 9,000. What were described as the 'the lapsed masses' amounted to nearly one half of the community.

Continued social progress depended on suitable educational provision, and this a far-sighted parliament implemented by the Education (Scotland) Act of 1872. The system of parish and burgh schools created by the old Scottish parliament had survived, but in an age of industrial towns and swollen population local initiative was needed to maintain them and supplement them, and this was seldom sufficient. Government, which hitherto had helped only by subsidising the building of elementary schools, now created at a stroke a new scheme of compulsory education in publicly maintained schools administered by local boards. Accordingly, at a local election in March 1873, from fourteen candidates were chosen the seven members of Irvine Burgh School Board. They included three councillors and four clergymen. Rev. David Wilson topped the poll, but George Brown was appointed as Chairman. Existing schools might apply to be taken over, and into the School Board's control thus passed Fullarton Quoad Sacra Parish School, the Free Church's Loudoun Street School, Irvine Public and Industrial School, and Irvine Academy. Roman Catholic schools, wishing to retain their denominational character, remained independent. Lyle's School and Lady Eglinton's School were taken over and soon after closed down. The funds of the various schools were transferred to the Board, the town council agreed to pay £115 per year in respect of its previous contributions to the academy, there were

Town plan, 1900. In the early part of the 19th century trade had languished despite railways to Ayr and Glasgow (1840) and to Kilmarnock (1848). An Academy was built (1816), as well as a widened bridge (1826), Bank Street (1828), and a gas works (1829), plus middle-class residential development. By mid-century there were fewer than 3,000 inhabitants in the royal burgh. Growth was taking place on the other side of the river, especially after 1871 south of the harbour; this area was added in 1881 to the burgh, whose population, thus augmented, was approaching 10,000 by 1900. The burgh acquired a new Town House (1862), additional churches including Trinity (1863), new schools and halls, and another railway station in Bank Street (1890). Although piped water was introduced (1878), housebuilding did not keep pace with the growth of population, and too many old properties degenerated into slums.

government grants, and a school rate of 6d in the £ was levied on householders.

There was some difficulty over the academy. Since government money was available only for elementary education, no support could be obtained for such a 'high class' school. There was no option but to raise fees. The roll dropped until in 1876 there were only 85 junior pupils and a handful of seniors. More younger children were going to the private schools run by Miss Wilson (79) and Miss Paton (49). In 1877 George Paulin resigned after thirty years' service — a pious and painstaking rector and a minor poet. The opportunity was taken to attempt some reorganisation. The rector would be paid £400, assistants £120, and a new Lady Superintendent at £60 would teach infants and look after all the girls. Fees would remain high — 3/- per quarter for infants, rising to £1.10/- for seniors. But a guarantee fund was to be raised, and Subscribers would collaborate with the Board in management. After a short spell with Zachary Ross as rector, the new era really began with the arrival in 1883 of Thomas Robert Stuart. This new rector was only twenty-four years old. He had come from Edinburgh to begin teaching in Kilmarnock three years before. Under Stuart (1883-1911) the fortunes of the academy began to revive. After Isabella Wilson took over as Lady Superintendent in 1884 more girls were enrolled. In 1889 David Gray bursaries were provided by the widow of the former town clerk. After the establishment of a County Committee for Secondary Education in 1892, annual government grants were obtained. By 1889 the School Board could begin planning a new academy building.

The number of children between five and thirteen for whom the School Board had to provide compulsory schooling was assessed in 1873 as 1324, of whom 371 were not yet at school. 966 from the town and 124 from the country were enrolled in the existing schools. The largest of them was the Public and Industrial School. Alexander Lumsden with a lady assistant and five pupil teachers had 396 pupils in 1876. He also instituted an evening school in 1873 to instruct young men in arithmetic and writing. The school was renamed East Road Public School in 1891. When Lumsden retired in 1893 after thirty years' service, his assistant John Miller succeeded him. Loudoun Street Public School, with 315 on its roll in 1876, was almost as large, run by James Miller till 1873, then R.C. Howie, Robert Selkirk 1875-78, and William Mitchell till 1902. Much smaller was Fullarton Public School, with 194 pupils under John Kerr Ferguson till his death in 1892.

Additional accommodation proved necessary. Those who wished to provide it by converting the academy into an elementary school were overruled, and a new school was planned. Designs of a local architect, John Armour, were accepted, and Bank Street School opened in 1875. Its first headmaster was William Mitchell from Airdrie and its roll was 333, taking in some of the 140 pupils from Lady Eglinton's School which was now closed. Mitchell had had a difficult task moving into a new school before the workmen had finished construction, and before all the necessary equipment was supplied — blackboards, slates, desks with inkstands. But even when things settled down, Her Majesty's Inspectors of Schools found progress in teaching unsatisfactory, discipline lax — there was a 'Stone battle' with boys from Mr. Lumsden's school one dinner hour in 1878 — and Mitchell incapable of instilling in his pupils the desired 'cheerful obedience'. In 1878 he was replaced by Robert Selkirk from Loudoun Street School, to which Mitchell was transferred. After Selkirk came there was a marked improvement. But here as elsewhere instruction had to be given to large classes. In 1890 Bank Street School had a roll of over 500 pupils, divided into four groups, for whom there were four certificated teachers, aided by young and inexperienced pupil teachers. One pupil teacher was responsible for a class of 79. Yet the basic subjects of arithmetic, spelling, grammar, composition, and reading were supplemented by geography, history, singing, sewing, and drill; Latin had been introduced for some older pupils too. Since government grants depended both on standards of performance and numbers in regular attendance, there was a constant pressure on teachers and pupils. To encourage the latter, prizes for perfect attendance were provided. The long and dreary school session was punctuated by a seven weeks' summer holiday from mid-July to early September, a week in the spring, and another at New Year; other breaks for Christmas, Bogside Races in April, Fast Days, and Sabbath School excursions on the Wednesday merchants' holiday in June; and half days for skating and special occasions like the Jubilee procession (1887), a circus (1891), the capture of Pretoria (1900), and the coronation of Edward VII (1902) when buns and milk were distributed. The academy still had its foundation-day holiday on 10th December.

Outwith the authority of the School Board was the Roman Catholic school. The new Church of St. Mary erected in 1883 had a schoolroom accommodating 250 plus a classroom for 76 infants. Government grant aid was awarded according to the number of pupils attending regularly, but (like the academy) there was no support from the rates. About half of the expense of upkeep had to be paid by the parishioners.

The triennial School Board elections were as urgently contested as those for the town council, so great was the interest in the provision of schooling, what was taught, how well — and at what cost. The early Boards, and the teachers they employed, had one particular difficulty. While education was compulsory for all children from five to thirteen, fees had to be charged. Alexander Lumsden found (in 1881) 'the same difficulties to contend with as when first I came, notwithstanding the institution of school boards: difficulty in getting fees, regular attendance, school books, and homework of any kind'. In exasperation he wrote in his logbook in 1888, 'Fees, fees, fees!' To begin with, these ranged from 1d to 3d per week, which was resented by parents of 'high fee' pupils. Even when a uniform 2d per week was substituted, there were always parents unwilling or unable to pay. Ultimately the problem was resolved in 1889 when free elementary eduation was instituted nationally. But the Board still had to rely on parents to supply slates, jotters, and books until 1908.

The School Board's main concern was the provision of elementary education — the three Rs of reading, writing, and arithmetic — to pupils progressing from Standard I to Standard VI. But with the promise of supplementary grants for pupils studying other 'Specific Subjects' in Standards IV, V and VI, some pupils over the age of ten were encouraged to take also English Literature, Domestic Economy, Mathematics, Latin and French. Thus the foundations were laid for the development of secondary education in the 20th century.

The character of the Irvine community at the end of the 19th century is revealed by the celebrations for the Queen's Diamond Jubilee in June 1897. There was a free dinner in the Drill Hall for four hundred of the deserving poor the previous Saturday. On Tuesday morning over a thousand children assembled at Bank Street School to receive bags of buns and sweets and sing the National Anthem. At noon there was a Reception in the magnificently decorated Town House, when Provost Breckenridge delivered a panegyric and an appropriate poem by George Paulin was recited. In the afternoon came a grand procession from the Golffields through High Street and Eglinton Street towards the Moor, for the cutting of a ribbon across the new Victoria Weir, followed by land and aquatic sports. The order of the procession and its composition is noteworthy: pipers of the 4th Argyll and Sutherland Highlanders; Irvine lifeboat and its crew; the Carters Society on horseback; the Boys' Brigade; Irvine Burgh Band; the burgh halberdiers; provost, magistrates, councillors, and officials; the clergy; the Incorporated Trades; the School Board; Irvine Parish Council; Irvine Gas Light Company; the Harbour Trustees; directors of the Literary and Social Institute; burgesses; followed by the Loyal Order of Shepherds, the Good Templars, Loyal Orangemen, Reformed Templars, and Rechabites.

Part Four
The 20th Century

SIXTEEN

A New Age

New inventions were beginning to make their impact in the early years of the 20th century. In 1907 the town council judged that 'the speed of Motor Cars through the streets of Irvine is excessive and dangerous and causing much alarm'. They petitioned the Secretary of State for a 10 mph speed limit and the exclusion of cars and steam threshing machines from East Road and side streets less than sixteen feet wide. In August 1910 some local folk went by train to the spectacular Aviation Show at Lanark. In 1911 there was a travelling cinematograph show on the Low Green, and the following year moving pictures were being shown upstairs in the Literary and Social Institute and in George Green of Glasgow's big new Picturedrome in Bank Street, able to accommodate 920 patrons. The *Irvine Herald* of 1911 was advertising 'Gramophones — all the latest models ... prices from 25s. Records — all the latest hits ... 2s 6d each'. In 1913 there were 4,000 soldiers in summer camp at Gailes; the Royal Flying Corps brought eight biplanes, and 'for the first time air ships were seen in the district'.

A changing way of life is suggested by other items. In 1904 the cleansing department became concerned at the disposal of 'old tin meat cans'. In 1908 there were four ice cream merchants — Luigi Croci (Bank Street), A. Dante (High Street), Pietro Pieroni (Loudoun Street), and Miss McCubbin (Montgomery Street). In 1911 the sale of chip potatoes on the street at Townhead on Sundays was authorised. And in the *Irvine Herald* a London mail order firm was offering 'General Drapery, Costumes, Shirts, Suits, Boots, Babies' Outfits, etc. Cash or Easy Payments. 1s weekly'. In 1904 the town council began seriously to think about acquiring a supply of electricity for the burgh; and in 1914 it began to plan for the construction of council houses.

By the beginning of the 20th century Irvine's population was rapidly approaching ten thousand — with 9,600 at the 1901 census. It was now far behind Kilmarnock's 35,000 and Ayr's 29,000, but the only other Ayrshire towns within reach were Saltcoats (8,100), Ardrossan (6,100), and Stevenston (6,000). And Irvine was perceptibly improving its status, its percentage of the Ayrshire population rising from 3.4 (1871) to 4.2 (1901). In these last three decades of the 19th century rather more people found homes in the congested old royal burgh — 4,300 increasing to 4,800. The main growth, however, was over the water in Fullarton and Halfway, where building beside the new industrial area provided for a massive increase from 2,600 to 4,800, making two equally populous districts on either side of the river. In the landward part of Irvine parish there were throughout the period around 1,600 people, most of them in the mining villages of Bartonholm, Sourlie, and Annicklodge. It remains to translate these bare statistics into a picture of the living community.

Early in the century Charles Murchland, editor of the *Irvine Herald* and provost 1898–1904, produced an *Irvine Post Office Directory* which offers a detailed insight into the town in 1908. He listed some two thousand householders, their occupations, and a wealth of supplementary information.

Prosperous local businessmen nearly all lived in Kilwinning Road or Bank Street. Professional people and what are now called white-collar workers were found mainly in Eglinton Street, Castle Street, West Road, Bank Street, and Annick Road. In High Street and the others in the centre of the old burgh there was a mixture of shopkeepers, tradesmen, and workers skilled and unskilled, often living as neighbours on different floors of the same tenements. In Glasgow Vennel, which was deteriorating into a slum, lived two builders, a fruiterer, a grocer, a dealer, a storeman, three carters, seven miners, six labourers, a chemical worker, and two others described as engineer and driver. Altogether in Irvine there were 154 householders who were miners. Most resided in East Road (45), Townhead (32), and in or adjoining High Street. Only twenty lived on the other side of the river. There, apart from occupants of the villas at Waterside, were skilled and unskilled workers, with shopkeepers in Fullarton Place, Loudoun Street and Montgomery Street. Beyond the railway, engineers and chemical workers predominated. By the harbour were seventeen fishermen, three sailors, a ships' chandlers, the customs and excise office, and a German consular agent.

In some places there were squalid slums, and overall

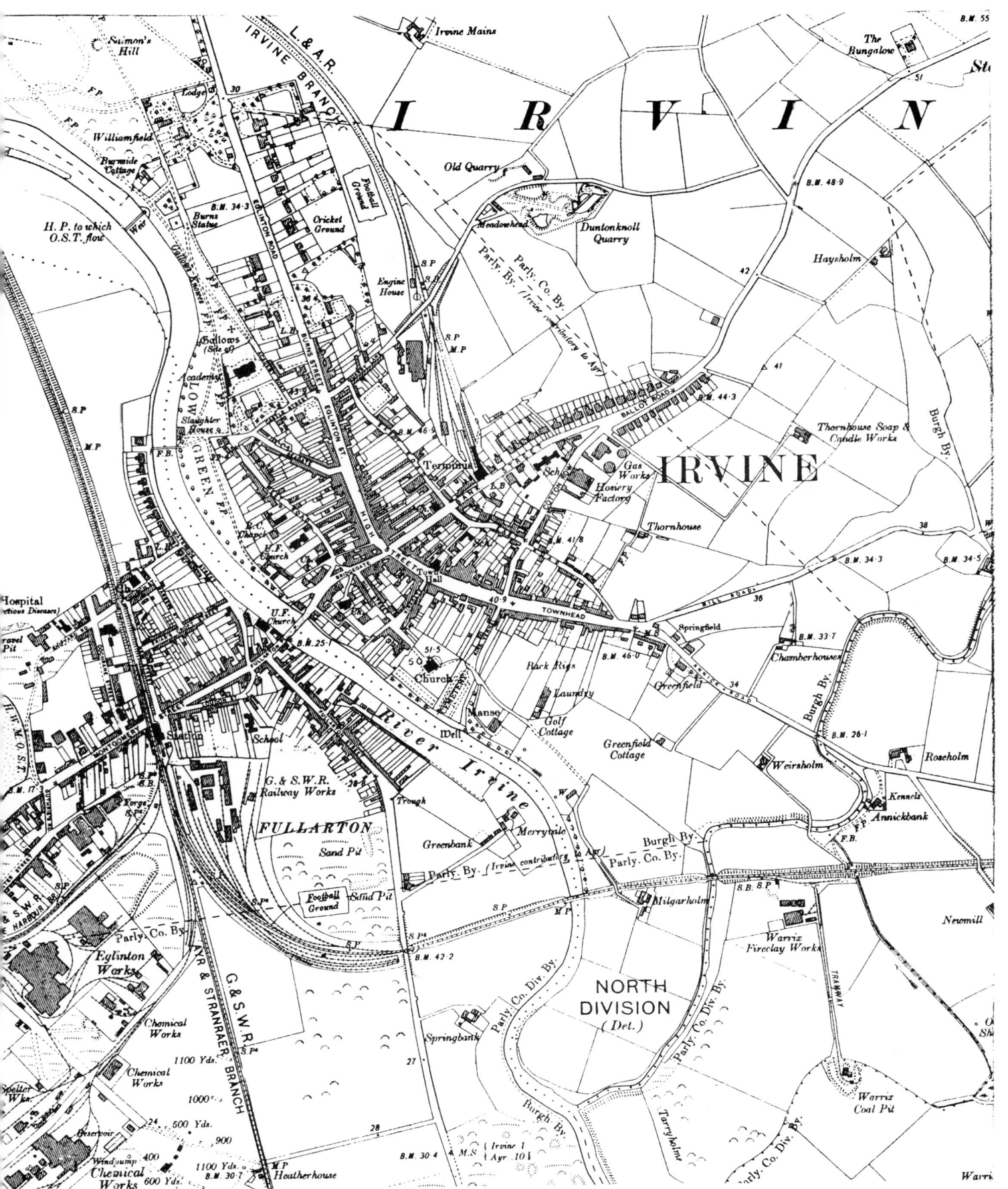

The Ordnance Survey map of 1908 shows many features which would remain unaltered for the next half-century.

High Street in the first decade of the 20th century, soon to be disturbed by motor traffic. There still survived, on the right, that gable-fronted building where, a century earlier, William Templeton had his bookshop.

there was gross overcrowding. In 1901 there was an average of 1.63 persons per room, and conditions were actually deteriorating, to 1.68 in 1911. Provost Charles Murchland wrote in his *Irvine Herald* about the insanitary localities of 1900. The 'plague spots in the burgh' were caused by proprietors who had evaded their responsibilities, letting rickety buildings without sanitary provision. 'Abominations which would have disgraced Omdurman fester in all their horrid obtrusiveness in the midst of a provincial town in enlightened and highly civilised Scotland.' Murchland cited Hamilhill Lane where 'the liquid filth and the stench was so horrible that the scavengers actually stated that they would not go into the place again'. What conditions were like in the mining villages is revealed by a report made in 1913 by the miners' agent, James Brown of Annbank. He describes Bartonholm, owned by William Baird and Co. Ltd.

'There were in all 57 families in Bartonholm with a population of 352. The houses for the most part consist of two apartments, with a few with three apartments. The rooms were very small, and the houses are of a poor type. They are built of stone, but many of them are very damp. Most of them are dingy and depressing. The pathways in front of the doors are unpaved, and the result that they are often in a bad state. The rent is 6s 5d a month. There is one ashpit and a dry closet with two entrances, with doors, and one washing house to every eight families. The washing houses and ashpits are built back to back, which leaves much to be desired.' With only seven dry closets (i.e. an average of fifty persons for each) conditions were worse than in the Greenwood Rows built by A. Kenneth and Sons in Dreghorn parish seven years earlier, with one dry closet for every four tenants. Fergushill nearby in Kilwinning parish was owned by A. Finnie and Son. Many of the houses in its seven rows were single-ends, none had been provided with coal houses or washing houses, and for the 363 occupants of the 78 houses the only water supply was a village pump fed by a spring. At least at Bartonholm, and within the burgh, there was a good supply of gravitation water.

The *Directory* of 1908 lists the principal industrial concerns, near the harbour in Gailes Road (later Portland

Bank Street, a thoroughfare created in 1828, provided sites for the Good Templars Hall (1871), the Baptist Church (1879), a Masonic Temple (1904), and Irvine's first cinema (1912).

Road). The United Alkali Co. Ltd. now controlled both Henderson's and the Eglinton Works. The Gas Residual Products Ltd. was joined by Metallic Oxides Co; Brand's Pure Spelter Works made zinc for galvanising; and Alexander Walker and Co. Ltd., formed in 1891, produced caustic soda, bleaching powder, and similar chemicals. In Guthries Road were the Block Works of Laird and Son who from ships' blocks had extended their range of products to include both thimbles and closet seats; John Stewart and Son's foundry; and that of Renfrew Brothers, who also began shipbreaking at the harbour. David Flanagan and Co., who had moved to Cochrane Street from Bridgegate in 1902, were making machinery castings in brass. Soon (1909) Henry Brown and Co. would form the Irvine Iron Works. Alongside the shipyard was the timber yard of Matthew Wright and Nephew, and in Fullarton Street Andrew Watt made ropes and twine until 1911. On the other side of the town in Quarry Lane, at the Caledonian Forge Robert Kerr and Son made engine and ship forgings in iron and steel.

In 1907 there was talk of a major development at the shipyard. By 1912 negotiations were finalised. The town council took over the old shipyard and additional land, for lease to Messrs. Mackie and Thomson of Govan who created four large building berths and a patent slipway and commenced extended operations. Over seven hundred men were soon employed, building ships up to 10,000 tons, larger than had ever been attempted locally, including vessels for the Clan line.

Though trade at the harbour was limited, a new dredger, the *Irvine*, was acquired in 1911, and the harbour master Martin Boyd had installed at the Pilot House one of his various inventions — a signalling apparatus which automatically showed the depth of water at the bar.

Irvine was still a fishing port. In July 1912 a record 73 boats landed herrings there. But only half-a-dozen of these were local boats. Just a handful of Irvine fishermen survived, taking herring in the summer months and haddock and white fish in the winter, unable to compete with the steam trawlers and the prohibition of hand

Irvine lost its lifeboat station in 1914. David Sinclair retired in 1898 aged seventy-five, after 32 years as coxswain. Most of the crew were his relatives, awarded Norwegian medals for rescuing the crew of the *Frey* in 1894.

trawling. As a result it became impossible to man the Irvine lifeboat, and the station was removed to Troon in 1914. The original RNLI *Pringle Kidd* (1861) had been replaced by the *Isabella Frew* (1874), *Busbie* (1887) and *Jane Anne* (1898). David Sinclair, Coxswain for thirty-two years, retired in 1898 at age seventy-five, and survived until 1913. He assisted at over fifty wrecks, saved forty-three lives, and was awarded a gold medal for rescuing the crew of the *Frey*, a Norwegian ship. At that time (1894) nine of the fourteen lifeboatmen were Sinclairs, and another three were related — the last of a dynasty of fishermen.

The miscellaneous other industries of the town included John Cowan's Thornhouse Works making hard and soft soaps, lubricating oils, and refined lard: 'Irvine Soap for Irvine Folk — Buy Cowan's Best Brown Windsor'. There were two makers of aerated waters: Andrew Braid in Fullarton Street, and Hugh Somerville who in 1888 had taken over the brewery beside the Low Green and added to his beer-bottling trade, but sold out to a Glasgow firm in 1911. A new enterprise was the Hosiery Manufacturing Company which James Watson opened in Cotton Row in 1900, employing a hundred girls, and extended in 1911 to supply shops throughout the West of Scotland. Another was the Irvine Steam Laundry in the Golffields, with delivery vans serving Glasgow, most of Ayrshire, and Arran. There were various small businesses — two coach builders, one umbrella maker, and a basket maker at Stanecastle; and there was one surviving cooper.

This industrial town was served by an appropriate range of shops. There were 12 bakers; 12 butchers; 2 fishmongers; 10 dairies — supplied from 12 registered cowsheds with 85 cows within the burgh; 44 family grocers, including 31 licensed grocers, plus 19 other spirit dealers; and 19 shops selling fruit, vegetables, and confectionery. There were 24 drapers and tailors; 15 dressmakers and milliners; 3 ironmongers; 5 china merchants; and 14 boot

Harbourmaster Martin Boyd with harbour employees in 1901.

and shoemakers mainly doing repairs. Among these merchants there was operating the Irvine and Fullarton Cooperative Society. It now had shops in Montgomery Street and Bridgegate, with departments for groceries, drapery, fleshing, china and hardware, coals, baking, tailoring, and shoemaking, and its annual sales (1908) were £25,000.

Other local businesses were builders (6), plasterers (2), house painters (5), plumbers and slaters (2), and joiners (9) who were also funeral undertakers. There were carters (7), carriers plying to Kilmarnock (2) and Glasgow (1), and blacksmiths (4). Some merchants dealt in ham curing (3), grain (4), eggs (2), and potatoes (1). At the harbour there were coal shippers (5) and ship brokers (5). There were seedsmen (3) and market gardeners (2). Various other services were catered for by hairdressers (7), chimney sweeps (2), washerwomen and manglers (9). An extended range of facilities was provided by hotels (9) and other eating places (3), watchmakers and jewellers (4), sewing machine agents (2), stationers and booksellers (10), tobacconists (2), cycle agents (3) — who would soon be dealing also in motor cars — photographers (1), teachers of music (14) and dancing (1), and ice cream merchants (4).

Five of the shops listed above were selling toys. Those energetic enough to analyse this long list will note that while some old trades had survived, the traditional markets had been superseded by a miscellany of retailers, some of whose wares reveal a new (though limited) affluence. Continuing poverty is instanced by three rag merchants, two pawnbrokers, and one debt collector. And a shortage of local work for girls is revealed by two servants' registry offices.

Professional services were provided by 4 doctors — W.A. Paterson, James Thomson, William and James Wilson — and H.R. Bower as surgeon dentist. There were no fewer than 58 teachers, 17 solicitors, 9 ministers, 2 trained nurses, 2 chemists, 2 veterinary surgeons, 27 insurance agents for 40 different companies, and the staff of 4 banks. These were branches of the Royal Bank of Scotland (Alexander Gilmour), Clydesdale Bank (A.T. Scott), and the Union Bank of Scotland (W. Hunter), all in High Street, while the British Linen Bank (A.C. McJannet) had moved to Bridgegate in 1905. The Irvine Savings Bank continued under the auspices of the Union Bank. The Post Office was in Bridgegate, with a sub-office at the harbour and nine collecting boxes throughout the

Boyd's Automatic System for indicating depth of water at the bar. The inventor appears on this postcard of 1906.

Town. There were three daily deliveries (7 a.m., 2 p.m. and 6.20 p.m.) and a Sunday delivery (8.20 a.m.) Letters posted still cost one penny (not exceeding 4 oz. in weight). Those for abroad cost more (1d per half ounce to British possessions, 2d elsewhere), and quick delivery was promised to Paris (1 day 8 hours), Moscow (4 days), New York (9 days), San Francisco (13 days), and Melbourne (32 days). The National Telephone Company's exchange was now upstairs within the Post Office, worked by batteries and manually controlled by a hand-operated dynamo. In 1910 a new Post Office was opened in High Street, and in 1912 the telephone service was taken over by the General Post Office.

From the *Directory* and other sources it is possible to sketch a picture of social life in the early years of the century. The Church of Scotland had its two congregations — Irvine Parish Church (Rev. Henry Ranken) and Fullarton (Rev. John Paterson). The town council was still responsible for the fabric of the parish church and the maintenance of the graveyard, which was again extended in 1911. And the council still chose each year a representative to attend the General Assembly as a burgh elder. But the members of the established church now constituted a minority. The United Free Church formed in 1900 had four congregations — Trinity UF (Rev. W.S. Dickie), Relief UF (Rev. James Winchester), Mure UF (Rev. James Cosh), and Fullarton UF (Rev. James Wishart). There were also the Baptist Church (Rev. Walter Millburn) and St. Mary's RC Chapel (Father Frederick Letters). There was a group of Christadelphians, and the Salvation Army was vitalised by a visit to Irvine in 1905 of General William Booth.

The School Board (with four clergymen among its seven members) began the new century by spending £16,000 building a 'palatial' new academy. The old one was demolished and pupils were accommodated in halls until completion of the new building, designed by local architect John Armour, and including science and arts rooms, workshops and a gymnasium all covering twice the area of the old academy. The new premises were formally opened on 27th December 1901 by the earl of Eglinton, great-grandson of the earl who had opened the first academy. And proudly the new school was designated Irvine Royal Academy, a title it had previously been given only occasionally by those remembering the royal grant to the burgh school in 1572 and the royal charter of 1818. By 1911 the roll had increased to 350, half of them seniors over the age of fourteen, including pupils from Kilwinning, Troon and the surrounding areas. Under its rector, Thomas R. Stuart, it now had a Lady Superintendent, teachers of English (4), Mathematics (2), French and German (2), Classics (rector and one other), Science (2), Art, Writing and Bookkeeping, Shorthand and Typewriting, Sewing and Fancy Work, Cookery and Laundry, Physical Instruction, Dancing and Calisthenics, Elocution, and tutors for piano, organ, violin, and singing. There was a renaissance of academic achievement. There was also an extension of athletics, football, and hockey, the formation of a school magazine, a debating society, a former pupils' society, and a kilted cadet corps. This last particularly appealed to the rector, who in 1888 had taken a commission in the local artillery volunteers and risen to become in 1905 Lieutenant-Colonel Stuart, commanding officer of the 2nd Lowland Brigade Royal Field Artillery of the Territorials.

After Stuart's early death in 1911 promotion came to Peter Monie, a former pupil who had been English master since 1877 and who concluded his career with three years as rector. During his term Sir David Paulin presented (1912) a bust of his father to the school; the windows were blown in by an explosion at Ardeer (1913); Miss Wilson retired (1914) after thirty-one years as Lady Superintendent and head of the junior department; and Will Templeton produced the school song.

The new Irvine Royal Academy opened in 1900.

The School Board was now responsible for a greater number of pupils than ever before with the raising of the school leaving age to fourteen in 1908. In preparation, the Board had opened its third new school building, this time making provision for the populous harbour industrial area. Montgomery School was opened in 1907 at a cost of £7,500. William Mitchell and his ten teachers were transferred from Loudoun Street to cater for 570 pupils (1913). At Loudoun Street School William Mitchell had succeeded his father as headmaster in 1902, and by 1905 this school was so overcrowded with 580 pupils that some had to be taught in the Cooperative Hall. It remained busy even after Montgomery School opened, with John Miller and nine teachers transferred from East Road School, and had a roll of 374 in 1913.

At this period there was inevitable rivalry between those on opposite sides of the river. The boys used to range themselves on either bank and shout across: 'The toon game cocks are locked in their box, And canna get out for the Halfway folks', with an answering chant: 'The Halfway cocks...' from children of the other two elementary schools east of the river.

Bank Street School continued to grow until it had 610 pupils in 1913. In that year Robert Selkirk retired, to be followed by R.M. Hogg. This Robert Hogg became a notable figure in the town. A native of Riccarton, he was educated at Kilmarnock Academy and came to Bank Street School from Galston as an assistant in 1891. He took charge of the evening continuation classes at the academy and became recognised as an authority on vocational education. He was also superintendent of the parish church Sunday school; helped found an Irvine Ramblers' Field Club, modelled on the Kilmarnock Glenfield Ramblers of which he had been a prominent member; became secretary of Irvine Burns Club; and entered the town council in 1908.

The nearby East Road School was never as popular, suffering from the stigma of its origin as a school for the poor. It had 300 pupils in 1906, and after the transfer of its staff to Loudoun Street in 1907 it was reduced to a junior school with 160 pupils under Miss E M. Ballantyne and four assistants. Meanwhile St. Mary's RC School was developed by the Sisters of St. Joseph of Cluny who came in 1906 and provided not only elementary schooling but taught some French and music, as well as attending to their

Montgomery School in Cochrane Street, shortly after its opening in 1907.

other responsibility of visiting the sick. But His Majesty's Inspectors felt that 'the premises are not at all well adapted for school purposes'. In 1906 there were only 176 pupils, increasing to 213 by 1913. In 1911 the parish priest, Father Letters, was able to get himself elected to the School Board. Another novelty was that for a short period before that a Mrs. McAllister was a member, the first local woman ever to be elected to a public body.

Well-established institutions continued their existence — the Burns Club and the Social and Literary Institute. So too did Lodge St. Andrew's No. 194, with their Masonic Hall built in Bank Street in 1904; joined by Irvine Harbour Lodge No. 676. For ladies, the Order of the Eastern Star was formed in 1908. The Incorporated Trades now held their Annual Social Function with the councillors as guests, who granted free use of the Town Hall. That members could no longer always attach themselves to an appropriate craft is revealed by the occupations of the office bearers in 1908: deacon convener (plumber), clerk (painter), deacons of squaremen (mason), hammermen (joiner), tailors (draper), shoemakers (bootmaker), and the obsolescent trades of coopers (hotelier) and weavers (fire clay manufacturer). The temperance movement continued to be active, with Free Gardeners, Foresters, Ancient Shepherds, Reformed Templars, Rechabites, two lodges of Good Templars, Sons of Temperance, and the Parish Church Temperance Society — but efforts to make Irvine 'dry' were successfully countered by Irvine Spirit Trade Defence Association. The Irvine Merchants' Association in 1908 chose George Rubie, later a prominent town councillor, as their secretary, a post he held for the next fifty years. Politically there was the Unionist Association (now with their own premises, rebuilt in 1913) and the Liberal Association (now without rooms). Ayr Burghs constituency had become predominantly Conservative. The Liberals just succeeded in recovering it briefly on two occasions — W. Birkmyre (1892-95) with a majority of seven, and Joseph Dobbie (1904-1906) with a majority of forty-four. The Conservative ascendancy of J. Somerville (1890-92) and C.L. Orr Ewing (1895-1904) was confirmed by George Younger (1906-22) despite the national swing to Liberalism. How keen was the fight is revealed in the second general election of 1910 when there was a 91% poll of the 8,230 electors of Ayr Burghs, 1,893 of them from Irvine.

Continuing cultural interests in Irvine are revealed by the formation of a Ramblers' Field Club, an Arts and Crafts Club (1903) and a Literary and Debating Club (1911). The brass band continued, though supporters failed to persuade the town council in 1901 to build a

Marymass 1906, with the Town Council, the Carters, and the Burgh Brass Band outside the Town House. Proclamation of the Fair here is still followed by procession to the Moor.

bandstand on the Low Green to 'encourage the Band to come out and play tunes in the Summer months'. The Irvine Choral Society in 1907 arranged an ambitious Burns Concert, putting on 'The Jolly Beggars' as a cantata. In 1911 a dramatic society was resuscitated and an amateur orchestra formed, and a new Gilbert and Sullivan Operatic Society presented 'The Mikado', with special late trains for patrons from adjacent towns. The next year they followed with 'The Yeomen of the Guard', but thereafter enthusiasm evaporated. 1913 was a bad year in various ways. In January an emigration agent organised a lecture in the Masonic Hall, and one Saturday three months later thirty persons left for Canada.

Nevertheless, recreational facilities were still widening. Irvine Golf Club was largely patronised by members from Glasgow, who took advantage of the railway station at Bogside. So in 1907 a municipal golf course was opened at Ravenspark. Councillor John Parker was the man who initiated and pushed through the scheme. The town had the ground, laying out and maintaining the nine-hole course was cheap (a single greenkeeper at 24 shillings a week), and it proved so popular (at 3d per round or ten shillings annual subscription) that it was extended to eighteen holes in 1912. Irvine Cricket Club continued at its Vineburgh Park (a curious abbreviation of Irvine burgh). Winton Bowling Club extended its facilities in 1907 by acquiring a drinks licence. A proposal in 1912 for alternative municipal bowling greens came to nothing. In 1903 a private tennis club was formed, with courts beside the Low Green. In 1911 the Irvine Curling Club created an artificial pond with five rinks on the south side of Bank Street, and the Vale of Clyde Works had a quoiting club. In 1908 an Irvine and District Angling Club was formed. In 1906 Irvine Bathing Club built a shelter for themselves at the shore. The beach was sufficiently popular for ice cream and aerated waters to be on sale there in 1912, and in 1914 the council contemplated erecting two bathing boxes. Not far from the shore were the ranges of the Ayrshire Rifle Association, and each year a number of gentlemen obtained permission to shoot over the town lands. The Volunteers (Territorials after 1907) had a drill hall for the infantry company of the RSF in East Road and a new one for the artillerymen (1911) in High Street. The annual flower show lapsed, and the old Ornithological Society was superseded by a Homing Pigeon Society in 1904 and a Cage Bird Society in 1911. In the winter, dancing was an increasingly popular activity for couples old and young. In November 1903 the bowlers abandoned their traditional annual 'smoker' in favour of a dance. In following weeks there was a Bachelors' Dance, a Steam Laundry Dance, and a Blacksmiths' Dance.

There was opportunity to play the now popular indoor sport of billiards in the Eglinton Arms, the Unionist Club, and the Institute Hall, and in 1914 Albert Strong installed six tables in the Albert Hall, which thus underwent another change of use. Football, of course, continued to be popular. Irvine Victoria, a second local junior team, from the other side of the river, was formed in 1904. But the older Irvine Meadow was more successful. In 1900, 1904, 1910, 1914, and 1915 it was champion of the Irvine and District Association — for which Provost Charles Murchland presented an *Irvine Herald* Trophy in 1902. And they brought back to Meadow Park the Ayrshire Junior Cup in 1899, 1901, 1904, and 1914. Also, in this period, a first abortive attempt was made to form an Ayrshire football league at a meeting in Irvine, at the Fullarton Hotel, in 1902.

The town council was adjusting itself to the new 20th-century situation. In 1901 and again in 1910 long-forgotten ceremonial had to be revived for the succession of new monarchs, with proclamations at the market cross, north and south ports, and the harbour. Then the councillors and officials had to swear a new oath of allegiance to the crown, and arrange appropriate coronation celebrations, with firework displays, and treats for schoolchildren and the aged poor. Routine business had to be attended to. The burgh's heritable properties, valued in 1908 at £55,221, had to be managed. The agricultural committee leased and supervised farms, conducted the annual roup of other fields, and still leased for pasture the Low Green and Gallowsknoll (at £15 per annum). A new turf committee administered the harbour flats. The council still provided coals for the poor; made annual donations (including the usual £20 towards Marymass races), established a labour bureau (1908), provided work for the unemployed making up Cochrane Street and Gailes Road, and organised two soup kitchens (1912); and continued to support good causes like the appeal from Luigi Croci and Pietro Pieroni for victims of an Italian earthquake (1909). The council in 1908 cooperated in forming a local committee concerned with the new old age pensions of five shillings a week for certain persons over the age of seventy. In association with the new Nursing Association (1903) it accepted the gift of a new ambulance wagon and an endowment to maintain it, raised by generous public subscription; and in 1909 it appointed a trained nurse. A local Red Cross Brigade was also formed (1911). A recreation committee was formed to manage the municipal golf course. Other innovations were the printing of the Council Minutes (from 1907), provision of a mortuary at Kirkgatehead (1908), tar-macadamising the streets (1909), purchasing a bicycle for the burgh surveyor (1909), and accepting from the local artillery volunteers (1908) two old muzzle-loading 32-pounder guns to be set up in concrete in front of the Town House. Discussions were afoot for important new public services, with decisions reached in 1914, as will be explained in the next chapter.

Some difficulties were caused to the burgh by the sudden death in 1906 of the town clerk, James Dickie. John Norval Murray who followed was an ill man who died in 1908, to be followed by David Gillies — too many changes after more than a century of long-serving continuity: James Innes (1779-1817), James Johnston (1818-53), David Gray (1853-77), and James Dickie (1877-1906). Other difficulties were emerging in administration. The council as local authority had successfully inaugurated a water supply, and indeed in 1902 commenced an additional Caaf Water reservoir also in the parish of Dalry. But in 1903 it had to agree reluctantly to the creation of an Irvine and District Water Board on which Irvine was the major partner, but its seven representatives were outnumbered by ten others from Kilwinning, Stevenston, and Saltcoats. Similarly the council as police commissioners had continued street improvements, introduced incandescent street lamps in place of the old flame burners (1902), and ordered the replacement of all thatched roofs (before Whitsunday 1903). But efforts to obtain a method of treating the raw sewage which was discharged into the river and the harbour proved fruitless. Plans for a new fever hospital in 1905 had to be postponed, and Irvine had to share in a joint smallpox hospital at Kilwinning and the county sanatorium for tuberculosis at Glenafton.

An important administrative reorganisation was effected in 1907 'to save time and unnecessary repetition'. The councillors had had to hold separate formal meetings as Local Authority and as Police Commissioners. Now under the provisions of the Town Council (Scotland) Acts of 1900 and 1903 these bodies could be dissolved and their functions made the direct responsibility of the council as such, to be administered through appropriate council committees. At the same time in 1907 Irvine Town Council decided on regular meetings on the first Tuesday of each month, at 7.30 p.m. Earlier these evenings the council would meet as Auditors of Accounts, and committees would be held on other Tuesday or Thursday evenings. Such committees from 1908 were: Agricultural; Recreational; Sanitary, Streets and Works; Hospital; Health; Law; and Turf. The various assessments were now consolidated into a general burgh rate, and a furious row ensued in 1909 regarding the proportions which should be borne by owners and by tenants of property.

The provost of the time, Archibald Kirkland, who supported the tenants' case, was one of the most radical councillors of this era. A baker and councillor from 1894, he claimed (at the Glasgow-Irvine Society dinner of 1909) to be 'a follower of William Morris, and he looked forward to the new Utopia when, instead of grinding under the stimulus of machinery, they would have happiness, and every man would till his own vine and sit under his own fig tree'. Soon after his election to the council he had proposed (unsuccessfully) the formation of an industrial committee, a labour bureau, and a minimum wage of £1.1/- for burgh workers. He was equally unsuccessful in 1896 in advocating a free library and the prohibition of drinking and gambling at Bogside Races. In the same year he pioneered the idea of council housing by suggesting 'working men's houses' to replace tenements demolished in the Bridgegate, and in 1897 he suggested a Model Lodging House to be provided by the council. In 1903 he revived the arguments for municipalisation of the local gas company. In 1903 he also put forward a scheme for an Electric Tramway System to connect Irvine with Ardrossan, Troon, and Kilmarnock. He did persuade the council in 1904 to accept in principle the desirability of lighting the town by electricity but, after two years of planning, the project was dropped 'until the advantages to be derived from Electricity are more fully appreciated', with Kirkland recording his dissent. Then in 1906, as member of the School Board, he advocated an extension of opportunities for secondary education. As it was, supplementary classes for older pupils had been formed in the elementary schools. Kirkland proposed 'that a proportion of the children entitled to enter the supplementary classes be drafted to the Academy'. The chairman, Rev. Henry Ranken, was afraid of 'inspiring young folks with the desire for professional life, who would be far better and happier as artisans'. The Board rejected the scheme of 'drafting' pupils in favour of providing more bursaries. But in 1911 a qualifying examination was introduced to select pupils for the academy. Thus were fulfilled Kirkland's requirements — as in due course were implemented nearly all the ideas he originally conceived. His appointment as provost in 1907 was unexpected. Support on the council for two rival candidates was fairly evenly divided. Seeking Kirkland's support, one faction formally proposed him, the other seconded him, each expecting him to decline. But he didn't, and found himself elected, for three awkward years. Even after he retired from the council in 1910 at the end of his provostship, he made one further contribution. When in 1912 the council was financing the new shipyard, Kirkland protested that under the terms of the 1881 Act the funds of the Common Good could not legally be expended outwith the area of the old royal burgh. A special clause had to be inserted into a new provisional order to allow the Common Good to be applied to any part of the extended burgh. When he died in 1913 in his sixty-second year the *Irvine Herald* commented on the breadth of his interests. He was a master baker who had lectured on and written a book on his craft. He had been an originator of the Arts and Crafts club. He 'did a very great amount of philanthropy in a quiet, unostentatious manner'. Politically, 'he allowed his sympathies, especially in connection with matters concerning the lower classes, to outweigh other considerations'. To sum up, 'in him the working classes had a warm-hearted friend'.

SEVENTEEN

The First War and After

In the months before the outbreak on 4th August 1914 of what became known as the Great War, newspapers were filled with talk of the Irish problem, House of Lords, tariff reform and suffragettes, and people were enjoying the sunshine of a glorious summer. Irvine Town Council had under consideration a number of weighty issues.

The shortage of houses had become critical, especially with an influx of workers to the new shipyard. Some had got accommodation in the new houses in Cochrane Street, or in the Trades Hotel opened nearby. But so desperate was the shortage that others were living in vans — 120 persons at a count made in 1912. What made matters worse was that the condition of some of the older tenements in the town was bad enough to force the council to place closing orders on them, under new statutory powers. A proposal that council houses should be built came from an unexpected source. Concerned at loss of trade if shipyard workers had to look outside Irvine for accommodation, in 1913 the Irvine Merchants' Association urged the council to erect dwellinghouses. Reluctantly, in the spring of 1914 the council unanimously agreed to exercise its powers under the Housing of the Working Classes Acts, 1890–1909. Possible sites were considered, and on Monday 3rd August 1914 the council met in committee to examine plans for houses to be erected in Ayr Road, Kirk Vennel, and behind Bank Street.

The extension of the shipyard required demolition of the old fever hospital. In 1905 it had been hoped to replace this with something better to be built at Duntonknoll. Now plans were made for an Infectious Diseases Hospital on the Moor near the Poorshouse. In the meantime fever cases had to be transported expensively to Kilmarnock Infirmary.

Another belated improvement was being implemented. In 1906 a scheme for a local supply of electricity had foundered. Now in 1913 negotiations were initiated with Kilmarnock Town Council which was undertaking to supply power for that burgh and a wide surrounding area.

The other issue which was agitating Irvine council was its unsuccessful efforts to prevent Messrs. Nobel from extending their Ardeer explosives works in the direction of Irvine. There had been worries since the commencement of the works in 1872 about ships transporting explosives through Irvine harbour; agitation against the building of a wharf in 1881 on the Garnock; and more recent alarm when the explosion of March 1913 broke many windows in Irvine. Reports which appeared in the American press that the whole of Irvine had been wrecked could be discounted; but another explosion in February 1914 which killed eight workers at Ardeer kept fears alive.

Other matters of interest were the receipt of a cheque from the Duke of Portland towards a proposed footbridge from Golffields to Ayr Road; a proposal to erect two bathing boxes at the shore; search for a site for a new burying ground; and the allocation to R. Johnstone of Fenwick of a stance in High Street near the weighing machine, at one shilling per annum, for a motor bus service between Kilmarnock and Irvine.

Irvine Town Council met on the evening of Tuesday 4th August 1914 for its regular monthly meeting, with Provost James Borland in the chair. Among thirty-one items of business, some were of special significance. The Kilmarnock Lighting (Extension) Order had received the royal assent. The Home Office would not prohibit the extension of Ardeer explosive works. The private road leading to the shipyard would be taken over as Boyle Street. There were other less important items — the greenkeeper, now responsible for an 18-hole golf course, a putting green and two clubhouses, sought an increase in wages; three sixty-foot lengths of hose were ordered for the fire brigade; no action was taken in support of a communication regarding Scots Home Rule. Nowhere in the minutes is there any hint of war. In the local press it was reported that news of the outbreak was received in Irvine 'in a very soberminded fashion', with 'quiet but determined patriotism'.

The first casualty was Marymass. The fair was cancelled for August 1914 and for the duration of hostilities. On 17th August the council held a special meeting to make allocations from the Common Good towards various relief funds — the Prince of Wales National Fund (£70), the Earl

A Burgh Hospital to replace the old Sickhouse by the Dockyard was built on the Moor. It had wounded soldiers as its first patients.

of Eglinton's County Fund for families of soldiers and sailors (£60) and the local Red Cross (£20). The Carters Society returned to the council its £20 annual award to augment these donations. At its September meeting the council agreed to co-operate with the Territorial Force Association in raising a reserve battery of artillery. In October 'the horrors of war were brought so near to us' by news of Irvine's first war casualty, Captain Harry Sherwood Ranken, RAMC, the parish minister's elder son. He died in France of wounds after gallantly continuing to care for others under fire when his own thigh and leg were shattered. He was posthumously awarded the Chevalier's Cross of the Legion of Honour, and the Victoria Cross.

For the next four years the War occupied the forefront of everyone's mind. The council instituted a Roll of Honour, and every month with monotonous regularity new names were added to the list of the fallen — reaching peaks of twelve in September 1916 and again in June 1917. Each week the local newspapers reported on those killed, wounded, or missing. By the end of 1918 there was a record of over two hundred who had been killed on the battlefield or at sea. Private Ross Tollerton, who survived to become Bank Street school janitor, had also the distinguished honour of winning the Victoria Cross for valour in 1915. At the Battle of the Aisne in September 1914 he had, though wounded, rescued an officer who was also wounded, staying with him for three days under heavy fire.

To begin with, the regular and territorial armed forces were augmented by volunteers. In November 1914 a first recruiting meeting was organised; in January 1915 the Royal Scots Fusiliers held a recruiting march; and in October 1915 the councillors constituted themselves as a Local Recruiting Committee. Conscription was introduced in 1916, and six councillors and one other formed a Local Tribunal which co-operated with a County Appeal Tribunal to consider exemptions on compassionate or conscientious grounds. The burgh surveyor was granted deferment, then when he was called up a temporary replacement was found, to be assisted by a clerkess installed in his office.

Patriotism had to be sustained. Flags of France, Belgium and Russia were purchased (October 1914) for display on Trafalgar Day and other appropriate occasions. A War Savings Committee (1916) encouraged financial contributions to the war effort. The War Charities Act (1916) regularised appeals for funds, and there were flag

A war memorial in the style of a mercat cross was unveiled in 1921. It was moved from the middle of the street in 1951.

days every other Saturday. To raise funds for YMCA huts there was a cycle and fancy dress parade in 1917, in which the Boy Scouts participated, and also the Carters in their Marymass garb. In the same year a contribution to war charities came from the Lawn Tennis Club which organised a new type of function — a whist drive and dance. Generosity exhausted the council's Common Good Fund, which remained in debit from 1917 until 1950.

War made further impact on Irvine. The shipyard and local industries were busy with war work. In 1917 a Royal Ordnance Factory was opened on a site near the shore — the 'Shell Work' or 'Lloyd George Factory', within a year employing over 1,500, 73% of them women. Irvine became a garrison town, with camps on the Moor and at Gailes, and with halls and schools commandeered for military purposes. Even the mortuary at Kirkgatehead was converted into a bath house for the Royal Engineers. Surprisingly, the illegitimacy rate remained low — 5.8% in 1916, 6.7% in 1918. Canteen and recreational facilities were provided by churches and other local organisations. Also on the Moor a Red Cross hospital was built for wounded soldiers and sailors. When the new Infectious Diseases hospital was completed in 1916, it was leased to the Red Cross for the duration.

Irvine being a coastal town, restriction was placed (October 1914) on elevated lights which might be seen from the sea, which affected the Academy and the Parish and Trinity churches. Street lighting had to be diminished (November 1914), and with only 53 of the town's 120 lamps lit, people walked into lamp posts and fell over ash buckets. Under the Defence of the Realm Act (1915) there was a temporary ban on travelling shows within ten miles at the coast. There was also prohibition (1916) of the ringing of bells or striking of clocks after sunset, which it was feared might be a guide to hostile aircraft — an unnecessary precaution. In November 1917, however, 'one of the Flying Corps gave a wonderful biplane exhibition over Irvine last Sunday forenoon'.

Bailie John Parker, joiner and inventor, turned his attention to devising contrivances some of which were taken up by the War Office and Admiralty: in 1914 a bullet-proof helmet; in 1915 a trenching tool with a rifle aperture used at Gallipoli; then ideas for protecting ships from mines, detecting submarines, and safeguarding tanks against land mines.

Everyday life was only marginally affected by the War. The Sunday delivery of letters was suspended (1915) and daylight saving introduced (1916) with summertime alteration of clocks. With many men on war service, including some of the younger ministers as chaplains to the forces, various organisations suffered. The debating club in the Social and Literary Institute ended and never revived. But football, golf, cricket, bowls, and tennis could be enjoyed; there were still pleasure boats on the river; and Bostock and Wombell's Circus on the Low Green in 1917. Green's Picturedrome and the Empire in Bridgegate offered films and variety shows at 4d, 5d, 7d and 11d, with penny Saturday matinees for children. By 1917 the U-boat campaign was having its effect on supplies. Sugar rationing had to be introduced. Food Control Committees were set up. The local body comprised seven councillors and five others, two of whom had to be ladies. Local trade unionists complained that there were only two 'Labour' representatives. This committee fixed maximum retail prices — 26/- per ton for the best house coal; Pope's Eye Steak at 2/2 per pound; sausages and mince at 1/3 per pound. Cream and ice cream could not be sold. There were queues for the four-ounce weekly ration of butter or margarine. In 1918 it was necessary to introduce fuel control. Allotments for growing vegetables were laid out; there were collections of scrap iron; and there was a shortage of paper for printing the new voters' rolls.

The War dominated the scene. Party politics seemed less important, save for the ILP, whose anti-war propaganda

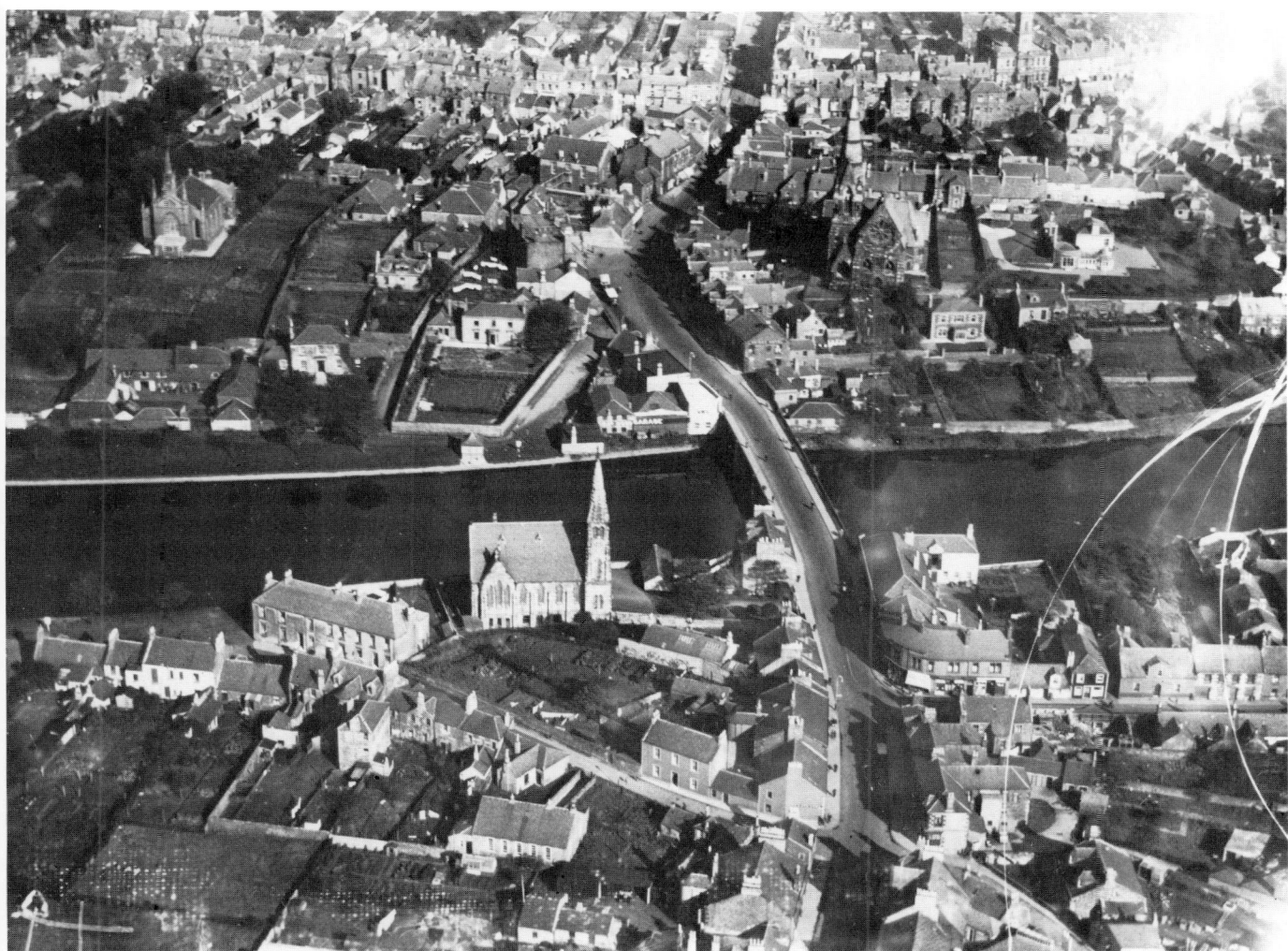

This aerial photograph of 1927 shows Fullarton Place at the nearer end of the bridge and the Bridgegate at the other. The three places of worship of the Free Church are seen — Mure, Wilson Fullarton, and Trinity.

had little impact. In 1915 the town council offered a vote of confidence to the new Coalition government. The *Irvine Herald* report in 1917 of 'certain recent disturbing events in Petrograd' left readers unaware of the importance of the impending Russian Revolution. Municipal elections were suspended for the duration of the War. Vacancies were filled by co-option — as when Councillor Green joined up in 1915, or when Provost Borland resigned in 1916, after the appointment of Walter Muir as a new provost. Routine work of the council continued as best it could. In 1915 three councillors were appointed as police judges to serve as additional magistrates. In 1916 additional committees were formed. Work proceeded with laying of the electricity cables. The first council houses in Ayr Road (Kyle Terrace) and Kirk Vennel (Johnstone Place) were completed in 1915, but plans for others had to be delayed. 'The much needed housing scheme in Irvine is now as far away as ever.'

When the Armistice came on Monday 11th November 1918, 'horns in all the public works in the town were in full blast, and the church and burgh bells were ringing'. Factories and schools closed for two days, flags and bunting were put up on buildings and ships, and at night bonfires were lit. In the Cotton Row, tar barrels were used to ignite the canvas and wood of the imitation tank which the Royal Engineers had paraded in the war savings campaigns. But there was an 'absence of the wild hilarity that marked some of the Boer War celebrations'. The end of fighting was welcomed with 'relief rather than jubilation'. At the council meeting of 12th November Provost Muir applauded 'the great victory of the Allied Forces' but reminded his colleagues of 'the large amount of work which lies before the town council'.

Peace was celebrated in April 1919 with a church service, procession, sports, and fireworks. Brigadier-General James Walker was presented with the freedom of the burgh in recognition of his services in the Territorial forces before and during the War. The widely representative committee which had been raising subscriptions for a war memorial planned to erect a reconstructed mercat cross in High Street outside the Town House. This was unveiled and formally handed over to the council in March 1921. It lists the names of 237 who 'gave their lives for their country'. Seventy-seven had served with the county regiment, the Royal Scots Fusiliers; only five with the navy; and fifteen with Canadian and ANZAC units.

Also, in 1920 the government presented to the town a captured German machine gun and howitzer as war relics. But disillusion was voiced by Councillor James Haggarty who noted 'plenty of relics in the town in the shape of disabled men'.

Problems of demobilisation, shortages, and profiteering merged into the greater one of post-war industrial depression. For a time the shipyard was kept busy, and the ancillary businesses supplying it. Indeed in 1919 Ayrshire Dockyard Company took over responsibility for the entire harbour, with its dredger, tug and wharf installations. In 1920 two Clan ships were launched, each of 7,600 tons, the largest ever built in Irvine. At its peak period, the shipyard employed between two and three thousand men. But shipbuilding was 'rationalised' and the Irvine yard taken over by Sir J. & H. Lithgow in 1928. Similar decay overtook the other major undertakings. The Royal Ordnance Factory ceased production and was dismantled in 1925. In that year, too, the Caledonian forge closed down. Imperial Chemical Industries, the combine formed in 1926, took over various works in Irvine. Those of the United Alkali Company were closed down; only their Walker Works and Scottish Tar Distillers continued. Also surviving in difficult circumstances were Laird's blockworks, Brown's iron foundry, Flanagan's brass foundry, Wright's sawmills, Cowan's soap works, and the Vale of Clyde railway works — which like other Glasgow and South Western properties was in 1921 incorporated in the LMS Railway Company. The only major new undertaking was the Portland Glass Company, set up in Gailes Road in 1920 on the site of the Metallic Oxides factory by Brigadier-General Walker. The Hosiery Manufacturing Company (1900) was joined by similar though small businesses — A. Cunningham, Greenbank (1914); A. & J. Wilson, Fullarton Street (1925); Walter Henderson, Bank Street (1926); British Textile Manufacturing Company, Cochrane Street (1929); and Eglinton and Star Hosiery, New Street (1933).

The general picture was of decline, and the virtual extinction of the north Ayrshire coalfield. William Baird and Co. Ltd. closed down the last three pits in Irvine parish — Bartonholm (1928), Bogside (1929), Eglinton (1930), and the adjacent Redburn (1930). A. Finnie and Son's Fergushill pits were abandoned by J. & R. Howie (1921). In Dreghorn, the Bourtreehill Coal Company ceased production at Broomland (1928). A. Kenneth and Sons alone survived at Montgomeryfield, Oldhall and Shewalton.

Depression inevitably brought distress. Despite the labour exchange established locally in 1919 by the Ministry of Labour for the distribution of unemployment benefits, there was necessary recourse to traditional measures. The annual distribution of coals for the poor continued. In 1920 two soup kitchens were established, this time on the initiative of the Co-operative Society. The council contributed £25 from the Common Good plus £14 left over from previous occasions. The council also provided work on the roads. Wartime neglect had to be repaired. The principal thoroughfares had to be improved to new Ministry of Transport standards. And the building of council houses gave employment not only to workers with local firms, but unskilled labour was required in making up new streets, at ten pence per hour in 1923.

The depression was punctuated by labour disputes. In 1920 the miners went on strike, and schoolteachers withdrew from evening classes for three weeks. In May 1926 came the General Strike, with the magistrates and an executive committee of councillors required by the government to handle any emergencies. In fact, as the *Irvine Herald* reported (after two weeks when it could not be issued), tempers remained calm. There were only two instances 'when transport buses were interfered with and windows broken — by a band of irresponsible rather than responsible trade unionists'. In the protracted coal dispute which continued after the General Strike collapsed, 'the behaviour of the local miners on strike continued to be exemplary... not a single untoward incident'.

During these years there were heavy demands on Irvine Parish Council which was responsible for poor relief. John Brown, a miner who lived in East Road, was an elected member for over twenty years, latterly chairman (1913-19). He declared that 'the aliment paid to the Poor of Irvine compared favourably with that of any other parish, though he had been frequently criticised on that point'. Betwen 1910 and 1920 the poors rate increased from 1/5 to 2/- in the £, and for some years thereafter it continued to grow, during the chairmanship of P.S. Clark (1919-30). Besides aiding the aged poor and contributing towards

In 1927 the harbour was busy, with three ships under construction at the dockyard, and others tied up nearby.

Cunninghame Poorshouse, assistance had to be given to those unemployed who did not qualify for benefit from the labour exchange, and to families of miners and others on strike. The General Strike required over £4,000 to be disbursed in relief payments in 1926/27, more than double the usual sum. The poors rate then was increased to 3/1 in the £, divided as usual between owners (1/6) and occupiers (1/7) of property. In the subsequent period of financial stringency the rate was reduced, to 1/3 by 1928/29, still rather more than the rate of 1/1½ for that part of the burgh for which Dundonald Parish Council was responsible. Distress among the growing numbers of unemployed resulted in the town council in 1928, on the advice of the Scottish Board of Health, forming a local Relief Committee comprising burgh and parish councillors and others immediately concerned. There followed an advertisement in the *Irvine Herald:* 'Owing to the severe unemployment in the town Messrs. Pieroni and Son will supply Fish Suppers on Tuesdays, Wednesdays, and Thursdays, at the reduced price of 4d'.

Coincidentally, these years of post-war depression marked also the end of Eglinton, whose feudal interests had so long dominated the local scene. Behind the facade of splendour there was a legacy of financial insolvency. As far back as the 18th century, the impressive improvements to the estate had left the 9th earl with a debt of £18,000, raised by his two successors to £40,000. In the 19th century the 12th earl's various ambitious projects increased the figure to £269,000. The 13th earl's expensive tastes could not be covered by the considerable new income from coal and iron. The 14th earl suffered in the Glasgow Bank crash of 1878, and lands had to be sold, including Coilsfield and the original family property of Eaglesham. Shortly after his death William Robertson's *History of Ayrshire* remarked that it 'need not do more than say that his lordship's inclinations did not lead him towards the discharge of public duties. He was famous as a fox hunter, and for many years rode at the head of the Eglinton Hunt'. His brother George succeeded as 15th earl (1892-1919), inheriting a diminished estate of 30,200 acres. He continued the Eglinton connection with Irvine by opening the new academy, the countess was active in the Red Cross and other local organisations, and together they played a prominent part in the county's war efforts, for the earl was Lord Lieutenant of Ayrshire. But when Archibald became 16th earl (1919-45), the estate was crippled by the death duties which now operated. Lands had to be put up for sale, including Bogside; in 1924 the race course was acquired by John Jackson of Carlisle (who managed it until his death in 1938). In December 1925 the pictures and furnishings in Eglinton Castle were sold off, the roof was stripped, and the magnificent edifice began to crumble into ruin. Later earls — Archibald William (1945-66) and Archibald George (since 1966) — inevitably had limited local connections.

All this was taking place in a new political climate. The Representation of the People Act of 1918 extended the franchise to all men over twenty-one and also women over the age of thirty. Numbers in Irvine eligible to vote increased to 5,000 for parliamentary elections (3,175 males, 1,816 females) and rather fewer with ratepaying qualifications for municipal elections (2,514 males, 2,163 females). At this time, too, the political scene was transformed with the emergence of the Labour Party. Locally councillors of radical views had been elected in the pre-war period, like Archibald Kirkland and John Johnston. But the Independent Labour Party — through whose branches the Labour Party was then organised — began to operate effectively in Irvine only after 1918. In the first post-war municipal election of November 1919 seven out of nine ILP candidates were successful in what the *Ardrossan and Saltcoats Herald* called 'a notorious Tory preserve'. They could celebrate with the first of their annual socials and dances in the Good Templars Hall. In 1925 they were able to open ILP rooms in Montgomery Street. Arthur Brady, their acknowledged leader, represented the First Ward (1919-20), then the Fifth Ward (1921-24, 1926-37), an indication of how fickle fortunes were in this transitional period. Nationally the Labour Party won power with a minority government in 1924, and another under Ramsay Macdonald in 1929. Ayr Burghs parliamentary constituency remained consistently Unionist in representation. This constituency was completely reshaped in 1918. It ceased to be a consortium of widely separated burghs. Campbeltown, Inveraray and Oban were removed, and it became that compact coastal part of Ayrshire extending from Irvine through Troon to Ayr. The result of the December 1918 election was delayed for a month to include the votes of absent members of the armed forces — 996 of them belonging to Irvine. Sir George Younger (who had been created baronet in 1911) retained the seat with 9,565 votes. The opposition was split between the Liberals with 5,410 and Labour's first candidate, Rev. Campbell Stephen, previously assistant minister in Ardrossan UF Church, with 4,534.

This pattern was repeated in 1922 when Sir John L. Baird won the seat, but his Labour opponent, John M. Airlie from Edinburgh, reached second place in 1923 and 1924. In 1927 Colonel Thomas Moore commenced his long tenure of the seat by defeating P.J. Dollan from Glasgow. In 1928 the franchise was extended to all over the age of twenty-one, giving Irvine 3,521 women voters, outnumbering 3,334 men. Hopeful of capturing the female vote, the Labour Party nominated Mrs. Clarice McNab Shaw of Troon, but at the 1929 General Election the Unionists retained Ayr Burghs with 16,974 votes against Labour's 13,429 and the Liberals' 6,479.

Although the Labour Party's advance was limited, its influence was notable in changing the composition and outlook of the town council. After the 1919 municipal election there remained nine councillors of the old regime — a saddler, two grocers, a potato merchant, hotelkeeper, publisher, schoolmaster, residenter, and the plumber John Johnston. Newly elected members included a drysalter and a spirit merchant, plus the seven Labour members — draper, tailor's cutter, another plumber, two miners, and two checkweighers. Provost Walter Muir was the saddler, working in the High Street shop where Provost Salmon had carried on the same trade nearly a century before. Dedicated to clearing the town of its slums, he died in office in 1923. His successor, R.M. Hogg, was able to continue that work, though also a traditionalist. In 1924, when the old washing house on the Golffields had to be demolished, he saved the slates for the restoration of the Powder House. In 1925 he had the Jockey Club's date for races at Bogside altered to avoid a clash with Marymass. That year there was a fire in the Glasgow Vennel house where Burns had lodged — with Constable Robert Barrowman earning a medal for lifesaving. When the house was repaired the next year, Hogg organised the presentation of a plaque from the Burns Club to mark the building, and the council recognised the Club's centenary by presenting the chairs once occupied by David Sillar and Dr. Mackenzie when councillors. In 1927 R.M. Hogg rectified a long omission by having the burgh coat of arms properly registered. When he retired in 1928, he was followed as provost by Peter Stuart Clark, of the Customs and Excise service, who was already serving as Chairman of Irvine Parish Council and as Deacon Convener of the Incorporated Trades, and

A rural setting in 1927 for Bank Street, adjoined by Bank Street School, the Gas Works, and the Hosiery Manufacturing Company. In the foreground Thornhouse farm, not yet aquired for council house building. In the background can be seen the Caledonian railway, the Caledonian foundry, and — beyond the open fields — Quarry Road leading to Duntonknoll quarry.

was an enthusiast for Marymass. He also absorbed much of Irvine's past from his mother, who had been a maid to Rev. Dr. Robertson, and who was the burgh's oldest inhabitant when she died in 1935 at the age of 97. When Clark died in 1953, he was described as 'the supreme Irvineite... there was not a nook or cranny in the town that he did not know'.

During the War, council committees had proliferated, and in 1922, with increased expenditure, the monthly examination of payments by the whole council was delegated to an accounts committee. In 1924 the whole system was tidied up, with duties allocated to six committees — finance, works, health, property, law, and recreation. In 1926 A.R. Wilson became town clerk, after serving six years jointly with David Gillies (1908-27). Much work continued to be routine. The Fever Hospital on the Moor was vacated by the Red Cross at the end of the War, and a matron and (when necessary) a trained nurse looked after its thirty-one beds. In 1925 the council recognised that it was no longer necessary to have the town bell rung at five in the morning and ten at night, and — another sign of changed days — accepted the abolition of Saturday afternoon delivery of letters. There were always unexpected outlays, in 1928 particularly. The council had then to contribute towards rebuilding the bridge over the Annick when mineral subsidence damaged the old one and closed the road. The Town House required repair, renovating the tower, renewing the vane, restoring eroded mouldings, and removing the old coat of arms for safety and preservation. And £570 was spent on the purchase of the old Loch Lomond Vaults in Bridgegate.

A sign that the council was bent on innovations appeared in 1920. Councillor Arthur Brady proposed the inauguration of a Municipal Bank. This idea was acceptable to the council, and a new institution was established, providing useful facilities for local depositors and cheaper capital for some of the municipal enterprises.

Priority was given to the provision of new housing. So desperate was the shortage in 1920 that military huts on the Moor were acquired to provide temporary accommodation. At the 1921 census Irvine, with a population of 11,826, was more overcrowded (1.73 per room) than at any time in the previous fifty years. That census, admittedly, was taken at an awkward time when numbers in some places were inflated by holiday visitors, but hardly Irvine. The town council in 1920 planned a major housing programme. The 32 houses in Ayr Road and 16 in Kirk Vennel had been built without state aid. Now government loans were available, and £50,000 was borrowed for the first phase of development — sixteen blocks with 54 houses at Thornhouse south of Bank Street costing nearly £1,000 each. When the 'New Houses' were completed in 1921, rents were fixed at £25 per year. This was high by existing standards, but the idea was that when better-off working-class families occupied them, the reasonably kept older houses they vacated would become available for those living in slum conditions. In 1923 another 64 were completed, and when Provost Muir died that year the council minuted that his contribution to housing had made Irvine 'the envy and wonder of neighbouring burghs'. This was surely too fulsome a tribute, for although there were now 166 council houses, many more were needed. In the next six years another 204 became available in the same area. But despite this, and grants which assisted the private building of around fifty houses for letting, and the use of new powers to force improvements on landlords of older properties, Irvine at the beginning of the '30s remained a particularly badly housed town. At the 1931 census, with an average of 1.55 persons per room, it was more overcrowded than any other Ayrshire burgh save Galston.

The streets of the new housing schemes required names. In 1922 the council chose Thornhouse Avenue (after the farm name), Dalrymple Drive (crossing the land of Dalrympleward), and Muir Drive (after the provost). There followed St. Inan Avenue (on the suggestion of Provost Hogg) and Galt Avenue and Allan Square (also of historical significance). Then Clark Drive established a continuing policy of naming most new streets after prominent members of the council. The opportunity was taken in 1922 to systematise some older street names. Boatstobs, Peter Street, and Guthries Road were included in Gottries Road, Alma Place in Shipyard Road, Hamilhill in West Road, Adam Square and Quarry Lane in Quarry Road, most of Ballot Road was added to Bank Street, and the remainder which was Cotton Row was designated Ballot Road. Later, Gailes Road would become Portland Road.

Electricity cables from Kilmarnock had reached Irvine in 1915, and several buildings including the new hospital were then lit. In 1919 the council began setting up electric lamps to light the streets, by annual stages. The new council houses were supplied, but the Town House had to wait till 1924. In that year the Kilmarnock generating station and its supply lines after twenty years' operation were taken over by the new Ayrshire Electricity Board. Gas remained the prinicipal fuel for cooking, but by the '30s most homes had electric lighting. Not until 1943, however, did Irvine Mains Farm obtain a supply.

Other plans delayed by the War were implemented. A road roller and motor lorry were acquired (1919). A child welfare clinic was opened, one afternoon each week, in Waterside Hall (1919). The old ford beside the bridge disappeared (1921) with renewed repairs to the river bank and the weir (1924). Pre-war plans for a new burying ground at Sandy Road beyond Ravenspark were revived, but an alternative site was chosen and Knadgerhill Cemetery opened (1926). Matters were less satisfactory in other respects. The local fire brigade was disbanded in 1922 and its appliances disposed of. The burgh came to rely on the services of Ayrshire Dockyard Company and other brigades from Kilmarnock and Ayr. The sewage problem also remained unsolved. River pollution was intensified with the new sewer from the housing scheme discharging into the Annick. In 1926 the Scottish Board of Health calculated a daily dry water flow of 424,800 gallons of sewage from two outfalls into the Annick, thirteen outfalls into the Irvine, and one into the Minister's Cast, plus discharges from the chemical works. An intercepting sewer was urgently required, the town council was informed.

More successful were the council's efforts to extend recreational facilities. The municipal golf course was supplemented by a putting course on the Low Green (1922), and courts for tennis (1926) and badminton (1928) were provided at Thornhouse Drive. A start was made to provide play parks for children, stimulated by an anonymous gift of £100 for swings on the Low Green (1928). But no special provision was made to develop Irvine as a holiday resort. A suggestion in the *Irvine Herald* of an esplanade at the shore was not taken up. Yet cheap railway tickets were bringing crowds of day trippers at the Glasgow Fair of 1925. 'Irvine, indeed, seems to have come into its very own as a coastal resort', announced the *Irvine Herald*. An editorial asked, 'why should the chemical works and bings be any deterrent to visitors?' but admitted it was a long walk to the shore and there were no buses. The council limited itself to converting the old lifeboat shed into a shop and bathing shelter (1927).

During the period when Irvine was continuing its modest growth, from 9,618 (1901), 10,179 (1911) and 11,826 (1921) to 12,032 (1931), the churches and schools were quietly adapting to new circumstances.

Throughout the period the parish church minister, Rev. Henry Ranken (1891-1928), 'not only filled the pulpit of that grand old kirk with great acceptance, but he enormously improved its amenities, and his interest in and enthusiasm for all the ancient privileges and rites of the burgh were as fervid as any native born and bred'. Like his predecessor, he had become a President of the Burns Club and he helped rescue the Powder House. Yet, a surprising example of older ecclesiastical manners, he continued the practise of private censure of erring parishioners until 1927. There survives his 'Private Record of Discipline', with those guilty of antenuptial fornication rebuked and absolved from scandal, and the names of persons concerned excised 'after a lapse of five years'. During his ministry the roll increased from 820 to 1170 members. Fullarton Parish Church also enjoyed the long and successful ministry of Rev. John Paterson (1903-37), who transformed a building which had been described as 'whitewashed brown and gey dirty'. Vitality was also evident in the four congregations which in 1900 became part of the United Free Church. The Relief Kirk extended its membership under Revs. Robert Pollock (1896-1903), J. Winchester (1903-19), James Graham (1920-25), and Samuel McNab (1925-51). At Trinity Church Rev. W.S. Dickie (1897-1931) continued another long ministry. The same was true of Wilson-Fullarton Church, with Rev. James Wishart (1902-47) doing valuable mission work in the harbour area. Only in Mure Church was there less continuity, with a succession of ministers — Revs. Donald G. Ross (1900-07), James Cosh (1907-16), C.R. Munro (1916-24) and R. Waldrum (1924-29). But here too membership increased, and changes were made with the building of a hall in 1903, installation of an organ in 1910, introduction of electric light in 1921, and the provision of individual communion cups in 1924. These churches all had their separate traditions — conservative in doctrine, strict in observance — as reflected by the United Free Presbytery in 1920 condemning whist drives and dances and advocating prohibitionism at the local veto polls. Yet when Union of the Churches came in 1929 there were no local difficulties among the six congregations of the new Church of Scotland. There had long been cooperation, and

Eglinton Castle was left vacant in 1926, marking the end of the long era of feudal power.

relations were good with the respected ministers of the old parish churches, and with Ranken's young and enthusiastic successor, Rev. Alexander Macara from Denny, who was ordained in 1928.

Outwith the presbyterian fold, the Baptists were served by a series of pastors. Rev. Walter Millburn was followed by Revs. John Climie (1909-13), Archibald Jack (1913-15), John Murphy (1915-19), A.H. Gammage (1920-28) and Neil McLachlan (1928-31). There were also the Salvation Army, Christadelphians, Christian Brethren in the Waterside Hall, and a Gospel caravan at the shore and Low Green in summertime. The 20th century brought welcome acceptance of the Roman Catholics. Father Frederick Letters (1897-1911) was able to win election to the School Board. Under Fr. Thomas Joyce (1911-18) their share in the war effort won respect. When Fr. Joseph Hogan followed (1918-36), he was provided with a series of curates to assist in extended activities. Sisters of the Cross and Passion acquired Williamfield, set up a convent, and took charge of the schooling. When the primary school moved out of the church in 1928, St. Mary's was renovated and enhanced.

The Education (Scotland) Act of 1918 brought a significant administrative change with the election of an Ayrshire Education Authority. To this new body the Irvine School Board before its dissolution handed over the schools it managed — Irvine Royal Academy (roll in 1917, 237), Bank Street (630), Montgomery (617), Loudoun Street (397) and East Road (229). Throughout this period the academy had as its rector J.W. Bryson (1914-30), under whom the roll increased as fees were reduced for secondary pupils and finally abolished in 1927. By 1930 a record 500 pupils were enrolled. Bank Street during this period continued under R.M. Hogg (1905-30), Montgomery under William Mitchell (1907-30), and Loudoun Street under William Miller (1902-15) then William McAngus, with Miss E.M. Bannatyne still at East Road. These were difficult times for the schools. During the War Loudoun Street school was requisitioned by the army and its scholars shared part-time education with those of Montgomery School, to which they were transferred. In 1920 huts had to be erected to provide extra accommodation needed after the school-leaving age was raised to fourteen in 1918. There were problems of the necessitous children in the depression and the provision of free school meals. The old Fullarton school was used as a soup kitchen.

Until the 1918 Act, St. Mary's had remained a private school, receiving only grant aid for its pupils (205 in 1917). Thereafter it became a 'transferred school' and came under the management of Ayrshire Educational Authority. Teaching was undertaken by the Sisters of the Cross and Passion. In 1921 secondary education was begun with seven girl pupils in the Convent at Williamfield, where additional building in 1923 created St. Michael's Secondary School, under Sister Mechtilde Joseph (1921-50). On an adjacent site a St. Mary's Primary School was opened in 1928, bringing children from the old church school under Sister Malachy (1921-33). Thus a modern system of education under centralised management was being evolved, despite the difficulties of the times.

There was a continued expectation that things should be better in this post-war era, and for those in work there was money to spend on new recreations.

We are now into the era of the cinema, which in the '20s and '30s became the most popular form of mass entertainment. Throughout the war civilians and servicemen stationed locally had enjoyed films and vaudeville shows in Green's Picturedrome, Bank Street, and Swan's Empire above the Literary and Social Institute in Bridgegate. In 1920 the latter under new management became the Picture Palace, and the Empire moved to new premises in the Gruip. A fourth cinema arrived when the Tivoli Theatre in the old Albert Hall in West Road began picture shows too. All continued to offer stage performances as well as the silent films which were accompanied by piano or a 'syncopated orchestra of Irvine musicians'. Then came the 'talkies', and Green's Picturedrome was first to introduce the new sound system in November 1929. Forthcoming attractions were prominently advertised in the local press, and the cinemas were always busy. In 1930 the Medical Officer of Health complained about 'the increasing custom of taking infants in arms to Picture Houses, etc. at night, particularly to "second houses" in the winter months'.

Another novelty was the 'wireless'. In 1922 the British Broadcasting Company was formed. Those who constructed their own receiving sets were catered for by an Irvine Radio Society and 'Radio Notes' in the local press. In 1926 the Poorshouse was supplied with a receiver, and eventually almost every home was equipped. In August 1929 they could listen to Provost Clark telling the story of Marymass from the BBC's Glasgow studio.

Transport developments brought a new mobility. The first bus service of 1914 between Kilmarnock and Irvine was followed in 1919 by others, and services were extended to Ardrossan and Ayr and (from Bank Street) to Glasgow. There was fierce competition among the rival operators. The most powerful challenge came from the 'Transport' — the Scottish General Transport Company which set up headquarters in Kilmarnock in 1925 and was merged into the SMT in 1932. This was answered by twenty-two small operators in 1926 forming the Ayrshire Bus Owners (A.1. Services) Ltd to compete on the Kilmarnock-Irvine-Ardrossan route; others in 1930 formed the A.A. Motor Services Ltd for the Ayr-Irvine-Ardrossan route, thus providing Irvine thereafter with a choice of three bus services. Local bus owners also offered summer day excursions. In 1925 three different firms advertised these. One was Alistair McPhail of Bank Street (an original director of the A.1.), who featured 'charabancs with pneumatic tyres' and a trip to the Three Lochs for 7/6. The railway had cheap day excursions to Glasgow (2/10) and Edinburgh (6/7), and that year the *Irvine Herald* noted that a few Irvinites were spending their holidays on the Continent. Though private cars were still few in number, the council in 1927 was already concerned about parking in High Street. Motor cycles were at the height of their popularity, and the Irvine Motor Cycle Club organised races. Other contact with the outside world was facilitated when the GPO erected a telephone kiosk in Bank Street in 1928.

Increased leisure facilities are indicated by the flourishing of local organisations. The football clubs could now afford regular travel, and a Western League was formed by fourteen clubs in 1919, including Irvine Meadow. Those too late in applying to join, including Irvine Victoria, revived the Irvine and District League. Irvine Meadow became Western League champions (1922, 1928), and winners of the League Cup (1928, 1929) and the new Moore Trophy (1929, 1930), although in this period they failed to recapture the Irvine District Cup or the Ayrshire Junior Challenge Cup. Bowling continued to be popular, and tennis on the private and municipal courts. The burgh Ravenspark golf course was improved, while at Bogside Sunday golf was introduced in 1928. But cricket collapsed after 1927. The Ramblers' Society still survived, but more outstanding was the revival of the swimming club (1927) with galas at the harbour, and a rowing club with a regatta opposite the Low Green (1928). The popularity of billiards was extended, with tables available in the Literary and Social Institute, the Albert Hall (until it became the Tivoli Theatre) and at halls in High Street (1924), Loudoun Street (1924) and New Street (1928). This last was converted in 1930 into the 'Star Roller Skating Halls and Palais de Danse'. Roller skating was a passing craze, but dancing was so popular that many local organisations featured it in special winter social functions. For the younger generation there was a proliferation of activities. The Boys' Brigade was resuscitated after the War, rivalled by the newer Boy Scouts, and the girls had Guides and Brownies. The YMCA, whose scope ranged from harriers to a choral club, had sections catering for boys, youths, and adults. Children in need were catered for by various charitable organisations, as well as Toc H, which also in 1928 built and handed over to the council an Old Men's Shelter in Kilwinning Road. The Cooperative Society, now firmly established as a thriving commercial concern, with the biggest dairy in town, a women's guild and educational lectures, entertained 150 old age pensioners in 1928. Established bodies continued to cater for fanciers of cage birds and homing pigeons. The Glasgow-Irvine Society was revived (1926). New bodies formed were the Thirty One Club for ex-servicemen, followed by the British Legion (1926); a Miniature Rifle Club (1927); and the League of Nations Union (1928). Cultural activities were still difficult to sustain. A musical association was resuscitated (1920) and a dramatic association (1921). The Burgh Band was reformed and shared with visiting brass bands summer performances on the Low Green.

Most remarkable was a renaissance of various long-established local institutions — the Incorporated Trades, the Carters Society, Irvine Burns Club, and Marymass.

That the Trades had managed to survive intact into the 20th century was due mainly to Thomas Hall who died in 1920. As their records state 'The revived interest in the Incorporated Trades of recent years and the continuance of all the old customs connected with the Trades was due in great part to Convener Hall's enthusiastic efforts to keep the old institutions alive. His mind was stored with much useful information concerning old craft and trading traditions of Irvine, and his influence over the Convener's Court where he presided so long, soon created that spirit of friendly rivalry which gave each of the Incorporated Trades a new life'. In 1922 a new constitution for the Convener's Court formalised the hitherto somewhat haphazard arrangements. At the same time the skinners' craft was reconstituted to join the surviving crafts of hammermen, weavers, tailors, cordiners, coopers, wrights and squaremen. The Trades could now be described as 'partly convivial, partly benevolent' in their function. The funds of each craft were augmented by the seat rents acquired from the Trades Loft in the parish church, but this ceased after the Church of Scotland (Property and Endowment) Act of 1925. Thus a scheme for providing technical bursaries had to be deferred. Each craft was expected to contribute towards the expense of the annual function, and the Deacon Convener was left to make up any deficiency personally. In 1929 it was decided that members of the craft should pay by ticket; and in 1930 it is recorded 'that the Annual Function this year should take the usual form of pies, and biscuits and cheese, and that it be held in the Eglinton Arms Hotel at a cost of 2/6d per Member, including one refreshment to be supplied to each Member'. Appropriately for this time of revival, a new Burgh Anthem was presented in 1929 — music by ex-Deacon Convener Harry Lumsden, lyrics by John N. Hall:

> Sons of this Royal and Ancient Town,
> Let love and honour spread abroad,
> As in the days of old renown
> When chivalry and glory rose.
> Then let the good cause triumph,
> For ever and for aye.

Although the trade of horse carter was destined to disappear in an era of motor transport, the Carters Society survived, welcoming into its ranks enthusiasts from other walks of life, and indeed by 1929 nearly all the members of the town council had been enrolled as members. Each Marymass Saturday morning the Carters continued to ride round the marches of the ancient burgh, led by a captain elected a week before. Captain James Sloan in 1925 and 1926 gave a 'new lease of life' to Marymass, and his worthy successor Sam Anderson shared with James Kyle — a predecessor from the beginning of the century — the record of being elected captain seven times.

Irvine Burns Club celebrated its centenery in 1926, with John N. Hall succeeding P.S. Clark as President, and R.M. Hogg continuing his long tenure as Honorary Secretary. Appropriately, a plaque was presented by John N. Hall to mark the house where Burns had lodged in Glasgow Vennel. This was followed by others — at the Drucken Steps, 1927, from Sir Andrew Duncan who presided that year; at Knadgerhill, 1929; and at Seagate Castle 1930. In 1924 the Club instituted prizes for pupils in local schools to encourage study of the life and works of the poet. This was more successful than a previous effort in 1874, which attracted only seven entrants — who were required to recite 'The Cottar's Saturday Night'.

At Marymass in 1913 there had been few carters, fewer councillors, a poor procession, and little public interest. The *Irvine Herald* concluded that 'if a step in the way of reform is not taken soon, the death knell of Marymass races will soon be heard'. After a period of abeyance during the war years, the omens did not appear auspicious in 1919. The Shows which had previously filled High Street from Bridgegate to the Kirk Vennel each April (for the Bogside Races) and at Marymass were banished to the Moor, then to the Golffields. The Board of Health persuaded the town council that shows in the main thoroughfare were a hazard as well as an inconvenience. This did not please the show people, nor various correspondents in the local press. 'Send the shows to Irvine Moor? They might as well have sent them to Timbuctoo!' 'An attempt to deprive us of the right and liberties of our Ancient and Royal Burgh.' 'Where were our Labour councillors?' Yet the council was sufficiently interested to donate the traditional £20 to the Carters Society in 1919. Treasurer John Johnston, whose sustained efforts over the years later won him the proud nickname of Mr. Marymass, made an important contribution in 1920: 'On a vote being taken by show of hands, it was decided that the Grant be unconditional', and so liquor was permitted to be sold at the Races for the first time in forty-two years. Local veto polls held under the Temperance (Scotland) Act of 1913 confirmed that Irvine was anxious to remain 'wet'. In 1920 those 1,470 persons who voted for 'no change' were outnumbered by 1,387 for 'no licence' and 153 for 'reduction', and the burgh's number of licensed premises was in fact reduced by thirteen. But in 1923 that limitation was repealed by a vote of 1,892 as against 1,216 for 'no licence', 134 for 'continued limitation', and 40 for 'further limitation'. Prohibition was losing its appeal.

In 1928 the council voted to increase its Marymass grant from £20 to £25, and to continue the usual £2 for ribbons, a modest augmentation but — as the first increase since 1866 — a token of greater enthusiasm. In 1925 Captain Sloan of the Carters had suggested associating the children more with this local tradition, and proposed a 'Marymass Queen'. It could not be left entirely to older residents, like Charles Arthur who in 1926 for the fiftieth time carried a carter's mallet. James Sloan, Sam Anderson and P.S. Clark planned a rejuvenated ceremonial for 1928. Martha McHarg of Bank Street School was crowned Marymass Queen before the Town House amid a crowd estimated at from seven to ten thousand. The bussing of the Carters' and the Town's flags with ribbons was revived, and a massed procession proceeded to the Moor for the Races. The celebration of Marymass was now to be closely associated with Mary Queen of Scots, for the 'Queen' was joined in the proceedings by her four Marys. In his BBC broadcast in 1929 Provost Clark told how 'Mary came to Irvine, landing at the old port at Seagate'. He also told how the Carters had formerly circled the Granny Stane where Wallace had crossed the river in 1297 to attack the English army. So from 1929 the Queen and her four Marys were supported by two boys representing Wallace and Bruce. Yet all this fiction was combined with the traditional ceremonies to create a colourful and popular pageant, successfully reminding the spectators of the burgh's history. By what the *Irvine Herald* described as 'a miracle' Marymass was saved, presented in 1930 with 'a solemnity which was almost uncanny', and children's sports were included, further to involve Irvine's rising generation.

EIGHTEEN

The Small Burgh and the Second War

With an unfeeling disregard for tradition, the Local Government (Scotland) Act of 1929 designated Irvine a 'small burgh'. What this meant requires some explanation. Burghs were henceforth to be of two kinds. Those with a population greater than 20,000 were allowed to retain most of their statutory functions. So Ayr and Kilmarnock became 'large burghs'. Ayrshire's other fourteen 'small burghs' had much diminished powers. The proud title of 'royal burgh' ceased to have administrative significance. In the new system the county council became the principal local authority. In the landward areas it was the sole agency now that parish councils were abolished, replaced by district councils with insignificant powers and subject to the county council. Irvine District Council comprised Dreghorn and the landward parts of Irvine and Kilwinning. In the burghs Ayr County Council exercised a new authority. Its previous interest in Irvine had been limited to policing it. Now it took from the town council control of main roads, planning, major public health functions and also responsibility for education (from the Ayrshire Education Authority) and poor relief (from the parish council).

From the beginning of the century expenditure by the town council in running the burgh and improving local services had grown. Annual assessments had increased from £5,710 (1904) to £7,706 (1914), with a significant leap to £22,382 (1924) and £23,382 (1930). To pay for this, rates levied by the council amounted to 3/6 in the pound in 1904 (shared equally by owners and occupiers), 3/10 in 1914 (from now on about two-thirds borne by occupiers), and 7/2 by 1930. This covered bills the council had to pay for its own services and for police and water. In addition the ratepayers had to pay separately for education and poor relief. From 1930 the town council became the collector of a consolidated rate, which was a tidier arrangement, and that rate was, to begin with, hardly more than the combined previous assessments. In 1931 the figures for Irvine were for owners $4/6\frac{1}{4}$ ($4/5\frac{1}{2}$ for that part in Dundonald parish), for occupiers $6/3\frac{1}{2}$ ($6/2\frac{3}{4}$), plus 6d each for water — a total of rather less than 12/- in the pound. But what irked was that from now on Irvine Town Council was responsible for collecting rates based on expenditure over which it had limited control. The total to be raised was £50,656 in 1932. The town council's own major outlays were on street lighting (£2,119), cleansing (£2,586), cemeteries (£1,784), minor roads (£1,496), sewers (£2,766) and housing (£3,545). The County Council requisition (£29,468) was more than twice as much, even with government grants, for such things as education (£13,896), major roads (£7,528), poor relief (renamed public assistance) (£6,909) and public health (£4,980). Another £3,545 was due to the Water Board. Among the ninety-one members of Ayr County Council, Irvine was represented by only four of its own members selected by the town council, plus Arthur Brady who was able to secure election as county councillor for Irvine landward area (1930–37). The Convention of Royal Burghs — which now included all burghs in its membership — provided a focus for complaints about reduced status and powers. And as the size of the county council requisition increased each year, there were criticisms of what in 1934 the *Irvine Herald* described as this 'too costly administration'.

It can be said, however, that the transfer of certain expensive responsibilities to a centralised authority left the town council free to concentrate on those functions it continued to administer. The most important of these was housing. The 1931 census report showed that over half of Irvine's 11,877 inhabitants were occupying 382 single-ends and 1,112 room-and-kitchen dwellings which formed the bulk of the burgh's 2,683 houses of all kinds. Twenty-five per cent of the population were living in grossly overcrowded conditions with three or more persons per room. Some people were living in huts and caravans in East Road, Fullarton Street, and Springbank. One family in 1929 was occupying 'an old wooden rabbit and canary house'. In 1932 it was calculated that 240 houses required major alterations and 193 others were beyond repair. But this was a time of financial stringency. The town councillors were most of them reluctant to commit themselves to heavy capital expenditure on slum clearance. But Labour's

Arthur Brady obtained a local inquiry by the Department of Health for Scotland which pushed the council into a massive programme of rehousing. Provost McKinlay later admitted (1937) 'that but for Dean of Guild Brady's efforts they would neither have had the quantity nor the quality of houses that they had'. The houses already built up to 1929, 370 in number, were followed by nearly a thousand more — 168 in 1932, 530 between 1934 and 1938, and another 264 completed by 1941. Of these, the major development of 476 houses began at Springbank over the river near the industrial area. This despite earlier fears of mining subsidence in that sector and now requiring, incidentally, a new football ground for Irvine Victoria. The other major scheme of 268 houses was at the opposite end of the town beyond Quarry Road, where new streets were created, and Winton Road and Wallace Road were given names from the burgh's past. Also 188 houses were added to those in the Thornhouse area south of Bank Street. The remaining 30 houses filled up small sites where old houses had been demolished. Among these was 173 High Street. That had comprised eleven single-ends and seven two-apartment dwellings, most occupied by families of five or more persons, one of them containing twelve in all — an example of the overcrowding which was being dealt with. In 1938 there were 111 unfit houses, plus 62 unfit and overcrowded and 682 overcrowded but fit. The council calculated that another 520 houses were needed. As owner of 1,332 houses built or building, Irvine Town Council was busier than ever. These houses had to be managed, older ones improved and allocations of tenancy made by the town chamberlain or by a letting committee from 1937. Rents of the newer slum clearance houses had to be cheaper than in the older council houses, and the council had to revise rents, trying to please all tenants, and ratepayers as well. In 1938 there were squatters to be removed from condemned houses, and some council tenants who were consistently falling into arrears had to be evicted.

The other major project of the '30s was sewage disposal. As population grew, action became increasingly urgent, and the Unemployment Grants Committee provided a welcome subsidy. Intercepting pipes were laid to carry all sewage downriver to an outfall on the shore south of the harbour. Screening plant was installed near the Blue Billy Bing, and the treated effluent discharged through a thirty-inch pipe into the sea below low water mark. The scheme was completed in 1932, though further work was necessary thereafter. Some corners of the town had to be linked up, including new houses built by the County Council at Girdle Toll (1934) and beside the old Slate Mill. There were continuing problems with pollution of the beach, aggravated by the County Council's Irvine Valley sewage scheme. Yet the town became a cleaner place, and the river too. A salmon ladder was installed at the weir (1936), and two years later a 21-pound salmon was caught at Shewalton dam.

The early '30s were difficult years. In the critical year of 1931 all local authority employees had to agree to a 'voluntary' reduction in salaries and wages. In 1932 there were over two thousand unemployed in Irvine. For reasons of economy various desirable projects had to be abandoned. Thomas Nisbet provided for an old Men's Cabin (1931) which the town council could afford to maintain. But plans for a hostel for elderly people were turned down by the Department of Health for Scotland (1935). Although the *Irvine Herald* hoped (1931) that 'Some day, we feel certain, Irvine will be the playground of Glasgow', suggestions for an outdoor swimming pool and a new road to the shore via Milgarholm came to nothing. Only minor improvements could be made at the shore. Brady's proposal for a municipal bus service (1933) encouraged private operators to provide additional local routes, including buses to the shore. Even council donations to deserving causes were more rigidly controlled in 1935 with a predetermined annual list. The Carters Society, which had had its Race contribution of £25 plus £2 for ribbons supplemented by £23 for the Marymass Queen ceremony, was consolidated at £50. The Nursing Association, RNLI, RSPCC, and six hospitals each received token donations. All other bodies had to rely on self-help and flag days (if approved by the magistrates). The longstanding annual awards to Irvine and Fullarton Coals committees were stopped. Some things could be accomplished cheaply or else had to be done. The statue of Lord Justice Boyle was removed (1929) from High Street to Seagatefoot, thus taking away the 'Black Man' which terrorised some children. The Gruip was pedestrianised (1930). Plans were shelved for a new slaughterhouse (1930), an aerodrome (1932), and a new town hall (1934). The old Slate Mill was sold (1932). When Duntonknoll quarry became filled up, a new rubbish coup was formed at Bowmans farm on the Moor (1935). One odd decision of 1935 by eight votes to five after a discussion 'in committee' was to refuse Arnold McJannet access to the burgh records for the burgh history he was writing.

There was some easing of financial restraints in later years. Ayr County Council set up traffic lights at Bridgegatehead in 1935, began building Ayrshire Central Hospital in Kilwinning Road in 1936, and planned an Irvine bypass road. Irvine Town Council could now afford in 1936 a salmon ladder at the weir, two motor tractors for the dust carts, an extension of the golf course, illuminations by fairy lights at Marymass, and restoring the annual donations towards coals for the poor. In 1937 it could light the streets all night from dusk to dawn — supplied both by

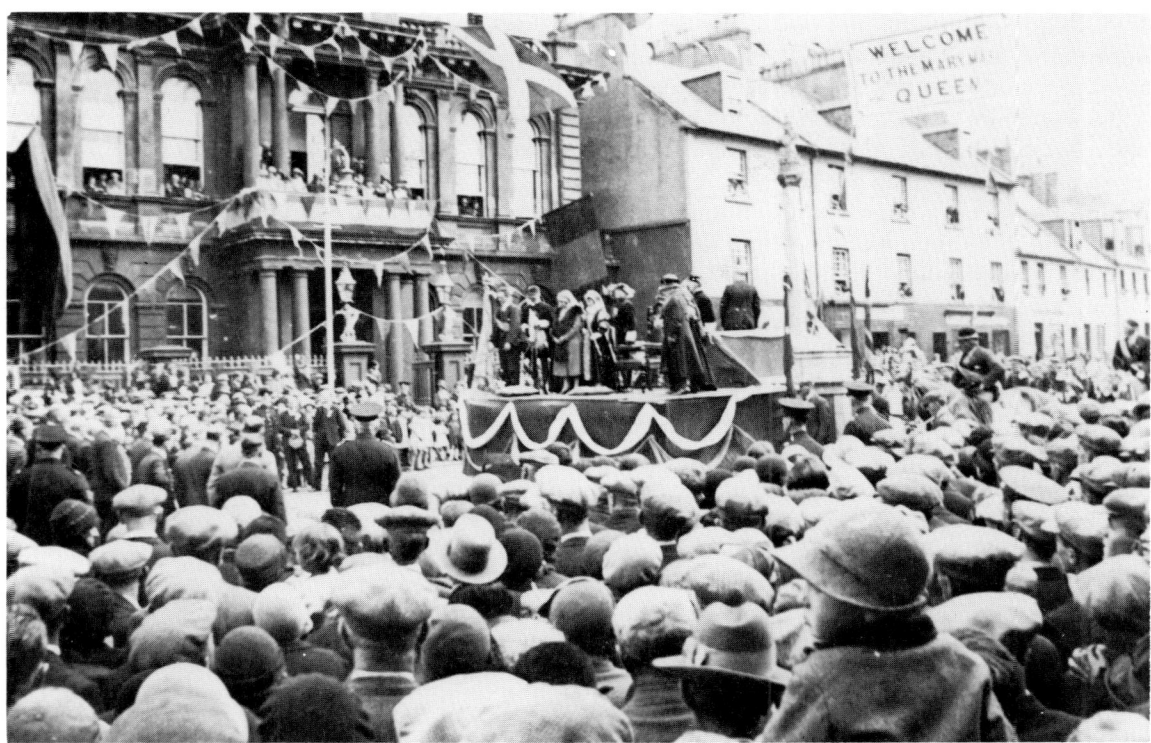

From 1928 the crowning of a Marymass Queen augmented the annual celebrations. In this photograph taken in the '30s, the Carters are in attendance (beside the War Memorial in the street), and the Town House is fronted by railings (removed during the Second World War).

the Ayrshire Electricity Board, and the Caledonian Gas Company which took over the local works in 1935. Also in 1937, £25 was spent on replacing the typewriter in the burgh surveyor's office, which had been 'in use for over twenty years'. In 1938 the council began laying out flower and shrub plots, and continued discussing the long-planned footbridge at the Golffields, which was eventually opened in 1940 and served especially the residents of the new Springbank housing scheme. The Glasgow Vennel was closed to bus traffic. Also in this period (1938) the GPO could afford to establish an automatic telephone exchange. And enough money could be raised by public subscription to replace (1937) the seventeen-year-old miners' ambulance — the only one available locally. Another important advance was made in 1935 when an Ayrshire General Medical Service was created by the county branch of the British Medical Association. Treatment and medicines were made more easily available to the mass of the people in return for small weekly family subscriptions. All the local doctors participated. Among them was Dr. James Thomson who had come to Irvine early in the century, going round his practice first on horseback, then in pony and trap. His death in 1943 would mark the end of an era.

The continued need for economy filled the minds of councillors. To ensure strict control, much of the work done by committees was considered in full council, or by newly constituted committees after 1933 on which all eighteen councillors were represented — law and finance, health and housing, works, property, recreation. The *Irvine Herald* of 1931 noticed that 'It is not so very long since Irvine Town Council was composed largely of men of leisure ... nowadays it is men of business who are in charge of the town's affairs'. To keep down the rates was a principal aim of those who were now known as 'the Moderate group'. As against them, the Labour Party urged a policy of providing work and improved services despite the cost. They failed to win support. Back in 1919 they had gained seven seats on the council, but by 1933 they were down to three. Nationally the party suffered from the collapse of the second Labour government when Ramsay Macdonald formed his National Government (1931). Locally the party organisation had to be reformed after the split when the ILP left the Labour party (1932). ILP and official Scottish Socialist Party candidates competed against each other in subsequent municipal elections. In 1935 there was a historic event when the Fifth Ward chose Mrs. Margaret Brady to become Irvine's first woman councillor. But she and her husband formed the entire Labour group, and when they left Irvine for Glasgow in 1937, their seats were taken over by Moderates. In the 1938 municipal election, so great was the demoralisation that there were no Labour candidates, and two Communists got minimal support. In national politics the 1935 general election confirmed Unionist control of Ayr Burghs, with Colonel Moore defeating Arthur Brady in a straight fight by 25,893 to 13,274 votes. When the Member of Parliament was knighted in 1937, Irvine Town Council granted Sir Thomas Moore the freedom of the burgh.

The drabness of so much everyday life in the '30s was lightened by extended recreation, even though in too many cases there was involuntary idleness. For those who could afford trips, the railway company offered cheap excursions in 1937 to Balloch (2/3 including a cruise on Loch Lomond), Largs (9d), and Campbeltown (via Fairlie, 6/6). The year before, over a thousand went by special trains to watch the new *Queen Mary* sail down the Clyde. Nearly everyone could afford the cinema shows at the Picturedrome, Picture Palace, the Empire re-opened in 1931 as the Regal, and the new Kyle Cinema in Bank Street opened by the Earl of Eglinton and Winton in 1937 — a 'super-cinema' accommodating 1,244 patrons at 3d to 1/- for matinees and 6d to 1/6 for evening shows. The Tivoli in West Road continued to provide variety shows, occasional repertory theatre, dances, and visits from celebrities like the tenor J.M. Hamilton and the illusionist Doctor Bodie (1936). The Saturday afternoon attraction of junior football continued, when Irvine Meadow topped the Western League (1933) and brought home a series of trophies — Ayrshire Junior Cup (1932), Consolation Cup (1933), Ayrshire Charity Cup (1935), Moore Trophy (1939), and Irvine and District Cup (1933, 1939). Irvine Victoria were also doing well, winning the District Cup (1935) and the Moore Trophy (1937). The indoor sport of billiards was still popular, joined (1932) by carpet bowling. There was outdoor bowling at Winton Club, plus a new Quoiting Club established (1931) in East Road. Two greyhound racing tracks were opened at Townhead and Bank Street (1932) — 'admission 2d, race cards 2d' — superseding the Sunday whippet racing at Stanecastle which had annoyed churchgoers in 1913. Horse racing at the Bogside meetings provided the other chance for the gambler to make a fortune. To encourage healthy recreation, the town council organised putting competitions and golf exhibition matches. This era produced the first of three famous golfers, all of whom came from the two rows of miners' houses at Bartonholm, conveniently next to the 16th hole of Bogside golf course. In 1937 Hamilton McInally won the Scottish Amateur Championship for the first of three times, followed later by Jimmy Walker and Jack Cannon. There was still a Hockey Club, and in 1931 cricket at Vineburgh Park was resuscitated by the Academy Former Pupils Club. For others with energy there were the YMCA Harriers, the Fullarton Wheelers Cycling Club formed in 1932, the Swimming Club with its annual gala, the Rowing Club with its regattas, and for the unemployed in particular an Allotments Association with plots at the curling pond off Bank Street. Additional recreational facilities were available in the Social and Literary Institute and the premises of the YMCA, the Territorials' two drill halls, the British Legion, and a rival Ex-Servicemen's Club formed in 1936. The Hosiery Manufacturing Club's new Welfare Club offered badminton and table tennis (1936). For young people this was the era of uniformed organisations — Boy Scouts with Wolf Cubs, two companies of Boys' Brigade with Life Boys, Girl Guides with Brownies and Rangers. For old folk, treats were provided by the Cooperative Society, Toc H and the British Legion.

On most weekday evenings the churches had their organisations for boys, girls, young people, women, and sometimes men. The churches' social functions were vastly extended to supplement their Sunday devotional purpose. Theological dissension had become a thing of the past, and disappeared within the six congregations belonging to the reunited Church of Scotland. The old parish church lost its former status as the burgh kirk. For a few years there was an attempt to rename it St. Inan's, but that name did not stick, and it became officially Irvine Old Parish Church. There was still an annual 'kirking of the council' and the council attended other churches to give a civic welcome whenever a new minister was inducted. From 1930 the long-established practice of royal burghs (and universities) electing members to represent them as elders at the General Assembly ended. Also in that year Irvine Town Council ceased to have the church bells rung each evening at six and eight o'clock. The magistrates, however, continued to have responsibility for the churchyard. The churches made their own way. The congregations of the Church of Scotland each retained something of their individual traditions and a variety of ministers. Two were long-serving: Wilson-Fullarton had Rev. John Wishart (1902-47); Fullarton had Rev. John Paterson (1903-37), to be followed by Rev. Angus Nicolson (1938-48). Two had young newcomers — St. Inan's with Rev. Alexander Macara (1928-78) and Trinity with Revs. Alexander King (1931-36) and Henry Ferrie (1936-47). The Relief Church was served by Rev. Samuel McNab (1925-51) and the Mure Church by Revs.

This photograph of Bank Street was taken before the Caledonian Railway Station was closed in 1930. The fine building remains intact.

John C. Hill (1929-37) and Alexander Greig (1937-46). St. Mary's Catholic Church suffered the loss by death of two priests, Canon Joseph Hogan (1918-36) and Martin Meagher (1936-37), which saw the return of Father Dermott O'Reilly (1938-49), who had been there before (1919-21) as St. Mary's first curate. The smaller denominations continued. The Baptist Church pastors were Revs. Neil McLachlan (1928-31), A.M. Cassells (1931-36), then Archibald Speed. The Church of the Nazarene set up a place of worship in Fullarton Street (1936). The Christian Brethren had assemblies at Waterside, also (from 1937) at Quarry Road, and a Sunday School (from 1933) at Slate Mill. There were Christadelphians meeting in the Cooperative Hall, and the Salvation Army in Glasgow Vennel. The Mure Mission — the Seamen's Bethel — at the harbour was visited in 1934 by the old miners' agent James Brown, a stalwart of the Ayrshire Christian Union who had become Lord High Commissioner to the General Assembly. The Mure Mission closed down soon afterwards, but a Railway Mission continued.

Ayr County Council Education Committee took over from the Ayrshire Educational Authority the management of all the schools, including 'transferred schools' like St. Mary's Primary and St. Michael's Secondary. Irvine Royal Academy under its rector James Porter (1930-53) had grown to a record roll of 500 pupils in 1931. In the following year there was built, on the academy's sports field in Kilwinning Road, an annexe specially designed to provide 'more varied fare' in the way of practical subjects for the 'non academic' pupils from twelve to fourteen years of age who were brought in to what was now the town's secondary school for all. Fees for secondary education had been abolished by the Education Authority, although they were still required from parents who wished to send their younger children to the primary department of the academy. In the elementary schools there had been no fees since 1889, and books were supplied free from 1908. The opening of the academy annexe in 1932 took away their older 'supplementary' pupils and helped relieve the pressure of overcrowding. When Bank Street got a new headmaster in William Thomson (1930-48), he took over from R.M. Hogg a school whose infants had since 1922 been accommodated in four huts in the playground, and some of whose senior classes overflowed into the Templars Hall, the YMCA, and even the waiting room of the now-abandoned Caledonian Railway Station. The school building itself was antiquated after a life of sixty years and was renewed and extended in 1937. It was then able to take in the pupils from the even older East Road School, which could now be closed down. Across the water there had been a similar amalgamation in 1934. Robert Stewart, who became headmaster of Montgomery School in 1930, also took over Loudoun Street School when William McAngus left in 1933, and continued in charge of this Loudoun-Montgomery School until 1946. The pupils began their schooling at Loudoun Street, and continued at Montgomery before going on to the academy. Both Bank Street and Loudoun-Montgomery schools engendered strong loyalties among their pupils. Though many of the children were poorly clad and ill fed, they could benefit from the new spirit which was enriching primary teaching, and football and other extra-curricular activities made school a pleasanter place than it had once been. Some still remember with affection John D. MacGregor, born in Halfway in 1899, who was a teacher in Loudoun-Montgomery School.

Irvine had become a more respectable place. When Piper Morton welcomed the New Year of 1932 at the Cross, the *Irvine Herald* recalled the erstwhile drunken crowds, noting that these 'scenes of former years seem to have departed'. Similarly Marymass since its reformation had become 'a people's festival'. Other occasions for communal commemoration were appropriately celebrated. At the Silver Jubilee of King George V in 1935 there were cinema shows for young and old, with bars of chocolate for children and pounds of tea for old age pensioners; a floodlit Town House; a beacon fire on Magistrates Hill lit by the Boy Scouts; and the usual church parade. After the Abdication of Edward VIII in 1936, George VI was proclaimed in traditional fashion in 'this Ancient and Royal Burgh'. The Coronation in 1937 was marked by gifts of a shilling to each child, two shillings to each old age pensioner, a service at the war memorial, sports, and a bonfire, and the town was illuminated and decorated. In 1936 there had also been a September Carnival at the Low Green, with dancing, floodlit putting, and various competitions.

These were special occasions requiring cooperation and effort. There was no comparable attempt in this period to revive any of the organisations which in previous generations had, so long as enthusiasm lasted, catered for music, drama, or the arts. Yet the churches, the Cooperative Society, and other local organisations were in the '30s all sponsoring amateur efforts in music and drama and providing a quite impressive range of cultural activities. Similarly, in this larger and more fragmented community, although a burgh band could not continue, the Salvation Army had a brass band, the British Legion and Boys' Brigade had pipe bands, and there was an Irvine Bluebell Flute Band. The County Council Education Committee's evening continuation classes now extended beyond practical subjects to provide lecture courses on a variety of cultural themes. The older organisations of the town — the Trades, the Carters, the Freemasons, the Burns Club — though catering specifically for their own members, were not inward looking. The Burns Club, for example, was planning a museum. A cheque from Col. Walter Scott of New York in 1933 formed the nucleus of a fund. The Secretary of the Club, John Hogg, set aside a room in his Bank Street home where were stored the books which his brother R.M. Hogg had bequeathed, where the precious Burns manuscripts could be kept in a safe, and where the directors of the club could meet. After his death in 1936 this arrangement was continued by the surviving sister, Miss Margaret Hogg, until her death in 1962. Literary interests were also encouraged by Ayr County Council which filled the long-felt want for a public library — in the Town House in 1932 until a year later the town council remodelled the Loch Lomond Vaults in Bridgegate as proper library premises. And in 1938 Arnold McJannet published his history of *The Royal Burgh of Irvine* at thirty shillings a copy.

One feature of the inter-war period was an increased awareness of international events — fostered by books, newspapers, radio, cinema, and adult classes in current affairs at the academy. Remembrance of what was still called the Great War was fostered each November by Poppy Day and the Armistice two minutes' silence and church services. Determination that war should never come again was expressed by the local branch of the League of Nations Union and confirmed by the film 'All Quiet on the Western Front' at the Palace cinema in 1931. Anti-militarist feeling was symbolised by the removal of the two old cannon from the front of the Town House and the two captured German guns from the parish churchyard in 1929. When the accession of Hitler to power in Germany in 1933 brought a renewed threat, and in 1935 a Scottish Office communication regarding Air Raid Precautions, Irvine Town Council — sympathising with an anti-war resolution from the local ILP — suggested that the government should appeal to the League of Nations for a ban on the use of aircraft in war. In an unofficial Peace Ballot in the town that year over four thousand electors overwhelmingly voted for disarmament and resisting aggression by economic and non-military means. In 1936 the town council by seven votes to six agreed to convene a meeting sponsored by the Irvine Peace Council and local branches of the League of Nations Union, National Unemployed Workers Movement, Communist Party, National Union of Railwaymen, and the National Council of Labour Colleges.

But a subtle change in public mood can be detected with the renewal of patriotic spirit associated with the Jubilee of 1935 — when the British Legion led the parade — and the Coronation of 1937 — when the local battery of territorials fired a twenty-one gun salute. The growing threat of war persuaded the town council in December 1937 to send (by the provost's casting vote) a delegate to a Scottish Peace

Traffic congestion became increasingly critical from the 1930s until the '60s, when this photograph of High Street was taken.

Council in Edinburgh; but it decided also to be represented at a county conference on Air Raid Precautions. Early in 1938 the council appealed for volunteers for an ARP service and provided the burgh workers with a course on dealing with poison gas. In the panic associated with the Munich crisis in September of that year, the council complained to Sir Thomas Moore, MP, about the government's failure to supply Irvine with adequate defence against air raids, and granted the town clerk powers to expedite ARP provision. In the same month John Smith from Irvine died fighting with the International Brigade in the Spanish Civil War.

Meanwhile recession was giving way to an industrial revival associated with rearmament. There were dark days in Irvine in the early '30s, with few businesses unaffected by the world economic crisis. Symptomatically, the Caledonian Railway Station in Bank Street (under the management of the LMSR since 1921) was closed from 28th July 1930, and the line used only occasionally thereafter, as for a Junior Football Special from Clydebank in 1936. The 'Riviera Express' of engine and one carriage which had supplied regular passenger services to Kilwinning became a memory. Not until 1936 did the *Irvine Herald* note 'a more hopeful spirit', and indeed during that year unemployment in the Irvine district (including Dreghorn and Springside) dropped from 1,520 to 1,050. The first step to recovery had been the establishment by ICI in 1935 of a new factory in Gailes Road for the manufacture of signal grenades. In 1936 two cargo ships which had been lying on the stocks for five years found purchasers and were launched. The *Coulmore* and the *Coulbeg*, each of 3,670 tons, were the last Irvine-built vessels. The shipyard, maintained by National Shipbuilding Securities Ltd. since 1930, was developed to carry out repair work on ships up to two thousand tons. In 1937 a major advance came with the reopening of the old Royal Ordnance Factory for the manufacture of munitions. ICI's Ardeer explosives works were also in process of massive expansion, providing more jobs for Irvine workers. So Irvine was preparing for war.

The declaration of war on Germany on 3rd September 1939 was not unexpected. Certain preparations were already in hand. Conscription had been introduced and the first 'militiamen' called up in July. When war came, the territorials were mustered, and in due course successive groups of young men were registered for military service.

Some volunteered in advance, particularly opting for the RAF, and the women's services relied on voluntary enlistment. In April the Home Office had instructed local authorities to give priority to civil defence over other business, in preparation for the massive air attacks which it was expected war would immediately bring. The issue of gas masks and identity cards, the enrolment of air raid wardens and special constables, installation of sirens, enforcement of total blackout, preparation of emergency mortuaries, obliteration of place names which might guide enemy agents — all were taken in hand. A nationally organised Auxiliary Fire Service was formed, and necessarily so, for, at the outbreak of war, as was later recalled, in the case of Irvine the only firefighting equipment was 'one stand pipe and that was out of order'. The town council cooperated by appointing a Firemaster (Malcolm Hume) and in 1940 belatedly acquired a 'peacetime fire brigade' emblazoned 'Royal Burgh of Fire Brigade', with the name 'Irvine' to be inserted at the end of the war.

In 1940 came the British Expeditionary Forces' evacuation from Dunkirk and the fall of France. The subsequent entry of Italy into the war was marked by rioting on the night of 10th-11th June and the looting of ice cream shops, aliens and British-born Italians being treated alike in 'a sorry outbreak of hooliganism' for which twenty-five persons were fined and which ultimately cost the town council £2,000 in compensation and another £1,000 in legal expenses. In 1940, to augment scrap iron supplies, railings were taken away, including those which embellished the front of the Town House. More serious was the imminent threat of air attack and the possibility of invasion. For civil defence, there were nine wardens' posts, controlled by two Chief Wardens, William Ross (Town) and John Lawson (Halfway). Inspector Tom Hood was liaison officer for the police and special constables. There were also Rescue and Decontamination parties and a Report and Control Centre. Static water tanks were set up for the National Fire Service (as it was designated in 1941), street air raid shelters were constructed, stirrup pumps issued and firewatching rotas in all premises arranged by a Fire Guard Staff Officer. The RAF provided barrage balloons to protect the munitions works. To counter the invasion threat, possible sites for enemy landings on the moor and shore were obstructed, boats were immobilised, and road blocks were set up by the hastily recruited Local Defence Volunteers. These formed 'C' (Irvine) Company of the 3rd Ayrshire Battalion of the Home Guard, under the command of Major D.M. Mackenzie, and there were other units connected with the Royal Ordnance Factory, the dockyard, and the LMS railway works. In 1941 war came very near with the Clydebank blitz of 13th-14th March,

and on Wednesday 7th May the Luftwaffe dropped bombs on Irvine. One hit the dockyard, but did little damage. A second landed near Heathfield. A third destroyed two council houses in Winton Road and killed four people.

Civilian life was disrupted more than in the previous war. Rationing was extended to include food, fuel, and clothing. The burgh slaughterhouse was taken over by the Ministry of Food. A British Restaurant at the Low Green (1943-45) provided three-course meals for one shilling (or soup 2d, meat 8d, pudding 4d) with tea, scones, buns and biscuits at one penny per item. War work absorbed older or unfit men and many women. The Royal Ordnance Factory employed nearly two thousand manufacturing TNT. At the shipyard, controlled by DEMS ('Defensive Equipment of Merchant Ships'), vessels were re-equipped and armed. As the war advanced a slipway was formed near the Wee Dock where landing craft were serviced. The local labour force had to be augmented by others directed to work in Irvine. Billeting officers had to find quarters for them and troops stationed in the town.

The first troops arrived in May 1940, French units returning from the unsuccessful Norwegian campaign. They were followed by Royal Marine Commandos who trained on the Ayrshire coast. Irvine Moor was requisitioned and hutted camps were established there and at Gailes, the two areas where the territorials had done their summer training — in the inter-war years 800 on the Moor, and 450 at Gailes. In 1942, when contractors were constructing huts on the Moor, quarrying of sand threatened the Magistrates Hill and it had to be restored. Later, tanks of the 6th Armoured Division devastated some areas. In Eglinton Park the derelict castle provided demolition exercises for the Royal Engineers. At the harbour from September 1943 the land-based *H.M.S. Fullarton* rehearsed on Irvine beach for the landings in North Africa and Normandy. A camp was constructed to accommodate Italian prisoners of war.

Canteen facilities for the troops were provided by the Women's Voluntary Services (chaired by Mrs. Cowan, then Mrs. McBain Stewart, with Mrs. Crawford as secretary); the ladies of six churches provided over a million cups of tea in the Wilson-Fullarton hall; and the Polish troops in particular were welcomed by their co-religionists at St. Mary's. Those local organisations which continued in being joined in the work of welfare. Groups like the Irvine Amateur Entertainers organised concerts which offered relief to servicemen and civilians alike during the blackout and also raised money for war charities and comforts funds. Sunday evening shows for similar purposes were provided by the four cinemas, outside which there were nightly queues for the latest Hollywood productions. The Tivoli abandoned its variety shows and became the

Bridgegate was particularly difficult for heavy traffic to negotiate. The photographer of 1963 waited for a quiet spell before taking his picture!

Ritz dance hall, and also there was dancing nightly in the Good Templars Hall.

For children, school life continued despite disruptions. The pre-war youth organisations contrived to continue despite difficulties, supplemented by an army cadet corps, an air training corps at the academy, and sea scouts in the old lifeboat shed, joined in 1945 by sea cadets. Young and old shared in the various campaigns organised for National Savings, with a Spitfire Fund, War Weapons Week, Warships Week, Tanks for Attack, Wings for Victory, Salute the Soldier, and Thanksgiving Week — well over a million pounds was raised locally. Less dramatically, there was salvage of paper, scrap iron, rags, bones, bottles and pig swill, and in 1941 the Social and Literary Institute supplied half-a-ton of discarded books.

As in the earlier war, elections were suspended for the duration, vacancies in the council were filled by co-option, and after the last batch of council houses was completed in 1941, only routine business could be contemplated. For each meeting there was a flood of government circulars to be attended to, and the town council's principal function was for the time being to act as local administrative agency for the Churchill government which took over the conduct of the war from May 1940. Matthew Lamont succeeded W.R. McKinlay as provost in November 1940, and the stringencies were such that when the town clock stopped in 1943 it was not repaired until the end of the war. By 1943, however, the tide of war was turning. After the American naval victory at Midway (June 1942), the British desert victory at El Alamein (October 1942), and the Russians' recovery of Stalingrad (January 1943), the Allies' unrelenting offensives promised ultimate victory. In 1943 Irvine town council set up a representative committee to raise funds to welcome homecoming servicemen. It was then assessed that 1,500 post-war houses would need to be built, and preliminary moves were made to take over army huts on the Moor as temporary accommodation. Also in 1943 Ayr County Council's planning department produced development proposals for Irvine. They envisaged the rebuilding of the town centre where 'the bulk of the properties are in a state of decay', clearing the river banks and Marress for recreational purposes, making 'a

An aerial photograph of 1936 reveals the decaying industrial area south of the harbour. At the dockyard is *S.S. Coulbeg*, the last Irvine-built ship, waiting to be launched.

clean sweep of the area south west of the railway' for industrial purposes, creating a new harbour on Bogside flats, and providing new through roads. In 1944, after Robert M. Whyte replaced A.R. Wilson as town clerk, the paper shortage was sufficiently relieved for councillors again to be issued with 'agendae' for all meetings. There was again talk of building a new town hall. Ayrshire Dockyard Company was able to turn from war work to the manufacture of steel sections for post-war houses. Irvine Town Council accepted the offer by the Scottish Special Housing Association Ltd. to supply houses — reversing a decision of 1937, confirmed earlier in 1944, that the council would 'prefer to build their own houses'.

In 1945, with the Allied armies advancing into Germany, it was possible to 'stand down' the Home Guard, disband the civil defence organisation, and reduce the National Fire Service. But so intimate had been the 'comradeship and association' that many members continued to meet thereafter for social and sporting activities. The end of the war in Europe (8th May) brought a spontaneous celebration, a service of thanksgiving with standing room only for some of those who crowded into the Old Church, the end of the blackout, and a trickle of liberated prisoners of war returning home. The Homecoming Fund was approaching £10,000. In the excitement of the time, the town council failed to note the death at Skelmorlie Castle in April of the 16th earl of Eglinton and Winton: in any case the old connection was now severed. But history was remembered in June when the council were guests of Glasgow University, in recognition of the hospitality it had obtained in the burgh three centuries before. Another tradition ended when the last burgh horse was sold — that Clydesdale gelding which just a year before had cost 'damages to the extent to fifteen shillings in respect of the value of vegetables destroyed in the allotments'. At this same time the burgh acquired that more lasting memorial of the past, Seagate Castle, as a gift from the late Mrs. Walker of Castlepark. Meanwhile during the summer there was boating on the river and pony rides on the shore. Could Marymass be revived? The Moor was still requisitioned, and the Carters Society suggestion that the municipal golf course might be used was impracticable, but it was possible to make do with sports and shows. By October the Incorporated Trades could resume their annual celebrations. Already the war had been ended with the dropping of atomic bombs on Japan (6 August), and victory was celebrated on 2nd September. Sirens hooted, bells rang, there were bonfires and fireworks, the council workmen had been able to prepare fairy lights for illumination of Waterside and the Low Green, and there were children's parties. The *Irvine Herald* noted that 'merrymaking went on until between three and four o'clock in the morning ... Relief that all was over was evident everywhere'.

There were public meetings throughout the year to discuss the future of the Royal Ordnance Factory and the burgh's industrial prospects. There were other massive problems to be faced — housing, food and fuel shortage, extending educational provision, and implementing the Beveridge plans for a welfare state. In July the parliamentary elections — the first for ten years — returned a Labour government to power. Sir Thomas Moore held on to Ayr Burghs with 22,593 votes, but he was closely threatened by 21,865 Labour votes for Major William Ross, later MP for Kilmarnock and Secretary of State for Scotland. In November, 68% of Irvine's 8,930 electors (including 824 service voters) participated in municipal elections to replace eight of the council's eighteen members. This resulted in the 'passing of some stalwarts'. By 'splendid organisation' five Labour councillors were elected, plus a Communist for Ward One. With their twelve Moderate colleagues they began the post-war development of an Irvine which had lost one hundred and fourteen on active service, and four in an air raid, plus one killed in the making of explosives.

NINETEEN

Mid-Century

In 1947 the town council accepted an invitation (from the present author) to participate in preparation of the Third Statistical Account of Scotland. Information on different aspects of Irvine life was assembled by seven committees of local persons, who were enthusiastic enough also to publish within the year a separate and fuller account of the Royal Burgh of Irvine, edited by William Phillips, teacher and secretary of the Burns Club for twenty-three years. That survey presented a picture of the community in mid-century when the scars of war were not yet healed, but when plans for social and economic reconstruction were being vigorously implemented. How successful these ventures were, in the twenty years leading to 1965, is explored in this chapter.

Nationally, in the immediate post-war period, Attlee's Labour government (1945-51) pursued a policy of nationalisation, which had its local impact. When the National Coal Board was formed to take over the mines (1947), it acquired Shewalton, soon to be closed down; and Warrix which had been re-opened in 1944 and employed 120 men working, under the burgh boundaries, the last exploitable seams of the north Ayrshire coalfield. Also in 1947 British Railways became responsible for the lines and stock which were formerly part of the LMS Railway. The local railway workshops were closed down, and ultimately after the Beeching Report the Kilmarnock Irvine-Ardrossan line was closed (1964), as was Irvine goods station (1965), and the halts at Gailes and Bogside (1966). In 1948 electricity and in 1949 gas were similarly brought under public ownership; with the introduction of piped gas, local production ended in 1964 and the gasworks were demolished in 1965. The creation of a National Fire Service on a peacetime basis meant Irvine's loss in 1948 of a full-time unit; part-time firemen at the Low Green station operated the fire engine which the town council had purchased in 1940, and which was not replaced until 1966. In 1948, with the formation of a National Health Service, doctors, dentists, and opticians became involved in the new welfare state, including the six doctors who served three practices in the town. Ayrshire Central Hospital, opened in stages from 1941, passed under the control of a Regional Board. The Burgh Fever Hospital, opened during the First World War, could consequently be closed by the end of the Second War. And what had been the Poorshouse became Cunnnghame Home, for helpless old folk in need of hospital care. Voluntary bodies like the Irvine Nursing Association could be dissolved. When the Ministry of National Insurance was formed in 1948, there followed decay or demise of those friendly societies which had previously been involved in distributing benefits. The National Assistance Board took over from the local authorities responsibility for what had once been called poor relief and would become known as social security. Ayr County Council among its varied continuing concerns had to provide for the raising of the school leaving age to fifteen in 1947. Irvine Town Council, like other authorities, had housing as its priority.

Meanwhile the economy was suffering from post-war dislocations and shortages. Wartime rationing of consumer goods continued; indeed had to be extended to bread between 1946 and 1948; and not till 1953 were ration books no longer required. It was a time of political excitement. The local Labour Party took five seats in 1945, another four in 1946, and for the first time won a majority in Irvine Town Council. At the formal meeting thereafter in the Town House 'a large number of members of the public desired admittance to the Council Chambers', and standing orders were suspended to allow the meeting to be adjourned to the hall of the Town House, where Archibald Green was elected provost — an engineer and ex-serviceman who had been wounded at Gallipoli in 1915. In traditional manner he took the oath of allegiance and the oath *de fideli administratione officii*. The council in 1947 was now composed of engineers (3), joiner, railway guard, craneman, shop steward, political organiser, miner, labourer, insurance agent, commercial traveller, retired civil servant, retired banker, grocers (2), works manager, and golf caddie master. Labour were also successful in the 1950 General Election when A.C. Manuel, a railwayman from Ardrossan, captured the new Central Ayrshire

A favourite view, first depicted in 1820, portrayed here on a postcard of 1950, before plans were made for drastic transformation.

parliamentary constituency to which Irvine was attached after its 243 years within Ayr Burghs. In closely fought elections the Conservatives won majorities in Parliament (1951-64), taking over Central Ayrshire briefly (1955-59), and there was a similar trend in municipal elections. In Irvine the Moderates organised themselves to recover their majority after only one year and the provostship in 1950. How closely the two parties were matched was obvious when in 1952 and again in 1955 equality of votes meant that the provost had to be chosen by lot. During this period, the Representation of the People Act of 1945 extended the municipal franchise from ratepayers to all who held a parliamentary vote, adults over the age of twenty-one; and municipal elections were moved in 1949 from November to May. In Irvine the number of magistrates was increased by the appointment of police judges (from 1955), and the council decided that a redistribution of wards was long overdue — by 1956 Ward One contained over 4,000 electors while Ward Six was left with fewer than 600, and each was represented by three councillors. Boundaries were redrawn, and in May 1957 all eighteen seats were declared vacant and a general local election (as in 1881) was called. This produced a woman councillor again after a twenty years' lapse, when Charles Bell and his daughter Susan Bell were both successful. It also produced, with nine Moderates, eight Labour and one Independent, a continuation of close party divisions on the council. Subsequent polls failed to end the deadlock: all that happened was fragmentation of political allegiances. By 1965 the membership of the council comprised six Labour, five Moderates, four Independents, two Scottish Nationalists, and one representing a Ratepayers' Association.

Although party politics occupied an essential place in municipal affairs, nevertheless personal worth did not go unrecognised either in elections or in the work of the council. Alexander Smith, a Communist, was well enough liked to be elected a councillor from 1945 to 1950, and able enough to be appointed as Treasurer. Douglas Clayton, an Independent councillor, persuaded the council to form a Town Development Sub-committee for the attraction of new industry, and was made its first convener in 1958.

Locally as nationally in this period, all parties were committed to measures of social advancement. So Irvine councillors were able to co-operate effectively — hopefully anxious to improve the town in various ways but realising that all available resources must be directed toward building the houses which were so urgently needed. The *Irvine Herald* acutely observed that all parties on the council agreed in spending hugh sums on building houses, and quarrelled only over letting them. The building programme was in the hands of capable men — first the Moderate ex-provost W.R. McKinlay, councillor for 43 years and Housing Convener 1939-52; then from Labour young Eric Dale, a joiner who was appropriately both Dean of Guild and Housing Convener 1952-60; followed by Wilson Muir whose father had as provost a generation before initiated Irvine's housing programme, and who in 1966 also became provost.

Emergency measures were neccessary to make up for the war years when no building was possible and, in the case of Irvine, to provide for a population which was steadily increasing. The Census reports recorded 12,032 (1931), 14,745 (1951), and 16,911 (1961). In 1946 Irvine Town Council acquired some 200 temporary prefabricated houses for erection at Ravenspark, Winton Place, the Glebe, and the Riggs to the west of Fullarton Street. Over a hundred Nissen huts left by the army on the Moor were converted to provide additional housing accommodation. A start was made by the town council and the SSHA building permanent houses in the Thornhouse area and planning a massive scheme beyond Winton Road on the land of Irvine Mains farm. In 1947 it was estimated that 1,300 houses were overcrowded, 480 families were quartered in other people's houses, and inadequate houses included 1,121 with only outside closets and 63 without an indoor water supply. There were squatters in huts at the Royal Ordnance Factory, at the Fullarton Prisoner of War Camp, and in 118 of the 155 condemned properties through the town. This lamentable situation was all the more tragic because the pre-war efforts of the council had gone far to counter what the *Irvine Herald* called 'the stigma so long attached to it that Irvine is a ramshackle old town'. Of Irvine's 3,682 inhabited houses in 1948, 47% were modern and less than twenty years old — only Cumnock and Kilwinning could beat that record with less rebuilding to do, and Prestwick which was one of those coast resorts with so much private building in the '30s. It was calculated that 1,500 new houses were required for Irvine.

Between 1946 and 1948 only 60 permanent council houses could be completed, because of the shortage of materials. In the next ten years 1,386 were built — more than in the twenty inter-war years, a considerable achievement. Fifty-one older houses were purchased, including the 34 built during the war adjoining Heatherhouse Road for Royal Ordnance Factory staff. Another 223 houses brought the total of post-war permanent council houses up to 1,669 by 1961, plus 513 others erected by the SSHA. It was possible from 1954 to begin demolition of the temporary post-war 'pre-fabs', which had all been replaced by 1970.

A vast new housing estate was created in the north of the town, stretching as far as the Red Burn burgh boundary, extending in a wide arc from Kilwinning Road across Quarry Road to Bank Street. It approached the pre-war Thornhouse scheme which was also augmented to a lesser extent, as was that other scheme across the river at Merryvale and Springbank, with parts of Fullarton Street cleared. Another corner was filled up between Golffields and Annick Road, involving the disappearance of the old country path known as Sliddery Lane or Skittery Wynd. Near the town centre some properties were demolished, the old Elephant Inn was replaced by two council houses, and new shopping premises were erected by local firms and chain stores to exploit the needs of this growing town — Woolworths arriving in 1957. The council was aware that Irvine was 'rotten at the heart', but plans for the systematic renovation of the town centre could not be implemented until 1965 when a start was made by clearing Kirkgate.

What progress was being made can be measured in the 1961 Census report. Of Irvine's 17,000 inhabitants in some 5,000 households, 71% or nearly 13,000 were tenants of 3,600 local authority houses; 2,000 others (14%) were living in 700 owner-occupied houses; another 1,200 were renting private houses plus 600 in 170 houses 'tied' to their employment; and around 80 families were renting furnished rooms. There were now only 90 single-end dwellings left in the burgh, only four households without a cold water tap and 35 without an indoor water closet, though still 545 without a hot water supply and 726 without a fixed bath. But 84% of the houses had all these four basic household requirements. Overcrowding had not disappeared, and the worst areas remaining were the 2nd and 3rd wards with 1.09 and 1.06 persons per room. But with a burgh average of 0.96 persons per room, for the first time ever Irvine had now more rooms than people!

One reason why provision of sufficient houses was difficult to achieve was that the population was being augmented: not only did a post-war boom in babies create 'the bulge', but a declining death rate produced a natural increase of 10% in the 1951-61 inter-censal period; and incomers added another 4%, outnumbering those who were leaving Irvine. While 13,000 or nearly 80% of the burgh's inhabitants in 1961 were Ayrshire born, there were 1,000 Glaswegians, 2,600 from other parts of Scotland, 370

Fullarton Place, busier since this early 20th-century view, remained intact — for the time being.

from England and Wales, 270 Irish, and 180 foreigners. The numbers of such incomers would continue to increase. Since many of them were workers with young families, this meant that Irvine had a large child population (27.4% under the age of 15 in 1961), while old folk, though growing in numbers everywhere would form a comparatively small fraction in Irvine (7.9% of 65 and over).

To cater for this busily growing community the councillors had to work hard, their evening meeting stretching out sometimes till after eleven o'clock. Agenda and minutes grew longer, and printing them was now too slow and expensive, so that an electrically operated Roneo duplicator was purchased (1947), and dictaphones (1958) for the town clerk's office. How the mass of business increased was painfully evident to the present researcher, faced with a formidable shelf of ever-thickening volumes until the Minutes for 1965-66 have 1,039 pages plus appendices and (thankfully) an index. The vastly increased work of management required the Burgh Chamberlain to shed part of his load to a Burgh Factor (1946), and a Burgh Architect was also appointed (1951). To provide office accommodation, Heathfield was purchased in 1946 and, in 1956, £135 was spent to provide the Chamberlain with his first calculating machine. For the fleet of motor lorries required for cleansing and transportation a new Caldon burgh yard was acquired in 1948. To these was added in 1954 'a car for use on offical occasions' — a Morris Oxford costing £737. The work of the council was expedited by a reorganisation of committees in 1950. These remained Finance, Health and Housing, Property, Works, Recreation and Parks, but — on the town clerk's suggestion — only eight or nine councillors were on each and not, as before, the whole council.

The housing and finance committees were of course the busiest. Not only had the building of houses to be planned and contracted out, but new streets had to be laid out, arrangements made for street lighting and provision of telephone kiosks by the GPO, sites had to be allocated for shops in the schemes and areas set aside for future schools, churches, and recreational areas, and negotiations entered into with Ayr County Council for planning permission and with government departments regarding design and finance. A direct labour repair squad was organised, and improvements were made in older houses, with bathrooms installed in 1952 in the original council houses of 1915. A points system for allocation of houses to tenants was introduced in 1946, rents had to be reviewed from time to time (posing difficulties for councillors who were themselves council tenants), and the council had to act as agents for SSHA houses. The system of door-to-door collection of rents was altered in 1958, regrettably after the tragic killing of a collector in the course of his duties; and after a brief reversion to that system in 1963 to try to deal with arrears, payments at a rent office were resumed. By 1965 a new type of problem emerged with increased ownership of cars, and congestion caused by parking in the streets of the housing schemes.

There was little time (or money) for anything else. The slaughterhouse was demolished (1953) and the bridge in Kilwinning Road over the derelict Caledonian Railway Line removed (1955). Street lighting was improved: in 1950, of the 418 lamps, 51 were still gas-lit but these were being superseded. The town clock was repaired (1946) and the spire of the Town House (1948 and 1961). But plans for a new and bigger town hall had again and again to be shelved. There was real need for a place which could accommodate larger functions, only partially met when the Cooperative premises in High Street were finished at the end of the war, with a Caledonian Hall commemorating the old Caledonian Arms on the site. The council was more successful in acquiring beside Quarry Road and laying out as a Recreation Park and sports ground that area of the old loch which was unfit for building upon, which critics of the scheme described as 'a swamp' and where old folks remembered skating when young. In 1950 a Parks department was formed. Children's playgrounds were provided in the housing schemes and at the Low Green. The tennis courts were maintained. The golf course was redesigned because part of the original course east of Kilwinning Road was needed for building; it was re-opened in 1955, and in 1957 Kidsneuk House was converted into a new club house. At the new Recreation Park, municipal bowling greens were obtained at last. But, as before, summer resort facilities amounted to no more than renting out the lifeboat shed as a shore cafe, ponies on the beach, McLean's boats on the river, and brassband performances on the Green. Irvine shore was becoming more popular, especially with car owners. But the council made limited improvements and was lukewarm about further developments. Holidaymakers who camped by the shore were evicted (1957). Messrs. Codona were able to set up amusements, but only on private ground. Yet by 1963 there was a civic welcome to a Caravan Club rally at the shore.

Even in this hectic modern era the past kept intruding and not just at Marymass. Customary donations to charities continued (including coal money), and the various bequests were administered. Queen Elizabeth was proclaimed in the traditional manner at cross, the old ports, and harbour, and the Coronation celebrated with the usual festivities (1953). The poet James Montgomery was remembered (1954); the old Powder House was repaired (1961); and the right of way at Puddleford was safeguarded (1962); other rights of way by the harbour and shore, however, tended to be forgotten. There were still the Common Good lands to be attended to: 200 acres of Moor and 200 other acres of farms to be let, with other fields rouped annually, and permits had to be issued for shooting over the harbour flats. Amid the plethora of more urgent business recorded in the council minutes appear fragmentary reminders of the disappearing rural past — complaints of cattle straying at the Golffields (1952) and piggeries at East Road and Thornhouse Avenue (1959). And while new regulations required protective clothing, holiday pay, and superannuation for burgh workmen — 73 of them in 1947 — the town's officers were still supplied with traditional livery of red coat, green vest, breeches, gaiters, and black silk hat.

The freedom of the burgh was awarded to distinguished persons. Sir Andrew Duncan (1884-1952) was, in the words of the *Irvine Herald*, 'without doubt the greatest Irvine man of this generation'. The son of a missionary at the Seaman's Bethel, from Loudoun Street School and Irvine Royal Academy he went to Glasgow University, then from teaching into law, becoming Secretary of the Shipbuilding Federation, war time Coal Controller, was knighted in 1921, then as President of the British Iron and Steel Federation was co-opted into Churchill's wartime government as President of the Board of Trade and Minister of Supply. He received the freedom of his native Irvine in 1948. Similar honour was bestowed (1949) on A.B. McDonald who returned from South Africa with benefactions for the town and its academy; on two ex-provosts, each of whom had given more than forty years of service on the council — Matthew Lamont (1953) and W.R. McKinlay (1956); and, as a tribute (1959), on the local territorial unit, Q Battery 279 (Ayrshire) Field Regiment Royal Artillery (T.A.) Several local persons were awarded burgess tickets, most notably in 1963 ex-Treasurer John Johnston, then in his 87th year, for 67 of them a 'brither cairter', and until his death in 1965 celebrated locally as 'Mr. Marymass'.

For the first time since Mary Queen of Scots passed by in 1563, the burgh was honoured by a royal visit. King George VI had inspected troops there during the war, but now came an official visit on a Royal Tour of several

Decent early 19th-century homes in Loudoun Street would soon be demolished.

Ayrshire towns. On 3rd July 1956 Queen Elizabeth and the Duke of Edinburgh made an eight-minute stop at the Town House to be greeted by Provost Donaldson. An even more fleeting visit by the Queen Mother followed in 1964 on her way to Hunterston power station.

Less happily, in the years between 1963 and 1965 memories were stirred of the corrupt practices of the old unreformed royal burgh of the 18th century. There were allegations of irregularities in housing allocations (1963), leaking of confidential information, impropriety over a contract (with ex-Dean of Guild Dale called in to make an inquiry), and complaints about councillors' expenses (all in 1964). In 1965 a burgh factor was jailed, and several other individuals were fined for defrauding the town council over housing expenditure.

In the immediate post-war years the industrial prospects of Irvine were uncertain. The contributors to the Third Statistical Account commented: 'As far as the future is concerned, the position of the Burgh with regard to industry and population cannot be gauged with any degree of accuracy. It would appear that no heavy industries will be established; the harbour has declined in importance, and the export of coal (to Northern Ireland, Eire, Spain, and France mainly) has dropped considerably, though it may be revived to some extent. It is true that in the plans for the Burgh under the various planning schemes provision is made for the establishment of new industries, but it could be argued with some measure of certainty that Irvine will remain a comparatively small town, of some 16,000 inhabitants'. Yet Irvine had a solid base in 'a fair variety of industrial activities'. Skilled workers, on a 44-hour week, were earning a basic £5.10/- (men) and £3.10/- (women). With easy public transport, workers from adjoining areas came in to make up 20% of those locally employed, with many residents also travelling out daily. There were only three hundred unemployed in 1947.

The principal industries were the metal working trades, employing over 1,000 workers in 1947. Although shipbuilding had ended, the Ayrshire Dockyard Company (with 525 employees) had widened its activities to produce light rolled steel sections used in prefabricated construction; indeed ship repairing was abandoned in 1959, and in 1961 the firm was renamed Ayrshire Metal Products Ltd. Laird's blockworks (208) was now forging and die-stamping light wrought iron goods. Iron founding was still carried on by Henry Brown's (122) and brass by David Flanagan's (24). The railway workshops (250) continued their specialised work, shortly to be transferred to Barassie.

Ardeer explosives works still employed 400 men and 200 women from Irvine. But the local chemical industry was dying — ICI's Walker Works (46) distilling sulphuric acid, Scottish Tar Distillers (30), and James Young and Sons who now owned the Thornhouse soap works (18) — all would disappear before 1965. The Portland Glass Company (249) would be taken over in 1957 by Rockware. The two timber merchants — Matthew Wright and Nephew (57) and Robert Glen and Son (64) — and a dozen small firms in the building and ancillary trades continued busy. 'Of paramount importance in the economic balance of the community' were those textile businesses where girls could find work, the Hosiery Manufacturing Company (470) and five smaller firms (373). There was also the Calder Glen Laundry (30) in Fullarton Street. This, however, closed in 1950, and its premises provided a garage for North Ayrshire Coaches Ltd. who operated a local bus service, later taken over by the AA bus company.

A question mark had hung over the Royal Ordnance Factory which had employed 1,730 at its maximum during the war, reduced to 400 by 1947, and later to 250 breaking up old ammunition. After closure, it had re-opened between 1952 and 1954, but finally shut down in 1959. To attract alternative employment an Industrial Development Council was formed in 1946 with equal representation of employers, trade unions, and councillors, but to little effect. In 1950 the abandoned Ministry of Supply store in Gailes Road was taken over by Wilson Pipe Fittings Ltd., and at Shewalton too were Eastwoods Cement and Pipe Works. Also outwith the burgh but near enough to benefit it the long-established Messrs. Robert Wilson and Son Ltd. in 1953 brought their food canning business to Eglinton Park. In 1958, with the closure of the Royal Ordnance Factory imminent, the town council took a bold step, and one which had dramatically successful consequences. A Town Development Committee was formed under Councillor Douglas Clayton who became 'Mr. Industry'. The Royal Ordnance Factory's 135 acres and 60 buildings were acquired for conversion into an industrial estate, with town clerk Robert Whyte masterminding the ambitious project. The premises, which he described as 'dolefully coated with camouflage paint ... with a Guard House at the entrance and enclosed by forbidding perimeter fences',

were transformed. The area was replanned and serviced, certain buildings were adapted and new ones built, and better access was provided by a bridge over the railway at Heatherhouse. A massive advertising campaign brought impressive results even before the official opening of the estate in September 1960. By the end of 1962, 342,400 square feet of factory space had been leased to seventeen new firms — five from Glasgow, six from other parts of Scotland, three from England, and three from the USA. In addition, four other new businesses were accommodated in 185,000 square feet outwith the estate, providing employment for 750 within and as many outside. The next year saw further welcome additions, and with business brisk among some of the older firms, the *Irvine Herald* in January 1964 could cheerfully announce that 'There was never a time when prospects for this locality looked brighter'.

Simultaneously the town council, in association with the SSHA, was building sufficient houses for incoming workers. The council itself erected 646 between 1962 and 1965, the SSHA another 426. From 1959 there was increased building of private houses, first in Annick Road, and speculative builders sought other sites. An overspill agreement arranged by the council brought 372 Glasgow families to Irvine. Only two did not remain, and for reasons which Robert Whyte explained: 'one because the dancing facilities in the town did not measure up to City standards, and the other one jump ahead of Summons for arrears'.

The facilities which Irvine provided for established residents and incomers were fully described in the Third Statistical Account. In 1947 there were 14 bakers, 15 butchers, 58 confectioners, 10 fish and chip shops, 15 cafes, 6 licensed and 87 unlicensed grocers, 5 chemists, 8 coal merchants, 15 drapers, 5 fishmongers, 3 ironmongers, 12 newsagents, 14 public houses, 6 hotel bars, 12 shoemakers, and 2 watchmakers. Most of these were in the centre of town, and most were owned and managed by local people. There were 15 multiple shops, and this number would increase. In addition there were branches of the main banks — British Linen, Clydesdale, Commercial, Royal, and Union. There was the Municipal Bank; Glasgow Savings Bank opened a branch in 1947; the long-established Irvine Savings Bank, latterly managed by the Union Bank, was dissolved in 1958. There were post offices in High Street and Harbour Street, four surgeries, a Social Welfare office, and a Labour Exchange.

The drabness of the immediate post-war years was relieved here as elsewhere by a renaissance of community activity. And as the town grew and its industrial prospects brightened, there was a fuller calendar of social opportunities.

The New Year of 1946 was ushered in at the Cross in a

Substantial tenements in Church Street west of the railway would eventually be demolished.

'quiet and orderly manner' by the Cadet Pipe Band. In succeeding years this public welcome to the New Year became a tradition in decline, replaced by more private first-footing celebrations.

At the end of January the annual celebration of Irvine Burns Club was now copied in a dozen other local Burns Suppers. In 1963 Irvine Burns Club inherited Wellwood in Eglinton Street from Robert and James Graham Paterson, bachelor sons of Provost John Paterson.

April brought Bogside Races, revived in 1947. There were seven days of racing in the year — two each in April, June and July and one day in September. The great day was the race for the Scottish Grand National, last run on 10th April 1965, after which the race course was finally closed, apart from February and March point-to-point meetings. But the April shows at the Goffields continued.

In May — from 1949 onwards — came the municipal elections. The long tradition of November polls was statutorily altered in hope of greater convenience on lighter nights. In 1949, 68.5% of Irvine's 9,652 electors turned out, high enough to signify considerable interest in local politics, which stimulated the formation for a few years of an unofficial junior town council.

Summer brought various festivities. Perhaps inspired by Victory Day in 1946, the following year the Ex-Servicemen's Club sponsored Highland Games in the new Park. The pre-war swimming galas at the harbour lapsed for a time, but regattas on the river were revived by the rowing and canoe clubs. New water sports came with an Irvine Cruising club and an Aqua Ski Club, and in 1964 the town council was considering the provision of an indoor swimming pool.

The highlight of summer was, of course, Marymass, revived with all its traditions after the War. The town council was vexed to have no longer a burgh horse to enter in the Carters Races, but it paid a burgh workman in 1947 to decorate a borrowed horse. And it was determined to extend the festivities. By 1952 the programme continued from Friday to Tuesday, including a flower show organised by the new Horticultural Society, and concluding with a gala ball (tickets, 12/6, from the town clerk). Local organisations were brought in to form a committee which from 1953 provided ten days of jollification. The Carters Society insisted on their special rights on Marymass Saturday, and after much argument a proposed introduction of 'mechanised vehicles' into the parade was disallowed. By 1974 the council expended £5,800 on Marymass.

In the autumn evenings various organisations resumed their winter programmes. As well as providing recreation for their members, many presented musical and dramatic performances. After the War older clubs were revived, and new ones were formed, some of which became firmly established. Special interests were catered for by the Horticultural Society, a Canine Club, Cage Bird Society, Homing Society, Riding Club, Judo Club, Camera Club, and a Model Aero Club; and archers resuscitated the Toxophilitic Society in 1964. Rather different in character were significantly new bodies — a Business Men's Club, Rotary Club, Round Table, and Toastmasters' Club; for the ladies, a Business and Professional Women's Club, Townswomen's Guild, Toastmistresses' Club, and an Inner Wheel — all formed in the '50's and '60's. Cultural horizons were widened when a Music Club was formed (1957), the Rotary Club organised art exhibitions, and an Arts Group set up what had become the Harbour Arts Centre (1965) in the old Harbour Mission. Youth organisations were also booming, encouraged by a District Youth Panel sponsored by the County Education Committee.

In October the Incorporated Trades held their annual functions — the 'Wee Pie' of each of the crafts, followed by the 'Big Pie'. In 1946 their tercentenary was celebrated. There were now 174 hammermen, 100 weavers, 10 tailors, 26 cordiners, 35 skinners, 22 wrights and squaremen, and 80 coopers. The wrights and squaremen, alone among the crafts, continued to demand an 'assay piece' before admission to membership and continued to provide small pensions for sick and aged members and dependants. For all the 'crafts' there was participation in golf and bowling sections (from 1949), and in the annual functions — from 1953 taking the form of a dinner though including the traditional pie. In 1955 a prize fund was formed to provide annual awards to secondary school pupils for specimens of good craftsmanship in metal, wood, and needlework. With this, and substantial donations to charity, the Incorporated Trades successfully justified their continued existence. In an appropriate verse from their 'Hymn':

> Gone the glory of old days
> When Trades were ruling,
> Now accept by God's grace
> New faith that's pulling.
> But let us keep our creed
> To succour those in need:
> So live, in word and deed,
> Craftsmen of Irvine.

With November came the annual Remembrance Day. There were services with wreaths laid at the War Memorial — which was re-sited in 1952 off the roadway. In 1952 a Memorial Garden for the dead of the Second World War was opened. This plot off Kilwinning Road was gifted by Mrs. A.M. Watson and laid out by the Ex-Servicemen's Club.

December brought Christmas, and more presents than ever in an increasingly affluent commercialised society.

Throughout the year a wide range of sports was available. There was golf at Bogside and Ravenspark — and Hamilton McInally won the Scottish Amateur Championship for the third time in 1947, followed by Jimmy Walker in 1961. Bowling at the Winton Club was now supplemented by new greens: Castlepark where the railwaymen took over from the Royal Ordnance Factory Works Club; and the Park bowling club under municipal auspices. Cricket was revived in 1948, and hockey for the ladies of the Academy Former Pupils Association. There were the Irvine Harriers and the Fullarton Wheelers cycling club, shooting with the West of Scotland Small Bore Rifle Association, and the water sports already listed. As well as horse racing at Bogside, there was greyhound racing attracting five hundred regulars to the Caledonian Stadium twice weekly and to Townhead once a week. Indoor sports were snooker, darts, and carpet bowls. A ten-pin bowling alley was opened at Townhead in 1964, and in the youth clubs table tennis and badminton were popular. The Social and Literary Institute — which had now lost all its literary aspects — continued as a games hall.

Pride of place among all sports continued to go to association football. Irvine Meadow celebrated their golden jubilee in 1948 by reaching the Scottish Junior Cup Final, an achievement repeated in 1951, while in 1959 the ultimate triumph was attained when they defeated Shettleston 2-1 to win the Cup. As the team returned from Hampden Park in an open-topped double-decker bus, through Girdle Toll to Irvine Cross, they were greeted by a crowd of ten thousand and received their second civic welcome. 'It was the greatest day, May 2, in the sporting life of Irvine.' They maintained their success, winning the Scottish Cup again in 1963 by defeating Glenafton. Over the twenty post-war years they were also Western League champions seven times, holders of the Western League cup four times, the Ayrshire Junior Challenge Cup twice, and the Irvine and District Cup six times. The other junior club, Irvine Victoria, had modest success, especially between 1952 and 1954 when three cups were won. In an attempt to emulate the juniors, there were a number of juvenile, amateur, and youth teams. And though Irvine Royal Academy introduced rugby, it remained a soccer playing school.

In general popular appeal, football was surpassed by films. In 1947 the four cinemas, with a combined capacity of over 3,000 were filled on Saturdays, and 80% full on weeknights. The Ritz in West Road presented variety shows on Fridays and Saturdays. But the coming of television on 14th March 1952, associated with the increased comforts of home life, presaged a new pattern in

Among activities which continued to flourish was junior football. Irvine Meadow won the Scottish Junior Cup in 1959, 1963, and 1973. The cup-winning 1972-73 team comprised — back row: Black (trainer), Lewis, Short, Renfrew, Hay, Bashford, O'Brien, Pinkerton, McIntyre (coach); front row: Hume, Johnstone, McCrorie (captain), McLaughlin, Gillespie, Morris.

social behaviour. The Palace closed in 1957 and the Regal became a bingo club in 1961. There continued in Bank Street the George (as the Kyle was named after 1946) and Green's (the Rex after 1965). Increased private ownership of cars was also changing social habits. And this was the era when holiday flights abroad became common. Among a series advertised locally in 1963 was fifteen days in Majorca for £51.

At the time of the Third Statistical Account minds were still concentrated on post-war difficulties of re-adjustment. Soldiers returning home, it is recalled, objected to local girls fraternising with Polish troops and Italian prisoners of war, and there was a 'serious disturbance' at the Ritz dance hall in September 1946. By the next year it could be recorded that immoralities associated with the war had diminished, and there was 'an improved sense of decorum and propriety'. But gambling was much more common, as was swearing, while vandalism and juvenile delinquency seemed to be on the increase. Drunkenness had shown a general decline since the beginning of the century, though in the '50's and '60's parties of inebriated visitors would give cause for complaint. The churches were particularly concerned at the disappearance of Sunday observance. There had been Sunday work during the war, and now the council allowed pony-riding and boating on Sundays in 1946 and Sunday golf in 1947. It was regretted that so few councillors bothered to attend the kirking of the council. Yet they continued to be officially represented at other church services, at Marymass, with the Trades, on Remembrance Day, at the induction of new ministers in the various churches, when the Moderator of the General Assembly visited Irvine in 1950 and 1961, and at a special service in 1960 to commemorate the anniversary of the Reformation.

The Church of Scotland continued to minister to a sizeable proportion of the community, with over 4,000 communicant members in 1947. At the Old Parish Church (1,160) Rev. Alex Macara exercised an effective ministry and cultivated the roses of which he was so fond. He caused a stir at the kirking of the council in 1965 by preaching against party politics in local government. Elsewhere there were changes. At Fullarton (660) Rev. J.P.E. Wightman (1948-52) was followed by Rev. Peter G. Thomson. Difficulties following a fire in the church in 1961 were successfully surmounted. At Wilson Fullarton (500), after forty-four years of service Rev. James Wishart was succeeded in 1947 by Rev. Robert Dougall. Similarly Rev. Samuel McNab who had served Relief (480) for 25 years had as successors Revs. Thomas Dick (1951-62), then J. Napier. New ministers came also to Mure (600) — Revs. A.A. Lawson (1947), George Corfield (1953), George B. Robertson (1961); and to Trinity (240) Rev. Joseph Hardie (1947-53). Efforts were made to combine smaller congregations. When Trinity became vacant in 1947, protracted negotiations for union with Relief proved abortive in face of congregational resistance. More successfully a joint ministry was arranged for Wilson Fullarton and Trinity under Rev. Alexander Burgess then Rev. Thomas Smail, and after ten years a union was concluded in 1963, with the new joint congregation of St. Paul's meeting in Wilson Fullarton Church under Rev. W. Lawrie Irvine, and the Trinity Church building was closed in 1966. This union made possible church extension into the new housing area. Worship began in a wooden hut off Caldon Road, then with aid from the trustees of the Ferguson bequest St. Andrew's Church was built. Under Rev. John Leckie (1957-60) and Rev. John Taylor (1960-70) its membership reached 1,100 by 1965.

Vitality was evident also at St. Mary's Roman Catholic Church. Father Dermott O'Reilly was followed by John Nicholas Murphy (1950-55) and Vincent Walker (1955-66). In 1947 there were 1,550 Catholics (of all ages) in Irvine. The church was severely damaged by fire in 1963, but the opportunity was seized not only to restore it but to improve. Smaller denominations continued to worship. The Baptists had 180 memebers in 1947, and Rev. A.J.R. Mackenzie (1948-62) was followed by Rev. Alexander Barbour. The Christian Brethren (150) had their Waterside Hall. Their Quarry Road meeting place was given up, but County Councillor Edward Adams continued Sunday School services at the old Slate Mill, and open-air services as well. The Church of the Nazarene (70), because of slum clearance in Fullarton Street, moved in 1956 to Eglinton Street. There also continued the Salvation Army (40), Christadelphians (35) and the Railway Mission. There were in 1947 also adherents of the Catholic Apostolic Church, Jehovah's Witnesses, Christian Scientists, and Episcopalians. These last in 1960 were able to begin regular services in the new Girl Guide hut in Kirkgate. It was calculated in the Third Statistical Account that in Irvine about two-thirds of the population had a church connection. If that estimate was correct, then Irvine was more religiously minded than the Ayrshire average, and indeed there were fewer without church affiliations than the 'lapsed masses' of previous generations. Certainly efforts were being made to attract youth. The six Church of Scotland congregations had together in 1947 nearly a thousand at Sunday school, another two hundred at Bible Classes, plus youth clubs and companies of Boys' Brigade and Girl Guides. The ministers acted as school chaplains and participated actively in the Education Committee's Youth Panel.

Although there were ambitious post-war plans for extending educational opportunity, resources were limited, and scarce building materials were devoted by Ayr County Council to building houses rather than schools. St. Michael's College, destroyed by fire in 1939, could not be replaced, and pupils (650 in 1956) were accommodated in primary classrooms and huts till 1965. Sister Mechtilde Joseph remained head until 1950, when she was followed by Sister Pauline. Irvine Royal Academy's roll reached one thousand after the raising of the school leaving age to fifteen in 1947. From 1952 no infants were enrolled, to implement the Education Committee's policy of closing down the academy's primary department, where fees had been abolished in 1947. Yet to accommodate the secondary pupils who came in from the two local primary schools, from Dreghorn, and (into the 4th year) from Kilwinning, huts had to be erected in the playgrounds in 1957. For James Porter, and Alex MacMillan who succeeded him as rector in 1953, there were other challenges. Junior secondary courses and vocational classes had to be devised for the majority of pupils who would leave at the statutory leaving age. Adademic standards had to be maintained for the 30-35% who continued into the senior classes. Extramural activities were extended. Tradition was maintained. The wearing of a school blazer was a mark of pride, and distinguished former pupils attended the annual prizegiving, like Sir Andrew Duncan in 1948 and Sir Hilary Blood, Governor of Mauritius, in 1952.

The closure of the academy's primary department increased pressure on the two primary schools. Bank Street School, with William D. Jardine as headmaster (1948-66), was crowded with 750 pupils. Things were even more difficult at Loudoun-Montgomery School with 900 pupils. The successive headmasters — James Climie (1946-50), William Irvine (1950-59), and George Donohoe (1959-74) — had special problems. The Loudoun Street building was burned down in 1946. Though numbers of children in the immediate area were fewer, others from distant housing schemes had to be sent here, which caused inconvenience and resentment. In 1960 the first of the town's new primary schools was built just beside where Duntonknoll quarry used to be, appropriately named the John Galt School. It is a measure of the urgency that it was 'built without planning permission having first been secured'. The new school under J.M. Wilson was itself soon overcrowded. By 1965 there were public meetings and a petition. More primary schools and a new academy were needed. The County Council requisition from Irvine Town Council was now half a million pounds annually, and most of that was devoted to education. But no Irvine councillor in 1965 had been chosen to serve on the County Education Committee. It seemed to indignant Irvinites that the County Council had a spite against Irvine.

At the time of the Third Statistical Account in 1947 only ten families sent their children to private or boarding schools, though Catholic boys still had to travel to Kilmarnock for secondary schooling. Almost all those who left school at the statutory leaving age could find local jobs then. To assist them, a Youth Employment Exchange in Waterside offered careers advice, directing keen applicants to pre-apprenticeship courses, day-release courses, and evening classes held locally or in nearby centres. The Youth Panel publicised social activies available in over a score of places — five companies of the Boys' Brigade, two of the Boy Scouts, Sea Cadet Corps, Air Training Corps, YMCA, Canoe Club and Rowing Club for boys; and six companies of the Girl Guides and Sea Rangers; also four church youth clubs and another at the academy. It was noted in 1947 that 'during the war and the immediate post-war years children and young adolescents seemed to grow up more quickly'. For this teenage population the favourite recreations included cinema, dancing, sports, and 'congenial company and a social atmosphere, against the almost constant background of the popular jukebox in the cafes of the town'.

The Town Clerk. From 1944 to 1972 Robert M. Whyte explored Irvine's past and contributed towards its future industrial growth.

TWENTY

From Burgh into New Town

The latest chapter of Irvine's history was prefaced by two Government White papers issued by Secretary of State Michael Noble in 1963. *The Modernisation of Local Government in Scotland* proposed radical alteration of the structure of local government. It would be followed by the Wheatley Commission in 1965, and a new Local Government (Scotland) Act in 1973 involving the abolition of town councils — and so would end the long history of Irvine as a burgh. The second, *Central Scotland: A Programme for Development and Growth,* hinted at the possibility of 'a fifth Scottish New Town in the Irvine area'. This exciting prospect of economic and social expansion overshadowed concern about the burgh's administrative future. What were to be the last ten years of the burgh as administered by a town council saw the establishment of an Irvine Development Corporation, which would lay the foundations of the New Town and build on these within the new local government framework created in 1975.

In 1964, meetings of the Scottish Development Department with Ayr County Council and the town councils of Irvine and Kilwinning resulted in a Draft Designation Order from the new Secretary of State William Ross, and the appointment of Messrs. Wilson and Womersley, consultant architects, to report on the feasibility of a New Town. Their interim plan was ready by May 1965, an Order was issued in February 1966 designating the New Town — to be called Irvine — and after a public inquiry the Order was confirmed. The proposals — the Wilson Plan — were published in May 1967. An area of 12,444 acres (reduced from 13,700 acres to meet objections from the farming community) would be developed to accommodate 55,000 new residents. In a wide arc extending from Kilwinning through Girdle Toll to Dreghorn and Drybridge along a 'neck-lace' of new communications would be formed 'beads' of industrial and residential growth. In June 1967 an Irvine Development Corporation (IDC) of nine members was constituted with A. W. Hardie as chairman. Among those nominated by the Secretary of State were two from Irvine burgh — Bailie Joseph Hunter and the former councillor Eric Dale. Dennis Kirby was appointed general manager, and Perceton House was acquired in September 1968.

It soon became obvious that the Wilson Plan required radical amendment. Geological surveys revealed extensive areas susceptible to mining subsidence. Existing populations had been underestimated. New proposals for the western expansion of Kilmarnock and for the development of a deepwater port at Hunterston had to be taken into consideration. Perhaps most important of all, the Wilson Plan involved too much destruction in Kilwinning and quite failed to integrate Irvine, with its extensive facilities and its coastal possibilities. Thus in September 1969 an Interim Revised Plan abandoned the concept of a new central area on a greenfield site east of Girdle Toll. The old burgh of Irvine was to become the focus of the New Town.

Following a series of consultations, public meetings, and exhibitions — all producing favourable reactions — helpful suggestions were noted and incorporated in *Irvine New Town Plan* published in January 1971. The existing population in the designated area of 40,000 (including 23,000 in Irvine burgh) would be expanded to 116,000 by 1986. Within Irvine would be formed a new shopping centre, and the shore and harbour would become a major sports and leisure area. The main industrial areas would be located east and south of Irvine at Newmoor, Shewalton, and Meadowhead. Irvine Development Corporation (IDC) would be responsible for overall planning and control, co-operating with local authorities and other agencies, itself investing in land purchase, building new houses and factories, providing roads and drainage, and co-ordinating the provision by others of necessary additional facilities for education, health, welfare, and recreation.

The drastic revision of the original plans produced delays, and natural local frustration at apparent lack of progress. In December 1968 the first housing development was inaugurated, at Pennyburn, Kilwinning. In May 1971 the extension of Perceton House was completed to provide headquarters for IDC's staff (whose members would rise to a peak of 368 in 1977). By March 1972, 3,799 acres — 30%

Over a period of sixty years Irvine Town Council built nearly 5,000 new houses, ranging from the first in Ayr Road (1915) to the 14-storey blocks (1968).

of the designated area — had been purchased, mainly in the landward area, and work begun making roads and building advance factories. Not till 1972 did Irvine itself feel the first impact of change. Then the whole of Irvine's central area was completely transformed.

1972 saw the whole north side of Bridgegate swept away for a complex of shops and offices in the new Bridgegate House. A new road was driven through the Low Green. At the same time Friars Croft, Montgomery Street, and Fullarton Place were cleared to make way for an improved road system west of the river. A southern crossing, making use of the old Kilmarnock railway line, had been provided in 1971; now a new road bridge at the Marress was completed in June 1973 to give access to Kilwinning Road between Heathfield and the Academy. The town centre could now be by-passed and the through traffic which congested it eliminated. The bottleneck which was Bridgegate could be pedestrianised and the way made clear for closure of Irvine's old bridge on 10 June 1973. This was demolished for the creation of a £5 million shopping centre spanning the river. The enclosed and air-conditioned Rivergate Mall with five department stores and 50 smaller shops was opened for business in October 1975. It was intended to extend it towards the railway station and beyond to the harbour area where Irvine Town Council in association with other authorities was constructing a new leisure and sports centre and IDC was planning a beach park and other ambitious developments.

The implementation of these major projects produced resentment. Members of Irvine Town Council, faced with sweeping and expensive changes over which they had no control, felt at times impotent and aggrieved. A 'vote of confidence in IDC', moved in the town council in January 1972, failed to pass, getting only seven votes. David Lambie, who in 1970 was elected Central Ayrshire's Member of Parliament as Labour's successor to Archie Manuel, fought a running battle with the 'New Town dictators' who were responsible only to the Secretary of State, whose nominees they were. Many persons had domestic, business, and financial interests disturbed by compulsory purchase orders. When part of the Low Green was taken over to form a new road, Ex-provost Wilson

Muir declared that 'the biggest mistake I made in my local government life was to welcome the New Town'. Some firms felt adversely affected by competition from the new shopping areas and — later in 1982 — by pedestrianisation of part of High Street. IDC's recreational plans led to cancellation in 1970 of the long-projected electricity generating station at the foreshore, and this met with criticism too. The work of demolition and reconstruction meant exasperating inconveniences, and for over two years the only direct way for pedestrians to cross the river was by an awkward and unsatisfactory temporary footbridge at the Puddleford. Even those who recognised the undoubted benefits of change nostalgically lamented what had been lost — the demolitions which removed for ever the birthplace of James Montgomery; Loudoun-Montgomery school; old Irvine bridge; and Saddlers Corner at the top of Bridgegate where lads and lasses used to meet. Surviving fragments of the past seemed out of place. Fullarton Church and its old school were isolated; Wilson Fullarton Church was dwarfed by the new bridge shopping edifice; the Relief Church was soon to be abandoned; the magnificent Trinity Church had been empty since 1966 and vandalised — 'the Shame of Irvine', 'the Building Nobody Wants'. Mae McEwan captured the feelings in verse:

> Irvine New Town wi' its changes — well, they say progress cannot rest,
> But I'm positive, you all, like me, loved oor auld Irvine best.

Not that IDC was unaware of the desirability of safeguarding what it could of Irvine's heritage. After all, in its first annual report it had wildly boasted that 'Irvine was an important settlement in Roman times'. James Marquis, its chief finance officer who succeeded as general manager in 1972, lovingly depicted the disappearing scenes of Old Irvine in pen and ink sketches. And in 1974 certain areas were designated as worthy of conservation, including Hill Street, Seagate, and Glasgow Vennel.

What made things especially difficult was that these were times of national and international unrest and uncertainty. Irvine, however, was a 'natural growth area'. The town council's Industrial Estate had by 1967 attracted a score of firms, including Plyglass Ltd., Bonney Forge (International) Ltd., Hyster Ltd., and Wilson Sporting Goods, to add to substantial existing firms like Rockware Glass Ltd., while nearby in the Shewalton area Skefco Ball Bearing Co. Ltd. and Chemstrand Ltd. were important acquisitions — all of which had persuaded central government that Irvine was eminently suitable for the creation of a New Town. In 1970 both Skefco and Rockware began major expansions. In 1973 there were two major developments: Beecham Pharmaceutical Divisions opened a plant at Shewalton; and the construction of Volvo trucks and buses was commenced in the old army depot at Eglinton, off Kilwinning Road. Altogether by 1975 a total of 51 firms had moved into new premises in the entire New Town area, providing just over 2,000 jobs. Some older local companies, however, were doing less well, and prospects were far from rosy. Various difficulties were inhibiting the growth of the New Town. Housing development at Bourtreehill was commenced in 1973, but progress was slow, and in 1975 there were 700 persons on the waiting list for rented accommodation. The New Town, planned to reach a population of 69,000 by 1976, had in fact reached only 50,700 ten years after designation: progress, though, substantial, had been less than anticipated.

Population growth required extended educational provision. In this respect Ayr County Council became a target for complaints, as its efforts were locally felt to be less than satisfactory. In 1966 provision was made of secondary schooling for Catholics by a new St. Michael's Academy, under Sister Pauline (1950-76), but this was in Kilwinning, and Williamfield was closed down. Irvine Royal Academy was old and overcrowded and a replacement was long overdue. In 1965 Irvine Town Council sold a site off Kilwinning Road for £9,870, and a massive block, the first Ayrshire school to cost over a million pounds, was opened in August 1969. But a storm broke earlier that year when Ayr County Council's arrangements were announced. Irvine Royal Academy staff and existing pupils would move into the new building, further pupils would be recruited from Kilwinning and the northern part of the town only, and the new school would be called Ravenspark Academy. All trophies, prizes, and funds would be retained in the old Irvine Royal Academy, which would be occupied by staff and pupils from Kilwinning and Dreghorn, and pupils from Bank Street and Loudoun-Montgomery primary schools would continue to be sent to this old school, with others from Dreghorn and Annick Lodge. An Irvine Parents' Association with 400 members was formed, but was unsuccessful in its efforts to have these complex zoning plans altered. At any rate, Irvine now had two secondary schools, comprehensive in character since primary promotion examinations were abolished in Ayrshire in 1967, and able to accommodate additional pupils following the raising of the statutory school leaving age to sixteen in 1973. Ravenspark Academy under its rectors Alexander MacMillan (1969-70) and Peter Milne (1970-74) provided modern facilities not only for pupils but recreational facilities for others in out-of-school hours. Irvine Royal Academy continued to operate effectively in the old building under John Hay (1969-72) and W. Iain Foulds (1972-84), celebrating in 1972 the 400th anniversary of the royal foundation of a school in Irvine. In 1973 a third

After more than seven centuries, Irvine ceased to be a burgh in 1975. The members of the last town council were — front row: Police Judge Joseph Hunter, Dean of Guild Hugh Howat, Bailie James Dick, Bailie George Donaldson, Provost Alex Rubie, Bailie Alex Burns, Bailie Joe Kerr, Treasurer Fred Loach, Councillor James Bilby; second row: Councillors Robert Neil, Mrs Mary Burns, George Hepburn, Jack Carson, Mike Regan, Mrs Elizabeth Herbertson, James H. Smith, Elliot Gray, James Smith. To the rear, the council officials: Ian Campbell, William Curdie, Martin Cameron, James Gordon, Robert Lindsay, William Cowan.

secondary school was opened between Irvine and Dreghorn, Greenwood Academy under William Cochrane, which to begin with had to provide temporary accommodation for displaced primary pupils from Irvine. Shortage of school places for the growing numbers of young children was evident. In 1966 there were some classes with up to fifty pupils, despite the recent (1960) opening of the John Galt School. Bank Street School continued under John Weir (1967-72), a national president of the Educational Institute of Scotland, then Hugh Drummond (1974-79), and Mrs. Agnes E. Carlyle (1979-82) who would be its last head teacher. Pressure was eased by a hutted Ravenspark Primary School in 1967 (renamed Recburn in 1969) under John Beattie; Castlepark Primary School in 1970 with John Reid as headmaster; and Woodlands (A.S. Chapman). Loudoun-Montgomery School, under George Donohoe until 1974, then Miss M.E.G. Livingstone, had to be closed to allow the bulldozers to clear a way for the new roads, and was not replaced until 1978. After the departure of secondary pupils to Kilwinning in 1966, St Mary's regained its premises, its title, and its first male head teacher with William Bennett. Ten years later he moved to the new St. Mark's. That was in 1975, when Ayr County Council handed over control of schools to Strathclyde Regional Council.

The growth and redistribution of the town population also involved the churches in inevitable change. The closure of Trinity Church in 1966 was followed by two others in the town centre. Wilson Fullarton Church, which had then become St. Paul's, was itself disbanded in 1974 to survive only as a social and recreational centre for the congregation of Fullarton Parish Church. The Relief Church was taken over in 1968 by Rev. Iain R. Munro, who had been born in the Kirkgate, son of a minister of Mure; plans for its demolition were averted in 1970; the congregation continued till 1977, when they sold the old building to the Royal British Legion and moved to a new church at Bourtreehill. Four Church of Scotland congregations remained. Irvine Old Parish Church enjoyed for fifty years the ministry of Rev. Alex Macara (1928-78). New halls were opened in 1968, and before going out of existence in 1975 the town council put into good order the steeple for which it had so long been responsible, and presented a window of commemoration. To the minister in 1967 was granted the freedom of the burgh, with a eulogy which noted how Rev. A. Macara had 'added a new lustre to his sacred calling; has splendidly upheld the ancient traditions of the said church; and by his compassion and charm has endeared himself not only to his congregation but also to the whole community'. Mure Church continued under Revs. George B. Robertson (1961-68) and Robert Sawers (1969-76). At Fullarton Church Rev. Peter G. Thomson, minister since 1953, shepherded those on the other side of the water. In 1972 this congregation commemorated James Montgomery whose Moravian birthplace was swept away in the demolitions. In 1974 they received into communion, when Wilson Fullarton Church was closed, the successors of those who had withdrawn from Fullarton Church with Rev. David Wilson in 1843. The youngest of the four congregations had become the largest, at St. Andrew's in the midst of the housing area. Rev. John Taylor went off to teach at Ravenspark, succeeded at St. Andrew's by Rev. J.W.F. Harris (1970-78)

St. Mary's, like Roman Catholic churches elsewhere, saw numerous changes after the Vatican Council of 1965 and the arrival of Father Thomas J. Murphy in 1966. Its newly formed parish council invited the town council, which attended St. Mary's in 1970 and subsequently, on a Sunday following the traditional kirking in the Old Parish Church. In 1975 there were some 3,000 Catholics of all ages in the area for which St. Mary's was responsible, as compared with around 5,000 adult communicant members of the Church of Scotland. Of the smaller protestant denominations, the Baptists worshipped in Bank Street under Revs. Alexander Barbour (1962-68), William S. Orr (1969-73), and D.M. Fraser; and the Church of the Nazarene continued in Eglinton Street. Demolition forced the Christian Brethren to move in 1967 from their Waterside Hall to Anderson Drive, then High Street in 1974. The Salvation Army had to move from Glasgow Vennel into Townhead. The Christadelphian Ecclesia and the Seventh Day Adventists were also displaced. The Episcopalians who lost their meeting place in Kirkgate were welcomed into St. Andrew's Church in 1973.

Despite disruptions occasioned by the New Town plan, the growing community was able to enjoy a widening range of facilities. In 1965 an Arts Group acquired the old Harbour Mission to form what became the Harbour Arts Centre. There provision was available for folk music, a film society, a record group, art exhibitions, and an intimate theatre seating one hundred, where the professional 'Borderline' company set up in 1974. A Rotary Club committee under Clement Wilson sponsored further development of the arts and the creation in 1973 of a Federation of Arts representing the Harbour Arts Centre, Irvine New Town Amateur Operatic Society, IDC Film Club, Ayrshire Metals Art Group, and the Abbey Society of Kilwinning. In 1966 a Folk Song festival was included in the Marymass programme, in 1967 a Choral Union of the churches was re-formed, and the Irvine Silver Star Accordian Band continued to thrive. Less successful meantime were efforts to form a Burgh Pipe Band or to revive the Burgh Brass Band.

Some older institutions disappeared. Demolitions in the Bridgegate brought closure of the old Social and Literary Institute in 1965, and the County Library had to find temporary premises in the Town House. From the Low Green had to be removed the Old Men's Cabin, also a hosiery firm operating in what had been built in wartime as a British Restaurant, and the old brewery where A.G. Barr & Co. Ltd. made aerated waters. In 1966 the old lifeboat shed at the shore was demolished. Other losses, in 1969, were the destruction by fire of the George, leaving Irvine without a cinema until the old Regal was re-opened; and the dredger *Irvine*, now 58 years old, was sent to the shipbreakers, signalising the virtual demise of Irvine as a commercial port. The *George Brown* had ended its long career (1887-1957) as the last paddle tug on the Clyde, replaced by the *Garnock* (1957-84). In 1973 the Shows ended their 54 years' use of the Golffields and were banished to the other side of the water until they could be accommodated on the Moor at Marymass.

The will to survival was strong. Marymass itself continued its annual success with an ever-widening programme of events. The Glasgow-Irvine Society celebrated its centenary in 1969. In that year sporting achievement was sustained when Jack Cannon won the Scottish Amateur Golf Championship, carrying on the Bartonholm tradition of Hamilton McInnally and Jimmy Walker. In 1973 Irvine Meadow won the Scottish Junior Cup for the third time, finally defeating Cambuslang Rangers after two drawn matches. The town continued to be served by its two weekly newspapers, the *Irvine Herald* passing its centenary in 1971 and the *Irvine Times* in 1973. Charles Ross, whose family had controlled the *Herald* since 1925, sold out in 1967 to George Outram and Co. Ltd.; in 1971 it was acquired by Scottish and Universal Newspapers Ltd., who in 1978 chose Irvine to establish modern printing works for their publications. The *Times* continued to be printed in Ardrossan by Arthur Guthrie and Sons Ltd., though this firm too was sold after the death in 1962 of George Guthrie, grandson of the founder. For long the *Times* reporter for Irvine was John S. Begg who set up a printer's shop at the corner of High Street and Bridgegate in 1873, continued by his son of the same name from the age

Following the establishment of an Irvine Development Council in 1967, the Bridgegate was cleared in 1972 and Irvine Bridge demolished in 1973 for the creation of a New Town Shopping Centre.

of seventeen till he retired in 1956 after fifty-nine years. New men and new methods brought a complete change in the character of these local papers. Tabloid format meant that events were reported in a more popular fashion, and with much less detail than before. Syndicated features sometimes meant less space for local news. Yet they continued to chronicle, and increasingly to portray in pictures, the changing pattern of social life. In 1966 the *Herald* had advertisements (still occupying the whole of the front page) for television rentals, vacuum cleaners, washing machines, house furnishings, taxis, driving lessons, and second-hand cars for sale. Among events there were reports (in 1967) of the demolition of Bourtreehill House, the opening of Stanecastle Hotel, the introduction locally of subscriber trunk dialling on telephones, the coming of colour television, and (in 1968) the opening of a Citizens Advice Bureau, restoration work at Eglinton by the Clement Wilson foundation, and news now on the front page. In 1970 Robert Cousar retired after 36 years as secretary and treasurer of the Carters Society; the following year his shop at Saddler's Corner was demolished. Yet old organisations like the Incorporated Trades, the Carters Society, and the Freemasons continued, joined by newer societies catering especially for business and professional people.

Perhaps most significant, in this decade of rapid change, was the realisation of Irvine Burns Club's long dream. Wellwood in Eglinton Street inherited in 1963, was opened in January 1967 by Sam K. Gaw, the Club's 141st president. These premises were a splendid acquisition for the club, and for the town, providing a directors' room, a library commemorating their former secretary R.M. Hogg, a graphic representation by Ted and Elizabeth Odling of Burns's stay in Irvine, and storage for the club's priceless manuscripts and its collection of autograph letters from those world-famous persons who annually were invited to become honorary members. Upstairs, bodies like Irvine Music Club could meet, and in 1975 a Royal Burgh of Irvine Museum was created, with the Club becoming custodian of the burgh's treasures.

In its last ten years the town council, despite the imminence of dissolution, energetically continued its operations. Housing was still a priority In that era multi-storey blocks were fashionable, if controversial, so after two

222 The History of Irvine

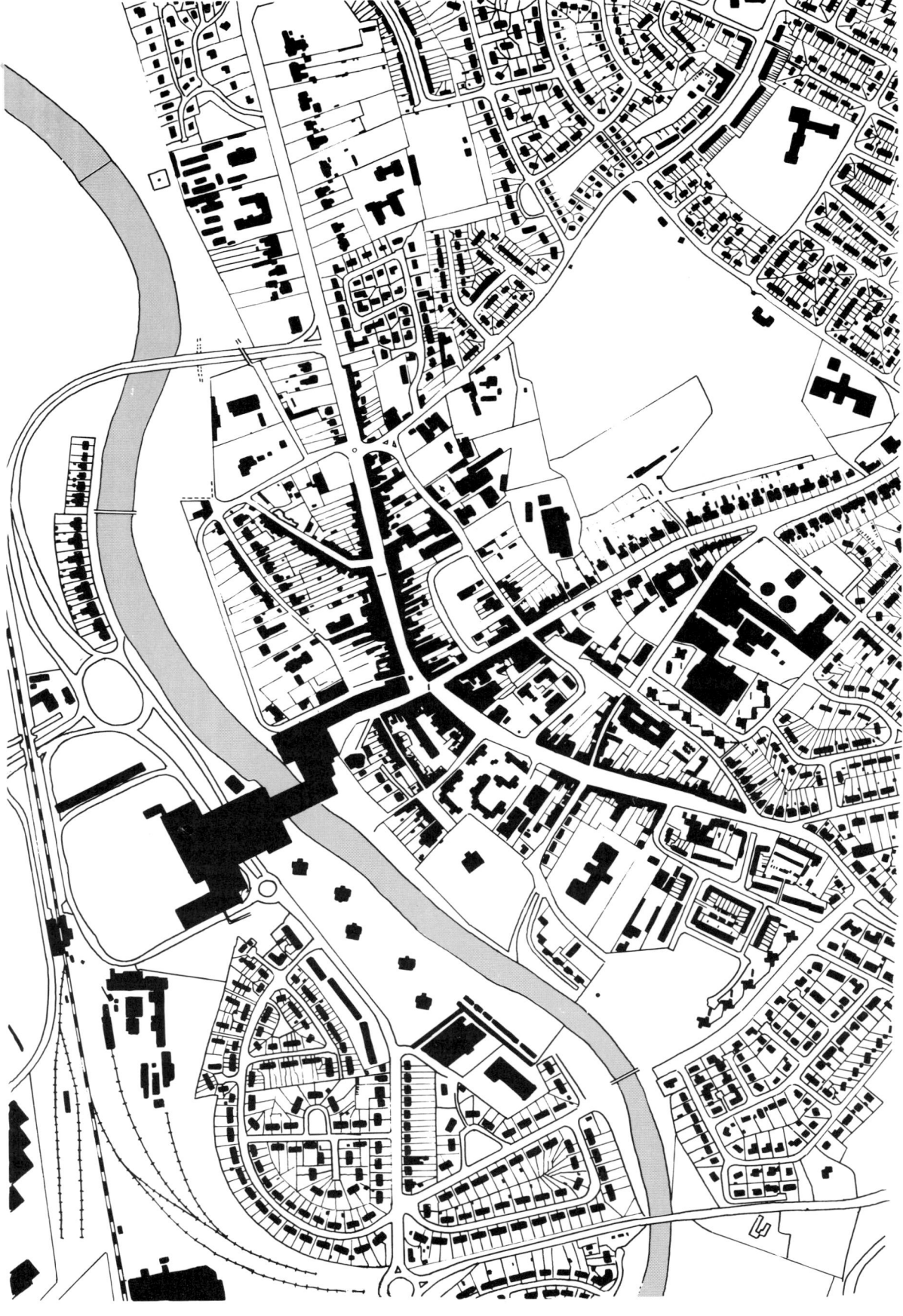

public inquiries five 14-storey blocks were erected in 1968, named Annick, Doon, Garnock, Lugton, and Afton Courts after Ayrshire rivers, providing 275 flatted homes. Sited between Fullarton Street and the river, they dwarfed the spires which had long dominated Irvine's skyline. Meanwhile council houses of traditional style continued to be built, some 700 by the council and as many by the SSHA, extending the built-up area beyond Irvine Mains to the burgh boundary of Red Burn. The old Burns walk to the Drucken Steps failed to survive, though commemorated by Steps Road; a stretch of the Red Burn became a piped culvert; and the Drucken Steps monument was relocated 700 yards to the south east in McKinnon Terrace (1976). In 1970 the council began its last major housing scheme, in Castlepark, with tenants segregated into what they felt was a 'ghetto' behind an eight-foot-high concrete 'Berlin Wall'. Altogether by 1975, after sixty years of endeavour, Irvine Town Council had the proud record of providing nearly five thousand new homes, supplemented by seventeen hundred belonging to the SSHA. Many of the older council houses were of course in need of renovation, and by modern standards the schemes formed 'undistinguished residential development' so that the town council in association with IDC began an 'Operation Facelift' in 1971. In 1972 the town council accepted the policy that any of its houses might be purchased by sitting tenants. And to meet the growing demand for private house-building it feued land it owned at Milgarholm and — beyond the burgh boundary —. at Newmoor. Only some fields for grazing at Knadgerhill were left for the traditional annual roup.

The council, benefiting from sales of land, was able to press ahead with ambitious plans. The Drill Hall in High Street was purchased in 1967 and renamed the Volunteer Rooms. Marress farm was acquired in 1971 for the creation of a new area for rugby and cricket. What were dreams in 1966 of a covered swimming pool and indoor bowling rink developed in the imagination of ex-provost Wilson Muir. Irvine and Ayr District Councils were involved, and in 1970 the harbour site was chosen for a massive multi-purpose recreation and leisure centre. The £3 million Magnum Leisure Centre would be opened in 1976, and beside it IDC would develop a Beach Park. Another development, less spectacular but also long anticipated, was special provision for old people. Plans for a hostel for the elderly had been turned down in 1935 by the Department of Health for Scotland. Now in 1967 a Senior Citizens Centre was opened at Woodlands in Kilwinning Road. In 1972 the council could begin the construction at Dalrymple Drive of sheltered houses for old people as part of its housing programme. The council also gave financial support to the six ward committee which provided winter socials and summer outings to 1,952 old folk in 1974. As always since 1814, aid was given to Irvine and Fullarton coal funds and the more recent 'All Electric' houses fund — and before dissolution of the town council all these were generously funded from the Common Good.

The Council continued its traditional policy of aiding other worthy causes including relief following disasters at Aberfan (1966) and Ibrox Park (1970). Routine business included the installation of telephones in councillors' houses (1967), repairing the spire and clock of the Town House (1968), supporting the new Citizens Advice Bureau (1968), co-operating with other authorities in providing a new coup at Bartonholm (1969), the magistrates refusing to license the showing of the film 'The Killing of Sister George' (1969), the dean of guild court approving the town's first Chinese restaurant (1970), repairing Seagate Castle (1971), purchasing the Co-operative yard at Golffields as a new depot for burgh vehicles (1971), initiating sale of council houses to sitting tenants (1972), and shifting the rent office from Heathfield back into High Street (1973). In 1968 contact was made with Irvine Ranch in California, and in years following there were exchanges of gifts and visits by selected young people. Participation in European town-twinning proved less successful, despite negotiations with places in France, Germany and Sweden. There was co-operation with authorities old and new. Irvine town council now had representation on no fewer than 27 other bodies, including Ayr County Council, and ranging from the Convention of Royal Burghs to Ayrshire Marriage Guidance Council. In addition, close association with IDC was maintained through a co-ordinating

Town plan, 1984. Within the 20th century the built-up area of Irvine was vastly extended until by 1984 there was an estimated population of 21,780 in the area of the former burgh out of a total New Town population of 57,150. After mid-century the townscape was transformed. Old school buildings were replaced — though Irvine Royal Academy (rebuilt 1901) remained intact. Three churches near the town centre (Relief, Wilson Fullarton, Trinity) were no longer required as places of worship. Two new road bridges (1971, 1973) and a bypass (1976) catered for through traffic. After the demolition of old Irvine bridge a New Town Shopping Centre was created (1975). New recreational facilities included the Magnum Leisure Centre (1976) near the harbour. With local government reorganisation (1975) the Town House in High Street was left vacant, and the new Cunninghame House in Friars Croft became the District administrative headquarters. Demolitions, rebuilding, and the new traffic system radically altered the old town centre. Seagate, Hill Street, and Glasgow Vennel were designated conservation areas (1974), but by 1984 only fragments of the old burghal pattern survived.

committee, dealing with the redevelopment of the town centre, providing a necessary drainage system for the whole area, and sponsoring 'Operation Beachcomber' in which young volunteers cleared the river banks and shore. When Cunninghame District Council was formed in 1974, advance arrangements had to be made for the eventual transfer of functions in 1975.

All this was successfully accomplished despite the continuing impasse of divided political representation on the council. The Labour Party continued to be frustrated. Though the largest group, it never held a majority of seats. Its greatest success was in 1972 with nine members. The other nine were divided among four Moderates, three Independents, one Conservative, and one Ratepayers Association. The Scottish National Party lost the representation they had had from 1964 to 1970. The Labour group now contained two women councillors, and in November 1972 one was absent from council for a reason unique in the burgh history, when Councillor Mrs. Mary Burns gave birth to a baby boy. In 1972 Joseph Hunter, a schoolteacher, concluded his three-year term as provost. With the council split, the provostship and other offices had to be determined by lot — as had also occurred in 1952 and 1955. Ironically the leader of the Labour group, James Bilby, failed in every draw. The man chosen to be Irvine's last provost was builder Alex Rubie.

One who sadly did not survive to complete his labours was town clerk Robert Whyte who died suddenly in 1972, aged 63, having served for 28 years under ten provosts. Provost Hunter summed up the feelings of all the councillors when he appropriately eulogised him: 'I cannot envisage a town clerk ever enjoying so much respect and so much confidence'. His close colleague, Burgh Chamberlain T. Martin Cameron, recalled the nature of his personality: 'He would listen to your doom-laden tale, hunched in his chair, faintly smiling at you over his specs. With a shaft of his droll Fife wit, he would demolish the villain of your piece, quietly outline the now so obvious solution, and most important of all, with the easy skill of the expert he would ensure that that solution was duly engineered'. James Gordon was appointed in his place to be Irvine's last town clerk. 1974 brought another loss by the death of John Doole who for 25 years had been burgh officer and chief halberdier.

The approach of local government reorganisation turned the council's mind to perpetuating the burgh heritage. In 1969 it was decided to award medals to all ex-provosts; a silver tea service which had been presented in 1845 to Provost Salmon was purchased by the council, with the expert co-operation of Harry Gaw; and Robert Whyte was invited to update McJannet's history of the burgh. From 1970 increased use was made of 'magistrates exercising their time-honoured right to appoint burgesses — one for each year of office'. Persons thus honoured included distinguished visitors, like the Moderator of the General Assembly (1970); individuals who had served the community well in various ways, like William Lockhart of the Incorporated Trades (1968), Mrs Tresia Reid, for twenty-seven years with the Girl Guides (1969), Douglas Clayton for service to industry (1970), Charles Ross whose family had run *Irvine Herald* from 1925 to 1967, (1970) Alexander MacMillan, academy rector and poet, (1971) and Mrs. Agnes Conway for long service with the Salvation Army (1973); and sporting personalities like Jack Cannon, Scottish Amateur Golf Champion (1970), and Bob Alexander, for twenty-five years secretary of Irvine Meadow football club (1973). In 1972 and 1973 civic receptions honoured others who had won national awards — Robert Affleck (boxing), Peter Bennie (judo), Jim Berry (athletics), Alistair McHarg (rugby), Ronald Ramsay (rifle and pistol shooting), and William Adrain and Mrs. Jenny McLellan (bowls). In 1975 the last burgess tickets were awarded to Martin Cameron, the Burgh Chamberlain who was retiring; and Andrew Hood, Secretary of Irvine Burns Club.

By other means the burgh heritage was visibly emphasised. In 1971, on the suggestion of the Rotary Club a film was produced by the town council and IDC. 'A Day in Irvine' showed a young Canadian from Galt, Ontario visiting the town whence his forbears had come. In 1972 opportunity was taken to mark the 600th anniversary of Robert II's charter to Irvine. A committee representing council, churches, schools and local organisations planned an impressive programme. It turned out to be something of a disappointment. There were criticisms of the £17,000 cost. The opening ball on 7 April at £4 a ticket was judged to be too exclusive. The grand parade on 8th April was spoiled by rain. For 15th-17th June an ambitious pageant was devised by Alex MacMillan, dramatically portraying the burgh history in ten episodes, with a commentary delivered by Sally Wallace as 'The Spirit of Irvine'. But bad weather recurred, attendances were poor, and the final performances had to be cancelled.

In its last year the council directed attention to possible means of securing the identity of Irvine in the coming local government system. There were hopes of some kind of continuing community council, financed by the Common Good Fund which, after lying empty from 1917 to 1950, had suddenly been massively augmented by land sales. But legal opinion advised that this could not be handed over to such a Trust. There could be 'generous but discriminating payments'. Handing out £5 to each domestic ratepayer was judged an 'illegal alienation'. Yet it was possible to present trophies to sporting organisations and approve some major

The New Town...

A

B

Irvine Bridge was demolished (A) in 1973 to make way for the Rivergate Mall shopping centre spanning the river (B, C). Bridgegate (D) was similarly and extensively renewed.

C

D

The Old . . .

A

Marymass is still celebrated each August. The fair is proclaimed outside the Town House (A). The Carters take their place at the head of the procession (B) which proceeds along High Street (C) towards the Moor for the traditional Races.

B

C

Part of the High Street (D) was pedestrianised in 1982.

D

C14

... And The New

New factories have been established on greenfield sites (A, B). Cunninghame House at Friars Croft (C) is headquarters of the Cunninghame District Council which took over from Irvine Town Council in 1975. New leisure facilities have been provided at the Magnum and the Beach Park (D) and new festivities organised at the Park and the Harbour (E, F, G, H).

A

B

C

D

E F

G

H

C15

...Conservation

A

B

C

D

E

The magnificent Trinity Church (A) has been saved from destruction. Hill Street (B) has been preserved. Kirkgatehead (C) retains a quiet attraction. Glasgow Vennel (D) has been effectively restored. Perceton House (E) has a new lease of life as headquarters of Irvine Development Corporation.

donations. Largest was £40,000 to Irvine Burns Club to set up and maintain a Burgh Museum. £5,000 went to the Carters Society to ensure the survival of Marymass. £23,000 was distributed among the churches and £11,000 to the schools in the burgh. £6,000 went to the three coal funds and £3,000 to the ward committees for old folk's welfare. There was naturally a good deal of argument outwith the council chamber about how the council thus distributed £100,000 from the Common Good Fund. There was inevitable misunderstanding, for that money could not legally be used to relieve the rates, subsidise council house rents, or support the five hundred unemployed in the burgh. There were further grumbles at the exclusive functions to mark the end of the burgh: entertaining the burgh's 150 manual workers in the Volunteer Rooms; and a dinner for 300 guests at Turnberry Hotel, requiring a police escort because of a rumoured protest by angry ratepayers. Thus, after more than seven hundred years the Burgh of Irvine ended its municipal existence.

The final meeting of Irvine Town Council took place on 13th May 1975. Some routine business had to be concluded: eleven deeds signed; the pedestrianisation of Hill Street authorised; bank and cash balances certified by the Auditor; certain donations approved — including support for Councillor Jack Carson on a sponsored walk for Christian Aid. Then Provost Rubie made a statement regarding the Common Good Fund. Capital assets were valued at £300,000, and Revenue Account after approved disbursements contained a further £220,000. A fund of over half a million pounds with an estimated annual income of £30,000 would be inherited by Cunninghame District Council 'for the benefit of the citizens of Irvine'. A letter from Secretary of State William Ross paid tribute 'to all those who have served with the authorities now about to go out of existence'. What the *Irvine Times* described as 'an emotional occasion' ended after the town clerk submitted a Scroll of names of the last town council:

Provost Alex Rubie; Bailies George Donaldson, James Dick, Alex Burns, Joe Kerr; Treasurer Fred Loach; Police Judge Joseph Hunter; Dean of Guild Hugh Howie; Councillors Robert Neil, James Bilby, Jack Carson, Mrs. Elizabeth Herbertson, Elliot Gray, Mike Regan, James Smith, James H. Smith, Mrs. Mary Burns, George Hepburn.

The chief officials were: Town Clerk James Gordon; Burgh Chamberlain Martin Cameron; Burgh Prosecutor William Curdie; Burgh Surveyor William Cowan; Burgh Architect Ian Campbell; Burgh Factor Robert Lindsay.

From 16th May 1975, new local authorities became responsible for the administration of Irvine's public affairs.

1984 Marymass Queen Lynn Coull escorted from the Town House by Captain of the Carters Bert Gibson, with visitors from Irvine in California looking on. The fair is celebrated annually on the third Saturday following the first Monday in August.

Irvine resumed its historic role as the administrative centre of Cunninghame. Most of the functions of the town council were transferred to the new Cunninghame District Council (CDC); most services provided locally by Ayr County Council (which also ceased to exist) were taken over by Strathclyde Regional Council. Irvine, for so long with its own municipal identity, found itself part of a District which included the Garnock Valley, the north Ayrshire coast, and the island of Arran; and within a massive Region which contained Glasgow and much of western Scotland.

For the ordinary person, perhaps already confused by the complexities of the change, that greater efficiency of a more centralised local government which justified the reform was less obvious than an increase in rates to pay, even though this might be attributed to inflation rather than administrative costs. In its last fiscal year Irvine town council had spent about £1 million on its own services (including £228,000 on parks and recreation, £193,000 on roads and sewers, £156,000 on cleansing, £65,000 on housing, £31,000 on lighting) plus a County requisition of over £2 million, counterbalanced by Exchequer grants of over £2 million. This required a domestic rate charged at

76p per £ of valued rent. The following year, for regional and district services, Cunninghame District Council had to levy 125p per £ on Irvine householders.

To prepare for the takeover, elections for the new councils were held in May 1974. Irvine was entitled to one member of Strathclyde's 103 and four of Cunninghame's 24. Robert Beattie joined the Labour Party majority on Strathclyde Regional Council. Cunninghame District Council was also won by Labour, although Irvine continued its traditional voting pattern. Labour took Irvine Mains and Irvine Eglinton with Jack Carson and Mrs. Elizabeth Herbertson; Townhead and Fullarton were won by Moderates Alex Rubie and Wilson Muir. A week after CDC's inaugural meeting on 21st May 1974, ex-provost Muir died, and the seat was then captured for Labour by Elliot Gray. All of these were members of the still-functioning town council, which eased the transfer of powers in 1975. There was, however, a spectacular turn-up to follow. In an upsurge of political feeling, the local elections of May 1977 were held — perhaps symbolically — on a day of heavy thunderstorms and torrential rain. The Scottish National Party emerged with eleven seats as the largest group in Cunninghame; in Irvine Sam Gaw took Fullarton and Matthew Brown took Eglinton. Matthew Brown, a local businessman, succeeded Dr. David White from Saltcoats as CDC Chairman. It was a brief interlude. After the abortive Scottish devolution referendum of 1979 came the 1980 district elections, and headlines could announce 'Labour Trounce the Tartan Army'. The Local Government Boundary Commission had increased the number of seats on Cunninghame District Council to 30, and 21 of them were taken by Labour. In Irvine two stalwart survivors from the town council continued: Alex Rubie holding Townhead for the Moderates, and Jack Carson holding Vineburgh for Labour. They were joined by three new Labour colleagues — James Farrell, North; Tom Dewar, Woodlands; David O'Neill, West. The election of 1984 confirmed these five in their seats and Labour continued to rule, with Tom Dickie from Kilbirnie succeeded as Chairman by Mrs. Teresa Beattie from Stevenston. Irvine's seat on Strathclyde Regional Council had been won at a by-election in 1976 by SNP Ian McLeod, but it was recovered by Labour's Elliot Gray in 1978 and held thereafter by him. Throughout the period David Lambie continued as Labour Member of Parliament. Elected in 1970, after the 1969 act which extended the franchise to all persons of 18 years and over, this schoolteacher from Saltcoats continued to represent the Central Ayrshire constituency, renamed Cunninghame South in 1983: on the back benches behind Wilson and Callaghan (1974-79) and opposite Heath (1970-74) and Thatcher (since 1979).

Irvine Development Corporation, constituted in 1967, changed only in membership. As Chairman, A.W. Hardie was followed by Sir William Gray (1974), J.H.F. Macpherson (1976), H.S. Whitson (1979) and Sir Charles O'Halloran (1983). The other eight members were replaced or given extended terms of office by successive Secretaries of State. By 1983 the membership had been completely renewed, after replacement of two members who had each served for the first fifteen years — William Paterson, last convener of Ayr County Council and IDC's Vice-Chairman; and Eric Dale from Irvine. There were also inevitable changes in staff. General Manager Dennis Kirby was succeeded in 1972 by James D. Marquis, Chief Finance Officer since 1967, who continued until Brigadier R.A. Rickets took over in 1981. Chief Architects were David Gosling, J.K. Billingham from 1973 to 1979, then Ian C. Downs.

The Corporation in 1975 had some fears of the impact of local government reorganisation on its plans, and was naturally concerned about its relations with the new authorities. Doing business with Ayr County Council and the town councils of Irvine and Kilwinning had not always been easy, but the atmosphere was amicable. This continued with Cunninghame District Council. CDC made its headquarters in a new office block, Cunninghame House, at Friars Croft in Irvine. Jim Miller, who was appointed Chief Executive, had been County Solicitor and Depute County Clerk with Ayr County Council. Among the other chief officials were some who had served Irvine Town Council — Depute Director of Administration, Jimmy Gordon, former town clerk; Director of Housing, Robert Lindsay, former Burgh Factor; Director of Cleansing, Bill Cowan, former Burgh Surveyor. Some CDC councillors were in due course nominated as members of the Corporation. Relations with Strathclyde Regional Council were in some respects less satisfactory. That council was, naturally, specially concerned with its most deprived areas. IDC's annual report for 1976 felt that consequently Irvine New Town suffered as 'falling victim to its own success'. Money was being devoted to Glasgow's derelict areas and Irvine was treated merely as 'one of Glasgow's overspill communities' (1977). The New Town needed roads, houses, and community facilities, but it was felt (1978) that 'the Regional Council is less than enthusiastic in its support for the New Town'. This was confirmed when the Regional Council Chairman in 1979 described Irvine New Town as 'a failure'.

Certainly Irvine was experiencing difficulties in a period of deepening economic depression, with rising unemployment, continuing inflation, and government cutbacks in public sector spending. As IDC noted in its 1976 report, it did not have 'an open-ended Government cheque'. The initial problems which had delayed developments were now overcome. 1975 saw the opening of the Rivergate Mall shopping centre; 1976 the Magnum Leisure Centre under CDC auspices, the beginning of a Beach Park, and the completion of an Irvine bypass. Yet industry inevitably was severely affected by the general recession. Although in 1977 Beecham Pharmaceuticals and Rockware Glass Ltd. began major expansions, a number of local firms were going into liquidation, and by 1980 closures followed at the Skefco factory in Shewalton and at Monsanto who had taken over the Chemstrand nylon works nearby beyond Drybridge. Unemployment within the old Irvine burgh area grew from 600 in mid-1975 to 1,500 a year after. By 1984 that figure had more than doubled, and by October of that year there were 3,250,000 unemployed nationally (13.6%), with nearly 350,000 in Scotland (15.5%). Irvine had 3,813 out of work, included in a New Town total of 5,693 — at 25% one of the worst-hit areas in Scotland.

Nevertheless, the number of industrial firms within the New Town had trebled, industrial space had doubled in area, and between 1969 and 1984 the numbers in employment actually increased from 14,800 to 16,100. In 1984 there were nearly two hundred industrial businesses. Most were quite small, but there were 27 employing from 51-100 persons, 13 with 101-200, and 8 with more than 200 employed. 161 of the firms were located in Irvine and its environs.

The largest concentration of 43 firms was in and around the burgh industrial estate which had been created in 1959. Here from 1950 Wilson Pipe Fittings Ltd. manufactured cast iron pipes and fittings and steel flanges and fittings, employing about 200 workers. In 1957 Rockware Glass Ltd. took over the Portland bottle-making factory and expanded to employ 400 making glass containers for the whisky industry. Hyster Ltd. came in 1960: after a rapid initial expansion this American company planned a reorganisation in 1982 which posed a threat, but the workforce accepted a package deal promising further development as the company's main European plant, and continued making fork-lift trucks. In 1962 Wilson Sporting Goods Ltd., another American company, began manufacturing golf clubs with 170 employed. They were followed by Flow Laboratories, with 110 producing laboratory, diagnostic, and research supplies.

In the harbour area 16 small firms carried on. The only large one was Ayrshire Metal Products Ltd., with 178 workers making cold rolled and pressed sections where the old dockyard had been. Two long-established firms survived. Matthew Wright and Nephew Ltd. employed 40 in the sawmills set up in the early 19th century. David Flanagan Ltd. had started brass founding in the Bridgegate in 1881, had moved to Cochrane Street in 1902, was forced out by the bulldozers in 1974, but set up in modern premises nearby in Ailsa Street, employing around 30 as non-ferrous founders and engineers.

East of the river were 34 industrial businesses dispersed through and beyond the old town, mostly small, but including Queen of Scots Knitwear Ltd. which set up in Sloan Avenue in 1958, and after 25 years was employing 480 hosiery workers. Nearby in Dalrymple Drive, Fullarton Fabrications made light gauge sheet metal products. In East Road, Fulton and Wylie Ltd., coachbuilders, after 20 years were employing 80 workers specialising in fire engines. North of the town two major firms had become installed in what had once been part of Eglinton estate. In Kilwinning Road from 1973, Volvo Trucks (G.B.) Ltd. constructed lorries and buses, employing 450. Earlier in 1953 the Adam-designed stable block in Eglinton Park was turned into a factory by Clement Wilson. He came from north Ayrshire farming stock. His father Robert Wilson had started a small ham-curing business, and Clement Wilson vastly expanded this by the manufacture of processed and canned foods. He chose Eglinton as the headquarters for 'Wilson's of Scotland' because he believed that work should always be done in a satisfying environment. Because he also believed that industry should play a significant role in improving that environment, this man of vision not only lavishly enhanced Eglinton Park but created in 1965 a Clement Wilson Foundation to support a variety of worthy causes locally and beyond. When he died in 1975, his son James W. Wilson continued to employ 350 at Eglinton in line with his father's philosophy.

Further away from Irvine there were 17 small businesses at Girdle Toll, but the main new developments were on the New Town industrial estates created east and south of Irvine. They provided facilities for an impressive range of 51 businesses, mostly concentrated at South Newmoor which held 37 of them. Beecham Pharmaceuticals came to Shewalton in 1973 to employ 650 producing semi-synthetic penicillin side chains and other bulk medicinal compounds. Scottish and Universal Newspapers Ltd. set up presses at South Newmoor in 1978, with over 100 workers printing six weekly papers and the *Paisley Daily Express*. In 1983 Prestwick Circuits Ltd. moved into Shewalton to print circuit boards and employ another 200. In 1984 S.C.I. Systems came from Alabama to employ 150 initially. Climax International, another manufacturer of computers — from Irvine in California — promised to join the growing range of electronic firms. Prospect of another 500 jobs came in November 1984 when Indy Electronics Inc., also from California, planned to begin assembly testing of integrated circuits in a new factory at Irvine.

Appropriately, Intec West Ltd. set up at South Newmoor an information and training centre for new technology and office techniques. With a variety of large firms securely established and a good number of smaller businesses managing to survive the recession, there was 'quiet optimism'.

In 1978 IDC realised that 'with changing conditions . . . the pace of its development needed adjustment', and in 1981 the continuing recession meant 'slower growth than the Corporation had hoped for'. The census of that year indicated a population of 55,400 with 17,000 jobs, and no chance of achieving the 116,000 population with 54,000 jobs set as a target in the 1971 Plan. Progress was made in improving the road network. The Irvine bypass was opened in 1976, allowing access to Irvine by the northern Eglinton interchange, with a southern link at the Warrix interchange added in 1981. 1983 saw completion of a dual carriageway A71 towards Kilmarnock and a similar continuation of the A78 towards Prestwick Airport and Ayr. But there remained little prospect of a direct connection to the national motorway system, which, as successive IDC reports lamented, inhibited the growth of Irvine New Town. Government cutbacks also restricted housing development to some building at Girdle Toll, and there was a general increase in rents. Phase Two of the Town Centre Shopping Development, to extend Rivergate as far as the railway station, and planned for 1980, was never started. A more limited scheme of smaller shops at the Forum in Bridgegate was completed in 1984. The ultimate plan of a covered complex extending from Rivergate right to the harbour to link with the Magnum Leisure Centre and the Beach Park was abandoned before 1979, when new safety regulations noted the potential danger from explosives at the Garnock wharf and required a limitation on numbers who could occupy the Magnum and the adjacent areas.

IDC had meantime to content itself with a series of more modest though praiseworthy projects. In 1975 a new Information Centre was opened in High Street. In 1976, in co-operation with CDC, work began on 'facelifts' for the old town centres of Irvine and Kilwinning. Parking was provided on the east side of High Street, where an experimental pedestrianisation began in 1982. A new short road diverted traffic from Townhead into East Road. Nearby at the Glasgow Vennel there was important restoration work. This historic street had sadly deteriorated, but plans for demolition had mercifully been postponed by Irvine Town Council. In 1980 a committee was formed, chaired by Lord Ross of Marnock, with representatives of IDC, CDC, the National Trust for Scotland, Scottish Tourist Board, Irvine Burns Club, and the Clement Wilson Foundation. Behind the scenes, IDC's Chief Architect Ian Downs had persuaded the authorities that conservation was feasible, and now made plans for renovating certain properties for sale, restoring no. 10 and the adjoining heckling shop where Burns had worked, and renewing no. 4 with its attic where Burns had lodged. The street was relaid with traditional stone setts, and the Vennel transformed for the official opening in January 1983 — a pleasing vignette of Scottish vernacular architecture. It won a prestigious 1984 Europa Nostra Award for conservation.

In its 1977 report IDC recognised Irvine's 'unique coastal location in the heart of a tourist area and attractive rural setting'. In 1976 the Magnum had been opened, and around it IDC was clearing the derelict old industrial zone to create a Beach Park of 150 acres. 'Facilities which had once been criticised as over-ambitious have, in many cases, proved to be too small to cope with the ever-growing demand.' Amenities in the harbour area were improved when Irvine Harbour Company (a subsidiary of ICI) rehabilitated the wharf, dilapidated houses were converted into attractive residences, and easier access was provided by a new bridge under the railway. The Harbour Arts Centre was extended. Laird's forge and other derelict premises were utilised in the creation of an impressive Scottish Maritime Museum, to be opened in 1985. In 1980, to advertise Irvine's new role, a cartoon seagull called 'Irwin' was created. In 1983 IDC could report that 'Irvine, the youngest of the Scottish New Towns, is beginning to develop its image and demonstrate its potential not only as an industrial growth area but also an important focus of leisure and sporting activity'. Appropriately the New Town was honoured by royal visits. In December 1978 Prince Charles inspected fork-lift trucks at Hyster. On 3rd July 1979 Queen Elizabeth and the Duke of Edinburgh visited two small and enterprising businesses — the local Craigie Carpets Ltd. and the Canadian Dominion Contact Lenses Ltd. — then toured the Town Centre, the Magnum, and the Beach Park. In an unofficial capacity, Princess Anne attended the Annick Lodge horse trials on several occasions.

Other facilities were being extended. Irvine, with a growing number of restaurants, but limited hotel accommodation, acquired in 1983 the new Skean Dhu hotel at Roseholm, with 128 bedrooms, covered swimming pool, and conference and banqueting facilities. In 1985 IDC opened Galt House in Bank Street to provide additional rented office accommodation.

Beyond the town, plans were made for an expansion of Eglinton Park. Here Wilson's food factory had been set up in 1953 and the owner, Clement Wilson, laid out the grounds, opened them to the public, and gifted them to CDC in 1978. Now IDC planned to extend them eastwards

The Carters Races at Marymass, with a concourse of spectators and bookmakers attracted by twelve races for horses, ponies, donkeys, and the traditional cart horses.

to provide nature trails, camping and caravan facilities, various other recreational opportunities, reconstructed historic farms, and parkland campus sites for high technology and science-based industries — much of this to await land reclamation, which would follow open-cast mining at Sourlie from 1983 to 1986. As well as providing such amenities, IDC was fostering the arts in the New Town.

An IDC brochure on 'The Arts in the New Town' not only lists Irvine's notable contributions of the past but also summarises the growing range of facilities and provides an 'Arts Trail' of places worth visiting. The literary traditions of Burns and Galt were of course conserved by Irvine Burns Club. The international Burns Federation came to the Magnum for its annual conference in 1981; Sam Gaw was Federation President in 1979, at forty-seven the youngest till then, as he had previously been Irvine's youngest-ever bailie; in 1984 John Inglis, another Burnsian from Irvine, also became the Burns Federation President. In 1970 a new poet appeared on the local scene. Henry Mair, a twenty-five-year-old factory worker, hailing from Kilmarnock originally, published *I Rebel*, followed in 1975 by *Alone I Rebel*, an autobiography with other poems, then *The Flowers in the Forest* in 1979. These lyrical pieces won acclaim, and in 1973 he initiated an annual Scottish Open Poetry Competition. A group of others in 1980 formed an Ayrshire Writers and Artists Society who, as custodians, acquired premises in the renovated house and heckling shop in Glasgow Vennel. One of their number, Mae McEwan, produced two collections of verse appropriately entitled *Let's Recall Auld Irvine* and *From Irvine with Nostalgia*. In music, the range was now extended — Irvine Youth Band, Irvine Pipe Band, Irvine Silver Star Accordion Band, Irvine Folk Club, various choirs and dance groups, and the New Town Amateur Operatic Society formed in 1971. The Harbour Arts Centre provided scope for the professional Borderline company and amateur groups, as well as promoting other cultural pursuits. In 1979 IDC and the Scottish Arts Council established a Town Artist Scheme, and for the successive artists-in-residence a studio was provided at Towerlands in 1981. The Water Wheel Sculpture installed in the Rivergate Mall was the first of a series of efforts to enhance the New Town with murals, stained glass, and sculpted items.

In so many of its ventures, Irvine Development Corporation was of course very much involved with, and often dependent upon, Cunninghame District Council and Strathclyde Regional Council.

The functions of Cunninghame District Council included housing, local planning and development, building control, cleansing, environmental health and food hygiene, libraries, community centre, parks and recreation. To administer these the Chief Executive and

Director of Administration (Jim Miller) was supported by Directors of Finance (Ian Herd), Technical Services (Charles Toner, then Lewis Dickens), Planning (Trevor Eaton, then Allan Reid), Housing (Robert Lindsay), Leisure (David Webster), Environmental Health (Tom Howie, then Bill Tulloch) and Cleansing (Bill Cowan). In housing, there was concentration now on provision for special needs, and co-operation with the other authorities. For example, CDC took over from Irvine Town Council sheltered houses for old people at Kiln Court and Dalrymple Drive, and built others, including some beside Kiln Court on the east side of Glasgow Vennel, and at Vineburgh. On the west side of Glasgow Vennel IDC built amenity houses for disabled persons in 1985, and also provided sheltered accommodation at Heathfield. Strathclyde Regional Council co-operated by appointing wardens to assist the old folk. In providing for leisure facilities, CDC could not afford capital expenditure on all that might have been desired. A new District library headquarters was built at Ardrossan, but Irvine had to make do with a branch library located in Cunninghame House, not all that convenient. No purpose-built community centres could be provided locally; premises were however available, as listed later. From Irvine Town Council CDC inherited golf course, playparks, open spaces for recreation, and control of the Magnum Leisure Centre. That outstanding facility could appropriately be advertised: 'Where in the world can you play badminton, squash, bowls, curling, watch a film, a play, a concert, cabaret, drink a pint, a cuppa, eat a burger, eat a meal, go skating, swimming, use a solarium, a gym and much, much more under one roof?' Nearby there was scope for putting, boating, and picnicking on IDC's Beach Park, mooring for yachts in the harbour, sea bathing at the beach — with an area in 1979 provided for nudists — and shooting on a new rifle range. An Irvine Water Sports Club formed in 1974 engaged in a range of activities, and in 1984 there was a first Harbour Festival which — despite some fears — did not detract from the continuing popularity of Marymass.

To ensure the survival of that ancient festival, Irvine Town Council had not only contributed generously to the funds of the Carters Society but had created an *ad hoc* committee under Councillor Jack Carson, which would continue under the auspices of Cunninghame District Council. At the 1978 celebrations, the 50th anniversary of the crowning of queens was marked by the presence of thirty of them. In 1984 the usual, ten to fourteen day-long series of events complemented those of Marymass Saturday, and the official programme note deserves recording:

'Every year for almost 1,000 years the festival has been celebrated on the third Saturday following the first Monday in August. On that day Irvine Moor becomes the stage for what is possibly the oldest horse racing event in the world to claim a continuous history stretching through the centuries. The actual proceedings on Marymass day are worthy of note in this Account because of the survivals of the ancient pageantry still incorporated and which doubtless will be maintained in all future celebrations.'

In the forenoon of the day itself the brothered Carters, led by their Captain elected a week before, rode the marches of the town. At noon the Fair was proclaimed in front of the Town House by CDC's Chief Executive, the queen was crowned and the flags of the Carters bussed. With music provided by five bands, a procession made its leisurely way to the Moor, led by the Carters; then the Queen, accompanied by William Wallace, Robert the Bruce, John Knox (an innovation that year); pages, equerries, and archers; the halberdier preceding Cunninghame's councillors, freemen, and officials; then the Incorporated Trades, Burns Club, Rotary, Round Table, Junior Chamber of Commerce, and guests; majorettes, horses and ponies; and a Carters rearguard carrying a mallet, symbolic of the trade. At the Moor the Carters greeted the others on Magistrates' Hill, CDC guests lunched in a marquee, the horse races followed, and there was climbing a greasy pole to win a ham. On the Moor now were stalls and the shows. Late in the afternoon the procession was reformed, to proceed to Seagate Castle for the singing of 'Auld Lang Syne'.

While Cunninghame District Council had those responsibilities already listed, Strathclyde Regional Council was concerned with major planning, regional industrial development, roads and transport, water and sewage, police, fire service, education, social work and other services. Although the Regional Council, with so many places crying for attention, could not immediately meet all the needs of the New Town, by 1984 IDC (for the first time) 'welcomes the Regional Council's approach'. The network of major roads was complete, and electrification of the railway line was anticipated by 1986. Between 1977 and 1984 extensive work had been undertaken in drainage and sewage disposal. A new fire station at Pennyburn (1970) was joined by another at South Newmoor (1980). There had been considerable expenditure by the Regional Council on these and other services, particularly in education.

In the seventeen years from the inception of the New Town, seventeen new schools were provided by Ayr County Council and (after 1975) by Strathclyde Regional Council. It was possible to dispense with older premises. The buildings of the old Loudoun — Montgomery school were demolished (1974), and Bank Street School was closed

(1982), as was St. Mary's (1984). But when Irvine Royal Academy was threatened, a vigorous local campaign in 1983 to 'Save I.R.A.' was successful in retaining this beloved institution which symbolised all that was revered in educational tradition.

Within the town there were now six primary schools — all new buildings. John Galt Primary School (1960) was joined by Castlepark (1970), Glebe (1974), Woodlands (1974), St. Mark's (1975) and a new Loudoun-Montgomery School (1978). Castlepark in Carron Place was the largest with 480 pupils under John L. Reid and eighteen teachers. Three others had each over 300 pupils. John Galt School in Tollerton Drive had as head teachers J.M. Wilson (1960–76), then Miss E.D. McTaggart. Woodlands School in Woodlands Avenue had Alexander S. Chapman. The Glebe School near Golffields was gutted by fire in 1981 but rebuilt, continuing under Miss J.P. Montgomery. Just under 200 pupils west of the river were taught in the new Loudoun-Montgomery School off Ayr Road. Soon after it was opened, Miss M.E.G. Livingstone moved to Fencedyke, one of four other new schools built for the Bourtreehill-Girdle Toll area. Here she was succeeded by Mrs. I.E. Brown till 1983, then Mrs. R. Dickinson. St Mark's Roman Catholic Primary School in Clark Drive opened under William Bennett who came from St. Mary's, followed in 1983 by Murdoch McGuire, responsible for 260 pupils. The basic primary school curriculum was still, in the words of Castlepark's head teacher, 'learning to read, write and count'. But there was the complementary aim of offering 'a broad-based experience of learning' including environmental and aesthetic subjects with opportunities for extra-curricular activities, and in each of the schools methods were such as to 'foster a love of learning' in 'a relaxed environment'. In all of them religious education had its place, with local ministers acting as school chaplains. At St. Mark's there were of course the special provisions usual in R.C. schools.

Within the New Town there were now five secondary schools. Eastern and northern areas were served by Greenwood Academy (1972) with 1,200 pupils and Kilwinning Academy (1977) with 1,300. St. Michael's Academy at Kilwinning (1966) catered for about 1,000 Roman Catholic pupils. Within the town of Irvine itself the Royal Academy with a roll of just under 800 took in pupils from Loudoun-Montgomery, Glebe, Woodlands, and John Galt primary schools. Ravenspark Academy's 850 pupils came from Castlepark, some from John Galt, the rest from Annick School at Girdle Toll. Irvine Royal's rector, W. Iain Foulds, was succeeded by A. Crawford in 1984, while Sam B. McCormack was rector at Ravenspark from 1974. In each case the rector was now supported by a depute, assistant head teachers, and principal teachers responsible for eighteen subject departments and for guidance — altogether a teaching staff of 56 (Irvine Royal) or 65 (Ravenspark) plus over a dozen non-teaching staff in each. In both schools the accepted system was followed of mixed ability classes following a common course for the first two years — all pupils taking English, Mathematics with Arithmetic, History, Geography, Science, French, Classical Studies, Art, Technical Subjects, Home Economics, Drama, Religious Education and Physical Education. In third and fourth years pupils followed chosen courses of seven or eight principal subjects which could lead to presentation at Ordinary Grade examinations for the Scottish Certificate of Education, with plans afoot for a new Standard Grade more appropriate for the whole range of abilities. A minority continued into fifth and sixth years — around 100 at Irvine Royal Academy, rather fewer at Ravenspark — preparing for Higher Grade and Sixth Year Studies Certificates. For all ages extra-curricular activities were fostered by enthusiastic teachers, Ravenspark with its modern facilities providing for over thirty different activities, Irvine Royal offering just as wide a range.

One feature of the new education was closer links between school and home regarding pupils' progress and any educational or disciplinary problems, with meetings formal and informal including parent-teacher associations and involvement in the local Schools Council. Strathclyde Regional Council continued to provide school meals, health inspections, and free bus transport for pupils living over a certain distance from school. The schools, both primary and secondary, strove to foster a sense of community by encouraging the wearing of a school uniform and by involving pupils in various charitable and worthy local projects.

How the range of educational facilities has been extended may be illustrated by a few examples. A first nursery school was opened in the grounds of John Galt School in 1975. In 1984 Bank Street School re-opened as an annexe to Kilmarnock Technical College to provide courses for 120 full-time and 80 other trainees. Further Education classes were developed by a Community Education Service. All the schools were made available for adult use, with social and recreational wings included in some of the newer buildings. At Castlepark there was a community centre, another when Redburn Primary School became surplus to requirements; even the old East Road School was converted into the Annick Centre, and use was made of Trinity Church. This endangered building was rescued and managed by a trust, with the Saltire Society and its local representative Knut Campbell of Ayr taking a prominent part. Strathclyde Regional Council provided also a Careers Office in Bank Street, and a Consumer Advice Centre in the new shopping area. Its Social Work department maintained within Irvine the Moor day nursery (in the old Burgh hospital), Burnside House children's home, and the Townhead Addiction Centre; it had responsibility for wardens in sheltered housing; and it supported CDC's Woodlands Day Centre for the Elderly.

Within the area which had formed the burgh of Irvine there was an estimated population of 21,780 in 1984. This was fewer than the figure of 23,019 recorded in the 1971 census, because the congestion of the old town centre had been relieved and some people rehoused outwith the old burgh boundary, but among the 57,150 resident within the New Town. Available to all were the services provided by Strathclyde Regional Council, Cunninghame District Council, and Irvine Development Corporation. There was other public provision. The Post Office in High Street, often overcrowded, was supplemented by sub-offices throughout the housing areas. The Health Service operated with nineteen doctors in three practices, the largest being a team of eleven based at the Porthead Surgery, headed by Dr. James Montgomery who had served the community since 1945. Ayrshire Central Hospital in Kilwinning Road was joined in 1982 by Crosshouse Hospital just five miles away.

Extended public provision was complemented by commercial and voluntary agencies. As well as 68 shops in the Rivergate Mall, there were 153 others within Irvine. There were branches of the Bank of Scotland, the Royal Bank of Scotland, the Clydesdale Bank, and the West of Scotland Trustee Savings Bank. Of 51 other commercial firms within the New Town, 32 were located in High Street or the new office premises in Bridgegate and Rivergate. The hotels included Annfield, Crosskeys, Eglinton Arms, Grange, King's Arms, Redburn, Skean Dhu, Stanecastle, Turf. The George Cinema in Bank Street, burned down in 1969, was able to continue in the old Regal in Chapel Lane until this was demolished in 1973. But the old Picturedrome in Bank Street was restored, and the George re-opened there in 1976 by showing — most inappropriately — the film 'The Towering Inferno'. There was continuing provision for bingo, and in 1983 and 1984 two snooker halls were opened. The New Town had over 400 clubs and societies, most of them in Irvine. These included sporting, social, charitable, and youth organisations too numerous to list.

The churches continued to play their part in the community. Four Church of Scotland congregations had nearly 4,000 communicant members in 1984: Irvine Old Parish (1,188) under Rev. James Greig since 1979; Fullarton (903) ministered by Rev. P.G. Thomson since 1953; Mure (607), with Rev. Hugh M. Adamson succeeding on the death of Rev. Robert Sawers in 1976; and St. Andrew's (1,146) under Revs. J.W.F. Harris, then Thomas S. Logan from 1978. The Relief Church had moved to Bourtreehill in 1977, and there was a smaller congregation also at Girdle Toll. St. Mary's Roman Catholic Church, under Father Thomas Murphy since 1966, was joined by St. Margaret's Oratory in Castlepark (1976) under Father Francis Moore, and a new parish of St. John Ogilvie Church at Bourtreehill. Each of these new congregations had over a thousand adherents of all ages, leaving St. Mary's with 2,200. The Sisters of the Cross and Passion, devoted to teaching and social work, moved in 1982 from Williamfield to Girdle Toll. There continued in Irvine the Baptist Church (Rev. A.V. Clark), the Church of the Nazarene (since 1948 under Rev. Leslie Hands), Christadelphians, Christian Brethren, Salvation Army, and a Church of Christ meeting in the Trinity Church community centre. The Episcopalian Church, from 1973, had obtained a place to worship, sharing St. Andrew's Church with its presbyterian congregation in ecumenical amity. Rev. David Goldie, their minister until 1982, was followed by Rev. A.T. Brown.

The *Irvine Times* (circulation 10,900 per weekly issue) and the *Irvine Herald* (2,350) reported not only progress but also occasional disasters and recurring difficulties. There were floods in 1974 when the temporary Puddleford foot bridge was awash, and again in 1978 when the Annick Water burst its banks. Instances of anti-social behaviour were attributed to lack of jobs. In 1971 there was a double murder in Winton Road; in 1975 police had to make a baton charge on the 'Apache' gang; there was continuing vandalism; in 1978 a score of teenagers were rounded up from a mob in Eglinton woods; there were packs of stray dogs (1975); and there was the vexed issue of finding a site for tinkers encamped near Redburn. The papers also reported on speculation that oil might soon be discovered under the Firth of Clyde.

Each week the local papers continued faithfully to record meetings and functions. Their columns feature names of prominent persons who have been mentioned in this book. Less newsworthy have been others, who are nevertheless familiar faces about the town. Irvine has always been not only a town of character but a town of characters — kenspeckle figures renowned in some cases for what they do or say, in other cases simply for what they are. Late one evening the author formed an *ad hoc* committee to compile a list of such persons. From that list an arbitrary and perhaps invidious selection of names has been made: Alex Bicker who treasures the Norwegian medal his father won as member of the lifeboat crew of 1894; Isobel Burns, that long and tireless worker for the Guides; the ubiquitous Joe Caldwell of the Eglinton Arms; Bob Campbell with his photographs of old Irvine; Mary Carnduff whose father worked with William Henderson in the Chemical Works;

Willie Freckleton, Entertainments Officer at the Magnum; Harry Gaw, retired Bridgegate jeweller; John Gray, walking daily from Ravenspark; ex-bailie Hugh Howat, renowned in song and story; Mrs Isa Mackie with her memories of the Eglinton family; Jean Mitchell who grew up in Glasgow Vennel and is today an authentic voice of old Irvine; Jack Ramsay, for many years Clerk to Irvine District Council and moving spirit of the Burns Club's Burgh Museum; David Shaw, man about town; David Shearer; Rose Stevenson; Jim Wales; and the indispensable Donald Wilson ... Such persons in their own way personify Irvine and its traditions.

In 1983 IDC produced a 'Development Profile' in which future prospects were assessed. It saw its two main concerns as the continuing high unemployment and the 'drab and unattractive gap sites and empty decaying buildings' which were unappealing to potential investors. The role of the Corporation must be 'to reinforce the economy by providing an environment in which industry can flourish'. A modified target population of 75,000 by the end of the century could be set, but this would require 10,200 additional jobs within less than twenty years. If this were possible, more factory space would be required, more houses would have to be built, and some roads would require realignment. Once a population of 70,000 was within reach, the interest of large retailers would justify extension of the Shopping Centre. While 'the fundamental purpose of the New Town continues to be the creation of jobs', meantime it would continue to improve 'the quality of the urban environment'.

Back in 1971 the 'New Town Plan' had succinctly defined its purpose: 'to build a town where people can lead happy, healthy lives with every opportunity for fulfilment of their diverse ambitions'.

Even further back in 1911 an observer provided what will be a fitting conclusion to this book:

'The history of Irvine is a fascinating theme ... There is, we think, no town in Scotland which for its size has so much to tell us of deepest interest ... The character of the people is one of the greatest assets of Irvine. They are canny, kindly, God-fearing, and actively-brained people from whom have sprung many uniquely gifted men and women.

'Its population may go up by leaps and bounds, and it may yet be the Eldorado of Ayrshire. We wish for it a prosperous future.'

Sources and Acknowledgements

Principal Printed Works

The history of Irvine has attracted a long succession of commentators. The principal contributors are listed here in chronological order of publication. Later, in the sections dealing with separate chapters, these are referred to by short titles (as indicated), and other specialist sources are noted.

Rev. James Richmond, 'The Parish of Irvine', in *The Statistical Account of Scotland,* Vol. 7, 1793 *(OSA)*. This has several passing references to the burgh's earlier history.

George Chalmers, *Caledonia,* 3 vols., 1810-24, described by one Ayrshire historian as 'probably one of the best and most reliable of all the local historian's handbooks', is a pioneer work which assembled references to the several counties and their parishes (references are to Ayrshire extracts in Robertson's *Historic Ayrshire,* 1891, 1894, noted below).

George Robertson, *Topographical Description of Cunninghame,* 1820. The author lived at Bower Lodge at Waterside on the Fullarton side of Irvine Bridge, and published, in Irvine, this and his next book which provide a great deal of historical material, including references to the burgh charters (cited as Robertson's *Cunninghame*).

George Robertson, *Genealogical Account of the Principal Families in Ayrshire,* 4 vols., 1824 (Robertson's *Families*).

Rev. John Wilson, 'The Parish of Irvine', in *New Statistical Account,* Vol. 5, 1842 (*NSA*). Historical material was included, and assistance acknowledged of J.W. Mackenzie; Robert Montgomerie; James Johnstone; J. Dobie; and David Gray.

James Paterson, *History of the County of Ayr,* in 2 vols., 1847-52; in 5 vols., 1863-66 (references are to the 5 vol. edition of Paterson's *Ayrshire*).

William Fraser, *Memorials of the Montgomeries,* 2 vols., 1859 (*Memorials of Montgomeries*) contains Irvine material. Also for the Montgomeries of Eglinton, *Report on the Eglinton MSS,* Historical Manuscripts Commission, 1885; *Scots Peerage,* ed. J. Balfour Paul, 9 vols., 1904-14; B.C. de Montgomery, *Origin and History of the Montgomerys,* 1948.

Topographical Account of Cunninghame about 1600 by Timothy Pont, edited by John Fullarton, 1858.

Cunninghame Topographized by Timothy Pont, 1604-1608, edited by J.S. Dobie, 1876, with extensive notes and continuations compiled by the editor's father, James Dobie (Dobie's Pont).

William Scott Douglas, *In Ayrshire: Cunninghame,* 1874, is a brief study.

Diocesan Registers of Glasgow, edited by Bain and Rodgers, Grampian Club, 2 vols., 1875, contain Irvine material for the years 1499-1513 (Protocol Book of Cuthbert Simpson).

The Muniments of the Royal Burgh of Irvine, edited by J.S. Dobie, Ayrshire and Galloway Archaeological Association, 2 vols., 1890, 1891, contain charters, church grants and miscellaneous documents (*Muniments*).

Ayrshire and Galloway Archaeological Association Collections, vols. 7, 8, 9, 1894-95; which are another three of the Society's eighteen massive volumes, these devoted to Irvine between 1613 and 1620 (Protocol Book of Robert Broun).

F.H. Groome's *Ordnance Gazetteer of Scotland,* 6 vols., 1882-85, supplies not only details of contemporary Irvine, but a historical summary.

William Roberstson, *Historic Ayrshire,* 2 vols., 1891, 1894, reprinted Pont, plus appropriate extracts from Chalmers, the two Statistical Accounts, Pitcairn's Criminal Trials, etc. William Robertson also wrote popular works including *Historical Tales and Legends of Ayrshire,* 1889, and *The Lords of Cunningham,* as well as a history of the county.

William Robertson, *Ayrshire: Its History and Historic Families,* 2 vols., 1908 (Robertson's *Ayrshire*). The first volume gives a chronological history of the county while the second deals with the leading families.

James D. Marwick, *The River Clyde and the Clyde Burghs,* Scottish Burgh Records Society, 1909.

Arnold McJannet, *The Royal Burgh of Irvine,* 1938 (cited simply as McJannet) is the culmination of a tradition of local enthusiasm. This is a splendid book by a local lawyer who combined local knowledge with a fully referenced acquaintance with the sources, though for some unaccountable reason the town council of the time denied him access to their records. McJannet diligently searched the printed public records for references to Irvine, which the present author has found most helpful. Too often, however, McJannet uncritically presumed that early legislation was immediately implemented locally.

The Third Statistical Account of Ayrshire, edited by John Strawhorn and William Boyd, 1951, and the associated pamphlet, *Third Statistical Account of Irvine,* edited by William Phillips, 1948, contain mainly 20th-century material.

John Strawhorn, *Ayrshire: the Story of a County,* 1975, provides an up-to-date survey of the development of the county, into which the present local study may be set.

Ayrshire Collections of the Ayrshire Archaeological and Natural History Society, vols, 1-13, since 1950, continuing, contain relevant new material. In particular, reference must be made to the essential study, George Pryde's 'The Burghs of Ayrshire', in vol. 4, 1958.

Irvine and its Burns Club, 1976, is a well-illustrated commentary on 19th and 20th-century social history.

Anne Turner Simpson and Sylvia Stevenson, *Historic Irvine: the archaeological implications of development,* Department of Archaeology, Glasgow University, 1980, is one of a series of reports based on burgh surveys.

Nicola Webster, *Irvine in Old Picture Postcards,* 1983, presents 76 pictures with comments.

Maps and Plans

The growth of Irvine can be graphically analysed in the various maps and plans which have been used to prepare for this volume a series illustrating (conjecturally for the earlier period) the development of the burgh. The method is outlined by M.R.G. Conzen in 'The Use of Town Maps', in *The Study of Urban History,* edited by H.J. Dyos, 1968; and the technique followed by William Dodd in 'Ayr: A Study of Urban Growth', *Ayrshire Collections,* vol. 10, 1972. Some of the original maps and plans listed have been reproduced — see later under *Illustrations.*

1654   *Scotia,* being volume 5 of the *Atlas Novus* published by W. and J. Blaeu, Amsterdam. This contains maps based on information collected locally by Timothy Pont, c.1600. That of Cunninghame has been reproduced in Dobie's Pont, with detail in McJannet; that of Kyle has been produced in facsimile by John Bartholomew and Son, Ltd., Edinburgh, 1967. The National Library of Scotland (NLS) possesses the surviving manuscript maps by Pont, which do not include those of Cunninghame and Kyle. NLS also has the surviving manuscript maps attributed to Robert Gordon who acted as editor and collator of the Pont manuscripts. Kyle is shown on the Gordon MS map 60; Map MS 59 covers part of Cunninghame, but lacks detail, the coastline is uncertain, and Irvine is inaccurately shown on the south side of the river. The assistance of Miss Margaret Wilkes, Superintendent of Map Room, National Library of Scotland, is acknowledged in supplying information and photocopies of these and other maps. Pont's work has been assessed in *Early Maps of Scotland,* ed. H.R. Inglis, 1936, and the extended edition, ed. D.G. Moir, Vol. 1, 1973; by Allan Findlay in *Scottish Geographical Magazine,* Vol. 94, 1978; David Stevenson in *Scottish Studies,* vol. 26, 1982; and by Dr. J.C. Stone, University of Aberdeen, who has supplied helpful comments.

1747-55   General William Roy's manuscript Military Survey Maps: scale approximately 1000 yards to 1 inch; originals in King's Collection, Map Room, British Library, London; photocopies in NLS and the Mitchell Library, Glasgow.

1776   'The Magistrates to employ a proper person to make out a plan of the whole of the towns property' (3rd October 1776); 'Account to the Amount of Twelve Pounds Six Shillings due by the Town to John Foulis of Roseholm for measuring grounds and making plans' (20th September 1771). These MS plans do not seem to have survived.

1775   *A New Map of Ayrshire* by Andrew and Mostyn John Armstrong: scale 1 inch to 1 mile in six sheets. Reprinted in facsimile for Ayrshire Archaeological and Natural History Society, 1959. They also had a version on a reduced scale of 3 miles to 1 inch, 1774 and 1783 editions.

1789-90   Eglinton Estate Plan Book. A magnificent series of 173 manuscript plans by John Ainslie, including the baronies of Stane and Armsheugh and a plan and drawing of Seagate Castle and Yard. Scottish Record Office, West Register House, Edinburgh. A companion volume covering other parts of the estate is held by Mrs. Isa Mackie, Southannan Estate Office, 28 West Road, Irvine.

1811   Map of Ayrshire, scale 3 miles to 1 inch, in William Aiton's *General View of the Agriculture of the County of Ayr.*

1819   *Plan of Irvine* by John Wood: scale 18 inches to 1 mile. Reproduced in two sections as appendix in McJannet but omitting that part showing the harbour. The entire plan is in Wood's *Town Atlas.*

1820   Map of Cunninghame in George Robertson's *Cunninghame*: scale approximately 2 miles to 1 inch.

1820   Plan of the Lands belonging to the Burgh of Irvine, signed Arch. Kennedy and Son. A reduced version, approximately 3 inches to 1 mile, 'by And. Laughlan' dated 1839. In Archivist's Office, County Buildings, Ayr.

1826   Plan for Improvement of Irvine Harbour and Bridge: $11\frac{1}{2}$ inches to 1 mile. Wood Memorial Library, Cunninghame District Library Headquarters, Ardrossan.

1828   *Northern Part of Ayrshire* and *Southern Part of Ayrshire,* by William Johnson: scale $1\frac{1}{4}$ miles to 1 inch. In John Thomson's *Atlas of Scotland,* 1832.

1829   *A New Parish Atlas of Ayrshire* by Robert Aitken. Part 1 only published, with fourteen sheets including Parish of Irvine: scale 2 inches to 1 mile. He produced also a single sheet *Map of Cunninghame,* 1830 — both printed in Beith.

1832 *Irvine:* Scale 6 inches to 1 mile. Parliamentary Boundaries Commission for Scotland; reprinted as frontispiece to McJannet.

1855-57 *Ordnance Survey First Edition Six Inches to One Mile* (1:10560), published 1857-60.

1857 *Ordnance Survey First Edition Twenty five Inches to One Mile* (1:2500), Irvine Parish in 12 sheets.

1859 *Ordnance Plan of the Town of Irvine,* scale 120 inches to 1 mile (1:500). 5 sheets plus title sheet, published 1861. No later editions on this scale.

1893-96 *Ordnance Survey Second Edition,* published 1896-99 (1:10560) and 1896-97 (1:2500).

1907-09 *Ordnance Survey Third Edition,* published 1909-12 (1:10560) and 1908-10 (1:2500).

All the Ordnance Survey series are held by the National Library of Scotland, Map Room; several are in Cunninghame House and local libraries. The Scottish Record Office, West Register House, Edinburgh, has other 19th and 20th-century items, dealing with railways, collieries, harbour, bridge, waterworks, church, manse, Seagate Castle and Eglinton Hotel. Those Irvine archives in the District Library Headquarters, Ardrossan, include plans of Gullilands and Golffields (1846), Marressfoot (1839, 1840), Burying Ground (1877), Plans of Irvine (1882), Bogside Flats (1889), and 20th-century items. In Cunninghame House, Irvine, see Planning and Estates Departments; also various harbour plans held by A. Weir, Leisure Department; Shewalton (1888) in Cleansing Department — William Cowan, Secretary of Irvine Burns Club. Geological maps, plans of coal workings and details of boring are held by Irvine Development Corporation at Perceton House, made available by K. Blair, who assisted in various ways, and confirmed that Magistrates Hill is *not* an old pit bing.

Archives
An enormous mass of archive material has been deposited in various centres:

SCOTTISH RECORD OFFICE (SRO): The Keeper of the Records, H.M. General Register House, Edinburgh, has a list of the main record groups concerning Irvine (Reference B 37), including the Council Records from 1593 to 1699; several 17th-century Protocol Books; Register of Sasines from 1721; various Registers of Deeds; also, separately, church and legal papers. At West Register House, Charlotte Square, Edinburgh, are the Eglinton Estate Plan Book, 1790 (RHP 3) and other plans earlier noted; also Irvine Outport records 1757-1862 (CE 71); and Board of Trade Defunct Company Files.

NEW REGISTER HOUSE: At the headquarters of the Registrar General for Scotland are registers of births, marriages, and deaths; also the confidential census returns to which access is allowed for 19th-century research.

IRVINE BURNS CLUB MUSEUM (BC) contains, in the Strongroom, the Burgh charters in four boxes; Council records 1593-1699, photocopies in 10 volumes of the SRO originals; Council records 1700-1975; Indexes for 1593-1700, 1700-1812, 1812-67; Minutes of Local Authority 1869-1907, Police Commissioners 1874-1907, and Council Committees 1875-1933; lists of burgesses from 1785; documents relating to harbour, colliery, academy, the hammermen, squaremen, and other societies. Also Burns Club records including 10 boxes with papers of Arnold McJannet, bundles of miscellaneous burgh documents, and press cuttings. There are also files of *Irvine Herald,* as listed later under *Newspapers.*

CUNNINGHAME DISTRICT LIBRARY HEADQUARTERS, ARDROSSAN (DL): The remaining documents from Irvine Town House have been deposited and catalogued here, including financial, legal, and other papers, and duplicate sets of certain Trades Council (TC) Minutes. There is also some material here in the Wood Memorial Library.

The Strathclyde Regional Archivist's Office, County Buildings, Ayr (SRA) and the Carnegie Library, Ayr (ACL) contain relevant items.

In private hands are the records of the Incorporated Trades and other societies; the parish church records from 1709 remain in the hands of the kirk session.

Full reference to the location of documents cited is given later.

Manuscript Material
Provost John Paterson's Notes c.1889: 'Original Scrap Book by J.P.' John Paterson, banker and provost from 1872-78, compiled this 376-page volume of extracts from various historical sources plus notes on persons and places. He mentions another 'two foolscap books' which have not been located. For his obituary, *Irvine Herald,* 4.12.1898.

Arnold McJannet's Notes and Historical Papers.

Robert Whyte, town clerk 1944-72: typewritten scripts of five lectures on Irvine and its records. Other Whyte documents are in the hands of the Chief Executive, Cunninghame House, Irvine. Whyte was invited by the town council to update McJannet's history, but regrettably died before this could be undertaken.

Sister Dominic Savio: well-documented typewritten articles on Irvine's 1372 Charter (1972), the Treaty of Irvine, 1297 (n.d.), Marymass (1970, 1974), Catholic Irvine (1978), *St. Mary's Church Centenary* (1975), and notes on the Medieval Town of Irvine and 17th-century Irvine crafts.

Notes of Alexander MacMillan and Andrew Hood: When Cunninghame District Council decided that there was a need for a new history to follow that of McJannet, the task was entrusted first to Alexander MacMillan, retired rector of Irvine Royal Academy; and then to Andrew Hood, for many years Secretary of Irvine Burns Club. In each case death prevented the completion of the work. Alexander MacMillan did prepare in two typewritten volumes a revised version of McJannet with supplementary material. He and Andrew Hood also assembled other materials, including notes supplied by J.R.D. Campbell, Depute Director of Finance, Cunninghame District Council.

These and other documents used in the compilation of this history have been deposited in BC.

Newspapers
The National Library of Scotland's *Directory of Scottish Newspapers*, ed. Joan Ferguson, 1984, gives precise details of repositories. In some cases the only surviving files are in the British Library Reference Division, Newspaper Library, Colindale Avenue, London NW9 5HE. Those locally available are listed:

Ardrossan and Saltcoats Herald since 1853: nearly complete series from 1857 microfilmed in DL, some missing issues in *Herald* Office, Ardrossan (cited as *ASH*).

Ayr Advertiser since 1803: complete series in ACL (cited as *AA*).

Glasgow Herald in Mitchell Library, Glasgow, which has manuscript and later printed indexes (*GH*).

Irvine Express 1884–86: in BL, odd copies in NLS and BC; incorporated in 1886 with *Ayrshire Post* whose files in ACL.

Irvine Herald since 1871: partly damaged series in BC till 1973, thereafter in Herald Office, Irvine (*IH*).

Irvine Journal 1826–27: copies in DL.

Irvine Times since 1873: only in British Library; from 1957 in NLS, from 1963 in *Times* Office, Irvine (*IT*).

Kilmarnock Standard since 1863: complete series in Dick Institute, Kilmarnock (*KS*).

Films
The Scottish Film Council, Victoria Crescent Road, Glasgow, holds in its Scottish Film Archive three-minute black and white film of Marymass 1931 made for Irvine Palace cinema; and a twenty-minute colour 'One Day in the Life of Irvine' (1971) which includes shots of traffic on the old bridge.

Oral Evidence
Over two and a half years, a considerable number of persons provided valuable information. Mr. and Mrs. Alex Bicker, Mr. Eric Dale, Mr. Tom Drape, Mr. J. Martin, and Mrs. J. Mitchell were interviewed and tape recordings deposited in the Ayrshire Sound Archive, Craigie College, Ayr.

Illustrations
Prints and documents from the following sources have been reproduced on the pages indicated.
Eglinton Plan Book, 1790, by permission of the Earl of Eglinton and Winton, with acknowledgement to the SRO — pp. 12, 41, 71.
Robertson's *Cunninghame* 1820 — pp. 81, 113.

Nixon and Richardson, *Views of the Tournament*, 1839 — p. 139.
D.O. Hill, in Wilson and Chambers, *Land of Burns*, 1840 — p. 88.
Dobie's Pont, 1876 — p. 133.
Muniments, 1 and 2 — pp. 23, 36.
McJannet — p. 45.
Irvine Burns Club — pp. 47, 80, 93, 102, 124, 126, 146.
DL Ardrossan — pp. 91, 92.
Mitchell Library Glasgow — pp. 97, 149.
Burns House Museum, Mauchline — p. 101.

Original maps and plans are taken from the following sources:
Pont 1654, from McJannet — p. 29.
Roy 1747, from the Map Room, British Library, London — pp. 72, 73.
Armstrong 1775 from Ayrshire Archaeological and Natural History Society — p. 77.
Wood 1819 from SRO — pp. 78, 110, 111, 112.
Aitken 1829 from DL — p.119.
Parliamentary boundaries 1832 from McJannet — p. 125.
Others reproduced with acknowledgment to the Ordnance Survey, Southampton, with Crown copyright subsisting on those less than fifty years old — pp. 70, 127, 128, 134, 150, 169.

The series of conjectural town plans was devised and prepared by the author in accordance with the concepts as noted earlier under *Maps and Plans* — pp. 10, 22, 32, 42, 52, 66, 96, 162, 222.

The line maps, devised by the author, were produced for publication by the Graphics staff of IDC, under the supervision of Tony Scott — pp. 5, 39, and all colour maps.

Photography reached Irvine about 1860. There is mention of a visiting professional, William Ligat (*ASH* 7.7.1860) and a local photographer Robert Burns Brown who died about 1873 (*IH* 1.7.1932, 22.7.1932). Like others later, they would specialise in portraits and family groups, and it is not easy to attribute authorship or date to those scenes of familiar places which have survived. Photographs of Irvine were also taken by Francis Frith (Frith Collection, Andover, Hampshire, not available for publication), George Washington Wilson (Aberdeen University Library), and for the Valentine postcards series (St. Andrews University Library). Three published books of views (as collected by Alex MacMillan) are listed, plus the sources for other photographs reproduced:

View Souvenir inscribed 'Photochrom Co. Ltd., London and Tunbridge Wells'. 6 photos approximately 8 x 4 inches pasted on brown pages $9\frac{1}{2}$ x $4\frac{1}{2}$ inches. c.1894–96 — pp. 11, 24.
Photographic Album of Irvine inscribed 'published by John S. Begg... Poulton's Collotype Series' in gilt lettering on red cover. 16 photographs 7 x 5 inches on 9 x 6 inch white paper pages. c.1896–1900 — pp. 55, 87, 100, 157, 159, 161, 197.
Irvine inscribed 'published by J. and G. Begg'. 15 sepia photos 7 x 6 inches attached to 11 x $8\frac{1}{2}$-inch brown pages with tissues. c. 1912–21 — pp. 138, 170, 171, 175, 207.

Other items from Alex MacMillan's collection — pp. 53, 57, 83, 121, 129, 172, 173, 174, 195, 215.
CDC Leisure Department — pp. 25, 98, 115, 145, 158, 177.
CDC Planning Department — pp. 17, 18, 43, 54, 90, 117, 209.
Mr. and Mrs. R. Campbell — pp. 59, 61, 89, 141, 160, 182, 189, 221.
John G. Hall — pp.140, 148, 153, 181, 213.
Irvine Herald — p. 14.
Irvine Times — pp. 219, 225, 229.
St. Andrews University Library, Valentine Series — pp. 16, 34, 199, 201, 205.
Aero Films — pp. 183, 185, 187, 202.
McJannet — pp. 68, 99, 100, 126.
IDC — pp. 3. 27, 33, 69, and all colour photographs.
Loudoun-Montgomery School — pp. 136, 176, 211.

Keith Gibson, with the cooperation of IDC, prepared some older prints and photographs for publication and was responsible for the following specially taken — pp. 4, 13, 15, 23, 30, 67, 135, 137, 147, 217.

Note on Dates
Before 1600 in Scotland the new year commenced on 25th March, which has required the conversion of certain dates to conform with modern usage. This calendar change proposed by Pope Gregory in 1582 was accepted in Scotland in 1600 but not in England till 1752, in which year throughout the United Kingdom another conversion from the Julian to the Gregorian calendar was adopted whereby 2nd September 1752 was followed by 14th September 1752, after which Old Style and New Style dates were sometimes quoted. Over a century later, in the Poors House, there was an entertainment on 'Old New Year's Night' on 13th January (*IH*, 16.1.1875).

Note on Spellings
'Cuninghame' was possibly the commonest early form, followed by the anglified 'Cunningham'. 'Cunninghame', given statutory authority for the district in 1975, has been used throughout for the place. For the family name in the days before standardised spelling, 'Cunningham' has been chosen.
Where it seemed appropriate, quotations from earlier periods have been given in the original spellings, to preserve the flavour of the times, but with occasional amendments for the sake of clarity.

Note on Currency
£1 Scots was valued at one twelfth of £1 Sterling. A mark was worth two-thirds of £1 Scots. It may now be necessary to inform younger readers that before decimalisation in 1971 £1 was divided into twenty shillings and each shilling contained twelve pennies. Thus £1.2.6, 12/6, and 10/- equalled respectively £1.12½p, 62½p, 50p.

To avoid overloading the text with detailed references, for each chapter there is a note of sources of information and sometimes supplementary details. Short titles are given of those main works previously listed.

Chapter 1 — Origins
The archaeological survey of the county made in John Smith, *Prehistoric Man in Ayrshire,* 1895, has never been repeated. Later discoveries and re-assessments have been included in the *Transactions of the Society of Antiquaries of Scotland* and *Discovery and Excavation,* annually. T.A. Hendry with his comprehensive knowledge of the county's early past has provided a list of sites in the area for the preparation of a map. See also A. Morrison, 'Mesolithic period in S.W. Scotland', *Glasgow Archaeological Journal,* Vol. 9, 1982. W.E. Boyd, 'Stratigraphy and Chronology of Late Quaternary raised coastal deposits in Renfrewshire and Ayrshire', unpublished Ph.D. thesis, University of Glasgow, 1982; and 'Archaeological Implications of a new palaeo-environmental model for part of the Ayrshire Coast', *Glasgow Archaeological Journal,* Vol. 9, 1982, offer new evidence on the prehistoric scene. Dr. Boyd has also assisted in estimating the recession of the sea since then. For the Whale at Warrix, see *Annals of the Kilmarnock Glenfield Ramblers,* Vol. 1, 1894. Dr. J.C. Stone, University of Aberdeen, is uncertain of the accuracy of the Pont-Blaeu map of 1654. For conjectured changes in the coast and rivers see also Robertson's *Cunninghame,* 164; *NSA,* V, 427, 620; Paterson's *Ayrshire,* 252, 257; Provost Paterson's Notes, 264; McJannet, 7, 39, 72, 337; Robert Whyte's lecture notes; *Scottish Geographical Magazine,* Vol. 94 (1978); also Maps and Plans listed above. There is no doubt about the significant 18th-century alteration in the course of the River Irvine near Warrix, but some uncertainty as to the precise date. In the Eglinton Plan Book (SRO, West Register House, RHP3/36) John Ainslie marked it as 1758. Provost John Paterson's Notes, 264, recorded it as 23rd November 1769. But earlier that year the Town Council (Minutes of Meeting of 28th July 1769) sought aid because of the 'great inundation which broke the neck of land at Tarryholm'. Early references to Irvine are given in A.O. Anderson, *Scottish Annals from English Chroniclers,* 1908, and McJannet, 65. Derivations of the name are discussed in Robertson's *Cunninghame,* 15; Chalmers' *Caledonia,* 446; Paterson's *Ayrshire,* 249; Smith's *Prehistoric Man in Ayrshire,* 125; McJannet, 21; and W.F.H. Nicolaisen, *The Names of Towns and Cities,* 1970. For the derivation of Cunninghame, see Robertson, 15, 16, and *Ayrshire,* 1, 2, 466, 467. For the de Morvilles and their successors see Robertson's *Cunninghame,* 46; Chalmers' *Caledonia,* 160; Paterson's *Ayrshire,* 216; McJannet, 3, 5, 27, 67; William Dillon, 'The Origins of Feudal Ayrshire', *Ayrshire Collections,* Vol. 3; G.W.S. Barrow, *Robert the Bruce,* 1976, and *Kingship and Unity,* 1981. For Christian origins in Irvine, McJannet, 10, lists all that is surmised, and A.P. Forbes, *Calendars of Scottish Saints* 1872, mentions Inan. Professor I.B. Cowan has made the most recent examination of the date of the foundation of Kilwinning Abbey. The foundation of the burgh has been considered in *OSA,* VII, 170; Robertson's *Cunninghame,* 412; Chalmers' *Caledonia,* 416; *NSA,* V, 621; Paterson's *Ayrshire,* 250; Dobie's Pont, 216; *Muniments,* I, xxix; Groome, IV, 325; McJannet, 56; notes of Robert Whyte and Sister Dominic Savio; George Pryde, 'The Burghs of Ayrshire', *Ayrshire Collections,* Vol. 4 (which disposes of the alleged agreement of 1205); and his *Burghs of Scotland,* 1965.

Registrum Monasterii de Passelet, Maitland Club, 1832, 48 refers to fishing 'inter castrum de Are et villam de Yrewin... anno regni domini Regis sextodecimo'.

Chapter 2 — Early Days in the Burgh
The various streets and places of the early burgh have been traced in *Muniments,* I, with its charters and church grants; *Muniments,* II, containing miscellaneous documents and extracts from 17th-century burgh records; the Protocol books of Cuthbert Simpson and Robert Broun; the notes of Provost Paterson and of Robert Whyte; these confirming and supplementing McJannet, 265 and elsewhere. Provost Paterson's Notes, 349-363, give details of particular localities. *Historic Irvine,* 1980, provides a useful summary. Reference may be made to the printed public records, viz. *Register of the Great Seal, Register of the Privy Seal of Scotland, Exchequer Rolls of Scotland, Accounts of the Lord High Treasurer, Records of the Convention of Royal Burghs,* their indexes, and particularly to those volumes published since McJannet. Paterson's *Ayrshire* supplies details not only of Irvine but also, under Parish of Dundonald, of Fullarton, for which see also J.H. Gillespie, *Dundonald,* 2 vols., 1939. For the landward part of Irvine parish, use has been made of Robertson's *Cunninghame,* Dobie's Pont, Paterson's *Ayrshire,* and for Armsheugh, Pryde's 'The Burghs of Ayrshire', *Ayrshire Collections,* Vol. 4.

Chapter 3 — The Burgh Council
The principal sources are the *Muniments* and other works listed for Chapter 2. The operations of the council of a nearby royal burgh have been vividly described in the introduction to *Ayr Burgh Accounts, 1534-1624,* edited by George S. Pryde, Scottish History Society, 1937.

Chapter 4 — Church and Castle
Muniments, I, listing the church grants, forms the main source for the medieval church. *Irvine Parish Church Magazine,* 1898-99, edited by Rev. H.R. Rankin, contained a series of articles (copies in DL — Wood Memorial Library) based on notes of Provost Paterson: there survives also a note book with a transcript and some additional notes (BC). 'The Ecclesiastical History of Irvine' was the subject of four anonymous articles in the *Kilmarnock Standard,* 1912, whose author may have been Frances H. Walker of Ayr (ACL 941.42, no. 68048), or more probably Charles Murchland of Irvine. Robert Reid of Balgray, *History of the Church of Irvine,* 1919, summarised the evidence, while McJannet has good chapters on 'The Pre-Reformation Church', 'The Officiating Clergy', 'The Carmelites', and 'The Temple Lands'. The Carmelites are dealt with also in Paterson's *Ayrshire* and Gillespie's *Dundonald.* See also William Dillon's *Catholic Ayrshire,* Catholic Truth Society pamphlet, 1958; his 'Spittals of Ayrshire' in *Ayrshire Collections,* Vol. 6, 1961, and his typescript of 'Ayrshire Clergy before 1600' (ACL). For some pre-Reformation clergy, *Papal Letters, 1394-1419,* edited by F. McGurk, Scottish History Society, 1972. Sister Dominic Savio's scripts and advice have also been most helpful. *The Knights of St. John of Jerusalem in Scotland,* ed. I.B. Cowan et al, Scottish History Society, 1983, lists Templar properties in 1539-40.

Seagate Castle was fully described in a detailed survey with drawings made in 1883 by William Galloway and included in *Muniments,* I. Provost John Paterson, in *Annals of the Kilmarnock Glenfield Ramblers,* Vol. 2, 1898, suggested 1565 as the probable date of reconstruction. McJannet deals not only with 'the Palace' but also with the office of Constable. Sister Dominic Savio's script on the Treaty of Irvine, 1297, is a reliable study, while McJannet, 80, gives the text of the document. For a vivid and imaginative fictional dramatisation see the novel by Nigel Tranter, *Robert the Bruce — The Steps to the Empty Throne,* 1969. The plaque commemorating the capitulation at Knadgerhill is a boulder of rough granite, 7 feet high, 3 feet broad, 2 feet thick, with 3 panels on the face. The top panel is inscribed: 'Site of Scottish Camp, War of Independence, 9th July, 1297. "Scots wha hae wi' Wallace bled, Scots wham Bruce has aften led".' The middle panel portrays the arms of Scotland, of the earldom of Carrick, of the Steward, and of Douglas. The bottom panel records the presentation of the memorial to the burgh on 7th June 1929 by Irvine Burns Club on behalf of the donor, Alexander B. McDonald, Plessie, Kenilworth, Cape Town, a native of Irvine. The plaque on Seagate Castle, presented by Irvine Burns Club, 25th January 1930, announces: 'Treaty of Irvine signed in the Old Castle, 9th July 1297. Mary Queen of Scots with her "Four Maries", Mary Beaton, Mary Seaton, Mary Fleming, and Mary Livingstone, visited the Castle 1st August 1563, and was entertained by Hugh, 3rd Earl of Eglinton, one of her most faithful adherents — "I was the Queen o' Bonnie France, And I'm the Sov'reign of Scotland".' Those who wish to pursue in further detail changes of ownership of properties in the landward part of the parish should refer to Robertson's *Cunninghame,* Robertson's *Families,* Dobie's Pont and Paterson's *Ayrshire.*

Chapter 5 — Feuds and Factions
For the feuds, see Chalmers' *Caledonia; Memorials of the Montgomeries;* Paterson's *Ayrshire,* especially the 'Historical Sketch' for Cunninghame; Dobie's Pont; Pitcairn's Ayrshire Criminal Trials as included in Robertson's *Historic Ayrshire;* Robertson's *Ayrshire;* and his *Lords of Cunninghame* for a fictional version. The Reformation and the religious conflicts of the 17th century have been dealt with in older works like Paterson's *Ayrshire,* especially the 'Historical Sketch' for Kyle; Robert Reid's *History of the Church of Irvine;* McJannet; the voluminous works of Robert Wodrow (who was a son-in-law of Rev. Patrick Warner of Irvine); and John Galt's *Ringan Gilhaize* which recreates imaginatively several local incidents. The *Muniments* contain much relevant material. But a clearer interpretation has been provided by more recent studies — Gordon Donaldson, *Thirds of Benefices,* Scottish History Society, 1949; and *The Scottish Reformation,* 1960; Ian B. Cowan, *The Scottish Reformation,* 1982; and *The Scottish Covenanters, 1660-1688,* 1976; David Stevenson, *The Scottish Revolution, 1637-44,* 1973; *Revolution and Counter Revolution in Scotland,* 1978; and *Government under the Covenanters,* Scottish History Society, 1982. For the ministers of this and later periods, *Fasti,* edited by Hew Scott, 1868. Regarding the Barclays, there is some uncertainty in Robertson's *Families,*

Paterson's *Ayrshire,* and Dobie's Pont; McJannet, 251, has become confused regarding Provost Mr. Robert Barclay, whose career I have elucidated with assistance from Dr. David Stevenson. There is one reference to him in the *Scots Peerage.* Barclay is listed, with other parliamentary commissioners, in an unpublished 'History of the Parliament of Scotland', proofs of which are held by the SRO.

Chapter 6 — Some Progress
For 17th-century developments, the printed *Muniments* include charters, writs, and excerpts from the council minutes and burgh accounts. Originals are in the SRO. Locally available are ten volumes of photocopied council minutes covering (incompletely) the period 1595-1699, together with a typewritten Index volume (BC). Some abstracts from these minutes and other 17th-century documents were included in Provost Paterson's Notes and utilised by McJannet, 349, 355. The first volume of the records of the Incorporated Trades, 'Conveners Court Minute Book 1673-1755', contains details of annual elections of boxmasters, acts anent the loft in the church, and notes of dues paid. Provost Paterson had access to other sources, whence the verses quoted (Notes 49-53). For various details see G.S. Pryde, 'The Burghs of Ayrshire', in *Ayrshire Collections,* Vol. 4, 1958; T.C. Smout, 'The Overseas Trade of Ayrshire, 1660-1707', *Ayrshire Collections,* Vol. 6, 1961; J.D. Marwick, *The River Clyde and the Clyde Burghs,* Scottish Burgh Records Society, 1909; Margaret Sanderson, 'Kilwinning at the Time of the Reformation', *Ayrshire Collections,* Vol. 10, 1972 and her *Scottish Rural Society in the 16th Century,* 1982; R.W. Clouston, 'The Church Bells of Ayrshire', *Ayrshire Collections,* Vol. 1, 1950; William Boyd, *Education in Ayrshire Through Seven Centuries,* 1961; James Coutts, *A History of the University of Glasgow,* 1909; J.D. Mackie, *The University of Glasgow, a Short History,* 1954, and *Munimenta Alme Universitatis Glasuensis,* 1854. Ramsay's 'Dundonald Regulations' are given in Paterson's *Ayrshire,* Gillespie's *Dundonald,* and in Boyd. The Council Minutes confirm Ramsay's scheme as being applicable to Irvine by reference to visitation of the school (1675), a scholars' seat in church (1670) holidays 'for a month or twenty days provided they keep the School during Harvest' (1678) and 'complaint against the bairns' (1677). For horse races see McJannet and document in BC (Bundle 44).

Chapter 7 — The Town Council and the 18th Century
The Council Minutes (BC) are missing for the years 1704-09, possibly abstracted for legal purposes because of the disputed election in 1702. Thereafter they form a principal source, supplemented by Provost Paterson's Notes which contain extracts from the Minutes with occasional annotations; by Robert Whyte's Notes which are based on them; and with John Galt's *The Provost* always to hand, for many of the incidents he recounts can be related to actual events in Irvine. For the 1756 election, 'James Boyle v. John Cumming et al.' (DL 1/32/1). For smuggling see Paterson's *Ayrshire,* 265-267, and McJannet, 319-325. John Strawhorn, 'Farming in 18th Century Ayrshire' and 'Industry and Commerce in 18th Century Ayrshire', in *Ayrshire Collections,* Vols. 3 and 4, provide details not only of smuggling but background material for other topics covered in this and the next chapter. For burgh finance, see Rental Books listing teinds, feu duties, and lotted lands, from 1771 (DL 1/10), Cessbooks listing levies on lands, houses, trade, and ships (DL 1/11), Factor's Accounts (1769-95 in BC Box 7/35, Box 5/24, Box 6/29; from 1795 in DL 1/19), Licensing Court Register from 1765 (DL 1/8).

Chapter 8 — Commercial Growth
T.C. Minutes for the 18th century are complemented by the Statistical Account (*OSA*) whose Irvine report by Rev. James Richmond, though published in 1793, was written in 1791. Our analysis of shipping has used particularly the Harbour Book 1769-70 (BC 18/15), Cess Book 1770 (DL 1/11/2), List of Vessels 1774 (BC Charter Box 4/E23), List of Vessels 1794 (BC Box 10/2(d)), Irvine Outport Books (SRO, West Register House, CE 71). Information on local industry comes from Baron Duckham, *History of the Scottish Coal Industry 1700-1815,* 1970; and two invaluable studies by C.A. Whatley, 'The Process of Industrialisation in Ayrshire 1707-1871' unpublished Ph.D. thesis, University of Strathclyde, 1975, (ACL), and 'A Fine Place for a Lasting Colliery', *Ayrshire Collections,* 1983. There are manuscript accounts for 'The Green Coals' 1762-67, 1767-68, and 'The Muir Coals' 1785-86 (BC 19/1, 1a, 2). The description of the Warrix pit appears in 'Charles Hutcheson's Journal, 1783' in *Scottish Historical Review,* XVI, 1919. For an earlier visitor to Irvine, Richard Pococke's *Tours in Scotland 1760,* Scottish History Society, 1887. For the Incorporated Trades, the two Minute Books of the Conveners Court, 1673-1755, 1756-1922, and other documents, are uninformative. Of the individual crafts, there are records (deposited in BC) of the hammermen from 1795, the squaremen from 1803, and the weavers from 1857 only. Paterson's Notes have abstracts from some records which have apparently not survived, and there was a Weavers Society Book covering the period 1649-1826. For the banks, McJannet, 279-281, and Paterson's Notes (374-376). Dr. John Hume, University of Strathclyde, supplied information relating to the mills.

Chapter 9 — Church and School
Robert Reid, *History of the Church of Irvine,* 1919; Rev. James Graham, *Relief United Free Church of Irvine,* 1923; *The Divine Dictionary,* 1785 (DL); John Train, *The Buchanites from First to Last,* 1883; John Cameron, *History of the Buchanite Delusion,* 1904, supplement McJannet on the church, while on the school his limited information is augmented by the TC Minutes and other papers including, for the books Maul requisitioned, Factor's accounts (DL 1B/3/1/16-29). For Maul see also Paterson's Notes, 260. The kirk session records cover the years 1709-32; 1732-50; 1771-78; 1784-1819. The one notorious career is recorded in *Memoirs of Major Semple, the Northern Impostor,* 1786 (copy in BC).

Chapter 10 — John Galt's Irvine
There are extensive Galt collections in DL (Wood Memorial Library) and in BC (Hogg Room). See John Galt's

Autobiography, 1833, and *Literary Life,* 1834; and *John Galt 1779-1979,* ed. C.A. Whatley, 1979. Mary Phillips, *Edgar Allan Poe the Man,* 2 vols., 1926, has information and illustrations of Irvine supplied by R.M. Hogg. Contemporary descriptions are now available in *OSA* (1791) and Robertson's *Cunninghame* (1820), in the maps of Armstrong (1775) and Wood (1819), and some details in William Aiton's wide-ranging *General View of the Agriculture of the County of Ayr,* 1811; while reference can be made to *Ayrshire at the Time of Burns,* ed. John Strawhorn, 1959. For the making of the turnpike roads see also Minutes of the County Road Trustees (SRA CO3/5/22). McJannet's index shows how well he has dealt with the important persons of this period, but much new material has been derived from the TC Minutes and other papers. Paterson's Notes, 250-264, contain original material on Burns's stay in Irvine, as used in Robert Chambers, *Life of Burns,* revised by William Wallace, 4 vols., 1896. Provost Murchland had different opinions, expressed in 'The Heckling Shop of Robert Burns', *IH,* 1.2.1907. Useful summaries are Rev. Henry Ranken, 'Burns and Irvine', *Burns Chronicle,* 1905, and Rev. John C. Hill, *The Life and Work of Robert Burns in Irvine,* 1933. Burns's autobiographical letter is No. 125 in *The Letters of Robert Burns,* ed. J. de Lancey Ferguson, 2 vols., 1931. For Jean Gardner see Train and Cameron (notes to Chapter 9) and the 1768 lawsuit (BC Box 5/22).

Chapter 11 — The Coming of Reform
This chapter is based largely on material not available to McJannet — the Town Council minutes (BC), the Burgh Letter Books from 1798 (DL 1/15), Memorial Book (DL 1/20/3), and their Report to the Parliamentary Committee on Royal Burghs (DL 1/32/5); minutes of provision for the poor (DL 1/33/9-11) and the unemployed (DL 1/33/5-7); Minutes of the Directors of Irvine Academy (BC/1/23/1); Minutes of the Harbour Trustees (EC/1/13), the Bridge Trustees (DL 1/20), the Board of Health (DL 1/37/1) and the Burials Register 1818-39 (DL 1/36/1) with the Register of Arrivals and Sailings from 1822 (BC 1/18/20). Also *Reports from the Commissioners on Municipal Corporations,* 1836: General Report, and Report on the Burgh of Irvine by John Cuninghame and J. Ivory. Robertson's *Cunninghame* is invaluable on social conditions, with some details from Aiton (as in Chapter 10). For friendly societies of this period see Ian MacDougall, *Catalogue of Labour Records in Scotland,* 1978, 5; also *Ayrshire Magazine,* December 1815, 200. Paterson's Notes supply details about the academy (132, 231, 282, 375), and the grave-robbers (146, 148), while McJannet tells of Neilson (231) and Maxwell Dick (234). For James Steadman, see James Nicol, *Who invented the Screw Propeller?* 1863 (BC, AT14). See also Thomas Hughes, *Memoir of Daniel Macmillan,* 1882, and C.L. Graves, *Life and Letters of Alexander Macmillan,* 1910. Whatley (as in Chapter 8) supplements the TC Minutes on coal. For the political events leading to reform, W.S. Brownlie, *The Proud Trooper,* 1964, outlines the part played by the Ayrshire Yeomanry, and McJannet's few details (170, 295, 344, 354) are filled out in Provost Paterson's Notes, 127, 130, 157, 320, and by the files of the *Ayr Advertiser. Irvine and County of Ayr Miscellany,* 1814-15, has little local information.

See also Alexander Wilson's 'Dr. John Taylor of Blackhouse, the Ayrshire Chartist, 1815-42', *Ayrshire Collections,* Vol. 1, 1950. Special note must be made of an unofficial local census of 1820. This unique manuscript source (BC, not catalogued in National Register of Archives Survey) is a large bound volume entitled 'Division of the Town and Parish of Irvine, Halfway, etc., into Districts with their Respective Deacons, 1820'. For each of 36 'Quarters' are listed: names of heads of families, numbers of males and females in each household, place of origin, occupation, religion, remarks. Though the entries are not always complete, sometimes intimate details of difficult family circumstances are given, and occasionally delightful comments like 'a happy looking new married couple'. For some Quarters there is a separate list of the poor who have badges, those receiving regular or occasional relief, and more likely to require relief. The decennial official *Census Reports* from 1801 supply more general statistics for this and subsequent chapters.

Chapters 12 and 13 — Little Change; Little Progress
These chapters analysing the period between the two Reform Acts, 1832-67, are based on TC Minutes, usefully complemented by Provost Paterson's Notes which contain for each year remarks on local events and, from 1854 (when he was elected a councillor), comments on council business. Other contemporary sources are the New Statistical Account (1840); the Ordnance Survey maps (1857); *Ayr Advertiser,* especially for parliamentary elections; the *Ardrossan and Saltcoats Herald* from 1853 reporting events in Irvine and (after 1864) town council meetings; there is a valuation roll for 1855 (BC). For matters ecclesiastical: Robert Reid, *History of the Church of Irvine,* 1919, and the Kirk Session records, still held locally; *Fullarton Parish Church 1838-1963,* 1963; *Wilson-Fullarton Church of Scotland 1843-1943,* 1943; Rev. A.A. Lawson, *History of the Mure Church, Irvine, 1849-1949,* 1949 — the records of this church are in SRO (CH3/1058); Rev. James Graham, *Relief United Free Church, Irvine,* 1923; James Brown, *Life of Rev. W.B. Robertson of Irvine,* 1888; Arthur Guthrie, *Robertson of Irvine,* 1884 and later editions; *Church of St. Mary Centenary Brochure 1875-1975,* 1975, has details of earlier Roman Catholic missions. Details of the various congregations are found in *Ardrossan and Saltcoats Herald* news items; *Kilmarnock Standard* (series of articles, 1912); and *Irvine Herald* ('History of the Churches', 5.3.1971); also *National Commercial Directories* of Pigot (1837) and Slater (1867), both in ACL. For schools, McJannet 212-238; Irvine Academy Minutes Book 1833-72 (BC 1/23/2); *Ardrossan and Saltcoats Herald,* especially for reports of annual examinations in July, and in particular 27.2.1858 for the Commercial Academy and 1.8.1863 for Dr. White's list of alumni; John Duncan, 'Education in Irvine Through the Centuries' in *Irvine Herald,* 5.3.1971. Many of the recreational activities are mentioned in the *Ardrossan and Saltcoats Herald.* Material relating to Bogside Races was assembled by Alex MacMillan. Contemporary descriptions, James Aikman, *Account of the Tournament,* 1839, J.H. Nixon and J. Richardson, *Views of the Tournament,* 1839, and James Paterson, *Autobiographical Reminiscences,* 1871, can be supplemented by Ian Anstruther, *Knight and the Umbrella,* 1963. Railway proposals and actual developments are referred to

in TC Minutes. For Maxwell Dick's experiments, see his *Suspension Railway,* 1830 (DL, Wood Memorial Library, Pamphlet box D1). W. McIlwraith, *Glasgow and South Western Railway,* 1880, has been followed by a useful brochure with the same title issued by the Stephenson Locomotive Society, 1950. For industries after the time of the New Statistical Account (1840) there are only passing references in TC Minutes, press, and directories cited above. For coalmines especially, see Ordnance Survey maps of 1857, and Barbara Paterson, 'Social and Working Conditions of the Ayrshire Mining Population 1840-1875' in *Ayrshire Collections,* Vol. 10, 1972. There are papers relating to Harbour Trustees (BC). Natives of Irvine who distinguished themselves, only a few of whom now seem worthy of note, are mentioned in McJannet, Paterson's Notes, and the *Kilmarnock Standard* series of 1912 and 1914. For the 'Mary of Eglinton' tradition of Marymass and 'St. Merri', see *Kilmarnock Standard,* 27.8.1910.

Chapter 14 — A New Beginning
The main sources are TC Minutes, also those of the Local Authority from 1870 and the Police Commissioners from 1874 (all in BC); Provost Paterson's Notes, especially 200-211, for water supply; Groome's *Ordnance Gazetteer,* 1886; and local newspapers, especially 'Irvine and Its Industries' in *Irvine Herald,* 22.8.1890; also a map of Shewalton estate (1888, in Cunninghame House), a burgh map (1892, in DL), and the O.S. maps of 1896 and 1910. S.G. Checkland, *The Mines of Tharsis,* 1967, explains William Henderson's important role in the development of the chemical industry. He was the subject of an article in *The Bailie,* No. 250, August 1877. See *Irvine Herald* also for Henderson (8.1.1881) and David Gray (15.1.1881). For coal, see Barbara Paterson, as above. Details of the Caledonian line are from *Railway Magazine,* March 1972.

Chapter 15 — Industrial Town
See minutes, maps, and other items cited for Chapter 14. The County of Ayr Constabulary Returns from 1862 supply details of police force, crimes and offences, and (for 1897) licensed premises. For other topics, *Scotland: Owners of Lands and Heritages, 1872-73* and *National Telephone Company's Directory for Scotland 1892-93,* both in ACL. See Provost Paterson's Notes for details of closes (362) and pools (227). For recreation, see local press, and Drew Cochrane, *The Story of Ayrshire Junior Football,* 1976. For churches, sources as for Chapters 12 and 13. For Census of Church membership, *IH,* 29.4.1876. The Minutes of Irvine School Board have disappeared. They were however used by McJannet, 239-240, and full reports of meetings appeared in local press. Also lost are the records of Lyle's School and the Public and Industrial School, which were consulted by McJannet. Extracts from the latter appear in William Boyd, *Education in Ayrshire Through Seven Centuries,* 1961. Still surviving are logbooks of Fullarton School 1897-1907 and Bank Street School 1875-1971, and other records of the latter — all in SRA. There are two well-illustrated school histories (copies in DL): *Loudoun Montgomery Primary School 1907-78,* Mary Livingstone et al; *Bank Street Primary School 1875-1982,* Agnes Carlyle et al. There are full reports of the Jubilee celebrations in *Ardrossan and Saltcoats Herald,* 25.6.97. For Dr. Agnes Smith Lewis and Dr. Margaret Dunlop Gibson see A. Whighorn Price, *The Ladies of Castlebrae,* 1964 (copy in DL) and other papers in BC. For various artists and musicians see IDC brochure on 'The Arts in the New Town'.

Chapter 16 — A New Age
Charles Murchland's *Post Office Directory 1908-09* (BC) is augmented by TC minutes; other TC papers including Abstracts of Accounts (DL); the files of the *Irvine Herald* (BC); *Ayr Advertiser* and *Ayrshire Post* for parliamentary elections (ACL); scrapbooks of newspaper cuttings, some assembled by R.M. Hogg (BC); *Census Reports* (sets in ACL); Drew Cochrane, *The Story of Ayrshire Junior Football,* 1976; Thomas McKerrel and James Brown's Ayrshire Miners' Union report to the Royal Commission on Housing reprinted as *Ayrshire Miners Rows 1913* in *Ayrshire Collections,* Vol. 13, 1979. Childhood memories of some of the older residents (listed above under 'Oral Evidence') provide an additional source of confirmatory and supplementary detail.

Chapter 17 — The First War and After
TC Minutes and papers (BC and DL) supplemented by data on council house building from CDC, Cunninghame House. McJannet's history, desultory in his treatment of the 19th century, virtually ignores the 20th: so the local press becomes of primary importance as a source. Charles Murchland, owner-editor of the *Irvine Herald,* died in 1926, praised for his 'great business capability, sound judgment, strong commonsense, and earnest desire for the public welfare... a delightful man with a fund of reminiscences especially of old Irvine' (*IH,* 21.5.1926). The *Irvine Herald* under W. & R.G. Ross continued his policy of providing editorials on local affairs and even livelier reports of council meetings — which serve to confirm the limitations of council minutes as a historical source. Minutes and Accounts of Irvine Parish Council for this period have been examined (SRA). Alex MacMillan's typewritten notes (BC) have information for this and later chapters on schools (with abstracts from the Academy logbooks), churches, the Incorporated Trades, bus services, the Royal Ordnance Factory, etc. There is oral evidence from surviving residents and participants. Useful details come from *Centenary Book of Irvine Burns Club, 1926; Robert Burns in Irvine: Guide to Irvine Burns Club and Museums,* 1968; and especially *Irvine and its Burns Club,* 1976. A copy of the Burgh Song is in BC (bundle 44).

Chapter 18 — The Small Burgh and the Second War
Sources as for Chapter 17 with some TC minutes in DL missing from BC; *Census Report* for 1931; plus Irvine District Council Minutes (DL). The closer involvement of Ayr County Council in the affairs of Irvine can be traced in County Council minutes and its departmental records (SRA). Oral evidence becomes increasingly valuable for the period of the Second World War when reasons of security inhibited reporting of certain events and incidents in the local press.

Chapter 19 — Mid-Century
Royal Burgh of Irvine: Third Statistical Account, ed. William Phillips, 1948; *Third Statistical Account of Scotland: Ayrshire,* ed. John Strawhorn and William Boyd, 1951; Correspondence and Papers relating to that survey (BC): these are augmented by the *Census Reports* for 1951 and 1961; TC Minutes (some only in DL) plus Whyte papers in hands of CDC Chief Executive, Cunninghame House; *Irvine Herald;* and increasing reliance on oral evidence.

Chapter 20 — From Royal Burgh into New Town
For the last years of the burgh, TC Minutes (series in BC incomplete but missing volumes in DL), and thereafter CDC Minutes (DL). The official *Annual Reports by Scotish New Towns* are complemented by numerous brochures published by Irvine Development Corporation, with additional information and help from IDC officials, in particular the Chief Architect Ian Downs, and Graeme Ballantine and Robert Orr of his staff. For the industrial situations in 1984, details were provided by some individual firms; and for schools, by the Divisional Education Officer, Ayr. The *Irvine Times* and the *Irvine Herald* continue as invaluable sources of major events, despite the changes (noted in the text) which eliminated the long and detailed report of earlier years. Oral evidence and comments by councillors, officials, and others have helped to provide a study of the contemporary situation which, it is hoped, will be of interest to those of the present and of value to future historians of Irvine.

Acknowledgements
To Cunninghame District Council who commissioned this history and financed its publication; to the local councillors — Jack Carson, Stewart Dewar, Tom Dewar, Jim Farrell, David O'Neill, Alex Rubie — for their enthusiastic support throughout; Chief Executive Jim Miller who guided the project; CDC officials and staff who provided facilities too numerous to mention individually save for Mrs. Irene McLellan and her assistants for long hours processing a difficult script; to other public authorities including Irvine Development Corporation and various members of its staff, with Tony Scott and Keith Gibson playing a major role in preparing illustrations.

To all those mentioned earlier in this appendix as supplying material — libraries, archivists, authors, specialists, experts, firms, organisations, local residents, and owners of copyright. Special note must be made of Irvine Burns Club, whose Wellwood premises contain a rich store of information, and whose custodian Mrs. Madge Smith deserves commendation.

To John Donald Publishers Ltd. for including this in their impressive series of books on Scottish history, and to John Tuckwell and Donald Morrison for their invaluable assistance.

To the people of Irvine whose company I have enjoyed over the last three years, whose traditions I have attempted to commemorate in these pages.

List of Provosts

First mention of a provost of Irvine was in 1539. Names and dates until the 18th century are based on a list compiled in 1896 by James Dickie, town clerk.

JOHN MURE 1540-42
ROBERT SCOTT 1542-43
STEPHEN TRAN 1551, 1557
ROBERT BARCLAY 1559
JAMES SCOTT 1561
JOHN PEEBLES OF BROOMLANDS 1570, 1596
HUGH SCOTT 1571
HUGH CAMPBELL OF LOUDOUN 1572-73, 1574, 1579, 1582, 1587
WILLIAM SCOTT 1583-84
JAMES McGOUN 1585
PATRICK TRAN 1591-93, 1600-01
HUGH NEVING 1594-95
ARCHIBALD GEORGE 1601-1603, 1608, 1611-12, 1613-14
NINIAN BARCLAY OF WARRIX 1602, 1616-17
WILLIAM SCOTT 1506
THOMAS BOYD 1608-10
HUGH SCOTT 1615
ANDREW TRAN 1617
ALLAN DUNLOP 1619-21, 1623-28, 1630-31, 1632-34, 1635-36, 1641-42
JAMES SCOTT OF CLONBEITH 1628-30, 1631-32, 1634-35
MR. ROBERT BARCLAY 1639-41, 1642-44, 1648-49, 1655-59
ALLAN DUNLOP OF CRAIG 1645, 1647, 1655, 1659-62
JAMES BLAIR 1646
JOHN REID 1648
JAMES BOYLE 1653-54
JOHN GUTHRIE 1663
ROBERT CUNNINGHAM 1664-68
JAMES BLAIR 1670-71, 1676-77, 1682
ALLAN CUMMING 1672-73, 1674-75, 1679
JAMES BOYLE 1680-82, 1683-85
JOHN MONTGOMERIE OF BEOCH 1685-86
WILLIAM WALLACE OF SHEWALTON 1687-88
ALEXANDER CUNNINGHAM OF COLLELLAN 1689-94, 1696-97, 1701-03
THOMAS McGOUN OF SMITHSTON 1695
WILLIAM CUNNINGHAM 1698-1700, 1710-11, 1712-13, 1715-17, 1719-21
ALEXANDER, 9th EARL OF EGLINTON 1702, 1709
WILLIAM MARSHALL 1711-12
WILLIAM McTAGGART 1713-15, 1717-19, 1721-23, 1726-27, 1730-31, 1733-38
JAMES MARSHALL 1723-26, 1727-29, 1731-33
WILLIAM BARCLAY OF WARRIX 1729-30
JAMES CUNNINGHAM OF COLLELLAN 1738-40
JAMES BOYLE OF MONTGOMERIESTON 1740-42, 1744-46, 1748-50, 1752-54
JOHN GLASGOW 1742-44, 1746-48, 1750-52
JAMES CAMPBELL 1755-56
JOHN CUMMING OF MILGARHOLM 1756-58
CHARLES HAMILTON OF CRAIGHLAW 1758-60, 1762-64, 1768-70, 1772-74, 1776-78, 1780-82
ALEXANDER, 10th EARL OF EGLINTON 1760-62, 1764-66
WILLIAM EWING 1766-68
ARCHIBALD, 11th EARL OF EGLINTON 1770-72, 1778-80, 1782-84, 1786-88, 1790-92, 1794-96
ALEXANDER MONTGOMERIE OF COILSFIELD 1774-76
JOHN FERGUSSON OF GREENVALE 1784-86
HUGH MONTGOMERIE OF COILSFIELD 1788-90, 1792-94, 1796-97, continuing as
HUGH, 12th EARL OF EGLINTON 1797-98, 1800-02, 1804-06, 1808-10, 1812-14, 1816-18
ARCHIBALD, LORD MONTGOMERIE 1798-1800, 1802-04, 1806-08, 1810-12
GENERAL JAMES MONTGOMERIE 1814-16, 1818-21, 1823-24, 1826-69
ARCHIBALD MONTGOMERIE OF STAIR 1821-23, 1824-26, 1829-31
WILLIAM MONTGOMERIE OF ANNICK LODGE 1831-33
WILLIAM GRAY OF BLACKLAW 1833-37
WILLIAM THOMSON 1837-39
WILLIAM GILLIES 1839-41
WILLIAM B. SALMON 1841-45
ALEXANDER ROBERTSON OF WHITEHIRST 1845-50, 1864-66
THOMAS CAMPBELL OF ANNFIELD 1851-64
GEORGE BROWN 1867-72, 1880-81
JOHN PATERSON 1873-78
J. GILMOUR 1879
JOHN WRIGHT 1881-88
ANDREW WATT 1888-91
JAMES ARMOUR 1891-94
WILLIAM BRECKENRIDGE 1894-98

List of Provosts

CHARLES MURCHLAND 1898-1904
JAMES BORLAND 1904-07, 1910-16
ARCHIBALD KIRKLAND 1907-10
WALTER MUIR 1916-23
ROBERT M. HOGG 1923-28
PETER S. CLARK 1928-34
WILLIAM R. McKINLAY 1934-40
MATTHEW LAMONT 1940-46
ARCHIBALD GREEN 1946-50
THOMAS BIMSON 1950-52
JAMES McDONALD 1952
HAMILTON STEWART 1952-55
GEORGE M. DONALDSON 1955-60
JOHN KERR 1960-63
JOHN R. ANDERSON 1963-66
WILLIAM WILSON MUIR 1966-69
JOSEPH HUNTER 1969-72
ALEXANDER M. RUBIE 1972-75

List of Events

IRVINE	ELSEWHERE
	1090–1153 Bernard of Clairvaux
	1162–1227 Genghis Khan in China
	1180 Burgh established at Prestwick
	1181–1226 Francis of Assisi
1184 Castle first mentioned	1184–89 Kilwinning Abbey founded
	1190 Richard I goes on Third Crusade
1230–49 Burgh established	1205 Burgh established at Ayr
1233 Church first mentioned	1215 John of England's Great Charter
	1263 Battle of Largs
1260 Market cross mentioned	1265–1321 Dante
	1275 Marco Polo in China
1297 Bruce's capitulation at Irvine	1291 Swiss Confederation formed
	1314 Battle of Bannockburn
1367 Stone castle built at Seagate	1338 Hundred Years' War begins in France
1372 Robert II's charter to Irvine	1339 Building of Kremlin in Moscow
1380 Sir John Montgomerie acquires Eglinton	1350 Black Death reaches Scotland
1386 Tolbooth erected	1368–1644 Ming Dynasty in China
1391 Mill mentioned	1381 Peasants' Revolt in England
1399 Carmelite friars now arrived	
1413 Common Good formed	1431 Joan of Arc burned
1430 representation in parliament	1445 Gutenberg prints first book
	1452–1519 Leonardo da Vinci
	1453 Constantinople captured by Ottoman Turks
	1478 First Czar of Russia
1488 Montgomerie-Cunningham feud begins	1492 Columbus crosses Atlantic
	1498 Vasco da Gama sails to India
	1513 Battle of Flodden
1533 Bridge first mentioned	1517 Martin Luther begins Reformation
1539 Provost first mentioned	1519–21 First voyage round world
1560 Church becomes protestant	1538 Henry VIII begins English Reformation
1563 Visit of Mary Queen of Scots	1564–1616 William Shakespeare
1565 'Palace' built at Seagate	1588 Defeat of Spanish Armada
1572 Burgh School endowed	1592 Burgh established at Kilmarnock
1609 Montgomerie-Cunningham feud ends	1603 Union of Crowns under James VI and I
1645 Glasgow University at Irvine	1606–69 Rembrandt
1646 Seal of Cause to Incorporated Trades	1639 National Covenant
1665 Postal service to Edinburgh	1649 Charles I executed after Civil War
1677 New Quay built	1653 Taj Mahal built
1691 Loch drained	1679 Covenanters in Drumclog Rising
1694 Meal market built: cross demolished	1688 Glorious Revolution: William and Mary succeed

List of Events

IRVINE

1702 Earl of Eglinton made provost
1747 Council in charge of Marymass
1748 Bridge rebuilt
1749 Linen company formed
1750 Largest Ayrshire town, pop. 3,000
1753 Carters Society constituted
1756 Old ports demolished
1760 Last execution in Irvine
1762 Burgh coal pits sunk
1773 Parish Church rebuilt
1773 Relief Church formed
1776 Fullarton Street built
1779 John Galt born
1781 Robert Burns in Irvine
1784 Buchanites expelled

1807 Bogside Race Course opened
1816 Irvine Academy built
1826 Burns Club formed
1828 Bank Street opened
1829 Gas Works established
1833 First municipal election
1839 Railway station opened
1839 Eglinton Tournament
1860 Police Station built
1862 New Town House
1863 Trinity Church built
1871 Chemical Works established
1878 Water supply introduced
1881 Burgh extension
1890 Bank Street Railway station opened

1901 New Irvine Royal Academy opened
1914 First bus service
1915 First Council houses built
1915 Electric lighting introduced
1928 First Marymass Queen
1936 Last ships launched at Irvine
1941 Four killed in air raid
1959 Irvine Meadow first wins Scottish Junior Cup
1960 Burgh Industrial Estate opened
1965 Bogside Race Course closed
1967 Irvine New Town established
1973 Irvine bridge demolished
1975 End of Irvine as a burgh
1975 New Shopping Centre opened
1976 Magnum Leisure Centre opened

ELSEWHERE

1707 Union of Scottish and English Parliaments
1715, 1745 Jacobite rebellions
1740–95 James Boswell
1752 Change in calendar
1757 Plassey: British defeat French in India
1759 Quebec: British defeat French in Canada
1759–96 Robert Burns
1767 Ayrshire Turnpike Act
1768 Cook in the Pacific
1769 Murder of the 10th Earl of Eglinton
1769 James Watt's steam engine
1770–1827 Beethoven
1772 Failure of the Ayr Bank
1776 Declaration of American Independence
1789 French Revolution

1808 Kilmarnock-Troon railway
1815 Battle of Waterloo ends Napoleonic Wars
1818–83 Karl Marx
1832 Great Reform Act
1837–1901 Queen Victoria
1840 Penny postage introduced
1843 Disruption and formation of Free Church
1854 Crimean War
1857 Indian Mutiny
1861–65 American Civil War
1869 Suez Canal opened
1871 German Empire formed
1872 Ardeer Works opened
1888 Dunlop invents pneumatic tyre
1899 Boer War begins

1903 Wright brothers' flight
1909 Introduction of old age pensions
1914–18 First World War
1917 Russian Revolution
1922 BBC begin broadcasting
1926 General Strike
1928 Fleming discovers penicillin
1939–45 Second World War
1948 Transistor invented
1951 First nuclear power stations
1956 Suez crisis
1957–73 Vietnam War
1962 Cuban missile crisis
1969 First landing on the moon
1973 Britain joins European Economic Community

Present-day street plan overleaf.

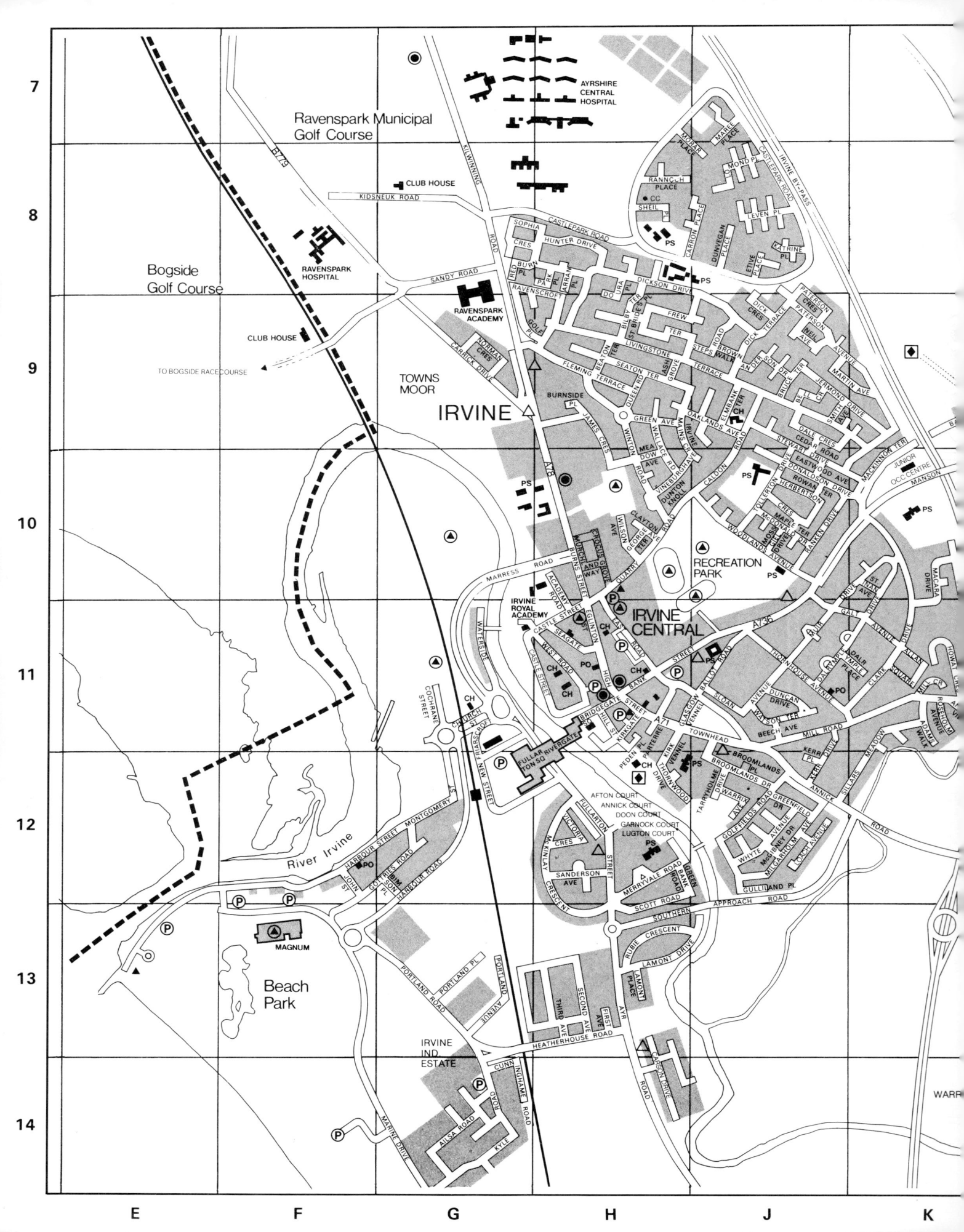

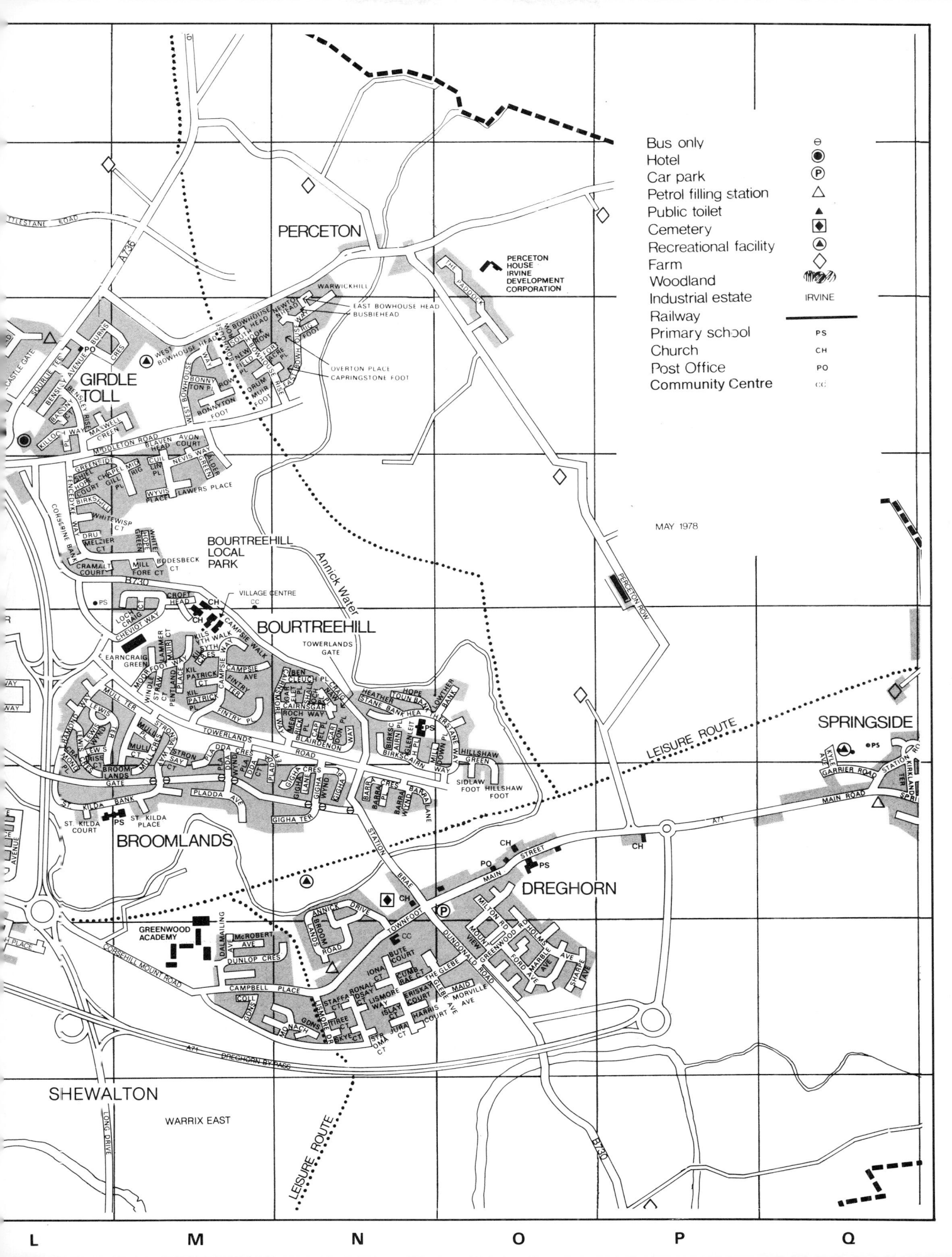

Index

Page numbers in *italics* refer to black and white illustrations and to Colour Sections *C1-C4, C5-C8, C9-C12, C13-C16*.
Places mentioned in the text may be identified from maps and plans on pages 5, 29, 39, 70, 73, 77, 78, 110, 111, 112, 119, 125, 127, 128, 134, 150, 169; the Street Plan on pages 248-249; and the Colour maps *C1-C12*, in particular *C6* for old place names.
Growth of the burgh is illustrated on the town plans on pages 10, 22, 42, 52, 66, 96, 162, 222.

A.A. Motor Services Ltd., 190, 210
A.1. Services Ltd., 190
Academy, 81, 97, 104, 109, 114, 117, 118, 122, 123, 124, 129, 132, 133, 136, 138, 156, 158, 163, 164, 174, 179, 182, 186, 189, 196, 197, 198, 201, 208, 212, 214, 215, 217, 218, 223, 224, 231, *113, 161, 175*
Adam Square, 188
Adams, Edward, 214
Adamson, Rev. Hugh M., 232
Adrain, William, 224
aerated water, 154, 156, 172, 177
Affleck, Robert, 224
Afton Court, 223
Ailsa Craig, 60
Ailsa Street, 227
air photographs, *3, 183, 185, 187, 202*
air raid, 200, 203
Air Raid Precautions, 198, 199, 200
Aird, Peter, 91
Airlie, John M., 186
Aiton, William, 116, 117
Albert Hall, 137, 138, 161, 177, 190, 191
alderman, 20
Alexander II, 5, 6, 7
Alexander III, 5, 30
Alexander, Bob, 224
Alexander, Friar, 30
Allan Square, 188
Allan, Alexander, 120
Allan, John, 74, 93, 101
Allan, William, 95
allotments, 182, 196
Alma Place, 188
ambulance, 149, 178, 195
America, 55, 59, 69, 77, 79, 88, 92, 93, 100, 101, 104, 128, 129, 142, 160, 180, 198, 210, 223, 227
Anderson Drive, 220
Anderson, George, 82
Anderson, Peter, 114
Anderson, Provost John R., 245
Anderson, Sam, 191, 192
Anderson, William, 113
Andrew or Andro, Mr. Thomas, 30, 41, 43
angling, 156, 158, 177
Annfield, 124, 232
Annick Centre, 231, *137*
Annick Court, 223
Annick Lodge, 95, 122, 130, 137, 154, 161, 168, 218, 228
Annick Road, 168, 206, 210

Annick School, 231
Annick Water, 2, 16, 17, 19, 21, 24, 30, 36, 40, 46, 58, 60, 83, 84, 94, 151, 156, 158, 187, 188, 232
Anti-burghers, 89
Apostolic Church, 131
archaeological sites, *C2*
archery, 60, 98, 117, 135, 136, 138, 139, 212
architects, 65, 114, 142, 164, 174, 207, 216, 228
Ardeer, 2, 4, 47, 74, 114, 149, 152, 174
Ardeer Explosives Works, 148, 152, 180, 199, 210, 228
Ardrossan, 6, 35, 38, 45, 65, 79, 109, 118, 140, 141, 142, 152, 168, 179, 186, 190, 204, 220, 230
Argyll, 5, 50
Argyll, Marquis of, 46
Armed Association, 108
Armour, Alexander, 104
Armour, John, 164, 174
Armour, Mrs. Jean, 104
Armour, Provost James, 244
armourer, 57
Armsheugh, 24, 30, 35, 39, 58, 114, 120, 154
Arran, 4, 83, 87, 101, 118, 172, 225
Arthur, 5
Arthur, Charles, 192
arts, 138, 157, 158, 176, 179, 212, 220, 229
Athenaeum, 138
athletics, 159, 224
Auchenharvie, 39, 55, 58, 79, 113, 117
Auld Dam, 156
Auld Water Gang, 2, 137
Auld, Sir Thomas, 30
Austin, Alfred, 156
aviation, 168, 182, 194
Ayr, 3, 6, 7, 8, 11, 14, 16, 20, 21, 26, 31, 34, 35, 46, 47, 50, 56, 57, 58, 59, 61, 64, 67, 70, 74, 76, 79, 82, 84, 85, 87, 92, 94, 95, 114, 118, 122, 126, 130, 131, 133, 140, 141, 142, 143, 146, 152, 154, 156, 158, 168, 186, 188, 190, 193, 231
Ayr Bank, 74, 85
Ayr Burghs, 64, 121, 124, 144, 176, 186, 196, 205
Ayr County Council, 149, 193, 194, 197, 198, 201, 204, 207, 214, 216, 218, 219, 223, 225, 226
Ayr Road, 146, 180, 183, 188, 231, *217*
Ayrshire, 7, 11, 54, 55, 56, 82, 122, 148, 154, 168, 172, 193

Ayrshire Banking Company, 119, 132
Ayrshire Central Hospital, 194, 204, 232
Ayrshire Dockyard Company, 184, 188, 202, 209
Ayrshire Educational Authority, 189, 190, 193, 197
Ayrshire Electricity Board, 188, 195
Ayrshire General Medical Service, 195
Ayrshire Metal Products Ltd., 210, 227
Ayrshire Writers and Artists Society, 229
Ayrshire Yeomanry, 108

Bachelors' Walk, 95
Back Riggs, 8, 21, 23, 24, 33, 71, 206
Back Road, 94, 116
badminton, 196, 212
Bailie of Cunninghame, 7, 20, 34, 35, 38, 40
bailiery, *see* Cunninghame
Bailiery court, 38, 65
bailies, of the burgh, 20, 21, 27, 43, 50, 51, 75
Baillie, James, 92
Baillie, Robert, 63
Baird, Sir John L., 186
Baird, William & Co. Ltd., 170, 184
bakers, 85, 172
Balgray, 24, 35, 114
Ballantyne, Ebenezer, 141
Ballantyne, Miss E.M., 175
Balliol, John, 6, 7, 31
Ballot Road, 58, 69, 95, 109, 188
Balsillie, Willis, 114, 120, 141
Baltic, 55, 79
bands, 118, 138, 158, 165, 176, 177, 191, 198, 208, 211, 220, 229, *177*
Bank of Scotland, 232
Bank Street, 85, 109, 116, 132, 135, 139, 141, 142, 154, 157, 160, 163, 168, 176, 177, 180, 184, 188, 190, 194, 196, 198, 206, 213, 220, 231, 232, *171, 187, 197*
Bank Street School, 156, 164, 165, 175, 181, 189, 197, 198, 214, 218, 219, 230, *187*
banks, 28, 29, 53, 74, 85, 95, 122, 123, 125, 132, 173, 188, 210, 232
Bannatyne, Miss E.M., 190
Bannatyne, Rev. Charles, 86, 87, 88
Bannockburn, 33
Baptist Church, 87, 89, 97, 116, 118, 131, 138, 147, 157, 160, 163, 174, 189, 197, 214, 220, 232
barbers, 84, 85
Barbour, Rev. Alexander, 214, 220

250

Index 251

Barclay family, 36, 45, 46, 116
Barclay, Alexander, 45
Barclay, Archibald, 45
Barclay, David, 45, 46, 62
Barclay, George, 87
Barclay, Hew, 46, 63
Barclay, John, 40, 45
Barclay, Margaret, 44, 45
Barclay, Provost Ninian, 40, 45, 46, 51, 244
Barclay, Provost Mr. Robert, 45, 46, 244
Barclay, Provost Robert, 41, 45, 244
Barclay, Provost William, 45, 46, 244
Barclay, Rev. George, 131
Barclay, Rev. Robert, 45
Barclay, Sir Robert, 46, 54, 56, 65
Barclaywards, 74
Barr, A.G. & Co. Ltd., 220
Barrowman, Robert, 186
Bartonholm, 2, 4, 25, 31, 35, 36, 37, 38, 74, 76, 83, 86, 94, 115, 116, 118, 120, 141, 142, 149, 154, 161, 168, 170, 184, 196, 223
bathing, 117, 137, 156, 177, 180, 189, 230
Baxter, Thomas, 8, 18, 28
baxters, 51
Beach park, 217, 223, 227, 228, 230, *C15*
Beattie, John, 219
Beattie, Mrs. Teresa, 226
Beattie, Robert, 226
Beaumont, John, 82
Beecham Pharmaceutical Divisions, 218, 227, *C15*
Begg, John S., 220, 237
Beith, 4, 26, 62, 68, 130, 132
bell foundry, 57
bell-ringer, 27, 51, 75, 114
Bell, Charles, 205
Bell, Susan, 205
bells, 54, 57, 86, 123, 146, 147, 148, 158, 182, 187, 196
Beltane, 44, 60
Bennett, William, 219, 231
Bennie, Peter, 224
Berry, Jim, 224
Bicker, Alex, 232, 237
Big Pie, 98, 212
beggit land, 9, 21
Bilby, James, 224, 225
billet master, 114, 123, 200
billiards, 177, 191, 196
Billingham, J.K., 226
Bimson, Provost Thomas, 245
bingo, 213, 232
Birkmyre, W., 144, 176
birleymen, 51, 69, 123, 146
Birrell, James, 62
Black Friars, 31
Black Hole, 70, 114
Black Man, 194
Blackie, Rev. James, 160
blacksmiths, *see* Smiths
Blackwood, James, 47
Blair, 122
Blair, Alan of, 36
Blair, Bryce, 37, 82
Blair, Colonel William, 122
Blair, Hugh, 37
Blair, Provost James, 40, 51, 91, 244
bleaching, 84, 103, 120, 141, 154

Block Works, 171
Blood, Sir Hilary, 214
Blue, Billy Bing, 152, 194
Board of Health, 113, 114, 118, 149, 192
boating, 147, 156, 157, 158, 182, 203, 208, 213
Boatstabs, 152, 188
Bodie, Doctor, 196
body-snatchers, 113, 118
Bog Ha', 102
Bogend, 2
Bogfaulds, Bogflatts, 24
Bogside, 13, 14, 25, 35, 37, 39, 56, 114, 140, 142, 154, 158, 177, 184, 186, 190, 202, 204, 212
Bogside Flats, 125, 137
Bogside Races, 98, 117, 124, 139, 147, 158, 164, 179, 186, 192, 196, 211
Bonney Forge (International) Ltd., 218
books about Irvine listed, 234
booksellers, 82, 100, 103, 118, 122, 173
Booth, General William, 174
Borland, Provost James, 180, 183, 245
Boswell, Sir James, 130
Bourtreehill, 35, 36, 86, 114, 154, 218, 219, 231, 232
Bourtreehill Coal Company, 154, 184
Bourtreehill House, 221
Bower Lodge, 116, 131, 234
Bower, H.R., 173
bowling, 98, 137, 155, 158, 177, 182, 190, 196, 208, 212, 224
Bowmans farm, 194
Bowmie's Close, 155
boxing, 224
boxmaster, 57, 84
Boyd of Kilmarnock, 18
Boyd, Edward, 30
Boyd, H.F., 158
Boyd, James, Lord, 38
Boyd, Martin, 171, *173, 174*
Boyd, Provost Thomas, 244
Boyd, Robert, Master of, 39
Boyd's Close, 155
Boyd's Hall, 131
Boyle Street, 180
Boyle, Colonel John, 99, 130
Boyle, David, Lord Justice, 93, 99, 141, 142, 152, 194
Boyle, Hon. Patrick, 99
Boyle, Patrick, 76
Boyle, Provost James, 46, 244
Boyles of Shewalton, 94
Boyll, Thomas, 40
Boyman, Adam, 18
Boyman, Robert, 18
Brady, Arthur, 186, 188, 193, 194, 196
Brady, Mrs. Margaret, 196
Brae, 76
Braid Close, 87
Braid Meadow, 24, 60, 71, 84
Braid, Andrew, 172
Brakanrig, John de, 35
Brand's Pure Spelter Works, 171
brandy, 55, 56, 58, 67, 68, 82
brass founding, 153, 171, 210, 227
Breckenridge, Provost William, 153, 165, 244

Brereton, Sir William, 15, 55
brewing, 57, 64, 83, 84, 120, 122, 141, 154, 172, 220
Bridge, 11, 12, 13, 14, 21, 26, 30, 43, 54, 58, 60, 68, 94, 95, 97, 109, 151, 163, 217, 218, 223, *81, 205, C13*
Bridgegate, 9, 11, 18, 19, 31, 43, 46, 86, 87, 94, 95, 109, 124, 131, 132, 139, 151, 153, 155, 156, 171, 173, 179, 182, 188, 190, 192, 198, 217, 218, 220, 227, 228, 232, *15, 99, 158, 201, 221, C13, C16*
Bridgegatehead, 85, 118, 139, 155, 194
Bridgend, 19
British Legion, 191, 196, 198, 219
British Linen Bank, 132, 173, 210
British Restaurant, 200, 220
British Textile Manufacturing Company, 184
British Workman's Public House, 157, 160
Brooks, Captain John, 113, 114
Broomlands, 35, 51, 74, 76, 81, 154, 184
Brougham, Lord, 129
Broun, John, 20, 40
Broun, Rankin, 28
Broun, Robert, 17, 21, 51, 55
Brown, Captain James, 129
Brown, Henry & Co., 171, 210
Brown, Hugh, 91, 139
Brown, James, 170, 197
Brown, James Lockhart, 92, 109
Brown, John, 82, 118, 184
Brown, Matthew, 225
Brown, Mr. Thomas, 30
Brown, Mrs. I.E., 231
Brown, Peter, 41
Brown, Provost George, 133, 147, 153, 163, 244, *148*
Brown, Rev. A.T., 232
Brown, Richard, 103
Brown, Robert, 46
Brown, Robert Burns, 139
Brown, Thomas, 65, 94
Browne, Johnne, 46
Browne, Rev. Andrew, 130
Brown's iron foundry, 184
Bruce, Mr., 109
Bruce, Robert, 6, 7, 31, 33, 34, 192, 230
Bruce's Close, 155
Brydeskirk, 4, 31, 36, 45, 46
Bryson, J.W., 189
Buchan, Mrs. Elspeth, 88, 89, 103
Buchanan, Archibald, 154
Buchanan, David, 56
Buchanites, 88, 89, 95, 103, 130, 131, 156, *91, 92*
burgage tenure, 8, 21
burgess fine, 21, 26
Burgess, Rev. Alexander, 214
burgesses, 8, 18, 20, 21, 23, 27, 41, 50, 51, 53, 57, 129, 165, 224
burgesses, honorary, 51, 54, 109, 129; *see also* freedom of the burgh
Burgh Anthem, 191
Burgh Architect, 207
Burgh chamberlain, 146, 207, 224
Burgh Court, 8, 20, 38, 51, 65
Burgh Factor, 69, 74, 75, 114, 123, 146, 207, 209, 226
burgh finances, 26, 74, 114, 124, 146, 178, 187, 193, 209, 225

252 *The History of Irvine*

burgh horse, 203, 211
burgh industrial estate, 227
burgh lands, 21, 23, 53, 71, 74, 79, 114, 118, 124, 142, 146, 178, 208, 223, *C7*
Burgh Mailes, 20, 27
burgh motto, 46
burgh of Fullarton, 59, 67, 135
burgh officers, 40, 51, 69, 75, 90, 113, 114, 123, 148, 156, 208, 224
Burgh Reform Acts of 1833, 123
Burgh School, *see* schools
Burgh Surveyor, 146, 151, 178, 181, 195
Burgher Kirk, 87, 89, 97, 113, 116, 118, 130, 136
Burn, Robert, 30, 43
Burns Statue, 148, 156
Burns Street, 84, 94, 132
Burns, Alex, 225
Burns, Isobel, 232
Burns, Lt. Col. William Nicol, 129
Burns, Major James Glencairn, 129
Burns, Mrs. Mary, 224, 225
Burns, Robert, 43, 63, 65, 68, 69, 88, 92, 95, 101-104, 129, 130, 137, 156, 160, 186, 191, 198, 221, 228, 229, *100*
Burns, William, 84
Burnside House, 232
Burrowland, 24, 41
bus service, 180, 189, 190, 194, 195, 210, 213, 218, 227
Busland or Bushlands, 24, 25
butchers, 85, 172
Bute, Marquess of, 163
butter, 25, 55, 81
bypass, 2, 194, 223, 227, 228

Cadgers Race Course, 98, 137, 154
Calderwood and Co., 141
Caldon Road, 214
Caldwell, 18, 19
Caldwell, Joe, 232
Caldwell, William, 40
Caledonian Arms, 208
Caledonian Foundry, 154, 171, 184
Caledonian Gas Company, 195
Caledonian Hall, 208
Caledonian Railway Company, 141, 153, 197, 199, 208
Caledonian Stadium, 212
Cameron, T. Martin, 224, 225
Cameronians, 89
Campbell of Loudoun, 18
Campbell, Bob, 232
Campbell, Colin, 46
Campbell, Ian, 225
Campbell, John, 44
Campbell, John, 74
Campbell, Knut, 231
Campbell, Lady Alice, 28
Campbell, Lord Neill, 46
Campbell, Mary, 104
Campbell, Miss, 116
Campbell, Provost Hugh of Loudon, 244
Campbell, Provost James, 65, 244
Campbell, Provost Thomas, 124, 140, 142, 160, 244
Campbell, R.F.F., 144
Campbell, Rev. Alexander, 87, 130
Campbell, Sir Archibald, 147

Campbell, Sir Hugh, 38
Campbell's Bridge, 140
Campbeltown, 64, 122, 186, 196
Canada, 100, 101, 147, 177, 224
Canadian Dominion Contact Lenses Ltd., 228
candlemaking, 123, 154
Candlemas, 91
Cannon, Jack, 196, 220, 224
Car ford, 58
Careers Office, 231
Carford, 12, 54, 58
Carfrae, James, 91
Carlyle, Mrs. Agnes E., 219
Carmelites, *see* friars
Carnduff, Mary, 232
carpenters, 26, 56, 114, 120, 156
carpet bowling, 196, 212
Carrick, 6, 31, 108
Carron Place, 231
Cars, 168, 173, 190, 207, 208, 213, 221
Carson, Jack, 225, 226, 230
Carters, 41, 58, 60, 77, 82, 84, 86, 90, 98, 113, 137, 138, 139, 147, 154, 165, 168, 173, 181, 182, 191, 192, 194, 198, 203, 208, 211, 221, 225, 230, *177, 225, 229, C14*
Carters Races, 98, 124, 137, 154, 211
Carters Society, 98, 114
Cassells, Rev. A.M., 197
Castle, 5, 6, 8, 11, 14, 31-35; *see also* Seagate Castle
Castle Street, 9, 84, 116, 168
Castlepark, 18, 203, 212, 223, 232
Castlepark Primary School, 219, 231
Cathcart, John, 37
Catholic Apostolic Church, 214
cattle, 15, 23, 24, 25, 59, 74, 95, 115, 126, 147, 208
cemeteries, 188, 193
Central Ayrshire, 204, 205, 217, 226
cess, 75, 114
Chalmer, James, 28
Chalmershouses or Chamberhouses, 35, 36, 115
chandlers, 85, 168
Channel Fleet, 138
Chapel Brae, 12, 19, 74
Chapel Lane, 9, 94, 232, *18*
Chapel Well, 4, 8, 12, 95, 113
Chapelford, 12
Chapelland, 24
chaplainries, 28, 41, 61
Chapman, Alexander S., 219, 231
chapter notes, 238-243
Charles I, 44, 45, 46
Chartists, 130
cheese, 55
Chemical Works, 142, 152
Chemstrand Ltd., 218, 227
cholera, 113, 114, 118, 120, 121, 125, 149
Christadelphian Ecclesia, 174, 189, 197, 214, 220, 232
Christian Brethren, 131, 160, 189, 197, 214, 220, 232
Christian Scientists, 214
Christmas, 44, 159, 164, 212
Christostome, Father, 44
Christy's Minstrels, 138

Churches and Religion, 4, 5, 6, 8, 11, 12, 27, 28-31, 41-45, 46-47, 51, 53, 57, 60-61, 70, 74, 75, 84, 85, 86-91, 95, 97, 103, 108, 109, 113, 114, 116, 123, 126, 130-31, 147, 158, 159-163, 174, 189, 196-97, 198, 213-214, 219-220, 225, 232
church discipline, 43, 44, 51, 61, 86, 89, 189
Church of Christ, 232
Church of the Nazarene, 197, 214, 220, 232
Church Street, *211*
churchyard, 43, 86, 104, 105, 109, 113, 125, 145, 146, 156, 174, 196, 198
cinemas, 168, 182, 190, 196, 198, 200, 212, 215, 220, 223, 224, 232
Circus, 138, 146, 157, 164, 182
Citizens Advice Bureau, 221, 223
Clark Drive, 188, 231
Clark, Ebenezer, 109, 135
Clark, Frances, 81
Clark, James, 109
Clark Marr and Co., 141
Clark, Provost P.S., 33, 184, 186, 187, 190, 191, 192, 245
Clark, Rev. A.V., 232
Clark, William, 93, 109
Clayton, Douglas, 205, 210, 224
cleansing, 124, 151, 168, 193, 207, 225, 226
Clement Wilson Foundation, 221, 227, 228
Clerici, Mr. John, 30
Clerk, Alan, 18
Clerk, Hugh, 18
Clerk, William, 62
Clerk's Acre, 69
Climax International, 227
Climie, James, 214
Climie, Rev. John, 189
Cloas, Barney, 87
clocks, 54, 70, 86, 87, 141, 182, 201, 208, 223
Clonbeith, 40, 51, 60
closes, 155
cloth, 15, 16, 26, 55, 85
Clydesdale Bank, 132, 155, 173, 210, 232
coach builders, 120, 172, 227
coaches, 95, 118, 154
coal mining, 15, 39, 55, 58, 60, 74, 76, 77, 79-83, 85, 118, 119, 120, 130, 132, 137, 141, 142, 145, 152, 154, 156, 158, 168, 184, 196, 204, 229, *80, C9, C10, C11, C12*
Coal road, 71
coastline, *C1, C2, C3, C4*
coat of arms, 27, 188
Cochrane Park, 157, 158
Cochrane Street, 153, 171, 178, 180, 184, 227
Cochrane, Benjamin and Joseph, 71
Cochrane, William, 219
Codona, Messrs., 208
Coffee Room, 117, 118, 138
Coker, William, 30
Commercial Academy, 135
Commercial Bank, 210
Common Good, 27, 53, 123, 153, 154, 179, 180, 182, 184, 208, 223, 224, 225
Common Seal, 27
common werkis, 21, 51
Communist Party, 196, 198, 203
Company of Scotland, 56, 64

Congregationalists, 131
Connel, Edward, 129
Conservatives, 144, 205, 224; see also Unionists
constables, 35, 37, 69, 75, 104, 114, 123, 130, 140, 146
constitution of the burgh, 50, 64, 120
Consumer Advice Centre, 231
Convalls Walls, 4, 18, 19
Convener of Trades, 105, 109, 122
Convent, 190
Convention of Royal Burghs, 53, 58, 76, 193, 223
Conway, Mrs. Agnes, 224
Cooperative Society, 156, 173, 175, 184, 191, 196, 197, 198, 208, 223
coopers, 16, 26, 56, 84, 85, 120, 137, 172, 176, 191, 212
Coopers Close, 155
copper, 85, 120, 152
cordiners, 16, 26, 56, 84, 191, 212
Corfield, Rev. George, 214
Corsan, Rev. George, 133, 135
Cosh, Rev. James, 174, 189
Cottagefield, 116
cotton, 77, 84, 120, 128, 141, 154
Cotton Row, 84, 87, 94, 95, 113, 128, 130, 149, 172, 183, 188
Coull, Lynn, 225
Council elections, 122, 123, 124, 144, 145, 147, 183, 186, 196, 201, 203, 204, 205, 211, 226
council houses, 168, 179, 180, 183, 184, 188, 193, 194, 201, 202, 206, 207, 208, 210, 221, 223, 225, 230, 217
council meetings, 51, 124, 178
councillors, 153, 186, 204, 225, 219
Couper, Matthew, 62
Cousar, Robert, 221
Cousin, Rev. William, 130
Covenanters, 35, 45, 46, 47, 47
Cow Fair, 88, 125, 146
Cowan, John, 154, 172
Cowan, Mrs., 200
Cowan, William, 225, 226, 230
Cowan's soap works, 184
Cowell, Sam, 138
Cowpers land, 25
craftsmen, 20, 26, 50, 56, 120
Craigens, 35, 37, 38
Craigie Carpets Ltd., 228
Craufurd of Giffordland, 18
Crawford, A., 231
Crawford, Archibald, 62
Crawford, David, 71
Crawford, E.H.J., 124, 144
Crawford, Archibald de, 30
Crawford, Isobel, 44
Crawford, Mrs., 200
Crawford, Rev. A.M., 130
Crichton, James, 85
Cricket, 136, 137, 154, 158, 177, 182, 190, 196, 212, 223
Crocefurd or Crossford, 25, 31
Croci, Luigi, 178
croquet, 137
Crosbie, 13, 43, 46, 54
Cross, 8, 11, 18, 19, 26, 51, 53, 54, 60, 95, 126, 184, 210, 212, 22
Crosshouse Hospital, 232

Crosskeys, 232
Crown Inn, 74, 98, 109
Cruickshanks, James, 122
Crumbie, William, 61
Culterland, 37
Cumbrae, 14, 54, 60
Cumming, Andrew, 62
Cumming, Patrick, 62
Cumming, Provost Allan, 244
Cumming, Provost Dr. John, 36, 62, 64, 65, 103, 244
Cumming, William, 91
Cummingfield, 36
Cundell, Anne Ross, 130
Cunningham family, 38, 39, 40
Cunningham, A., 184
Cunningham, Archibald, 39
Cunningham, Edward, 39
Cunningham, John, 40
Cunningham, Margaret, 37
Cunningham, Provost Alexander, 38, 40, 51, 56, 69, 85, 244
Cunningham, Provost William, 35, 37, 38, 40, 56, 57, 65, 91, 92, 244
Cunningham, Robert, 40, 55, 58, 117, 244
Cunningham, Sir Alexander, 40
Cunningham, Sir Richard, 38
Cunningham, Sir Walter Montgomerie, 95
Cunningham, Sir William, 144
Cunningham, Cunninghame, 3, 5, 6, 7, 8, 15, 18, 21, 25, 26, 28, 31, 35, 37, 44, 50, 58, 59, 63, 64, 65
Cunninghame District Council, 224, 225, 226, 228, 229, 232
Cunninghame House, 30, 140, 223, 226, 230
Cunninghame Poorhouse, 90, 120, 180, 185, 190, 204
Cunninghame South, 226
Cunninghame, William of, 28
Cunninghamhead, 40
Curdie, William, 225
curling, 98, 117, 137, 158, 177, 196
Currency, Note on, 328
customs, 14, 19, 20, 26, 27, 51, 55, 65, 67, 68, 74, 93, 132, 142, 186
custumars, 14, 20
cycling, 158, 159, 173, 196, 212

Dailly, 92
dairies, 172
Dale, Eric, 206, 209, 216, 226, 237
Dalry, 26, 131, 141, 149, 178
Dalrymple Drive, 188, 223, 227, 230
Dalrymple Wards, 24, 74, 115, 146, 188
Dalrymple, Charles, 65
Dalrymple, James, 63
dancing, 137, 142, 173, 177, 189, 196, 198, 201, 212, 213, 215, 229
Darleith, John, 13
Darnshaw, 113
darts, 212
Dates, Note on, 238
David I, 5, 6
Davidson, Major, 116
Davidson, William, 62
Deacon Convener, 56, 57, 62, 84, 98, 176, 182, 186
Dean of Guild, 51, 69, 95, 123, 125, 223
Dean, Alexander, 44
Dean, John, 44

Department of Health for Scotland, 194, 223
Derby, Earl of, 129
Dewar, Tom, 226
Deyn, Robert de, 29
Dick, Dean and Co., 141
Dick, James, 109, 225
Dick, Maxwell, 118, 120, 122, 137, 140, 148, 156, 100
Dick, Rev. Thomas, 214
Dickens, Lewis, 230
Dickie, Adam, 79
Dickie, Andrew, 40
Dickie, James, 146, 178, 244
Dickie, Rev. W.S., 160, 174, 189
Dickie, Tom, 226
Dickie, William, 91
Dickinson, Mrs. R., 231
Dickson, Rev. David, 45, 47, 63
Divet Park, 25, 71, 74
Dobbie, Joseph, 176
Dobie, James, 132, 234
Dollan, P.J., 186
Donaldson, Provost George, 209, 225, 245
Donohoe, George, 214, 219
Doole, John, 224
Doon Court, 223
Dougall, Rev. Robert 214
Doura, 24, 58, 76, 79 113, 114, 118, 120, 140, 141, 154, 161
Downs, Ian C., 226, 228
drainage, 113, 125, 151
drama, 55, 59, 60, 157, 158, 177, 190, 191, 196, 200, 211, 220, 229
Drape, Tom, 237
dredger, 151, 171, 184, 220
Dreghorn, 13, 17, 30, 31, 45, 76, 83, 94, 116, 138, 151, 170, 184, 193, 199, 214, 216, 218
Drill Hall, 158, 165, 177, 196, 223, 225
Drucken Steps, 4, 31, 58, 95, 103, 191, 223
druggist, 85, 95
Drumclog, 47
Drummer, 27, 47, 51, 69, 74, 114, 123
Drummond, Hugh, 219
Drummond, Margaret, 34
Drummond, Rev. James, 130
Drybridge, 216, 227
Duke of Edinburgh, 228
Duncan, Sir Andrew, 191, 208, 214
Dundonald, 4, 6, 12, 14, 17, 21, 28, 30, 34, 35, 51, 62, 77, 128, 130, 145, 146, 149, 151, 185, 193
Dunlop, Provost Allan, 46, 244
Dunlop, Robert, 114
Dunlop's inn, 114
Duntonknoll, Duntonknowe, 17, 23, 53, 60, 71, 74, 94, 120, 141, 146, 148, 154, 180, 194, 214
Dunwodyes, 46
Dyets Temple, 30, 31
Dykehead, 149

Eaglesham, 35, 38, 185
East Road, formerly East Backway, East Back Road, 8, 9, 23, 58, 87, 92, 94, 104, 115, 117, 135, 136, 137, 141, 151, 155, 158, 168, 177, 184, 193, 196, 208, 227, 228
East Back Road School, 136

East Road Public School, 164, 175, 189, 197, 231
Eastwoods Cement and Pipe Works, 210
Eaton, Trevor, 230
Eckford, Henry, 93, 100
Edinburgh, 9, 14, 20, 38, 40, 45, 46, 55, 58, 63, 104, 126, 149, 164, 186, 190
Edward I, 7, 31, 33
Edwards, Alexander, 83
Eglinton Arms, 98, 124, 133, 137, 151, 155, 177, 191, 232, *121*
Eglinton Castle, 39, 65, 117, 139, 149, 186, *41, 138, 189*
Eglinton estate, 21, 35, 37, 38, 41, 46, 50, 60, 65, 81, 95, 103, 105, 114, 116, 120, 154, 184, 185, 186, 218, 221, 227, 232
Eglinton Hunt, 139, 147, 186
Eglinton Iron Works, 141, 171
Eglinton Park, 200, 210, 227, 228
Eglinton Street, 9, 11, 63, 132, 149, 151, 165, 168, 211, 214, 220, 221, *25*
Eglinton Tournament, 139, 140, 141, *139*
Eglinton Trophy, 140
Eglinton, Bryce de, 24
Eglinton, Hugh de, 6
Eglinton, Lady Mary, 139
Eglinton, Ralph, 24
Eglinton, Robert, Master of, 40
Eglinton, Sir Hew of, 7, 24, 34, 35, 38, 63
Eglinton, 1st earl, 35, 37, 38, 39, 40
Eglinton, 3rd earl, 17, 26, 34, 39, 40
Eglinton, 4th earl, 40, 41
Eglinton, 5th earl, 18, 36, 44
Eglinton, 6th earl, 40, 44, 45, 46, 58, 60
Eglinton, 7th earl, 44, 54, 61
Eglinton, 8th earl, 40
Eglinton, 9th earl, 47, 64, 90, 185, 244
Eglinton, 10th earl, 35, 65, 71, 87, 93, 98, 244
Eglinton, 11th earl, 65, 76, 82, 88, 93, 94, 244
Eglinton, 12th earl, 36, 65, 86, 95, 98, 105, 108, 109, 114, 116, 117, 118, 122, 139, 185, 244
Eglinton, 13th earl, 37, 109, 125, 130, 136, 139, 140, 142, 154, 160, 185
Eglinton, 14th earl, 129, 139, 154, 155, 157, 160, 185, 186, *C12*
Eglinton, 15th earl, 147, 174, 181, 186
Eglinton, 16th earl, 186, 196, 202
Eglinton, countesses, 44, 136, 147
Eglinton, family, 18, 34, 35, 36, 116, 233; *see also* Montgomerie family
electric lighting, 151, 168, 179, 180, 183, 188, 204, 218
Electric Tramway proposed, 179
Elephant Inn, 63, 149, 206, *61*
Elizabeth, Queen, 208
emigration, 141, 154, 177
Empire Cinema, 182, 190, 196
epidemics, 21, 46, 63, 95, 102, 113, 149
Episcopalians, 214, 220, 232
Evangelical Union, 160
Ewing, C.L. Orr, 144, 176
Ewing, Provost William, 244
Ex-Servicemen's Club, 196, 211, 212

Factory Park, 84

Fairlie, Alexander, 82
fairs, 26, 40, 51, 53, 85, 95, 125, 139, 146, 147
farming, 25, 50, 71, 115, 125, 145
Farrell, James, 226
Fast Days, 160, 161, 163, 164
Fencedyke, 59, 74, 231
Fencibles, West Lowland, 69
Fergushill, 58, 76, 79, 140, 141, 154, 161, 170, 184
Ferguson Bequest, 129, 133, 136, 214
Ferguson, John, 129, 133, 142, 164
Ferguson, Provost John, 244
Ferrie, Henry, 196
feu-ferme, 20, 27
feuing, 24, 26, 30, 50, 53, 64, 74, 76, 97, 115, 116
Finnie, A. & Son, 170, 184
fire brigade, 71, 75, 95, 124, 149, 151, 158, 180, 188, 200, 204, 227, 230
fires, 17, 21, 53, 90, 94, 95, 97, 186, 231
Fiscal, 51, 123, 145, 146
fishing, 13, 14, 15, 16, 25, 27, 35, 53, 56, 64, 67, 77, 120, 135, 171
Fishmarket, 53
Fitzalan, Walter, 5, 6
FitzGerald, Father William, 131
Flanagan, David, 153, 171, 184, 210, 227
flax, 84, 85, 102
Fleming, Dr., 75, 82
Fleming, John, 18
Fleming, Rev. Archibald, 130
Fleshmarket, 19, 31, 53, 69, 74, 130, 136, 142
Fletcher, John, 113
Flodden, 38
floods, 76, 83, 99, 109, 124, 232, 238
Flow Laboratories, 227
football, 109, 158, 177, 178, 182, 190, 196, 198, 199, 212, 224
footbridges, 33, 151, 180, 195, 218
forces, military, 67, 146, 149, 155, 182, 200, 206
fords, 12, 54, 188
foresters, 69, 123, 146, 176
Forum, 228
Foulds, W. Iain, 218, 231
Foulis, John, 235
Foullartoun, John, 14
Foullertoun, Adam, 30
Foullertoun, George, 13
Foullertoun, Rankin, 30
Fowlertoun, Alan de, 12
France, 5, 15, 19, 55, 56, 59, 131, 181, 200, 209
Frances, Joseph, 102
franchise, 20, 122, 130, 144, 186, 205, 226
Francis, William, 24, 35
Frank, James, 57
Fraser, Rev. D.M., 220
Freckleton, Willie, 233
Free Church, 130, 132, 147, 159, 160, 163
Free School, 109, 135, 136, 138
freedom of the burgh, 109, 118, 129, 130, 147, 184, 196, 208, 220, 230; *see also* burgesses, honorary
Freemasons, 98, 103, 120, 137, 138, 176, 198, 221

Frew, Robert, 82
friars, 12, 13, 30, 41, 61, 130
Friars Croft, 12, 13, 30, 33, 74, 84, 97, 113, 116, 217, 223, 226
Friars Ford, 12, 30, 33
Friarsgate, 9
friendly societies, 90, 118, 119, 137, 165, 176, 197, 204
Friersmill, 17, 24, 30
Fullarton, 4, 12, 13, 30, 31, 43, 46, 68, 74, 83, 84, 87, 89, 94, 116, 132, 140, 141, 144, 145, 146, 149, 151, 152, 154, 168, 226
Fullarton burgh, 59, 67, 135
Fullarton Chapel of Ease, 130
Fullarton Church, 130, 136, 140, 161, 163, 189, 196, 213, 218, 219, 220, 232, *135*
Fullarton Fabrications, 227
Fullarton Free Church, 130, 136, 139, 160, 163, 174
Fullarton Hotel, 178
Fullarton Mill, 17
Fullarton Old Place, 33
Fullarton Place, 13, 163, 217, *207*
Fullarton Prisoner of War Camp, 206
Fullarton schools, 136, 163, 164, 190, *135*
Fullarton Street, 94, 97, 129, 135, 141, 149, 154, 171, 172, 184, 193, 197, 206, 210, 214, 223, *83, 160*
Fullarton Works, 153
Fullarton family, 11, 12, 13, 14, 30, 37
Fullarton, Adam, 37
Fullarton, Bailie Robert, 89, 101, 123, 142, *102, 124*
Fullarton, Colonel Stewart Murray, 94, 115, 142
Fullarton, Colonel William, 94, 97
Fullarton, George, 43, 74
Fullarton, James, 46
Fullarton, John, 30, 91
Fullarton, William, 54, 59, 67
fullers, 16, 56
Fulton and Wylie Ltd., 227
Fulton, John, 154

Gailes, 13, 31, 94, 118, 120, 140, 149, 155, 182, 200, 204
Gailes Road, 151, 170, 178, 184, 188, 199, 210
Galloway, 5, 6, 34, 35
Gallowmure, 24
Gallows Well, 155
Gallowshill, Gallowsknoll, Gallowsknowe, 11, 20, 31, 44, 82, 83, 94, 108, 178
Galt Avenue, 188
Galt House, 228
Galt, Alexander, 91
Galt, John, 31, 69, 70, 74, 84, 88, 90, 93, 94, 95, 100, 101, 105, 108, 118, 123, 132, 156, 229, *69, 98, 102*
Galt, John, 98
Galt, Mary, 101
Galt, Robert, 17
Galt, William, 100, 101
Gammage, A.H., 189
gaoler, 70, 114, 123
Gardner, Jean, 103, 104
Gardner, John, 103

Garnock Court, 223
Garrick, David, 99
Garven, Hugh, 40, 51, 84
Garven, Janet, 57
Garven, Thomas, 62, 122
Gas Residual Products Company, 152, 171
gas works, 104, 109, 116, 148, 151, 163, 165, 178, 179, 188, 204, 208, *187*
Gaw, Harry, 224, 233
Gaw, Sam K., 221, 226, 229
Gemmel, John, 83, 91
Gemmell, George, 35
Gemmell, Zacharias, 56
General Assembly, 45, 86, 116, 123, 147, 174, 196, 197, 213, 224
General Strike, 184, 185
George Cinema, 213, 220, 232
George V, 198
George VI, 198, 208
George, Provost Archibald, 14, 244
ghost, 16
Gibson, Bert, *225*
Giffen, 6, 40
Gilkinson, Thomson & Co., 120
Gillies, David, 178, 187
Gillies, Provost William, 119, 122, 132, 244
Gilmour, Alexander, 173
Gilmour, J.H., 153
Gilmour, Provost J., 244
Girdle Toll, 2, 194, 212, 216, 227, 228, 231, 232
Glasgow, 15, 17, 28, 58, 59, 77, 79, 82, 83, 91, 94, 95, 109, 113, 114, 118, 120, 137, 140, 141, 152, 158, 168, 172, 177, 186, 190, 210
Glasgow and South Western Railway Company, 141, 153, 154, 184
Glasgow Bank crash, 185
Glasgow Herald, 118, 135, 139
Glasgow Savings Bank, 210
Glasgow University, 45, 46, 63, 113, 135, 203, 208
Glasgow Vennel, 9, 58, 65, 84, 87, 88, 94, 95, 102, 103, 132, 138, 148, 155, 160, 168, 186, 191, 195, 197, 218, 220, 223, 228, 229, 230, 233, *100, C16*
Glasgow-Irvine Society, 147, 157, 178, 191, 220
Glasgow, Provost Jean, 64, 244
Glasgow, Robert, 115
Glasgow, 2nd earl, 99
glass, 17, 60, 152
Glassauch, John of, 20
Glassites, 131
Glebe, 41, 44, 116, 206
Glebe Aiker, 25
Glebe Primary School, 231
Glen, Robert, and Son, 210
Glencairn, earls, 18, 38, 40, 41, 50, 63
Glengarnock Iron Company, 141
glover, 26
Glover, Jean, 104
Goatfields, Gottfields, Goalfields, Golfhills, *see* Golffields
Goddard, Harry, 157
Goldie, Rev. David, 232
golf, 158, 177, 178, 180, 182, 188, 190, 194, 196, 203, 208, 212, 224, 230

Golffields, 12, 25, 33, 57, 74, 84, 87, 95, 98, 136, 137, 142, 154, 165, 172, 180, 186, 192, 195, 206, 208, 211, 220, 223, 231, *88*
Good Templars, 157, 160, 165, 176, 186, 201
Gooslone, 25
Gordon, James, 224, 225, 226
Gosling, David, 226
Gottries, 94, 120, 151, 171, 188
Goudie, Bailie, 144
Graham, Father Ambrose, 163
Graham, James, 189
Graham, John, 30, 63
Graham, Lieutenant Nicol, 129
grain, 15, 53, 55, 67, 68, 79, 84, 126, 142, 146
gramophones, 168
Grand National, 158
Granny Stane, 2, 12, 156, 192, *4*
grassum, 53, 74
Gray, Bailie, 79
Gray, David, 120, 122, 123, 132, 141, 146, 164, 178, 234
Gray, Dr. William, 148
Gray, Elliot, 225, 226
Gray, John, 91, 92
Gray, John, 233
Gray, Provost William, 244
Gray, Rev. John, 160
Gray, Sir William, 226
Gray, William, 122
Green, 9, 12, 25, 26, 43, 59, 79, 81, 82, 120, 124, 137, 141, 146, 156, 157, 168, 172, 177, 178, 182, 188, 189, 191, 198, 200, 203, 208, 217, 220
Green, Councillor, 183
Green, George, 168
Green, Mrs., 158
Green, Provost Archibald, 183, 204, 245
Greenbank, 184
Greenfield, 115
Greenock, 76, 77, 79, 93, 100, 101, 118, 158
Greenvale, 95
Greenwood Academy, 219, 231
Greenwood Rows, 170
Gregor, Rev. John, 161
Greig, Alexander, 197
Greig, Rev. James, 232
greyhound racing, 196, 212
Grip, Groop, Gruip, Grupe, 9, 12, 29, 53, 94, 116, 131, 157, 160, 190, 194, *18*
Grip Gutter, 9, 53, 60
Groatholm, 24, 71
guild brethren, 20
Guild Closs, 87
Gulden Wells, 156
Gulliland, 24, 74, 91, 156
Gulliland, Bryce, 101
gunpowder, 57
gunsmith, 120
Gushet House, *159*
Guthrie, George, 220
Guthrie, Provost John, 244

Haggarty, James, 184
Hair, John, 36
Hair's mill, 36
Hairsmill, 16

halberds, 27, 40, 51, 98, 123, 165, 224, 230
Halfway, 54, 67, 87, 94, 95, 97, 99, 113, 114, 116, 129, 132, 135, 140, 145, 149, 151, 168, 175, 198, *57*
Hall, John N., 191
Hall, Thomas, 191
Hallowe'en, 60, 159
Hamilfield, 116, 158, *117*
Hamilhill, 9, 53, 87, 188
Hamilhill Academy, 136
Hamilhill chapel, 130, 131, 135, 136, 161
Hamilhill Lane, 170
Hamilton, Alexander, 58
Hamilton, Arthur, 40
Hamilton, David, 109, 114
Hamilton, Gavin, 44
Hamilton, J.M., 196
Hamilton, John, 63, 79, 103
Hamilton, Provost Charles, 65, 71, 76, 84, 103, 244
Hamilton, Robert, 36, 41
Hamilton, William, 56, 63, 65, 93
Hamilton, Rev. William, 47
hammermen, 16, 26, 56, 85, 120, 176, 191, 212
Hands, Rev. Leslie, 232
hangman, 46, 51, 70
harbour, 3, 4, 8, 13, 14, 15, 20, 21, 27, 46, 53, 54, 58, 60, 67, 74, 76, 77, 79, 81, 94, 95, 109, 113, 114, 118, 119, 140, 141, 142, 151, 152, 153, 154, 155, 156, 163, 165, 168, 170, 171, 173, 184, 189, 190, 194, 197, 202, 209, 211, 216, 217, 220, 227, 228, *55, 78, 128, 129, 148, 150, 157, 173, 185, 202, C15*
Harbour Arts Centre, 212, 220, 228, 229
Harbour Festival, 230
Harbour Flats, 208
Harbour Force Company, 153
Harbour Mission, 197, 208, 212
Harbour Street, 120, 160
harbourmaster, 69, 76
Hardie, A.W., 216, 226
Hardie, Rev. Joseph, 214
Harperland, 146
harriers, 196, 212
Harris, Rev. J.W.F., 220, 232
Hay, James, 62
Hay, John, 218
Hayholm, 23, 74, 115
Headless Lady's Gott, 16
Heatherhouse, 210
Heatherhouse Road, 206
Heathfield, 20, 44, 116, 200, 207, 217, 223, 230
heckling shop, 53, 104, 228, 229, *100*
hemp, 79
Henderson, Mr., 91
Henderson, Rev. James, 116
Henderson, Walter, 184
Henderson, William, 152, 171, 232, *149*
Henry, George, 158
Hepburn, George, 225
Herbertson, Mrs. Elizabeth, 225, 226
Herd, Ian, 230
herds, 23, 24, 69
heritors, 60, 86, 108, 126, 146
herring fishing, 15, 16, 56, 77, 120, 171
hides, 15, 26, 79, 152

Index 255

Hiemyre, 24, 59, 74
Higgins house, 74
High Street, 4, 9, 17, 18, 23, 24, 26, 31, 45, 46, 53, 65, 85, 88, 95, 98, 99, 100, 102, 103, 104, 105, 113, 116, 117, 118, 124, 129, 131, 132, 137, 140, 142, 146, 151, 155, 157, 165, 168, 173, 174, 177, 180, 184, 186, 190, 191, 192, 194, 208, 218, 220, 223, 228, 232, *16*, *17*, *24*, *25*, *27*, *33*, *42*, *68*, *98*, *121*, *133*, *145*, *170*, *199*, *C14*
Highland Games, 211
Highlands, 15, 16, 65, 139
Hill Street, 8, 9, 92, 94, 101, 115, 132, 218, 223, 225, *14*, *C16*
Hill, John C., 197
Hinchcliffe, Joseph, 161
Hirun, 4, 5
Hislop, James, 91
hockey, 196, 212
Hog, Mr. William, 30
Hogan, Fr. Joseph, 189, 197
Hogg, John, 198
Hogg, Miss Margaret, 198
Hogg, Provost R.M., 175, 186, 188, 189, 191, 197, 198, 221, 245
Hoggarth, John, 115
Holehouse, 24, 30, 35
holidays, 156, 188, 189, 190, 208, 213, 228
Holland, 47, 55, 59, 79
Holmes, James, 131
Holmes, Robert, 146
Holmes, William, 154
Holms, Robert Rankin, 129
Holy Trinity, 28
Home Guard, 200, 202
Hood, Andrew, 224, 236
Hood, Inspector Tom, 200
horse fair, 85, 125, 146
horse racing, 60, 98, 117, 139, 158, 186, 196, 212, 228, 230, *229*
horses, 55, 59, 147
Horssey, Philip de, 35, 37
horticulture, 139, 142, 158, 211, 212
hosiery, 184, 227
Hosiery Manufacturing Company, 172, 184, 196, 210
Hospitallers, 31
hospitals, 113, 114, 128, 149, 151, 178, 180, 182, 187, 188, 194, 204, 232, *181*
hotels, 221, 228, 232
housing, 17, 60, 94, 115, 116, 132, 149, 151, 155, 156, 163, 180, 218, 223, 232; *see also* council houses
Houston, Gavin, 62
Houston, William, 23
Howat, Hugh, 233
Howden, Rev. R. Cassels, 131
Howe Mill, 16, 17, 33, 36, 83, 115
Howie, Hugh, 225
Howie, J. & R., 184
Howie, Jonet, 19
Howie, R.C., 164
Howie, Tom, 230
Hume, Malcolm, 200
Hunter, James, 85
Hunter, John Kelso, 118, 126
Hunter, Mrs., 89
Hunter, Patrick, 88, 103

Hunter, Provost Joseph, 216, 224, 225, 245
Hunter, W., 173
Hunter's Bank, 119, 132
Hunterston, 209, 216
Hurlingford Pool, 156
Hutcheson, Charles, 83, 99
Hutcheson, Rev. George, 47
Hutchison, John, 57
Hutton, Allan, 114, 118
Hyster Ltd., 218, 227, 228

ice cream, 156, 168, 173, 177, 200
illegitimacy, 155, 182
Imperial Chemical Industries, 184, 199, 210; *see also* Ardeer
Incorporated Trades, 26, 50, 56, 57, 58, 64, 65, 67, 82, 84, 85, 86, 90, 98, 104, 119, 120, 121, 122, 129, 137, 157, 165, 176, 186, 191, 198, 203, 212, 213, 221, 224, 230, *53*
Independent Labour Party, 144, 182, 186, 195, 198
Industrial Estate, 218
Industrial School, 104, 136, 160, 163, 164
industries, 79, 118, 120, 141, 142, 152-154, 155, 171-173, 182, 205, 209, 227-228, 233, *202*, *C15*
indwellers, 8, 14, 21
Indy Electronics Inc., 227
Information Centre, 228
Inglis, John, 229
Ingram, James, 142
Innes, Andrew, *92*
Innes, James, 123, 178
Innes, John, and Co., 84
inns, 117, 135, 155
Insch, Isobal, 44
insurance agents, 173
Intec West Ltd., 228
Inveraray, 64, 122, 186
Ireland, 5, 15, 46, 47, 50, 54, 55, 59, 67, 68, 69, 76, 79, 87, 104, 131, 139, 142, 152, 154, 163, 209
iron, 55, 79, 141, 152, 171, 210
Irvine and District Water Board, 178
Irvine and Fullarton Property Investment Building Society, 156
Irvine Burns Club, 104, 105, 118, 130, 137, 157, 175, 176, 186, 189, 191, 198, 204, 211, 221, 224, 225, 228, 230, 233, 236, 239
Irvine Development Corporation, 216, 217, 218, 220, 223, 224, 226, 228, 229, 232, 233
Irvine Express, 156
Irvine family, 4
Irvine Forge Company, 153
Irvine Foundry, 141
Irvine Herald, 148, 151, 152, 153, 156, 220, 232, 237
Irvine in California, 223, 227
Irvine Iron Works, 171
Irvine Mains, 74, 115, 142, 154, 188, 206, 223, 226
Irvine Meadow, 159, 178, 190, 196, 212, 220, 224, *213*
Irvine Orator, 144
Irvine Shipbuilding and Engineering Company, 153

Irvine Smith and Machine Works, 153
Irvine Spirit Trade Defence Association, 176
Irvine Times, 156, 220, 232, 237
Irvine Victoria, 177, 190, 194, 196, 212
Irvine, earl of, 46
Irvine, Viscount, 46
Irvine, William, 214
Irvingites, 131
Isle of Man, 67, 68

Jack, Archibald, 189
Jack, Rev. James, 87
Jack, William, 91, 135
Jackson, John, 186
Jacobites, 46, 65
Jail Close, 155
James I, 28
James II, 21
James IV, 21, 30, 40
James V, 21, 40
James VI, 24, 26, 40, 44, 57, 61
James VII, 47, 51
Jardine, William D., 214
Jehovah's Witnesses, 214
Jenny's Burn, 60
John Galt Primary School, 214, 219, 231
John Street, 151
Johnston, James, 123, 178, 234
Johnston, John, 186, 192, 208
Johnston Place, 183
Johnstone, R., 180
Jones, John Paul, 69
Joseph, Sister Mechtilde, 190, 214
Joyce, Fr. Thomas, 189
judo, 212, 224

Kairde's Yairds, 25
Kanest, 18
Keane, Father Thomas, 161
Keir, David, 158
Kelly, Rev. James, 160
Kempt, Mr. James, 92
Kennedy, Alexander, 40
Kennedy, James, 56
Kennedy, Sir Thomas, 38
Kennedy, Thomas, 121
Kenneth, A. & Sons, 170, 184
Kerr, Edward, 56
Kerr, Joe, 225
Kerr, Provost John, 245
Kerr, Rev. Archibald, 160
Kerr, Robert, 154
Kerr, Robert & Son, 171
Kerr, William, 154
key-masters, 85
Kidsneuk, 25, 37, 74, 82, 115, 142, 208
Kilbirnie, 26, 43, 45, 65, 226
Kilmarnock, 6, 26, 31, 44, 46, 56, 57, 58, 59, 63, 76, 77, 79, 88, 91, 94, 101, 114, 118, 121, 133, 140, 141, 142, 143, 144, 154, 164, 168, 175, 179, 180, 188, 190, 193, 204, 215, 216, 217, 228
Kilmaurs, 6, 26, 28, 38, 54, 60, 77, 83, 87
Kilmaurs, Lord, 38
Kiln Court, 230
Kilwinning, 3, 4, 5, 6, 9, 24, 38, 51, 58, 60, 63, 76, 81, 82, 84, 131, 140, 141, 149, 151, 154, 155, 161, 170, 174, 178, 193, 199, 206, 214, 216, 218, 220, 226, 228, 231

Index 257

Kilwinning Abbey, 6, 28, 36, 41, 44, 220
Kilwinning, Abbot of, 18
Kilwinning Academy, 231
Kilwinning Road, 94, 116, 125, 129, 151, 162, 168, 191, 194, 197, 206, 208, 212, 217, 218, 223, 227, 232, *115, 117*
King, Dr., 114
King, Rev. Alexander, 196
Kings Arms, 98, 102, 124, 131, 138, 147, *121*
Kirby, Dennis, 216, 226
kirk session, 43, 44, 56, 61, 74, 86, 89, 91, 130
Kirk Vennel, 9, 85, 113, 116, 132, 180, 183, 188, 192
Kirkgate, 8, 9, 11, 12, 18, 19, 29, 30, 31, 38, 45, 46, 85, 94, 113, 132, 137, 163, 206, 214, 220, *23, 33*
Kirkgatehead, 53, 62, 91, 93, 95, 108, 113, 120, 124, 135, 136, 178, 182, *C16*
Kirkland, Provost Archibald, 151, 178, 179, 186, 245
Knadgerhill, 24, 25, 31, 33, 58, 59, 71, 74, 79, 95, 115, 124, 125, 142, 188, 191, 223, 239
Knights Templars, 31
Knowe, 9
Kyle, 3, 5, 6, 7, 11, 12, 13, 18, 108
Kyle Cinema, 196, 213
Kyle Terrace, 183
Kyle, James, 191

Labour Party, 186, 195, 196, 203, 205, 224, 226
Lady Eglinton's School, 136, 163, 164
Lady Sophia Pit, 154
Ladyland, 45, 63, 65
Laird's blockworks, 153, 171, 184, 210, 228
Lambie, David, 217, 226
Lammas, 26, 44
Lamont, Provost Matthew, 201, 208, 245
land tax, 75
Lang Calsay, 54
Landsborough, Rev. David, 133
Langhurst wood, 24
Langlands, Alexander, 126
Langside, 41, 98
Lapraik, John, 92
Largs, 3, 6, 7, 21, 26, 31, 65, 68, 117, 196
laundries, 154, 172, 177, 210
Lawson, John, 200
Lawson, Rev. A.A., 214
Lawthorn, 2, 31, 120
lawyers, 85, 120
leather, 16, 26, 55, 57, 152
Leckie, Rev. John, 214
Lee, Robert, 161
Leechman, Rev. John, 131
Leslie, Bishop, 15
Leslie, James, 149
Leslie, Mr. George, 92
Letters, Father Frederick, 163, 174, 176, 189
Lewis, Mrs., 158
Liberals, 144, 155, 176
libraries, 118, 138, 157, 163, 179, 198, 220, 230
lifeboat, 142, 147, 165, 172, 189, 201, 208, 220, 232, *172*
lifeboat shed, 189, 201, 208

Lindsay, J.B. and Co., 132
Lindsay, Matthew, 62
Lindsay, Robert, 225, 226, 230
linen, 53, 57, 64, 84, 85, 102, 120
Linen Company, 64, 84
liquor, 82, 139, 147, 172, 192
Literary and Social Institute, 138, 147, 157, 160, 165, 168, 176, 177, 182, 190, 191, 196, 201, 212, 220
Lithgow, Sir J. & H., 184
Littlestone, 120
Livingstone, Miss M.E.G., 219, 231
Lloyd George Factory, *see* Royal Ordnance Factory
LMS Railway Company, 184, 199
Loach, Fred, 225
Local Authority, 145, 148, 149, 151, 152, 178
loch, 2, 8, 11, 17, 23, 25, 31, 43, 58, 59, 60, *C3, C4, C6*; *see also* Scottish Loch, Trindlemoss
Loch Lomond Vaults, 188, 198
Lochmill, 16, 17, 58, 60, 79, 83, 84, 95
Lochwards, 16, 24, 74, 105, 115
Lockhart, William, 224
Lodge Irvine St. Andrews, 98, 137, 157, 176
Logan, Rev. Thomas S., 232
Longford, 142
Lople, 18
Lorne, Lord, 46
Loudoun, 3, 6, 18, 28
Loudoun Street, 94, 168, 191, *209*
Loudoun Street School, 136, 163, 164, 175, 189, 190, 197, 198, 208, *136*
Loudoun-Montgomery School, 198, 214, 218, 219, 230, 231
loupingstanes, 95
Low Green, *see* Green
Lugton Court, 223
Lumsden, Alexander, 136, 164, 165
Lumsden, Harry, 191
Lyle, William, 135
Lyle's Free School, 136, 163

McAllister, Mrs., 176
McAngus, William, 190, 197
Macara, Rev. Alexander, 189, 196, 213, 219, 220
Macaulay, Rev. R.S., 130, 160
McClintock, Mr., 141
McConnel, James, 109
McCormack, Sam B., 231
McCoul, John, 47
McCririck, William, 120
McDonald, Alexander B., 208, 239
Macdonald, Lord of the Isles, 114
McDonald, Provost James, 245
McDougall, Duncan, 120, 141
McDougall, Malcolm, 153
McEwan, Mae, 218, 229
McFade's Rigg, 25
McFarlane's Hill, 9, 71
McGavin, Robert, 141
McGill and Co., 153
Macgillivray, Pittendreigh, 156
McGorran, James, 126
McGoun, Provost James, 244
McGoun, Provost Thomas, 51, 56, 244
MacGregor, John D., 198

McGuire, 126
Maguire, Father Osmund, 131, 136
McGuire, Murdoch, 231
McHarg, Alistair, 224
McHarg, Martina, 192
McInally, Hamilton, 196, 212, 220
McIver, John, 91
McJannet, A.C., 146, 173
McJannet, Arnold, 5, 6, 11, 31, 33, 194, 198, 224, 234, 236
McJannet, William, 132, 138, 146, 157
Mackaile, Hew, 46
Makeachne, Martin, 38
McKelvie, Mary, 92
Mackenzie, Alexander, 147
Mackenzie, Dr. John, 104, 113, 115, 186, *101*
Mackenzie, J.W., 234
Mackenzie, Major D.M., 200
Mackenzie, Rev. A.J.R., 214
Mackie and Thomson, Messrs., 171
Mackie, Mrs. Isa, 233, 235
McKinlay, Provost W.R., 194, 201, 206, 208, 245
McKinnon Terrace, 223
McKnight, Rev. William, 47, 86
McLachlan, Father John, 131
McLachlan, Rev. Neil, 189, 197
McLaren, Rev. Archibald, 130
McLauchlan, Walker, 137
McLean's boats, 208
McLellan, Mrs. Jenny, 224
McLeod, Ian, 226
Macluskie, Rev. James, 160
McManus, Private John, 114, 118
Macmillan, Alexander, 147, 214, 218, 224, 236
Macmillan, Daniel and Alexander, 118
Macmillan, Duncan, 118
McMillanites, 89
McMusarthill, 25
MacNab, Allan, 109
McNab, Samuel, 189
McNab, Rev. Samuel, 196
McNab, Rev. Samuel, 214
McPhail, Alistair, 190
Macpherson, J.H.F., 226
Macreadie, Patrick Mure, 141
Macredie, John, 142, *C12*
Macredie, Robert, 115
Macredie, William, 116
McTaggart, Miss E.D., 231
McTaggart, Provost William, 56, 79, 244
McUnstanhill, 25
macer, 51
Madras school, 136, *135*
Magisterial Bench, 139
Magistrates' Hill, 126, 139, 198, 200, 230, *67*
Magnesia House, 120
Magnum Leisure Centre, 223, 227, 228, 229, 230, 233, *C15*
Mair, Henry, 229
Malachy, Sister, 190
malt, 30, 63, 67, 84, 85, 87, 102
manse, 44, 60, 116
Mantell, Robert Bruce, 158
Manuel, A.C., 204, 217

258 *The History of Irvine*

maps and plans of Irvine listed, 235-236
Market House, 53
markets, 25, 26, 51, 53, 85, 125, 147
Marquis, James, 218, 226
Marress, 13, 14, 25, 30, 43, 54, 94, 95, 118, 201, 217, 223
Marress ford, 12, 146, 151
Marressfoot, 3, 53, 74, 81, 82, 140, 152
Marschale, sir John, 29
Marshall, Provost James, 46, 244
Marshall, Provost William, 244
Martin, J., 237
Mary Queen of Scots, 21, 35, 41, 98, 139, 192, 208, 239
Marymass, 26, 28, 40, 44, 58, 60, 65, 75, 82, 84, 85, 98, 103, 104, 114, 118, 124, 125, 135, 139, 146, 147, 155, 156, 178, 180, 182, 186, 187, 190, 191, 192, 194, 198, 203, 208, 211, 213, 220, 225, 230, *97, 145, 177, 195, 225, 229, C14*
mason, 95
Masonic Hall, 137, 176, 177
masons, 57, 60, 85, 95, 120, 156
Mauchline, 31, 88, 92, 105
Maul, Benjamin, 92, 93, 100
Maybole, 31, 57, 85
Meadowhead, 216
Meadowpark, 158, 178
Meagher, Martin, 197
Mealmarket, 53, 60, 67, 71, 74
Medical Officer, 146, 190
medical service, 57, 64, 69, 83, 85, 91, 92, 95, 104, 113, 114, 120, 126, 195, 204, 232
Menagerie, 157
Mennons, John, 118
merchant guild, 20
merchants, 15, 16, 20, 26, 53, 64, 109, 122, 173
Merchants' Association, 176, 180
Merchants Holiday, 139, 164
Merry and Cunninghame, 154
Merryvale, 206
Metallic Oxides Co., 171, 184
Methodists, 86, 89, 116, 131
Michaelmas, 20, 26, 50, 51, 64, 123
Milgarholm, 16, 35, 36, 64, 83, 84, 91, 103, 115, 156, 194, 223
Militia, 69, 99
Millar, John Fulton, 158
Millburn, Rev. Walter, 174, 189
Miller, Helen, 105
Miller, James, 164, 226, 230
Miller, John, 164, 175
Miller, William, 190
Milliken, Thomas, 95
mills, 16, 17, 36, 53, 60, 74, 83, 84, 114, 125, 145, 151
Milne, Peter, 218
miners and miners' rows, *see* coal mining
Minister's Cast, 60, 74, 84, 156, 188
Misk, 77
Mitchell, J., 237
Mitchell, Jean, 233
Mitchell, William, 164, 175, 189
Moats Hole, 2, 156
Model Lodging House, 179
Moderate group, 195, 196, 203, 205, 224, 226

Monie, Peter, 174
Monkredding, 154
Monro, Bailie George, 56, 64
Monsanto, 227
Montaber, 24, 31
Montgomerie, family, 38, 39, 40, 74; *see also* Eglinton
Montgomerie, Alexander, 63
Montgomerie, Alexander, Lord, 35, 38
Montgomerie, Barbara, 120
Montgomerie, Charles, 36
Montgomerie, Dr. William, 120
Montgomerie, Hugh, Lord, 38, 40
Montgomerie, John, 18, 39, 40
Montgomerie, John, Master of, 38
Montgomerie, Lady Jane, 108
Montgomerie, Master Matthew, 39
Montgomerie, Neil, 39
Montgomerie, Provost Alexander, 244
Montgomerie, Provost Archibald, 244
Montgomerie, Provost Hugh, 244
Montgomerie, Provost James, 244
Montgomerie, Provost John, 244
Montgomerie, Provost Lord Archibald, 244
Montgomerie, Provost William, 122, 130, 244
Montgomerie, Robert, 31, 46, 85, 132, 234
Montgomerie, Sir John, 35, 38
Montgomerie, Sir Robert, 40
Montgomerie, William, 36, 39, 40
Montgomery Boyd's Close, 104
Montgomery School, 175, 189, 190, 197, 198, *176*
Montgomery Street, 151, 168, 173, 186, 217, *57, 90, 159*
Montgomery, Dr. James, 232
Montgomery, James, 87, 99, 138, 142, 208, 218, 220, *90*
Montgomery, John, 87
Montgomery, Miss J.P., 231
Montgomeryfield, 184
Montgreenan, 40, 76
Monti, Joseph De, 158
Montmisarthill, 19
Moody and Sankey, 160
Moor, 2, 21, 23, 25, 31, 59, 64, 65, 71, 74, 81, 82, 84, 95, 117, 120, 126, 132, 137, 139, 141, 146, 147, 149, 154, 155, 156, 158, 165, 180, 182, 187, 188, 192, 194, 200, 201, 203, 206, 208, 220, 230, 232
Moor, Samuel, 70
Moore, Father Francis, 232
Moore, Sir Thomas, 186, 196, 199, 203
Moravian Brethren, 87, 99, 220
Morton, Piper, 198
mortuary, 178, 182
Morvilles, family, 5, 6, 23, 35, 37, 38
Motor cycles, 190
mottes, 31
motto, 27
Mount Musart, 9, 43, 94
Mowat's Hole, 156
Mr. Marymass, 192, 208
Muir Drive, 188
Muir, David, 86
Muir, James Robertson, 92
Muir, John, 16
Muir, Provost Walter, 183, 186, 188, 245
Muir, Provost Wilson, 206, 217, 218, 223, 226, 245

Municipal Bank, 188, 210
Munro, C.R., 189
Munro, Rev. Iain R., 219
Murchie, Peter, 141
Murchland, Provost Charles, 148, 156, 168, 170, 178, 242, 245
murders, 65, 114, 118, 126, 133, 232
Mure Church, 160, 174, 189, 196, 214, 219, 220, 232
Mure, Margaret, 19
Mure, Misses, 90, 160
Mure Mission, 160, 197
Mure, Provost John, 19, 20, 26, 37, 64, 244
Mure, Quintin, 19
Mure, Sir William, 63
Mures of Caldwell, 19
Murkland, Charles, 62
Murphy, Father Henry, 163
Murphy, Father John Nicholas, 214
Murphy, Father Thomas, 220, 232
Murphy, John, 189
Murray, John Norval, 178
Murray's Land, 25
Musart, 9
Museum, Burgh, 221, 225, 233
Museum, Maritime, 228
music, 135, 137, 142, 157, 158, 173, 177, 191, 198, 211, 212, 220, 221, 229
mussels, 146

naphtha, 141, 152
Napier, Rev. J., 214
Napoleon, Prince Louis, 140
National Shipbuilding Securities Ltd., 199
National Telephone Company, 151, 174
Nechell, John, 30
Neil, James, 109
Neil, Robert, 225
Neilson, James Beaumont, 120
Nesbitt, Alexander, 46
Nethermains, 140, 142
Neving, Provost Hugh, 244
New Street, 184, 191
New Town, 6, 8, 216, 218, 220, 226, 227, 228, 229, 230, 232, 233
New Year, 81, 104, 137, 138, 164, 198, 210
Newhouse, 118
Newmill, 2, 17, 83
Newmilns, 21, 26, 130
Newmoor, 24, 58, 59, 71, 74, 79, 141, 142, 146, 154, 216, 227, 230
newspapers, 124, 138, 156, 198, 220, 221, 232, 237
Newton-upon-Ayr, 7, 84
Nicolson, Rev. Angus, 196
night watch, 51
Nisbet, Alexander, 65
Nisbet, John, 62
Nisbet, Thomas, 194
Niven, John, 142
North Ayrshire Coaches Ltd., 210
North Port, 11
Norway, 15, 31, 55, 59
Nursing Association, 178, 194, 204

Olding, Ted and Elizabeth, 221
O'Halloran, Sir Charles, 226
old folk, 191, 194, 207, 220, 223, 225, 230
Old Place of Fullarton, 30, 33

Oldhall, 118, 184
O'Neill, David, 226
Orange Hall, 155, 163, 165
Orangemen, 131, 144, 163
O'Reilly, Father Dermott, 197, 214
Ornithological Society, 147, 158, 177
Orr, Alexander, 62
Orr, Bailie, 121, 144
Orr, Rev. William S., 220
Orr, Scott Munro, 158
Oswald, Richard, 122
outintoun burgesses, 21
oven soles, 141
overcrowding, 149, 156, 170, 180, 188, 193, 206
Overwards, 24

Paisley, 40, 77, 79, 118
Paisley Bank, 85, 119, 132
Paith, 9
Palace, 31
Palace cinema, 198, 213
papingo, 60
Parish of Irvine, 21, 24, 168, 184, *C5*
Parish Church, 130, 132, 146, 147, 158, 160, 161, 163, 174, 182, 189, 191, 196, 202, 213, 219, 232, *11, 87*
parish councils, 128, 144, 149, 165, 184, 186
Park, Finlay, 28
Parker, John, 177, 182
parks, 177, 188, 196, 208, 211, 212, 225, 230
parliament, 21, 41, 46, 64, 120, 126, 129
"Parliament House", 71
parliamentary elections, 122, 130, 144, 155, 176, 186, 203, 204, 205, 217, 226
parochial boards, 128, 144, 149
Parterre, 99, 113, 140, 142
Paterson, Alexander, 85, 132
Paterson, Dr. W.A., 173
Paterson, James, 140
Paterson, John and Co., 154, 158
Paterson, Provost John, 23, 86, 87, 113, 123, 131, 132, 133, 144, 148, 156, 211, 236, 244, *146*
Paterson, Rev. John, 130, 174, 189, 196
Paterson, Rev. Robert, 160
Paterson, Robert and James Graham, 211
Paterson, William, 226
Paton, Rev. Joseph, 161
Patons Thorn, Patoun's Thorne, 24, 44; *see also* Thornhouse
patronage of the church, 44, 60, 116, 130, 160
Patterton, 24
Paulin, George, 133, 135, 161, 164, 165
Paulin, Sir David, 174
Pauline, Sister, 218
Pawkie Close, 155
Peace Ballot, 198
Peacock, Alexander (or Samuel), 102, 104
pearl fishing, 56
Peat Hole, 156
Peebles, Provost John, 36, 51, 244
Perceton, 31, 45, 46, 54, 65, 116, 141, 142, 151, 154, 216, *C16*
Peter Street, 151, 188
Phillips, William, 204
photography, 139, 173, 212, 237

Picture Palace, 190, 196
Picturedrome, 168, 182, 190, 196, 231
Pieroni, Messrs., 185
Pieroni, Pietro, 178
Pilkington, T.F., 131
Pilot House, 171
piper, 51
pirates, 56
place names, 4, 5, 9
plague, 21, 46, 63
plasterers, 120, 173
Plyglass Ltd., 218
Pococke, Richard, 3, 35, 76
Poe, Edgar Allan, 93, 101
Police Commissioners, 123, 145, 148, 149, 151, 156, 178
police force, 130, 142, 146, 155, 163, 193, 225, 232; *see also* constables
police judges, 183, 205
Police Station, 130, 142
Pollock, Rev. Robert, 160, 189
Pont, Timothy, 3, 12, 13, 14, 16, 17, 25, 30, 35, 36, 37, 50, 54, 234, 235
pony-riding, 212, 213
poor relief, 29, 61, 70, 75, 85, 89, 90, 91, 92, 108, 116, 124, 126, 128, 129, 146, 165, 184, 193, 204
Poorshouse, 90, 120, 128, 180, 185, 190, 204
population, 8, 50, 76, 79, 94, 116, 118, 132, 142, 154, 168, 170, 188, 189, 193, 206, 207, 216, 218, 223, 228, 232, 233
Porteous, Dr., 160
Porter, James, 63, 197, 214
Porter, William, 40
Porthead, 65, 139, *68*
Porthead Surgery, 232
Portland Glass Company, 184, 210, 227
Portland Road, 151, 170, 188
Portland, dukes of, 118, 140, 180, 228
ports, 9, 60, 95, 98, 178, 208
postal service, 58, 104, 131, 174, 182, 190, 195, 210, 221, 232
potatoes, 74, 115, 128, 168
Powder House, 57, 69, 87, 120, 146, 186, 189, 208, *54*
precentor, 62, 86, 91, 130, 139, 161
Presbytery of Irvine, 44, 53, 63, 91, 142
pressgangs, 69, 95
Prestwick, 7, 31, 156, 206, 228
Prestwick Circuits Ltd., 227
Prince Charles, 228
Princes Anne, 228
prison, 11
Proc, 5
procurator, 20, 146
propellor, screw, 120
provostship, 20, 21, 19, 20, 21, 43, 50, 51, 65, 123, 179, 205, 224
Public and Industrial School, 104, 136, 160, 163, 164, *137*
Puddleford, 8, 9, 12, 13, 23, 33, 84, 95, 124, 156, 208, 218, 232, *11*
Puddle-deidly, Puddliedoodly, 12, 33
punishments, 20, 114
Purdie's Close, 155
putting, 188, 196, 198

quarry, 17, 35, 53, 54, 60, 74, 94, 120, 141, 148, 154, 238
Quarry Lane, 132, 140, 151, 154, 171, 188
Quarry Road, 58, 60, 188, 194, 197, 206, 208, 214
quartermaster, 69, 75, 104
Queen Elizabeth, 209, 228
Queen of Scots Knitwear Ltd., 227
Queen's Bridge, 140
quoiting, 137, 177, 196

Raa, Hugh, 30
rabbits, 117, 146
Radical Association, 130
radio, 190, 198
Railway Mission, 197, 214
railway workshops, 141, 153, 184, 200, 204, 210
railways, 118, 120, 139, 140, 141, 142, 154, 157, 158, 163, 177, 188, 190, 196, 202, 204, 217, 228, 230, *140, 153, 197, C8*
Ramblers' Field Club, 175, 176, 190
Ramsay, Jack, 233
Ramsay, Mr. Thomas, 30
Ramsay, Robert, 62, 63
Ramsay, Ronald, 224
Randall, Donald, 30
Ranken, Captain Harry Sherwood, 181
Rankin, Rev. Henry, 160, 174, 179, 189
Rankin, Robert, 115
Rankine, J.A., 132
Rankine, John, 39
Ratepayers' Association, 205, 224
rates, 129, 178, 184, 185, 193, 225
rationing, 182, 200, 204
Ravenscroft, 98, 116, 142, 154
Ravenspark, 177, 188, 206, 212
Ravenspark Academy, 218, 220
Ravenspark Primary School, 219
Reading Room, 142, 163
recreations, 136, 157, 165, 177, 188, 190, 191, 196, 212, 225, 230; *see also* arts, music, water sports, *etc.*
Red Burn, 21, 25, 31, 74, 206, 223
Red Cross, 178, 181, 186, 187
Redburn, 25, 31, 37, 58, 71, 81, 82, 94, 118, 141, 154, 184, 232, *71*
Redburn Primary School, 219, 231
Redmeadow or Roodmeadow, 24, 31, 46, 74
Reformed Presbyterians, 89
Regal Cinema, 196, 213, 220, 232
Regan, Mike, 225
regattas, 147, 158, 190, 196, 211
Reid, Allan, 230
Reid, John, 40, 81, 219, 231
Reid, Mrs. Tresia, 224
Reid, Provost John, 45, 224
Reid, Rev. Henry, 160
Reid, Thomas, Robert and William, 114
Relief Church, 87, 89, 93, 97, 103, 116, 130, 131, 160, 163, 174, 189, 196, 214, 218, 219, 223, 232, *89*
Renfrew Brothers, 172
Renfrewshire, 5, 15, 65
repledging, 20, 67
restaurants, 223, 228
resurrectionists, 113, 218
Rex Cinema, 213
Riccarton, 33, 77, 175

Richmond, Rev. James, 76, 79, 85, 88, 90, 94, 97, 103, 116, 118, 130, 234
Rickets, Brigadier R.A., 226
rifle shooting, 138, 147, 158, 177, 199, 212, 224
right of way, 208
riots, 64, 68, 84, 90, 98, 118, 200
Ritz dance hall, 201, 212, 213
River Garnock, 2, 3, 4, 13, 35, 37, 54, 77, 118, 146, 152, 158, 180, 225, 228
River Irvine, 2, 3, 4, 5, 6, 8, 12, 13, 16, 31, 54, 58, 60, 68, 76, 83, 84, 94, 115, 142, 151, 156, 175, 188, 208, 211, 217, 218, 223, 238
Rivergate Mall, 217, 227, 228, 229, 232, C13
Riviera Express, 199
roads, 58, 94, 95, 124, 144, 145, 184, 193, 202, 217, 219, 225, 230, C7
Robert I, 6, 7, 31, 33, 34, 192, 230
Robert II, 7, 8, 11, 21, 26, 33, 34, 35, 224
Robert III, 21
Robert the Steward, 6, 7
Robertson, George, 116, 117, 118, 234
Robertson, Provost Alexander, 124, 244
Robertson, Rev. George B., 214, 220
Robertson, Rev. Peter, 87, 130
Robertson, Rev. W.B., 130, 131, 132, 138, 142, 155, 159, 160, 187, *126*
Robertson, Tinkler, 114
Rockware Glass Ltd., 210, 218, 227
Roddinghill, 24, 30, 35
roller skating, 191
Roman Catholics, 87, 89, 116, 131, 136, 161, 164, 189; *see also* St. Mary's
Romans, 2, 3, 5, 218
Rood Meadow, 24, 31, 46, 74
ropeworks, 84, 113, 120, 141, 171
Roseholm, 228, 235
Ross, Charles, 220, 224
Ross, Hew, 62
Ross, Marion, 46
Ross, Rev. Donald G., 189
Ross, Sir Godfrey de, 24
Ross, William, 200, 203, 216, 225; Lord Ross, 228
Ross, Zachary, 164
Rotary Club, 212, 220, 224, 230
Rothesay, 64, 122, 123
Rotten Bog, 25, 53
Rotten Row, 9, 155
Rottenbog, 25
rounders, 137
rowing, 190, 196, 211, 215
Roxburgh, 18, 46
Royal Bank of Scotland, 132, 173, 210, 232
Royal Ordnance Factory, 182, 184, 199, 200, 203, 206, 210, 212
rubber, 120
Rubie, George, 176
Rubie, Provost Alex, 224, 225, 226, 245
rugby, 212, 223, 224
Russel, Jas., 87

saddlers, 50, 85, 120
Saddlers Corner, 218, 221
Sailors Society, 86, 90
Sakeschaw, John, 20
salmon, 13, 15, 16, 56, 194

Salmon, Provost William, 126, 139, 186, 224, 244
Salmon's Hill, 126, 139
salt, 15, 55, 56, 67
Saltcoats, 3, 26, 55, 56, 59, 60, 67, 76, 79, 117, 118, 120, 149, 156, 168, 178, 226
Salvation Army, 160, 174, 189, 197, 198, 214, 220, 224, 232
Samson, Charles, 141, 142, 153
Sandgate, 9, 60
Sandierig, 25
Sandy Potts, 116, *147*
Sandy Road, 188
Sandyhill, 9, 23
Sanitary Inspector, 146
sasine, 21
Savings Bank, 119, 132, 173, 210
Savio, Sister Dominic, 236
Sawers, Rev. Robert, 220, 232
sawmills, 141, 153, 171, 227
say-masters, 85
schools and education, 27, 53, 61-63, 65, 74, 91-93, 97, 104, 108, 113, 114, 124, 136, 161, 163-165, 174-176, 179, 189-190, 193, 201, 214-215, 218-219, 225, 230-231
School Board, 163-165, 174-176, 179, 189
schools, private, 92, 109, 135, 164, 190, 215
SCI Systems, 227
Scot, Mr. Thomas, 29
Scot, Walter, 70
Scott, A.T. 173
Scott, Alexander, 28
Scott, Col. Walter, 198
Scott, Frances, 91
Scott, John, 38, 51
Scott, Mr. Thomas, 30
Scott, Provost Hugh, 244
Scott, Provost James, 244
Scott, Provost Robert, 19, 26, 244
Scott, Provost William, 244
Scott, Walter, 60
Scott, William and Hugh, 14
Scottish and Universal Newspapers Ltd., 220, 227
Scottish General Transport Company, 190
Scottish Grand National, 211
Scottish National Party, 205, 224, 226
Scottish Socialist Party, 196
Scottish Special Housing Association Ltd., 202, 206, 208, 210, 223
Scottish Tar Distillers, 184, 210
Scotts loch, 31, 51, 58, 60, 74, 115; *see also* loch *and* Trindlemoss
Scottswards, 24, 46, 74
Scoular, Rev. John, 130
Scrimgeour, William, 44
Seagate, 8, 9, 11, 14, 16, 17, 19, 31, 33, 88, 95, 103, 104, 113, 132, 192, 218, 223, *34*
Seagate Castle, 13, 18, 31, 33, 34, 35, 53, 95, 138, 139, 155, 191, 203, 223, 230, 239, *12, 34, 36*
Seagatefoot, 79, 84, 113, 114, 116, 124, *30*
Seagatehead, 11, 43, 47, 53, 58, 85, 95
Seal of Cause, 50, 56, 63, 85
Seamen's Bethel, 197, 208, 212
Secretary of State, 144, 168, 203, 216, 217, 225, 226
Seggans Bank, 135

Semple, James George, 93, *93*
Senior Citizens Centre, 223
sergeant, 51
Service, Mary, 129
session clerk, 62, 91, 132
Seton, Alexander, 40, 45
sett, 50, 64, 120
Seventh Day Adventists, 220
sewage disposal, 113, 148, 151, 178, 188, 193, 194, 225, 230
Seymour, Lady Jane, 139
Shambles, 74
Shaw, David, 233
Shaw, James, 74, 82, 98
Shaw, Mrs. Clarice McNab, 186
Shaw, Rev. Mr., 47
Shearer, Isobel, 44
sheep, 30, 59
Shewalton, 2, 3, 13, 14, 51, 76, 77, 79, 93, 99, 118, 120, 130, 142, 152, 154, 184, 194, 204, 210, 216, 218, 227
Shewalton Mill, 17
Ship Inn, 65
shipbuilding, 76, 84, 120, 141, 149, 156, 171, 179, 180, 182, 184, 199, 200, 209
Shipmill, 120
ships, 15, 19, 44, 55, 56, 69, 75, 76, 77, 79, 120, 131, 151, 171, 172, 182, 196, 199, 200, 220
Shipyard Road, 188
Shoarmaster, 76
shoemakers, 26, 85, 121, 122, 176
shops, 18, 53, 71, 74, 85, 120, 156, 172, 173, 206, 210, 217, 232
shore, 189, 194, 208, 220
Short, Rev. George, 160
Shows, 192, 210, 220, 230, *145*
Sickhouse, 149
Siddons, Mrs., 99
Sillar, David, 75, 92, 99, 103, 104, 186
silversmith, 120
Simpson, Alexander, 154
Simpson, Cuthbert, 21
Sinclair, David, 172, *172*
Sinclair, Rev. J., 144
Sisters of St. Joseph of Cluny, 175
Sisters of the Cross of Passion, 189, 190, 232
Six Riggs and a Half, 71
skating, 158, 208
Skean Dhu Hotel, 232
Skefco Ball Bearing Co. Ltd., 218, 227
skinners, 15, 26, 56, 84, 191, 212
Skinners Close, 155
Skittery Wynd, 206
Sklate Hall, 17, 18
Slate Mill, 16, 17, 83, 194, 197, 214
slaters, 57, 79, 120, 173
slaughterhouse, 113, 114, 124, 194, 200, 208
Slaughterhouse Well, 95
Sliddery Lane, 206
Sloan Avenue, 227
Sloan, Captain James, 191
Sloan, James, 192
Sloan, Jamie, 144
Sluices, 141
Smail, Rev. Thomas, 214
Smeaton, John, 76
Smiddy Close, 155
Smiddybar, Smithy Bar, 9, 24, 31, 58, 94

Index   261

smith, 50
Smith, Alexander, 205
Smith, Betty, 104
Smith, James, 91, 225
Smith, John, 2, 65, 90, 158, 199
Smith, Rev. Robert, 131
smiths, 16, 26, 50, 56, 58, 84, 85, 120, 173, 177
SMT buses, 190
smuggling, 35, 67, 68, 95
Smyth, John, 54
Snodgirs, Thomas, 39
Snodgrass, 2, 114, 142
snooker, 212, 232
snuffmill, 83
soap, 154, 172, 184, 210
Social and Literary Institute, *see* Literary
Sodgers Plumb, 156
soirées, 138, 157
Somervill, Hugh, 172
Somerville, Rev. James, 130, 160
Somerville, William, 147
Sommerville, J., 144, 176
Sor Milk Raw, 94
Sourlie, 116, 118, 120, 168, 229
Spain, 15, 152, 199, 209
Spark, James and Thomas, 60
Spark, John, 38, 91
Spark, Patrick, 37
Spark, Thomas, 35, 37
Speirs, John, 147, 156
Spellings, Note on, 238
Spenshill, 104, 108
Spiers, John, 146
Spittal Meadow, 31, 24, 31, 71
Springbank, 114, 151, 156, 193, 194, 195, 206
Springfield, 44, 115, 139
squaremen, 16, 26, 56, 57, 113, 120, 176, 191, 212
St. Andrew's Church, 214, 220, 232
St. Anne, 95
St. Bride or Bridget, 4, 5, 31
St. Bryde's well, 4, 103
St. Christopher, 28
St. Columba, 4
St. Conval, 4, 5, 28
St. Inan, 4, 5, 28, 95
St. Inan Avenue, 188
St. Inan's Church, 196
St. James land, 24, 46
St. John, 28
St. John Ogilvie Church, 232
St. John's land, 25
St. Katherine, 28
St. Margaret's Oratory, 232
St. Mark's School, 219, 231
St. Mary, 28, 29
St. Mary's Church, 161, 163, 174, 189, 197, 200, 214, 220, 232
St. Mary's RC School, 175, 190, 219, 231
St. Mary's Well, 30
St. Merri, 139
St. Michael, 28
St. Michael's School, 190, 197, 214, 218, 231
St. Mungo, 4
St. Nicholas, 28
St. Ninian, 4, 5, 28
St. Paul's Church, 214, 219

St. Salvator, 28
St. Sebastian, 28
St. Stephen, 28
St. Thomas, 28
St. Wissing, 18
Standing Stones, 4, 12
Stane, Stanecastle, 2, 3, 4, 16, 18, 24, 31, 35, 36, 39, 58, 71, 74, 92, 94, 95, 114, 137, 149, 172, 196, 221, 232
Steadman, James, 120
Steelle, John, 142
steelyard, 85, 126
Stein, Robert, 113
stentmasters, 27, 51, 69, 75, 123, 146
Stephen, Rev. Campbell, 186
Steps Road, 223
Stevenson, Rose, 233
Stevenston, 2, 4, 14, 58, 77, 82, 149, 151, 168, 178, 226
Stewart, Daniel, 109, 122
Stewart, James, 91
Stewart, John, 36, 44
Stewart, John & Sons, 141, 171
Stewart, Mr., 91
Stewart, Mr. John, 29
Stewart, Mrs. McBain, 200
Stewart, Provost Hamilton, 245
Stewart, Robert, 197
Stewart, Thomas, 115
Stewarthall, 116
Stewarton, 6, 31, 40, 94, 121, 135
Stewart's Iron Works, 153
Stirling, Rev. John, 47
Stirling, Maria, 56
Storm, Robert, 30
Stoupishill, William, 28
Strang, Rev. John, 63
Strang, Rev. William, 143
Strathclyde, 5
Strathclyde Regional Council, 219, 225, 225, 229, 230, 231, 232
Strawhorn, John, 204
street lighting, 97, 109, 114, 116, 151, 182, 188, 193, 194, 208, 225
streets, 53, 58, 75, 94, 95, 114, 116, 124, 132, 145, 151, 155, 168, 178, 188
strikes, 147, 184, 185
Strong, Albert, 177
Stuart, Lord James, 124
Stuart, Thomas R., 164, 174
Superintendent of Cleansing, 151
Superintendent of Works, 151
Surgeon's Acre, 69
Sutherland, William, 46, *47*
Swan Close, 155
Swan Inn, 155
Swan, Jean, 133
Swan's Empire, 190
swimming, 158, 190, 194, 196, 211, 223
Symington, 31
Sympill, Gabriel, 39
Syriac gospel, 158

table tennis, 196, 212
tailors, 16, 26, 51, 56, 84, 85, 122, 137, 172, 176, 191, 212
Tailor's Straun, 11
tambour works, 84
tanning, 84, 95, 114, 120, 152

Tarbolton, 94, 102, 103, 104
Tarry Plumb, 156
Tarryholm, 31, 77, 81, 83, 156, 238
taverns, 56, 57, 58, 62, 74, 79, 95, 98
taxation, 20, 21, 27, 51, 53, 75, 114
Taylor, Dr. John, 122, 130
Taylor, Isobel, 44
Taylor, Rev. John, 214, 220
Taylor, William, 118, 120
tea, 67, 68, 113
Technical College, 231
teinds, 60, 74, 116
telegraph, 120, 141, 152
telephones, 151, 174, 221, 223
television, 212, 221
Temperance, 130, 147, 155, 157, 160, 165, 176, 186, 192, 201
Templar tenements, 31, 38
Templedean, 31, 102
Templeton, John, 118
Templeton, Will, 174
Templeton, William, 75, 82, 93, 100, 103
Tennant, Sir Charles, 152
tennis, 177, 182, 190, 208
Tent Question, 147
Territorials, 174, 181, 184, 196, 198, 199, 208
thatched roofs, 178
theatre, *see* drama
thesaurer, 26
Thirty One Club, 191
Thomson, Dr. James, 173, 195
Thomson, Father William, 131
Thomson, John, 56
Thomson, Mr. John, 91
Thomson, Provost William, 197, 244
Thomson, Rev. P.G., 213, 220, 232
Thornhouse, 154, 188, 194, 206, *187*; *see also* Patons Thorn
Thornhouse Avenue, 188, 208
Thornhouse Drive, 188
Thornhouse soap works, 172, 210
Thornliebank, 36
timber, 24, 55, 142, 152, 153, 171
Timmerland, 18, *45*
tinkers, 85, 120, 232
Tivoli Theatre, 190, 191, 196, 200
tobacco, 56, 77, 79, 83
Tobias, 57
Toc H, 191, 196
tofts, 21
Tolbooth, 11, 18, 20, 21, 26, 33, 38, 40, 46, 47, 50, 51, 54, 57, 60, 64, 67, 69, 70, 71, 74, 86, 95, 97, 104, 114, 118, 126, 142, 146, *23, 70, 133, 141*
Tollerton Drive, 231
Tollerton, Private Ross, 181
tollgates, 94
Toner, Charles, 230
Tourlands, Towerlands, 35, 36, 40, 83, 115
Town Clerk, 20, 27, 40, 46, 51, 63, 65, 69, 71, 75, 105, 114, 123, 132, 145, 146, 178, 202, 207, 210, 211, 224, 226, 244, *215*
Town House, 31, 142, 145, 146, 155, 157, 163, 165, 178, 184, 187, 188, 192, 198, 200, 204, 208, 209, 220, 223, 230, *141, 177, 195, C14*
Town Mission, 116

town officers, *see* burgh officers
town pyper, 44
Townend, 95, 109, 137, 146
Townend Port, 11
Townhead, 16, 17, 19, 23, 44, 53, 67, 90, 94, 95, 115, 118, 120, 123, 124, 132, 141, 168, 196, 212, 220, 226, 228, 232, *27*
Townhead Addiction Centre, 232
Townhead Port, 9
Towns Herd, 23, 24, 69
trade, 7, 15, 16, 26, 54, 55, 56, 58, 67, 75, 77, 79, 81, 94, 109, 118, 119, 151
Trades Hotel, 180
traffic lights, 194
Train, Sir Lawrence, 30
Tran, Provost Andrew, 15, 19, 44, 244
Tran, Provost Patrick, 19, 244
Tran, Provost Stephen, 19, 26, 244
Tran, Robert, 19, 62
Trans, Robert, 19
treasurer, 51, 123
Treaty of Irvine, 33, 35, 239
Trinder, J. Colbourne, 157
Trindlemoss, 31, 43, 51, 60
Trinity Church, 130, 159, 163, 174, 182, 189, 196, 214, 218, 219, 223, 231, 232, *126, 221, C16*
Tron, 11, 70, 103, 114, 142, 180, *23*
Tron, Robert, 62
Troon, 3, 13, 14, 54, 65, 67, 68, 79, 118, 140, 141, 142, 152, 154, 156, 172, 174, 179, 186
Tucker, Thomas, 14
Tulloch, Bill, 230
Turf Hotel, 232
Turner, Mary, 63
Turnpike Acts, 94, *C7*
Twa Faulds, 24
Twibill, Joseph, 141

unemployment, 108, 109, 116, 120, 126, 128, 141, 147, 178, 184, 185, 194, 196, 198, 199, 225, 226
unfree traffiqueris, 51
Union Bank, 132, 173, 210
Unionists, 155, 176, 177, 196; *see also* Conservatives
United Alkali Co. Ltd., 152, 171, 184
United Gospel Church, 131
United Presbyterian Church, 131, 159
unlaw, 20, 26, 51
uplandis men, 8
Urry, Adam, 18
Urry, Reginald, 18

Vale of Clyde, *see* railway workshops
vandalism, 109, 137, 155, 218, 232
vane, 114, 142, 146, 188
Vauce, Thomas de, 35
Victoria, 123, 124
Victoria Cross, 181
Victoria Weir, *see* weir
Vindogara, 3, 4
Vineburgh, 158, 177, 196, 226, 230
vines, 30
visitors for inspecting, 51, 69, 123, 146
Volunteer Rooms, *see* Drill Hall

Volunteers, 65, 69, 86, 98, 138, 147, 158, 174, 177, 178, 181, 223, 225
Volvo Trucks (G.B.) Ltd., 217, 218

Wackmil, 17
wages, 81, 86, 92, 156, 179, 180, 184, 194, 209
waggonways, 76, 79
Waldrum, R., 189
Wales, Jim, 233
Walker, Alexander, 152
Walker, Alexander & Co. Ltd., 171, 184, 210
Walker, Brigadier-General James, 184
Walker, Dr., 114
Walker, Father Thomas, 131
Walker, Father Vincent, 214
Walker, Jimmy, 196, 212, 220
Walker, Mrs., 203
Walker, William, 137
Wallace Road, 194
Wallace, Edward, 14, 94
Wallace, John, 14, 30, 58
Wallace, Provost William, 47, 51, 244
Wallace, Rev. William, 62
Wallace, Sally, 224
Wallace, William, 11, 12, 23, 33, 93, 192, 230
wappin schewings, 21
war, 8, 21, 31, 69, 79, 92, 128, 147, 180-184, 186, 187, 188, 198, 199-202, 206, 211, 213
war memorial, 11, 184, 198, 212, *182*
wards, 145, 205, 223, 225
Warner, Patrick, 74, 114, 115
Warner, Rev. Patrick, 47, 56, 59, 239
Warrix, 2, 45, 46, 51, 76, 82, 83, 156
Washing House, 74, 136, 148, 186
watchmakers, 120
watchman, 114
Water Mill, 16
water sports, 147, 158, 190, 196, 211, 215, 230
water supply, 53, 95, 113, 146, 148, 149, 151, 156, 163, 170, 178, 193, 206, *147*
Waterside, 97, 113, 116, 168, 197, 203, 215, 234
Waterside Hall, 160, 188, 189, 214, 220
Watson, James, 172
Watson, Mrs. A.M., 212
Watt, Hugh, 146
Watt, John, 86, 98
Watt, Provost Andrew, 147, 171, 244
waulking, 16, 17, 56, 83, 84
weavers, websters, 2, 16, 26, 51, 56, 84, 85, 109, 113, 120, 122, 128, 136, 176, 191
Webb, John, 76, 115
Webster, David, 230
weddings, 139, 161
Wee Dock, 200, *129*
Wee Grip, 9, 155
Wee Pie, 98, 211
Wee Plumb, 156
weir, 2, 137, 151, 156, 158, 165, 194
Weir, James, 14
Weir, John, 219
Weirisholme, 24
wells, 53, 75, 86, 95, 113, 114, 124, 137, 142, 145, 148, 149, 155

Wellwood, 211, 221
Wesleyan chapel, 131
West Port, 9, 11
West Road, West Back Road, West Backside, 8, 9, 23, 25, 71, 74, 87, 89, 113, 116, 130, 131, 135, 137, 151, 155, 163, 168, 188, 190, 196, 212, *13*
Western Bank, 132
Western Iron Works, 141
Wheatsheaf Inn, 98
whippet racing, 196
whisky still, 84
whist drives, 182, 189
White Friars, 30
White, Dr. David, 226
White, Dr. John, 133, 135
White, Rev. Hugh, 87, 88
Whitefield, George, 86
Whitson, H.S., 226
Whyte, Robert M., 13, 202, 210, 224, 236, *215*
Wightman, Rev. J.P.E., 213
wigmakers, 84
William IV, 121
William of Orange, 47
William the Lion, 5, 6, 7, 34
Williamfield, 60, 94, 116, 152, 189, 190, 218, 232
Williamson, John, 18
Wilson, A. & J., 184
Wilson, A.R., 187, 202
Wilson and Womersley, 216
Wilson, Clement, 220, 221, 227, 228
Wilson, Donald, 223
Wilson, Dr. James, 146, 173
Wilson, Dr. William, 146, 173
Wilson Fullarton Church, 189, 196, 200, 214, 218, 219, 220, 223
Wilson, Isabella, 164
Wilson, J.M., 214, 231
Wilson, James, 62, 113, 227
Wilson, Michael, 18
Wilson, Miss, 174
Wilson Pipe Fittings Ltd., 210, 227
Wilson Plan, 216
Wilson, Rev. David, 130, 160, 163, 220
Wilson, Rev. John, 116, 130, 234
Wilson, Robert and Son Ltd., 210, 228, 229
Wilson Sporting Goods, 218, 227
Wilson, Thomas, 18
Winchester, Rev. James, 174, 189
windmill, 83, 84
wines, 15, 56, 67, 71
Winton Bowling Club, 137, 158, 177, 196, 212
Winton Place, 206
Winton Road, 194, 200, 206, 232
Wintun, Alexander, 58
Wishart, Rev. James, 174, 189, 196, 214
witchcraft, 44, 45
Witches Plumb, 44, 156
Withrington, John, 118
Women's Voluntary Services, 200
wood, 57, 79
Wood of Langhurst, 24
Woodlands, 223, 226
Woodlands Avenue, 231
Woodlands Day Centre, 232
Woodlands Primary School, 219, 231

Woods, Father John, 163
Woodside, John, 62
wool, 55, 57, 84, 85, 120
Workman, Rev. William, 161
Wright, Matthew and Nephew Ltd., 153, 171, 184, 210, 227
Wright, Provost John, 153, 244

wrights, 16, 26, 56, 57, 84, 85, 120, 191, 212
Wyllie, Bailie, 144

Yeomanry, Ayrshire, 130
YMCA, 160, 182, 191, 196, 197, 215
Young, James and Sons, 210

Young, John, 41, 43
Young, Thomas, 20
Young, William, 82
Younger, Sir George, 176, 186, 212, 214, 215
Youth organisations, 159, 165, 182, 191, 196, 198, 201, 205, 212, 214, 215, 224, 232

Jim Miller, Chief Executive of Cunninghame District Council from 1975, who helped so much in the making of this book, died suddenly on 14th August, 1985.